Soviet Politics in Perspective

'What Sakwa has given us is a bold, thought-provoking and often brilliantly insightful analysis of the Soviet experience.'

Robert F. Miller, *Australian National University* [from the first edition]

'The first author to produce an after-collapse, full, up-to-date, analytically-orientated politics text geared to the rise and fall of the Soviet regime.'

Jeff Gleisner, *University of Leeds*

Soviet Politics in Perspective is a new edition of Richard Sakwa's successful textbook *Soviet Politics: An Introduction*. Thoroughly revised and updated it builds on the previous edition's comprehensive and accessible exploration of the Soviet system, from its rise in 1919 to its collapse in 1991.

The book is divided into five parts, which focus on key aspects of Soviet politics. They are:
- historical perspectives, beginning with the Tsarist regime on the eve of revolution, the rise and development of Stalinism, through to the decline of the regime under Brezhnev and his successors, and Gorbachev's attempts to revive the system;
- institutions of government, such as the communist party, security apparatus, the military, the justice system, local government and participation;
- theoretical approaches to Soviet politics, including class and gender politics, the role of ideology and the shift from dissent to pluralism;
- key policy areas: the command economy and reform, nationality politics, and foreign and defence policy;
- an evaluation of Soviet rule, and reasons for its collapse.

Providing maps, key texts and bibliographies, this book offers the complete history and politics of the Soviet period in a single volume. It will be indispensable to students of Soviet and post-Soviet politics as well as the interested general reader.

Richard Sakwa is Professor of Russian and European Politics at the University of Kent at Canterbury. His publications include *Soviet Politics: An Introduction* (1989), *Gorbachev and his Reforms* (1990), and *Russian Politics and Society* (second edition, 1996). His research now focuses on problems of democratisation in Russia.

Soviet Politics in Perspective

Second edition

Richard Sakwa

London and New York

First published 1989
Second edition published 1998
by Routledge
11 New Fetter Lane, London EC4P 4EE

Simultaneously published in the USA and Canada
by Routledge
29 West 35th Street, New York, NY 10001

Typeset in Baskerville by
Ponting–Green Publishing Services, Chesham, Buckinghamshire
Printed and bound in Great Britain by
T.J. International Ltd, Padstow, Cornwall

British Library Cataloguing in Publication Data
A catalogue record for this book is available from the British Library

Library of Congress Cataloging in Publication Data
Sakwa, Richard.
 Soviet politics in perspective / Richard Sakwa. – 2nd edn.
 Rev. ed of: Soviet politics. 1989.
 Includes bibliographical references and index.
 1. Soviet Union – Politics and government.
 I. Sakwa, Richard. Soviet politics.   II. Title.
 DK266.S2363   1998
 947.084 – dc21   98–16760

ISBN 0–415–16992–5 (hbk)
ISBN 0–415–07153–4 (pbk)

**For my mother, Andrée,
and the memory of my father, Zenon**

Contents

Figures

Tables

Preface to the second edition

When the first edition of this book was published in 1989 the Soviet Union was engaged in a monumental act of self-discovery and reorganisation. Mikhail Gorbachev had come to power in 1985 and launched a programme of reform under the slogans of *glasnost* (openness) and *perestroika* (restructuring) that promised to renew the Soviet Union by drawing on its economic, social and human potential to create a new, more democratic and dynamic country. This would be a society that remained loyal to the socialist idea but would no longer be in competition with the West but engaged in peaceful development on a parallel track. Coercion would give way to democratic consensus, and the humanistic potential identified in the writings of the young Marx would allow alienation to be overcome and a new society born.

In the event, already by 1989 it was clear that this vision of a renewed socialist society was facing challenges that would ultimately bring it down. The attempt to shift the source of authority away from the Communist Party of the Soviet Union (CPSU) to society in the form of soviets, and to a renewed non-party executive in the form of a strengthened presidency, had provoked a growing crisis of governance. The old economic and political administrative institutions had been dismantled but no effective and legitimate new ones had been created to replace them. The failure to tackle economic reform in a considered way had brought out all the latent crises within the system. The relaxation of central authority revealed the myriad tensions in the country's multinational structure. Above all, the revelations of *glasnost* had revealed Stalin's crimes in all their awfulness and had begun to chip away at the sacred aura surrounding Lenin, the founder of the Soviet system. The ideological glue of Marxism–Leninism lost its cohesive qualities. Soviet authoritarianism appeared to give way to 'democratic' anarchy. By 1991 the communist system of government had dissolved, and in December of that year the Union of Soviet Socialist Republics (USSR) followed the Soviet communist party into oblivion.

We can now take stock of the whole period of Soviet politics from October 1917, when the Bolsheviks seized power, to the fall of the regime in 1991. Rather than becoming the first step in the world communist revolution that would have put an end to capitalism in its entirety, the Soviet experiment can now be seen to have been no more than an interlude in the larger history of Russia and in the broader pattern of world history. With the benefit of hindsight we can more clearly see the features of the system created by the application of Marxist–Leninist ideas to Russia. The story has an end.

We can now place Soviet politics in perspective, and this is the aim of this book. We can see more clearly what was important, and what was not. The work is designed for the general reader and for students of politics seeking an introduction to the Soviet system. The overall shape of this new edition follows that of the first, although with some modifications, and the text has been modified and updated where appropriate. An analysis of the history and institutions of the Soviet Union is followed by a discussion of how the system worked in practice and some of the main policy issues it confronted, and the book ends with a brief consideration of the reasons for the fall and the place of the Soviet experiment in a broader perspective.

As with the first edition, the intellectual debts to generations of scholars who have offered their knowledge and insights on the Soviet Union are far too numerous to be individually acknowledged. Footnotes have been kept to a minimum to avoid interrupting the flow of the narrative. At the end of each chapter there is a list of works with the key texts identified separately, and at the end of the book there is a bibliography of the major English-language general works on Soviet politics. My special thanks to Ann Miller in the library at the University of Kent, who unfailingly provides support and help when most needed. I would like to thank all those involved in the progress of this work at Routledge, and in particular the patience and encouragement of Patrick Proctor. I am grateful to the Nuffield Foundation for the support that has helped provide time and space to complete the revised edition of this book.

Canterbury
January 1998

Figure 1 USSR: administrative divisions

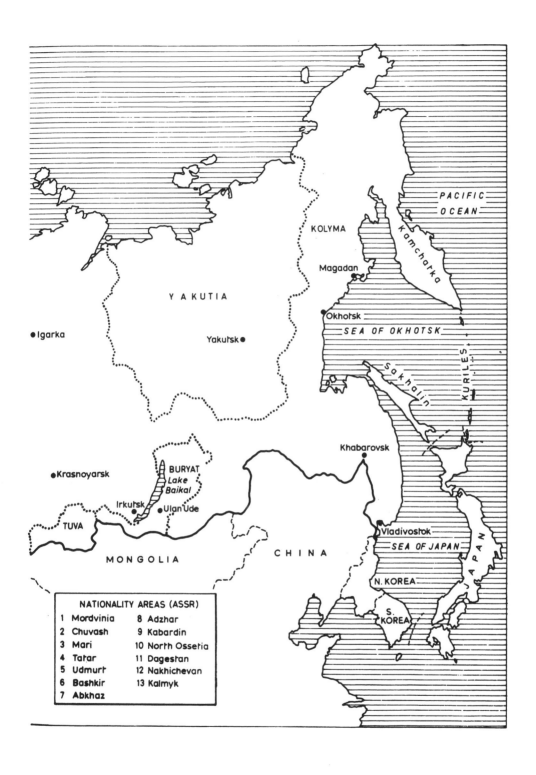

PACIFIC
OCEAN

Kamchatka

KOLYMA

●Magadan

Y A K U T I A

●Igarka

Yakutsk●

●Okhotsk

SEA OF OKHOTSK

Sakhalin

K U R I L E S

Khabarovsk●

●Krasnoyarsk

BURYAT
*Lake
Baikal*

Irkutsk● ●Ulan Ude

TUVA

●Vladivostok

SEA OF JAPAN

J A P A N

C H I N A

M O N G O L I A

N. KOREA

S.
KOREA

NATIONALITY AREAS (ASSR)

1	Mordvinia	8	Adzhar
2	Chuvash	9	Kabardin
3	Mari	10	North Ossetia
4	Tatar	11	Dagestan
5	Udmurt	12	Nakhichevan
6	Bashkir	13	Kalmyk
7	Abkhaz		

Part I

History

1 The Russian legacy

Revolutions destroy the old and yet are forced to build on the foundations established by their predecessors. The Bolshevik revolution was unprecedented in its depth and its explicit repudiation of not only the Russian past, but much of the European tradition as a whole. The rhythms of time, of geography and of peoples, however, stamped the communist regime that came to power in October 1917. Russian traditions and communist innovation fused in unexpected and disturbing ways. The attempt to build a society on new foundations in Russia profoundly affected the course of the twentieth century and shaped the destiny of the planet.

THE OLD REGIME

The adoption of what was to become the Orthodox form of Christianity by Prince Vladimir in Kiev, then the centre of the Russian lands, in 988 stamped Russia with a Byzantine form of religiosity which stood in sharp contrast to that of the Roman Catholic countries of Europe. The capture of Constantinople in 1453 by the Ottoman empire isolated Russia from its religious roots, and the Mongol occupation for some 240 years from about 1240 to 1480 further estranged Russia from the West and contributed to the creation of a unique culture. The struggle against the Mongols contributed to the emergence of the strong centralised state of Muscovy. Religious and political isolation encouraged ideas of Russia's unique mission in the world, manifested in the concept of Moscow as the 'third Rome', to supplant Constantinople and Rome itself. Under Ivan the Terrible (1533–84) the power of the monarch was extended in a system termed an 'autocracy' to emphasise the personalised system of rule. The fusion of temporal and secular power in the person of the emperor as head of both church and state, avoiding the conflicts between the two that were typical of Europe, gave rise to a distinctive Russian form of 'caesaropopism'.

The dominance of the state was to remain and gave rise to another distinctive feature of Russian history. Russia's geopolitical location on the vast Eurasian landmass with few natural frontiers other than the Volga River and the Ural Mountains encouraged a preoccupation with defence and the maintenance of a powerful army. Russian history was marked by national consolidation and the occupation of adjacent territories or, as the great Russian historian Vasilii Klyuchevskii put it, 'Russia's history is that of a country colonising itself'. From the conquest of the khanates of Kazan and Astrakhan in 1552 and 1556, respectively, Russia expanded at the astonishing rate of about 50 square miles a day for some three centuries across Siberia as far as the Pacific Ocean in the east, into Central Asia in the south, and pushed back the borders of the Turkish Ottoman empire to reach the Black Sea and the Balkans to the south-west. European fears of Russian expansionism provoked the Crimean War of 1854–56, when Britain and France sent their troops in defence of an increasingly decrepit Ottoman empire. At the onset of the Second World War in 1939–40 Soviet territories were further extended to the west with the incorporation of parts of Finland, the three Baltic republics (Estonia, Latvia and Lithuania), eastern Poland and Bessarabia. At its peak the Soviet state covered 8.6 million square miles, or one-sixth of the world's land surface, extending over eleven time zones stretching 5,600 miles from east to west.

The Mongol occupation turned Russia on to a divergent path of development from that pursued in the rest of Europe. In economic and administrative terms Russia lagged behind the more developed countries. As if to compensate, Russian history was punctuated by periodic attempts to catch up. Peter the Great (1682–1725) launched a development programme designed to graft on to Russia the latest technological developments of England and Holland. Peter established a precedent for furious state-sponsored modernisation imposed on a battered society, which (as Lenin put it later) tried 'to defeat barbarism by barbaric means'. The pattern was established of a Russia selectively borrowing from the outside world while jealously defending its independence and uniqueness. The West was, on the one hand, a model of development and a source of ideas and, on the other, a warning and a potential threat to the Russian state. The receptivity of Catherine the Great (1762–96) to the ideas of the Enlightenment can be understood in these terms. The concept of enlightened despotism in particular combined Russian hopes for social development while preserving the powers of the monarch and the state. The ideas associated with the revolution in France from 1789, however, posed a much more formidable threat. Victory over Napoleon in 1812 boosted the monarchy's self-confidence but unleashed forces that the autocracy ultimately could not contain. The nineteenth century for Russia was a period of great achievements, especially in the industrial and cultural fields, but also one of accumulating tensions that were ultimately to destroy the old regime.

The dominance of the state was accompanied by the weakness of social estates. Western feudal ideas of the rights and duties of monarchs as well as of subjects made little headway in Russia. Max Weber talked of certain countries where there was a patrimonial relationship between the state and society in which the rights of sovereignty and the rights of property became indistinguishable. The land and the people were treated as the property of the monarch or, in modern parlance, the property of the state. The Russian patrimonial state stood in sharp contrast to the Western system where feudalism stressed a sharp demarcation between the state and society, expressed in conflicts between the monarch and the aristocracy. The counterpart of the dominance of the state was the weakness of representative institutions. Their development was stifled by the Mongol invasions and in their place the cruel tyrannies of the type of Ivan the Terrible emerged. It was Ivan who in the 1580s put an end to the alternative pattern of development represented by the Novgorod republic and its popular assembly, the *Veche*. The germs of Russian representative institutions such as the Duma of Boyars, the *Veche*, and the broader body, the *Zemskii Sobor* (Assembly of the Land), had disappeared by the end of the seventeenth century. The rapid advance of serfdom further undermined the roots of popular representation.

A ubiquitous state bureaucracy was created which tried to run society as the general staff runs an army. Peter the Great systematised the Russian scheme of government into an elaborate Table of Ranks, with carefully defined gradations for government officials, and at whose head stood the autocratic monarch. The centralised Tsarist bureaucracy exerted a powerful influence on the country's social, political and economic life. The Russian nobility was never able to establish a degree of autonomy based on independent land ownership or administrative authority but instead was bound to the monarch. Furthermore, the state stifled the emergence of an indigenous mercantile bourgeoisie by relying on state monopolies. From the time of Peter the Great the Russian Orthodox Church was thoroughly subordinated to the crown, with its Patriarch abolished and affairs run by a synod responsible to the Tsar. According to Richard Pipes the patrimonial state was converted into a 'bureaucratic-police state' from the reign of Nicholas I (1825–55).[1] The dominance of the Russian state hampered the development of civil society, the social arena of independent economic activity, social movements and civil associations. The distinctive pattern of Russian development also hindered the emergence of a middle class, or indeed of a bourgeoisie, that could effectively challenge the state. There was little tradition of autonomous group activity, including trade union activity. The conduct of politics, defined as the attempt to influence the distribution of power, was forced into oblique if not into outright subversive forms.

Alexis de Tocqueville in his *The Old Regime and the Revolution* pointed out the continuities in French political culture after the revolution of 1789. Similarly, in Russia these six features of Russian political culture – a distinctive religion, isolation, an expansionist drive, the dialectic between backwardness and modernisation stimulating the dominance of the state, the weak development of representative institutions and society, and the bureaucratic attempt to replace politics by administration – to varying degrees link the Soviet regime with its Tsarist predecessor. As we shall see, however, 1917 marked a sharp break in continuity and the roots of the Soviet system were to be found as much in the ideological and organisational principles of Marxism–Leninism as in the patterns of history or of a distinctively Russian political culture.

Not least of the differences were the strict limits to autocratic power, termed 'constrained autocracy' by Nicolai Petro.[2] Tsarist authoritarianism was limited by private property, foreign travel and the inhibitions of the government itself. Klyuchevskii pointed out that the Tsars of Moscow might well have been all-powerful with regard to the people but they had no power to modify social relations. The Bolsheviks, on the other hand, set themselves precisely the task of remoulding all of society. Furthermore, the traditional picture of the 'peculiarities of Russian history' was changing rapidly in the half-century before the revolutions of 1917. The legal reforms of Alexander II (1855–81) of 1864 established an equitable system of courts and provided for independent judges and a twelve-person jury, although the peasantry retained its customary law. In the same year Alexander systematised the system of local government with the creation of *zemstvos* (representative institutions responsible for local health, education and so on) in rural areas. However, the great reforms in the era of Alexander II were limited, and in some cases rolled back in his later years and by his successors Alexander III (1881–94) and the last Tsar, Nicholas II (1894–1917). In political trials there were major violations of the principles of the 1864 reform, prompted in part by the terrorism launched by sections of the radical intelligentsia. In nationality policy the earlier 'imperial' or supranational approach to the non-Russian nationalities in the 1880s changed to a more narrow 'Great Russia' policy of Russification. The Poles, Jews and Muslims were especially harshly treated.

Not all was lost of the great reforms, and Alexander III came into sharp conflict with his own officials when he attempted to reverse them. The bureaucracy and the government were able to resist the monarch's authority because of respect for established traditions and the monarch's need for professional expertise. The *zemstvos* and municipal authorities survived the reaction, though not unscathed, and were responsible for a wide range of medical and social improvements by the eve of the revolution. An educated and critical public opinion emerged, symbolised by the spread of 'thick journals' (*tolstye zhurnaly*), read throughout the empire by concerned citizens. The last years of Tsarism were marked by a religious renaissance and a cultural 'silver age' whose luminaries included Andrei Bely, Alexander Blok, Anna Akhmatova and Marina Tsvetaeva. The system of orders was disintegrating to be replaced by the emergence of distinct social classes. Russian society was looking more and more modern on the eve of the revolution.

SOCIAL AND ECONOMIC DEVELOPMENTS TO 1917

The Crimean War starkly revealed the disparity between Russia's great power pretensions and its actual military and economic capacities when faced with more modern armies. Russia's defeat demonstrated that its great power status could not be sustained without the modernisation of the economy, and in a sense this was the theme of Russian and Soviet history thereafter. However, the options open to a country on the verge of reform are never so clear-cut as they appear to posterity. Three times in modern Russian and Soviet history the government and intelligentsia have been racked by a debate about the means and paths of economic modernisation. The first was in the second half of the nineteenth century, the second was in the 1920s, and the third rumbled on from the death of Stalin in 1953 to the collapse of the Soviet Union in 1991, and in a sense is not yet resolved.

The basic questions in the nineteenth century were a combination of economic and political issues: the nature of the Russian state and its role in economic development; the degree of capitalist development in Russia; did Russia have to undergo the transitional phase of a bourgeois system or could it pass directly to socialism; what role could the Russian peasant commune (the *mir*) play in this transition; and could the peasantry, rather than the working class, act as the major revolutionary class? Underlying our understanding of these debates is the question of the prospects for an evolutionary outcome to Russia's development if the country had not entered the First World War in August 1914. Would Russia have been able to settle down to a path of capitalist development and bourgeois dominance? The debates over the nature of the Tsarist economy and over appropriate economic policies had a continuing relevance as the peasant societies of the 'Third World' sought viable patterns of development.

Russia in the nineteenth century was balanced between capitalist development and the patriarchal economy. The chief feature of Russia's economic retardation was the large and unproductive agricultural sector. Serfdom, long a symbol of Russia's backwardness, had been consolidated by the state in the seventeenth century as a military and civil measure rather than as a privilege granted to the nobility. The peasant emancipation of 1861, introduced in response to the shock of defeat in the Crimean War, was only partial and did not bring into being a prosperous peasantry which could have stimulated economic development. Its economic effects were largely negative: either the peasant received too little land or was burdened by redemption payments on a larger parcel. The peasantry received only about half of the land that it had cultivated earlier. The emancipation depressed the peasant's purchasing power and hence undermined the development of a domestic market for manufactured goods. It failed to provide a cheap mobile labour force for the factories. A key anomaly of the emancipation was the retention of the communal system, the *obshchina*, organised on the basis of the *mir*. Most peasant land was held collectively and periodically redistributed to take into account changes in the size of a family. The communal structure discouraged the development of modern farming methods and depressed productivity. By the turn of the century the shortage of land, caused by a rapidly expanding population, generated enormous social discontent.

Effects of the Crimean War ; the peasant emancipation of 1861

The pattern of industrialisation which followed the Crimean War was designed, in part, to enhance Russia's military potential. The involvement of the state in the industrialisation process was a legacy of the Russian tradition of state prominence, but it was also a sign of backwardness. The only way for Russia to catch up with the advancing economies of Western Europe was for the state to take a leading role. There was considerable economic development from the 1830s with the construction of the railways, designed primarily to export grain. In a programme devised by the minister of finance, Sergei Witte, in the 1890s Russia embarked on a vigorous attempt to stimulate industrial expansion by liberalising credit facilities, allowing expanding state budget deficits, taking foreign loans (especially from France), and imposing protectionist tariff barriers. The casualty of industrial expansion was, as usual, the peasantry as they were 'squeezed' ever harder through heavy taxes and high grain exports, even when famine struck the villages in 1891 and 1896, to service the debt and loans and maintain Russia's credit-worthiness. A massive state-sponsored industrialisation was grafted on to a peasant economy, causing untold social strains. The economic results, however, were impressive, with an average annual growth rate of over 8 per cent in the 1890s.

Economic and social developments began to change the old pattern of autocracy to allow the emergence of a quasi-capitalist state. An essential feature of modernisation theory is the stress on the links between self-sustaining economic growth, reforms favouring social mobility and political modernisation incorporating the aspirations of groups in society. These conditions were developing, if only slowly, in Tsarist Russia. Private initiative played an important and often underrated part in Russian economic development. The role of the state was balanced by a strong autonomous domestic contribution to economic development. Paul Gregory has provided higher estimates of the independent contribution of agriculture to the industrialisation process, while Olga Crisp demonstrated that from the eighteenth century there was a spontaneous stream of industrialisation, notably in the textile and food industries. Furthermore, the degree to which Witte's industrialisation drive was consciously state sponsored has often been exaggerated. There is much evidence of bitter conflict in the government, and the industrialisation-inducing measures were not so much part of a consciously planned programme but the result of bureaucratic in-fighting. The state played a key role, but the pattern of industrialisation differed markedly from that established by Stalin from the late 1920s. The consumer-goods industries developed together with heavy industry, and the municipalities took an increasingly important role. By 1914 only 8.3 per cent of total estimated wealth was in the state sector, whereas over a quarter was in the public co-operative sector.

Alexander Gerschenkron argues that after the state-sponsored industrialisation drive of the 1890s the state could afford to take a less prominent role. Reforms from 1907 pushed through by the prime minister, Peter Stolypin, allowed peasants to move out of the communes to set up separate farms to create an expanding domestic market to stimulate manufacturing industry. The emerging commercial banking network could take over from the state the financing of investment. For Gerschenkron, the outbreak of the First World War interrupted an otherwise successful process of economic modernisation in Russia. This schema shares some features with Walt Rostow's modernisation theory where economies pass through five stages: traditional; preconditions for take-off; the economic take-off phase itself; the drive to maturity; and finally the onset of the age of mass consumption. The take-off period, according to Rostow, lasts about twenty years and in Russia took place between 1890 and 1914.

In *The Development of Capitalism in Russia* (1899) Vladimir Ilich Ulyanov, known to posterity as Lenin, argued that capitalism had made major inroads into the Russian economy and agriculture. The country, he asserted, was acquiring the economic preconditions for socialism, and in addition the social strains generated by industrialisation created the political conditions for revolution. A large class of peasants was losing its land and being forced to become wage labourers whom he expected to ally with the urban workers. Economic development saw the emergence of a significant working class, although the common practice of locating factories in the countryside blurred the distinction between peasants and workers. By 1913, 3.5 million were in the factories out of a total population at that time of 150 million. Most retained some contact with the villages and kept their land within the communal system. The pattern of Russian industrialisation has been called uneven development, where backward countries skip stages to catch up with the more advanced, This leads to the insertion of advanced capitalism into agrarian societies, and to a high degree of concentration of the labour force. In Petrograd, for example, huge factories such as the Putilov metal plant employed about 50,000 workers in 1914.[3] Despite vigorous attempts by the municipal authorities to improve living conditions, often provoked by scathing reports by the government factory inspectorate, workers' living conditions, especially for the unskilled, remained appalling and marked by long hours, crude barrack-type housing, poor hygiene, low wages and an exceptionally high accident rate.

Despite major economic and social advances prior to the First World War, Russia's 'backwardness' still consisted of two key features: a large peasantry only loosely integrated into a national market and culture; and a weak entrepreneurial class still stifled by state tutelage. The patrimonial legacy of the Russian state became modernised in the form of its conversion to state paternalism designed to restrain the bitter class conflicts and contestatory politics typical of Western European and American industrialisation. Following the eruption of the first major workers' strikes in the 1880s the autocracy was unable to develop an effective response which could have secured the loyalty of the working class to the monarchy and capitalism. The autocratic state clung to the bureaucratic image of itself as being above contending social forces and the ultimate arbiter of all political affairs. The state tried to protect the interests of both the employer and the employees. Its policies veered between the repressive and the paternalistic. Police trade unions were formed under S. Zubatov – a former revolutionary who came to head the Moscow Okhrana (secret police) from 1896 to 1902 – who pioneered brilliant counter-insurgency techniques designed to convert socialists into monarchist trade unionists.

The ten years from 1905 were marked by astonishing economic progress, with extensions to the railway system and the doubling of its traffic and revenue. Consumption statistics show great improvements in the standard of living, and the production of consumer goods was higher than in Germany. The industrial sector represented not so much an enclave, as is common in developing countries, but was organically linked to the rest of the economy through market and financial ties. By 1914 the vigorous social and economic developments of the past half-century had closed the gap between Russia and the more developed countries and had elevated it to fifth place in the league of industrial powers. Hegemonic strategies of rule were being devised that sought to bridge the gulf between state and society, the privileged and the outcast, with developments in the old capital of Moscow standing in sharp contrast to the polarisation in St Petersburg.[4] However, while socio-economic progress was encouraged, the autocracy tried to retain its political pre-eminence. The shooting of workers in the Lena River gold mines in 1912 precipitated a surge of industrial unrest that lasted until the outbreak of war. Powerful social and political conflicts remained unresolved.

REVOLUTIONARY MOVEMENTS AND BOLSHEVISM

During the nineteenth century the crown's claim to a monopoly of power in the state was increasingly challenged. With only decreasing justification could Russia fulfil Weber's definition of a state as 'a community that (successfully) claims the monopoly of the legitimate use of physical force within a given territory'.[5] The old regime came to be challenged by three major social philosophies: the liberal, the populist and what came to be known as Marxism–Leninism. These political challenges were interwoven with alternative economic programmes.

French revolutionary ideas were transmitted back to Russia by the officers of the imperial army who had helped defeat Napoleon in 1815. A period of revolutionary debate and plotting climaxed with a rising, sometimes called the first Russian revolution, on Senate Square in St *Decembrists* Petersburg on 14 December 1825 against Nicholas I. The Decembrists, as the movement became known, aimed to establish a democratic 'republic'. Although divided between Southern and Northern groups, the quality of their thought, the emphasis on establishing a constitutional system and their qualms over spilling blood mark them out as imaginative, if hesitant, revolutionaries. The uprising signalled the onset of a century of revolutionary activity in Russia.

The liberal view of development took England as its model in which economic and political advances reinforced each other. Economic modernisation, the development of a capitalist agriculture and industrialisation, they hoped, would promote and sustain a democratic govern- *Liberals* mental system. The reforms of the 1860s buoyed their hopes for such an evolution, but their *or the* spirits were dampened by the reaction that set in under Alexander III. The liberals were par- *Constitutional* ticularly active in local self-government (the *zemstvos*), where they were able to achieve 'small *Democrats* deeds' in education, welfare and administration. Nicholas II's inaugural speech of 17 January *(Kadets)* 1895, however, dampened hopes of reform by talking of the 'senseless dreams' of liberals who hoped to raise their perspectives from local to national concerns. The torch of liberalism gradually passed from gentry activists to the intelligentsia, and in the process took on a more challenging guise which George Fischer dubbed 'have-not' liberalism typical of underdeveloped countries. This was increasingly willing to challenge the existing illiberal regime and to demand a constitutional government bounded by laws and institutional liberties. Deprived of effective political and institutional channels to advance their cause, liberals turned to the press to argue their case. Only in 1905 were they able to create the natural vehicle for liberalism, a political party. The career of Paul Milyukov, the leader of the Constitutional Democrat (Kadet) party, was symbolic of the fate of liberalism in Russia as a whole, inclined to extremism and lacking firm social roots. The weakness of liberalism in Russia reflected the underdeveloped tradition of autonomous group movements.

A marked feature of the Russian democratic intelligentsia borne of the gentry was that it tended towards illiberality from the outset. The democratic movement in Russia was consistently anti-capitalist and anti-bourgeois, perhaps because it began as a movement of nobles, and their philosophy was opposed to Western individualism and materialism. Alexander Herzen, the finest example of this proto-populist tendency, forged the strivings and hopes of the intellectuals into an effective anti-government political ideology in which they would lead the people to a better future. The radical intelligentsia held to abstract ideals that became ever more suffused with the spirit of grandiose social engineering and not with the liberal principles of freedom and democracy. This spirit was taken to the extreme by Lenin, who came from a rising intelligentsia family in Simbirsk (Ulyanovsk). Lenin always displayed a profound contempt for liberalism and all its works.

Russian and Soviet history was marked by a profound ambiguity over Russia's Europeanness. Echoes of the controversy in the 1830s between the Slavophiles and the Westernisers can be heard throughout later debates to this day. The Slavophiles contended that each country should follow its historic mission and that Russia's path diverged from that of the West. The Westernisers insisted that Russia was a European country and that its uniqueness represented backwardness, and hence the major task for Russia was to modernise on the Western pattern. The Slavophiles condemned Peter the Great for having undermined traditional Russian life, for having humbled the Orthodox Church and for having imposed an alien Western culture on the upper classes, whereas the Westernisers praised him for attempting to modernise the country. The Westernisers lauded the rationalism, individualism and legal formalism of the West, whereas the Slavophiles extolled the mystic inner truth of the Russian people and the Orthodox religion. Their social ideal focused on a paternalistic government, communal landholding and the peasant collectivist tradition of self-government.

After the failure of the liberal 1848 revolutions throughout Europe, sections of the Russian intelligentsia abandoned hopes for liberalism and parliamentary reform and placed their hopes on the peasantry. This vast mass, which comprised 90 per cent of the population, seemed to represent a dormant power that only needed to be roused in order to shatter the autocracy. It was from this point that the Russian intelligentsia took on an increasingly authoritarian and illiberal guise. Its passion for justice took precedence over liberty, and it was increasingly willing to use violence to achieve its aims. The Russian Populists (or *Narodniks*) were a diffuse tendency whose programme found a ready response among the intelligentsia. They echoed Herzen's suggestion that Russia represented a special case and could escape the capitalist phase of development. They rejected the need for capitalist industrialisation in Russia and instead placed their hopes on consolidating the land commune (the *mir*) and its collective way of life. Russia could evolve its own form of socialism without undergoing the preliminary capitalist phase of exploitation and wage slavery. They shared the Slavophile contempt for European constitutionalism and stressed the moral duty of the intelligentsia to enlighten the people.

The Land and Freedom (*Zemlya i Volya*) movement from the 1860s represented a back-to-the-land movement expressed through good works and urban benevolence to the exploited peasant. The programme was as fundamentally misconceived as it was clumsily executed. In summer 1874 the Populists tried to 'go to the people': an army of young people dressed up as peasants went to live in the villages to learn popular wisdom and instruct the peasants. In some places the villagers were bemused, in others they contacted the police leading to the arrest of over 800 activists. In 1876 a new Land and Freedom Party demanded that land be given to the peasants and that the state should be destroyed in the name of collectivism. The weakness of the programme was compensated for by a growing reliance on strong organisation. For the first time a revolutionary party no longer based itself on the mass of the people and began a programme of terrorism. In 1878 Vera Zasulich shot and wounded the governor of Petersburg, General Trepov. In 1879 a secret organisation called People's Will (*Narodnaya Volya*) was created to fight for political freedom. The campaign of bomb-throwing and assassination culminated in March 1881 with the murder of Alexander II, the 'Tsar liberator'. The foundation of the Socialist Revolutionary (SR) Party in 1900 represented a fusion of terroristic principle with the practice of mass agitation. The SR leader, Victor Chernov, insisted that the solution to peasant grievances lay in the redistribution of state and gentry land to the peasants, and not so much in the abolition of the commune or industrialisation. The party was essentially a loose coalition of anti-bourgeois forces and, although it re-

nounced utopian socialism in favour of so-called 'scientific socialism', the party remained
resolutely opposed to Marxism.

The evolution of the Populists illustrates a major theme in the development of the Russian
revolutionary movement: the increasing emphasis on conspiracy and the principle of the small
number exerting leverage at the crucial spot to effect major changes. S. G. Nechaev in the late
1860s advocated terror and was the first to use cells and conspiracy. A much more sophisticated
version was developed by Peter Tkachev, a follower of the French revolutionary August Blanqui,
and one of the leaders of the People's Will party. He insisted that only a tightly knit group of
professional underground revolutionaries could evade the police. Nechaev and Tkachev represented a shift not only in organisational tactics, but also in theoretical principle. They required
the absolute subordination of the individual to the revolution, a belief in the conscious minority who would remould the world, and argued that in service of the cause the end always
justified the means. The terror campaign, however, only succeeded in making the autocracy
more obdurate and repressive. The accession of Alexander III in 1881 saw a more mystical if
no less vigorous assertion of the power of the throne summed up by the slogan developed by
Count Sergei Uvarov in the 1820s of 'Autocracy, Orthodoxy and Nationality', a policy continued by his successor Nicholas II. He supported the Union of Russian People organised in
'Black Hundreds' who used the Jews and foreigners as scapegoats to compensate for what they
considered the declining cohesion of Russian society. The blockage of reforms 'from above'
only intensified the struggle for change 'from below'.

The third major challenge to the autocracy came from the Marxists. Marx argued that 'the
more developed society shows to the less developed the image of its own future', and yet even
he was willing to countenance the Populist belief that Russia could avoid the Western path of
capitalist development and move directly to socialism on the basis of peasant collective traditions. In 1878 he wrote that 'if Russia continues along the road she has followed since 1861, she
will forego the finest opportunity that history has ever placed before a nation and will undergo
all the fateful misfortune of capitalist development'.[6] In a series of draft letters to Vera Zasulich
in 1881 he explored the possibility that under certain conditions the commune might become
the kernel of a regenerated Russia.[7]

Marx's followers in Russia, however, insisted that capitalism was as much an essential stage
of development for Russia as it was for the West. Marx's late thoughts on the communal option
were ignored, or not known. George Plekhanov, the 'father' of Russian social democracy and
one of the founders of the Emancipation of Labour group in Geneva in 1883, together with
Pavel Axelrod and Vera Zasulich, insisted that the immediate future belonged to capitalism.
Plekhanov argued that the peasant commune was no more than a fiscal device used by the
government to obtain taxes, and Lenin and he ridiculed the Populist belief that the *mir* could
form the basis for socialism in Russia. The Marxists supported the Tsarist efforts to industrialise since it was creating the economic base for socialism. Moreover, according to their theory
of class conflict, it was developing its own gravedigger, the proletariat. From the 1890s a number
of so-called 'Legal Marxists', most notably Peter Struve, argued that the development of capitalism was in the long-term interests of the labour movement. Such 'economism' emphasised
that Russia would have to go through the economic stages outlined by Marx, and yet the
question remained whether it would have to go through the same political stages: the ascendancy of the bourgeoisie and only then the socialist revolution carried out by the proletariat.

In a process which has often been seen as the assimilation of Marxism to Russian traditions,
Lenin tried to weld the Russian Social Democratic Labour Party (RSDLP), founded in Minsk

in 1898, into a single organisation. He attacked the Economist argument that the working class should restrict its struggles to economic rather than political issues while waiting for the economy to develop. The newspaper *Iskra* (*Spark*), founded by Lenin, Julius Martov, Plekhanov and others in 1900, helped bridge the gap between the workers and the intelligentsia, but served to divide the social democratic movement. In 1902 Lenin published his crucial pamphlet *What Is To Be Done?* which outlined his concept of a tightly knit organisation of dedicated revolutionaries who would lead the class struggle of the proletariat. Somewhat reminiscent of the Tkachev principle of the small number, Lenin wrote 'Give us a revolutionary organisation and we will turn Russia upside down.' At the second congress of the RSDLP in 1903 in London Martov defended a broader definition of party membership. The division was over Lenin's wording in the party programme of 'personal participation', in contrast to Martov's looser 'personal support'. The actual vote on the party statutes was lost by Lenin, but his group achieved a majority of two in the elections to the editorial board of *Iskra* and hence adopted the name Bolsheviks ('the majority') and Martov's group was left with the inglorious name of 'the minority' (Mensheviks).

The focus of Lenin's political thinking was opposition to passivity and wishful hopes for the spontaneous development of the revolution. Lenin argued that the working class on its own could only develop a trade union consciousness (i.e. would only concern itself with wages, conditions and so on, and not with changing the fundamental exploitative structure of society) and hence needed to be guided from outside by the revolutionary party. The critical role of the intelligentsia in devising the revolutionary programme and leading the masses was clearly reminiscent of the Populists, and indeed Lenin drew many of his ideas, including some of his thoughts on party organisation, from them. Lenin modified Marx's thinking about revolutionary organisation, which had stressed that the liberation of the working class would be achieved by the working class itself: it would first become a class 'in itself', and then a class 'for itself'. In Lenin's theory, as Trotsky (who was not yet a Bolshevik) prophetically pointed out, there was the danger of the party substituting for the working class, and the process would not stop there: 'The party is replaced by the organisation of the party, the organisation by the Central Committee, and finally the Central Committee by the dictator.'[8]

The problem still remained of how to make the revolution in Russia. The theory of autocratic power increasingly came into conflict with the modernising impulse of the Russian state. There was a fundamental incompatibility between imperial ambitions and the existing structure of power in a world undergoing a technological transformation. Could this transformation be grafted on to the autocratic system? Russian defeats in the Russo-Japanese War of 1904–05 confirmed the lessons of the Crimean War a half-century earlier: substantial reforms were required for the Russian state to meet the heavy demands of modern warfare. The Japanese were themselves a good example of how this grafting could be achieved, as was Germany. But could Russia emulate their achievements in assimilating technological modernisation and economic change to a conservative social and political framework?

For a number of reasons Russia was not able to achieve this in time and in the short term Russian failures in war abroad led to social revolution at home. On 9 January 1905 a demonstration led by Father Gapon, an Orthodox priest and labour organiser, demanded food and workers' rights. They were gunned down outside the Winter Palace by Cossacks, thus precipitating widespread worker and peasant unrest. In the October Manifesto of that year the monarchy was forced to concede a State Duma (parliament), unions and elements of the rule of law. Juridically a constitutional monarchy came into being. The year also witnessed the formation of soviets, organisations which began as workers' strike committees but which were to evolve into the constitutional basis of the communist state. Peasant discontent erupted in uprisings that dragged on into 1907 and which were suppressed by summary trials and executions. The monarchy was saved by the fact that the army as a whole remained loyal, yet the revolution was a clear warning that the survival of the autocracy was at stake. As Lenin put it, 1905 was a 'dress rehearsal' for 1917.

The 1905 revolution focused on a liberal programme of political demands, but already it was clear that the dynamism of the revolution came from mass action. The revolution demonstrated that the Tsar was no longer the unique source of authority and that society was capable of making and sustaining demands on it. As yet, the organisation of these demands was weak. The parties played little role in 1905, and the differences between the Bolsheviks and the Mensheviks were little understood, and their rivalry was unpopular in working-class circles. Events seemed to show that, contrary to Lenin's inclinations, spontaneity did indeed have a role to play in the Russian revolution.

For a brief period following the 1905 revolution it appeared that a path could be found between the demands of the revolutionaries and the resistance of the autocracy in a Russian form of constitutionalism represented by the State Duma. However, the Russian constitution (or Organic Laws) of 1906 placed few restrictions on the powers of the monarch, and failed to provide for a broad suffrage and a parliament to which governments would be responsible. The First Duma met in the spring of 1906 and saw the crystallisation of a number of parties. On the right the Octobrists, named after the Tsar's manifesto, were a loose grouping of business interests, conservative noble landowners and *zemstvo* gentry moderates. The Constitutional Democrats (Kadets), formed in 1905, were the major standard-bearers of the liberals, representing the more progressive intelligentsia of the capitals, the *zemstvo* gentry constitutionalists and the moderate intelligentsia in the provinces. They held the single largest block of seats in the First Duma, 196 seats out of 478. The Duma was boycotted by the SRs and the Social Democrats, and lasted two and a half months before it was dissolved on 20 July 1906, the government considering it too radical as the opposition was desperate to prove itself irreconcilable. The Second Duma, however, proved little less oppositional, and while the Kadet's total of seats fell to 92, the socialists, having given up their boycott, gained an impressive 113 seats. The Second Duma survived barely three months, from March to June 1907.

Gradually the Tsar restored order and could take back his concessions. In June 1907 Nicholas's most able prime minister, Stolypin, manipulated the electoral system to allow the gentry, whose economic power had been declining, to dominate the legislature. The Third Duma from 1907 to 1912, the 'landowners' Duma', proved amenable to the Tsar. The government did not restrict itself to a policy of repression. The Stolypin reforms in the countryside were attempts to buttress the Tsarist social system by the creation of an independent peasantry. Stolypin argued that the peasantry could be used to defeat the revolution, and to do this the government must free them from the commune and permit them to acquire private property. The principles of economic liberalism were introduced into peasant agriculture. This 'wager on the strong' only made the weak even more aware of the shortage of land, and in the short term did not markedly improve the technological level of Russian agriculture. Only a small minority of peasants by 1914 had established the Western-style farm (*khutor*). At the same time the regime shed some of its paternalistic ethos and took the first steps towards the liberal approach to labour. A law of March 1906 permitted the creation of trade unions to defend workers' interests. The monarchy tried to remove some of the causes of unrest by enacting some social legislation, as in the rather modest Social Insurance Laws of June 1912. The reforms fell short of the German social insurance laws promoted by Bismarck or the social legislation passed by the Liberal government in Britain from 1906. The development of a peculiarly Russian labour policy lacked sufficient vision and energy to divert the working class from its increasingly revolutionary path.

The Tsar alienated most of his sources of support. His relationship with the growing industrial middle class, for example, was not, as Soviet historiography tends to suggest, an easy one. The industrialists were unable to get their way in 1913 in their plans to replace the system of indirect taxation, which disadvantaged the industrial sector, in favour of a single progressive income tax. The alliance between the government, the landed classes and the bourgeoisie was strong enough to neutralise the forces of change, but not flexible enough to develop a programme of positive development. Liberal forces, it appeared, were simply too weak to sustain the Russian constitutional experiment. The major paradox is that as Russia modernised, the retention of a monarchical form of personalised rule inhibited the development of effective political institutions worthy of a modern state – a problem that faced the Soviet regime in its declining years. The incompatibility of the two created an almost permanent governmental crisis in the last years of the autocracy.

Learning from 1905 and its aftermath, Lenin insisted that the Russian middle class would not have the strength to make a bourgeois revolution (as in England, France or America). Instead, the working class, in alliance with the peasantry, would have to take the lead. Following the onset of severe repression in 1907 the Bolsheviks conducted both legal and illegal activity. This was the period of the spectacular expropriations, some of which were organised by Joseph Vissarionovich Djugashvili, who was to enter history under the name of Stalin. Lenin insisted that the Bolsheviks should take advantage of the opportunities allowed by the law and defeated 'recallism', the movement to recall deputies from the Duma and other bodies. In January 1912 at the Prague Congress the Bolsheviks constituted themselves as a separate party. They were just in time to take advantage of the massive upsurge in the workers' movement provoked by the shooting of unarmed workers in the Lena River gold fields on 4 April 1912. The incident provided the spark for the wave of labour unrest that lasted until the outbreak of the war in August 1914. The strikes gradually became 'political' in character, to which the employers responded with lockouts, fines and closures. Whether Russia entered the war in part to divert attention from the strikes is a moot point, although it appears that by the eve of hostilities the strikes were waning.

The consolidation of Russian constitutionalism was dealt a fatal blow by participation in the war. The Russian leaders, motivated by considerations of national prestige and trapped in the system of international alliances, entered the war on the side of Britain and France. Russian leaders had failed to learn that military adventures placed Russia's political system under intolerable strain and exacerbated the discontents smouldering in Russian society. An extensive moderate liberal opposition emerged. In the Fourth Duma (1912–17) opposition to the monarchy coalesced in August 1915 in a 'Progressive Bloc' of liberals who urged the creation of a responsible government, that is, one accountable to parliament. The Kadet leader Milyukov is a classic example of a liberal who virulently condemned the abuses of the monarchical system and yet defended the monarchical principle to the end. The inability of the monarch to work with the legislature ultimately provoked even his natural allies, the Octobrists, to join forces with the Progressive Bloc in demanding a responsible ministry. Outside the Duma liberal hopes focused on the national association of town and *zemstvo* unions (*zemgor*). The *zemstvo* union was formed during the Russo-Japanese War of 1904–05, and the union of towns in 1914, to assist the Tsar in prosecuting his wars. By 1916 they had become more hostile to the autocratic regime which they increasingly saw as one of the major obstacles to victory. Another centre of opposition was in the War Industry Committees, concentrated more narrowly on industrialists who sought to further the war effort. A debate continues over whether these three forces together made up the kernel of a 'bourgeois revolution', or whether, as Lenin and the Bolsheviks insisted, their own fear of popular movements ultimately transformed their temerity into cowardice, and hence undermined attempts at moderate reform.

During the war the Bolsheviks were isolated and persecuted. The party was mostly abroad and maintained only a vestigial presence underground in Russia. Severe repression destroyed internal organisation and sent worker activists to the front. In 1914 the majority of parties in the Second International, the grouping of European social democratic parties, put nation over class and voted for war credits, with the notable exception of the Russians and the Serbians. From the first Lenin insisted on a policy of defeatism and called for the transformation of the 'imperialist' war into a civil war which he hoped would lead on to revolution. Despite the signs of political and social crisis, however, as late as January 1917 Lenin admitted that it would be unlikely that he would see the revolution in his lifetime and left it as a bequest to the younger generation. A few weeks later the revolution broke out in Petrograd.

KEY TEXTS

Carr, E. H., *The Bolshevik Revolution, 1917–1923*, Vol. 1 (Harmondsworth, Pelican, 1966).

Kochan, L., *The Making of Modern Russia*, 2nd edn (London, Macmillan, 1983).

Pipes, R., *Russia under the Old Regime* (Harmondsworth, Pelican, 1974).

Raeff, Marc, *Understanding Imperial Russia: State and Society in the Old Regime*, trans. Arthur Goldhammer, foreword by John Keep (New York, Columbia University Press, 1984).

Riasanovsky, Nicholas V., *A History of Russia*, 4th edn (Oxford, Oxford University Press, 1984).

White, Stephen, 'The USSR: Patterns of Autocracy and Industrialism', in Archie Brown and Jack Gray (eds), *Political Culture and Political Change in Communist States* (London, Macmillan, 1979), pp. 25–63.

2 The creation of the Soviet state

Tsarism fell because of military reverses and war weariness, social strains sharpened by economic dislocation and incompetence, and the failure to create a government in which the Duma and the people could have faith. The influence of the drunken debauchee Grigorii Rasputin on the court further discredited the monarchy. The war acted as a catalyst, bringing out the underlying social and political tensions. Nicholas II's weak and vacillating character only exacerbated the political crisis at the heart of the Russian polity and thwarted the development of rational administration. Rather than making possible the consolidation of constitutional government, however, the removal of Tsarism only unleashed the social conflicts that had precipitated the revolution. After a mere eight months Russia's first experiment with democracy under the Provisional Government was brutally terminated by the Bolshevik seizure of power and the country was launched on a profound socialist experiment.

THE REVOLUTIONS OF 1917

From 23 February 1917 (Old Style, thirteen days behind the Western calendar until February 1918) strikes in St Petersburg protesting against food shortages gradually developed into wide-spread disturbances. The fate of the monarchy was sealed once mutinies broke out in the garrison as soldiers joined the demonstrators. On 3 March Nicholas II abdicated, bringing an end to the Romanov dynasty after 304 years. The revolutionaries had played little part in its fall. Power passed to a 'Provisional Committee' of the Duma which, indirectly, became the first Provisional Government headed by Prince G. E. Lvov, head of the union of *zemstvo*s and towns (*zemgor*), and based on the Kadet party. At the same time, power was shared with a hastily formed 'Provisional Executive Committee of the Petrograd Soviet', meeting in the Duma building, which energetically set about organising the revolution. The age of mass politics was thrust upon Russia in February 1917 with little preparation. The problem was how to reconstitute central authority in a society riven by class divisions and national jealousies while trying to conduct a war against a powerful antagonist. Ultimately the task proved impossible for the Provisional Government.

For most of 1917 Russia in effect had two governments sustained by antagonistic though not necessarily mutually exclusive ideologies. For the liberals and the bourgeoisie, and indeed for a large segment of the socialist leadership, the February events represented primarily a political revolution. Its tasks were seen as establishing a constitutional parliamentary system on the principles of universal suffrage, equality before the law and private property. A so-called bour-geois democratic republic was established amid scenes of national rejoicing in the days after the overthrow of the monarchy. The Provisional Government promised general elections to a Constituent Assembly which would adopt a constitution that would determine the structure of government. By April Lenin was able to declare that Russia was 'the freest country in the world'. There was a tremendous explosion of social organisations and popular political activity. These months showed that despite Russia's relatively backward socio-economic development and the restrictions imposed by the Tsarist regime on political life, there was a great capacity for the development of a vigorous public sphere. Everywhere one looked a committee was being formed and people were being drawn into struggles of one form or another. A distinctively Russian form of liberalism struggled to emerge which could combine social justice with political rights.

The second view of the revolution stressed its social character, an interpretation taken to the extreme by the Bolsheviks. The Provisional Government remained fundamentally out of step with the popular forces that had generated the revolution in the first place and which continued to propel it to the left until the denouement in October of that year. From the first the political revolution of February 1917 had the capacity of being transformed into a socialist revolution. The system of 'dual power' inaugurated in February meant that the government had to share power with the resurgent soviets, which were being formed the length and breadth of the country. The famous Order Number One of 1 March of the Petrograd Soviet called for the election of committees in all military units and contributed massively to the disintegration of the Russian army. The order deprived the government of control over troop dispositions. The soviets in 1917 were organised loosely, but soon their executive committees, composed of socialist politicians and intellectuals, came to dominate the rank-and-file delegates in the plenums.

Dual Power

The Provisional Government failed to consolidate its power for a number of policy and organisational reasons. Above all, the first Provisional Government considered the February revolution a protest against the inept conduct of the war by the Tsarist regime and not directed against the war itself. Foreign minister Milyukov's note to the Allies in April promising to fight until 'decisive victory' led to the fall of the government and the creation of the first coalition government, still under Lvov, which lasted from May to July. The new government included liberals and socialists, with the SR Alexander Kerensky as minister of war. The moderate socialists took a 'defensist' position in the war: insisting on the defence of Russian territory but rejecting any annexations or indemnities from the defeated powers. In June, under pressure from the French to divert German forces from the hard-pressed Western Front, Kerensky launched an ill-fated offensive in Galicia, hoping to take advantage of the expected revolutionary enthusiasm. He soon discovered that the concept of national defence was losing its meaning to hungry and exhausted soldiers and workers. Kerensky had fatally misinterpreted the French revolution where, as it has often been pointed out, the revolutionary war was launched three years after the revolution, whereas in Russia the revolution took place three years into a disastrous war. Lenin understood that war weariness was at the root of the revolution and Bolshevik anti-war agitation found a receptive audience. The failure of the offensive undermined the government's authority and led to the fall of the first coalition government; as John Bright remarked, 'war destroys the Government that makes it'. On 15 July tensions between the moderate socialists and the bourgeois parties led to the resignation of Lvov and four Kadet ministers and a second coalition government was formed, headed by Kerensky.

Lenin & the socialists

The unity of the multinational empire was undermined by the revolution and a number of peoples took advantage of the temporary weakness of central authority to break away. Finland declared itself independent, and the Ukrainians set up their own government in the form of the Rada. Disagreements over recognising the autonomy of the Ukraine led to the fall of the Lvov government. Muslim national movements developed rapidly in the course of 1917, while in the Caucasus the foundations were laid of an independent Georgia and Armenia. Nationalist demands within a multinational empire, in which Russians made up barely half of the population, were to remain a constant source of tensions for the Provisional Government and its successor.

missed opportunity by the government

The decline of Russia as a military force was hastened by the agrarian crisis. From May 1917 soldiers left the fronts to participate in a spontaneous and escalating wave of land seizure. The peasant communes in conjunction with the newly elected district committees became the *de facto* rulers of the countryside. Chernov, head of the SR party and now also minister of agriculture, was in a unique position to implement his party's land programme. This called for the socialisation of land, its transfer to the peasant communes to be distributed equally for personal use, and the banning of the hire of paid labour. However, wary of encouraging further desertions from the army by peasants eager to take part in land redistribution and intimidated by the complexity of land reform, the government made the fatal mistake of refusing to implement this programme in its entirety until sanctioned by the Constituent Assembly. The government thereby failed to gain the support of the peasantry, who ultimately simply took the land.

In industry, workers began to organise factory committees to defend themselves and to keep the factories open in the face of economic disruption and lockouts. The principle of private property and the power of the industrialists were challenged. The government was faced with a dire choice between supporting the workers' control movement or enforcing the principles of bourgeois democracy and private property, and hence the rights of the factory owners. The Bolshevik party supported the workers' but did not control what in effect constituted a revolution within the revolution. It is important to realise that the workers' movement in 1917 was not a homogeneous movement manipulated by a tightly organised Bolshevik party. The party itself was divided over policy, while there were major divisions within the working class, especially between skilled and unskilled, male and female, hereditary and new workers. The worsening economic crisis of 1917 was accompanied by a deepening radicalisation of the working class to which the Bolshevik party responded. By October 1917 the Bolsheviks appeared to be the only party offering a viable economic and social alternative to economic catastrophe and bourgeois dominance. The simple and basic issue of food shortages in the towns came to fuel the political struggle.

The rivalry between two sources of authority in 1917 was a contest between two philosophies and by October 1917 was transformed into a second revolution. On a range of issues the Provisional Government found itself not flowing with the current of demands and social pressures, but attempting to obstruct, divert or suppress them. The cumulative nature of these issues ultimately overwhelmed the government. The Kadets strove for a constitutional system and looked to the West for models, but they failed to tackle the key problems facing them. These were accurately reflected by the Bolshevik slogan of 'Peace, Bread, Land'. Lenin himself

Lenin's April Theses

returned from exile in Switzerland in a sealed railway carriage with the help of the Germans in April 1917. The Bolsheviks were by no means united over policy and Lenin was forced to wage a vigorous struggle to obstruct the natural inclinations of many moderate Bolsheviks to enter into coalition with other socialists like the Mensheviks or to give critical support to the government. In his April Theses Lenin sharply condemned the moderation of the leaders in Russia such as Stalin and L. B. Kamenev who prior to his return had been carried away by the general rejoicing at the fall of the autocracy. The theses sharply rejected as outmoded the orthodox social democratic advocacy (to which the Mensheviks remained loyal) of a two-stage revolution: the 'bourgeois' revolution had to be completed before socialism could be considered. Lenin insisted that a socialist revolution was on the agenda in Russia on the grounds that: first, alliance with the peasantry would give the working class strength to overthrow the old system; and second, theory of imperialism saw the revolution as only the first step in the world revolution, which would then come to the assistance of backward Russia. The first all-Russian conference of Bolsheviks (7–12 May 1917) adopted, though against considerable opposition, Lenin's views on the transfer of power to the soviets, the immediate giving of land to the peasants, workers' control in industry and the end of the war by spreading the revolution.

On 3–5 July a spontaneous revolution of exasperated workers and soldiers broke out in Petrograd. Bolshevik activists at the grass roots were heavily involved in transforming the accumulating tensions into a challenge to the government itself, a step which the Bolshevik leadership only reluctantly endorsed and which Lenin considered premature. The Bolsheviks had provoked but did not lead the 'July Days'. The moderate socialist leadership of the soviets categorically refused to take power. The government suppressed the disturbances at the cost of some 400 killed or wounded. Lenin and his colleague G. E. Zinoviev were forced to go into hiding, Kamenev was arrested and *Pravda* banned. [handwritten margin note: *Lenin goes into hiding 'July Days'.*]

In late August 1917 the military high command under General L. G. Kornilov moved to restore order by establishing a military dictatorship. The attempt met with no more success than Russian arms at the front and was repulsed by the Petrograd Soviet and the city's workers organised in Red Guard units. The Bolsheviks took the credit, however, and were rescued from the crisis in which they had languished since the July Days. In September they gained majorities in the Petrograd and Moscow city soviets. Kerensky's attempts to broaden the base of the regime by forming a third coalition government in late September failed to overcome the alienation of left and right. Driven by Lenin's urgings and against the warnings of Kamenev and Zinoviev, on 24 October the Bolsheviks organised by Trotsky moved to take power. Against weak resistance and with the majority of the population passive, the Bolsheviks took control of Petrograd and the Winter Palace. On the night of 24–25 October they presented the second congress of soviets with a *fait accompli*: power belonged to the Bolsheviks and the soviets. An exclusively Bolshevik government headed by Lenin called the Council of People's Commissars (Sovnarkom) was formed. The Bolsheviks in October 1917 were the beneficiaries of a broad coalition united only in despair at the ineffectiveness of the Provisional Government. [handwritten margin note: *Lenin & Bolsheviks take power once again*]

The nature of the October revolution has been hotly debated. This was the classical Leninist revolution, with small bodies of armed men waving red flags seizing power against the background of a cowed and frozen city. Only a relatively small number of people were involved in the fighting; the rest of the population looked on passively. The revolution did not overthrow a fully fledged bourgeois democratic state but one that was only beginning to develop. As in Weimar Germany after the First World War, a republic had emerged without republicans, a democracy without democrats. The Provisional Government lacked the time to establish the institutions of constitutional democracy, and its popular support was still weak. A new administrative machinery was only gradually emerging and the government was dependent on the voluntary co-operation of various agencies. In other words, the Bolsheviks struck not against a liberal democratic capitalist system but against one in the act of creation. [handwritten margin note: *October Revolution*]

The failure of the Provisional Government was as much the responsibility of the moderate socialist parties, the Mensheviks and the SRs, as it was of the liberal parties, primarily the

Kadets. All were increasingly tainted with the government's inability to deal with the problems facing the country. The moderate socialists failed to seize the initiative in policies. Their ideological dogmatism confined them to the pre-arranged scenario that capitalist development and the bourgeois revolution must precede socialism. The liberals understood but failed to define an adequate response to the fact that the Russian revolution was as much a social as a political revolution. Given a different set of circumstances – an end to the war, some economic stability, a unified revolutionary movement – then the February 'bourgeois' revolution might have survived. In the event the problems that had overwhelmed the Tsarist government engulfed the Provisional Government as well.

Neither the February nor the October revolution was caused by rising social classes bursting into prominence (the Marxist view); rather, a specific set of conjunctional factors was abetted by long-term social and political strains. The weakness of the Provisional Government might not have mattered so much if it had not had the misfortune of having its own resolute executioners to hand, the Bolsheviks. Only they offered a clear political and social alternative, however demagogic in detail it might have been. The demand to transfer power to the soviets offered the prospect of a break with old patterns of authority. It appeared to present an opportunity of improving their economic conditions and status. In October 1917 the aims of the social movements and that of the Bolsheviks coincided; together they swept away the old government and took the destiny of Russia into their hands.

THE FORMATION OF THE SOVIET STATE, 1918–21

The dictatorship of the proletariat and commune democracy

The revolution was tactically brilliant: Lenin admitted that an attempt a few days earlier might well have failed, a few days later and it would have been crushed. Theoretically, the revolution was justified by the theory of imperialism. Capitalism had become a world system and would not be able to survive once its weakest link, in this case Russia, was broken. In an early version of the domino theory, for Lenin the Russian revolution was only the beginning of the world revolution. It would set all of the developed world alight and Russia's own backwardness would be offset by foreign assistance. As it turned out, there was no successful general European revolution and Russia was forced to rely on its own resources.

The Bolshevik seizure of power was both a *coup d'état* and a revolution with a clear social and political logic of its own. The social demands reflected the fact that what had taken place was not simply a workers' revolution but also a peasant one. The Bolshevik decree 'On Land' of 26 October 1917 implemented the SR land programme, giving legal status to the wholesale redivision of land on egalitarian principles carried out by the village commune. The Bolsheviks were forced to compromise on their aim of introducing what they considered more modern forms of large agricultural holdings. The size and productivity of peasant allotments fell sharply but the neutrality, if not the loyalty, of the peasants had been secured, one of the essential conditions for Bolshevik victory in the Civil War.

The social demands of the workers focused on the defence of employment and ensuring food supplies. In the first months the regime conducted a 'Red Guard attack against capital'. The factory committees were given a juridicial status in a decree of 14 November 1917 to 'control' (supervise) the capitalist managements. The run-down in war orders in late 1917 provoked a massive economic crisis and growing unemployment. The factory system came to be maintained only through state support and subsidies. In the short term at least, rather than solving the economic crisis, the revolution only made things worse and by the spring of 1918 the inhabitants of the capital cities were on the verge of starvation.

The political concerns of the revolution were focused on the integration of the soviets into a new system of state power and an end to the war. The Bolsheviks on coming to power had no political blueprint which they proceeded to implement. As the first successful Marxist revolution they were forced to adapt their ideas to circumstances. The new government never pretended to favour generalised (liberal) freedom, but insisted that freedom was only for the working class and its allies. According to Marx, the period after the revolution was to be the dictatorship of the proletariat, a phase in which the working class was to maximise the use of state power in order to crush its enemies. Since the revolution would in principle be supported by the majority this period was expected to last merely a short time as it completed its unpleasant task, and then the socialist state could begin to wither away.

The key point in this theory was that the bourgeois state was to be smashed, and with it all the alleged left-overs from the past such as the rule of law, courts and the separation of powers. Power was to be consolidated on the model of the Paris Commune of 1871, extolled by Marx in his *Civil War in France*. The central features of commune democracy were the fusion of executive and legislative functions, the conversion of deputies from representatives to delegates who could be recalled by the electorate at any time, and a thorough-going egalitarianism in which no delegate was to be paid more than workmen's wages. Lenin took up these ideas in his *State and Revolution*, completed in September 1917, maintaining that in the post-revolutionary system there would be a great simplification of administrative functions so that a cook would be able to manage the affairs of state. The soviets were to act as the basis of this new system. Liberal democracy was to be replaced by a commune democracy which promised to end the division between state and society and to permit the broad participation of the people in public affairs. The model, however, was flawed since, as society develops, instead of becoming simpler administration becomes more complex and the division of labour intensifies. Little was said about who would do the managing in these circumstances. The fundamental problem was that no mechanism was established to ensure popular control over executive bodies. The commune model was an inclusive rather than contestatory type of democracy which denigrated the role of politics and independent associations in society. The absence of checks and balances allowed an enormous concentration of power, which when combined with the Bolshevik definition of themselves as 'doers' encouraged the growth of an unchecked dirigisme (commandism or leaderism). In 1916 Nikolai Bukharin had warned Lenin of the massive authoritarian potential of the modern state. Lenin preferred to believe that the destruction of the bourgeois state and the creation of the proletarian dictatorship based on commune democracy would solve the problems. It was an act of faith that was to have momentous consequences.

The Bolshevik party itself was not a united body on coming to power. It had grown from a small group of about 25,000 in February 1917 to something around 300,000 in October. Part of the perennial fascination of the early years of Bolshevik rule is the interaction between Bolshevik ideological principles and the realities of power. The collision gave rise to a series of vigorous controversies over policy and organisation.

The first major debate was over the organisation of Soviet power. The creation of an exclusively Bolshevik government in the Sovnarkom headed by Lenin on 25 October shocked and disappointed many radicals. The formation of Sovnarkom took power away from the Central Executive Committee (VTsIK) of the soviets in whose name the revolution had been made.

Power was transferred to a body responsible to no one but the Bolshevik party itself. A group including Kamenev, Zinoviev and A. I. Rykov insisted on the formation of a coalition government with some of the anti-war moderate socialists and envisaged a role for some organisations in addition to the soviets in the new system. They felt so strongly over the issue that they resigned from the new government, warning that Lenin's policies would lead to civil war. Lenin, inspired by the idea of commune democracy, insisted that power was to be based on the soviets alone, now dominated in the major cities by the Bolsheviks. Only a month later Lenin agreed to share power with the Left SRs, a group which constituted itself as a separate party in November. After a bitter struggle the coalitionists were defeated. This was the first instance of a major debate in a revolutionary party in power.

Their defeat opened the way for the destruction of the long-awaited representative assembly. In the elections to the Constituent Assembly in November 1917 the Bolsheviks maintained their hold on the cities of Petrograd and Moscow and gained almost a quarter of the total seats (147), but in the country as a whole the peasant-based Socialist Revolutionaries gained a large majority (410 delegates). It is difficult to gauge how different the results might have been if the elections had been held a month later, after the formal split of the SRs and when the Bolshevik land decree had become better known. The Assembly met on 5 January 1918 only to be dissolved that same day. Bukharin read a declaration stating that the Bolsheviks 'declare war without mercy against the bourgeois parliamentary republic'. Soviet Russia's constitutional experiment had come to an end before it had begun. Lenin claimed that a far higher form of democracy had been instated in Russia: commune democracy and the dictatorship of the proletariat. The shooting of workers demonstrating in favour of the Assembly illustrated the country's slide into civil war and gave notice that the coincidence of the social and political revolutions of October was beginning to unravel.

Civil War and armed peace

Soviet Russia's attempt to withdraw from the Great War nearly tore the Bolshevik party apart. Negotiations were begun at the border town of Brest-Litovsk in November 1917. Trotsky hoped to force concessions by threatening revolution behind German and Austrian lines, yet the Central Powers proved stubborn. With the Russian army disintegrating, due in part to the success of their earlier propaganda, the Bolsheviks were forced to concede vast territories containing some of the most valuable industries. The Treaty of Brest-Litovsk in March 1918 was bitterly opposed by a group of so-called Left Communists led by Bukharin who asserted that a revolutionary war should be waged to defend Russia and take the revolution to the 'imperialists'. The peace did not entail a rejection of the Bolshevik commitment to internationalism but it did represent a shift of emphasis to communist nationalism. The defence of the solid achievement of the Soviet revolution was regarded as the priority rather than the intangible benefits of trying to spread the revolution militarily. A by-product of the peace was the resignation of the Left SRs from the government to leave the Bolsheviks to rule alone.

In the 'breathing-space' following the Brest-Litovsk peace Lenin developed a strategy for Russia's development based on what he called *state capitalism*. Aware that the revolution had taken place in a relatively underdeveloped country and not in a mature capitalist society as anticipated by Marx, Lenin argued that the socialist state should compromise with elements of capitalism in order to further Russia's economic development. Lenin sought to emulate the successes of the German war economy based on the emergence of gigantic cartels but stripped off the bourgeois political system – the Krupp empire without the Krupps. Lenin negotiated with certain capitalists to form trusts through which he hoped that the enormous potential of modern industrial organisation could be harnessed to serve the socialist state. The compromise was to be with capitalism, not with the bourgeoisie or with bourgeois democracy.

The state capitalist period of April–May 1918 was accompanied by attempts to restore labour discipline and raise labour productivity in the factories, attended by enthusiasm for Frederick Taylor's time and motion studies on Ford production lines. For the first time a socialist state was forced to face up to the problem that egalitarianism in an industrial society tends to undermine labour productivity. The factory committees were subordinated to the Bolshevik trade union structure as the party sought to weaken syndicalist tendencies. Lenin's policies enraged the Left Communists. They insisted that the peace of Brest-Litovsk was economically disastrous, that the compromise with capitalists represented a betrayal of the interests of the working class and that any labour discipline should begin with the workers themselves. The debate was cut short by the onset of full-scale civil war from May 1918. On 28 June 1918 the bulk of Russian industry was nationalised, putting an end to state capitalism and compromises with capitalists.

The Civil War, from 1918 to 1920, was not an elemental disaster visited upon the Bolshevik state but was a logical consequence of Bolshevik policies, as the coalitionists had warned.[1] The Bolsheviks never denied that their seizure of power represented an act of war against the 'exploiting' classes and the 'imperialist' nations. During the Civil War fourteen countries intervened but in most respects it was a real civil war. The 'whites' were hampered by Bolshevik control of the centralised railway network focused on Moscow, by a divided command structure, relegation to the peripheries of the empire, the absence of a single inspiring alternative to the Bolsheviks, and the lack of support from the peasants accompanied by the hostility of the working class. They were unable even to harness the discontent of the nationalities to their cause since they were in favour of reconstituting the Russian empire.

In military affairs the Bolsheviks rapidly sloughed utopian visions of collective decision-making and reconciled themselves to the use of former Tsarist officers, known euphemistically as 'military specialists' (*spetsy*), thousands of whom were drafted to provide military expertise as commanders under the supervision of Bolshevik commissars. The war was fought by the Bolsheviks largely as a traditional war, with centralisation and military discipline. A regular army was recreated by Trotsky which was very different from the militia army long hoped for by Marxists, and indeed very different from the egalitarianism of the People's Liberation Army during the Chinese civil war. Opposition to traditional standing armies, however, was very much a Marxist conviction. The idea of a militia army lingered on into the 1920s as a way of integrating the army into society. Trotsky's attempt to militarise labour in 1920 was designed to redeploy the massive Red Army of 5 million created by that time to reconstruct the civilian economy. Instead of integrating the army into society, Trotsky sought to remodel society on the pattern of an army. The legacy of the Civil War was a militaristic approach to social and political administration.

War Communism

The Civil War was accompanied by War Communism, which lasted from mid-1918 to March 1921. War Communism represented the massive consolidation of state power and the extension of the revolution to all spheres of the economy and society in the belief that a rapid transition to socialism could be achieved. The concentration of national resources in the hands of central authority and their military disposition is called a mobilisation regime, the attempt by government to rule society directly.[2] It represented the apogee of nineteenth-century sociology with its utopian belief that a direct leap could be made into socialism by enacting social measures. The degree to which War Communist policies can be attributed to the pressures of fighting a war or to the intrinsic ideological convictions of the Bolshevik regime has been the subject of sharp controversy. In practice the Civil War acted as the catalyst which brought out the most radical features of Bolshevik ideology. War Communism was a distinctive blend of revolutionary enthusiasm and pragmatism. Some War Communist policies were not destined to outlive the Civil War, but others were to become a permanent part of Bolshevism in power.

In the countryside War Communism represented a system of transferring grain from the peasantry to the hungry urban working class. Armed detachments left the cities to take the alleged 'surpluses' from the peasantry, and at the same time to foment class war against the richer peasants, the kulaks. From May 1918 committees of the poor (*kombedy*) were established which attacked not only the kulaks but the middle peasants. By late 1918 the excesses and negative impact of such policies on the amount of grain available to the regime, accompanied by peasant uprisings, forced Lenin to modify the policy and make peace with the middle peasants, a foretaste of the compromise made with the peasantry as a whole in 1921. The requisitions were the characteristic feature of War Communism and continued until March 1921. Lenin called them a 'loan' from the peasantry to the working class, who were in no position to supply the countryside with much needed manufactured goods. Relations between the Soviet government and the peasantry were to remain uneasy.

In industry War Communism was marked by the gradual elimination of private property and enthusiasm for such schemes as the abolition of money. Mass nationalisation was provoked by the onset of war in June 1918, and was then extended to cover not only large plants but even the smaller ones, culminating in a decree of November 1920 nationalising the remaining small enterprises. The management of nationalised enterprises was not vested in the workers' collectives or the trade unions, but in special economic councils (*sovnarkhozy*), rising in a pyramidal structure to the Supreme Economic Council (Vesenkha) in Moscow. This system in effect represented a giant corporation divided into an ever-increasing number of branches (*glavki*). It held the whole economic life of the country in its hands but was not able to organise effectively even the smallest plants.

The rights of workers' organisations, the trade unions and workers' control commissions, were limited. In the chaotic circumstances of 1917 and early 1918 the workers' control commissions played a vital part in maintaining industry, but the role of workers' control was ambiguous from the start. After the October revolution there had been high hopes that the trade unions, incorporating the workers' control movement, would take over as the managers of the economy. The eighth party congress in March 1919 resolved that this would indeed ultimately be the case, but as the years passed this goal receded ever further into the future. The factory committees were gradually divested of any major supervisory role and were restricted to agitational functions. The tripartite system of factory management established in the first period after full-scale nationalisation, in which power was shared by the economic councils, the trade unions and the technical and managerial staff of plants, gave way by late 1920 to the imposition of one-person management.

This was a period of terrible economic decline. Industrial output by 1920 had fallen to only 15 per cent of the 1913 level while the harvest of 1921 was only 43 per cent that of 1913. The working class was drained by military mobilisations, and weakened by hunger and cold in the grim and unlit cities. Unemployment gave way to labour shortages and a system of compulsory labour conscription.

In the political sphere War Communism saw the consolidation of power in the hands of the communist party. The Kadet and other 'bourgeois' parties were outlawed in the days following the revolution. The press was from the first severely controlled by the Bolsheviks. Following an abortive uprising in July 1918 the Left SRs were outlawed. The position of the Mensheviks was more ambiguous since they refused to declare themselves in outright opposition to the Bolsheviks. They retained a lingering presence in the soviets until their destruction in the early 1920s.

The role of the Bolshevik party following the victorious revolution was ambivalent. In principle, once it had helped organise the revolution, power could be transferred to the working class organised in the soviets. But how was this to work in practice? As far as the Bolsheviks were concerned the soviets were unreliable since not only did they contain (a few) non-Bolshevik deputies, primarily Mensheviks, but they also represented the peasantry. Only the Bolshevik party represented the proletariat alone and hence was entitled to primacy. They were the repository of the higher revolutionary consciousness. This was the theoretical basis for the emergence of the one-party state and party control over the soviets. However, the practical implementation of these relations between the party and the state was a contentious one from the start. How could the party's 'leading role' be reconciled with meaningful political functions for the soviets? In a major debate over this issue a group of Bolsheviks, known as the Democratic Centralists from late 1918, insisted that the relationship should be based on a division of labour: the party would provide the ideological leadership; but the soviets should be respected as institutions representing the working class. The eighth party congress agreed that the party should 'guide' the soviets, and not 'replace' them, though this formulation left the details vague and the problem of substitutionalism (*podmena*) remained to the end. In effect a novel form of dual power was established which retained a revolutionary potential, one that was exploited by Gorbachev's reforms in the form of a revival of the slogan 'all power to the soviets'.

After the revolution the party sent its best cadres to work in the soviets and the commissariats, and as an organisation began to 'wither away' while the state expanded. The party committees, however, remained the kernel of the new political system. In 1918 there had been moves to restore organisational coherence to the party, and these attempts were intensified during War Communism. By March 1921 a uniform network of party committees had emerged under the central party secretariat in Moscow. The principles of democratic centralism, with the subordination of lower to the higher bodies, was established as earlier federal forms of organisation were undermined. The party cells in the factories and the army lost their earlier direct control over their respective institutions. War Communism saw the elimination of mass independent associations in society as they were replaced by special groups like the Komsomol (Communist League of Youth). All organisations were to be imbued with the 'party spirit' (*partiinost*), a fundamental principle of Soviet political life.

The War Communist political system was not internally coherent. On the organisational level it was riven not only by divisions between the party, on the one hand, and the soviets and the state mechanism in general, on the other, but the state organisations themselves were locked in struggle with each other. This was a period of massive institution-building: the economic ministries expanded their ambit; other commissariats, such as those of the interior and justice, sought to establish unchallenged authority in their spheres. These two commissariats in particular were challenged by the security police, the Cheka, established in December 1917, one of the most ambitious and uncontrollable bodies spawned in the early period of Soviet power. The Cheka represented a force to impose not only organisational unity but, and this was its original feature, ideological conformity. Attempts to establish effective party control over the Cheka failed.

While bureaucratic conflict between various institutions was rife, the whole problem of rampant bureaucracy was an obsession of the period. Its manifestations were legion: red tape, corruption and inefficiency. As the functions of the state expanded so the bureaucracy mush-roomed. Everywhere new committees and commissions were born regulating ever smaller segments of life. The fact that the whole vast apparatus did not work very well was usually attributed to 'minor inadequacies of the mechanism', and just one more reorganisation, it was asserted, would improve matters no end. The numbers employed in bureaucratic administra-tions swelled to make up over a third of the labour force. The Bolsheviks were at a loss to comprehend the omnipotence of bureaucracy, all the more so since the theory of commune democracy held that bureaucracy would disappear in its entirety. Lenin insisted it was a social problem and reflected the lack of culture of Russia. Others insisted that it was a legacy of the Tsarist regime that would be overcome in time. Such responses were rejected as inadequate by the perceptive Moscow Bolshevik E. N. Ignatov and the Democratic Centralists who insisted that structural factors were at work. The very fact that the Bolsheviks tried to run the whole life of the country from Moscow gave rise to the bureaucracy, they argued. The responses to the emergence of a native Soviet bureaucracy merged with the ideological debates of the period.

The oppositions

Bureaucratic conflicts were paralleled by ideological rifts. The coalitionists have already been mentioned, and the Left Communist critique of Bolshevik centralisation without adequate worker representation was to give rise to a series of oppositional groupings. Trotsky later in-sisted that during the Civil War the political culture of the Bolsheviks had become militarised, but it should be noted that there were powerful anti-militarisation forces in such oppositions as the Democratic Centralists and the Workers' Opposition. This was a period of profound ideo-logical restructuring as Marxist abstractions and Leninist organisational nostrums encoun-tered the harsh realities of building socialism in a war-torn country. The Democratic Centralists, as we have seen, fought for a partnership between the party and the soviets. The first Soviet constitution of July 1918 was long on declarations of principle (see Chapter 7), but left the institutional arrangements for the actual organisation of power extremely vague. The Demo-cratic Centralists hoped to remedy the situation by revising the constitution to safeguard the rights of lower-level bodies from the encroachments of the centre. By 1920 they insisted that the temporary infringements of lower-level rights, which they had been willing to tolerate during the Civil War, now had a tendency to become permanent.

In 1920–21 two interrelated but separate debates challenged the whole structure of power as it had taken shape during War Communism. The first issue focused on inner-party democ-racy and can be labelled the party debate. This covered such issues as free speech within the party, the rights of party cells, the functions of the committees and the role of leadership. The polarisation of society in 1917 between the *verkhi* (upper classes) and the *nizy* (lower classes) was by the end of the Civil War thoroughly internalised within the Bolshevik party, but now the *verkhi* were represented by higher party officials, and the *nizy* by the party's rank and file. The second debate focused on the trade unions. The Workers' Opposition led by Alexander Shlyapnikov and Alexandra Kollontai insisted that more rights should be vested in the direct expression of workers' organisation. The stifling of worker initiative in the economy should be replaced by a national congress of producers. Kollontai criticised the bureaucratic regulation of all aspects of social existence, which included the attempt to instil *partiinost* in dog lovers' clubs! Trotsky, on the other hand, took War Communist practices to their logical conclusion and insisted that the unions should be incorporated into the economic apparatus. Lenin ultimately took a middle path: the unions should remain independent and act as educators of the working class rather than the organisers of production.

By early 1921 War Communism was in crisis. Peasant revolts in the countryside, notably in Tambov, against the forced requisitioning were compounded by urban unrest. The protests climaxed in March 1921 with the revolt of workers and sailors at the Kronstadt naval fortress in the Gulf of Finland, formerly one of the strongholds of Bolshevism. The insurgents rallied under the slogan of 'soviets without Bolsheviks', denouncing the Bolshevik usurpation of the rights of the soviets. At the tenth party congress in that month economic concessions were balanced by the intensification of War Communist political processes. The first measures that were to lead to the New Economic Policy were launched, and in particular forced requisitioning from the peasantry was replaced by a fixed tax in kind. Lenin admitted that the attempt to continue the organisation of the economy by wartime means had been a mistake. War Communism, he insisted, had been necessitated by the war and dislocation but it was not a viable long-term policy. Lenin hoped to justify both the necessity of War Communism and its repeal.

The party debate was, as such, never resolved. A cosmetic programme of reform under the label of workers' democracy was instituted, but its effect was only to consolidate the powers of the committees and the party leadership in a process which first saw the use of the term *perestroika* (restructuring) in the Soviet context. The challenge to War Communist political relationships was not met by compromise but by repression. At the congress two decrees condemned the oppositional groupings and imposed a 'ban on factions', a 'temporary' measure which long remained a cardinal principle of Soviet rule.

The eight brief months of the Provisional Government proved to be a mere interregnum between two repressive systems. By 1921 a powerful new state had emerged in Russia following the virtual collapse of authority in 1917. Its grip on political life was almost total, even though its ability to govern the country was yet to be proved. All intermediary organisations in society, including working-class and non-Bolshevik socialist ones, were subordinated to the new authorities. Organised opposition within the party was no longer tolerated. A system based on hierarchy and coercion had become consolidated. This outcome was not an inevitable result of the pattern of Russian history with the veneration for the Tsar simply shifted to the Bolsheviks, and the ideology of absolutism drummed into the people over the ages transferred from one subject to another. Some of the problems faced by the Bolsheviks were similar to those of the Tsars, such as governing a vast territory, but their responses were very different. Tsarist authoritarianism cannot be held responsible for Bolshevik dirigisme since the Bolsheviks had come to power with the idea of achieving a certain programme, however much the precise speed and details of that programme were open to discussion. The new regime's own social base was weak, the political relationship between the party and class was ambiguous, and the institutional arrangements of the dictatorship of the proletariat and commune democracy made no provision for institutional or ideological bulwarks against authoritarianism. There was a tendency to reduce every sign of opposition to class contradictions. No distinction was made between opposition *within* the revolution and opposition *to* the revolution. Political debates were not integrated into the structure of Soviet power, though of necessity they were tolerated in the early years. The result was a peculiarly Leninist definition of socialism. The defeat of the oppositions in 1921 meant the end of the chance of the emergence of social bodies independent of the state under Soviet socialism. It was not so much Tsarist political culture but the new regime's own contradictions and ideological convictions that help explain these developments.

The Leninist revolution had a double – and contradictory – objective. The first concentrated on overthrowing the Europeanised elite and the destruction of Westernising social and political processes, a project justified by the attempt to smash the bourgeois state and to extirpate alienating capitalist relations. The second objective, however, ran counter to the first. In attempting to transform Soviet Russia into a modern industrial state the Bolsheviks required the technological sophistication of the West, a scientific rationality and political modernity. The West was both a model and anti-model: its productive capacities were to be emulated but its political system decried. As with Peter the Great and other Russian modernisers, they hoped to take Western technology without Western values.

The various oppositions of the Civil War years tried to answer the fundamental conundrum of why there was such a discrepancy between Marxist expectations of socialism and the realities of the Soviet republic. One approach was to lay responsibility on the fact that the revolution lacked the conditions laid down by Marx and instead took place in a relatively underdeveloped country with a small proletariat. The military demands of the Civil War and economic collapse further eroded the social basis of the regime. This led to the party-state massively expanding and ultimately acting as a substitute for the social movement that should have made and sustained the revolution. A second approach, favoured by Trotsky, held the absence of a world revolution responsible for domestic distortions. Isolation added force to later arguments in favour of accelerated industrialisation to provide a defensive base for the regime. A third view holds the Bolshevik ideology itself responsible. The critical dynamic between a relatively backward country and the distinctive ideology and mentality of the Bolshevik party was to have momentous consequences for the country and the revolution.

KEY TEXTS

Acton, Edward, *Rethinking the Russian Revolution* (London, Edward Arnold, 1990).
Carr, E. H., *The Russian Revolution from Lenin to Stalin, 1917–1929* (London, Macmillan, 1979).
Fitzpatrick, Sheila, *The Russian Revolution, 1917–1932* (Oxford, Oxford University Press, 1982).
Keep, John L. H., *The Russian Revolution: A Study in Mass Mobilisation* (London, Weidenfeld & Nicolson, 1976).
Kochan, Lionel, *Russia in Revolution* (London, Paladin, 1970).
Service, Robert, *The Russian Revolution: Culminations, Beginnings, Disruptions* (London, Macmillan, 1986).
Von Laue, Theodore H., *Why Lenin? Why Stalin?*, 2nd edn (Philadelphia, PA, Lippincott, 1971).
White, James D., *The Russian Revolution 1917–1921: A Short History* (London, Edward Arnold, 1994).
Wood, Alan, *The Origins of the Russian Revolution*, 2nd edn (London, Routledge, 1993).

3   Stalin and Stalinism

The New Economic Policy (NEP) was introduced in March 1921 in response to peasant hostility, worker unrest and political fragmentation within the communist party. The NEP was a concession but it soon gained adherents who argued that it was a system which could lay the basis for the transition to socialism in Russia. NEP represented another version of Soviet politics in contrast to the harshness of War Communism, and in some ways it took up the ideas of the state capitalist period of early 1918. Lenin personally was not long to preside over the new system. He suffered a stroke in May 1922 and after two more in late 1922 and March 1923 he died on 21 January 1924. The fate of the NEP became bound up with the succession struggle. Although Lenin had insisted that the 'NEP would last a long time and seriously', he added the ominous words – 'but not for ever'. Although Bukharin sought to transform the NEP into a long-term strategy for socialist development, others opposed its concessions to 'alien class forces' and by the end of the 1920s it was dead. The militant revolutionary strategy of Stalinism emerged, combining frenetic industrialisation, total collectivisation and cultural revolution, accompanied by the intensification of coercion and the elevation of the Stalinist personality cult to unprecedented levels. The Soviet Union triumphed in the Second World War, partly as a result of the industrial foundations laid in the 1930s, but the system bequeathed by Stalin proved fatally flawed.

THE NEP COMPROMISE

In 1921 the Bolsheviks found themselves in the position forecast by Plekhanov in 1883 when he argued that a socialist party would find itself in enormous difficulties if it took control in the absence of the necessary economic conditions for the realisation of its programme. Given such a premature revolution the party would be obliged to grant concessions to the very forces that socialism was pledged to eliminate. This is just what the Soviet government was forced to do. The enormous central economic monopolies were broken up, market relations were restored between the peasant villages and the urban economy, and free exchange and private enterprise were tolerated. Underlying the NEP was a compromise with the peasantry justified by the idea of a link (*smychka*) between them and the proletariat. The peasants were allowed to sell their surpluses on the market after having paid their tax in kind, usually grain, to the state. This was converted to a monetary tax in 1925.

NEP was not accompanied by a new political policy, and indeed Lenin insisted that, during a retreat, discipline was at a premium to avoid a rout. In the early 1920s the vestiges of non-Bolshevik parties were effectively eliminated. The trial of a group of leading Socialist

Revolutionaries in mid-1922 presaged the show trials of the 1930s. To compensate for the real and imaginary threats to Bolshevik rule the mystique and power of the party were enhanced all the more. The introduction of the NEP was accompanied by what was called a 'restructuring' (*perestroika*) of the party. The Bolshevik committees tightened their administrative control over local party organisations. Centralisation and conformity within the party were intensified just as they were being relaxed in the economy. In April 1922 Stalin became General Secretary of the party, a post at the time regarded as no more than that of a glorified filing clerk. In a consummate manner he consolidated the party machine and his own power over that machine. His ability to appoint, dismiss and transfer party officials prefigured the ubiquitous *nomenklatura* mechanism of later years and gave him a powerful weapon in the inner-party debates. A 'circular flow of power' (R. V. Daniels) was established whereby Stalin's appointees became beholden to him for their positions. Stalin became the beneficiary of a process of restructuring that had begun quite independently of him.

The struggle for Lenin's succession took the form of a personalised contest between Stalin, Trotsky and other leaders. At first Stalin cloaked his ambitions behind the triumvirate of Zinoviev, Kamenev and himself, which assumed the leadership at Lenin's request in late 1921, but gradually Stalin was able to dispense with subterfuge. The Lenin succession was complicated by the fact that no one knew what formal post constituted the leadership. As the Democratic Centralists had earlier charged, the system of government under Lenin was chaotic in the absence of the formal delineation of functions. Lenin himself was head of the government (Sovnarkom) and held no official party post, although dominating the party through his immense personal prestige.

In December 1922 Lenin, recovering from his first illness, dictated his 'Testament' which characterised the leading contenders. Bukharin's intellectuality was criticised, while the hesitations of Kamenev and Zinoviev in October 1917 were branded as not having been 'accidental'. Trotsky was accused of 'excessive self-assurance' and a 'preoccupation with the purely administrative side of work'. Stalin, rather surprisingly, was elevated as Trotsky's equal (Lenin had always worked much better with Stalin than with Trotsky), but Lenin noted that 'Comrade Stalin, having become General Secretary, has concentrated enormous power in his hands, and I am not sure whether he will always be capable of using that authority with sufficient caution'.[1] Lenin was dismayed by Stalin's rudeness at this time towards the Georgian communists, reflecting his lack of respect for nationalities, which reminded Lenin of the worst traditions of Russian chauvinism. The Testament exacerbated personal conflicts by drawing attention to the weaknesses of all the major leaders. Hearing of a personal affront to his wife Krupskaya, Lenin dropped his even-handed approach. In a postscript of 4 January 1923 Lenin accused Stalin of intolerable rudeness and urged his colleagues 'to think of removing Stalin from that post'. Trotsky's failure to make known Lenin's condemnation of Stalin's behaviour over the nationality question at the twelfth party congress in 1923 destroyed one of the best chances of suffocating Stalinism at birth. Lenin's failure to nominate his own successor or a replacement for Stalin was understandable but did not help matters.

The *perestroika* of the party following War Communism prompted forty-six leading party members in October 1923 to write a letter protesting against the suppression of party democracy. Trotsky took the opportunity to write his famous letter, known as *The New Course*, to the Central Committee warning against the consolidation of the party bureaucracy spawned during the Civil War. Tactlessly, he spoke slightingly of most of the Bolshevik leaders of 1917. Stalin's fellow triumvirs, Zinoviev and Kamenev, launched a ferocious attack, and both Trotsky and the forty-six were condemned by the thirteenth party congress in May 1924. Trotsky not only accepted the congress decision, but went so far as to support the assault against the opposition. Trotsky's behaviour between 1923 and his expulsion from the party in 1927 was contradictory, torn as he was between loyalty to the party and opposition to Stalin. His vacillations and appeasement actually disarmed and confused the anti-Stalin opposition; at the thirteenth congress he argued 'the party is always right … We can only be right with and by the party',[2] a statement that devalued any objective truth and undermined resistance to the ever-growing power of the Stalinist bureaucracy.

Lenin's last year was taken up by concerns over the succession and the formation of the USSR (see Chapter 15), but above all by the problem of bureaucracy. His last article, *Better Fewer, But Better*, was a bitter denunciation of the morass of bureaucratism in which the Soviet government found itself, but could suggest no effective solution. The great expansion in the Lenin Enrolment following his death and the continued recruitment swept a mass of new untested communists into the party. Between 1924 and 1928 party membership nearly trebled from 472,000 to 1,304,471, swamping the old generation of Bolsheviks. Trotsky later insisted that the mass recruitment of this time rendered the party machine, dominated by Stalin, almost completely independent of the rank and file.[3]

In late 1924 Trotsky's *The Lessons of October* was attacked by Zinoviev and Kamenev. Stalin in the guise of a moderate accused them of going too far: 'The policy of cutting off heads is fraught with dangers for the party.' In January 1925 Trotsky was deprived of his post as commissar of war, and 'Trotskyism' was officially condemned. At the fourteenth party congress in December 1925 Stalin appeared for the first time as *rapporteur* of the Central Committee, on which he now enjoyed a majority. Stalin's policies were endorsed by the congress, which had been packed with his supporters. Alarmed, Stalin's erstwhile co-leaders Zinoviev and Kamenev, who had been hopelessly outmanoeuvred, were even prepared to attack the NEP as part of their campaign against him. They joined forces with Trotsky in a United Opposition, which did little to enhance their reputations for integrity. Bukharin, the key supporter of the NEP, rallied to Stalin in defence of moderate economic policies. The opposition's appeal to the party's rank and file contravened the rules on party discipline and they were easily crushed by the Stalinist machine. In July 1926 Zinoviev was expelled from the Politburo, followed by Trotsky and Kamenev in October. In November 1927 the opposition in desperation took to the streets, and thus played into Stalin's hands. They were expelled from the party on 15 November 1927 and denounced by Bukharin at the fifteenth party congress in December 1927. Having defeated the United Opposition with Bukharin's assistance, Stalin moved to defeat Bukharin and what he called the Right Deviation. The succession struggle entered its final phase.

The NEP has often been seen as a golden age, a period of communist liberalism coming between the harshness of War Communism and the brutality of Stalinism in the 1930s. The NEP did indeed see an effervescence of cultural life, with a brilliant age of film-making by the likes of Sergei Eisenstein and Dziga Vertov. The *Smenavekh* (change of landmarks) movement from 1922 was an attempt by various intellectuals to act as a mediating force between the regime and cultural interests, a project which met with little success. Compared to what came later it was a period of cultural diversity, but already the empire-building of Soviet institutions that had begun during War Communism was being extended to the cultural sphere. The suicide of Sergei Yesenin in 1925 prefigured the despair that led to the death by his own hand of Vladimir Mayakovskii in 1930. Nadezhda Mandelstam has dismissed the myth of the 'happy twenties' as serving to disassociate contemporaries from the rise of Stalin, who alone is blamed for putting an end to the flowering of the arts, sciences and literature.[4]

THE GREAT INDUSTRIALISATION DEBATE

The tensions generated by the conflict between political concentration and economic liberalisation provided the context for the rise of Stalinism. The debate in the 1920s over the means to achieve the industrialisation of the Soviet Union represented the second phase of a controversy that had begun in the nineteenth century. At issue was the question of whether the NEP was a temporary expedient to allow the Soviet regime and economy to recuperate from the travails of the Civil War before launching a new offensive, or rather a more permanent attempt to establish a system appropriate for the long-term development of socialism. Like his evaluation of War Communism, Lenin's position on this question was open to opposed interpretations. At first, as noted, he insisted that it would last for a long time 'but not for ever', but by the end of his life he appears to have changed his mind. Instead of viewing the NEP as a tactical retreat, Lenin began to see it as lasting a considerable period and acting as a 'bridge into socialism'. Lenin hoped that by entering co-operatives and other joint endeavours the peasantry would gradually be won over to socialism. If he had lived his views might well have changed yet again, but it appears that he died convinced of the value of gradualism in Soviet economic policy.

The NEP had many achievements to its credit. In 1923–24 financial stability was restored following the hyper-inflation of the Civil War. By 1926–27 pre-war levels of agricultural and industrial production were achieved, although the urban economy lacked dynamism. The restoration of market relations in the countryside allowed the peasant economy to strengthen. However, the NEP was accompanied by major social problems such as unemployment and gross inequalities symbolised by the so-called NEPmen, who were regarded as 'speculators' peddling wares at inflated prices.

In foreign affairs the Soviet revolution remained isolated (see Chapter 16). In the 1920s the world revolutionary movement suffered a series of reverses. The conclusive defeat of the German revolution in autumn 1923 alarmed the Bolshevik leadership, while the massacre of Chinese communists in 1927 by the nationalist Guomindang illustrated the pitfalls of alliances with 'bourgeois' revolutionary forces. The international revolution, on which the Bolsheviks had staked so much, was clearly delayed and therefore help would not be immediately forthcoming from abroad. Capitalism, it appeared, had entered upon a period of stabilisation. Indeed, by May 1927 a war scare with Britain suggested that capitalism was prepared to launch a new offensive.

A mood bordering panic circulated among the leadership. Several times Trotsky related that the Soviet government was hanging by a thread. Trotsky's views on the precariousness of the Soviet regime were coloured by the slow advance of the collective farms (*kolkhozy*), which the Soviet government neglected. Furthermore, the weakness of state rural administration (rural soviets) was notorious, and for most of the 1920s communist influence over the countryside was minimal. The relationship between the peasant soviets and the state can be characterised by Robert Redfield's terms of the 'little community', and the 'big community'.[5] The majority of the population lived in the villages in the little community, with its own rituals and patterns. Even after the launch in 1925 of a vigorous 'face to the countryside' campaign to strengthen the rural party, the number of communists in the villages only rose from 153,000 (31 per cent of total membership) to 333,000 (25 per cent) in 1929. The quality of the new recruits left much to be desired.

Stalin offered an alternative to alarmist and gloomy prognoses. From 1924 he challenged the pessimists and declared that it would be possible to 'build socialism in one country' with or without foreign assistance. Underlying the debate over the economy lay political issues which became bound up with the factional infighting for the succession. Yet Stalin's victory was assured by more than his mastery of the Bolshevik political machine. His policies had a broad political appeal. Stalin's concept of 'socialism in one country' held that Russia could not only *begin* the building of socialism, but could on its own resources go on and *complete* the process. The theory of socialism in one country, as opposed to its *de facto* practice since the establishment of the Bolshevik regime, constituted a major revision of Marxist theory and made a virtue out of necessity. Socialism gradually became identified with the national interests of the Soviet Union. In contrast, Trotsky, while agreeing that Russia could begin to build socialism, from his theory of permanent revolution argued that the process could be completed only after the revolution had spread to other countries. It implied that the Russian revolution was dependent, and in a sense hostage, to the revolutionary process elsewhere.

The NEP stabilised the Soviet regime but the question remained of how to build socialism in a relatively backward country. The Soviet regime became a 'modernising' one (as most Marxist regimes have), but the commitment to industrialisation was above all vexed by the 'peasant contradiction'. The free market in agricultural products seemed to stymie the Soviet government's urge to industrialise. The Bolsheviks had come to power and established the political system of socialism, but in the countryside the capitalist system in effect still reigned. Bukharin stressed reformist gradualism, an agrarian co-operative socialism whereby socialism would be reached on the 'peasant nag' eschewing social conflict and securing marketable surpluses through allowing the kulaks, who were more efficient, to expand their holdings. One of the major problems of the NEP, however, was illustrated by the 'scissors crisis' of summer 1923, the discrepancy between agrarian and industrial prices. The 'scissors' were never completely closed, meaning that the terms of trade remained skewed against the countryside. Bukharin's strategy called for low industrial prices to increase demand which could be taxed for further development. He admitted that this would be a long path. Once again, as with Stolypin, it was a 'wager on the strong' which increased inequality in the countryside.

Bolshevik radicals increasingly perceived the peasants as an obstacle to their hopes of rapid industrialisation. For many the NEP could be tolerated as no more than a temporary expedient. The left accused it of betraying working-class interests in favour of the 'petty-bourgeois' peasantry. The NEP was unadventurous, and to those nurtured on the revolutionary enthusiasm of the fight against Tsarism and the heroism of War Communism it appeared a decidedly poor substitute for the vision of the socialist society to which they had devoted their lives. The NEP's emphasis on educational work, long-term cultural improvement and gradualism contrasted with the Bolsheviks' image of themselves as the masters of social and political forces. The institutional tensions inherited from War Communism also played their role in undermining the consensus over the continuation of NEP. Above all, this centred on the state bureaucracy which thrived under the NEP in the towns. This powerful bureaucracy, Trotskyists argue, was irked by the existence of spheres beyond its immediate control, above all by market relations among the peasantry and parts of the economy. For the leftist oppositions the NEP itself was responsible for providing an atmosphere conducive to the growth of the bureaucracy as revolutionary methods gave way to routine administration. Lenin's position was sufficiently ambiguous to allow the view to flourish among Bolsheviks that the NEP was a 'retreat', and that as soon as the state became strong enough the advance would continue.

Opposition to the NEP focused on the danger of the restoration of capitalism through the nefarious activities of the NEPmen and the kulaks. Trotsky and the United Opposition condemned the idea of socialism in one country and feared the moment when the bastions of the nationalised economy would be swept away by the petty-capitalist tide led by the peasants. The strategy, they argued, should be to build up the state-run industrial economy as fast as possible. But where would the necessary funds be found? The answer was provided by Yevgenii Preobrazhenskii in his concept of 'primitive socialist accumulation', a 'feudal exploitation of the peasantry' mimicking the process described by Marx of capital formation in Britain. The state was to accumulate the resources for accelerated industrial investment at the expense of the peasantry by demanding high prices for industrial products and by high taxes. The market was to be suppressed in the industrial sector and relations with agriculture were to be highly controlled. This programme relied on a series of fiscal measures, and not on direct coercion. Condemned at the time by Bukharin and Stalin, it was this programme, stripped of its subtleties, that was later implemented.

Stalin's position, which in the period after Lenin's death seemed to coincide with that of Bukharin, gained the support of the majority of party leaders. Rejecting Trotsky's views on the necessity of a combined strategy of intensifying the class struggle between workers and peasants while simultaneously pressing for world revolution, Stalin argued that the peasants could be won over to socialism by opening up the private market and improving supplies of industrial goods. Yet Stalin increasingly revealed an enthusiasm for accelerated industrialisation incompatible with the maintenance of NEP. The sixteenth party conference in November 1926 resolved on 'catching up and then overtaking the level of industrial development of the advanced capitalist countries in a relatively minimal historical period'. At the fifteenth party congress in December 1927 even Bukharin was willing to accept an ambitious programme of industrial investment and the voluntary collectivisation of agriculture.

The congress met against the background of a threatening international climate. There were growing food shortages in the cities. Peasants were reluctant to part with their grain since prices were low, and in any case there was a scarcity of industrial goods for them to purchase as a result of Bukharin's policy of low industrial prices. Stalin identified the 'kulak hoarder' as responsible for the shortfall in procurements and he reacted by launching a series of 'extraordinary measures'. In one of his rare departures from Moscow in late 1927 Stalin travelled to the Urals and Siberia to obtain the planned amounts of grain through coercion, bypassing the regular procurement agencies. The 'Urals–Siberian' method of grain requisitioning signalled the breakdown of the will to keep the NEP in operation.

Bukharin accepted the necessity for more rapid industrialisation but he urged that this should be kept within the bounds of a balanced economic programme. In his *Notes of an Economist* Bukharin insisted that sustained industrial growth could best be achieved within the framework of the NEP and with the balanced development of agriculture.[6] His condemnation of the leftists' arguments for super-industrialisation as constituting a 'feudal–military exploitation of the peasantry' was an oblique attack on Stalin himself. Defeat of Bukharin now denoted the end of the NEP compromise as Stalin adopted the arguments, though not the means, for rapid industrialisation from Preobrazhenskii.

The fundamental question in understanding the end of NEP is whether there were real economic alternatives to the policies adopted by Stalin. The Bukharin approach has been held up as a viable alternative which would have achieved strong economic results while avoiding the political brutalisation of the Stalin years. Distrust between the party leadership and the peasants, ideological hostility to the market and co-operatives, political manoeuvring to succeed Lenin, and the lack of political will to maintain the NEP were the causes of its demise as much as any inherent flaws. As a mechanism, NEP might well have survived with some fine-tuning of the exchange mechanisms between town and country, such as in setting industrial prices and the level of the agricultural tax, and with more far-sighted investment to provide the peasants with the means of production.[7] The debate, however, was not only concerned with the development of the socialist economy but with the definition of socialism itself.

THE REVOLUTION FROM ABOVE

Between 1929 and 1932 the NEP was reversed as the Soviet Union witnessed a veritable 'revolution from above' consisting of three main aspects: accelerated industrialisation; rapid compulsory collectivisation; and the cultural revolution.

The state took a leading role in the industrialisation process, but this was in marked contrast to the 1890s. In the earlier period state intervention to obtain foreign loans and to promote the capital-goods sector had been accompanied by the vigorous development of commercially based capitalism and consumer goods. Stalin's industrialisation, on the other hand, was accompanied by the elimination of the capitalist sector in its entirety and by a great concentration on heavy industry (known as sector A) as opposed to consumer goods (sector B). As if to echo Stalin's own name (which means 'man of steel'), this was an epoch of the 'metal-eating' industries. Consumption was reduced to an absolute minimum to permit greater investment in heavy and associated defence industries. The Stalinist definition of 'industrialisation' was a narrow one aimed at maximising development through national programmes of economies of scale. This super-industrialisation represented a complete rupture with Bukharin's gradualism.

The key to the whole period was the idea of planning. The State Planning Committee Gosplan (Gosplan) had been established in 1921 and by 1925 was issuing 'control' figures for industries, which in 1929 were to become the plan target figures. In 1928 the first five-year plan (FYP) was introduced which substantially raised the tempos hitherto achieved for industrial development. Within a few weeks of its adoption the key targets were revised substantially upwards to begin a headlong spiral of ever-rising goals. The establishment of targets became not so much a 'control figures' function of planning but a way of accelerating growth. There was chaos within the plans since, as Alec Nove pointed out, any plan which aims towards overfulfilment undermines the very notion of planning. The plans were determined by considerations other than the rational attempt to harmonise economic targets with resources. This 'willful' planning system, G. Grossman argues, was not so much a planned economy as a 'command economy'.[8] The first FYP engendered the massive expansion of the administrative apparatus. The system of ministries respon- command economy sible for branches of Soviet industry born during War Communism became universal, with ministries controlling not only plants but also housing, various ancillary networks, quite apart from the labour force. The management of industrial plants was strictly centralised under one person responsible to the relevant ministry.

The speeded-up industrialisation was accompanied by intensified pressure on the peasantry. The *smychka* between the peasantry and the proletariat was a fragile one, marked by suspicion on the side of the party authorities afraid of the luxuriant capitalism in the countryside. Above all, hostility was directed against the kulaks. Economic means of obtaining grain gave way to direct political and administrative coercion reminiscent of War Communism. Food shortages in the towns led to the tightening of rationing in February 1929 and the 'Urals–Siberian' method of compulsory grain requisitioning was intensified. Wholesale collectivisation became increasingly attractive to a section of the party to solve the problem of grain supplies and peasant autonomy once and for all. Stalin took advantage of the discrepancy between Bolshevik ideology and the peasant realities of the countryside. The urban-based Bolsheviks were no longer prepared to accept a situation in which the peasants could apparently hold the revolution hostage through the operation of the market in grain. We cannot really know whether Stalin shared or manipulated the party mood to his advantage. Bukharin's moderate line gained much support, and the views of the party on developing the economy were far from unanimous. At the very least we can say that most Bolsheviks shared the Marxist contempt for the peasant ('the idiocy of the countryside') and were convinced that collective agriculture was preferable to individual peasant farming.

Of more immediate concern were Bolshevik views about the class structure of the countryside. During the early years of the revolution there had been a profound levelling process as the large farms were divided and the poorer peasants gained land. Little had changed during the NEP, and the Bolshevik class analysis of the countryside as divided into kulaks, middle peasants and poor peasants (and a group of itinerant workers, *batraki*) was artificial. Of the Soviet Union's 125 million peasants no more than 2.3 million were hired farm hands (poor peasants), and the kulaks owned no more than 750,000, or 3.4 per cent, of all farms. Most kulaks employed nobody, and even the most prosperous peasant in 1927 had no more than three cows and three working animals, with about 10 hectares of sowing area to support an average family of seven.[9] The Bolshevik definition of the kulak was imprecise and transformed a statistical category into a social class.

Bukharin had argued that the process of collectivising agriculture should be voluntary, extend over a long period and be based on the gradual mechanisation of agriculture. Attempts during the NEP to encourage peasants to join the collective farms (*kolkhozy*) and state farms (*sovkhozy*) were half-hearted. By 1928 97.3 per cent of the total sown area was still being farmed by individual peasants. The voluntary collectivisation of the peasantry gradually gave way to coercion as armed detachments were sent to the countryside. It was suddenly discovered that, even without mechanisation, the small and medium peasants were ready to join. In November 1929 Bukharin was removed from the Politburo, opening the way for Stalin on 27 December to decree 'the liquidation of the kulaks as a class'. The dekulakisation programme was to provide the other peasants with the kulaks' land, animals and tools in the absence of machines. Violent social conflict was unleashed as the poorer sections of the village community were set against the kulaks and old scores were settled. The so-called kulaks (and the term was used indiscriminately to brand anyone remotely critical of collectivisation) were not allowed to join the collective farms.

War was declared against the private peasant as they began to be forced off their 25 million family holdings and on to the collective farms. A desperate civil war broke out as kulaks and other sections of the rural population, notably peasant women in the so-called 'women's riots' (*bab'i bunty*), resisted wholesale collectivisation.[10] Particularly detested were the 'twenty-five thousanders', an urban invasion of factory workers and urban party activists sent to organise the *kolkhozy*, even though they knew little about agriculture.[11] By March 1930 over 55 per cent of the peasantry had been collectivised. In that month Stalin called a temporary halt to the blood-letting in his speech 'dizzy with success' which held the overenthusiasm of the activists responsible for the 'excesses'. By the end of the year about half of the recently collectivised peasants drifted back into private production. But the pressure was sustained and 90 per cent of all farms were collectivised by 1936. According to official statistics 115,200 kulak families were deported in 1930 and 265,800 in 1931.[12] Unofficial statistics suggest that 15 million were left homeless by collectivisation, a million of whom were sent to labour camps and some 10 million deported to Siberia, a large proportion of whom perished.[13] Rather than donating their livestock to the collective farms peasants preferred to kill their animals. The results were catastrophic. Between 1928 and 1934 the number of horses declined from 32 to 15 million, cattle from 60 to 34 million, pigs from 22 to 11.5 million and sheep from 97.3 to 32.9 million. Heavy compulsory deliveries coupled with the slaughter of animals led to a famine in 1932–33 over the South Ukraine, the North Caucasus and other traditional grain-producing regions. About 5 million died in the famine, and throughout the land there was unimaginable misery.[14]

Collectivisation and industrialisation were accompanied by a cultural revolution, which it is argued by revisionist social historians owed as much to dynamism from below as initiatives from above. The targets of the cultural revolutionaries were bureaucratic administration and the old intelligentsia. In their place they propounded utopian visions of collective life with new approaches to education, architecture, law and social relations in general. The elements of utopianism in effect represented a cultural purge as the social and natural sciences were bent towards a dogmatic leftism. Experimentation in literature, for example, was ended as the Russian Association of Proletarian Writers (RAPP), founded in 1928, sought to destroy various bourgeois and other cultural organisations to establish its dominance in the literary field. David Joravsky speaks of a 'great break' (*velikii perelom*) in 1928–29 as the old intelligentsia lost out to a new generation who had been emerging in various professions during the NEP.[15] The cultural revolution was not simply imposed by the party but represented the partial resolution of tensions within the society of the NEP period. The pressure came from sectors of the party, the youth movement (Komsomol) and the working class for more radical policies. However, by mid-1931 Stalin repudiated some of the excesses of the cultural revolution and began what Timashev has labelled the 'great retreat' of the 1930s towards more conservative cultural and social attitudes.[16]

Cultural Revolution

Were forced collectivisation and rapid industrialisation the only options open to the Soviet regime in 1929? The cornerstone of the government's strategy was for agriculture to finance industrial development. Yet the search for a steady supply of grain or more efficient farming barely figured in the collectivisation process. If there was not a direct economic logic to the process, then one has to look at political reasons. Mass collectivisation had always been an integral component of the Bolshevik programme in line with Marx's bias against peasant individualism. When combined with Bolshevik political culture, which encouraged a lack of restraint when dealing with social forces, the scene was set for conflict. War Communism left a legacy of Bolshevik enthusiasm and maximalism that was not satisfied by the gradualist programmes of the NEP.

The arguments of Bukharin and the right were not defeated on rational grounds but as part of political struggle. The revolution from above was a way of consolidating Stalin's own position and destroying the bases of opposition influence. Stalin himself justified his policies on nationalistic grounds, in terms of the need to make up the lag compared to the advanced countries and to secure Soviet defences:

> To slacken the tempo would mean falling behind. And those who fall behind get beaten. But we do not want to be beaten. No, we refuse to be beaten! One feature of the history of old Russia was the continual beatings she suffered because of her backwardness. She was beaten by the Mongol khans. She was beaten by the Polish and Lithuanian gentry. She was beaten by the British and French capitalists. She was beaten by the Japanese barons. All beat her – because of her backwardness, military backwardness, cultural backwardness, political

backwardness, industrial backwardness, agricultural backwardness ... We are fifty or a hundred years behind the advanced countries. We must make good this distance in ten years. Either we do it, or we shall be crushed.[17]

Political competition with the West was now transformed into an economic race, but one whose standards and measure of achievement were set in the West. Furthermore, the Bolshevik leadership was increasingly dissatisfied with having to 'bribe' the peasants to part with their grain. There was a fundamental contradiction between a socialist political 'superstructure' sitting uncomfortably on top of the peasant economic 'base'. The second revolution was a way of integrating the two and of securing the social foundations of the Bolshevik regime.

COMMAND ECONOMY AND SOCIETY

The central question of the 1920s had been how agriculture could contribute to industrialisation. There was no essential economic connection between forced collectivisation and rapid industrialisation, contrary to the views of advocates of the latter, although without collectivisation the industrial growth rate of that period would not have been quite so high.[18] Collectivisation freed the government from having to buy off the peasant producer and allowed resources to be concentrated in industrial investment. The harvest in 1933 at 5 million tons was less than in 1928, but the state's share had doubled, some of which was exported for hard currency to purchase machinery for the first FYP. Cheap food to feed the expanding labour force in the towns allowed wages to be kept low. Gains were offset, however, by the need to divert resources into accelerated tractor building to make up for the huge losses of livestock and horses.

The *kolkhozy* were forced to fulfil extremely high delivery quotas at low prices in a state-directed system of peasant exploitation. In addition, prices for industrial goods were set so high that they amounted to a further onerous tax on the peasantry. As Khrushchev later admitted, for long periods the peasantry were unable even to cover production costs. The peasantry descended into a 'state of semi-serfdom'[19] and were forced to fulfil high labour norms in return for a share of the usually non-existent profits. Personal plots were legalised in 1932 to stave off generalised famine and perhaps as a concession to defuse the unrest in the countryside. The *kolkhozy* did not own the machinery but had to hire them from Machine-Tractor Stations (MTS), which acted as both economic and political centres of control. The result of such policies was the sustained impoverishment of the peasantry and the extended debilitation of the agricultural sector of the Soviet economy.

Despite the catastrophic losses sustained by the agricultural sector, Soviet industry was able to maintain impressive development. By the time of the German invasion of 22 June 1941 the Soviet Union was one of the world's major industrial powers and the foundations had been laid on which to fight the war. Accompanying the industrial expansion there were massive changes in society (see Table 1). This was the 'quicksand society', as Moshe Lewin dubbed it. To escape from the poverty and violence of the countryside in 1931, 4.1 million peasants moved to the cities, a total which by 1935 had risen to 17.7 million. Between 1926 and 1939 the cities gained some 30 million people. Urban dwellers as a proportion of the total population increased from 18 to 24 per cent. During the first FYP the salaried labour force (workers and officials) virtually doubled from 10.8 million to 20.6 million, with the bulk of this growth coming from the peasantry. By 1940 the number had increased to 31.2 million.[20]

Table 1 Class composition of the population (%)

	1913	1928	1939	1959	1970	1979	1985
Workers and employees	17.0	17.6	50.2	68.3	79.5	85.1	87.9
Manual workers	14.6	12.4	33.7	50.2	57.4	60.0	61.7
Employees	2.4	5.2	16.5	18.1	22.1	25.1	26.2
Collective farmers	–	2.9	47.2	31.4	20.5	14.9	12.1
Individual peasants	66.7	74.9	2.6	0.3	–	–	–
Property owners	16.3	–	–	–	–	–	–

Sources: *SSSR v tsifrakh v 1985 godu* (Moscow, 1986), p. 13; *SSSR v tsifrakh v 1986 godu* (Moscow, 1987), p. 6.

The first five-year plans were marked by enormous upward social mobility as peasants moved to join the industrial working class, and skilled workers were promoted into white-collar and managerial positions. One of the major aims of the cultural revolution was to replace the old intelligentsia by new cadres. This was achieved through a massive programme of 'proletarian advancement' (*vydvizhenie*) whereby workers and working-class communists were promoted to fill the expanding ranks of engineers and administrators. The educational system was re-formed to allow workers maximum access to the expanded classes in technical subjects. Universities were opened to adults even if they had not completed a full secondary education. A generation stamped by the crash industrialisation programme was rapidly trained and promoted under the auspices of the party (the 'thousanders'), a total of about 110,000 communist adult workers and 40,000 non-communist ones. This cohort of 'red specialists' remained the dominant generation of economic and political leaders until the 1980s.

There was massive labour turnover among the vast intake of new factory workers, seeking desperately to improve their appalling conditions. The free market in goods had been abolished but the labour market remained. Labour discipline and productivity were low. In response the authorities introduced a system of internal passports in December 1932 in an attempt to decrease mobility, and in 1938 labour books were issued recording an individual's work record and without which they could not be employed. The labour books symbolised the irrevocable gulf between the social aspirations to free labour of the 1917 revolution and the actual development of party dictatorship. The Stakhanovite movement, named after the legendary Donbass miner Alexei Stakhanov who allegedly far exceeded existing norms to cut 102 tonnes of coal in a single shift in 1935, introduced yet another cycle of administrative pressure in the workplace, further disrupting production. After collectivisation standards of living fell sharply. The urban workforce was incapable of any but the most inchoate resistance against state and factory authorities. Real wages had fallen by at least half by 1932, and workers were only sustained by general rationing in force from 1928 to 1935. The housing stock lagged far behind the tripled urban population, which rose from 22 million in 1922 to 63 million in 1940. The meat consumption of urban and country dwellers alike declined to reach only a third of the 1928 level in 1932. The peasantry were denied the benefits of social security and were not issued with internal passports. They responded by working badly and devoting their energy to their personal plots.

The end of the cultural revolution in 1932 was marked by the great retreat which permitted the consolidation of a conservative society. The educational system took on a more traditional look, and from 1931 engineers and other sections of the old intelligentsia were once again in favour. Experimentation in the arts gave way to the stifling orthodoxies of 'socialist realism'. The beneficiaries of the crash educational programme, the worker *vydvizhentsy*, consolidated their gains in 1937 as the great purge carried off the old managerial and administrative elite. The stress was increasingly on conservative marriage laws, restrictions on divorce and the banning of abortion except on medical grounds. Under Stalin a new hierarchy of inequality emerged together with an overbearing officialdom, but the position of this group, dubbed by Milovan Djilas a 'new class', was insecure. They could never be sure that the early morning knock would not one day sound for them. Even under Stalin social laws operated with a degree of independence, but individuals remained at the mercy of the political system. At the base of Stalinism were those who profited from it in one way or another. Vera Dunham has identified a postwar 'Big Deal' between the Stalinist system and the rising middle class of Soviet functionaries. In return for loyalty and labour they were rewarded with privileges, responsibility and the opportunity to pass on their advantages to their children. The mores of the new Soviet middle class simulated those of the bourgeoisie but lacked any dynamism in contributing to economic development. The price of the Stalinist model of industrialisation was a parasitic 'new class', inefficiency and low labour productivity. As radical economic reformers later admitted, only so much could be achieved through planning, commanding and storming. Above all, the creation of a massive state and party bureaucracy to run the economy was to have a baleful effect on the quality of Soviet political life for several decades.

THE GREAT PURGES

The concept of the purge was familiar to the Soviet citizen from the periodic campaigns within the party to expel so-called careerists, hangers-on and other undesirables. The Civil War had been accompanied by annual re-registrations of communists to screen the party, but the campaign of 1921 was the first occasion on which the term 'purge' (*chistka*) was used to describe the process. The rapid recruitment of 1924 following Lenin's death continued into the the early 1930s and raised new concerns about the quality of party membership. A purge in 1930 saw over 100,000 communists expelled, and this was repeated in 1933–34 when over a million were expelled. In the exchange of party cards in 1935 about half a million members were expelled, and by this time expulsion from the party was almost automatically accompanied by arrest. According to Brzezinski, the ruling party required a permanent purge to maintain its own internal discipline and to prevent its degeneration into a corrupt self-serving body. However, in the 1930s the idea of the purge was extended to the rest of society, and the cleansing of the party was no longer restricted to the expulsion of undesirables but to their elimination.

Stalin's fiftieth birthday in 1929 was celebrated by the massive inflation of his personality cult. The powers of the secret police, the OGPU (as the Cheka was now known), headed by V. R. Menzhinskii and later G. G. Yagoda, had been steadily increasing. A series of trials selectively attacked important groups. In June 1928 the trial of fifty-three engineers and technicians in the Shakhty district of the Donetsk Basin set the pattern for the trial in late 1930 of eight high economic officials who had allegedly formed an Industrial Party. The whole technical intelligentsia inherited from Tsarist times came under threat. Accounts were settled with the Mensheviks in a trial of March 1931. The brutality of collectivisation infected the whole political system with a lust for blood and any criticism came to be identified with the sabotage and 'wrecking' of class enemies.

Despite the risks there were attempts to limit Stalin's powers. In late 1930 two leading party figures, S. I. Syrtsov and B. Lominadze, were demoted for privately criticising the damage caused by crash industrialisation and collectivisation. In 1932 M. Ryutin in Moscow went further and called for a change in priorities from industry to agriculture and consumer goods, demands which prefigured the concerns of the post-Stalin leadership. Stalin personally was severely criticised. Apparently Sergei M. Kirov, the head of the Leningrad party organisation since 1926, led the group in the leadership who resisted Stalin's demands for Ryutin's death. They were unwilling to set the precedent of executing leading party figures, and Ryutin was merely exiled. The discontent reportedly culminated at the seventeenth party congress in January 1934, dubbed the 'congress of victors'. The abasement of defeated oppositionists like Bukharin, Zinoviev and Kamenev can be interpreted as an attempt to remain in the party and resist Stalin from within. The desire for a relaxation, now that the foundations of the socialist economy had been built, focused, allegedly, on Kirov. He seemed to represent a reaffirmation of the leading role of the party as opposed to the dominance of the informal structures around Stalin, compromises with the intelligentsia and a relaxation in the countryside. It should be stressed, however, that Kirov was no liberal: he headed Leningrad during the brutalities of collectivisation and repressed religion and alleged communist oppositionists with a vigour that equalled if not surpassed his predecessor, Zinoviev. According to Anastas Mikoyan 300 votes at the congress were cast against Stalin and only 3 against Kirov out of 1,225 voting delegates.[21]

Alarmed by Kirov's popularity and the tactics of the Old Bolsheviks (those who had been Lenin's comrades), Stalin struck first in a brilliant double blow that eliminated one and brought down the others. The assassination of Kirov in Leningrad on 1 December 1934 by Leonid Nikolaev in the corridors of the Smolny party headquarters was blamed on a conspiracy of Trotsky and, in time, Zinoviev, Kamenev and others. Khrushchev and Medvedev claimed that Stalin was behind the murder and much circumstantial evidence points in this direction.[22] The assassin, Nikolaev, had been released in suspicious circumstances by the NKVD (the new name for the OGPU) after earlier trying to approach Kirov with a pistol, and he appears to have been assisted by Genrich Yagoda. On that very day Stalin launched a wave of terror with the implementation of legislation that had obviously been prepared beforehand. A system of closed hearings was introduced presided over by three-person commissions (the infamous *troiki*) which routinely applied the death penalty. Nikolaev himself was executed after a short interrogation, but the main victims were the old leaders of the communist opposition, in particular Zinoviev and Kamenev who were the centrepiece of the first 'show trial' in August 1936. After a brief hiatus in 1935, from 1936 there was a steady escalation of the great terror which culminated in the *Yezhovshchina* (named after the head of the secret police, Yezhov, who replaced Yagoda in 1937). The repressions of 1937–38 comprised a series of centralised and carefully planned state terrorist actions. With the partial exception of the war there was barely a halt in the mincing machine up to Stalin's death in 1953.

The purges were remarkable for several reasons. In the first place, their scale was unprecedented. The precise figures have been the subject of vituperative exchanges between historians whose major result has been less to establish precise numbers than to force a thorough review of the available evidence. Steven Rosefielde argues that the average Gulag forced-labour population in the years 1929–53 was about 8.8 million, and that the total adult losses attributable to forced labour, collectivisation and the purges was over 20 million.[23] Stephen Wheatcroft argued that these figures were exaggerated owing to misinterpretation of the evidence. There was a shortfall in the Soviet population from various causes, including dekulakisation,

[handwritten margin notes: "Assassination of Kirov ↓ Purge? Show Trials"]

famine and a decline in the birth rate, from 1930 to 1937 of about 15 to 16 million. Medvedev estimates that up to 1937 Stalin's policies had claimed some 18 million victims, of whom 10 million died. The 'great terror' of 1937–38 itself saw some 5 to 7 million arrested, most of whom went to the Gulag but about a million may have been shot. Some 10 to 12 million suffered deportation or arrest during and after the war.[24] It is estimated that there were some 12 million deaths between 1936 and 1950 attributable to persecution.[25] The labour-camp population reached about 8 million in 1938, roughly 5 per cent of the population, who were contracted out by the NKVD as slave labour for the regime's building projects.

A further notable feature was the use of show trials. There were three main ones presided over by Andrei Vyshinsky. The first in August 1936 starred Zinoviev and Kamenev and saw their names joined in death as in life. The second in January–February 1937 featured Radek and Pyatakov, and the third in March 1938 put an end to Bukharin, Rykov and Yagoda. Vyshinsky, a former Menshevik who in Moscow in 1917 had called for Lenin's arrest, considered the confession 'the queen of evidence'. He ended the prosecution cases with the words 'Shoot the mad dogs', which became the catchphrase of the purges. No more than about seventy people were involved in the trials but they acted, as foreign observers put it, as latter-day witch-hunts. They were literally 'shows' directed at the population and were apparently masterminded by Stalin personally. They were designed to illustrate the penalties of deviation from Stalinist orthodoxy and demonstrated that enemies could be found in the very highest circles. Their crude populism sought to drive home the lesson that unceasing vigilance was required and that justice could strike down even the great. A striking aspect of the terror, displayed during the show trials, was the forcing of 'confessions' from the victims. Moral debasement was added to physical destruction. The torture and confessions lent credence to another feature of the terror, the forging of great chains of conspiracy. The friends, relatives and workmates of a victim were often caught up in the whirlwind.

An astonishing feature was the secrecy surrounding the whole process. A few show trials were publicised, but behind them the mincing machine ground down millions of victims. The scale of the purges was unknown within the USSR, let alone abroad. Most contemporaries believed the confessions and in the existence of the conspiracies. Gradually information did filter to the West through such publications as Trotsky's *Bulletin of the Opposition* but it had little impact. The publications of eye-witnesses went largely ignored. Western socialists argued that such 'rumours' were slanders against the Soviet system; right-wingers had been talking about the atrocities of the Soviet regime for so long that their warnings came as yet another 'cry of wolf'. Stalin's purges were particularly unsettling since they took place at a time of peace. The Bolshevik Red Terror of 1918 or the Jacobin terror of 1793 in France could at least be justified on the grounds of military emergency. Like the Jacobin terror, however, the operation of revolutionary justice focused on social and class factors rather than on any proof of having committed an offence. Such attitudes were not born under Stalin but had typified Lenin's dealings with recalcitrant social groups from the first days of Soviet power. However, the dekulakisation campaign had so brutalised Soviet life that justifications could be found even for the scale of Stalin's purges.

Successive waves of 'fifty-eighters' (those convicted under Article 58 of the Criminal Code, covering political offences) filled the 'labour-extermination camps', as Solzhenitsyn terms them. The police powers that had previously been employed against people outside the party were now turned against Bolsheviks themselves. Some 60 per cent of the party activists of 1931 were purged by 1937. The purges destroyed the majority of the Old Bolsheviks. Of the 139 members of the Central Committee elected by the seventeenth congress in 1934, 110 (79 per cent) had been arrested before the next congress in 1939; as had 1,108 (56 per cent) of its 1,966 delegates. Rank-and-file communists were not immune: members of previous oppositions were swept up together with thousands of ordinary party members.[26] The leaders of the national republics were purged almost in their entirety, amid accusations of bourgeois nationalism and other crimes. The purges led to the wholesale destruction of the old managers who had led the first phase of Soviet industrialisation. Exhausted, they were replaced by a vigorous younger generation trained in the school of Stalinism. Following the cultural revolution the old intelligentsia and technical specialists were rehabilitated and became a privileged group, but as individuals they suffered particularly badly. All the professions were hit, and in particular those individuals who had had any contact with the outside world. Understandably, diplomats suffered a particularly high casualty rate.

One group of special significance was the military leadership purged in 1937–38. On the eve of the war Stalin dealt the Soviet Union an almost mortal self-inflicted blow by striking down over three-quarters of the Soviet High Command and the officer elite.[27] The victims included Marshal Tukhachevskii, one of the most talented Soviet officers.

The sufferings of the mass of the Soviet population, Russians and non-Russians, should not be forgotten. The victims were random, often the object of anonymous denunciations as neighbours sought a few extra metres of living space. The chains of conspiracy and denunciation caught up relatives and friends in arbitrary patterns, with names often chosen to fulfil the local police quotas. The leadership of the NKVD itself was periodically purged: Yagoda in 1937 gave way to Yezhov, who himself fell victim in 1939 and was replaced by Lavrenty Beria, who put an end to the first phase of the great terror.

The purges did not end with the onset of war and final victory, the only difference being that their scope was now extended to the international stage. Already in the 1930s groups behind the lines in the Spanish Civil War had been purged. The war saw a certain degree of liberalisation and was fought under nationalist rather than socialist slogans. The central political structures had their roles redefined, especially the secret police and the party, which witnessed a massive recruitment. However, victory in the war was not accompanied by a relaxation of the terror, and the relative liberalism of the war years was reversed. The *Zhdanovshchina* (named after Andrei Zhdanov, the Leningrad party boss) of 1946–48 was an attempt to eradicate laxity in culture and the economy, and to reassert the 'party line' through discipline and central control. It was in these years that the poet Anna Akhmatova suffered exile, the writer Mikhail Zoshchenko was persecuted, and the outstanding Jewish actor Solomon Mikhoels was murdered. This period was marked by conflicts at the top, especially between Beria and Malenkov, leading a state faction against Zhdanov's 'party revivalism'. The formulation and implementation of major policies were frequently the result of compromise between contending factions both inside and outside the Politburo.[28] Zhdanov's death in 1948 was followed by a purge of the Leningrad party organisation. Campaigns of an anti-Semitic nature continued in the form of a struggle against 'cosmopolitanism'. Beria's own position came under threat in 1951, and it appears that he was due to become a victim of his own machine. At the nineteenth party congress in 1952 the Politburo and the Presidium were united to form the Presidium, now enlarged to thirty-six members. This seemed to imply that some of the old 'deadwood' could be cut away as soon as their replacements were ready. The so-called 'Doctors' Plot' in early 1953, in which a group of doctors with Jewish-sounding names were allegedly plotting to eliminate the entire Soviet leadership,

Reason's for the Purges under Stalin

presaged a new round of blood-letting. With the axe poised for yet more purges Stalin died on 5 March 1953 and only then was the terror machine stilled.

There are constant attempts to look for rationality in the purge process in general and in the great terror of 1936–38 in particular. The easiest explanation is to look to Stalin's own personality, his paranoid mentality, which sought to destroy all opposition to himself and the regime that he created. Out of a sense of inadequacy, it is argued, he destroyed all those who had known Lenin or could be judged his equal. Some have sought to enhance this psychological model by showing that there was a logic to the purge of Old Bolsheviks, with all those against whom he had a grudge dating back to 1917 and earlier falling victim. Moshe Lewin points out that the endless purges may have reflected Stalin's fear of becoming the prisoner of the bureaucratic machine that he had nurtured. There is no doubt that Stalin personally was the greatest beneficiary of the purges, with his opponents eliminated and his subordinates cowed. Without Stalin, it is argued, there would have been no purges.

To counter this, a second type of explanation focuses on the legacy of Bolshevism. From this perspective Stalinist terror was no more than the logical outcome of trends begun under Lenin. Political life since October 1917 had been marked by narrow sectarianism and intolerance for conflicting views. Even within the party the scope for debate had become limited to a narrow circle of leaders. Solzhenitsyn points out that the terror machine was created by Lenin and began its work under him. With collectivization the whole political elite became accustomed to routine violence. Both these types of explanation, the one which holds a single individual responsible and the other which blames the system, must be modified. Stalin's personality was important, but it could only operate in interaction with a system prone to violence.

A third set of explanations places the purges in a developmental perspective. The revolution from above was a way of concentrating all resources, human and material, on industrialisation. The destruction of the old managers and intelligentsia and their replacement by a new generation trained by Soviet power ensured a loyal managerial class. Modernisation required an elite, but subordinate to the leadership and to Stalin personally. This is associated with a fourth type of explanation which places the purges in the international context of the 1930s. All Bolsheviks were in favour of industrialisation, but the frenetic pace of Stalinist development focusing on defence heavy industry was, it is argued, determined by the hostility of Western capitalist powers and later by the threat posed by Nazi Germany. Both of these types of explanations take a short-sighted view since they leave out of the analysis, first, the damage inflicted on Soviet development by the extraordinarily wasteful pattern of Stalinist industrialization and the destruction of qualified workers and engineers by the purges, and, second, the distortions imposed on Soviet foreign policy by Stalin's vengeful, manipulative and secretive diplomacy. Foreign-policy factors clearly played a role and could be used to justify clearing of the country of all possible sources of opposition in case of war. This does not explain the destruction of the best officers which lowered Hitler's estimation of Soviet military power and may well have hastened the war. It certainly contributed to Nazi military successes in 1941.

A fifth view sets the purges of the 1930s in the context of domestic politics and challenges some of the conventional wisdom. J. Arch Getty argues that the purges were more than a result of Stalin's megalomania, and that the centre had remarkably little say in their conduct at the local level. He insists that even in the mid-1930s there were factional conflicts among the leadership, particularly between Molotov and Orjonikidze. Given our knowledge of Soviet politics in other periods this is a reasonable supposition. Getty restores the original sense of the concept of the purges by firmly locating them in the context of a cleansing of the party of undesirable elements, and sees the 1935 verification of party documents as an opportunity for officials to settle personal scores at the local level. He takes issue with the view of the party as being a totalitarian monolith and stresses the degree of lively politics and debates over indus-trialisation. Above all he focuses on conflicts between the centre and the localities, Moscow and the regional party organizations. Stalin is exonerated from personally initiating the purges and the link with Kirov's assassination is dismissed. The fundamental logic of the purges is seen to be less of a central bureaucratic process swallowing up the old revolutionaries than a grass-roots reaction against party bureaucracy. The consolidation of Stalin's personal rule is seen as part of the process of establishing order amidst chaos.

Getty's interpretation derives from a misreading of the course of the Bolshevik revolution from 1917. While he is undoubtedly correct in stressing the chaotic elements in Soviet administration in the early years, his characterisation of party organisation as inept, corrupt, badly organised and with poor communications between the centre and the locality is exaggerated. At its worst and in many rural districts this was the case, but a feature of Soviet rule was the coexistence of pockets of strong organisation with poor integration between them. To characterise city party organisations as he does is absurd, and yet the purges were no less violent in Moscow than in Smolensk region, his major source of information. Getty's interpretation adds much to our understanding of the dynamics of the purges but not to the processes that gave rise to them.

'STALINISM'

The ambiguities in Lenin's legacy, the tensions within the NEP and the isolation of the revolution allowed Stalin to consolidate his power. A decisive 'man of action' capable of mobilising the revolutionary elite and drawing on the unfulfilled aspirations of the revolution was able to launch a new revolution which transformed the face of the country. However, while the term 'Stalinism' is useful for describing a particular phase of Soviet history, it is misleading if the features of that period are assigned to the doings of one man. The problem of defining Stalinism, and hence combating the legacy of the man, haunted the Soviet system to the end. There is much that we do not know about the period, including the precise role played by Stalin personally in policy-making, the operation of the political and economic systems at the local and national levels, the economic and political dynamics of the purges and the social basis of the regime.

Any evaluation of Stalinism depends on when it began. Khrushchev dates the beginning of Stalinism as 1934, after the horrors of collectivisation and with industrialisation in full swing. His view accepts the sacrifices of those years as emanating from party policy. Only after 1934 was Stalin able to attack the party itself and hence became transmuted into 'Stalinism'. Others trace the origins back further: to 1929 and the defeat of the last serious alternative in the form of Bukharin and the rise of Stalin's personality cult; to 1921 and the 'ban on factions' and the crushing of the Kronstadt insurgents; to the revolution in 1917 and the way that the Bolsheviks seized power; and even back to Marx, laced as his works are with a primitive fury, saturated with a violence of language and dedicated to the destruction of civil society and the market.

Was Stalinism the inevitable outcome of Soviet development as charted by Lenin and Bol-shevik ideological and organisational traditions and distinct from what preceded and suc-ceeded it? Stalin himself never claimed that his regime differed from that of Lenin. Indeed, the basis of the legitimacy of Stalin's rule was that it was a continuation of Lenin's policies. Solzhenitsyn argues that:

> We may justifiably wonder whether 'Stalinism' is in fact a distinctive phenomenon ... Stalin
> himself never tried to establish any distinctive doctrine (and given his intellectual limitations
> he could never have created one), nor any distinctive political system of his own ... he was
> a faithful Leninist and never in any matter of consequence diverged from Lenin.[29]

Solzhenitsyn argues that all of the following began under Lenin: the Stalinist horror, with its
camps, the use of the death penalty against ideological opponents (be they of the left or right),
the willingness to use coercion against sections of society, the arbitrariness of the secret police,
the ban on factions within the party (albeit as a 'temporary' measure), and the accumulating
power of the leadership. The only major departure, according to Solzhenitsyn, was Stalin's
treatment of the party.

Trotsky tried to salvage Lenin's reputation by talking of the party as the repository of a
higher democracy, and implying that the society was to be held responsible for what the party
brought upon it. He cultivated the myth of a 'democratic party in an undemocratic society'.[30]
Trotsky's description of Stalinism as 'Marxism reflected in a samovar' emphasised the continuity with Russian political culture. Trotsky radically rejected the idea that there was any essential
link between the October revolution and the emergence of Stalinism, which he saw as the
outcome of social rather than political forces and stimulated by such factors as the experience
of the Civil War, the smallness of the working class, Russia's low level of culture, the capitalist
elements released by the NEP and the emergence of the bureaucracy. For Trotsky's biographer
Isaac Deutscher, Stalin fulfilled elements of Russia's historical destiny. The socialist revolution
came about in an isolated backward country and so forced the bureaucracy to industrialise and
carry out defensive preparations. The inevitable, but fundamentally necessary, cost was the
wholesale destruction of civil liberties and socialist democracy. A geopolitical and cultural
determinism permeates the Trotskyist view.

Roy Medvedev argues that Stalin's was only one possible route of Soviet development.
Stalinism emerged because of a series of unfortunate circumstances, amongst which Lenin's
death in 1924 was crucial.[31] R. C. Tucker supports the view that there was no causal connection between Lenin and Stalin. The latter's own particular personality was a crucial factor.
Tucker insists that the NEP course laid out by Lenin, with all its defects, was a far cry from the
totalitarianism of Stalin.[32] Stephen F. Cohen's argument that Stalinism differs from Leninism
because of the difference of scale, the sheer excess of Stalin, is true but does not reveal the
source of excess.[33] Morally, it might be argued, there is little difference between the murder of
one person or a hundred.

What are the distinguishing features of Stalin's rule? War Communism was full of ideological and institutional tensions and left a disputed legacy to the next period. These tensions
increased steadily during the NEP as the debate over industrialisation became bound up with
the contest for the succession. Bolshevik ideology did not offer a blueprint for the government
to follow, and the rise of Stalin to supremacy from 1928 brought about a significant change to
the Soviet polity. It was the metamorphosis of the original Bolshevik movement into a leader-
dominated 'mass movement regime' (Tucker). It was not accompanied by any change in the
regime's self-definition but it marked a shift in its ideological emphasis and institutional arrangements.

Under Stalin the teleological elements of Bolshevism were taken to the limit. The utopian
belief in the rapid move to socialism ensured the dominance of the end justifying the means.
As a young power the ideology was marked by a revolutionary idealism which craved the

immediate creation of a secular version of the New Jerusalem. Under mature Stalinism this chiliasm was accompanied by a powerful vulgarisation of the ideology and its reduction to a number of basic propositions, and the stifling of intellectual debate. This did not exclude some policy disagreements among the leadership, especially in the period following the Second World War, but for the mass of the population adherence to the single ideology and acceptance of cultural conformity were conditions of survival. The primary allegiance, however, was to the party line as interpreted by Stalin, however much it might change. Stalin intensified Lenin's habit of reducing the ideas of his theoretical protagonists to pronouncements of the class enemy. There could only be one truth, and that was the current line being put out by the party. The Stalinist system was permeated by a hyper-rationalism, which Karl Mannheim described as the ability to justify the consequences of actions taken on pragmatic grounds, however unprincipled they may be. Any action, however deplorable, could be rationalised in terms of service to the revolution. Society itself lived in a horrendous informational vacuum of the true state of affairs, both within the country and beyond. The lack of feedback in the political system reached such a pitch that Stalin himself apparently even began to believe his propaganda films of a well-nourished and contented peasantry!

Stalinism rested on a realignment of the major institutions making up Soviet power. Lenin's legacy of a polity governed more by convention and his personal charisma than by rules was intensified. The party suffered a dramatic decline in relation to the other main institutions. The party survived as a mass movement and as a power machine, but as a functioning political organism it was gutted. No party congress was convened between 1939 and 1952, and the Central Committee did not meet once during the critical years of the war. From 1941 Stalin headed both the party and governmental hierarchies, and played one off against the other with the help of the secret police. Stalin's power derived less from any formal office but from his undisputed personal dominance. He ruled both through the party and over it as the party's decision-making functions were usurped by a small coterie of leaders. Even at the trough of its fortunes, however, the party remained the principle symbol of legitimacy.

If the party was the greatest loser under Stalin, the secret police was one of the greatest beneficiaries. A powerful security police had already emerged under Lenin and now the terror machine consolidated its dominance over society. The theory justifying the purges was one of Stalin's few original contributions to Bolshevik ideology, namely the belief that the class struggle intensifies as society approaches socialism. The security police, however, was not allowed to achieve an independent institutional legitimacy and was always subordinated to Stalin personally. Towards the end Stalin was obviously irked by Beria's power and it appears that the Doctors' Plot was partially directed at him. Rumours that Beria struck first by allowing Stalin to die following a stroke by preventing medical assistance reaching him in time add an element of poetic justice to the dictator's death.

There was an enormous expansion of state power and the bureaucracy, but the government itself was 'shapeless' (Bialer). The system was rigidly hierarchical and worked 'bureaucratically', in the sense that it was plagued by paper-pushing, buck-passing and procrastination, but it can hardly be described as bureaucratic in the Weberian sense. It did not operate according to a binding set of rules with steady aims and targets and, as noted, the purges prevented the system settling down into bureaucratic routine. Stalin's rise was as the archetypal 'organisation man', yet he loathed organisations that could not be bent to his service. His paranoia in this respect was perfectly rational in that he achieved his aim of subordinating the party-state bureaucracy that had brought him to power.

The trends of War Communism concerning mass organisations were intensified. The soviets, the major instruments of popular participation, underwent a long period of stagnation. All non-Bolshevik intermediary organisations in society were eliminated and in their place 'transmission belt' mass organisations mobilised the population to build the new society. For Rigby the USSR under Stalin emerged as a tyranny exercising its power over a mono-organisational society in which everything was directed from above through an organic system of control.[34] As we shall see, according to totalitarian theory society was atomised as the state expanded to become the universal employer.

The institutional framework of Stalinism was integrated by a dirigisme that took the leadership principle espoused by Lenin to the absolute limit. Soviet dirigisme was personified by Stalin himself who was venerated as the *vozhd*, the leader or *führer*. Stalin's charisma was like Lenin's in that it operated in a modern scientific context, that is, the ability to understand and apply the laws of history to specific circumstances, but differed in that it was consciously cultivated in a manner which Trotsky called 'Asiatic'.[35] Stalin's charisma derived from the movement that he led, and it was the creative tension between the movement and the leader that raised both to unprecedented heights. Districts and factories were run by powerful bosses whose powers often appeared unlimited until they themselves perished in the purges. Merle Fainsod's work on Smolensk in the 1930s has shown that arrests and deportations could be ordered at fairly low levels by these 'little Stalins'. The Stalin cult found favour with the 'new' members of the urban working class and the rapidly advanced working-class intelligentsia who were emerging to make up the new Soviet middle class. The mass mourning at his death illustrates a high degree of veneration, and there remains a solid bedrock of support for Stalin even after the denunciation of his excesses. Stalin's extraordinary powers emerged out of his ability to manipulate the relationship between the emerging elite and popular forces, together with his dominance of the security police and the party.

Following Stalin's death the political system was given some stability in the abandonment of further revolutions from above, but this had already been prefigured by an increasingly conservative social ethos. The institutions that Stalin moulded in the 1930s became synonymous with the concept of communism itself. The achievements in industrialisation and war laid the foundations of the Soviet Union as a 'superpower'. In the context of socialism in one country Stalinism was primarily a war machine with the emphasis on heavy industry, a way of industrialising the country to sustain its military potential. Bukharin's view that the same ends could have been achieved at less cost has been much debated, but there is no doubt that the view of Stalin as a traditional nationalist, a ruthless moderniser in the tradition of Peter the Great, assumes a fairly simplified notion of what modernisation entails. The Stalinist legacy was a distorted modernisation in which some features were highly developed whereas others, like responsiveness in the political sphere and criteria for rational decision-making, were grossly underdeveloped. Stalinism can be defined as an 'anti-social' socialism. The cost of the 'externalities' of the Stalinist command economy, the terror, the stifling of initiative, the excess losses during the war, the loss of labour power, low labour productivity, poor quality of consumer goods, and the slow uptake of new technology in production must all be weighed in the balance. The Soviet polity and economy were endowed with a legacy of inflexibility, in particular in agriculture and industrial management, that came to haunt later generations of Soviet leaders. Stalinism can be seen as a distinctive mutation of the Soviet system, neither inevitable nor immutable, but not necessarily avoidable either.

KEY TEXTS

Carrère d'Encausse, H., *Stalin: Order through Terror* (London, Longman, 1981).

Deutscher, Isaac, *Stalin: A Political Biography* (Harmondsworth, Penguin, 1966).

Dunmore, Tim, *Soviet Politics, 1945–1953* (London, Macmillan, 1984).

Medvedev, Roy, *Let History Judge: The Origin and Consequences of Stalinism* (Nottingham, Spokesman Books, 1976).

Tucker, R. C., *Stalinism: Essays in Historical Interpretation* (New York, W. W. Norton, 1977).

Von Laue, T. H., *Why Lenin? Why Stalin?*, 2nd edn (Philadelphia, PA, Lippincott, 1971).

Ward, Chris, *Stalin's Russia* (London, Edward Arnold, 1998).

Wood, Alan, *Stalin and Stalinism* (London, Routledge, 1990).

4 Khrushchev and destalinisation

The Stalinist system placed enormous strains on the social and political cohesion of Soviet society. As Gorbachev put it, in Stalin's later years there arose 'a contradiction between what our society had become and the old method of leadership'.[1] Everything had to be decided at the top and the Stalinist state became heavily overloaded through its extirpation of initiative from below. The challenge facing Stalin's successors was to find new ways of achieving the integration of the system once terror and personal dictatorship had ended.

THE NEW COURSE

Lenin's decline and death in the early 1920s were accompanied by vigorous policy debates, and similarly Stalin's death in March 1953 allowed suppressed policy divisions to emerge. A number of outstanding issues urgently required attention. The Korean War was dragging on into its fourth year and the Cold War confrontation with the West was at its height. The economy had been restored to pre-war levels but agriculture continued to languish and there were few consumer goods in the shops. The immediate issue was the succession itself. Beria held the most effective card through his dominance of the vast security apparatus, and in the weeks following Stalin's death it was clear that he was prepared to make use of it. But his very identification with the axe ensured his downfall. His colleagues in the Politburo, united on little else, conspired to secure his arrest in June 1953 and his execution in December of that year. The military, led by Marshals Zhukov and Konev, played a key part in Beria's demise and helped bring the KGB under party control (see Chapter 8).

At Stalin's death G. M. Malenkov was simultaneously both First (later General) Secretary of the party and Chairman of the Council of Ministers. In other words, he held both posts at the summit of the Soviet political system. His colleagues, worried about this concentration of power and with recent memories of dictatorship, insisted that he choose between them in order to instate a system of collective leadership. Malenkov's decision to divest himself of the party leadership illustrates the low status of the party at this time. Nikita S. Khrushchev became First Secretary, and from that position was able to consolidate his own powers while restoring the party to the centre of the policy-making process. The struggle between Khrushchev and Malenkov was also a conflict between two competing bureaucracies, the party and state. As in the 1920s the post of party secretary was the crucial one in the succession struggle because of its powers of appointment. Khrushchev nominated his supporters to key positions, especially in the republic and regional (*oblast*) levels of the party, who in turn elected delegates who voted for the top party bodies, all of whom became beholden to him for their jobs and security in the process noted above of the 'circular flow of power'.

The contest between Malenkov and Khrushchev was fought in terms of policy issues. The debates of Stalin's last years were no longer waged as murderous faction fights with the losers being dubbed counter-revolutionaries. With Stalin dead it would have been absurd to insist on a single line of absolute correctness. Differing ideas over such issues as industrial policy, agriculture, culture and foreign policy now openly competed. In the cultural world a 'thaw' began to push back the icy wastes of Stalinist orthodoxy. However, the debates were conducted within the terms of the system established by Stalin. At issue was the 'fine tuning' of Stalin's mechanism, not its abolition, and hence this period differs significantly from the great debates of the 1920s when the very future of the country and society was at stake; 1953 did not represent quite such a radical break in Soviet history as Khrushchev liked to believe.[2]

The first years of the post-Stalin era witnessed remarkably open discussion over policy. Malenkov proposed what was called a New Course, arguing for the redirection of investment from heavy to light industry to provide the long-suffering Soviet population with consumer goods. Khrushchev called for greater investment in agriculture, and in particular proposed to plough the 'virgin lands' of Kazakhstan and South Siberia for grain. The plan would once again divert scarce resources into heavy industry to produce the necessary agricultural equipment. The debate over the sowing of an area of 30 million hectares of virgin and idle lands, an area greater than that covered by Austria and Switzerland combined, acts as a famous case study of policy formation, from policy initiation to adoption and implementation, in the early post-Stalin years. The prominent role of the agriculturalists signalled the increased scope for specialist input in policy-making in the post-Stalin era. The debate was launched by Khrushchev in September 1953 when he argued that there was a grain shortfall, while Malenkov insisted that the situation was not critical. The programme encountered the resistance of the Kazakhstan party organisation, who feared an influx of Russians. In February 1954 the Kazakhstan first and second party secretaries, Zh. Shayakhmetov and I. I. Afonov, were dismissed by the Khrushchev-dominated four-person Secretariat of the Communist Party of the Soviet Union (CPSU) and replaced by Russians, P. K. Ponomarenko and L. I. Brezhnev, respectively. The programme was then adopted by the Central Committee in March 1954. Khrushchev had been obliged to work hard to obtain approval for his policy, and the resolution of the issue in his favour revealed the power of the party Secretariat.

In foreign policy Malenkov recommended lower spending on defence and a revived policy of peaceful coexistence. In a Stalinist manner he insisted that the changes taking place in the Soviet Union should be adopted across the board in Eastern Europe. Defeat over the Virgin Lands Scheme, however, sealed Malenkov's fate and in February 1955 he was replaced as Prime Minister by N. A. Bulganin. No executions followed and a non-bloody precedent had been set for leadership change. In keeping with tradition, however, the whole affair was kept secret. Malenkov's demotion did not remove all opposition to Khrushchev, and in the Politburo he was confronted by a phalanx of dedicated Stalinists: V. M. Molotov, L. M. Kaganovich, M. Z. Saburov and K. E. Voroshilov.

DESTALINISATION

Malenkov's reappraisal of Stalinist policies focused on economic issues, whereas with the passage of time Khrushchev's criticisms became more and more political. At this time there were approximately 8 million people in the labour camps, about 15 per cent of the entire male adult population. This represented a massive drain on the economy, compensated in part by the use of German and Japanese prisoners of war until 1955 for construction work. After Stalin's death a trickle of prisoners was released, including some relatives of leaders, such as Molotov's wife. A Central Committee commission established in 1954 under P. N. Pospelov was horrified by what it discovered during its investigation into Stalin's persecution of leading party figures. The fundamental problem was what was to be done about the crimes and how to analyse the political system that had given rise to them. How much could be revealed without undermining the stability of the Soviet state? As Gorbachev discovered during *glasnost*, if too much was made known there was a risk of an outburst of mass anger against the system which had permitted the crimes; and the dangers were all the greater for leaders of Khrushchev's generation who were personally implicated in those crimes.

One option was to maintain a stolid silence, the tactic pursued by Brezhnev for so many years. The twentieth party congress, the first since Stalin's death, meeting from 14 to 25 February 1956, at first took this course. The official party report delivered by Khrushchev concentrated on foreign and economic policy and said nothing about the purges. A new Central Committee was chosen which contained only 79 (63 per cent) of the 125 elected at Stalin's last party congress in 1952. Khrushchev was re-elected First Secretary, and his position was consolidated by the election of 54 (41 per cent) new members on to the enlarged 133-person Central Committee. With the business of the congress over, the delegates were preparing to leave when in the late evening of 24 February they were called back to attend a closed session where they were informed Khrushchev would deliver a speech. At the time Khrushchev was 62 years old, a colourful personality made all the more unique when set against the drab *apparatchiki* of the Stalin years. He had been an enthusiastic young communist in the 1920s, the head of the Moscow party organisation in the 1930s and leader of the Ukrainian party in the 1940s. For over two decades he had been one of Stalin's closest colleagues and therefore had a unique vantage point to observe the inner workings of the regime.

Khrushchev addressed the gathering for four hours until late into the night. The delegates listened in amazement to his extraordinary revelations about Stalin's crimes. There were occasional shouts of anger or ripples of laughter when Khrushchev employed a particularly vivid turn of phrase. Khrushchev accused Stalin of having breached the 'Leninist' principle of collective leadership and of covering his rise by suppressing Lenin's Testament. He had developed a 'personality cult' with its attendant 'loathsome adulation' and had falsified history by claiming that he had been Lenin's main helper. Khrushchev's main indictment was that he had 'victimised' innocent people. His condemnation on this score was mainly restricted to Stalin's attack on the party after 1934, accusing him in effect of the murder of Kirov and the majority of delegates to the seventeenth party congress. A large part of the speech was devoted to the rehabilitation of party and military people. He denounced the continuation of the purges after the war, in particular in Leningrad, and the preparations for a new purge in 1953 (the 'Doctors' Plot'). Moreover, Khrushchev condemned the theory behind the purges, the Stalinist principle 'that the closer we are to socialism the more enemies we will have'. This was absurd, he argued, especially after 1934 when 'the exploiting classes were already liquidated and socialist relations were rooted in all phases of the economy, when our party was politically consolidated'. Closely linked to this was the further charge that Stalin had allowed the party to decline as a functioning institution. This was a matter particularly close to Khrushchev's heart, and not only because he used it as a vehicle in the factional infighting of the 1950s. Khrushchev's whole life had been sincerely devoted to the party and its ideology, and this perhaps more than anything else marked him out from those whose lip service to the party covered a primary allegiance to Stalin himself.

Stalin was accused of the misconduct of the war, especially the woeful misreading of Hitler's intentions and ignoring warnings. The lack of preparations were compounded by the slaughter of military leaders in 1937–38. Khrushchev's emotion here revealed itself in the intensely personal way that he tried to destroy Stalin's reputation as a war leader. Stalin's psychological collapse in the first days of the war was followed by the grossly wasteful use of men as Stalin planned operations on a globe. Khrushchev summed up: 'This is Stalin's military "genius": this is what it cost us.' Furthermore, Khrushchev condemned the wholesale deportation of peoples towards the end of the war who had been under German occupation and who were accused of collaboration – the Chechen, Ingush, Kalmyks and others, but he notably failed to mention the Crimean Tatars: 'The Ukrainians avoided meeting this fate only because there were too many of them and there was no place to which to deport them.' Among the other charges were Stalin's mishandling of foreign policy and in particular his high-handedness which provoked the break with Yugoslavia in 1948. Khrushchev touched on one of his pet themes in criticising Stalin's neglect of agriculture.

The speech was a broad attack on the personality and some of the policies of Stalin. What became known as the 'Secret Speech' did not remain a secret for long. It was initially circulated among party activists and then in all workplaces and thus became quickly known at home and abroad, although it was not actually published in the Soviet Union. The means of its broadcasting was as much of a compromise as its contents. Despite its limitations, owing partly to the fact that it had evidently been prepared in haste, the speech was a courageous and important event. Never before had the policies of the regime been the target of such sustained criticism by one of its leaders. However, the speech restricted itself to describing the Stalinist horror and failed to analyse how it had come about. The indictment was restricted to the years after 1934 and hence forced collectivisation and industrialisation were accepted, as were the ways in which they were conducted. Khrushchev was careful to present the party as the victim and as somehow disassociated from Stalin's crimes. All that was positive under Stalin came from the party, all that was negative from Stalin: 'Our historical victories were attained thanks to the organisational work of the party.' Just as Khrushchev's reforms were in the main limited to adjusting the operation of the system established by Stalin, based on collective farms and enterprises responsible to state organisations, so his speech was largely concerned not with the Stalinist system itself but its excesses. Khrushchev said little about the sufferings of the peasantry and ordinary people and he was selective in his choice of victims to rehabilitate. The losers in the power game following Lenin's death, dubbed oppositionists, such as Trotsky, Bukharin, Rykov, Zinoviev and Kamenev, were only mentioned to be condemned. The victory of Stalin personally and his policies were therefore condoned, but the way he misused his power was condemned.

In a perverse inversion of the Stalin cult the entire responsibility for the negative features of the Stalin years was placed on Stalin personally, whereas previously all the victories were his own doing. As Palmiro Togliatti, the leader of the Italian Communist Party, pointed out, 'All that was good used to be attributed to the superhuman qualities of one man; now all that was evil is attributed to him.'[3] The responsibility of Stalin's associates, including Khrushchev himself, for the crimes was evaded. Togliatti insisted that it was un-Marxist to seek the explanation of a major historical phenomenon in the evil of an individual, not in economic or social circumstances. The exposure of Stalin was partial and left many areas in the dark. If the party had retained its basic correctness, why had it, and indeed Stalin's colleagues, not resisted his reckless policies and the purges? The speech failed to provide any theoretical or historical explanation for the emergence of the Stalin phenomenon. There was no analysis of the legal, political, ideological or institutional foundations of Stalinism.

Instead of providing a systemic analysis, the criticisms were moral rather than political. The aim was to condemn Stalin rather than to provide a political explanation of Stalinism. The system that Stalin nurtured was forcefully distinguished from what was termed Leninist social-ist legality. The 'back to Lenin' theme (one that Gorbachev was to revive later) served impor-tant functions in the adjustment of the Soviet system but it was only a partial retreat from Stalinism. In displacing Stalin's personality cult on to an inflated cult of Lenin, Khrushchev was guilty of a Stalinist practice. Khrushchev argued that if the matter were analysed seriously 'we may preclude any possibility of a repetition in any form whatsoever of what took place during the life of Stalin'. However, the basic apparatus created by Stalin continued to rule and no institutional or political barriers were erected against a revival of Stalinism.

In the circumstances Khrushchev's victory of the half-truth over the unmitigated lie was a major victory. Stalin's crimes and personality were disassociated from Soviet socialism. To have gone much deeper into the roots of Stalinism in a forum attended by Mao Zedong and other international communist leaders, with Stalin's henchmen such as Molotov and Kaganovich present, may well have been bravery taken to the point of folly. The speech was undoubtedly partly motivated by the desire to discredit the Stalinist hardliners, who earlier in 1956 had rallied against Khrushchev, though it was much more than this. Stalin's betrayal of the loyalty and idealism of his generation made Khrushchev's denunciation of Stalin a personal mission as much as an act of political calculation. From a Marxist perspective Medvedev argues that Khrushchev denounced Stalin's crimes in order to rationalise the system of bureaucratic gov-ernment and to consolidate the privileges and power of the class of office holders, the *nomenklatura*.[4] This class had developed under Stalin, and now the lifting of the terror allowed them to enjoy their rewards. By 1964, having consolidated the rule of the party and the existence of the bureaucratic system, Khrushchev became expendable.

For many the speech came as a great shock. The idol of a generation was deposed from his pedestal. Supporters were forced to face up to what had been suppressed for so long. In the West there were major debates in the communist parties, and by the end of the year mass desertions. A New Left, more critical of the Soviet Union, emerged. The Italian Communist Party under Togliatti now publicised the idea of national roads to socialism under the term 'polycentrism'; while in China Mao advanced his own critique of the Stalinist developmental model. Moscow was no longer the Rome of the world communist movement.

In Eastern Europe the shock was all the greater since the Stalin cult had been imposed together with Soviet power as an act of faith for a decade. In 1955 Khrushchev had conceded the principle of national roads to socialism during his reconciliation with Tito's Yugoslavia. The succession struggle in Moscow and ideological divisions had a profoundly destabilising effect. Khrushchev's victory over Malenkov in 1955 saw the fall of the Hungarian reformer Imre Nagy, who had proposed similar reforms to Malenkov's. In June 1956 a Declaration on Relations between the Soviet and Yugoslav parties was followed a week later by strikes in Poznan in western Poland. In October a potentially disastrous political confrontation between hardliners and reformers was only averted after Khrushchev's personal intervention and by the return of the 'national communist' Wladyslaw Gomulka to head the communist party to im-plement the 'Polish road to socialism'. The Polish party was granted a degree of autonomy in domestic policies in return for political loyalty to Moscow and the maintenance of the leading role of the party. The Soviet economic model was swiftly discarded as a wave of decollectivisation swept 85 per cent of Polish agriculture back into private hands. The factory councils established in 1956 were gradually undermined, but some of the achievements of the 'Polish October' remained in a fairly relaxed censorship, relatively free travel and a concordat with the church.

In Hungary events took a far more explosive turn. Destalinisation sparked off a challenge to the very existence of communist rule. Nationalist themes merged with factional struggles over the Hungarian road to socialism. The major difference with Poland was the greater degree of disunity at the head of the Hungarian party and the absence of a sufficiently forceful leader who might have controlled the destalinisation process and facilitated an internal solution to the challenges. The Stalinist Mátyas Rákósi and his supporters clung to power for too long, and once belatedly returned to power late in 1956 Nagy was always one step behind the demands for popular government, full freedom of speech and publicity, and ultimately for national independence and withdrawal from the Warsaw Pact, the military alliance of Soviet bloc countries established the previous year. In the last days of October the crisis developed into a full-scale revolution. The Soviet ambassador Yurii Andropov lulled Nagy into a false sense of security as Soviet troops prepared to invade. From the Soviet point of view, the benefits of intervention far outweighed the costs, especially since world attention was distracted by the disastrous Israeli, British and French attack on the Suez Canal, recently nationalised by the Egyptian leader, Gamal Abdel Nasser. After several days of street fighting in early November 1956 the Hungarian revolution was crushed. The clear lesson was that destalinisation would not be allowed to threaten the Soviet bloc in Eastern Europe, although some latitude was permitted in domestic policies. The declining ideological unity and the absence of Stalin's personalised leadership were compensated for by increased institutional ties through the Warsaw Pact (officially known as the Warsaw Treaty Organisation, WTO) and by rejuvenating the Council for Mutual Economic Assistance (CMEA, known as Comecon), formed in 1949. The events in Poland and Hungary illustrated that the thaw would not be allowed to bloom into spring.

Within the Soviet Union responses to the speech were more muted as the years of suppressing independent thought had left their mark. Destalinisation was at its most explosive when combined with nationalism. Only in Georgia, Stalin's homeland, did the speech lead to disturbances when in June 1956 demonstrations protested against the debunking of the local hero, even though the republic had suffered particularly harshly during the purges. Khrushchev himself began to backtrack in the face of a conservative backlash. In June 1956 he declared that Stalin was 'a great Marxist–Leninist' and condemned the concept of 'Stalinism', which he alleged to be the invention of anti-Soviet propaganda. The major result of the speech was the creation of commissions to visit the labour camps. Between 1954 and 1958 they authorised the rehabilitation and release of over 2 million political prisoners. Throughout the summer ragged and emaciated camp inmates struggled home, witnesses to the crimes and living testimony of the need for reform. However, those most closely responsible for the Soviet holocaust remained unpunished and still held responsible posts.

The thaw was taken furthest in the cultural sphere. The poet Alexander Tvardovsky had been appointed editor of *Novy Mir* (*New World*) in 1950, and now this 'thick journal' became the forum for the best contemporary literature. Unofficial free thought blossomed in a movement that became a 'cultural opposition' as it sought to probe the origins of the Stalin phenomenon beyond the official limits. These years were a time of relative cultural and intellectual liberalism as censorship became less heavy-handed and the cultural intelligentsia began to participate more fully in political and intellectual life.

The inconsistencies of Khrushchev's speech were reflected in the sharpening of the inner-party struggle. His opponents focused on the alleged economic and political deficiencies of Khrushchev's leadership (see below), but fears of the pace of destalinisation played their part. They opposed what they considered an excessive relaxation of Soviet controls over the international communist movement, especially in Yugoslavia, and condemned Khrushchev's policy of peaceful coexistence. A grouping of Malenkov, Molotov, Kaganovich and the foreign minister D. T. Shepilov launched an attack in June 1957. They obtained a majority in the Presidium (later renamed the Politburo) of seven to four and denounced the whole gamut of Khrushchev's policies. They demanded his resignation, but Khrushchev argued that only the Central Committee could dismiss him. A Central Committee plenum was hastily convened with the assistance of Zhukov and the military, who flew in members. Khrushchev's earlier appointments now stood him in good stead and he obtained an overwhelming vote in his favour, the tradition of unanimity still exercising its power. His policies in agriculture and destalinisation commanded more support than the alternative put forward by the hardliners. He followed up this victory by dismissing his opponents, dubbed the 'anti-party group'. Molotov was sent as ambassador to Mongolia and Malenkov to manage a power station in Siberia. Zhukov's support was cruelly rewarded by his demotion and replacement by Marshal Malinovskii. Zhukov's popularity and independence had weakened one of the basic principles of the Soviet Union: party control over the army. In 1958 Khrushchev further consolidated his position by replacing Bulganin as premier, and he therefore combined the two key posts as Stalin had done in 1941.

However, while Khrushchev's formal power continued to grow, his personal popularity was in steep decline as his policies caused confusion. It was partly this which prompted Khrushchev to raise the Stalin question again in 1961 at the twenty-second party congress. In many respects this congress represented a more radical destalinisation than the twentieth. On 17 October 1961 Khrushchev addressed an open session of the congress, naming Stalin's accomplices and launching an attack on Stalin himself. His scope was broader than in 1956, criticising parts of Stalin's strategy for economic development, in particular condemning the 'steel-hungry' heavy industrial programmes. Once again the major charge against the personality cult was that it had raised itself above the party. Khrushchev's tone was much more bitter than it had been in the Secret Speech, although the level of analysis was not much deeper. With the congress still in session, on the night of 31 October, Stalin's body was removed from the Mausoleum where it had rested next to Lenin. It was buried by the Kremlin Wall marked by a plain slab, 'J. V. Stalin', and covered by tons of concrete as if the leadership feared his resurrection. Soon after, his name was removed from thousands of towns and streets.

The condemnation of Stalin was now conducted in open and the congress speeches were published in the press. A pent-up flood of revelations about the Stalin period was released. A genre known as 'camp literature' burgeoned as books and articles described Stalin's atrocities. In 1962 Khrushchev personally authorised the publication in *Novy Mir* of Alexander Solzhenitsyn's *One Day in the Life of Ivan Denisovich* which described life in the camps. Yevgenii Yevtushenko's poem *The Heirs of Stalin* warned against the survival of the spirit of Stalinism. However, as after the twentieth congress, Khrushchev became alarmed about the outpouring of this literature and began a retreat. Extremely conservative culturally, Khrushchev was disturbed by the potential of the revelations to destabilise the system. One of the shortcomings of destalinisation under Khrushchev was that it was partly a function of Khrushchev's struggle to retain the leadership. Indeed, the lack of a structural analysis of Stalinism allowed Khrushchev to develop a minor personality cult of his own. With his ouster in October 1964 destalinisation swiftly lost momentum.

The main achievements of destalinisation were the termination of twenty-five years of mass terror and the limitation of the powers of the security police. Millions of prison-camp survivors were released, many administrative and bureaucratic abuses were curbed, and the role of charismatic one-person rule was reduced. But the whole Stalinist phenomenon remained a festering sore in the absence of a credible official structural analysis of the phenomenon. The failure of the regime itself to come to terms with Stalinism now meant that later, under Gorbachev, society itself would take up the task, this time implicating the Soviet system in its entirety in Stalin's crimes.

ECONOMY AND SOCIETY

Stalin laid the foundations of the Soviet Union's modern economy. Certain sectors, however, such as agriculture, had been woefully neglected and new technologies, such as plastics, were almost completely ignored. His centralising zeal meant that the ministries in Moscow were responsible for overseeing the smallest operational details of plants perhaps thousands of miles away. Plan targets were set in terms of quantity rather than quality. The problem now was how to devise a strategy to capitalise on the achievements of the Stalinist system while inducing a new dynamism to the economy, a combination which was still being sought thirty years later. Possible solutions were as familiar to Stalin's immediate successors as they were later: greater reliance on the market, more decentralisation, more and better consumer goods, greater private initiative within the collective system, and economic incentives for the introduction of new technology.

Malenkov's New Course of 1953–54 had shifted the emphasis to more consumer goods for Soviet citizens, though his cuts in retail prices went too far and led to shortages. Malenkov, however, was unable to gain sufficient support for his reform programme. Khrushchev led the assault, but having wrested the leadership from Malenkov proceeded to implement the latter's economic policies. The most pressing problem was in agriculture, a sphere that Khrushchev made his own. The wartime destruction of villages and shortages of labour were exacerbated by the continued high-delivery obligations and high taxes. Agricultural productivity stagnated under the authoritarian collective-farm structure. Khrushchev continued Malenkov's long-overdue payment of higher procurement prices for agricultural products, relaxations on the peasant's personal plot, and higher investment, which quadrupled between 1953 and 1964. Apart from these sensible reforms many of Khrushchev's policies were ludicrously over-optimistic. The Virgin Lands Scheme ignored ecological factors and, after some years in which grain output increased, the region began to suffer from severe erosion and dust-storms. Another of Khrushchev's 'hare-brained schemes' followed his visit to Iowa in 1959 when he seized on maize as a fodder crop to increase meat and dairy production. Farms were forced to grow maize irrespective of local conditions, and in general the livestock campaign was conducted in a hopelessly inept manner. His forceful methods were often reminiscent of Stalin's.

In 1958 he dissolved the machine-tractor stations (MTSs), which acted as political centres and supplied the farms with machinery. Khrushchev's policy veered from one extreme to the other. Previously farms had been forbidden to own their equipment, but now they were forced to own the machinery even if they did not want to and lacked service facilities. The abolition of the MTSs allowed the revival of the 'link' system, which had been abolished in 1950, whereby groups were allowed to work a piece of land for extended periods and even to own machinery. It was a concession to personal agriculture, but despite much talk the system was not allowed to make the contribution it was capable of until the 1980s. After the initial easing of restrictions on the personal plot Khrushchev began to take fiscal and administrative measures against private livestock. The restrictions were imposed on ideological grounds and were designed to discourage private farming. They contributed to declining productivity as the peasants once again found themselves under attack. Agriculture did show some improvement as grain output increased, but Khrushchev's enthusiasms led to disruption. Increases in food prices in 1962 led to unprecedented riots and to workers' protests in Novocherkassk which were crushed by tanks. Bad weather in 1963 exacerbated the poor harvest and Khrushchev was forced to spend scarce foreign currency to import grain.

Khrushchev moved to tackle a problem highlighted by the anti-party group. The industrial ministries were carving out empires which were becoming increasingly independent of the bodies responsible for co-ordinating economic plans. Khrushchev proposed a radical solution by abolishing the central ministries and transferring their responsibilities to over a hundred regional economic councils (*sovnarkhozy*) which were to be co-ordinated by larger republican bodies and the central planning agencies. The change was accompanied by the first major economic debate since the 1920s. The reform proved flawed since it was difficult to combine central planning with regional authority. The plethora of sectoral state committees established to reconcile the demands of the centre and the localities failed to prevent economic chaos. In response the number of councils was reduced, but when such measures as merging several republics to create larger economic units were proposed national sensitivities were provoked. The duplication of tasks at the local and national levels only increased the bureaucracy. Following Khrushchev's ouster the councils were abolished and the central ministries were re-established in Moscow.

In 1957 Khrushchev asserted his authority over economic policy and scrapped the sixth five-year plan, adopting an ambitious new seven-year plan which attempted simultaneously to increase consumer satisfaction and to achieve high economic growth rates. The result inevitably was high-handedness and centralisation as agencies desperately sought to fulfil their part of the plan by applying administrative pressure. Khrushchev's enthusiasms offended many key groups and threatened to unbalance the economy. There was a marked slowing down of economic growth after 1958 as his administrative methods led to disorganisation. Khrushchev's reforms relied more on organisational changes than on changes in economic mechanisms themselves. Khrushchev's tragedy was not that he tried to tackle the real economic problems, but that his education, background and personality did not provide him with the ability to achieve his aims.

In the summer of 1957 the USSR hosted the sixth world youth festival. Moscow had not seen so many visitors since before the revolution as Soviet citizens and foreigners met and exchanged ideas in what was called 'the spirit of the twentieth congress'. This was a period of great Soviet achievements. The first Sputnik circled the globe in October 1957; a month later the dog Laika was the first living creature in space; and on 12 April 1961 Yurii Gagarin was the first man in space in a 108-minute flight. These events made a great impression on the rest of the world and signalled that the Soviet Union had come of age as a technological power. Of greater concern for the military planners of the West, it demonstrated that the USSR had the capacity to launch inter-continental ballistic missiles (ICBMs).

In social policy Khrushchev's ascendancy was marked by the extension of social security benefits. Stalin's legacy in the field of housing was years of neglect and crowded communal apartments. As workers crowded into the cities from the 1930s to work in industry Stalin concentrated resources on building yet more factories and grandiose housing projects. Khrushchev achieved a doubling of the housing stock between 1955 and 1964, typically five-storey blocks not requiring lifts but not built to last. The Khrushchev era saw a notable improvement in the standard of living, especially in the countryside. No longer did heavy industry absorb all the available resources.

Under Khrushchev the educational system witnessed a major expansion. He attempted to remedy the problem of social inequality which had become such a pronounced feature of Stalin's rule. Between 1955 and 1957 Khrushchev tried to undermine educational privilege and the advantages of the elite in their access to higher education by combining education with labour. This culminated in 1958 with his plan to abolish the upper classes at school and to force all children over 15 to enter the labour force for at least two years and to learn a trade. Access to higher education would be through part-time programmes of evening or correspondence courses. It amounted to a 'polytechnisation' of education through work training harking back to some of the educational experiments of the early Soviet years. The debate over the reform provides a second good example, together with the Virgin Lands Scheme, of policy formation in the post-Stalin period. It provides one of the clearest examples of resistance from an interest group to the policies of the government. Khrushchev's plans were based neither on the advice of educational specialists nor on the experiments tried since 1955. He underestimated the value of full-time education in secondary schools and the problems facing youngsters of 15 in choosing a profession. Khrushchev was thwarted in his plans by a coalition of vested interests. After a brief discussion a milder version of his plans was adopted in December 1958 but even this was never fully implemented and the reform was quietly dropped in 1965.

In the legal sphere Khrushchev tried to establish certain basic rules and procedures. The principle that only properly constituted courts could pass sentences was enshrined in the new Russian Criminal Code of 1961. Khrushchev, however, undermined the principles of legality that he himself had set. The Code had limited the death penalty to treason alone, yet in 1961 some black marketeers were shot after its retrospective extension, a procedure against all accepted norms of justice. The terms of the 'anti-parasite laws' of 1957 were cast so broadly against those not in official gainful employment that officials frequently used them as a catch-all statute against individuals guilty of a range of offences including 'dissent'. The commitment to the restoration of socialist legality was undermined by the fact that Khrushchev did not renounce force to impose his will on specific issues. As Breslauer points out, Khrushchev based his authority on achieving impressive results in a short time, the politics of 'pressure', hence the tendency to resort to coercion to overcome resistance. Mass terror was ended, but coercion remained embedded in the operation of the system.

AUTHORITY AND IDEOLOGY

The zigzags in policy between 1953 and 1964 and the erratic style of Khrushchev's leadership reflected the enormous power vacuum created by the end of dictatorial rule and mass terror. Stalin's successors were forced to devise new patterns of power and authority. Khrushchev's economic policies had been maturing within the Stalinist shell, but in the spheres of authority patterns and ideology Khrushchev's approach did contain some genuinely novel features which

Mary McAuley called the 'Khrushchev alternative'.[5] The aim was to overcome the political ossification imposed by Stalin. At the centre of Khrushchev's approach was a Leninist fundamentalism adapted to new conditions.

The novel feature of Khrushchev's rule was the attempt to revitalise political participation, amounting to a Soviet form of populism. Under both Lenin and Stalin mass popular participation had been encouraged as one of the fundamental principles of commune democracy. Participation, however, can be divided into two types: the managerial approach, adopted by Malenkov and practised by Brezhnev, channelling participation into safe paths which would not threaten the political and bureaucratic prerogatives of Soviet officials; while the populist approach challenges their autonomy and exposes bureaucrats to effective criticism. Khrushchev adopted the second type and despite equivocations he led a determined assault against elitism and bureaucratism somewhat reminiscent of the workers' inspection movement (Rabkrin) during War Communism. Khrushchev tried to draw the population into the building of socialism. His populism was more than a tactic in the factional struggle but was conceived as part of a strategy to improve economic and political efficiency.[6] Khrushchev sought to supplement political controls from above by expanding the bounds of decision-making. He did this by seeking the advice of specialist groupings, such as scientists, and by extending popular participation in political processes. This was to be achieved by drawing (*privlechenie*) new social activists, known as *obshchestvenniki*, into public life by massive recruitment to the party, expanding the rights of the soviets and the trade unions, and the transfer of some state functions to public or social organisations. In the factories, for example, the penal system was to be supplemented by the establishment of comrades' courts, which tried minor offences. The work of the militia was bolstered by the creation of volunteer patrols (*druzhiny*) in the streets. The creation of a centralised Joint Committee of Party and State Control in 1963 had the potential of acting as a powerful means of control over party and state bureaucrats, giving official sanction to popular supervision. Khrushchev sought to use the masses to control the state and economic bureaucrats.

Khrushchev's Leninist fundamentalism was particularly apparent in religious affairs where he revealed himself to be a 1920s type of militant atheist. He was more of a 'conviction politician' in this respect than Stalin, whose religious policy was extremely pragmatic. Stalin's persecution of religion during the collectivisation campaign had been accompanied by the closure of churches, but during the war many had been given permission to reopen. Whenever Khrushchev found himself in a strong political position he initiated an anti-religious campaign. In December 1958 he launched a major offensive which resulted in the closure of most of the churches reopened during the war, and of many more churches, mosques and synagogues. They were converted into government stores or left to rot, thus destroying a priceless cultural heritage. His aim was to remedy the perceived ideological laxness of Stalin's last decade, and in this respect continued the tradition of 'party revivalism' pursued by Zhdanov. He placed the churches under a far more invidious system of state supervision than Stalin ever had. For him religion was antithetical to the values of communist society and its scientific-materialist basis.[7]

Under Stalin the government bureaucracy dominated the party and became the main institutional expression of power. Khrushchev's defeat of the anti-party group in 1957 ruined the collective leadership and he emerged as the single most powerful figure. However, Khrushchev did not attain a position above the party and state comparable to Stalin's. He governed through the party, and not over its head. The party was restored to the position it had enjoyed under Lenin as the ruling political organisation. Its institutional life was revived with regular congresses, and its central and local committees functioned according to the party rules. The Presidium (Politburo) became the central political arbiter in the Soviet Union. But Khrushchev, having raised the status of the party as an institution, did his best to ensure that it did not function as such. The decline in collective leadership after 1957 was accompanied by Khrushchev's strengthened personal dominance over the party machine. No party secretary or official could withstand the First Secretary's imperious will. The growing economic problems from 1960 encouraged Khrushchev to broaden his assault on the bureaucracy to encompass party officials. In the purge that followed nearly half of provincial and territorial party first secretaries lost their jobs in the space of a year. It became clear that party officials owed their jobs to the First Secretary and not to an anonymous bureaucracy. This was a measure of how little had changed since Stalin had used these methods to consolidate his power in the 1920s.

In addition to continuing the destalinisation campaign the twenty-second party congress in 1961 adopted a new party Programme to replace the 1919 one. It summed up the party's achievements and outlined highly ambitious plans for the future. According to the Programme the Soviet Union would catch up and overtake the USA economically by 1970, and within twenty years (1980) the USSR would 'in the main' be a communist society. The economic objectives were ludicrously optimistic, but the Programme's main interest lies in its attempt to provide a theoretical restatement of the historical stage reached by the USSR. The Programme argued that the economic, social and international achievements of the Soviet Union, the new and higher stage of the Soviet material base, necessitated corresponding theoretical developments. It reflected Khrushchev's own beliefs concerning the role of the party and the nature of Soviet society. It also advanced the theory of peaceful coexistence with the West, put greater stress on equality and foresaw the emergence of a 'new Soviet person', ideologically conscious, skilled and politically active.

The Programme's major novelty was the assertion that socialism had already been constructed in the Soviet Union. Contradictory classes had disappeared and therefore the state was no longer the dictatorship of the proletariat: it was now viewed as a 'state of all the people' engaged in building communism. In 1936 Stalin had argued that socialism had been built, but to justify the purges had insisted that the state grew stronger as it approached its end because of the intensification of the class struggle, a theory repudiated by Khrushchev in his Secret Speech. The new Programme was an attempt to remove Stalin's inconsistencies. Its major emphasis was on the withering away of the state, which it argued could now commence. This was to take place through the transfer of the coercive power of the state and its functions to such public organisations as the trade unions, popular militias and comrades' courts. Bureaucratic organisations like ministries were to disappear while the soviets were to be revitalised to stimulate communist self-government. Reflecting the usual Khrushchevian ambivalence, the Programme argued that the withering away of the state would be a protracted process and that the party, as a social organisation, was to expand its functions. The question of the role of the party in the future communist society had always been left vague yet it had always been assumed, and Stalin concurred, that the party would wither away at the end of the dictatorship of the proletariat. Now Khrushchev proposed its consolidation. The ringing utopias of earlier years gave way to an image of communist society as a consensual, depoliticised, limited participatory socialist democracy dedicated to the welfarist improvement in standards of living. The charge of revisionism levelled at Khrushchev by Mao Zedong and others rested on the Programme's assertion of the ending of the class struggle: the Chinese declared that all states are class states until the final establishment of communism.

The twenty-second congress proceeded to implement some of the Programme's doctrines. The principle of rotation of offices within the party was established: for Central Committee members four terms of four years each (a maximum of sixteen years, unless they were especially good, a flattering loophole utilised by Brezhnev); members of the Presidium for no more than three years; and shorter periods lower down the hierarchy. In effect, Khrushchev abolished tenure in the party. The shock to those used to a lifetime job can be imagined. It provoked widespread discontent since party officials now faced the possibility that they would have to readjust to a new job at some point in their careers.

Khrushchev's economic problems of this period encouraged him to look to the party, his favourite body, for a solution. The division of the party in 1962 into industrial and agricultural sectors at the provincial and lower levels was designed to integrate it more closely into economic administration. Separate agricultural and industrial hierarchies were established and party officials had to decide which to join. The reform only exacerbated the chronic ambiguity over the functions of the party official in production. To what extent was their role to be advisory, or should they rule directly, thus replacing the responsible official? Khrushchev was trying to cut the number of salaried party officials by increasing the number of voluntary and part-time staff to stimulate the involvement of rank-and-file party members, yet the division further expanded the bureaucracy by having two of everything.

Khrushchev's populism inevitably encountered the opposition of those with vested interests in maintaining their positions and accustomed authority. Attempts to open up administration inevitably engendered the hostility of the bureaucrats themselves. They considered themselves the masters of a narrowly defined political sphere in which they brooked no interference.[8] Their priority was the smooth management of state and economic affairs rather than the extension of democratic self-management. They shared the bureaucrat's traditional antipathy to popular government and mass participation which threatened their political autonomy. The underlying assumption of Khrushchev's destalinisation campaign and the promulgation of the theory that the class struggle had ended in the Soviet Union was that the Soviet people could now be trusted to manage their own affairs to a greater extent than before. The strategy sought to bring administrative and political processes within the ambit of popular control.

Yet Khrushchev's populism was contradictory. The party Programme had compromised on the question of popular initiative by channelling it through state agencies. Despite the proclamation of the 'state of all the people', with the emphasis on volunteers and standing commissions, after 1961 the authority and functions of the soviets continued to decline and the government and party still maintained their 'petty tutelage' over them. It would take more than exhortations to revive the soviets. The greater respect shown to specialists was balanced by Khrushchev's support for the biologist Trofim Lysenko, whose insistence on the ability of species to assimilate rapidly to new circumstances (Michurinism) represented the triumph of Bolshevik voluntarism over nature. Lysenkoism set back by a generation the study of genetics in the USSR. It was at this time that a campaign was launched against unofficial art and literature. Khrushchev's populism did not amount to a liberalisation of the system as a whole. His attempts to achieve greater social homogeneity through his anti-corruption drive, the assault against 'parasitism', and his heavy-handed campaigns against religion and cultural non-conformity all revealed a high degree of authoritarianism. The opposition of officialdom to his programme was bolstered by a great degree of popular resistance. It proved impossible to reconcile the contradictory aims of maintaining the centralised managerial administrative mechanism with the attempt to expand public influence on the operation of the system. This remained a problem for post-Khrushchev reformers.

KHRUSHCHEV'S FALL

Khrushchev had been able to impose his policies in investment priorities, administrative reform, political participation and foreign policy, but from 1962 his authority weakened. By October 1964 Khrushchev's power seemed to be at a peak but his authority, the ability to initiate and see through policies, had crumbled. Problems in all fields mounted and Khrushchev lacked a coherent strategy to deal with them. His colleagues in the leadership increasingly saw him as a liability. Moreover, he had gratuitously weakened his position by attacking his natural power base, the party officials. On 12 October 1964 Khrushchev was summoned to a meeting of the Presidium and the twenty-two people present were unanimous that Khrushchev had to go. He was replaced by a collective leadership of Leonid Ilich Brezhnev (First Secretary, soon after renamed General Secretary) of the party, Aleksei Kosygin (Chairman of the Council of Ministers) and Nikolai Podgorny (Chairman of the Presidium of the Supreme Soviet, in effect president). Khrushchev was accused of infringing the principle of collective leadership and returning to the style of the personality cult, though the very fact that he was ousted reveals the limits to his power.

The Central Committee next day confirmed his ouster and Mikhail Suslov outlined the main charges against him. They included precipitate decision-making, nepotism (his son-in-law A. I. Adzhubai had been appointed editor of *Izvestiya*), causing administrative confusion by splitting the party, foolish 'campaigns' in agriculture which led to the agricultural crisis of 1963–64, and pursuing an adventurist foreign policy which had led the world to the brink of nuclear war over Cuba in October 1962. Khrushchev was stripped of his posts and retired. No punitive actions were taken against him and the peaceful nature of the transition was a measure of the changes wrought by him. It is for this reason that Mark Frankland paradoxically calls the moment of Khrushchev's humiliation his 'finest hour'.[9] After the bloodthirsty years of Stalin's rule Khrushchev had restored basic civilised norms to the conduct of Soviet politics.

The accusations levelled against Khrushchev were on the whole justified, but they were not the whole reason for his dismissal. On the social level Khrushchev's ouster can be seen as a bureaucratic counter-revolution. The recruitment of specialists into the party, government and management undermined the rough and ready politicians drawn into the leadership in the 1920s and 1930s. Khrushchev's style jarred with their sense of decorum and procedure. The political elite objected to the introduction of the principle of the rotation of offices. The division of the party gave Khrushchev massively expanded powers of patronage and introduced an intimidating new form of 'permanent purge'. His populist measures prevented the consolidation of managerial autonomy and production efficiency in industry. His leadership style, tempered in the various campaigns of Stalinist industrialisation, was cast in the mould of storming rather than settled routines. In the name of stability and order the political and economic bureaucracy rallied in October 1964 and ousted Khrushchev.

Under Khrushchev an alliance for reform was to some extent created, but it came up against the social realities of an entrenched bureaucracy who fought hard to preserve their privileges and power. His overthrow marked the end of a sustained period of reform and inaugurated two decades of conservatism. As Stephen Cohen points out, 'Change in the Soviet system, and resistance to change, have been the central features of Soviet political life since Stalin's death in 1953.'[10] It was a conflict between 'innovation' and 'tradition', or between 'reformism' and 'conservatism', a split which to some extent coincided with the division between anti-Stalinists and neo-Stalinists. The battle between the two tendencies was fought on many grounds, including the evaluation of the Stalinist past, Russia's historical role and the potential for socialist development in the Soviet Union. The reformists insisted that the system and the ideology were capable of indefinite development, whereas the conservatives focused on the defence of past achievements. Khrushchev's reforms were imposed from above, and attempts to generate a self-sustaining movement of continuing reform from below, as with the cultural opposition, were repressed. The reforms therefore lacked either an institutional base to continue them once he was gone or a social constituency strong enough to influence the new leadership. The reformism of the Khrushchev years, Cohen argues, was not an organic outgrowth of the system but only a reaction to the long period of Stalin's tyranny. In other words, reform was sustained by a relatively small constituency and was permitted for a time by the revulsion against some of Stalin's excesses. Following the stabilisation of the system, the end of the terror and the restrictions on arbitrary police power, the forces of reform were left with few powerful allies. Put another way, and from the totalitarian point of view, Khrushchev never got beyond the 'struggle for succession' phase of dictatorships. The cause of destalinisation was allied to his political struggle against the conservatives and the Stalinists.

Stalinism represented the period of 'system-building', whereas Khrushchev's rule established the framework for the 'system-management' phase of the governance of the USSR. Khrushchev's aim was to achieve the maximum viability of the regime. He hoped to reduce coercion as standards of living increased, to decrease the scope of administrative agencies as the public became more involved, and to improve the efficiency of the economic system as workers became more conscious. The ideological legitimacy of the system was to be bolstered by its practical achievements in the sphere of social consumption and political interaction between regime and society. Stalin's revolution from above had laid the foundations of a more educated and complex society, and it was left to Khrushchev to devise a strategy to find a means of integrating this into the political regime bequeathed by Stalin. The destalinisation campaigns, administrative reforms and populism were all responses to the problem. However, while rejecting the excesses of Stalin, Khrushchev returned to the Leninist system that had provided the ground for them to emerge in the first instance.

His rule was marked by a degree of continuity with the preceding period, such as the unprincipled struggle to come to power against Malenkov, his clear discomfort with the limitations of collective leadership and the emergence of a mini-personality cult of his own, the sacrifice of Imre Nagy in Hungary, and the struggle against the peasants' personal plots. His commitment to sustained social changes spoke of his refusal to allow the regime to make peace with society. His rule was distinguished by populist strategies for mobilising the citizenry against the office-holders and the erratic nature of policy formation and implementation. His ideological ardour represented a genuine return to Leninist fundamentalism. There was of course no suggestion of introducing some form of political pluralism either in the party or society. On a very general level two basic patterns of Soviet power can be identified, the War Communist and the NEP. Khrushchev's reforms represented no more than the modification of the War Communist model, marked by state domination of the economy and permeated by a high level of ideological and social coercion but stripped of some of its more violent characteristics. Khrushchev did not so much represent an alternative to the long-term pattern of Soviet politics as an attempt to infuse the existing practices with some life.

The Stalinist regime, with its purges and wars against its own people, its economic storms and social catastrophes, could not continue for ever. Khrushchev's major achievement was to accept the need for change and to set the mould for post-Stalinist governance. The net effect of his policies was to alienate most of his former bases of support since the reforms threatened the power and privileges of the very people he was forced to rely on to implement the changes. Khrushchev was not ousted because of any fundamental policy disagreements, but over the manner of their implementation and the challenge that his methods posed to officialdom. Under Khrushchev the provisional period was ended and he began the task, completed by Brezhnev, of putting post-Stalinist administration and its relationship to society on a firmer basis.

KEY TEXTS

Bialer, Seweryn, *Stalin's Successors: Leadership, Stability and Change in the Soviet Union* (Cambridge, Cambridge University Press, 1980).

Breslauer, George, 'Khrushchev Reconsidered', *Problems of Communism*, Vol. 25, No. 3 (September–October 1976), pp. 18–33; also in S. F. Cohen, A. Rabinowich and R. Sharlet (eds), *The Soviet Union since Stalin* (London, Macmillan, 1980).

Cohen, S. F., 'The Friends and Foes of Change: Reformism and Conservatism in the Soviet Union', in S. F. Cohen *et al.* (eds), *The Soviet Union since Stalin*; revised version in S. F. Cohen, *Rethinking the Soviet Experience* (Oxford, Oxford University Press, 1985).

McCauley, Martin (ed.), *Khrushchev and Khrushchevism* (London, Macmillan, 1987).

McCauley, Martin, *The Khrushchev Era, 1953–1964* (Harlow, Longman, 1995).

Medvedev, Roy, *Khrushchev*, trans. Brian Pearce (Oxford, Basil Blackwell, 1982).

Tompson, William, J., *Krushchev: A Political Life* (London, Macmillan, 1995).

5   From Brezhnev to Gorbachev

Khrushchev was overthrown by an alliance of interests threatened by his erratic behaviour and populist impulses. By contrast, the Brezhnev years were marked by a stability which imperceptibly degenerated into stagnation. An unprecedented degree of security of tenure for office-holders was established, known as the policy of 'stability of cadres', whereby an increasingly stable elite could enjoy the fruits of office. The new leadership consolidated a pattern of post-Stalinist politics developed by Khrushchev but shorn of his populism. Khrushchev's rule had been stamped by bold policy initiatives and institutional innovation, whereas Brezhnev's rule was characterised by a timidity and conservatism that evolved into a prolonged period of drift and the accumulation of problems. His two successors, Andropov and Chernenko, lacked the time to consolidate their positions, and it was left to Gorbachev to overcome the inertia by injecting into the system leadership dynamism, a renewal of the elite, a flurry of policy initiatives and increasingly radical institutional change. While stagnation might have been dangerous for the system, radical reform proved fatal.

CORPORATISM AND COMPROMISE

The Brezhnev approach was marked by a limited and pragmatic view of social engineering, an end to revolutions from above, continued restraints on mass terror, a commitment to improved social welfare and a broadening of consultation with specialist groupings and the political elite. Brezhnev decisively rejected tempestuous mass mobilisations or the encouragement of mass initiatives from below. The period was a modest Soviet equivalent of the 'Great Society' programme of the 1960s in the United States. The utopian vision of communism was pushed into the distant future and domesticated to suit the regime's mediocre tastes.

The Brezhnev period was based on a type of social compromise, a social compact or contract. Its fundamental principle was that if the state did not make excessive demands of the population, but provided a steadily improving standard of living and a degree of private autonomy, then the population should not make excessive demands of the state such as calling for political involvement, self-governance, or other aspects of Khrushchev's populism. Victor Zaslavsky characterised the system as a 'neo-Stalinist compromise' since the essentials of a modified Stalinism were retained without the personality cult.[1] Millar called the bargain a 'Little Deal' whereby the people gave their political rights to the party in exchange for the promise of consumerism and improved welfare.[2] Breslauer denoted the compromise as welfare-state authoritarianism, marked by a distinctive approach to political participation, social transformation and material welfare. It was based on a 'contract', not in the classical political philosophy sense of an agreement between bargaining equals, but as a *quid pro quo*.[3] For the first time since its inception the regime as a whole (the NEP had always been opposed by part of the leadership) set aside its mobilisational impulse and established a degree of peace with society. Janos Kadar, party leader in Hungary, captured the new mood in 1962 by the phrase 'He who is not against us is for us'. Political conformity ensured physical security. However, by the late 1970s the compromise had given rise to complacency, decay and corruption. The fallacy of the assumption that economic development could be achieved without modifying the social and political system endowed the Brezhnev era with an increasing air of unreality. The bargain was undermined by faltering economic performance and social alienation.

Khrushchev's ouster was not followed by any dramatic changes in policy or personnel. The great majority (83 per cent) of the members of Khrushchev's 1961 Central Committee remained on the one elected in 1966, and of the latter 80 per cent were again re-elected in 1971. The provisions of the 1961 party Programme for the rotation of offices were quietly forgotten, as were some of its other more ambitious targets. The division of the party into industrial and agricultural wings was abolished in November 1964. Khrushchev's spate of reorganisation was now followed by a lengthy period of administrative stability. Almost for the first time since the formation of the Soviet state emergency gave way to settled routines and procedures. The requirements made of officials were known and not too demanding. Officials were now able to enjoy the physical security achieved under Khrushchev with the job security established under Brezhnev. The stability of cadres policy, however, resulted in the increasingly geriatric Brezhnev leadership. By 1982 the average age of the Politburo members was 71, and if Gorbachev is excluded the average rises to 74, only two years younger than Brezhnev himself. The period cannot quite be called petrification since there remained considerable turnover at intermediate and lower levels. Nevertheless, the political system under Brezhnev became transformed into a relatively stable oligarchy.

The consolidation of Brezhnev's personal dominance took several years as the collective leadership established in 1964 died a lingering death. Brezhnev brought in personal associates such as K. U. Chernenko to buttress his position. In May 1977 he replaced Podgorny as President, and in October 1980 the last of the triumvirate that had come to power in 1964, the ailing Kosygin, was replaced as Prime Minister by the octogenarian N. Tikhonov. Elements of the old collective leadership did not altogether disappear, as Mikhail Suslov retained his stifling guardianship of Soviet ideological orthodoxy. His death in January 1982 presaged the end of the Brezhnev era.

The role of leadership underwent a change. Even more than under Khrushchev the leader's authority was based on his administrative abilities and success as an economic manager. The heroic image gave way to a more practical exercise of leadership. In this respect Khrushchev represented a transitional period. His personality and schooling in the shadow of Stalin encouraged elements of charismatic leadership, giving rise to 'hare-brained schemes' and lack of consultation with colleagues. Brezhnev acted as a political broker rather than as a charismatic leader. He ruled with his colleagues and did not appeal to the masses over the leaders' heads as Stalin and Khrushchev had done.[4] Like Khrushchev, however, he held a belief in the party as the ideal instrument of rule.

Having consolidated his position, Brezhnev enjoyed considerable power over policy. In contrast to Khrushchev's confrontational style, Brezhnev preferred to rule in a consensual manner by coalition-building. Since he never challenged the establishment, the limits to his personal power over policy are unknown. His policy priorities, such as agriculture, defence and détente were for the most part those of the majority. However, his actual method of implementing policy was his own. This amounted to an expensive capitulation to a multitude of demands, placing a heavy strain on financial resources. Brezhnev's policies included many of the major planks of the reformers' economic and social programmes, such as a commitment to consumerism and light industry, high investment in agriculture, the espousal of increased social spending and improved standards of living, scientific management and legal proceduralism. These policies, moreover, were politically expedient since they helped consolidate the new leadership in power.

The major economic question of the Brezhnev years was not the general direction of policy, over which there was a large degree of consensus, but the means of achieving the goals. Economic reform figured largely in official debate from 1964 but in practice it came to be stripped of the essential elements of any genuine reform, an increased role for the market and decentralisation (see Chapter 14). The reforms favoured by Brezhnev focused on institutional reorganisation and exhortation, rather than on structural change. He worked within the terms of the basic Stalinist economic model, marked by a high degree of centralisation, tight and detailed planning, the stress on quantitative outputs, the absence of autonomy for lower economic tiers or managers combined with the dominance of the ministries, and the lack of any self-regulating or self-generating mechanisms. More rational economic and administrative policies did expand the scope of consultation with interested groups and specialists before decisions were taken. Nevertheless, the Brezhnev era never capitulated to a technocratic ethos of depoliticised decision-making.

In the 1970s Khrushchev's peaceful coexistence policy was transformed into a period of agreements with the West denoted by the term détente. This had major economic implications as foreign and domestic policy became entwined. In spite of early optimism, administrative reorganistion failed to substitute for more thorough-going economic reform and created a unique situation in the early 1970s. Like American presidents, Brezhnev became increasingly conservative at home while innovative abroad. The strategy of satisfying major economic and political interests through an expanding welfare state has been seen as a Soviet type of corporatism. The main ideological concept of the Brezhnev era was 'developed socialism'. It represented 'a corporate vision of a consensual society, in which conflict would be managed by deals struck between the state and functionally-based interests'.[5] The high level of defence expenditure, the enormous drain of agriculture, the highly centralised administrative system, the slow rise in productivity, and the massive and inefficient economic apparatus all placed excessive demands on the system and heavy burdens on the domestic consumer. Brezhnev sought to pay for these 'deals' by improving foreign ties to provide a rapid transfusion of technological know-how, consumer goods and credits. For the first time the Soviet Union became closely associated with foreign economic and political systems as Brezhnev went abroad to finance the corporatist deal.[6] Instead of engaging in effective economic reforms, which might have threatened the sovereignty of the party and the planners, the viability of the domestic impasse was to be maintained by Western assistance. Brezhnev broadened support for détente in 1973 by co-opting key figures on to the Politburo; the foreign minister Andrei Gromyko, the defence minister Marshal Grechko (on his death in 1976 replaced by Dmitrii Ustinov), and the head of the KGB Yurii Andropov.

Brezhnev's ascendancy marked an elitist reaction, though it was not a return to Lenin or Stalin but represented a new pattern. Khrushchev's populism was not abandoned but redefined as it became attuned to the managerial approach to political participation. There was little attempt to redefine authority relations as trust in society gave way to trust in cadres. Order and discipline became the watchwords of the regime. The sphere of the political became very much the preserve of elite groups and their trusted allies, and only routine matters were delegated. Non-political forms of participation were encouraged, but the choice of what was political and what was routine, not surprisingly, was kept firmly in the hands of the leadership.[7]

The conservatism of the Brezhnev years manifested itself in the consolidation of due process rather than in challenges to the entrenched elites. Participation in policy debates within the government was broadened as the authority of specialist groupings rose.[8] Contrary to the long-standing ideal of Soviet policy-making, interest groups began to assert their own 'departmental' interests over those of an 'objective' national interest. A secure class of *apparatchiki* was consolidated as political officials became relatively autonomous.[9] Appeals over the heads of the elite to the people were discouraged. The dismantling of the party-state control commissions in December 1965 removed an important channel of popular supervision. Much weaker separate control commissions for the party, state and people were established. The concept of the state of all the people, and with it the idea of ever-increasing mass involvement which would ultimately lead to the withering away of the state, was played down, though it was revived in a weaker form in the 1970s. Discussion of the theoretical distinction between state and society was discouraged. Lenin's fulminations against bureaucracy in *State and Revolution* and in his later works such as *Better Fewer, But Better* were forgotten. The inculcation of civic pride and Soviet nationalism were to compensate for the absence of democratisation. The Soviet victory in the Second World War, and Brezhnev's own modest role in that victory, became obsessive themes of the agitprop apparatus. The period appealed not to a sense of dynamism but to the yearning for stability and enjoyment of past victories.

There was no full-scale return to Stalinism but the conservatism of the period was marked by a partial restalinisation. From 1965 a movement began for the reconsideration of the two destalinisation congresses. On the eve of the twenty-third party congress in 1966 a letter of twenty-five leading intellectuals protested against the creeping rehabilitation of Stalin. The leadership clearly realised that the political costs of rehabilitation would be high, and the issue was left vague at the congress. By 1968 the neo-Stalinists were gaining ground, and sensed victory with the intervention in Czechoslovakia in August to crush the reforms introduced by party leader Alexander Dubček. In 1969 the conservatives planned to erect a statue on Stalin's grave and to celebrate his birthday on 21 December with a laudatory article in *Pravda*. Only the warnings of the Polish and Hungarian communist parties, and it was rumoured the personal visits of Gomulka and Kadar to argue against rehabilitating Stalin, led to the last-minute cancellation of the article – but too late to prevent it being published in Ulan Bator. Western communist parties would undoubtedly have protested. The episode highlights the international context of destalinisation and illustrates what effect association with other socialist countries might have had during Stalin's rise in the 1920s. After 1969 Brezhnev checked those in favour of a complete rehabilitation of Stalin, but the battle between the two forces continued. Brezhnev's rule became increasingly heavy-handed as he permitted a series of trials against dissenters, even though they undermined his own détente policy. The social sciences, particularly historians dealing with sensitive episodes in the USSR's past, were subject to increasing restrictions. There were, however, major novelties in style. Greater individual autonomy was permitted as long as it did not pass beyond the bounds and become an open challenge to the regime. The Brezhnevite compromise was reflected in the muted celebration of Stalin's centenary on 21 December 1979, with *Pravda* praising Stalin's leadership during the war but noting the excesses of the personality cult. There was no mention of the purges, and indeed the very existence of the labour camps was officially ignored.

THE DECLINE OF THE REGIME

The Brezhnev era is now fated to pass into history as the 'era of stagnation', and yet it was a time of great successes for the country. The Soviet Union achieved strategic parity with the United States; it rose from being a regional to a global superpower; and the détente process culminated in the Conference on Security and Co-operation in Europe in Helsinki in August 1975 which ratified Soviet wartime territorial gains and its status in Eastern Europe. Agricultural output, the standard of living, and housing all improved significantly. Under Brezhnev it appeared that the USSR had finally achieved a rational approach to policy-making and had made peace with society. Brezhnev's rule marked a period of tranquillity after decades of turbulence. But while the stability was based on solid achievements, the fundamental structural reforms needed to deal with the accumulating problems of the Soviet economy and society were deferred. Already in 1976 Hough pointed out that Brezhnev was emulating Louis XIV with his attitude of 'after me the deluge'.[10] The problems were bequeathed to his successors. The administration was increasingly unable to achieve even relatively simple goals. Brezhnev's last years were marked by political stagnation and leadership immobility. It was not clear whether this reflected the leadership's own particular failings or a more general shortcoming of the system. Was the twenty-year stagnation a personal, social, economic or political phenomenon, or a combination of all four? Brezhnev's gradual political death between 1979 and 1982 in some ways parallels Lenin's between 1921 and 1924, and reflects the general rule that in the absence of constitutional limitations leaders are unlikely voluntarily to resign. Brezhnev loved the trappings of power, but reconciled himself to his inability to exercise that power.

The Brezhnev period appeared to represent the natural state of equilibrium of the Soviet system, a type of neo-feudal patron–client society. The historic failure of the Brezhnev era consisted of several related aspects. The prestige of the Soviet model of development in the world at large was eroded. The apparent inability to move beyond a stiflingly self-satisfied appraisal of political performance and coercive social integration undermined the ideological and moral cohesion of society. This was made all the more acute by the declining vigour of Soviet economic performance. Growth rates fell as capital investments and inputs gave a declining rate of return. The introduction of new technology remained partial and labour productivity stubbornly refused to increase as rapidly as planned. The sense of stagnation was exacerbated by the decay of Soviet ideology to dogmatic utterance. The Brezhnev period increasingly lived on the political capital accumulated during earlier periods of Soviet power.

The compromises of the social compact between the regime and society were mirrored by a number of unresolved contradictions within the polity itself. Among them was the balance to be struck between traditional party interventionism in economic and social life and the technocratic demand for a depoliticised sphere of administrative competence. Similarly, the balance between the use of material incentives and ideological exhortations to stimulate performance under developed socialism remained unclear. What was to be the relationship between participation from below and orders from above? Economic reform was left hanging in the air as an unfinished item on the agenda for nearly twenty years. Even the direction of change was not clear as in some spheres the market emerged while the economic and planning organs lost few of their powers. Would managers finally be allowed to encroach on the job security of their employees in order to attain economic efficiency? To what extent would the *de facto* administrative devolution of power to the ministries and a range of monopolies be allowed to continue? The social costs of the stability of cadres policy were becoming increasingly glaring. Corruption was rife with leaders beginning to act as petty princelings within their fiefdoms. The political role of the party was undermined as informal and unofficial contacts between officials increased. Above all, systemic integration was beginning to take place through social rather than political mechanisms.

Brezhnev himself was well aware of the shortcomings and tried to deal with them in so far as he knew how. From 1972, coinciding with the golden period of détente, new acts were passed enforcing social discipline and tightening censorship. A sustained campaign was waged to impose labour discipline through legal measures, social pressure and exhortation. This was accompanied by a renewed stress on social conformity. Brezhnev's twilight years were attended by his increasingly bitter but thoroughly impotent denunciations of ministerial officials. He was unable to move beyond an analysis which contrasted the failings of individuals to the basic soundness of the system itself.

By the late 1970s it was clear that Brezhnev's compromise would not work. A combination of foreign and domestic problems saw the disintegration of the corporatist deal. What had made corporatism possible in the first instance, détente, with which Brezhnev was so closely identified, appeared to be running into terminal difficulties (see Chapter 16). The level of assistance from abroad was not as extensive as Brezhnev had hoped and he was forced to consider domestic solutions to economic problems. From 1976 Brezhnev's health rapidly deteriorated and the succession issue became all the more pronounced. The jockeying for power, the building of alliances, and the undermining of opponents began in earnest. Furthermore, the Soviet economy's poor performance after 1978 became critical after a series of poor harvests and harsh winters. The social manifestations of the long stability became increasingly alarming to the leadership. There was a general sense that Soviet society was suffering from an unspecified malaise marked by the rapid growth of official corruption, the perceived decline in labour discipline and youth rebelliousness.

Under the superficial tranquillity of the Brezhnev integument, however, it increasingly became clear that a new style of politics was being born. A new approach was maturing which proposed alternative solutions to Soviet problems. Leaders since the death of Brezhnev reflected various facets of this new approach. One of the major elements in the new Soviet politics became identified with the name of Brezhnev's successor, Andropov, but had begun even while the former lived. Andropovism meant the enforcement of social discipline through authoritarianism and KGB activism, attempts to raise productivity, reduce corruption, enforce discipline in the workplace, and encourage the party apparatus to improve its work. This approach began to be applied from 1969 in Azerbaijan, when as part of a drive against corruption Geidar Aliev, the former head of the KGB in the republic, came to head the party organisation. In 1972 in Georgia the corrupt Brezhnev protégé V. P. Mzhavanadze was replaced by the republic's minister of the interior, Eduard Shevardnadze. These two leaders revived the 'permanent purge', though with a minimum of bloodshed, as key figures were dismissed, some of whom were tried for corruption and other offences. Lacking the ability to introduce substantive political reforms, the political and economic elites in the two republics were purged and purged again. The process revealed the limits to reform under the Brezhnev system, with its emphasis on the quality of cadres within immutable structures.

The anti-corruption campaign became prominent nationally in September 1978 when the involvement of deputy fishing industry minister Rytov in the great 'caviar scandal' led to his disgrace and execution. It became clear that hundreds were involved in the spectacular economic crime of exporting caviar in cans labelled herring. The investigation, led by the KGB, implicated such high party figures as S. Medunov, Brezhnev's associate and first secretary in the Krasnodar region. The 'fish case' strengthened the hand of those in favour of greater discipline and probably prompted the August 1979 Central Committee decree on the need to strengthen law and order. Brezhnev paid lip service to the campaign, but he was well aware that it threatened his own position. Just as with the party purges from 1920, there were attempts to make the anti-corruption campaign a public movement, though this did not get very far. The party's bureaucratic procedures and personnel prerogatives were being undermined by corruption, clientelism and the abuse of power. As informal practices weakened the party's ability to act as the leading force in society, Andropovism appeared to offer a way of reviving the system.

By 1979 Brezhnev's political position had been much weakened under the impact of cumulative policy failures. The year in many ways represents the real end of the Brezhnev era. Stable leadership patterns and policies gave way to a series of major initiatives. With considerable personal misgivings, Brezhnev approved the invasion of Afghanistan in December 1979; despite the warnings of academics and some top officials the leadership as a whole clearly believed that they had little to lose since détente lay in shreds. Similarly, the decision to step up the pressure on non-conformity and ultimately to eliminate dissent was precipitated by the forthcoming 1980 Olympic Games, to be held in Moscow. Brezhnev acquiesced in the law and order campaign, and from late 1981 the anti-corruption campaign struck at the very roots of his personal and political power. A politically astute campaign masterminded by Andropov exposed the sordid underside of Brezhnevite stability. Brezhnev's own daughter, Galina, was harassed by the KGB, and his ally Medunov was demoted amidst a political scandal. Brezhnev died in November 1982, but he had already outlived the 'Brezhnev era' by two to three years. A change in the political terms of reference had taken place that comes about but once a generation.

THE FINAL SOVIET POLITICS

Andropov: the struggle for discipline

The Brezhnev era began with the slogans of stability and order but ended in intrigues and crises. The absence of a clear succession mechanism and the jostling for power revived the Kremlinological approach to Soviet politics, the detailed and necessarily arcane analysis of power struggles within the leadership. It was an extraordinary finale to the Brezhnev years. His death was followed by a rapid sequence of leadership changes. However, contrary to the expectations of some, the long-awaited succession was not accompanied by a new 'time of troubles'. The interregnum was relatively brief and ended peacefully.

A new style in Soviet politics had emerged to accompany the decline of Brezhnev. One of its major expressions was the enhanced role for the KGB, headed since 1967 by Andropov. The basic principle of Andropov's policing was to achieve the maximum effect with the minimum violence. Although the KGB was restrained by the rules established at Stalin's death and remained under party control, during the Brezhnev era its influence and prestige rose. Andropov's accession to the Politburo in 1973 marked the first occasion that a KGB chief had achieved full membership since the death of Beria in 1953. From 1974 there were increasing numbers of

KGB personnel in the Central Committee, and in February 1981 at the twenty-sixth party congress Brezhnev paid elaborate, though not necessarily sincere, compliments to the KGB. In May 1982 Andropov replaced the deceased Suslov in the party Secretariat in charge of ideological affairs, and thus distanced himself from the KGB. As a member of the Politburo and Central Committee Secretariat Andropov was ideally placed to succeed Brezhnev as General Secretary. It is clear that in addition to being the choice of the police and the army, Andropov carried the hopes of certain economic reformers. His bid was aided by the brilliant cultivation of his image, projecting himself as dynamic and, indeed, as a man of culture. His experience in foreign and domestic politics was stressed, as was his reputation as being uncorrupted and blameless for the failings of the Brezhnev years.

Andropov's appointment was greeted, on the one side, with hopes that some major economic, or even political, reforms would be carried out by someone who appeared a pragmatist and in favour of greater debate; on the other side, by those who with much greater vehemence condemned Andropov as the redoubtable police chief and the representative of the rising tide of KGB influence and authoritarianism in Soviet politics. In fact, Andropov combined these images as he broke with Brezhnev's consensual politics and established a distinctive style of rule which sought to integrate the reformist and conservative strands in Soviet political life. His short tenure seemed to establish him as a bureaucratic authoritarian reformer rather than a reformer in the sense of a decentraliser and liberaliser. As during the transition to the NEP, economic reforms were to be balanced by political consolidation.

Not surprisingly, given his background, Andropov turned first to an extensive anti-corruption campaign whose roots went back at least to the early 1970s. The programme was presented as coming as much from below as from above. Some of the reputed thousands of letters complaining about corruption were now featured in the press and on television. Early 1983 was marked by a spate of dismissals of corrupt, and usually elderly, officials who had benefited from the lax political and moral atmosphere of the Brezhnev years. Brezhnev's close associate Nikolai Shchelokov was dismissed as police chief and the MVD itself came under the influence of the KGB with the appointment of V. V. Fedorchuk, Andropov's replacement as head of the KGB. The campaign succeeded in discrediting the Brezhnev elite and achieved a significant consolidation of the KGB's institutional position. It alone emerged unscathed and even in the post-Andropov period the KGB escaped with remarkably little criticism.

Along with the battle against corruption came a new emphasis on discipline, in both political and social life. After 1961 Khrushchev had dropped the stress on discipline in line with his idea of the state of all the people. Discipline allowed officials broad discretion to exercise their powers, whereas Khrushchev's populism stymied their rights in this respect. The term was revived in 1965 by Brezhnev and signalled the decreased emphasis on changing patterns of authority.[11] Under Andropov the concept of discipline was expanded to become the cornerstone of his rule. Khrushchev-type social controls were intensified, accompanied by the more scientific application of discipline by the government. As a harbinger of the *glasnost*, or openness, to come, the tone of the press changed with less eulogies and more straightforward criticism of shortcomings. The party reins were tightened over institutional interests. A programme of labour discipline tried to reverse the habits of a labour force that had become used to slackness, moonlighting and an easy-going attitude to plan fulfilment. The Andropov period opened amid extraordinary scenes of people being pulled out of bath-houses and snatched from queues during working hours to be charged with absenteeism. In August 1983 harsh new penalties for labour indiscipline were announced which cut a day off holidays for every day absent from work, penalised late arrival, and introduced the concept of compensation for loss of production resulting from absenteeism. The campaign launched in 1979 to eliminate the vestiges of dissent was continued with great vigour and was extended to the cultural sphere.

Like all new Soviet leaders, Andropov sought to consolidate his own position through a series of personnel changes in the party and state apparatuses. Brezhnev's close group of colleagues, known as the 'Dnepropetrovsk mafia', was broken up. By June 1983 Andropov felt strong enough to take on the post of President in addition to that of General Secretary and thus continued the Brezhnev tradition of combining both posts. Andropov's changes focused on strengthening his team concerned with economic affairs. Yegor Ligachev, the incorruptible party leader in Tomsk *oblast*, was brought on to the Politburo and Secretariat in charge of personnel affairs, and Nikolai Ryzhkov, a former director of Uralmash (one of the largest engineering complexes in the Soviet Union) was appointed to the Secretariat and later replaced Tikhonov as Prime Minister. Both represented the new technocratic bias of appointments favouring people who had risen through economic lines rather than through party appointments. M. S. Gorbachev, Central Committee secretary in charge of agriculture since 1978, was given overall responsibility for the economy.

Andropov's economic programme did not change Brezhnev's basic priorities, retaining the emphasis on agriculture and accepting the need to maintain the output of high-quality consumer items, but it did try to come to terms with the challenges posed by a mature economy. A limited experiment launched in July 1983 aimed to encourage greater managerial autonomy by reducing the number of instructions from the central ministries. The limited decentralisation permitted a greater proportion of profits to remain in the plant to be used at the discretion of the manager. The aim was to encourage the introduction of new technology and to improve labour productivity by shedding surplus labour within the framework of an improved planning mechanism. Andropov did not put forward any far-reaching solutions or any major structural changes. The problem remained of introducing real incentives for genuine improvements in labour productivity. This was tackled in July 1983 by a Law on Labour Collectives, promoting a limited form of self-management which extended the scope for organised groups of workers to discuss questions concerning their work. The law encouraged the use of the brigade system whereby groups of workers themselves decided on the allocation of tasks and distribution of pay, although they were unable to appoint their own leaders or to encroach on the rights of managers. It was an attempt to introduce self-policing mechanisms on to the shopfloor by instilling a greater sense of responsibility. In agriculture there was a renewed emphasis on the 'link' system, known later as the 'collective contract', in which a group of fifty to a hundred agricultural workers were offered a piece of land, equipment, seeds and so on, and were paid by results. They were allowed to keep any profit on crops produced over and above the plan, although this was capped to prevent the re-emergence of a class of rich peasants (kulaks). The plan's greatest proponent was Gorbachev, who saw greater local initiative and decentralisation as a possible alternative to Brezhnev's wasteful investment strategy for improving agricultural productivity.

In foreign policy Andropov's rule coincided with the second Cold War following the decline of détente, the imposition of martial law in Poland and the banning of Solidarity, the continuing war in Afghanistan, and the imminent deployment of Cruise and Pershing II missiles in Western Europe to counter the Soviet SS20s. The shooting down of the civilian South Korean airliner KAL 007 with the loss of 269 lives in September 1983 led to a twenty-year low in East–West relations. The mismanagement of that affair was partly due to Andropov's poor health.

He suffered kidney failure in February 1983, and his increasing absence from public view from August 1983 meant that his period in office declined into a time of drift, rather like Brezhnev's, brought to a close by his death on 9 February 1984.

Andropov's period in office signalled a reversion to the tradition of authoritarian reform that had emerged victorious in 1921 over the trend of 'democratic reform' proposed by the various oppositional groupings of that time. Andropov's policies were a combination of martial law and economic reform. He began to curtail the expanded privileges of the elite and to limit corruption, and promised to clip the powers of the institutions and interest groups. His rule witnessed an institutional shift of emphasis away from the party to operating other levers of power. This does not mean, however, that he accepted that power should be more diffuse. The increased role for the KGB was designed to buttress not to supplant the party's leading role.

Chernenko: the struggle for conformity

The remarkable feature of Chernenko's rule is that he was chosen to be General Secretary at all. Aged 73 and suffering from emphysema, his appointment at a time when the country faced critical challenges seemed a singularly short-sighted act by his peers. They appeared more intent on saving themselves than the country, a desperate attempt to hold back the tide of personal biological decay and political change. Chernenko's accession can be seen in terms of a backlash of the party old guard, which was threatened by the Andropov discipline and anti-corruption campaigns and worried about his economic reforms. They were forced, however, to concede certain powers to the representative of the new politics, Gorbachev, who acted as an unofficial deputy general secretary.

According to Ligachev, 'Chernenko was a classic apparatchik – from head to toe, to his very marrow. He'd spent decades working in offices, at a respectful distance from real life.'[12] His appointment revealed the strength of the Brezhnev approach in Soviet politics. Brezhnevism cannot be simply equated with the resistance of entrenched office-holders to the encroachments of political and economic reform. The Brezhnev system satisfied a range of concerns, including officialdom, and gave them powerful vested interests in the maintenance of a relatively *laissez-faire* approach to social and political management. Reform not only challenged the privileges of the powerful, but exposed the thousand little strategems devised by individuals to survive under Soviet conditions. Overt dissent was crushed under Brezhnev only to reappear in myriad acts of social non-conformity. The new Soviet politics associated with Andropov threatened not only the privileges of the powerful but the exigencies of the weak.

Chernenko's rise under Brezhnev's patronage revealed the worst features of Brezhnevite political cronyism. Chernenko continued the anti-corruption drive but deflected some of its force to social deviancy and non-conformity and relieved the pressure against political corruption. Coming to power at a time when relations with the West were extremely poor, he concentrated on imposing ideological conformity through such petty acts as banning the importation of foreign pop music and unlicensed videos. His thought was imbued with notions of ideological pollution and noxious Western influences that harked back to the worst features of the Cold War under Stalin. Chernenko became the guardian of dogma: 'There are some truths that are not subject to revision, problems that were solved long ago and once-and-for-all. The basic principles of dialectical materialism cannot be forgotten.'[13] The second Cold War as far as Soviet domestic policies were concerned was indeed a farcical rerun of the tragedy of the first. Only Gorbachev's intervention prevented Chernenko restoring the name of Stalingrad to the city that Khrushchev had renamed Volgograd. He did, however, make some gestures towards reviving détente and obtaining an arms-control agreement. An article by Chernenko in September 1981 insisted on the need to avoid antagonising any social groups and to obviate social tension.[14] This blast against the politics of discipline, judging from his performance in office, appears to have been an attempt to establish his 'liberal' credentials in opposition to Andropov in the struggle for power. Chernenko's assumption of the presidency together with the post of party General Secretary may have given him the illusion of great power but it certainly did not endow his leadership with authority. There is insufficient evidence to establish the direction that Chernenko might have taken given better health and a longer period in office. It is probable that he would have tried to combine the Brezhnev approach with some of Andropov's initiatives in the economic and social spheres. His long-expected death on 10 March 1985 brought an end to the interregnum between Brezhnev and Gorbachev.

Gorbachev: the struggle for change

While Chernenko was clearly an interim leader, the selection of Gorbachev as General Secretary broke the mould of Soviet politics and established a new tone for Soviet leadership. Economic and political factors propelled Gorbachev to challenge the social contract policies of the neo-Stalinist compromise to stimulate the economy and to tackle grave social problems. Gorbachev argued that the later Brezhnev years were marked by a 'pre-crisis', which would have become a full-scale crisis if timely action had not been taken. In addition he questioned Andropov's authoritarian approach to reform and returned to the traditions so sharply truncated in 1921 of democratic and even liberal reform. Gorbachev joined the long Russian tradition of reformers from above, but at the same time the novelty of his reforms was that they offered some real scope for initiative from below.

Mikhail Sergeevich Gorbachev was born of peasant stock on 2 March 1931 in the agricultural Stavropol region (*krai*) of south Russia. He graduated with a degree in law from Moscow State University in 1955, and in 1967 he passed a correspondence degree in agronomy. At Moscow University he met his wife Raisa, who holds a doctorate in Marxist–Leninist philosophy. He spent most of his early career in his native Stavropol *krai*, rising from Komsomol chief to the party leadership. His career was that of a typical party official. It was advanced by his association with Fedor Kulakov, the first secretary of the party in the region, and with Suslov, the guardian of Brezhnevite ideological orthodoxy, who acted as Gorbachev's patrons. When Kulakov was appointed minister of agriculture in 1970 Gorbachev replaced him and in the next year became a full member of the Central Committtee. He achieved significant successes with his policies of agricultural innovation and support for greater individual initiative. On Kulakov's death in 1978 Gorbachev, at the youthful age of 47, replaced him as Central Committee secretary responsible for agriculture. Gorbachev's reputation emerged remarkably unscathed from the series of poor harvests from 1978, and he rose to become a candidate member of the Politburo in November 1979 and a full member in October 1980. Promoted by Andropov and in effect sharing power with Chernenko, his election as General Secretary was nevertheless no foregone conclusion. He was opposed by the Brezhnevites V. Grishin and G. Romanov, and a large number of the Central Committee apparently had misgivings. At the decisive 11 March meetings, however, they kept silent and after a firm statement in his favour by the veteran foreign minister, Gromyko, Gorbachev was elected unanimously by the Politburo and the Central Committee. On coming to power in March 1985 he was 54 years old, the youngest

Soviet leader since Malenkov (51 in 1953). His experiences were mostly of the post-war era, and for him the traumas of collectivisation, purges and war were history.

Gorbachev came to power when there was an unprecedented desire for change in the Soviet Union. There was a sense that the country faced a mounting and intolerable 'lack of order' (*bezporyadok*), as manifested by alcoholism, corruption, and ineffective party and police mechanisms. The political climate was more conducive to reform than at any time since the early years of Khrushchev. And it appeared that Gorbachev was the man to face up to these challenges. His relative youth, his education and his lively and enquiring mind all marked him out from his predecessors. The accession of Gorbachev as a reform-minded leader seemed to confirm the hopes of those, like Roy Medvedev, who had long argued that the most realistic prospect for change in the Soviet Union was from within the system itself, a new leader supported by reforming officials and sections of society.[15] Gorbachev revived the revisionist approach of inner-party renewal last practised in the USSR by Khrushchev and thought to have died with the crushing of the Prague Spring in Czechoslovakia in 1968.

He signalled his intentions straight away at the April 1985 plenum of the Central Committee (CC), which advanced a critique of 'Brezhnevism' that was to become the hallmark of his rule. The launching of the policies of restructuring (*perestroika*) of the economy, of acceleration (*uskorenie*) and of openness (*glasnost*) all indicated the advent of a serious reformer. The Andropov leadership shared the belief in the need for economic reform but this was to be based on greater discipline. Under Gorbachev the realisation increasingly came to the fore that the technocratic approach was inadequate and that economic reform could not be achieved by administrative measures alone. The reform process would have to tackle the roots of the problem by 'democratisation'. A link was forged between further economic development and political modernisation; otherwise the Soviet Union was in danger of sinking in the world economy to the economic status of a third world primary-materials exporter. No longer were the legacy of Tsarist backwardness and the destruction of the Second World War convincing excuses to explain the USSR's continued relative backwardness in most spheres other than the military. Gorbachev argued that *perestroika* was placed on the agenda by the entire course of social development, and that minor repairs were no longer enough. His maiden speech to the CC in April 1985 stressed the objective need for reform since there was 'no other way'. The remoralising strain in *perestroika* was crucial. Gorbachev later noted that the decision to launch *perestroika* was prompted in part by 'our troubled conscience'.[16]

Gorbachev's ambitious early programme, reflected in the goals outlined in the twelfth (and last) five-year plan (1986–90), was geared to the year 2000, by which time he hoped the economy would have been successfully restructured and society democratised. He defined *perestroika* at the twenty-seventh congress of the CPSU as not only raising the rate of economic growth but as a qualitatively different type of growth: the intensification of production on the basis of scientific and technological progress, the structural reorganisation of the economy, improved management and better incentives for labour. He had no illusions about the magnitude of the task facing him. The entire overhauling of the system was required. In a break with the Andropov approach, political *glasnost*, criticism and democracy were seen as essential facets of economic *perestroika*. He also talked about the need for a 'psychological restructuring' entailing a spiritual reformation away from Stalinist authoritarianism towards individual initiative and the 'human factor' operating within effective structures. *Glasnost* was designed to permit the greater democratisation of society and the extension of socialist self-management and popular initiative. As Gorbachev insisted at the June 1987 CC plenum, the command and administrative approach to managing society put a brake on development and could only be remedied by promoting democracy.

The leadership changes of the early 1980s were remarkable for the almost complete absence, at least explicitly, of the issue of destalinisation. With the leadership question settled by the accession of Gorbachev, *glasnost* permitted a re-examination not only of the person of Stalin but of his policies. This was no longer part of a destalinisation campaign from above but was accompanied by a reappraisal from below. At the Writers' Union Congress of the Russian Republic in December 1985 Yevtushenko returned to the theme that had made him famous under Khrushchev: the issue of Stalin's crimes. The debate was taken up in literary journals, and once again the 'blank pages' in Soviet history were under discussion. The film *Repentance* by Tengiz Abuladze exposed the characters of Stalin, Beria and the Stalinist period. Anatolii Rybakov's *Children of the Arbat* painfully revealed the reality of life and suffering in the 1930s. In February 1988 Bukharin was at last rehabilitated, signalling that the NEP alternative to War Communist policies could now be openly discussed. The scale of rehabilitations indicated the degree to which party policy had changed but it had nothing to do with redressing injustice until law could exist independently of party policy. Destalinisation challenged the Soviet regime to face up to its own past, and when the test came at this time the system failed critically to acknowledge its own crimes or to express genuine repentance for the horrors it had inflicted on its own people. This failure, perhaps more than anything else, undermined the bonds of trust between the government and people that Gorbachev had begun to create.

Although initially marked by a return of optimism and belief in the reformability of the system, by 1989 darker shadows had begun to haunt the reform process. It appeared that *perestroika* was dominated by a negative destructive logic, and was unable to build a coherent set of political institutions to replace the declining role of the communist party or to devise an effective economic policy to negotiate the traumatic passage from the plan to the market. These frustrations finally boiled over into the attempted coup of 18–21 August 1991. There remain numerous questions over what the State Committee for the State of Emergency, which was established on 18 August, sought to achieve, since its members were already the embodiment of power, but above all they were concerned with maintaining the unity of the country and an authoritative central authority (not necessarily the communist party). The resistance by the Russian authorities led by Boris Yeltsin led to the coup swiftly unravelling, but when Gorbachev returned from vacation in the early hours of 22 August he entered a different country. Soviet politics was effectively finished, and by the end of the year the Soviet Union no longer existed.

Gorbachev's reform programme represented a return to some of the themes of Khrushchev's rule, such as the need for popular initiative, an understanding of the past, new approaches to economic and political organisation, and a 'back to Lenin' motif. However, whereas Khrushchev's reforms were predicated on overcoming the baleful consequences of the doings of one man, Joseph Stalin, *perestroika* recognised that the problems went much deeper, but then failed to devise an adequate programme in response to what it acknowledged. The problems and achievements of Gorbachev's struggle for change will be dealt with in the following chapters.

KEY TEXTS

Bialer, Seweryn, *Stalin's Successors: Leadership, Stability and Change in the Soviet Union* (Cambridge, Cambridge University Press, 1980).

Brown, A. and M. Kaser (eds), *Soviet Policy for the 1980s* (London, Macmillan, 1982).

Brown, Archie, *The Gorbachev Factor* (Oxford, Oxford University Press, 1996).

Hewett, E. H. and Victor H. Winston (eds), *Milestones in Glasnost and Perestroika: Politics and People* (Washington DC, The Brookings Institution, 1991).
Hewett, E. H. and Victor H. Winston (eds), *Milestones in Glasnost and Perestroika: The Economy* (Washington DC, The Brookings Institution, 1991).

Part II

Government

6 The communist party

The Communist Party of the Soviet Union (CPSU) was the linchpin of the Soviet political system. What we shall call in the next chapter the 'unwritten constitution' of Soviet government was generated by the existence of a party with great but undefined powers. This endowed the system, however well ordered it might have looked superficially and from the perspective of the formal constitution, with an arbitrariness that became the hallmark of the entire regime. The party acted as a 'ministry of politics', claiming a monopoly on organised political life. The Bolshevik party was indeed, as Lenin claimed, a 'party of a new type', a unique combination of organisational and ideological innovation.

But what happens when a party of this type begins to decay? Under Brezhnev the party's authority was eroded as its ideology stagnated, trust in cadres gave way to corruption, and policy stability to immobility. The political dictatorship of the party began to give way to the social dominance of a new class. It was against this social degeneration, marked by corruption, that Andropov set his face, and which Gorbachev sought to reverse by opening up the sphere of politics to include popular oversight over the political class. Gorbachev's ambitious intention was to restore the authority of the party through real moral leadership, renewed policies and identification with the aspirations of the population. Not for the first time a communist party sought to redefine its relationship with society while stopping short of full pluralism, and in this Gorbachev followed in the tradition of Khrushchev, the Czechoslovak reformers of 1968, and the attempts at the internal renewal (*odnowa*) of the Polish party in 1980–81. Gorbachev's reforms of the party, however, precipitated its collapse.

RECRUITMENT POLICY

Recruitment from 1917 alternated between periods of intensive growth and renewed restrictions. The early years saw a rapid expansion as the party acted as a massive conveyor belt of workers into administration and military posts. During the Civil War the party's elect membership was diluted by the influx of 'Soviet bureaucrats' and illiterate workers and peasants, evoking fears about its degeneration and precipitating the first national purge (*chistka*) of party membership in 1921 that sought to screen out undesirables. Lenin's death in 1924 was followed by the mass influx of the 'Lenin Enrolment' (*Leninskii prizyv*), a process that allegedly allowed Stalin to swamp the more independent-minded older generation of communists by a mass of raw workers beholden to him for advancement. The industrialisation drive from the late 1920s was accompanied by a major enrolment drive, halted by the party purge of 1933. If membership (with candidates) stood at 472,000 on 1 January 1924, just before Lenin's death, by early 1933 there were 3,555,338, the vast majority of whom were workers or peasants when they joined.[1] The late 1930s and the war years once again witnessed expansion which slowed down after the war.

Under Khrushchev there was sustained growth, especially in the years after 1957. The party grew by 65 per cent, with an annual growth rate of about 5 per cent, as Khrushchev attempted to catch up with population growth, the enlargement of the working class and educational progress. Excessive growth appeared to threaten the party's vanguard role and the growth rate was halved after 1965, and once again halved in 1971–76. The decline also reflected demographic patterns, with a low birth-rate during the war and again after the immediate postwar baby boom. Growth fell from an average of 762,000 per annum between 1962 to 1965 to 311,000 in 1981–86, an annual average of 1.7 per cent. The slowdown was a response to what John Miller called the 'dilemma of party growth' whereby rapid increases undermined the party's vanguard position.[2] While the party tried to ensure that its membership was representative of society at large, the principle of 'strict individual selection' remained the dominant entrance criterion. By 1988 the rate of membership growth had fallen to a minuscule 0.1 per cent, and then in 1989 membership actually fell, for the first time since 1954.[3] In 1990–91 the party lost about a quarter of its membership,[4] a large proportion of whom were industrial workers and young members.

In earlier years a decline in growth usually coincided with a campaign to check the credentials of the existing party membership. During the Civil War these campaigns were called reregistrations. They were systematised in 1921 when the party underwent the first full-scale purge, and the party purges of the early 1930s merged into the great purge of the entire society. In 1971 the twenty-fourth party congress sanctioned a new purge, once again described as a reregistration, which in three years saw 347,000 communists expelled. Even when no reregistration campaign was in progress there was a steady stream of expulsions. Between 1981 and 1986 about 430,000 communists were reportedly expelled, reflecting attempts to reimpose discipline following the Solidarity crisis in Poland and Brezhnev's death. Party discipline collapsed in the final years, with over a million members overdue with their membership dues by October 1990, contributing to the major financial crisis in the party itself, a crisis exacerbated by the sharp decline in subscriptions to the party press.

By 1986 the CPSU had achieved a membership of 19.04 million members and candidates, representing 9.7 per cent (nearly one in ten) of the adult population (see Table 2), or 6.8 per cent (one in fifteen) of the entire population of 284 million. Recruitment policy was based on the idea that the party represented the cream of Soviet society, the most dedicated and the most able, who wished to serve their country. It was on this principle that the legitimacy of the party's dominance of Soviet political life rested. Increasingly, however, the party was perceived to be made up of time-servers and careerists while its leadership appeared resistant to change. Recruitment among the groups it claimed to represent, moreover, was declining, particularly with respect to young workers. The rationale for its 'vanguard' role was undermined and the way out appeared to lie either in full pluralism or a reassertion of party rule through coercion.

Party membership can be divided into three categories. The first group comprised the party *apparatchiks* who worked full time in the party's own bureaucracy. Their precise number is unknown but they made up a fairly small proportion, about 2 per cent of total party membership. Some of them are included in the second category, the party activists. In February 1986 there were 5.3 million elected officials, most of whom were part time, representing 29 per cent of total CPSU membership.[5] The third group was made up by the rank-and-file membership. Some of

Table 2 The CPSU in figures

	1971	*1976*	*1981*	*1986*
Total membership	14,455,321	15,694,187	17,480,768	19,037,946
Full members	13,810,089	15,058,017	16,763,009	18,309,693
Candidates	645,232	636,170	717,759	728,253
Population 20+	152,281,000	165,767,000	178,874,000	196,267,800
Communists as % of				
adults 20 and over	9.4	9.4	9.4	9.7
Social composition				
Workers	5,759,379	6,509,312	7,569,261	8,551,779
%	40.1	41.6	43.4	45.0
Peasants	2,169,437	2,169,813	2,223,674	2,248,166
%	15.1	13.9	12.8	11.8
Employees	6,443,747	6,959,766	7,637,478	8,204,433
%	44.8	44.5	43.8	43.2
Sexual composition				
Women	3,195,556	3,793,859	4,615,576	5,475,145
%	22.2	24.3	26.5	28.8
Recruitment (%)				
Workers		57.6	59.0	59.4
Peasants		11.3	10.3	9.9
Technical intelligentsia		24.5	25.4	26.1
Administrators		5.2	3.8	3.2
Students		1.4	1.5	1.4
Women		29.5	32.2	34.1
Education				
Higher	2,819,642	3,807,469	4,881,877	6,045,653
%	19.6	24.3	28.0	31.8
Incomplete higher	337,995	385,556	391,216	398,059
%	2.4	2.5	2.2	2.1
Secondary	4,932,958	6,022,397	7,297,089	8,451,480
%	34.3	38.5	41.9	44.5
Incomplete secondary	3,573,368	3,175,163	2,973,839	2,601,613
%	24.9	20.3	17.1	13.7
Primary	2,708,600	2,251,306	1,886,392	1,507,573
%	18.8	14.4	10.8	7.9

Note: The columns represent changes over the five-year period between congress. The twenty-fourth party congresses met in March 1971, the twenty-fifth in February 1976, the twenty-sixth in February 1981, and the twenty-seventh in February 1986.
Source: *Partiinaya zhizn*, No. 14 (July 1986), pp. 19–24.

these were recruited not because of any particular dedication to the party but because they represented the elite in their professions. They fulfilled the 'cadre' role in their chosen field, representing the party and its policies in their place of work. Their role was that of mass leadership, a channel for the transmission of influence and information to and from their colleagues.

Lenin's ideal of the communist as a dedicated revolutionary remained in force until the end, and there were constant attempts to maintain a level of *aktivnost* (activity), contrasted to *passivnost* (passivity), in all spheres of a party member's life. While the CPSU was traditionally a cadre party, one made up of dedicated activists, it had also become a mass party. The distinction between the two became blurred, although it was clearly a mass party run by a cadre core. The fundamental dilemma was how to reconcile its mass functions with its vanguard, or leading, role. The party's size was limited to about 10 per cent of the adult population to maintain the balance between its cadre and mass roles and to guard against its 'dissolution' into society.

Membership in theory was open to any citizen of the USSR but there were various screening processes. Prospective members had to be invited to join: the decision was not so much the individual's as that of the party organisation. Recruitment became an extended system of co-optation. The checks consisted of references from communists of not less than five years' standing, approval by a party meeting, usually at the place of work, endorsement by party officials at the next highest administrative level, and a probationary period (candidature) of twelve months during which the candidate had to prove her- or himself worthy of membership by attending party meetings, working well, and showing the requisite political consciousness. The system was a legacy of pre-revolutionary procedures designed to avoid infiltration by police spies. About 5 per cent of candidates failed to graduate to full membership. During *perestroika* the conditions became more exacting to screen out unworthy elements, with a preliminary discussion of the merits of candidates at workplaces. Recruitment began to be democratised, accompanied by an influx of political activists (like Anatolii Sobchak, later mayor of Leningrad), who once again saw the party as a vehicle for political change.

The party stressed the duties associated with membership rather than the privileges. Yet there were advantages, above all the opening up of career opportunities and access to what was called party information, news about the world outside and domestic political concerns that was not readily available to ordinary citizens. There was also the prestige of being one of the chosen few, but by the end this factor had given way to the prevalent cynicism. The use of party membership to advance one's career was condemned, yet under Brezhnev the dangerous tendency emerged for party membership to be associated with particular jobs. Officials stressed that membership was not automatic simply because a person held a certain post or as a family tradition. The personal qualities of the applicant were what counted, although certain social or national categories, such as industrial workers, found it easier to join in line with attempts to prevent the party becoming one of white-collar workers and the intelligentsia. On the other hand, certain top posts were almost always reserved for party members. This was particularly the case in the diplomatic service and for senior military officers, where party membership was a prerequisite for promotion.

The party's social composition was always a matter of prime concern, although it is difficult to judge the question since statistics usually described a member's status on joining the party and not subsequent changes. In 1986, 45 per cent were described as workers, 11.8 per cent as collective farmers, and 43.2 per cent as employees or in the army.[6] Figures on employment status released in 1990 revealed a somewhat different picture (see Table 3). The party now claimed to be not only the vanguard of the working class but of the whole society, in line with the concept of the state of all the people, and this justified the recruitment of employees. Despite the fact that since 1918 the working class never comprised an absolute majority of membership, the party still claimed to have a special relationship with the workers. Khrushchev's policy of increasing the proportion of workers was continued by his successors. By 1986, 59.4 per cent of new members were workers, compared with 26.1 per cent employees, 3.2 per cent administrators and managers, 9.9 per cent collective farmers and 1.4 per cent students[7] in a society made up of 61.7 per cent workers, 16.2 per cent employees and 12.1 per cent collective farmers. Given rising educational levels, the increased proportion of new party members designated 'worker' does not necessarily mean that they were manual workers or employed in traditional manufacturing or extractive industries. The emphasis shifted to the recruitment of

Table 3 The social composition of the CPSU, 1990

CPSU	Number	Percentage
Total membership	19,228,217	
Candidates	372,104	1.9
Women	5,813,610	30.2
Age groups		
20 and under	38,553	0.2
21–25	645,091	3.4
26–30	2,001,936	10.4
31–40	5,001,311	26.0
41–50	3,682,076	19.1
51–60	3,844,212	20.0
over 60	4,014,038	20.9
Education		
Higher	6,808,715	35.4
Incomplete higher	358,350	1.9
Secondary	8,605,207	44.7
Primary	1,154,880	6.0
Less than primary	54,570	0.3
Employment status		
Workers	5,313,524	27.6
Collective farmers	1,466,361	7.6
White-collar staff	7,793,048	40.5
Students	101,415	0.5
Pensioners and housewives	3,344,981	17.4
Others	1,208,888	6.3

Source: *Izvestiya TsK KPSS*, No. 4 (1990), pp. 113–15; adapted by Stephen White and Ian McAllister, 'The CPSU and its Members: Between Communism and Postcommunism', *British Journal of Political Science*, Vol. 26, No. 1 (January 1996), p. 110.

workers employed in the leading-edge industries of electronics, communications, energy and engineering.

Some professions were greatly over-represented, especially ideologically sensitive posts or the armed services. Three out of four journalists were party members, but only one artist in five and one in four engineers and teachers. Party 'saturation' of those with higher education was higher than the population at large. The typical party member was better educated than the average citizen and better qualified, with over 78 per cent of communists having completed secondary or higher education. About 12.5 per cent of the employed population had higher education whereas in the party they made up 32 per cent. Three-quarters of employees joining the party were skilled professionals, such as agronomists, engineers, teachers, doctors and cultural figures. As the party became more solidly white collar, better educated and more urban than the population as a whole, there was the danger that certain sections of society, in particular the poor and under-educated, would find themselves unrepresented.

Party membership, especially at higher levels, can be broken down into generations. Recruitment went through successive phases and these remained as geological layers in the party. The leadership cohort schooled under Stalin remained in command until the early 1980s but was gradually diluted by the postwar generation. Andropov appealed both to the conservative authoritarianism of the old generation and to the younger technocrats, while Gorbachev's rise to the top represented the much-delayed change of generations. From a party of youth in the early years, the party under Khrushchev was only slightly younger than the national average and thereafter stable recruitment patterns allowed the party to mature in keeping with the general ageing of the population. The legal minimum age for joining was 18, but under Brezhnev recruitment tended to be delayed for at least five years. Nearly three-quarters of those recruited in the early 1980s were Komsomol members, that is, under 28 years old, and four-fifths were under 30. In 1986 17.6 per cent of membership was under 31, 23.7 per cent between 31 and 40, and 22.3 per cent between 41 and 50.[8] The proportion of long-term members rose, with 68 per cent having been in the party for over ten years in 1986 compared to only about 50 per cent in 1967.

The national composition of the party was as much a matter of concern for the leadership as was social composition, and it was equally sensitive. Ethnic Russians officially made up just over half (51 per cent) of the total Soviet population, but in 1986 they comprised 59.1 per cent of the CPSU. This disproportion represented a decline from 66 per cent in 1961: the non-Russian republics maintained a high recruitment rate in an attempt to equalise representation – Uzbeks, for example, were joining the party at an annual rate of 3 per cent, while the national average was 2 per cent, and the RSFSR rate was only 1.6 per cent. The five titular Central Asian peoples together made up only 5.7 per cent of the CPSU while in 1979 they represented 9.9 per cent of the total population (see Tables 4 and 9, below).

Great variations between republics remained, with the rate of increase the highest in Moldavia, at 3.1 per cent per annum, and lowest in Georgia, possibly to offset earlier over-representation. There was a higher representation of Jews than any other single nationality in the CPSU at about 20 per cent of those over 20 years old. The Georgians were the next highest to be represented at 11.6 per cent of the total adult population, the Russians at 10.3 per cent, down to 3.5 per cent for Moldavians. A marked feature was the falling recruitment of ethnic groups without national republics, such as Tatars and Jews, while those with union republics consolidated their positions. The CPSU gradually lost its Russian face but its features remained predominantly Slavic: the Slavic peoples (Russians, Belorussians and Ukrainians) in 1986 together

Table 4 National composition of the CPSU, 1986

Nationality	Number	Percentage
Russians	11,241,958	59.1
Ukrainians	3,041,736	16.0
Belorussians	726,108	3.8
Uzbeks	465,443	2.4
Kazakhs	387,837	2.0
Azerbaijanis	337,904	1.8
Georgians	321,922	1.7
Armenians	291,081	1.5
Lithuanians	147,068	0.8
Moldavians	110,715	0.6
Tajiks	87,759	0.5
Latvians	78,193	0.4
Kyrgyz	78,064	0.4
Turkmens	76,786	0.4
Estonians	61,277	0.3
Others	1,550,527	8.2
Total	19,004,378	100.0

Source: Partiinaya zhizn, No. 14 (July 1986), p. 24.

made up 79 per cent of membership (see Table 5). It is clear that the leadership was unable to control ethnic recruitment quite so closely as it could social composition.

Women were always greatly under-represented (see Table 2). This might be understandable when the party claimed to represent the industrial working class, but was less so as the society modernised. In 1920 women made up only 7.4 per cent of membership, rising to 22.2 per cent in 1971 and peaking at 30.2 in 1990.[9] Policy clearly aimed to redress the imbalance and the proportion of women among those joining the party rose from 29.5 per cent in the early 1970s to 34.1 per cent in the 1980s. With women outnumbering men in the population (53 per cent), the under-representation was more severe than the above figures suggest, a pattern even more marked in the higher echelons of the party.

The party acted as a system-regulating mechanism for the incorporation of society into political society. Stable recruitment policies and patterns in the Soviet system's last decades sought to iron out inherited disproportions in keeping with the managerial approach of 'developed socialism'. Some new imbalances, however, crept in, such as the under-representation of nationalities without their own republics and the poorly educated. Recruitment was never left to the market and remained a matter of concern to the party leadership.

ORGANISATION

The CPSU was organised as a pyramid with the central bodies (the Central Committee, Politburo, and Secretariat) rising above successive stages of party committees from the primary party organisations. With the exception of the RSFSR until the very last days, every union

Table 5 Membership of the CPSU in the union republics, 1971–86

	1971	Growth %	1976	Growth %	1981	Growth %	1986
USSR	14,455,321	8.6	15,694,187	11.4	17,480,768	8.9	19,037,946
RSFSR	9,253,243	6.7	9,875,562	10.2	10,885,704	7.7	11,730,254
Ukraine	2,378,789	10.1	2,625,808	11.7	2,933,564	8.7	3,188,854
Belorussia	434,527	16.5	506,229	17.6	595,311	12.2	667,980
Moldavia	115,164	17.5	135,303	21.1	163,902	15.6	189,403
Transcaucasia							
Azerbaijan	258,549	11.3	287,823	14.8	330,319	14.1	376,822
Georgia	296,375	7.4	318,371	10.1	350,435	9.4	383,472
Armenia	130,353	9.7	142,959	15.2	164,738	13.3	186,637
Central Asia							
Uzbekistan	428,507	13.8	487,507	16.6	568,243	13.0	642.025
Kazakhstan	575,439	14.2	657,141	11.0	729,498	11.1	810,776
Tajikistan	86,491	11.8	96,716	12.7	108,974	12.9	122,985
Kyrgyzstan	104,632	4.9	109,746	15.2	126,402	14.3	144,466
Turkmenistan	69,862	11.5	77,910	20.1	93,556	17.7	110,141
Baltic							
Lithuania	122,469	18.8	145,557	17.4	170,935	15.4	197,274
Latvia	127,753	12.2	143,305	12.5	161,264	9.9	177,258
Estonia	73,168	15.2	84,250	16.2	97,923	11.9	109,599

Note: There was no republican party organisation for the RSFSR: the figures given are the remainder after the subtraction of the fourteen other republics. Growth rates calculated from the table.
Source: Partiinaya zhizn, No. 14 (July 1986), p. 20.

Figure 2 CPSU: organisational structure

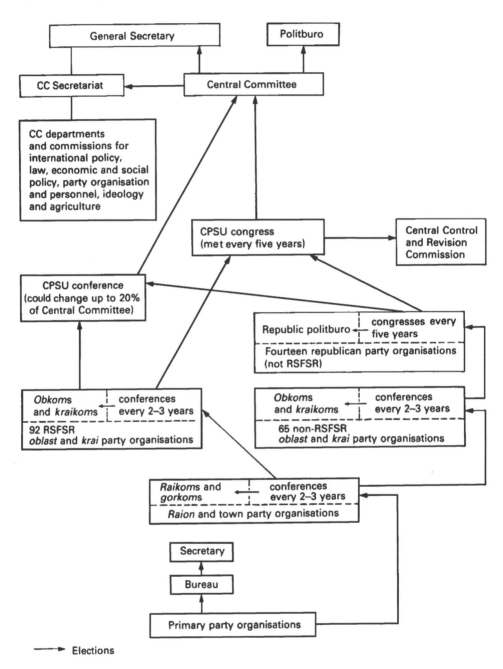

republic had its own communist party. It must be stressed, however, that while the state system was federal, the CPSU was unitary (see Figure 2).

The ideological perspectives of the party were contained in the party Programme. It summed up the tasks and nature of a given period. The first Programme was adopted at the second party congress in 1903, the second at the eighth congress in 1919 to reflect the coming to power of the Bolsheviks, and the third in 1961 to reflect Khrushchev's 'state of all the people'. The new edition of the third Programme adopted by the twenty-seventh party congress in March 1986 held out few promises for the future, dropping the utopian aspirations of Khrushchev's text, such as the promise that 'this generation of Soviet people will live under communism', and some of the more bombastic assertions that the USSR would overtake the USA by 1970 and attain communism by 1980. The twenty-eighth (and last) party congress in July 1990 drafted a radical programme entitled *Towards a Humane, Democratic Socialism*, but the fall of Soviet power prevented its implementation.

The organisation of the CPSU was governed by its statute or Rules, modified occasionally to reflect the concerns of the Programme. The 1961 Rules were amended in 1966 and 1971 to eliminate Khrushchev's 'excesses', like the obligatory turnover of personnel. The last Rules were adopted in March 1986. Democratic centralism was the key principle governing the organisation of the CPSU, and indeed of the whole polity. The concept was formulated by Lenin as one of the fundamental principles of party organisation. It claimed to combine effective central control with democratic practices from below. The 1986 Rules listed the five key elements of democratic centralism (Rule 19):

> (a) the election of all leading bodies, from the lowest to the highest; (b) periodical reports of party bodies to their organisations and to higher bodies; (c) strict party discipline and subordination of the minority to the majority; (d) the obligatory nature of decisions by higher bodies for lower bodies; and (e) collective spirit in the work of all organisations and the personal responsibility of every communist for the fulfilment of his [or her] party assignments.[10]

The last point was a new addition reflecting the spirit of *perestroika*. In practice, centralism had always predominated over democracy; the election process was governed from the top down as part of the 'circular flow of power'. Democratic centralism served to prevent the mass of the party membership controlling its own leadership. All party bodies were subordinated to the decisions of party congresses and conferences as interpreted on a day-to-day basis by the Politburo and lower-level party committees. Democratic centralism kept certain questions off the agenda and banned groups within the party, so-called factions, from developing. The 1986 Rules explicitly stated that 'any manifestation of factionalism or group activity is incompatible with Marxist–Leninist principles and party membership'. Democratic centralism inhibited interest group politics and justified the 'monolithic unity' of the party, guaranteeing that lines of communication within the party remained vertical, from top to bottom, rather than horizontal, between like-minded individuals, groups or committees.

The base of the party was the network of primary party organisations (PPO, formerly called party cells), numbering 440,363 in January 1986. All party members had to belong to a PPO and participate in its activities. Reflecting the Soviet conception of the individual primarily as a worker, PPOs were organised mainly in workplaces and only rarely on a territorial basis. In 1986, 25.6 per cent were located in industry, 17.4 per cent in offices, 11.3 per cent on farms and 16.7 per cent in colleges. They varied greatly in size, with 39.8 per cent having the minimum of three to fifteen, and 7.1 per cent ranging from 101 to several thousand. Average membership in industry was ninety-five, and about sixty on farms. All PPOs had a secretary, a bureau if the organisation was large enough, and a committee in the 45,000 very large organisations. Officials were formally elected by members, but the initial candidature before the onset of *perestroika* was usually proposed by a higher party committee and then merely ratified by the membership. Party meetings at which new members were admitted and disciplinary measures passed were usually held once a month. The PPO was responsible for recruiting, training and disciplining its members. Individuals were assigned responsibilities, and the cell as a whole mobilised the population for the various campaigns that were launched from time to time. The PPO's committee or bureau in workplaces acted as a type of board of directors, taking part in decision-making although it was formally subordinated to the manager. There was always great scope for conflict owing to the ambiguous relationship between the party cell and management, described in terms of the 'right of supervision' (*pravo kontrolya*, but not 'control' in the English sense).

The next stage consisted of 3,550 *raion* (urban borough or rural district) committees. The *raikom* (*raion* committee) of between eighty and one hundred members was elected by a conference of delegates from all the PPOs in the area. It met in plenary session about six times a year, leaving the running of current affairs to a bureau of about a dozen, most of whom were full-time officials. This bureau met much more frequently than the plenum, usually about two or three times a month. The *raikom* oversaw a number of party departments, established to supervise the affairs of the district and the local soviet, reflecting the major industries of the area. In the countryside, for example, an agricultural department supervised the affairs of the local farms to ensure that plans were fulfilled, and indeed this interest often virtually replaced the functions of local managers, the process known as *podmena*. All *raikom*s had an agitprop department to run local ideological work of meetings, clubs and lectures. The organisation department was the focus of local personnel placement; no significant appointment in a given locality could take place without its sanction.

Above the *raikom*s there were 889 city committees (*gorkom*s), 10 area (*okrug*) committees, 2 city committees (*gorkom*s – Moscow and Kiev) with the rights of *obkom*s, 151 regional or *oblast* committees (*obkom*s) (92 of which covered the RSFSR), 6 *krai* committees (*kraikom*s) and 14 republican party committees. In addition, separate revisional commissions without overlapping membership were elected at the same conferences as the party committees to oversee the latter's work and to ensure financial, moral and organisational probity. The *obkom*s were larger versions of the *raikom*s, with the exception that they usually had a secretariat of full-time party workers (*apparatchiki*) distinct from the bureau. *Obkom*s had between 100 and 150 members and met perhaps once a quarter, with day-to-day affairs run by a bureau. Most *obkom*s had separate departments for industry, agriculture, health, education and so on. Duplication between party and state bodies was rife, with the relationship between the two ruled, as elsewhere, by convention. Of the 5.3 million party activists, 4.9 million were found in the PPOs, 407,000 in *gorkom*s and *raikom*s, and 31,900 in *obkom*s, *kraikom*s and republican committees.

Party committees were responsible to party conferences, held every two to three years. The elections were indirect, with PPOs electing delegates to *raion* conferences, which elected the local committee, and so on up through a series of conferences to the national party congress. The voting at party gatherings (until the final period) was carefully controlled and took place by show of hands. The individual merits of particular candidates were not scrutinised; once nominated from above, they were confirmed from below. At the top the national party congress after 1961 met every five years, usually gathering for about a week and timed to coincide with the adoption of the five-year plan. The twenty-seventh congress in February 1986 had 5,000 delegates, 76.5 per cent of whom were elected for the first time, representing top party officials from the centre but also some rank-and-file delegates from the localities. The Central Committee ensured that the proper mix of delegates was selected, with a certain proportion of women, minorities, soldiers, intellectuals, workers, officials and so on. The party congress elected a Central Auditing Commission to ensure correct procedures in the party and the investigation of abuses.

The leadership's policies for the succeeding five years were legitimised as fulfilling the programmes outlined by the party congress. Under Brezhnev congresses became the scene of orchestrated unanimity, with all major speeches approved in advance by the Secretariat. This had not always been the case, and some congresses before Stalin stifled debate were the scenes of bitter controversy. Against the backcloth of vigorous debate the tenth congress in March 1921 imposed the ban on factions which allowed Stalin to consolidate his administrative control over congresses. By the time of the seventeenth congress in 1934 (the 'congress of victors'), celebrating collectivisation and the completion of the first five-year plan, criticism of Stalin could at most be oblique. Few congresses met under Stalin, and none in the crucial war and reconstruction years between 1939 and 1952. Congresses met regularly in the post-Stalin period, though tended to become professional affairs, managed to ensure the smooth progress of earlier decided motions. Echoes of controversies, however, slipped in and careful analysis of speeches can reveal subtle differences of emphasis. Under Gorbachev more open debate was permitted culminating in the bitter but ultimately futile exchanges at the twenty-eighth congress in July 1990.

National party conferences met frequently under Lenin, but died out completely under Stalin following the eighteenth in 1941. Conferences provided a forum for debate and the discussion of policy options, although their precise powers with respect to electing the Central Committee were unclear. By reviving the body in June–July 1988 with the convocation of the nineteenth party conference, Gorbachev hoped to achieve consensus for reform and to institutionalise his strategies of *perestroika* and democratisation.

Congresses leave one of their most important tasks until the end, namely the adoption of the list of Central Committee (CC) members put to it by the leadership. Under Lenin it was the equivalent of the later Politburo, a compact group of ten to twenty members. As the CC grew in size to become a condensed party congress its authority declined. The CC elected in March 1986 had 307 full members and 170 candidates (or non-voting members), a total of 477. Of the full members, 30.6 per cent were new, reflecting Gorbachev's unusually rapid personnel turnover. The CC represented the key sections of society and co-opted various notables – for example, Valentina Tereshkova, the first woman in space. Members were usually selected because of the particular job that they held, with CC membership only confirming the importance of the other job. The CC elected in 1986 contained no fewer than 104 regional party chiefs, half of whom were new to the CC; 31 came from the CC apparatus itself; 56 from the governmental ministries; 24 from the armed services; and 5 from the KGB.[11] The CC was the high gathering of the Soviet elite and became a type of social parliament representing various institutions rather than individuals.

The Central Committee was the source of official legitimacy for policies between congresses, but it was far from being an autonomous policy-making body. Its political decline dated from the early 1920s, with the majority elected in 1934 falling victim to Stalin's terror; and between 1945 and Stalin's death it met only twice. After 1953 the CC plenum was restored as the supreme authority in the country between congresses. Khrushchev appealed successfully to the CC against the anti-party group's vote in the Politburo to oust him in 1957. It was the CC, however, that in 1964 confirmed his dismissal. Under Brezhnev the CC tended to act as the platform for the announcement of policies and to ratify changes in personnel. According to the party Rules the CC had to meet at least once every six months with an agenda typically limited to one or two questions (it did not usually discuss military policy). The CC organised a Party Control Committee to ensure the observance of party discipline and rules, and to consider appeals against expulsion from the party. One of the key functions of the CC was to approve changes in the membership of the Politburo and the Secretariat.

The CC played the key role in confirming the successors to Brezhnev chosen by the Politburo in the early 1980s. Gorbachev used CC plenums to launch major policy initiatives and debate, but not without a struggle. Freed from the stifling restrictions of his predecessors the CC became the forum for more open debate. New rules governing plenary sessions permitted interventions from the floor during debates that were entered into the official minutes. The January 1987 plenum, which Gorbachev used to launch his proposals for democratisation amid lively debate, was three times postponed. As Gorbachev cut through what he perceived as the deadwood among office-holders, he was left with the problem of 'dead souls' in the Central Committee, people who had lost the job that originally entitled them to membership but who could not be dismissed until the next congress.

The Politburo was usually elected by the Central Committee at the end of a party congress, and further changes between congresses were ratified by a CC plenum. Established in 1919 to reach quick decisions at a time of civil war, the Politburo came to dominate party congresses and the CC until in turn it was subordinated to Stalin. Under Khrushchev the Politburo (called the Presidium until 1964) became the main policy-making body, the focus of the Soviet system of government. No longer terrorised by a single individual, it collectively decided policies, allocated resources and appointed key personnel. The Politburo was not impregnable, as evidenced by the role of the CC in 1957, but it certainly represented the super-elite. The Politburo typically consisted of about a dozen voting members and half a dozen alternating or candidate members. The CC elected a General Secretary who theoretically was no more than 'first among equals' in the Politburo. In contrast to Khrushchev's adversarial style, his successors tried to rule by consensus rather than imposing decisions through voting. This was made easier by the detailed preparatory work carried out by the CC Secretariat. On most items there was no discussion and Politburo members simply appended their signatures to a prepared file. An average four-hour Politburo meeting could thus deal with a great number of issues without overloading the highly centralised system of decision-making.

Under Brezhnev the Politburo began to take on the features of a cabinet, that is, representing the major departments of state, the military, security apparatus, heavy industry and some key geographical areas like Ukraine and Central Asia. It became, as Rigby put it, a 'self-stabilising oligarchy', balanced to avoid conflict. The Brezhnev Politburo was marked by the gradual ageing of its members as stability gave way to senescence, oligarchy to gerontocracy. However, the principle of *ex officio* membership was never conceded and therefore it was far from being a genuine cabinet system of rule. Membership was formally at the discretion of the CC but was in effect controlled by the Politburo and the General Secretary. Only in 1990 at the twenty-eighth party congress was the Politburo's status radically changed, with fifteen of its twenty-five members *ex officio* the leaders of the union republics. Gorbachev was freed from Politburo control, and the once-mighty body sank into desuetude.

The CC Secretariat itself was headed by the General Secretary and consisted of about ten full members and half a dozen candidates elected by the CC, some of whom were also members of the Politburo (the so-called super-secretaries). Leadership of the Secretariat buttressed the General Secretary's position in the Politburo. The Secretariat drafted proposals for Politburo meetings and was dubbed by Yegor Ligachev as 'the operations staff of the Party leadership'.[12] Secretaries were powerful officials responsible for several key areas of policy covered by the CC departments. A secretaryship was often a stepping stone to Politburo membership, and joint membership was conventionally an essential condition to becoming General Secretary. The reorganisation of September 1988, when six new policy commissions were created (see below), put an end to the Secretariat's effective role.

The Secretariat traditionally headed the *apparat*, the vast Central Committee apparatus of appointed officials divided into about twenty-five departments, each of which was led by a departmental head, a first deputy and a number of other deputies. Groupings of departments were headed by a secretary. The key departments were administration, party organisation, ideology, defence industries and international (foreign affairs), with a special department for the KGB. The general department acted as the General Secretary's personal administrative office. In effect, the Secretariat was a shadow ministerial system assisted by a staff of *apparatchiki*, the party's civil service (or, indeed, a state within the state) which oversaw the implementation of Politburo decisions. This was the party machine, the full-time salaried party functionaries controlled by the General Secretary and the Secretariat. In Moscow the *apparat* was based in the Central Committee building not far from the Kremlin in Old Square. Each level in the giant pyramid, from the republics, *oblast*s and down to the *raikom*s had their own staffs, estimated to number about a quarter of a million. The great majority (83 per cent) of party functionaries were employed by *gorkom*s and *raikom*s. The apparatus played an important role not only in the party but in the whole Soviet political system. The Secretariat departments had close links with the ministries and acted as a vast supervisory mechanism. Policy was determined by the Secretariat departments in conjunction with the ministries. The Secretariat hosted conferences at which party policy was hammered out.

The Central Committee Secretariat was the nerve centre of the vast system of centralised appointments, the *nomenklatura*. It appointed officials to key bodies such as the Komsomol, trade unions, and myriad other state and public organisations as well as to the party itself. Local party secretariats also had their *nomenklatura* lists. To put it simply, at each level there was a list of posts to be filled (considered to be in a particular committee's *nomenklatura*); and a second list of people suitable to fill them. The *nomenklatura* of the Central Committee, for example, was managed by the Politburo and included the top positions in the party, the soviets, the ministries, the armed forces and the leading scientific, academic and cultural institutions. The *nomenklatura* of a *raikom* would include the secretaries of the party cells, the chair of the village soviet, the chair of the *kolkhoz* and the director of the local factory. The *nomenklatura* system was a vast system of patronage exercised by the party. Those on the *nomenklatura* lists constituted the top people in the Soviet system, although those on the list of the Central Committee were clearly very different from those at borough level. Those whose *nomenklatura* was held by a department of the CC were considered to have broken through into the inner circle. The very peak was made up of those whose *nomenklatura* was held by the Politburo or the Central Committee itself. The number of people on these lists is not known. Estimates vary from 750,000 to 3 million, including posts in the party itself.[13] There was a certain amount of personnel movement between the party, state and ministerial hierarchies, but the system was clearly conducive to confused lines of command.

Appointment to posts did not take place through open advertisement or competitive recruitment but through this system of extended co-optation. Political as much as professional factors were taken into account in making appointments. This more than anything revealed the Soviet system as an imperfect bureaucracy, not based on clear performance criteria as in the Weberian model but on a variety of informal practices. Under Brezhnev the incompetent and corrupt were shielded from the consequences of their actions. The system of patronage and the extended development of patron–client relations began to challenge the *nomenklatura* system itself. Corruption allowed favouritism and bribery rather than political qualities to determine appointments. Even more alarming from the CC's point of view, patronage bypassed the Secretariat and the official system of appointments. One result of the anti-corruption campaign launched by Andropov was to re-establish the Secretariat's control over the party machinery. A marked feature of appointments from the mid-1980s was the 'parachuting in' of newcomers untainted by local networks.

The system of party organisation as developed in the first years of Soviet power and consolidated by Stalin allowed little scope for democracy in the party. The 'circular flow of power' established in the 1920s inverted democratic centralism so that, in place of elections from the bottom up, the party's electoral system was fused with the party apparatus, which proceeded to 'select' suitable candidates from the top down, who were then 'elected' by the body concerned. Instead of the Central Committee electing the Politburo, the Politburo chose the membership of the Central Committee, which was then confirmed by the party congress. Under Gorbachev these patterns began to change as the emphasis shifted from centralism to democracy. The introduction of elections in the appointment of party and other posts challenged the *nomenklatura* system. Moreover, democracy within the party was no longer considered a substitute for democracy in society; it soon became clear that one could not survive without the other.

PARTY, STATE AND GOVERNMENT

Article 6 of the 1977 constitution provided a succinct formula for the role of the communist party in the Soviet state:

> The leading and guiding force of Soviet society and the nucleus of its political system, of all state organisations and public organisations, is the Communist Party of the Soviet Union. The CPSU exists for the people and serves the people.
>
> The Communist Party, armed with Marxism–Leninism, determines the general perspectives of the development of society and the course of the home and foreign policy of the USSR, directs the great constructive work of the Soviet people, and imparts a planned, systematic, and theoretically substantiated character to their struggle for the victory of communism.
>
> All party organisations shall function within the framework of the Constitution of the USSR.[14]

This provided a general indication of the powers of the party in the government and society, but the details were left vague. The ambiguity of Soviet constitutionalism meant that from the very beginning, much to the anger of the Democratic Centralist opposition in 1919–20, the party–state relationship, as in other spheres of Soviet life, was governed more by convention than by statute. The relationship between the party and the state was a complex one: not only was the CPSU the kernel of the state, it was potentially the state itself. The Soviet Union, in effect, had two operative governments, the party and the state system. The party, however, is not to be identified with the government or state despite its close links with them. The standard formulation is that the communist party ruled but did not govern. The party was in effect the senior executive branch of Soviet government where decisions were made or confirmed. The Supreme Soviet and the Council of Ministers acted as the junior administrative branches, implementing decisions taken within the appropriate party committee. This overlapping of functions was a natural consequence of the constitution's rejection of the separation of powers.

The relationship between the party and state was the crucial one, changing over time, level in the hierarchy and area of the country. The system of power was both fused and confused. In keeping with the notion of 'developed socialism', the 1977 constitution moved somewhat away from the standard Soviet notion of a 'state structure' towards the idea of a 'political system', implying a more subtle relationship between the constituent parts of the Soviet polity.[15] The party was not meant to act either as an organ of state or as an alternative to state structures, although in practice this injunction was not always upheld. Party control over the state and governmental systems was achieved through six main mechanisms.

1   The use of party groups in the soviets, institutions and mass organisations. The party faction acted as a caucus directing the work of the host body. In the smaller soviets the party faction was often a minority (in over 43 per cent of soviets in 1980), but at higher levels communists were always in the majority; the higher the body, the greater the percentage. In 1979 the percentage of communists in village soviets averaged 41 per cent, in *oblast* soviets 55 per cent, at the republican level some 65 per cent, while in 1984 (its last convocation) 71.7 per cent of the 1,500 Supreme Soviet deputies were communists. These proportions were bolstered by Komsomol members, acting as a junior version of the party. The factions ensured the dominance of communists on soviet executive bodies. In 1979, 12.1 per cent of the 2,229,785 deputies at *oblast* level and lower were members of executive committees, and of these 71.6 per cent were communists. At *oblast* level communists comprised 93 per cent of executive committees, and in villages 68 per cent. The party caucus in a soviet usually met prior to sessions to agree on co-ordinated policies and was, it goes without saying, subordinate to the local party committee. The caucus system was the heart of classical Leninism and ensured that party policy decided elsewhere was adopted by the host institution. Non-party deputies did not have the right to met separately beforehand and therefore, even if they so desired, could not put up coherent opposition.

2   The party's influence was channelled through the vast network of primary party organisations. The PPOs in factories, farms and institutions performed a variety of functions, supervising the local managements, disseminating the latest political directives and ensuring the fulfilment of plans. The party secretary in any enterprise was an important figure, and although limited to a one-year occupation of the post they were usually re-elected year after year. Their precise rights with respect to management were always unclear. Essentially, they enjoyed the right of supervision (*pravo kontrolya*) over management, but, as noted above, this did not mean control in the English sense. Since managers were usually communists, too, they would in any case try to ensure that their decisions were in conformity with party directives. In undoing the Khrushchev reforms, party dominance under Brezhnev was somewhat undermined by the devolution of authority to the ministries, a trend that from 1971 was countered by the reassertion of party authority. Party organisations in ministries and departments were mandated to ensure the implementation of policy in the light of party directives.

3   All important posts were appointed through the *nomenklatura* system. In this way the party ensured the loyalty both of the people appointed and the organisation in which they worked. The system allowed the communist party to use its members to the maximum effect by placing them in strategic positions.

4   The system of appointments was reinforced by extensive interlocking membership. Senior party figures in a locality were often the same people who led the soviets or other public bodies. Following the defeat of the anti-party group in 1957 Bulganin was replaced as Prime Minister by Khrushchev, who retained his post as head of the party. On Khrushchev's ouster in October 1964 it was decreed that in future no individual could occupy both posts simultaneously. However, no such stipulation regulated the other link in the triad, the party leadership and the presidency. Brezhnev's elevation to the presidency in 1977 while remaining General Secretary was the most spectacular instance of interlocking membership and established a precedent followed by Andropov, Chernenko and Gorbachev. There was, however, no overlap between the Council of Ministers and the Presidium of the Supreme Soviet.

5   The party was the ultimate decision-making body. Hill and Frank dubbed the party Programme the 'ideological constitution' of the country in which the key theoretical principles of a given stage were outlined and out of which detailed policies were developed. The Central Committee apparatus maintained an extensive shadow ministerial network, reproduced on a smaller scale down through the system. The party was not meant to engage in the direct administration of industry or agriculture but to supervise the work of the relevant bodies. Its decisions were usually enacted through the relevant soviet or governmental machinery and thus gained the force of law.

6   Responsibility for making policy was closely associated with accountability for ensuring its implementation. Local soviet or ministerial officials learned to live with the interference of party officials in their work, and since most shared a common allegiance to the party the relationship was not unduly adversarial. The local party organisations and their secretaries were the cornerstones of a powerful system of party supervision (*kontrol*) from the highest to the lowest level. The republican, *obkom* and city first secretaries were powerful officials in their districts. Hough has compared them to the French prefects, acting as the plenipotentiaries of central power to ensure the execution of economic and political programmes.[16] The purpose of an *obkom*, for example, was to direct (*napravlyat*) the activities of the state, economic and public organisations, exercising executive leadership (*rukovodstvo*) over the life of the locality. It maintained *kontrol* over factories, but tried not to replace one-person management by a form of collective leadership. The party had an auxiliary role intended to settle questions of political principle but not day-to-day management policy. In the unreformed system everything was subordinated to plan fulfilment and even the party sometimes had to accede to the demands of local managers. In places 'company towns' emerged dominated by one factory or industry and where the responsible ministry wielded enormous power.

The detailed involvement of party officials in administration through these six mechanisms suggests that the country was over-governed. Local party secretaries were responsible for effective economic performance and political stability, appointing personnel and supervising the performance of industry and agriculture. The 'prefects' were encouraged to take the broader view to ensure that the general conditions of workers, food supplies and so on did not reach crisis point. Under Brezhnev the system on the whole worked effectively and there was no major confrontation with workers like the one in Novocherkassk in 1962. At all levels local party organisations maintained departments staffed with their own experts, ensuring a high degree of detailed supervision. Party and state structures were maintained in parallel, giving rise to the duplication of knowledge and expertise. The theoretical demarcation of party and state spheres of competence was increasingly blurred as the role of experts increased. The party was meant to act as the supreme rational co-ordinator. However, the rationality was conditional upon a variety of considerations which were often at variance with the achievement of maximum economic efficiency. The party–state administrative structure under Brezhnev did not always generate, in Habermas's words, a sufficient 'quantity of rational decisions'.[17]

The lack of precise definition of the party's leading role and its extensive powers tended to convert its guiding functions into substitution: *podmena* was a permanent feature of Soviet life. The party's involvement with local soviets could not but take the form of 'petty tutelage' or 'parallelism', condemned since the first days of Soviet power. As we saw above, the eighth party congress in March 1919 warned that the party should lead but not merge with the state administrative system. For over seventy years it was difficult to establish a workable balance since the problem was a structural one and could not be overcome by decrees alone. *Podmena* reflected the underlying power relationship. Given the political weakness of the soviets and the politicisation of economic management, such 'parallelism' was not surprising. Local party secretaries, moreover, were judged by their performance in ensuring social order and the fulfilment of economic plans, hence their careers depended on detailed involvement in affairs that properly lay in the domain of state or governmental officials.

The role of the local party organisations changed over time but their prefectorial role remained constant. As Rigby put it, they became officers of a 'ministry of coordination', a system that under Brezhnev achieved its peak of stability. Although the system wastefully duplicated administrative resources, it worked effectively to achieve certain goals. The prefectorial system oversaw the industrialisation of the country and the maintenance of social peace in the post-war years. The question increasingly arose, however, whether such a system, developed in different times and with different aims, was suitable for a developed society and economy. The accustomed definition of the leading role of the party was increasingly challenged.

THE LEADING ROLE OF THE PARTY

Party, state and government were locked into a complicated relationship, governed, as elsewhere in the Soviet polity, by informal relationships. The party's leading role was ensured by its dominance in defining policy, personnel appointments and supervision of implementation. The political levels of decision-making (legislation) and the administrative level of decision-implementation (administration) became thoroughly entwined. For this reason Kassof labelled the polity an 'administered society' where politics gave way to expanded administration. The origins of the system lie in the Leninist ideal of a self-administered commune state with a high level of public participation guided into politically correct channels by the party. The model excluded the possibility of antagonistic conflicts once the old exploiting classes had been eliminated, and therefore there appeared no need for mechanisms to adjudicate between competing interests and policies. The emphasis was on social and political unity, which too often came out as conformity. The party acted as the gatekeeper in a literal sense in establishing policy options and determining access to decision-making. To paraphrase Marx, the communist party was nothing more than an executive committee for managing the collective affairs of the socialist state.

The nature of Soviet-type parties was long a matter of debate. Could a party be a party at all in a one-party state? The absence of free competition with other political organisations and internal domination by small leadership groups (and often by individuals) suggested the rule not of a political party but of a hybrid 'state-party'. The party lost some of the attributes of a political organisation, although in the post-Stalin era the party was re-established as a functioning political body, with regular party congresses and the whole panoply of political agencies and reports. The party retained its separate organisational identity and formally it did not take over the functions of the state and nor was it captured by the state. Yet the party's monopoly over politics and administration did indeed make it a unique organisation: it was more than a ruling party in government and indeed became a 'state-party', the nerve centre of the whole Soviet state structure without which the whole system would collapse.

The CPSU was at one and the same time a mass party, a revolutionary party, a cadre party and something on the Mexican model of the Party of the Institutionalised Revolution. This was reflected in several layers of membership performing different functions. The party maintained its revolutionary role in society and abroad, and at the same time performed a cadre role in society. The identification of the entire party with the new ruling class is clearly misleading given the size of its membership. The party member working in the dairy of a *kolkhoz* or in the machine room of a factory was hardly a member of the social elite, though it would be fair to say that they perceived themselves as members of the political elect. The party was clearly an elite body in that it had selective membership and proclaimed its higher status through a greater devotion to duty. The division of the party into a small inner corps and a much larger mass membership is useful, with the inner party broadly corresponding to those holding *nomenklatura* posts. There was, however, great variance in the importance of these posts also.

The party's functions included socialisation through a vast agitation and propaganda (agitprop) network operating through the media, local party organisations and special agitprop bodies. In 1986 there were over a million propagandists working with about 2.5 million agitators. The malaise and corruption of the later Brezhnev years suggested that much of this vast effort was ineffective. It did little to eradicate the alleged ills of Soviet society such as passivity, consumerism, narrow-mindedness and philistinism, let alone averting the corruption of the political leaders themselves.

In a vast country covering eleven time zones and with dozens of languages and nationalities the CPSU acted as a massive integrating force. The party was as active in an economically backward region as in an advanced one. Its influence was exerted through the mechanisms described above, but it also acted as a symbolic unifying force with which all classes and nationalities could identify. The centrifugal tendencies of the federal state structure were countered by the centralised and unitary communist party until Gorbachev's reforms paralysed the party. Information from communist party organisations from all over the country arrived daily at the Central Committee headquarters in Moscow and provided the leadership with its own source of information about conditions in the country. The party in the Soviet Union was effectively embedded in its society, whereas in Poland, and to a lesser extent in Czechoslovakia, a gulf remained which can be expressed as one between the *pays légal*, the official system, and the *pays réel*, the actual operation of society.

This difference derived largely from the way that party rule was established in Eastern Europe after the war and from differing political cultures, but it also owed something to the fact that the Soviet party was until the end a relatively effective political and economic manager, within the framework of its self-proclaimed tasks. The CPSU was able to sustain itself as a hegemonic force and only relied on coercion in extreme instances. Melvin Croan argues that the party was not only 'well-rooted' in Soviet society, it was the basis of that society.[18] The power relations of the Tsarist regime were not simply transferred to the Bolsheviks but were thoroughly remoulded. The party generated a new political society to replace the one it destroyed.

The history of the post-Stalin era was the story of the party's defence of its 'leading role' in society, as the guiding force in Soviet-type political systems. Under Stalin the party as a functioning political institution waned, although as we have seen it remained the source of legitimacy. Khrushchev's most durable achievement was the reconstitution of the leading role of the party, while Brezhnev's definition of developed socialism consolidated the theoretical basis for the party's dominance. While Marxism talked of the ultimate withering away of the state as class contradictions disappear, and elements of this were reflected in the idea of the state of all the people proclaimed in 1961, there was no equivalent theory for the ultimate withering away of the party to allow genuine popular self-management freed of the incubus of a self-proclaimed revolutionary knighthood.

The Soviet political system without the communist party would have been something entirely different. Khrushchev's restoration of the party, however, could not go back to Lenin altogether since conditions had drastically changed. The quickening pace of advances in science and technology increasingly raised the spectre that the party's leading role would itself obstruct the further development of society. Already some of the attempts at economic reform, as in 1965, were aimed at substituting some of the administrative controls exercised by the interlocking administrative apparatus with economic mechanisms operating through elements of the market. The first steps were taken towards reducing the direct economic role of the party by warning against 'petty tutelage' over enterprise affairs. Opposition to decentralising reforms was in part resistance to the implicit downgrading of the role of the party in a more marketised economy. The threat was not only to the privileges of the bureaucratic elite, but ultimately to the political dominance of the party. Reform of the centralised command economy threatened the whole machinery of the command society.

In 1968 the Czechoslovak communist party tried to broaden the definition of its leading role in order to establish an interactive relationship with diverse social forces. The party's Action Programme of April 1968 accepted that its authority derived not from the once-and-forever act of taking power but that it was based on performance and had to be fought for and won daily. The party's leading role was to remain, not in the form of a monopolistic concentration of power in its hands but through hegemony. Communist absolutism was tempered as the party renounced its divine right to rule. This was not a new idea, having been proposed by the Democratic Centralists in 1919–20 when they railed against the petty tutelage of the party, and it was taken up by the Workers' Opposition as regards the trade unions, but under Stalin the issue was taboo. Dubček's 'socialism with a human face' dismantled censorship of the press, but the reform that really precipitated the Warsaw Pact invasion of 21 August 1968 concerned inner-party organisation. The party Rules were democratised to allow internal elections to be held by secret ballot; the regular turnover of party officials was envisaged. The Czechoslovak party attempted to repeal Lenin's 1921 ban on organised factions. Democratic centralism was in effect discarded as minority views were allowed within the party even after decisions had been taken.[19] The invasion took place not to restore the party's leading role, for that was not in doubt, but to ensure that it operated in the old way. Under Brezhnev the Soviet party resisted the ideas of the Action Programme and vigorously reaffirmed its prerogatives over society. Thereafter the absence of serious economic reform reflected the Brezhnevite political impasse. Those reforms that did take place focused on the introduction of new technology, improving planning techniques and extending the powers of central government. It was the blockage on evolutionary political reform (as with the Tsarist regime earlier) that precipitated a revolutionary outcome.

The Leninist system was a highly effective mechanism for retaining a monopoly on power but lacked the flexibility to adapt to more complex ways of governing. The Soviet party was too successful in resisting domestic and external challenges and failed to learn from the experience of other communist systems, above all the reform attempts of the Eastern European communist parties. Although the Soviet party successfully resisted the advance of political pluralism, it found it necessary to reconcile itself to elements of social and institutional pluralism. Pyramidal lines of command covered the polity in a dense network of controls over functionally differentiated groups and institutions. The charismatic leader gave way to settled routines and the institutionalisation of power.

Richard Lowenthal described the modification in the party's role in terms of a shift from a mobilisation phase, when the industrial foundations of socialism were laid, to a post-mobilisation phase when the era of major transformations came to an end. The political monopoly of the party was more difficult to justify in the second phase and had to be placed on a different footing.[20] The stages, according to Samuel Huntington, were 'transformation', 'consolidation' and 'adaptation', the last stage being variously called the 'post-mobilisation phase' or David Apter's 'reconciliation system', in which the regime gradually draws in the various strategic sectors of society and ultimately incorporates dissent to establish a politically stable system.[21] Kenneth Jowitt was less sanguine and argued that after the mobilisation and adaptation phases the process of inclusion was neither inevitable nor irreversible, and in any case took place on the regime's terms.[22] The Soviet communist party was unable to find a stable type of 'inclusion' phase, despite Gorbachev's desperate attempts to find a formula that could have achieved inclusion while preserving the party's leading role. Zygmunt Bauman insisted that there was a long-term systemic crisis and not long-term political stability.[23] Stagnation and not political development were indeed prevalent under Brezhnev. The historian Mikhail Heller talked of the party as a parasite on society which was not necessary but justified on ideological grounds.

The polity centred on the party was increasingly challenged to adapt to the society that it had created. The challenge was not a new one, since in many respects the problem of greater inner-party democracy, though for long periods suppressed, never entirely disappeared. The relationship between the ideology of socialist development and the Leninist theory of party organisation was a problematical one from the outset. Lenin's theory of 'consciousness', the preserve of an enlightened elite, imposed certain patterns on party organisation and on the party's relationship with society that suffocated the latter and stifled the creative development of the former.

The alternatives to ideologised party control appeared to be either the emergence of a technocratic ethos of public administration or some form of (socialist) democracy. The party acted as an obstacle not only to democratisation but to the emergence of an independent technical sphere dominated by the rule of the 'experts'. The technocracy itself, it should be stressed, was increasingly dominated by party members and there was no stark distinction betwen 'red' and 'expert' as there had been in the USSR's early days. Technocratic party and governmental officials gradually merged into a managerial view of politics, yet points of tension remained, above all the censorship imposed by the party that isolated the development of Soviet science from mainstream developments elsewhere. The alternative proposed by some of the leading exponents of reform in the Soviet Union, like Roy Medvedev, argued for a clear definition of the leading role within the context of socialist democracy. This would have allowed for particularities within the framework of the dominant party whose powers were defined and therefore limited. The party was to make more use of the state, soviets, mass organisations like Komsomol and the trade unions and a variety of special interest organisations, both as instruments of administration and opinion formation and as means of sounding opinion and generating support, within the context of greater trust for non-party people and organisations. There would be legal guarantees against the arbitrariness of the authorities.[24] However, the programme of 'socialist legality' advanced by Medvedev entailed only a partial re-evaluation of the role and nature of politics in the Soviet polity.

The party was closely involved in administration but it was more than a 'political broker' between various competing groups. Like the Bonapartist state, it 'stood above' warring interests. Under Brezhnev the party lost its dynamism and in practice some of its authority devolved to powerful specialist and interest groupings in society. Andropovism was in part a response to the social effects of this trend but did not tackle its political roots. The party under Gorbachev tried to remain the dominant political force but to shed some of its administrative functions. At a time of reform it faced a fundamental dilemma: on the one hand it needed to maintain its dominance over state and economic bodies in order to force through reforms; on the other, these reforms could only succeed if the party allowed groups and forces in society to enter into a dynamic relationship with each other, and to do this the party's role had to be fundamentally redefined. The experience of NEP in the 1920s illustrated some of the issues involved. The relative autonomy granted to the market and social forces led to accumulating frustrations among sections of the leadership who felt that the party's role as the chief 'doer' was being undermined. Either there had to be a breakthrough to democracy or there would be a reversion to authoritarianism.

THE END OF PARTY RULE

By the 1970s several Western European communist parties, notably the Italian and Spanish, rejected Leninist vanguardism in favour of a Eurocommunism which explored the possibilities of a shift to more hegemonic forms of rule, of the type that had been outlined in Czechoslovakia in 1968. In the Soviet Union itself the question became ever more urgent, but in the last years before Gorbachev was suppressed ever more vigorously. The 'temporary' ban on factions, imposed in 1921, appeared ever more anachronistic. Why should party members not meet together to discuss matters of common interest? For how long could the party hold back the tide of social pluralism that was inextricably a part of modern industrial society?

Dubček's socialism with a human face under Gorbachev became *perestroika* through the human factor, reviving some of the ideas of the Action Programme in linking economic reform to *glasnost*. Reform entailed fundamental changes for the party. The most urgent was the party's retreat from detailed supervision of local economic management as greater autonomy was conceded to factories. Reform also required a reappraisal of the basic relationship between the party and the soviets, together with greater independence of the government from party supervision. Chinese experience demonstrated the importance of separating the functions of the communist party from that of the government, transferring power to lower levels and reforming administration and management. The Chinese party leader, Zhao Ziyang, in 1988 argued that the monolithic party-state would eventually be replaced by 'a mechanism of checks and balances' operating in the context of a strengthened legal system and a marketised economy. These aspirations ended in the bloodshed of Tiananmen Square as the democracy movement was crushed in June 1989, but in the USSR they were implemented with increasing boldness.

Gorbachev's reforms called for the separation of the functions of party and other bodies while exhorting active party involvement to ensure the implementation of reforms. The party apparatus and the *nomenklatura* were forces which for a time at least had to remain outside the reform process in order to generate the desired changes, and yet their presence inhibited the development of self-sustaining and irreversible reforms. In 1987 competitive elections were introduced to party posts, and by the end of the year over a hundred local party secretaries had passed through this unaccustomed procedure.[25] At the nineteenth party conference in mid-1988 Gorbachev admitted that there had been deformations in the work of the party, leading above all to a loss of contact with society as a whole and the dominance of the bureaucracy within the party ruling over the membership and society on the basis of directives and commands; democratic centralism, he argued, had become bureaucratic centralism.[26] The conference resolutions called for the 'profound democratisation' of the party, including more independence for local branches, recruitment on the basis of the personal qualities and not quotas, more freedom in party meetings for the rank and file to express their views, and above all competitive elections to all posts up to Central Committee level for a maximum of two five-year terms.[27] The aim was to expand the rights of rank-and-file members and to weaken the prerogatives of the party apparatus. Despite the heady rhetoric of this time, the attempt to reform the Soviet system while retaining many of its key features led to compromises that satisfied no one. *Perestroika* represented a hybrid form of democracy and one-party rule that proved unviable.

The fall of the CPSU came with brutal swiftness. A reorganisation in September 1988, designed to shift the balance of power away from the party machinery to ordinary members, and from the party to the state, began the process whereby the party was stripped of its supervisory machinery. As noted, six new commissions responsible for party affairs, ideology, social and economic policy, agriculture, international affairs and legal reform were created, and following their reorganisation in October the powers of the CC Secretariat were effectively transferred to them. The vast apparatus of the Central Committee was drastically reduced. In the March 1989 elections the party was humiliated, and then at the first convocation of the Congress of People's Deputies the party's record was condemned by many radical deputies. In the final speech to the Congress Andrei Sakharov outlined a 'decree on power' that would repeal the party's constitutionally guaranteed right to a leading role, enshrined in Article 6 of the Soviet constitution, and would invert the relationship between the centre and the localities to guarantee that the laws of the former could only be implemented in the latter with their explicit authorisation.[28] The February 1990 CC plenum acknowledged that it could no longer maintain its constitutional monopoly on power, an act formalised in March when Article 6 was amended to remove its guaranteed right to a 'leading role'. Russia's Declaration of State Sovereignty on 12 June 1990 adopted many of Sakharov's ideas, stipulating the separation of the communist party from state management.

In the run-up to its twenty-eighth (and final) congress in July 1990 the party split into numerous factions, including a Democratic Platform calling for the party's transformation from a vanguard to a parliamentary organisation, and a Marxist Platform demanding a reassertion of the interests of the working class. On the eve of the congress a Russian communist party was established, indicating that in future politics would be focused on the republics – although the party never formally federalised itself and remained a unitary body. The congress itself moved a long way towards democratising the party's own operation, allowing 'platforms' if not 'factions' which guaranteed the rights of minorities to advance their own views.

On the eve of the attempted coup of August 1991 the CPSU published its draft party Programme that indicated the way that it hoped to develop.[29] The document developed the themes of the draft party platform, *Towards a Humane, Democratic Socialism*, that had emerged after the February 1990 plenum (ending one-party rule) and the twenty-eighth congress in July of that year. The draft programme accepted that mistakes had been made from the very first days of Bolshevik power in 1917, but insisted that the October revolution (now described as a 'popular revolution') remained a major turning point in world history. The NEP and the Khrushchev periods were evaluated positively, while Stalinism was condemned:

> the creative energy of the liberated people was fettered by an impersonal state ownership alienated from the producer, the political omnipotence of the party and state bureaucracy, the monopoly position of vulgarised Marxist ideology and intolerance of democracy and *glasnost*. Mass punitive measures became the principal means of preservation of the regime.[30]

The party now appealed not to a specific class but to all of society. It sought to create a Western-style democracy based on the rule of law and the development of democratic institutions. Gorbachev hoped to convene a twenty-ninth party congress later that year to confirm the CPSU's turn towards social democracy. The coup, however, intervened, and the communist party in Russia was first suspended in late August, its financial assets and property were confiscated, and then the party was outlawed on 6 November 1991. Thus communist party rule came to an end just at the time when the popular aspirations of 1917 finally appeared close to fulfilment.

KEY TEXTS

Gill, Graeme, *The Collapse of the Single-party System: The Disintegration of the Communist Party of the Soviet Union* (Cambridge, Cambridge University Press, 1994).
Hill, R. J. and P. Frank, *The Soviet Communist Party*, 3rd edn (London, George Allen & Unwin, 1986).
Schapiro, Leonard, *The Communist Party of the Soviet Union*, 2nd edn (London, Methuen, 1970).
White, S. and D. Nelson (eds), *Communist Politics: A Reader* (London, Macmillan, 1986), pp. 135–56.

7   The structure of power

The Soviet polity was made up of a unique blend of institutions and procedures which were later adopted by some sixteen countries which proclaimed themselves to be Marxist–Leninist states on the road to communism. There were three interlocking hierarchies of power: the Communist Party of the Soviet Union (CPSU), which we examined in the previous chapter; the state system of soviets crowned by the Supreme Soviet; and the governmental system of ministries, headed by the Council of Ministers. They operated in a markedly different way from the practices of liberal democracies but confusion is often caused by the use of similar terminology. Hence for convenience the Chairman of the Presidium of the Supreme Soviet was often called 'President', and the Chairman of the Council of Ministers was called 'Prime Minister', although neither office officially existed until the last days in the Soviet Union. The apparent clarity of the threefold division between party, state and government in fact covered a highly complex power structure in which a series of institutions competed for influence.

CONSTITUTIONS AND POWER

The party, the economic apparatus, the secret police, the military, the economic and political bureaucracy, and the leaders in the various Soviet republics made up a delicate balance of power acting directly and indirectly to constrain the powers of the central leadership. At various times one or other of these, either singly or in concert, dominated. Overall, it was the communist party that acted as the source of legitimacy and power, albeit within the context of a fragmented politics. The fundamental political relationship between the power centre and the mass of the population was subject only to slow modification as the society and the system matured.

The Soviet constitution gave little indication of the relationship between the party, soviet and governmental hierarchies; nor did it give precise details on the relative powers of the centre and the republics in the federal framework of the USSR. Soviet constitutionalism differed significantly from that in the West. The aim of each of the four Soviet constitutions, promulgated in 1918, 1924, 1936 and 1977, was less to define the functions of political institutions or the relations between them than to act as a general ideological statement. They reflected Marxist–Leninist concepts on the role of popular sovereignty and the scope of politics in socialist society. The rights granted to individuals were limited by catch-all general phrases such as the 'interests of the people' and were primarily defined in social rather than political terms. The constitutions reflected the collectivism of the Soviet system in stressing that the interests of the individual were subordinate to those of society as a whole, and in the emphasis that individual rights were inseparable from duties. There was no higher court of appeal against infringements of constitutional rights. The constitutions only hesitantly moved away from the view that the need for 'politics' itself had been transcended, with no contestatory political parties, hence no open competition for power, and no overt conflicting social or national interests. For long periods the tautology that the state can do no wrong in a people's state dominated.

There was no formal separation of powers either between the three major structures of power or within the soviets, where executive and legislative powers were merged. The American constitutional concept of checks and balances was alien to Soviet practice and there was little of the Madisonian attempt to restrain the exercise of power. The Supreme Soviet itself, the highest state body according to the constitution, enjoyed no independent legislative powers and its political role was dependent on decisions taken elsewhere. The constitutions did not set limits to state power, and above all there was little attempt to define the powers of the communist party. The operation of the Soviet political system was always a matter more of convention and informal practices than the legal definition of prerogatives. Above all, the Soviet constitutional order (particularly in the Stalin period) is best understood in terms of personalities rather than institutions: as Sheila Fitzpatrick says, 'it was not the institutional position that conferred power on the man, but the man whose status determined the fortunes of the institution he headed'.[1] Power in the Soviet Union was not defined and was therefore not limited, although informal restraints, as in Britain, increasingly came to the fore.

Constitutionalism, together with legalism, is foreign to the Russian political tradition. The Decembrists in 1825 failed to achieve the creation of a constitutional system, and no popular movement ever managed to force Tsarism to concede limits to its authority or to ensure the rights of citizens. Only after the revolution of 1905 was a Fundamental Law (constitution) adopted in 1906, but Nicholas II insisted that Russia was still an autocracy. The powers of the four pre-revolutionary State Dumas (parliaments) were limited and ministers remained responsible solely to the autocrat.

The four Soviet constitutions each marked a new stage in the development of the political system: the foundation of the Soviet republic in 1918; the creation of the USSR in 1924; the claimed achievement of socialism in 1936; and the alleged onset of developed socialism in 1977. They reflected the regime's own assessment of the achievements and perspectives of the system at the time. They ratified the gains and established a programme for further developments rather than giving details of the operation of the political system. They had a declarative rather than a defining function.

The first Soviet constitution of 10 July 1918 established the pattern for the future. It summed up the experience of the first eight months of Bolshevik power but left the details of government uncertain. The document reflected commune democratic concepts of state organisation outlined in Marx's *Civil War in France* and Lenin's *The State and Revolution*: no separation of powers; the fusion of executive and legislative functions; a bias in favour of working people; the right of recall of deputies to soviets who thus became delegates rather than representatives; and the use of open rather than secret voting. Marx had called for the conversion of representative institutions from the 'talking shop' politics of parliamentarianism to 'working bodies', while for Lenin the soviets represented the mechanism whereby this could be achieved. However, the soviets failed to play this role in the first seventy years of Soviet power, not only because of adverse economic and international circumstances, but because of flaws in the very theory of unified executive and legislative power. The lack of checks and balances and the absence of the separation of powers allowed the enormous accumulation of power in the hands of executive bodies.

The first part of the 1918 constitution consisted of a 'Declaration of the Rights of Toiling and Exploited Peoples', rather like the French Declaration of the Rights of Man. The communist party was not mentioned and its role was unclear. The constitution applied the principles of the dictatorship of the proletariat in its open class discrimination against property owners and in the differential voting for workers and peasants. There was no attempt to establish a framework for the defence of individual rights against the state: laws were to serve the interests of class justice. The absence of a delineation of functions led the Democratic Centralist group within the Bolshevik party from late 1918 to demand revisions to the constitution to define the powers of the party, soviets and other bodies. The group alleged that decisions were being taken by small coteries of people in *ad hoc* groups. The Central Executive Committee (VTsIK) of the soviets was nominally the highest state body yet it was constantly undermined by the Council of People's Commissars (Sovnarkom), the forerunner of the Council of Ministers, which was permitted at a time of war to enact 'measures of extreme urgency' without reference to VTsIK, to which it was constitutionally responsible. Once again, as in the last years of the autocracy, the opposition demanded a ministry responsible to the legislature, and thus to the people. The defeat of the group in early 1921 and its dissolution marked the end of attempts to define the powers of the elements of the Soviet state. The tradition of constitutional chaos was thus perpetuated.

On 31 January 1924 the second Soviet constitution came into force to mark the creation of the Union of Soviet Socialist Republics (USSR) on 30 December 1922. With victory in the Civil War and Soviet power consolidated over the greater part of the old Tsarist empire, the shape of the new multinational Soviet state had to be decided. The Bolsheviks had always proclaimed the rights of nations to self-determination (see Chapter 15) but were reluctant to adopt the principles of federalism. From the first there were powerful pressures in favour of extreme centralisation, and the independence of Russia's peoples was made conditional on the class struggle. The 1924 constitution defined the Soviet system as federal yet said little about the highly centralised power system in the country dominated by the unitary communist party. It allowed each republic to maintain the trappings of nationhood and permitted some variations in legal practices but, as with the internal governmental arrangements, the precise rights of the national republics were left vague. The Central Executive Committee elected at a Congress of Soviets was now to be bicameral. One chamber was to be elected on the basis of population representation alone; the other was to be based on representation from each nationality group in the USSR. This concession to the nationalities reflected the belief that, as the revolution spread, other countries would be incorporated into the Soviet constitutional framework.

The so-called 'Stalin Constitution' of 5 December 1936 remained in force for over forty years. It consolidated what had been achieved rather than striking out in new directions: its ethos was conservative rather than revolutionary. A commission had been established in February 1935, in the hiatus between the assassination of Kirov in December 1934 and the onset of the great terror in 1936, to draft a new constitution which would register the progress made since the industrialisation and collectivisation drives of 1929, and which would, through its humanistic and progressive principles, stand in stark contrast to the fascist order that had come to power in Italy in 1922 and Germany in 1933. Bukharin played a leading role in drafting the document and sought to enshrine legality to restrain the Stalinist terror. For the first time the constitution mentioned the party as uniting the 'leading forces' in the country, but its precise role remained vague. The constitution registered that socialism had been built in the USSR and that antagonistic classes had been eliminated. Private ownership, in particular of land, had been abolished, and a socialist economic system had been established. The constitution was extremely democratic in its provisions, although Bukharin knew better than anyone that no legal resources were available to ensure their fulfilment. The whole population was enfranchised and the legal distinctions between workers and peasants dropped. The old system of elections through the pyramidal structure of the soviets gave way to universal, direct, equal and secret voting for delegates to a new bicameral Supreme Soviet. The drafting commission claimed to be adapting the Soviet political structure to the successful construction of the socialist base. However, under conditions of terror the social relationships in society were as far from socialist as ever and the absence of legal guarantees reached its tragic denouement in the purges.

The 1977 'Brezhnev constitution' underwent a long period of gestation. The idea for a new constitution was first mooted in 1959 to reflect the emergence of a 'state of all the people' and Khrushchev's ambitious plans for the 'full-scale construction of communism'. Brezhnev's proposal for a new constitution to mark the fiftieth anniversary of the October revolution in 1967 fell by the wayside, and only in 1972 was the project taken up. In June 1977 a draft appeared, followed by a four-month nationwide discussion until its adoption on 7 October. According to official figures a total of 140 million people participated, 80 per cent of the total adult population, and 400,000 amendments were proposed leading to some minor changes to the final version. The campaign was a well-publicised discussion of great noise and little content, a typical Brezhnevite exercise to demonstrate the legitimacy of the new constitution and its provisions.

The new constitution's long preparation indicated disagreements over the formulation of ideological and institutional programmes, yet when it appeared it did not differ in any fundamental way from the 1936 constitution. The introduction once again summed up the stage through which the country was passing. It called the Soviet Union a 'developed socialist society' and argued that a state of all the people had been created with no antagonistic classes. There was more on the role of the party (see Chapter 6), but as usual the details of governmental relationships were kept vague and the constitution placed few limits on the party's freedom. It made explicit the party's leading role in Soviet society (Article 6) and thus moved away from Khrushchev's long-term aim of creating a self-managed society. The concept of the withering away of the state was quietly shelved; the state, and with it political conformity, was rehabilitated. Indeed, in some respects the new constitution brought theory more into line with practice in its insistence that 'A citizen of the USSR is obliged to safeguard the interests of the Soviet state and to help strengthen its might and prestige' (Article 62). A new section discussed foreign policy and combined peaceful coexistence with declarations of support for wars of national liberation. There was a slight shift of power to the centre from the union republics, although they were still declared to be 'sovereign' (Article 76) and retained 'the right freely to secede from the USSR' (Article 72). This constitution, as with the three others, once again illustrated that while constitutions were ubiquitous in communist states, the systems were governed less by statute than by an 'unwritten constitution' of informal rules and conventions.

The nineteenth party conference in June–July 1988 outlined a programme of political change that took concrete form in the constitutional amendments of December 1988 (with further amendments in December 1989 and March and December 1990), in effect creating the fifth and final Soviet constitution. A new two-tier parliament was created (see below) and the principle of socialist legality was to govern the new system. A Constitutional Court (formally known as the Constitutional Oversight Committee) was established (coming into operation in April

1990) to ensure compliance with the revised constitution. Faced with the challenge of the August coup, however, the Court temporised and soon after was abolished, together with the new Soviet legislature in its entirety.

THE NATIONAL LEGISLATURE

According to all the constitutions the soviets (literally meaning 'councils') were formally sovereign, and indeed gave their name to the state itself, and yet their role was from the outset severely constrained by the powers of the two other networks of power, the party and the ministries. Only with the development of *perestroika* were there serious attempts to establish a responsible legislature with some scope for independent activity. We will first examine the traditional Supreme Soviet and then the later USSR Congress of People's Deputies.

The Supreme Soviet

Created by the 1936 constitution and later regulated by the 1977 constitution, the Supreme Soviet was the highest body of state power in the USSR. It was the legislative authority, and as a representative institution endowed the system with formal legitimacy. The Supreme Soviet consisted of two chambers with an equal number of deputies (750) in each. The Soviet of the Union was elected directly by the population through universal suffrage, with about 300,000 electors per constituency. The Soviet of Nationalities was elected from the various federal and national units with a fixed number of deputies from each. The two chambers had equal rights and usually met together. By law the Supreme Soviet had to meet at least twice a year, and between sessions its affairs were conducted by a presidium, usually of thirty-nine people. Plenary sessions were generally very short, lasting some two or three days, and infrequent, usually no more than the stipulated two times a year. The main work of the December session was to adopt the budget for the following year. The Supreme Soviet elected a chairman for its Presidium who was commonly known as President of the USSR. Mikhail Kalinin filled this post for many years under Stalin. Brezhnev, Andropov and Chernenko all took on the post in addition to their leadership of the party and obviously thought it important, if only for reasons of prestige when meeting foreign leaders. From June 1985 the post was held by Andrei Gromyko; Gorbachev at first preferred to concentrate on policy and devolved some of the ceremonial duties to the head of state until he, too, became President in 1988.

The Supreme Soviet appointed the government of the USSR, the Council of Ministers, many of whom were also members of the Supreme Soviet. Soviet government therefore had the appearance of a classic parliamentary system with the principle of ministerial responsibility to a legislative assembly. The Supreme Soviet also elected the Supreme Court and appointed the Procurator-General, the post which supervised the Soviet legal system. The Supreme Soviet played little role in initiating policy but it did perform several important functions. The legislative function was evident in its participation in drafting complex legislation, and indeed the drafting of new laws moved to some extent from the Council of Ministers to the Supreme Soviet. This allowed more scope for the incorporation of a wide range of specialist opinion. The supervisory, or *kontrol*, function over the state apparatus was achieved through thirty-four standing commissions (seventeen in each house). They reviewed legislation, oversaw its implementation and audited the work of state bodies. Over 80 per cent of deputies were members of standing commissions such as agriculture, health, foreign affairs and so on. Since most deputies had full-time jobs elsewhere (a principle of commune democracy), the standing commissions usually met no more frequently than the full plenary sessions, about twice a year. The commissions of both houses usually met together. The ombudsman function allowed deputies to pursue citizens' grievances against governmental or local state bodies.

The representative function allowed the Supreme Soviet to project the image of mass involvement and the smooth operation of socialist democracy. Deputies were selected to represent the key sectors of society such as workers, peasants, women, minorities and various professions, undermining any serious selective role for elections. The party leadership, especially Central Committee members, were traditionally over-represented. The so-called barometer function allowed deputies to indicate the mood of the population. In foreign policy major treaties were ratified by the Supreme Soviet. It provided weight to Soviet foreign policy initiatives and lent prestige to Soviet leaders in the international arena. The Supreme Soviet provided a useful channel for contacts with other political systems through parliamentary delegations and direct links between Soviet deputies, East European assemblies, Congressional representatives and Members of Parliament, linked in particular through the Interparliamentary Union. Gorbachev's first major public visit abroad, during which Mrs Thatcher discovered that he was a man with whom she could 'do business', was as a member of a Supreme Soviet parliamentary delegation to London in December 1984.

It was anticipated that the role of the Supreme Soviet would increase as the principle of popular sovereignty in a communist context was revived and political decision-making broadened. However, up to the mid-1980s one of the most remarkable features of Soviet politics was the slow adaptation of political structures to developments in society and the economy. In particular there was no evidence of a secular trend for the Supreme Soviet to become more active, to meet more frequently or for longer. The Brezhnevite stagnation in Soviet political development refuted the optimistic hopes of those who believed that Soviet social developments would be reflected in political changes. There was little evidence of an 'iron law of pluralism' and, on the contrary, on several counts the activity of the Supreme Soviet declined, such as in the frequency and length of sessions and the number of speeches, while the volume of legislation passed remained fairly constant.[2] In some East European countries the parliaments became more active than in the Soviet Union. By the 1980s the Polish Sejm and the Hungarian Diet made important political interventions and witnessed the revival of wide-ranging and critical debates.

The Congress of People's Deputies and the Supreme Soviet

Major changes were introduced by the constitutional amendments passed by the Supreme Soviet on 1 December 1988 after a short but vigorous debate. Of the 174 articles of the 1977 'Brezhnev' constitution, 55 were changed. The constitutional amendments began to put an end to the rule by party committees by empowering a reorganised two-tier legislature (see Figure 3). At its base a new supreme organ of Soviet power, a tricameral Congress of People's Deputies of 2,250 members, was created: 750 deputies were elected in general national elections to form a Soviet of the Union; 750 in direct elections from the federal units to form a Soviet of the Nationalities; and the remaining 750 were nominated by a variety of 'social organisations', including 100 by the communist party, to form a Soviet of Representatives. The 1,500 were elected in national elections in March 1989, while the rest were nominated at that time.

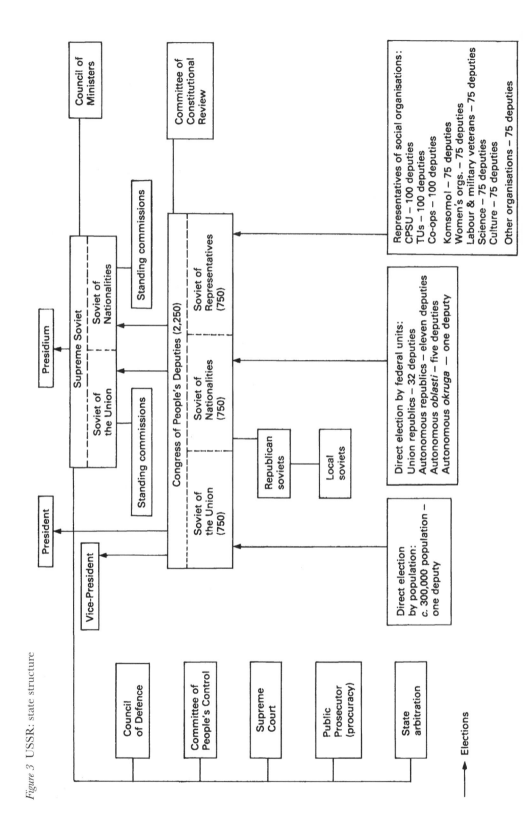

Figure 3 USSR: state structure

During its short existence the Congress of People's Deputies met on average twice a year for about two weeks each time. It convened for the first time for fifteen days from 25 May to 9 June 1989 with its main task the election of a 542-member Supreme Soviet. Despite the radicals' insistence that membership should be more than a preordained choice of the Politburo to be rubber-stamped by the assembly, the Supreme Soviet on 27 May was in fact elected from pre-arranged lists for every region, which in most cases numbered exactly the same as the number of places. Thus there was great scope for bureaucratic manipulation. Moreover, the system of negative voting meant that instead of voting *for* someone, deputies voted *against* by crossing out names on the ballot paper. Hence there was a structural bias in favour of the obscure since those who were well known were more likely to be crossed off, leading to the emergence of what was called a 'parliament of mediocrities'. As the most famous politician after Gorbachev, Yeltsin failed to win one of the eleven places out of twelve candidates for the Russian republic in the Soviet of Nationalities, but later took the place of a deputy who made way for him by resigning.

The amendments stipulated the obligatory turnover of up to a fifth of Supreme Soviet deputies every year to provide fresh energy between elections, but this was not fulfilled in practice. Deputies were elected for a maximum of two five-year terms, and could theoretically be recalled at any time. The Congress also elected the Constitutional Oversight Committee with the crucial task of deciding whether acts were constitutional or not. Only the Congress could dismiss the President, modify the country's frontiers, or repeal laws of the Supreme Soviet. It appointed the Procurator-General of the USSR and the supreme command of the armed services as well as electing the Supreme Court.

The Supreme Soviet was a full-time parliament on the Western model, holding three or four two-month sittings a year. Half of its members were picked on a regional basis, with, for example, each of the fifteen union republics having an entitlement of eleven seats each, to make up the Soviet of Nationalities. The other 271-member house, the Soviet of the Union, was chosen taking into account the distribution of the population. The responsibilities of the Supreme Soviet included appointing the Prime Minister and approving his or her ministers. The Supreme Soviet became a parliament with full-time paid MPs who, for the first time since the 1920s, freely used their right to vote against government programmes.

The radicals were severely disappointed by the composition of the new Supreme Soviet, and many echoed Yurii Afanasev's sentiment on 27 May that a 'Stalinist–Brezhnevite' body had been chosen. Those who shared his view about the 'aggressive and obedient majority' in the Congress went on to found what was in effect a separate faction, the 'inter-regional group'. This group could count on a maximum of a fifth, some 450 deputies, out of the 2,250 at the Congress. The division had a class aspect, since the majority of the radicals were intellectuals, whereas the 'obedient majority' tended to be workers by origin, though often bureaucrats by profession. These could barely restrain their animosity towards the 'Moscow intellectuals'.

Gorbachev was elected the nation's first executive President (officially titled Chairman of the Supreme Soviet) on the first day with minimum debate and no alternative candidate (although eighty-seven voted against him), thus perpetuating the lack of choice that he had so much criticised in the country at large. As President, the constitution granted him the exclusive right to nominate a candidate for the post of First Deputy Chair of the Supreme Soviet, in effect Vice-President. He proposed his close ally, Anatolii Lukyanov, who was duly elected, but only after severe questioning by other deputies. On 8 June Nikolai Ryzhkov was reconfirmed in his post as Prime Minister.

The status of the Congress remained unclear. Nominally the supreme authority, it appeared to duplicate the Supreme Soviet. The Congress granted itself the power to review and amend all laws passed by the Supreme Soviet and thus acted as a second chamber. The functions of the four-fifths of the deputies not in the Supreme Soviet at any one time were also unclear. It was conceded that any deputy, not only those in the Supreme Soviet, could be members of standing committees, allowing a broader range of specialist input. Half the places on the committees would be reserved for them, and indeed the work of the twenty-three parliamentary standing committees was assisted by 250 members of the Congress who were not members of the Supreme Soviet. Congress delegates argued that not only those elected to the Supreme Soviet but all 2,250 deputies should become professional politicians and give up their jobs. On 26 May the Congress decided that 'as a rule' Supreme Soviet deputies, in keeping with the professional nature of the new body, would have to give up their former jobs. This formulation allowed party officials, with Gorbachev at their head, to keep their second jobs while simultaneously acting as deputies. Once again, the party's leading role allowed it to flout the rules it imposed on others.

The debates of the Congress, which were televised live, enthralled the nation. The populace did not remain passive, however, and Yeltsin's initial failure to be elected to the Supreme Soviet was protested by a mass demonstration on 28 May at the Luzhniki Stadium in Moscow. Voters, moreover, inundated deputies with requests and instructions. The heated debates reflected the growing gulf between radicals and conservatives. Most remarkable of all was the sight of Sakharov, who only three years earlier had languished in exile in Gorkii (now Nizhnii Novgorod), at the podium of the nation's supreme assembly. Under the cover of parliamentary immunity the deputies enjoyed to the full their new rights to freedom of speech and day by day pushed back the frontiers of *glasnost*. Yeltsin on 31 May once again proposed a radical programme of reform, including a new law to define the powers of the party, limits to the powers of the head of state, for all privileges of the *nomenklatura* to be abolished, and he held Gorbachev personally responsible for many of the failures of the first four years of *perestroika*.

The new Congress was a far cry from the old ceremonial rubber-stamp legislature typical of communist systems and on several occasions showed a new self-confidence in calling the government to account. The Congress marked a turning point in Soviet politics and established a counterweight to the party apparatus and the governmental bureaucracy. The Soviet Union could never be ruled as before. The debates at the Congress, with their fearless denunciations of corruption, the bureaucracy, shortages and much more besides, encouraged the public to become politically active. In particular, the debates acted as the catalyst for miners' strikes over grievances that had been long suppressed.

However, the hopes of some that the Congress would act as a type of constituent assembly and place the Soviet Union on a new road were disappointed. The reform programme of the radicals, which included such elements as full-scale marketisation of the economy, changes in the electoral law, the repeal of restrictive decrees on demonstrations, decentralisation of powers to the republics, and a calling to account of those responsible for the foreign policy errors of earlier governments, failed to be adopted. Many of the aspirations of deputies from the Baltic and elsewhere were not realised. Above all, no clear decisions were taken on the separation of the functions of the party and state. This prompted Sakharov on the last day of the Congress to announce his 'Decree on Power' which warned of the excessive power in the hands of the President, called for the annulment of Article 6, the subordination of the Supreme Soviet to the Congress, the transfer of the power of appointments from the party to the

Congress, the transition to a professional army, and the creation of a 'federal ethnic constitutional structure' to create a 'union of equal republics joined by a federal treaty'.[3] In short, he called for the genuine implementation of the slogans of 'all power to the soviets' and the creation of a law-governed state. While this might not feed the people, only this, Sakharov insisted, could 'create political guarantees for the solution of these problems'.

The new Supreme Soviet had a supervisory capacity, especially in overseeing the budget, checking the ministries and their agencies, and reviewing legislation. Fears voiced in the debates on the amendments on excessive centralisation were tempered by attempts to establish some control over power. The Supreme Soviet was given the right to repeal decrees of its own presidium and instructions of the President, to recall any elected or appointed officials if they failed in their duties, and it was made mandatory for the government to report back to the assembly at least once a year. In an attempt to avoid another Afghanistan, or indeed Czechoslovakia, the Supreme Soviet reserved to itself the exclusive right to authorise the use of Soviet troops beyond the country's frontiers. The system of standing committees was much strengthened, including the right to summon and interrogate ministers and officials. Despite this, the absence of real control over finances, coercion and the much strengthened executive allow us to dub it a 'premature legislature', marginal to the operation of the real levers of power.

As long as a 'leading role' continued to be reserved for the party or enhanced executives, the revival of the soviets as effective decision-making centres remained in doubt. The constitutional amendments of 1988 provided no clear delineation of the functions of party and soviet bodies despite the constant calls for this to be addressed. In rather traditional language the party was urged to promote the development of the soviets, but not to substitute for them (the process known as *podmena*) or to interfere in their work.[4] The amendments gave legislative force to the division of functions between legislative and executive bodies. Drawing on American rather than British constitutional practice, members of the executive, including ministers, were prohibited from being deputies to soviets. This, of course, diminished the effect of parliamentary accountability, but was designed to enhance the independence of deputies. All state bodies, including the Council of Ministers, were to be accountable to the Supreme Soviet. The legislature and the government emerged as separate centres of power, and government appointees now needed the ratification of parliament rather than approval from the party alone. The amendments at last tried to give institutional force to the democratising reforms and to establish a state governed by law.

The communist party retained a guiding role in the Supreme Soviet, with many Politburo and Central Committee members holding key positions, and about two-thirds of the deputies were communists who held official positions of one sort or another. The acceptance of checks and balances in the Soviet system broke with the tradition of Marxist commune democracy, which stipulated the fusion of executive and legislative powers. However, the problem remained of how a system of checks and democratic proceduralism could be established against the power of the communist party or the strengthened executive.

THE GOVERNMENT

The governmental system as Stalin left it was an enormous bureaucratic complex responsible for the planning and administration of the whole economy and society from the farms, shops and factories to the armed forces and the education system. Every ministry was an administrative empire, a vast realm of bureaucracy. The ministry of one of the heavy industries such as

Figure 4 USSR: governmental structure

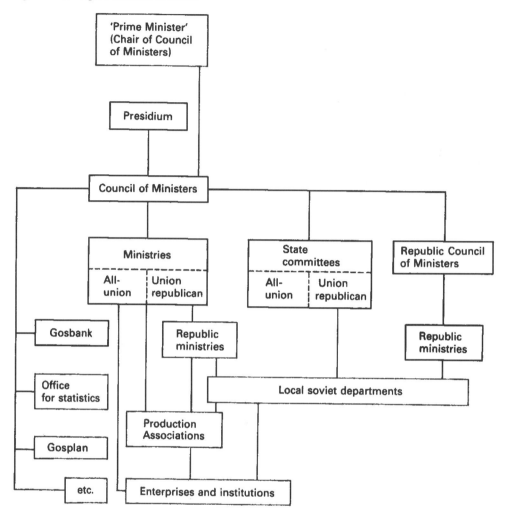

steel was like a giant monopolistic concern with its own housing, transport and shops in addi
tion to the steel mills themselves. The common Soviet quip was that their ministries were the
equivalent of giant Western multinationals, with the difference that Soviet ministries provided
housing, a political focus, holidays, and much more not usually catered for by Western compa-
nies. Alfred Meyer talked of 'USSR Inc.' to highlight the integrated bureaucratic system of
economic and political power. The ministries and the bureaucratic empires they spawned were
the source of much of the inertia of the Soviet system. Each ministry represented an island of
power stretching across the land. Khrushchev's deconcentration of the ministries to the regions was a brave but poorly executed attempt to tackle the problem. Brezhnev's consensual
style of politics once again allowed the ministries to consolidate their power (for a general
model of the ministerial system, see Figure 4).The number of ministries and state committees
changed, with a rising trend following the recentralisation of the ministries in 1965 until the
accession of Gorbachev in 1985. In 1984 there were fifty-nine ministries and twenty-two state

committees, and some other committees responsible for sport, religious affairs, state prizes and so on. A ministry was usually responsible for one vertically organised branch such as agriculture or defence, while a state committee usually cut across several branches such as prices, planning or science and technology. A typical ministry was fairly small with about 1,000 officials, but under Gorbachev there was some merging to create so-called 'super-ministries' (see below). The ministerial network in total employed hundreds of thousands of trained officials, although staff were not selected according to strict civil service criteria but largely through informal networks. Elements of competitive entrance had evolved but were still rudimentary. Most of the senior officials were trained in their fields, and even the ministers themselves were not usually politicians but specialists who tended to remain in their jobs for extended periods. The creation of super-ministries and the relaxation of central economic management were accompanied by the vigorous shedding of staff.

It should be stressed that Soviet governmental practice did not distinguish between the permanent bureaucracy responsible for the implementation of policies and the politicians who established the policies. The concept of a permanent civil service that survives changes of government is anathema to commune democracy principles. The Soviet system was a single bureaucratic chain with no constitutional division between the Politburo or ministerial policy-makers and the lower officials who executed the policies.

The ministerial system came to a head in the USSR Council of Ministers, made up of a chair, eight deputy chairs, over fifty ministers, the heads of the state committees and the chairs of the councils of ministers of the union republics, a total of about 120 people in 1987, over half of whom were involved in the management of the economy. According to the 1977 constitution it was 'the highest executive and administrative organ of state power' (Article 128) and was responsible to the Supreme Soviet. It dealt with a large amount of legislative activity and was the source of the majority of decrees in the country, but its sheer size prevented it becoming an effective cabinet. The 1977 constitution (Article 132) for the first time identified a presidium which acted as an inner cabinet. In late 1985 the aged Tikhonov was replaced as Chair of the Council of Ministers by the more reform-minded Nikolai Ryzhkov. Under Gorbachev the Council of Ministers rose in political weight, but it still by no means outweighed the Politburo or the Central Committee Secretariat. The Council of Ministers and its executive bodies were responsible for the day-to-day running of the country and represented the executive branch of the government. They were traditionally more involved with policy implementation than policy origination.

The state committees and ministries themselves fell into three categories: all-union, union republican, and republican. The all-union ministries were responsible for all aspects of their brief throughout the country. Defence, transportation and most heavy industrial concerns came into this category. The union-republican group, which included education, culture, finance, health, justice and internal affairs (MVD), directed its subordinate units through affiliate ministries of the same name in the capitals of the union republics. There was a tendency for union-republican ministries, such as coal and geology, to be reorganised into all-union ministries. The affiliated ministries operated according to the principle of 'dual subordination': subordinate both to their local council of ministers and to the Moscow ministry.

Each of the fifteen union republics had its own local council of ministers and its own supreme soviet. The governmental institutions of a union republic and an autonomous republic duplicated on a smaller scale those of the national government. The republican supreme soviets, as nationally, acted as the legislative arm, and had their own presidiums to serve as legislative organs between plenary sessions. The republican executive branch, as at the national level, was represented by a council of ministers which oversaw the ministries of local significance and included the top officials in the republican government. The republican ministries worked under the direct control of the local council of ministers.

Under Stalin there was extreme centralisation of power in Moscow. Official jargon represented Moscow as the 'centre' and all the rest of the country as the 'periphery' or the 'localities'. The reality of Soviet federalism was an extremely centralised political system with little authority vested in the republican capitals. In the soviets, the ministries and the party, actual authority was consolidated to a large extent in small and interlinked presidia: the presidium of the Supreme Soviet, the presidium of the Council of Ministers, and the Politburo of the CPSU Central Committee. In practice the three hierarchies combined to form a unified power structure but it would be misleading to call it a party-state monolith because of the tensions engendered by the fragmentation of responsibilities. The departments of the CC Secretariat, for example, had an ambiguous relationship with the ministries. They were supervisory and policy-making and yet (as in the United States), the regulatory bodies tended to coalesce into policy communities with the organisation they supervised. The Council of Ministers had several commissions overlapping with the departments of the party Secretariat, giving scope for conflicts. Brezhnev's relaxed administrative style put the premium on formal unity, but behind the scenes it permitted departmental interests to coalesce. The system, however, tried to ensure the primacy of the general interest as defined by the party. The unified structure emerged out of the centralised system of appointments and the integrating role of the party. However, the system remained in a condition of tense equilibrium, profoundly stable in normal circumstances but brittle in crisis. The inertia of the ministerial system made reforming the Soviet Union a gargantuan task and one which the party ultimately failed to achieve.

Gorbachev's reforms tried to develop an effective government responsible to parliament and thus to the people. This entailed the creation of ministries which were no longer extensions of party organs, which at its crudest meant that ministries were not much more than the executive agents of departments of the Central Committee. The number of ministries was reduced in Gorbachev's early years by the creation of the 'super-ministries'. In October 1985 a Bureau for Machine Building was created to co-ordinate the eleven civilian ministries in the field, and in November the five ministries and two state committees concerned with agriculture and its equipment were united to form a state agro-industrial committee ministry (Agroprom). The amalgamated ministries shed up to a third of their staff.

The Council of Ministers was drastically reduced in size, due, in part, to the merging of ministries into larger bodies. The Council of Ministers was appointed by and formally responsible to the new-style Supreme Soviet. It became the effective government of the USSR, performing executive and administrative tasks. It remained, however, the primary organ of the state bureaucracy and as such came in for special criticism. Its role as a policy-making body, however, was limited both by the existence of the party's Politburo and by the reactivated Supreme Soviet, its presidium, president and committees. Prospective ministers had to demonstrate their competence and be recommended by the relevant standing committee of parliament. In June 1989 confirmation hearings began for the new government presented by Ryzhkov, made up of fifty-seven ranking ministers and thirteen deputy premiers. The number had fallen sharply from the old 115-member Council of Ministers, with the greatest fall in the number of economic portfolios, down from fifty-two to thirty-two. Only ten of the ministers in office in 1984 survived. Leonid Abalkin was confirmed as a deputy premier in charge of a new state committee for economic reform. The first non-communist minister since the 1920s was Nikolai Vorontsov, in charge of the state committee for nature conservation. Those who were confirmed often had a stormy ride, as in the case of the defence minister, Yazov.

The constitutional changes of 1988 elevated the status of the government in relation to the party. This was reflected in the new prominence given to the role of the Prime Minister, and Ryzhkov's own personal profile was raised sharply; in effect he became second only to Gorbachev himself. This recreated something like the situation obtaining at the close of Stalin's era, when Georgii Malenkov felt confident that the prime ministership was enough to ensure his succession to Stalin, only to be outwitted by the party's First Secretary, Khrushchev, who went on to establish a thirty-five-year dominance for the party. In December 1990 the Council of Ministers was renamed the Cabinet of Ministers, and at the same time Ryzhkov was dismissed, to be replaced by a moderate reformer, Valentin Pavlov. At the same time, the December 1988 constitutional amendments had created what was in effect the presidency (formally Chairman of the USSR Supreme Soviet), and in March and December 1990 Gorbachev's presidential powers were increased – an attempt to impose a caesarist solution on the country's growing crisis of political authority.

From the above account it is clear that Walter Bagehot's distinction between the dignified and efficient parts of government is as applicable, if not more so, to the USSR as it was to nineteenth-century Britain. In the Soviet Union the dignified part of the constitution was represented by the network of soviets, the Council of Ministers, the adoption of constitutions and the declaration of a range of rights that prompted Stalin to argue that the 1936 constitution was 'the most democratic in the world'. The dignified façade, however, masked the efficient parts of the Soviet constitution, the Politburo and the Central Committee Secretariat shrouded in a dense network of party control and democratic centralism. Gorbachev's attempts to reconcile dignity with efficiency, however, provoked the collapse of both.

KEY TEXTS

Barry, Donald D. (ed.), *Towards the 'Rule of Law' in Russia?: Political and Legal Reform in the Transition Period* (Armonk, NY, M. E. Sharpe, 1992).

Hough, J. and M. Fainsod, *How the Soviet Union is Governed* (Cambridge, MA, Harvard University Press, 1979).

Kiernan, Brendan, *The End of Soviet Politics: Elections, Legislatures, and the Demise of the Communist Party* (Boulder, CO, Westview Press, 1993).

8   Security and justice

The military and the security police played important roles in Soviet politics, reflecting the insecurities of a power born in revolution with the explicit aim of revising the traditional system of international relations abroad and of destroying opposition at home. The judiciary played a smaller role than in liberal democratic states, with law always subordinated to political expediency. Under Lenin the party apparatus presided over the soviets but never really gained a hold over the secret police or the vast economic commissariats spawned by War Communist centralisation. Under Stalin the major coalition was the economic apparatus, the security police and the leadership principle. With Khrushchev the party once again dominated but its rule was tempered by an element of populism and headstrong leadership. Brezhnev's rule saw the emergence of a broad coalition comprised of the party apparatus, the administrative bureaucracy, the economic ministries, the military and increasingly the security apparatus. During Andropov's brief ascendancy the security apparatus was more prominent than at any time since the death of Stalin. Under Gorbachev the military's influence waned and soviets and professional groups were encouraged within the context of revived political activism inspired by the leader. These shifts gave Soviet politics its dynamism and allowed each successive leader to stamp a period with his name. Throughout, however, Soviet society was unable to establish direct legal or political restraints on the exercise of power.

THE MILITARY AND SOVIET POLITICS

Born in revolution and war, the Soviet regime always placed a strong emphasis on its armed forces. The Red Army was formed in the spring of 1918 to defend the infant Soviet regime from foreign intervention and domestic enemies. It was moulded by the military genius of Leon Trotsky, the military commissar, during the Civil War of 1918–21. The system of dual control whereby military officers inherited from the Tsarist regime (the so-called *spetsy* – specialists) were supervised by political commissars survived in a modified form to the end. Despite the traditional Marxist antipathy to standing armies, the failure of the revolution to spread undermined hopes after the Civil War that a militia army would be created. Paradoxically, a system born in hostility to standing armies became one of the most militarised in the world. This in part explains why the party leadership was haunted by the ghost of 'Bonapartism', the military strongman coming to power and ousting the civilian leadership at the end of a revolutionary period. In the Soviet system the spectre took on a novel twist, and instead of the general appearing on horseback (or in a tank), he emerged as the staff officer intent on maintaining the dominance of the 'metal-eating' industries supplying the armed forces with military hardware. Bonapartism with a briefcase posed no less of a challenge than the horseback version and ultimately brought the system to its knees.

The party established an elaborate mechanism to forestall any Napoleonic urges within the military. The fear that Trotsky might play that role as head of the army in the early 1920s significantly weakened his position in the struggle against Stalin, and his own misgivings that he might fulfil such a destiny paralysed his will. Once in power Stalin was careful to insure against a military challenge to his rule, culminating in the bloody purge of the military in 1937–38. The destruction of the army high command led to the USSR's poor performance against the Finns in the Winter War of 1939–40, and to the initial defeats following the German invasion of 22 June 1941. The struggle was accompanied by a relaxation of the system of dual command, allowing officers a degree of operational autonomy. The military emerged from the war with their prestige greatly enhanced. This alone was enough to unsettle Stalin, and soon after he pointedly demoted Marshal Georgii Zhukov, the captor of Berlin. Zhukov fared little better under Khrushchev despite his assistance in defeating Beria in 1953 and the anti-party group in 1957. Khrushchev was intent that no rival would emerge to challenge either him or the party. Furthermore, his belief that nuclear weapons made ground forces obsolete led to drastic cuts from 1959 in the conventional military budget for both soldiers and the 'metal-eating' military supply industries. Khrushchev's overthrow in 1964 was therefore, not surprisingly, welcomed by the military, particularly after his nuclear adventurism that had provoked the Cuban missile crisis of October 1962.

Brezhnev removed the challenge to the ground-forces budget while maintaining the strategic-missiles programme and thus guaranteed that the military became one of the main supports of his rule. The elevation of Marshal Andrei Grechko to full membership of the Politburo in 1973, to consolidate support for détente, underlined the importance of the military as an interest group. The defence budget grew steadily, with a sustained 4–5 per cent annual increment in the decade up to 1976, falling off to about 2 per cent thereafter. The figures have been disputed, but at least 15 per cent (and some estimates during *perestroika* suggested that the figure was closer to a third) of GNP was devoted to military expenditure, double that of the USA, whose economy was at least 40 per cent larger. There were an estimated 5 million men under arms (excluding KGB and MVD troops) in the conscript army, compared to 2.2 million in the US armed forces, although many were employed in labour battalions and suchlike rather than in directly military activities. One of the most spectacular results of the spending was the expansion of the Soviet Navy under Admiral S. G. Gorshkov from a fairly modest coastal defence force to a powerful strategic, submarine and high-seas fleet capable of projecting Soviet power worldwide.

The principle of party leadership over the armed forces remained central in Soviet civil–military relations. Party control was ensured through the Defence Council, whose existence was only acknowledged in 1976 when Brezhnev was chair, and its position was formalised by the 1977 constitution (Article 121). The Defence Council was chaired by the General Secretary, and included the Premier and the defence and foreign ministers. It was one of the most important decision-making bodies in the fields of foreign policy, military affairs and the domestic economy through the defence industries. Party influence over the military was directed by the Main Political Administration of the Armed Forces. It paralleled the military command structure with a vast network of agitators, instructors and propagandists that sought to inculcate the military with communist values. Its role had changed from the Civil War years when the loyalty of officers was in doubt, and it was now mainly concerned with political education and socialisation. Since the overwhelming majority of top officers were party members, the residual system of dual control was rather anachronistic. The actual management of the Soviet military was the responsibility of the General Staff, which oversaw the running of the five services (Ground Forces, Strategic Rocket Forces, Navy, Air Forces and Air Defence Forces) as well as the intelligence directorate, the GRU.

The military professionalism of the Soviet Army rose steadily. More and more the premium in modern warfare is on scientific skills, and no army can afford to lag behind its adversaries, especially in microelectronics and communications. In some areas the technological sophistication of the Soviet forces was second to none, yet the problems here were the same as in the economy as a whole: the lack of initiative in routine matters, the slow rate of innovation, the shortage of technicians and poor maintenance in a system which stressed political reliability rather than technical ability. This induced some of the more forward-looking generals to support the modernisation of the Soviet economy to provide the technological basis for an advanced defence industry. The head of the General Staff from 1977 to 1984, Marshal Nikolai Ogarkov, noted the advantage that sophisticated high-technology weapons had given the United States, and advocated increased defence spending to allow the Soviet Union to develop its own 'smart' weaponry.[1] The poor performance of Soviet weaponry in the June 1982 fighting in the Lebanon demonstrated that today's wars are won as much in the scientist's laboratory as on the field of battle. The threat of US President Ronald Reagan's Strategic Defence Initiative (Star Wars) in the mid-1980s lay not so much in the budgetary challenge it posed to the Soviet Union (the high command was well aware that there was no immediate need to respond in kind) but in its exploitation of American technological superiority.

The final generation of Soviet officers had less personal experience of the Second World War, but had been tested in the Horn of Africa and in Afghanistan. The professional military became an increasingly distinctive caste in society, with recruitment coming largely from within its own circles. Some no doubt sought to defend the privileges gained under Brezhnev, but others were more open to the need for change. The military ethos became part of the political culture of the Soviet Union, with all men at the age of 18 having to serve two years in the army. The gulf between the officer elite and the mass of the Soviet Army, raw and often ill-educated conscripts from villages and factories, should be stressed. The demographic rise of Central Asia meant that every year a growing proportion of recruits did not have Russian as their primary language. The time spent in the army was designed to inculcate Soviet youth with patriotic and party values, and yet the military was not insulated from the problems facing Soviet society. Alienation and indiscipline were as rife in the forces as in the factories, exemplified by the prevalence of bullying (hazing, in Russian, *dedovshchina*) among recruits that led to several hundred deaths a year, including many suicides.

The Soviet military was the cornerstone of the Warsaw Treaty Organisation (WTO), established in 1955 to integrate the command structures of the Soviet Union and its allies in Eastern Europe. In 1987 the USSR had thirty-one divisions based in Eastern Europe (twenty in the GDR, known as the Western Group of Forces, five in Czechoslovakia, four in Hungary and two in Poland). The supreme commander was always Soviet. The WTO was as much responsible for maintaining Soviet power in the area, as in Czechoslovakia in 1968, as it was for countering NATO. The army had a dual role in Soviet-type systems: defence against external aggression; and to act as the ultimate domestic arbiter. Eastern European armies were both national institutions and acted, as General Wojciech Jaruzelski did in December 1981 in imposing martial law in Poland, in the Soviet interest. The sight of generals in power in Poland clearly evoked shades of the Bonapartist nightmare as party governance gave way to military rule.

The growing power of the military in Soviet domestic affairs up to 1985 was seen as posing a challenge to the hegemony of the party. Despite the elaborate mechanisms of party control, Roman Kolkowicz argued that under Brezhnev the military as an interest group gained prominence at the expense of civilian party leaders. The increased routinisation of government allowed the military to consolidate its position in leading bodies, and the Soviet Union's growing global ambitions frequently took on a military form. Both Brezhnev in his last speech and Andropov in his first sympathised with the vigorous demands being put forward at the time by Ogarkov for further expenditure on conventional forces, but Chernenko lost patience and dismissed him in 1984. The military played an important part in foreign policy formation and foreign relations, with a broad military assistance programme including a high level of arms transfers which made the USSR the world leader in arms exports. Flushed by their successes in the Horn of Africa, the military overestimated their capacities and moved into Afghanistan in December 1979. The baleful consequences of the growing military role in Soviet foreign policy formation committed the USSR to its longest war – one which it did not lose but which it also did not win, but that had a terribly demoralising impact on the military and society.[2]

Stalinist industrialisation focused on heavy industry to create a powerful defence sector. By Brezhnev's time the defence industry had achieved a rare degree of privilege in the Soviet economy, even though it was not only responsible for supplying weaponry but provided some consumer durables for the domestic economy. This distorted pattern of Soviet development led to claims that the Soviet Union had a military-industrial complex which dominated the political system. To this Seweryn Bialer retorted that the Soviet Union *is* a military-industrial complex.[3] Quincy Wright observed long ago that socialism had proved to be 'the war organisation of capitalism'.[4] Gerner called it a 'militarised industrial state'.[5] While highlighting an important facet of Soviet politics, the concept of a military-industrial complex is somewhat too narrow to describe the complex interpenetration of Soviet military, political and economic concerns.

It would be an exaggeration to talk of a struggle between the military and the party. With 96 per cent of senior Soviet officers belonging to the communist party, the military was thoroughly imbued with the party spirit (*partiinost*). The party and the military shared a common ethos and both for long were imbued with a military perspective on decision-making. The shared values included a respect for hierarchy and discipline, a strong sense of Soviet patriotism and Russian nationalism, and a campaigning and storming mentality. The civilian and military elites were barely distinguishable and shared a common militaristic perception on global affairs. The career of the former defence minister Dmitrii Ustinov, who had enjoyed a long career as a civilian administrator in the defence industry before becoming the party's choice as military leader, illustrates the close relationship between sectors. The absence of a department for military affairs in the Secretariat of the Central Committee indicated the party's readiness to rely on the advice of the professional military in debates over Soviet military policy. The traditional premium on secrecy gave the General Staff broad discretion in shaping the policy options. The Soviet slogan of the 'unity of the party and the army' reflected the reality.

This is not to suggest that the relationship was always a smooth one. Gorbachev was well aware that the military represented one of the most significant drains on investment and hoped to divert some of these resources to his programme of domestic restructuring. The conventional Soviet view that technological developments and production innovations would somehow spill over to invigorate the domestic economy palpably failed to materialise. Apart from investment priorities, another issue on which Gorbachev found himself at odds with them was military doctrine. The Soviet military until the mid-1980s had never fully accepted the doctrine of Mutually Assured Destruction (MAD) and retained a belief in the concept of limited nuclear war. In 1977 in Tula Brezhnev accepted that this was not the case, and yet the military fought a long rearguard action to sustain the belief that a nuclear confrontation could be fought and won.[6] Clearly, such arguments ran counter to Gorbachev's deeply held beliefs on disarmament and the lunacy of nuclear war. Gorbachev conducted his bold arms-control initiatives in the face of the military's misgivings; but, it might be added, his failure on occasion even to forewarn them of a new initiative (as in his announcement of a cut of half a million soldiers announced at the United Nations in December 1988) did not help build confidence in his leadership abilities.

Under Gorbachev there was a marked decline in the status of the military. He all but removed them from the Mausoleum on ceremonial occasions. Following Ustinov's death in December 1984 his successor (nominated by Chernenko), Marshal Sergei Sokolov, a man in his seventies, obtained only consultative (non-voting) status on the Politburo. The flight of Matthias Rust to Red Square in 1986 permitted Gorbachev to change key figures in the military, including the replacement of Sokolov by Yazov. The military, however, was still well represented on the Central Committee. Gorbachev's references to the military were usually pointedly short and often critical. Military power remained a high priority under Gorbachev, but he began the arduous task of reconstructing the Soviet military away from its traditional belief that the *only* way to maintain peace is to prepare for war. His successors were left to grapple with the problem of a monstrously bloated military establishment who believed that any attack on them represented an assault on the very idea of Russia.

THE KGB

The establishment of a security police force was always to be one of the first acts of a Marxist–Leninist revolution. Shortly after the Bolsheviks came to power, Lenin systematised the struggle against 'counter-revolution'. On 20 December 1917 the All-Russian Commission for the Fight Against Counter-revolution, Sabotage and Speculation was created, known from its acronym as the 'Cheka'. The Cheka's first leader F. E. Dzerzhinsky gained for his organisation the right not only to hold prisoners, but to judge and execute them. The Red Terror of September 1918, following the attempted assassination of Lenin by the SR Fanny Kaplan on 30 August, saw the powers used to such an extent that even many Bolshevik leaders, such as Lev Kamenev, were horrified and sought to bind the actions of the Cheka in some form of legality. This was the intention of the reforms after the Civil War, with the creation in February 1922 of the State Political Directorate (GPU). Soon after, in November 1923, this name was restricted to local organisations, and the central body became officially the Unified Political Directorate of the USSR, the OGPU. In 1934 the security police was further restructured by merging it with the interior ministry to create the People's Commissariat of Internal Affairs, the NKVD. A huge bureaucratic nightmare machine had been created, waiting only for the signal from Stalin to be unleashed. Following the assassination of Kirov on 1 December 1934 special enabling legislation (above all, the creation of the *troikas*, three-person commissions that could pass sentences *in camera*) turned the NKVD into the potent weapon of the great purges. Stalin's power came to rest on his personal dominance of the police apparatus.

Following the death of Stalin the Politburo sought to restrain the security police and thus remove the danger to themselves. The police system was split so that one part could restrain the other, a primitive version of checks and balances. The security police was demoted in status from a ministry to a state committee, becoming the Committee for State Security (KGB). Various ministries took over the NKVD's economic functions, and its legal functions, such as the Special Boards and the running of the labour camps, went to the Ministry of Justice. The MVD (Ministry of Internal Affairs) became responsible for the militia, which conducted routine police business against crime, controlled traffic and administered the internal passport system. The principle of 'socialist legality' was established and normal judicial proceedings replaced secret trials. The KGB was brought under strict party control and loyal communists were appointed to run it: Ivan Serov (1953–58); followed by two men from the Komsomol, A. N. Shelepin (1958–61) and V. E. Semichastny (1961–67); then Yu. V. Andropov (1967–82); V. V. Fedorchuk (1982); and Viktor Chebrikov (1982–88). The surprise appointment of the hardliner Vladimir Kryuchkov to head the KGB in September 1988 (joining the Politburo at the same time) left Gorbachev's reforms exposed to the machinations of the security police. Kryuchkov went on to participate in the attempted coup in August 1991.

The KGB became part of the governmental network but in addition it was responsible to the General Department of the Central Committee Secretariat. The reversal of destalinisation under Brezhnev was accompanied by a growing role for the KGB in Soviet society. Under Andropov's leadership the KGB became a much more professional organisation and its prestige rose. It reasserted itself as a relatively independent centre of political power, a position it had lost with the death of Stalin. Andropov was ultimately able to use this power base to launch his bid for the party leadership in November 1982. His accession was accompanied by the promotion of KGB personnel to top party and government posts. In 1982 Fedorchuk, head of the Ukrainian KGB, was brought in to replace Andropov and then to lead the corrupt MVD. The division between the MVD and the KGB was in effect undermined. The KGB took the lead in the anti-corruption campaign, putting political leaders once again at the mercy of the security police. The KGB consolidated its hold on the OBKhSS, the Bureau for the Prevention of the Pilfering of Soviet Property, as part of the anti-corruption campaign. In the midst of a sea of corruption, only the KGB appeared to stand as an island of incorruptibility.

The Soviet Union was a controlled society and hence the role of the security apparatus was commensurately prominent. The KGB was structured into a number of Chief Directorates, the most important of which were the First (foreign relations), the Second (responsible for domestic counter-espionage), the Fourth (responsible for border controls and several categories of forces including the border guards and internal security troops), while the Fifth dealt with internal subversion. It had offices throughout the country with a staff of some 700,000 and at least an equal number of informers. The KGB was represented on the bureaus of all the republican party committees, and its leaders after 1973 had full membership of the national Politburo. The republican heads of the KGB were usually Russian, acting as a powerful integrative force in the polity. The personnel office in most enterprises had a special department run by the KGB to maintain surveillance over the workforce. The secret police was not restricted only to malevolent tasks but, in line with Lenin's initial idea, had an important part to play in maintaining the civilian economy through the battle against corruption and the enforcement of labour discipline.

The KGB was an influential political actor in its own right and represented an important interest group in both foreign and domestic policy. It had its own sources of power which operated relatively independently of the party-state structures; and it was a vast bureaucratic organisation with files on everything and almost everybody. The reality of the neo-Stalinist compromise was of a sustained low-level terror practised in the context of a culture of informers and betrayal. The lesson of Jaruzelski's coup in Poland seemed to be that while the party was dispensable, the security apparatus was not. However, in the Soviet Union the secret police remained under party control until the party itself decomposed in the final years. Andropov was always careful to present himself as a loyal party official rather than as a policeman, and it was this that allowed him to become General Secretary in 1982. The KGB provided an alternative source of information to the party leadership and, as witnessed during Andropov's rule, could be an important means of implementing policies beyond its immediate sphere of concerns, such as the anti-corruption campaign. The modern KGB stood in relation to the party as the state-party stood to the state apparatus. It placed its operatives at all levels of the party and maintained extensive files on party officials, although (with memories of Stalin) it was not able to act against them directly. It acted as an important pillar complementing the state and party hierarchies.

The KGB had an important part to play in the reform process initiated by Gorbachev. While it appeared to support moderate economic *perestroika*, it clearly had major reservations about political *glasnost*. The KGB was one of the few organisations to escape criticism at the twenty-seventh party congress, yet after a long period when it appeared to be the only organisation in the Soviet Union above criticism, in January 1987 Chebrikov was forced to apologise in *Pravda* for the unlawful persecution by the KGB of V. Verkhin, the editor of *Soviet Miner*, following his exposé of poor safety conditions for miners. Chebrikov promised that 'the organs of state security will act in complete accordance with the law',[7] yet the delay in investigating the case, in which Verkhin died, revealed the limits of *glasnost*. The incident not only showed that under Gorbachev no organisation could consider itself immune from criticism, but also that the road to Canossa also led away from it.

JUSTICE

Soviet constitutional practice recognised no role for an independent judiciary. The ambiguous role of law in the Soviet state derived from the belief that both the 'state' and 'law' would wither away with the development of a self-governing and self-regulating communist society. At first the system was defined as a 'dictatorship of the proletariat' in which the proletarian state would have to consolidate itself for a short time while it carried out the unpleasant task of eliminating bourgeois and capitalist opposition. This entailed a massive consolidation of the state and necessarily made any laws regarding personal inviolability redundant. The institutions of the class dictatorship were unregulated, since they were destined to disappear, and were considered mere epiphenomena to the overriding struggle between the proletariat and its enemies. As a Soviet text put it in 1928:

> The undisguised and deliberate use of state institutions as an instrument in the class struggle is fully in accord with the Marxian doctrine of the State, namely, that it is a class organisation. In this case it is an instrument of the ruling proletarian class.[8]

Justice was dependent on the nature of the case and in class terms objective guilt or innocence was meaningless. The state would wither away only when the exploiting classes had been eliminated, and in the meantime its powers had to be strengthened. The state remained the basic form of socialist society, and gradually there came the recognition that its practices would have to be defined by laws and some sort of balance struck between state power and the rights of society.

In the first years of Soviet power there was no theoretical or practical role for law and lawyers: they simply did not fit into the political project of the Bolshevik revolution. The leading exponent of this 'legal nihilism' was E. B. Pashukanis, who argued in favour of the rapid withering away of traditional civil and criminal law. With the onset of NEP, law was partially rehabilitated, including the restoration of the Defence Bar, a reform regarded with hostility by communist ideologues since most lawyers were trained by the Tsarist regime. A renewed offensive against law accompanied the cultural revolution of 1928–32. However, from 1932 Vyshinskii headed the theoretical re-evaluation that led to official recognition that a stable legal framework was essential for the operation of government. The 1936 constitution restored the concept of law in socialist society, perhaps in part due to Bukharin's desperate attempt to avert the purges. It is ironic that this re-evaluation coincided with the mass lawlessness of the great terror. It reflected the dualism of a legal system comprised of what has been called 'prerogative law', used against dissidents, and the 'due process of law' approach applied to judging ordinary criminality and regulating economic and social affairs. The restoration of law in the 1930s was not simply a façade for terror but an attempt to constitute a centrally directed legal system that could operate in parallel to the terror. Due process, of course, could not be totally insulated from prerogative law.

The introduction of the concept of state of all the people by Khrushchev made possible the systematisation of Soviet governance. As the Soviet system matured the elements of order and constitutionalism were strengthened, although legal arbitrariness remained deeply rooted in the system. The 1977 constitution further rehabilitated law in socialist society and tried to provide a framework for its stable operation. However, while the duties of Soviet citizens were specific, their political rights were general. According to Soviet theory law served to protect the system itself rather than the rights of individuals. The regime never fully accepted the proposition that it should obey its own laws and integrate prerogative law with due process. General slogans of revolutionary legality gradually gave way to a more settled system where in theory and mostly in practice the concept of 'Soviet legality' came to dominate. The scope of arbitrary police actions was severely curbed. To overcome Stalin's dominance of the judiciary and the security police, the party brought the former within its own jurisdiction. The crucial further step was to free it from party tutelage and allow it a degree of independence within the Soviet constitution – but this was never done.

Criminal Codes were adopted by each of the republics, but differed little from each other and were closely co-ordinated with Soviet constitutional principles. The revision of the Russian Criminal Code in 1961 formalised many innovations stretching back to the early years of Soviet power. The Soviet legal system was administered by the Procurator-General, who ensured that state bodies remained within the law. The judges of the Supreme Court of the USSR, and of the supreme courts of the union republics, together with the Procurator-General, were elected by the respective supreme soviets for five-year terms. The USSR Supreme Court acted as the final court of appeal for cases coming up from the people's courts. These lower courts were presided over by a professional judge and two lay assessors formally elected for two-year terms by workplace meetings. The procuracy acted as the state prosecution service. Official policy proclaimed that sentencing was not only guided by a retributory impulse but was designed to reform and re-educate offenders to deter them from committing further offences. The system emphasised not so much the trial itself as the pre-trial investigation, often without adequate representation by a defence lawyer who until the late 1980s was not allowed to interview clients until after the police and counsel for the prosecution had done with them.

Among his many initiatives, Gorbachev urged legal reform. The motive for this was a shift from the 'utilitarian' basis of the rehabilitation of law of the 1930s to the theoretical 'humanitarianism' basic to Western law. Debate over attempts to establish a 'socialist legal state' focused on the following issues: greater powers for defence lawyers; a review of sentencing procedures, with an improved quality of judges and people's assessors, and possibly the reintroduction of twelve-person juries abolished in 1917; less political interference, dispensing with 'hot lines' between local party bosses and the courts; greater protection for those accused of crimes; rewriting the Criminal Code to make it more humane; revising the notorious Articles 70 and 190 dealing with political offences; decreasing the number of offences punished by the death penalty; and judicial review of legislation in the light of the constitution. In short, the aim was to develop greater independence for the judiciary and to end 'prerogative law'. The problem was not the often-asserted claim about the lack of a legal perspective in Russian political culture or the absence of a presumption of innocence (the case also in the French system), but the demands of the Soviet political system which saw law as a branch of the state. The protection of citizens from the state was regarded as anathema. The obstacles to achieving a strongly rooted legal system defended by an independent judiciary in a system where even overt political conduct had little relation to the provisions of the constitution were ultimately insuperable.

KEY TEXTS

Butler, W. E., *Soviet Law* (London, Butterworth, 1983).
Colton, Timothy J. and Thane Gustafson (eds), *Soldiers and the Soviet State: Civil–Military Relations from Brezhnev to Gorbachev* (Princeton, NJ, Princeton University Press, 1990).
Knight, Amy, *The KGB: Police and Politics in the Soviet Union* (London, Unwin Hyman, 1988).

9 Local government and participation

The slogan of 'all power to the soviets' was one of the most effective in the Bolsheviks' political armoury in 1917. Nevertheless, following the July events of that year, when Bolshevik dominance in the soviets seemed unattainable, the slogan was shelved. It appeared that the soviets were dispensable in the Bolshevik vision of the future. In October 1917 Trotsky led the Bolsheviks to military victory in Petrograd and only then presented the second Congress of Soviets with a *fait accompli*. The soviets became the basis of the legitimacy of Bolshevik rule but soon lost any residue of autonomy. Within five years of the Bolsheviks coming to power no representatives of other parties remained in them. The soviets were transformed from revolutionary organisations into the kernel of the administrative system. The party continued to rule in their name, accompanied by periodic attempts to 'revive' them, particularly under Khrushchev and Gorbachev.

LOCAL SOVIETS AND ADMINISTRATION

The 1918 constitution vested power in the soviets headed by an All-Russian Congress of Soviets, which elected a Central Executive Committee (VTsIK) to manage current affairs. However, effective power lay with the Sovnarkom, which had the right to issue decrees without consulting VTsIK. From the first there emerged a gulf between the theory and the practice of Soviet government, complicated by the undefined though dominant role of the party. Under Stalin the representative role of the soviets declined as they became almost purely administrative bodies, and even this function was severely limited by the burgeoning ministerial apparatus. The soviets were limited politically by the party and administratively by the ministries. Following Stalin's death the new leadership led by Khrushchev launched a campaign for the revival of 'Soviet democracy' and in particular of the soviets themselves. The attempt, significantly, began not with the soviets but with the party leadership. Khrushchev's policy was continued by his successors but with a diminished vigour until the accession of Gorbachev.

The 1977 constitution (Article 2) stated: 'All power in the USSR belongs to the people. The people exercise state power through soviets of people's deputies, which constitute the political foundation of the USSR.' From 1977 they were called 'soviets of people's deputies' in line with the concept of the all-people's state, no longer distinguishing between workers, peasants and intelligentsia. As part of the rhetoric of returning to Leninist practices there was a new emphasis on public or mass participation. The stress was on the professionalism of soviet bodies, with more formal procedures and observance of rules within the context of the restoration of Soviet legality.

The soviet network in 1985 was made up of the USSR Supreme Soviet, 15 supreme soviets of the union republics, 20 supreme soviets of autonomous republics, 129 *krai* and *oblast* soviets, 8 soviets of autonomous *oblast*s, 10 soviets of autonomous *okrugs*, 3,113 *raion*, 2,137 city, 645 town-*raion*, 3,828 urban-type settlements and 42,176 village soviets; a total of 52,074 soviets of people's deputies.[1] The soviets were the major link between the regime and the population, acting to implement the policies of the political leadership, and at the same time enabling them to keep in touch with grass-roots opinion. The tension between the maintenance of party leadership and the attempt to upgrade the quality of mass involvement, however, was never resolved. As Khrushchev discovered, the attempt to convert managerial participation into populist participation encountered resistance from the party and ministerial bureaucracy. Participation without power too often in the Soviet context became plain mobilisation. Despite the limitations, a large proportion of the adult population was drawn (a process known as *privlechenie*) into local administration. The number of deputies at all levels from the Supreme Soviet to the smallest village increased from 1.5 million in 1957 to 2.3 million in 1985. Of these, 44 per cent were classified as workers, 25 per cent collective farm peasants and 31 per cent employees. Overall, 43 per cent were full party members or candidates, 34 per cent were under 30 years old, and 89 per cent had higher or secondary education.[2] There were, in addition to these elected representatives, some 30 million activists associated with the standing commissions of the local soviets, in electoral commissions, or involved in some other local public organisation, such as the comrades' courts, the people's guards (*druzhiny*), street and house committees and other largely voluntary bodies.

The structure of the soviets reflected their debt to the theory of commune democracy, the principle of participatory rather than representative democracy. The notion of direct democracy was reflected in the soviets as 'working bodies' rather than parliamentary 'talking shops'. Most soviet deputies had full-time jobs in addition to their electoral responsibilities. In contrast to the principle established in Western democracies, deputies were not representatives but delegates. They were issued binding instructions (*nakazy*) by voters, and if they deviated from them they could in theory be recalled. In the early days of Soviet power this was frequently used as a stratagem to remove Mensheviks and others, but by the last years the power was rarely used. Deputies were obliged to give periodic reports (*otchety*) to their constituents on their work in the soviet and their fulfilment of the *nakaz*. To prevent a recurrence of Stalinist terror a system of 'parliamentary' immunity had been introduced that protected deputies from arrest, fines or administrative actions without the agreement of the body to which they had been elected.

The principles of commune democracy were combined with the practice of democratic centralism to create the unique Soviet system of government. Soviets fused both legislative (making policy) and executive (its implementation) functions in one body. This classic Marxist principle dispensed with the liberal notion of the separation of powers and instead focused authority in a single unitary body. Medvedev argued that the combination encouraged the concentration of power while undermining popular accountability.[3] In practice, Soviet local government was less about politics than administration: the executive bodies were strengthened at the expense of the legislative.[4] The Soviet system of integrated power assumed a congruence of interest between the constituent elements of society and thus there appeared to be no need for the conflicts and negotiations typical of an open-ended political process. In Lenin's commune, ideal political conflict would be replaced by administration guided, it was implied, by the leading role of the party. Any conflicts that might emerge would be not so much political as technical or departmental.

The theory of commune democracy proved an effective weapon against residual notions of the separation of power and allowed the extension of democratic centralism from the party to the rest of society. Soviet governmental and administrative procedures reflected unitary organisational practices. Although formally federal in structure, local administration represented the single, indivisible authority of the state in a particular locality; all Soviet institutions functioned as part of a single giant bureaucracy. At the heart of this was dual subordination: soviet executive committees were directly accountable both to the plenum of the soviet which elected them and to higher executive committees, which could annul the decisions of lower bodies (see Figure 5). Dual subordination operated within the framework of strict hierarchical divisions accompanied by overlapping control by state and party bodies.

Local soviets had departments coming to a head in an executive committee, and in larger areas a presidium. Each local soviet had a single chamber whose membership averaged 33 deputies at the village level, 78 in the *raions*, 134 in the cities and 218 in the *oblasts*. Ordinary deputies were seldom involved in policy formulation since plenary sessions met on average only about six or seven times a year for sessions that usually lasted no more than a day each. The day-to-day running of affairs was left to the executive bodies, and all attempts to revive soviet plenums vis-à-vis executive committees met with little success: decisions taken by executive bodies in the morning were voted on by the legislature in the afternoon. The communist party dominated the legislative proceedings, with the party caucus bound by the directives of the local party committee. There was usually unanimous approval of all legislation, with voting taking place by a show of hands.

The shift from Khrushchev's confrontational and politicised leadership style to Brezhnev's consensual and managerial leadership style was accompanied by greater emphasis on achieving a level of public consensus and the satisfaction of social needs. Central party direction of soviets did not always guarantee uniformity in their operation. Away from the gaze of international scrutiny local soviets could be more lively than central bodies. There was more scope for initiative in the choice of topics to be discussed and they were more representative of the local population. They contained a greater proportion of women and shopfloor workers. The 337,000 standing commissions in local soviets and in the Supreme Soviet assisted the executive bodies in their work. Locally they met more frequently than their national counterparts and thus allowed more consultation with deputies. The budget commissions, in particular, gained influence over financial affairs. Committees like housing, industry, education, health and agriculture, as in the Supreme Soviet, had a supervisory function. About 80 per cent of local soviet deputies were members of standing commissions, and this high level of involvement to some extent offset the infrequency with which soviets met.

Local soviets were authorised to carry out a wider range of functions than their counterparts in the USA or Great Britain. However, in practice their real powers were much more circumscribed. This was partially due to the system of dual subordination, with all officials subordinate to the next rank in the chain as well as to the plenary session of their soviet. The powers of local soviets varied greatly depending on the field since much was beyond the local soviet's purview, such as enterprises under all-union ministries and research institutions, and much heavy industry, defence establishments and national transport and energy utilities. Until Gorbachev there was little fundamental change in the highly centralised system bequeathed by Stalin in which the lowest state farm or factory was run by a ministry in Moscow.

Figure 5 USSR: local government

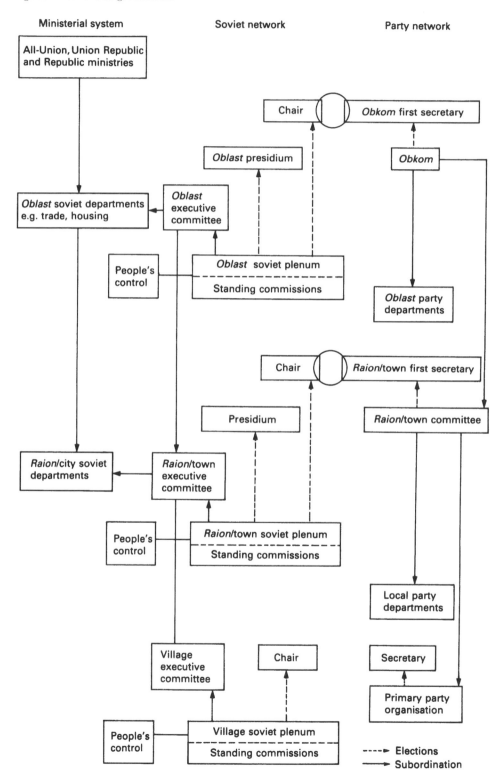

Local soviets were severely weakened by tight central control over finances and their inability to raise taxes. Their main source of income came from the sales tax, which was collected locally but distributed nationally. The dominance of the all-union level in the allocation and distribution of resources deprived local politics of much of its excitement. The all-union centre argued that the limited financial autonomy of the republics would ensure an equitable distribution of funds between richer and poorer areas, and to some degree this was justified. Local soviets played a pivotal role in the local economy. They were responsible for ensuring that local economic plans were fulfilled and that the decisions of higher authorities were implemented. Job placement programmes had been developing since the 1960s and, with the development of plans in the 1980s to allow enterprises to shed workers, local soviets gained primary responsibility to find the displaced workers new jobs. Local soviets were responsible for running local transport, municipal shops, mains supplies, some industrial and construction enterprises, and cultural, welfare and health services. The weakness of local soviets, however, was revealed by the generally poor level of infrastructural development. Under Gorbachev local soviets were much criticised for their failure to use existing powers to improve local services.

Housing provides the most dramatic example of the problems encountered by the soviets in their attempted revival. In 1936 the state devolved primary responsibility for housing to enterprises, which could use this as an inducement to attract and keep scarce labour. Effective city planning was undermined, leading to unbalanced development. To compensate, local soviets after 1957 were made responsible for the co-ordination of local building, with all new land use having to be approved by them and the ownership of all public housing concentrated in their hands. However, the attempt to encourage more rational local planning and the revival of the soviets was stymied by the government bureaucracy. Ministries and plants themselves still built housing for their workers and controlled their allocation, often with little or no consultation with the local soviet and its planning department. The problem was part of the larger one of controlling the vast centralised economy and the ministries, with vested interest groups fearing the loss of their economic and political power. In a highly centralised system there was the paradoxical problem of power being diffused among a multitude of agencies. As Taubman pointed out, theoretically the Soviet system should have been ideal for extended urban planning, but surprisingly enough it resulted in the worst of both worlds: it 'managed the twin feats of reproducing the distortions of free enterprise under socialism and the pitfalls of pluralism in a centralised state'.[5] Despite strict controls Soviet urban expansion was unbalanced, with country towns denuded of services and facilities while Moscow, Leningrad and the other big cities acted as irresistible magnets. The population of Moscow by 1985 exceeded the planned target for the end of the century, while thousands of Russia's villages disappeared and the rest languished in a pitiful state.

The Brezhnev years saw attempts to balance enhanced central control over policy-making with greater initiative for local administration, and yet the local soviets failed to achieve a breakthrough into a sustained sphere of independent action. Rather than the decentralisation of power there was a degree of deconcentration unaccompanied by any expansion in local autonomy. The chief features of the revival were the increased competence of local government bodies, strengthened budgetary rights, an increased role for the soviet plenums as distinct from their executive committees, and an improvement in the role, status and quality of the individual deputies. Despite their large cachet of responsibilities local soviets lacked real powers in managing local affairs and tended to act as agencies of the central authorities with little real independence. They were effectively bound by the principles of democratic centralism and dual subordination. The central government bureaucracy continued to dominate the local consumer and producer economy. Urban points out that even on a technical level the qualitative indicators of soviet performance were unimpressive. In the absence of ready access to technical information, elected delegates were unable effectively to partake in government. The stress on professionalism under Brezhnev meant that standing commissions as much as individual deputies were unable to challenge their own administrative bodies owing to the lack of detailed information.[6] The obstacles to greater deputy involvement in policy formation and supervision proved formidable. As in other countries this was compounded, despite the rising educational level of deputies, by the lack of experience and expertise of most elected officials.

The dominant role of the party prevented the soviets from becoming fully developed agencies of local government. The counterpart of dual subordination was the dual allegiance of state officials to their immediate superiors in the state hierarchy and to the parallel party organisation. The *nomenklatura* system applied to local administration as to all other Soviet organisations. The local party committee oversaw elections, established local priorities and ensured that centrally adopted policies were carried out. Taubman calls the party the 'supermayor', represented above all by the party first secretary. The party was intended to work through the soviets and governmental agencies, but since local party officials took ultimate responsibility for plan fulfilment they had a tendency to take direct charge of economic affairs. The local party had the right of supervision (*pravo kontrolya*) over the local soviet, its departments and the enterprises it managed. It is not surprising that the sixfold mechanism of supervision (see Chapter 6) often led to substitution (*podmena*).

The soviets were overshadowed by so many bodies that one can talk of their 'multisubordination'.[7] However, several Western analyses of local government in the final years stressed that when viewed in detail there was a degree of liveliness in local politics. For example, Hill challenges the view of the state apparatus as merely a façade for complete communist party control. He saw the overlapping membership of party and state organs at the local level as ensuring ultimate party control but providing the potential for more effective local political decision-making. One of the paradoxical features of 'totalitarian' administration was its chaotic character. The two major interests in the locality, the party and the industrial managers, sometimes cancelled each other out to permit a limited amount of local pluralism.[8] The 1970s saw much discussion over the extent of 'pluralism', 'participation' and 'feedback loops' as part of a unique Brezhnev system of power. However, Gorbachev's *glasnost* in the 1980s convincingly demonstrated the inability of Brezhnevite mechanisms to overcome the distortions within Soviet administration caused by overcentralisation of planning and governmental processes.

Local deputies acted as barometers of public opinion, but local administration as a whole was not constrained by any effective system of public accountability. The deputies' tenuous hold on some freedom of manoeuvre did not negate their weakness. The revival of the soviets as a party-directed process meant that they were necessarily limited. They were prevented from developing any autonomous and genuinely representative role. The regeneration of commune democracy proved impossible under conditions of party dominance. In 1968 the Czechoslovak Action Programme argued that to avoid an undue concentration of power a division of power was required whereby one agency could be checked and supervised by another agency of equal standing.[9] Both democratic centralism and commune principles were modified. In the USSR, however, despite Gorbachev's rhetoric, the party still dominated local soviet affairs and determined the main lines of policies. Only at the very end did the politics of departmentalism give way to a vigorous public life. For most of the Soviet period public officials were in constant struggle with each other for resources and favourable policy strategies, with debate confined to the administrative system as part of bureaucratic pluralism. Internal communications did play an important role at the local level, and, indeed, informal communication, in which the party usually played a minimal role, did reduce many of the frictions and irrationalities that persisted in local administration, but 'bureaucratic crypto-politics' (to use Rigby's term)[10] did not give way to what Habermas calls communicative action where an interactive relationship is established to produce rational outcomes.

Since the actual powers of local soviets fell below their legal rights there remained much scope for the expansion of their activity. Gorbachev returned to Khrushchev's policy of revitalising the soviets, and changes in central authority and in the principles of federalism were accompanied by the reform of local government. At the January 1987 Central Committee plenum Gorbachev argued that elected bodies should have greater authority over executive ones. To make soviets more accountable to the electorate and to avoid the traditional dominance of legislative bodies by their executives, most full-time soviet officials were prohibited from standing in elections to soviet executive committees. The aim was to improve their work and to remove 'formalism and show' (*paradnost*), to make soviets businesslike and more effective in *perestroika* and to eliminate 'paper' methods of management.[11] Gorbachev insisted on 'the need to restore completely the role of the soviets as bodies of political power and as the foundation of socialist democracy'.[12] The cardinal task of political reform, he insisted, was to breathe new life into the soviets, for them to be able to decide on all local affairs and become fully fledged bodies of people's self-government.[13] The link between the deputy and the electorate was to be strengthened by more feedback mechanisms, legislative bodies were to be given more rights to offset those of executives, and their budgetary rights and control over local economic life were to be increased.

The slogan of 1917, 'All power to the soviets', was resurrected, but this very formulation, quite apart from its threat to party rule, once again suggested the concentration rather than the separation of powers. At the nineteenth party conference Gorbachev hoped to avoid the emergence of dual power between the party and the soviets by making the local party and soviet leaders one and the same person, an idea condemned by a number of speakers, including Yeltsin. The measure ran counter to the leadership's intention of separating the functions of party and state, but was justified as a way of avoiding conflicts. The institutional tensions between the party and the soviets remained to the end. It proved impossible to separate the party and the state in a one-party state.

ELECTIONS

Elections reflect the quality of citizen participation in community decisions. Participation in the Soviet Union was mostly organised from above, but to a large extent it was voluntary. Elections to soviets had a special importance since they involved citizens directly. Deputies to local soviets were elected for two and a half years, as opposed to five years for republican and higher soviets; from 1989 all deputies were to serve five-year terms. The widening role of local soviets in managing the local economy and services made the choice of candidates increasingly important, and yet until Gorbachev the electoral system stagnated. Under Brezhnev the single-candidate system was refined to an art; it was choiceless 'voting' rather than the choice implied in the term 'election'.

In 1936 discrimination against 'anti-soviet' classes was dropped and from that time elections were open to all. Voting was direct in state elections, whereas in the communist party it was indirect. Direct elections revealed the leadership's confidence in its ability to 'manage' the results. A secret ballot was used whereby the voter simply dropped the printed ballot paper, on which there was usually only one name, into the box. Curtained booths were provided but their use was suspect. Many voters under Brezhnev displayed ostentatious loyalty by simply folding the paper and dropping it into the urn in full public view. If the booth was used, the person was suspected of crossing the name out, the way of registering a vote against the candidate. The premium was on unanimity, and as in the soviets (where a show of hands was used), there were social pressures to conform. A candidate was elected if they obtained the support of more than 50 per cent of the registered voters in the constituency (not just 50 per cent of those voting on the day). Between 1937 and 1981 about 30 million candidates had run in elections to soviets at all levels, and until 1987 none faced an opponent. Remarkable turnout figures were officially claimed. In the 1984 Supreme Soviet elections it peaked at 99.99 per cent – and with nowhere else to go, the system collapsed.

With the result not in doubt, the focus shifted to the nomination process. Not only was the CPSU the only political party, but until the final years there was no choice within that party. The CPSU was involved at all stages, with the party's *raion* committee overseeing the local voting process. The 1977 constitution (Article 100) permitted a range of social bodies to nominate a candidate, including the CPSU, trade unions, co-operatives, the Komsomol and 'other social organisations'. The electoral law was revised in 1978 to prevent dissident groups constituting themselves as 'social organisations' and proposing their own candidates. Candidates thereafter could only run if they were nominated by a recognised institution. Nominations to the soviets at local level could sometimes permit local initiative, such as when there was a problem in finding a suitable candidate, but the final choice lay with the local party organisation. All candidates had to be acceptable to the party, and while they could be *non*-party they could not be *anti*-party.

The party established central guidelines in selecting candidates to obtain a desirable mix reflecting not so much the local population as national objectives. The actual competence of the candidate was often only a secondary consideration with relatively strict central quotas applied for sex, Komsomol and party membership, age, occupation, education and nationality. In national areas care was taken to ensure fair representation of ethnic groups. Local soviet elections had a tendency not to produce individual candidates but groups of deputies (women, communists, workers and so on). Attempts to revive the soviets were accompanied by campaigns to improve the quality of the candidates. The proportional principle lost force further up the hierarchy as individuals were predominantly chosen for their competence and loyalty.

In the absence of a free press and free speech, and with restrictions on printing and meeting, there was no adversarial election campaign. Soviet commentators stressed the element of popular choice in selecting the candidates, but the choice was not made openly by the general public. In the local elections of 1980, 77 out of 2.27 million candidates failed to get elected because the number of scratched ballot papers exceeded those simply placed in the boxes. This was a very small, and declining, proportion and usually occurred in remote villages or when the official candidate was particularly obnoxious. A negative vote did not usually constitute a rejection of the Soviet system but reflected a local grievance and local solidarity. However rare, the authorities tried to avoid such incidents and aimed to find acceptable candidates. A defeated candidate could not be nominated a second time. If a person once elected proved to be particularly inept, or suffered from some personal problem, the nominating body of that deputy had the right to recall them. This was a cumbersome procedure and the candidate was usually induced to resign.

The actual conduct of an electoral campaign revealed the organising abilities of the system at its best, but the whole process under Brezhnev was imbued with formalism and cynicism. The heart of an election campaign was the agitation group, the *agitkollektiv*, which conducted the campaign at the grass roots. It was a permanent institution which was revived about two or three months prior to an election. At the base of its hierarchical structure was the agitator who was allocated fifteen to twenty electors and was instructed to ensure that they voted. About 7 per cent of the electorate actively participated in the campaign as members of the *agitkollektiv*. An equal number were involved in the district electoral commissions responsible for the formal registration of voters and for the counting. Hence a total of about 15 per cent were directly involved. Much of this activity was purely formal as workers were delegated by enterprises or institutions as part of their social obligations, and participation was rarely marked by great enthusiasm.

The aim was to ensure that the voter registered at the offices of the district electoral commission. An individual could refuse on various grounds, including citing a specific grievance, or stating that they would be away on election day. Those claiming prior commitments obtained an absentee certificate, and in some urban areas up to a quarter of voters received such certificates. They were readily granted because it avoided forcing overt expressions of dissatisfaction. The much-quoted majorities of 99 per cent should therefore be seen in perspective. The figure excludes the significant minority of the population who had registered their absence and those who refused to register or in any way have anything to do with 'voting'. The 99 per cent represents those who register and turn out to vote; hence the percentage of dissatisfied people was considerably higher than 1 per cent.

If elections did not perform the selective function typical of liberal democracies, why then were they held? Elections served several practical functions. They permitted the population to bargain with the authorities over matters of local significance, such as housing, broken pavements and poor lighting. The local agitator's job was to listen to these complaints and report them to higher authorities. Workers sometimes even bargained for higher stakes. Party loyalists and potential deviants could be identified during the voting process. Zaslavsky and Brym point out that this was particularly important in universities, where potential troublemakers could be identified early on in their careers. Elections were also a channel for upward political mobility, with canvassers able to display their public-spiritedness and bring themselves to the notice of local officials. Voting also served general social control functions and helped to expose infringements of internal passport and registration regulations. Elections were also a useful pretext for periodically mobilising the population behind the government and providing an opportunity for a ritual display of loyalty. Elections served as a socialising device and enabled the leadership to claim popular support. Electoral politics, moreover, were colonised by the regime and inhibited the slogan of free elections becoming the rallying call of a potential opposition grouping. Soviet elections traditionally served as a form of plebiscitarian democracy. The inescapable conclusion is that the voting was less important than the campaign which preceded it. As Hough puts it, election day was merely the pretext for the election campaign.

It was often argued that Soviet elections performed a legitimating function, and this was certainly the case under Stalin. But under Brezhnev it became clear that elections actually delegitimised the system by being so patently meaningless. There was much evidence of disillusionment with the system. In a sociological survey of the ZiL factory in Moscow in the early 1970s, 18 per cent of respondents expressed outright dissatisfaction with the electoral system.[14] Despite widespread criticism of the single-candidate elections, Brezhnev set his face resolutely against electoral reform and indeed strengthened the system. Zaslavsky and Brym explain this in terms of the actual conduct of elections. Elections buttressed the existing distribution of power in the USSR; they reinforced the recruitment of new people to the ruling elite; and they defined the map of political consciousness of the citizen by engaging in the pseudo-democratic process. By participating in hollow elections people displayed an act of consent or submission to the institutions and rituals of the political system and thus became party to its preservation. In certain respects the system resembled the eighteenth century in Britain before the formation of organised parties, allowing the legislature to renew itself and its legitimacy while not not threatening the existing balance of power. Soviet 'elections without choice' were a parody of pluralist democracy and, according to Sakharov, were 'an insult to commonsense and human dignity'.

Perestroika forcibly raised the issue of electoral reform. Possible changes were already apparent by the reforms introduced in some other socialist countries. Elections in Hungary in 1985 for the first time gave voters the choice of two or more names rather than a single take-it-or-leave-it candidate, although none of the thirty-five independent candidates was elected.[15] In Poland, the GDR and Cuba more than one candidate were sometimes nominated for office. Individual competition did not mean political opposition, but it helped achieve the regime's aim of improving the quality of the candidates. Obviously, a multi-choice electoral system would undermine the *nomenklatura* system of appointments. In his programme for the extension of 'socialist democracy' announced at the January 1987 CC plenum Gorbachev accepted the logical consequence that soviet multi-choice elections would raise the question of elections in factories for managerial and representative bodies and within the party. He called for greater use of the 'electoral principle' in soviets, the party, administration and industry, with greater popular involvement in all stages of electoral campaigns.

Gorbachev's initial proposal for reforming elections to the Supreme Soviet was for larger multi-member constituencies. Voters would have a choice of candidates from an approved list. The element of competitive electoral choice remained minimal and campaigns were to focus on personalities rather than policies: the option was to cross out the name of an individual against whom there was an objection. The June 1987 local elections allowed a limited and experimental choice of candidates in about 5 per cent of seats.[16] Gorbachev's early plans for choice of candidates and secret balloting in the party applied only to the election of secretaries within committees, and not to the election of the committees themselves by the mass of party membership. In 1987 experiments began for the election of enterprise managers by majority vote in secret ballots. The aim was to increase the authority of factory directors by making them more than simply the nominees of a distant ministry in Moscow. The opportunities for loyal non-party people were extended, but early experiments showed the limits to such developments. Officials, used to organised elections, placed restrictions on who could vote, the choice of candidates, and procedures (secret or open voting). It was only with the March 1989 elections to the Congress of People's Deputies that a genuinely competitive election was held with numerous candidates for most constituencies, but at all stages, from nomination to the voting itself, old habits of administrative interference remained. This did not prevent, and probably provoked, the defeat of many leading communist officials. The elections to the Russian Congress in March 1990 was a far more open and democratic process.

PARTICIPATION AND SOCIALISATION

The meaning of participation

Classical democracy is usually judged by the extent of participation, and there is no doubt that on a range of indicators the USSR was a highly participatory society. The nature of this participation, however, was ambiguous. It became more than what used to be called mobilisation, the bureaucratic organisation of consensus and enthusiasm, but less than voluntary effective public involvement in self-administration. Soviet participation had little to do with Western notions of participation as a form of control over political leaders conducted by rational and informed citizens.[17] Pre-Gorbachev elections illustrated that the effective choice functions of participation had been overshadowed by the control functions of institutions and structures generated elsewhere in the political system. Participation was often little more than an exercise in political socialisation.

The Soviet regime always stressed the principle of direct participation in the belief that the division of political labour between the rulers and the ruled could be transcended. In contrast to liberal democracy, the Soviet commune view of democracy insisted not only that everyone *could* but that everyone *should* take part in the management of the new society. The people (society) would take back the power hitherto delegated to special bodies. Mass involvement and the rotation of offices, Marx argued, would replace conventional parliamentary democracy.[18] State and society would become reintegrated and the state, Engels added, would gradually wither away. In practice, exactly the opposite took place under the centralised system of the dictatorship of the proletariat. The state was massively strengthened and the individuals making up society were left defenceless. In addition to the class functions of the proletarian dictatorship the power of the state was bolstered by the economic programme of the Bolsheviks. While Lenin constantly urged maximum participation his period in power saw the emergence of a powerful state separate and distinct from society in which even the mass participatory bodies, such as the trade unions and Komsomol, became thoroughly bureaucratised. The institutions of participatory democracy could not operate effectively in the absence of open debate in society. The institutions designed to draw people into the building of communism and to extend party influence in society were dubbed by Lenin 'transmission belts', and they reached their peak of mechanical efficiency under Stalin.

The totalitarian implications of theories of direct democracy have been denounced ever since Jean-Jacques Rousseau in *The Social Contract* first condemned the alienating and formal process of parliamentary democracy.[19] Theories of totalitarianism have traditionally emphasised the conjunction of tight controls from above with the stimulation of mass participation from below. Stalin's mobilisation of the Soviet population was not satisfied with passive acquiescence but demanded active enthusiasm. In the post-Stalin era enthusiastic mobilisation gave way to routine participation – a half-hearted plebiscitary vote of confidence in regime policies and institutions. The transition from the terminology of the dictatorship of the proletariat to the state of all the people reflected this shift. Khrushchev's populist attempt to transform managerial participation was designed to control the bureaucracy. Under Brezhnev popular participation remained important but with a change of emphasis; participation was no longer set against bureaucratic rule but was defined as its complement. The concept of developed socialism played down conflictual elements in Soviet society and the stress on professionalism undermined the scope for popular checking of bureaucratic activity. Formal procedures and

rule observance replaced Khrushchev's *ad hoc* frontal assaults against bureaucratic prerogatives. The cybernetic challenge of the 'scientific management of society' provided for so-called
'feedback loops' whereby society could influence the leadership. The Brezhnev era saw the
consolidation of formalised participation through greater public debate and debates within
administrative apparatuses, select academic institutions, specialist groupings and party offices.

Rather than resurrecting populism, Andropov relied on one section of the administrative
apparatus (the secret police and militia) to combat the deficiencies in another (the corrupt
officials in state and party posts). The post-interregnum leadership, however, sought to redefine
participation away from Brezhnevite formalism to a more active form of commune democracy. The trajectory of Gorbachev's reforms transformed participation from the routine and
managerial towards something closer to the liberal democratic model, eschewing populist
exhortations of mass control over established procedures, and ultimately would have allowed
greater self-management of society. This participation was less than the grandiose ambitions
of transcending the gulf between state and society of early Bolshevism, but more than hollow
transmission-belt politics.

The 'democratic' participation in the West has been contrasted with the 'pseudo-participation'
in Soviet-type systems. Studies from a comparative perspective, however, have blurred such a
sharp distinction. Little, for instance, argued that most popular participation in the USA and the
USSR is unconnected with policy outcomes or leadership recruitment and hence a similar qualitative approach can be adopted. In both systems participation was argued to have little impact on
elite decision-making or on the satisfaction of popular demands.[20] While the argument was
clearly overdrawn, it did draw attention to some of the positive features of managed participation. In the workplace, while economic self-management remained distant, the trade unions did
(in addition to their welfare functions) provide some services to workers. The soviets combined a
governing role and one of integrating citizen's demands, being at the same time both state organs
and popular participatory bodies, the kernel of community self-management. Contrary to the
Leninist theory of public administration in the commune state, which assumed the simplification
of administrative tasks, Max Weber argued that modern industrial society leads to an increasing
division and specialisation of labour. There remained some scope, however, for the extension of
popular participation and democratic supervision of administrative procedures. Habermas distinguishes between practical-democratic decisions, such as whether to build a road, and technical-
administrative issues, such as the question of what the road should be made of, a technical
question which can be dealt with in the realm of administration. In the Soviet Union democratic
centralism conspired with commune practices to remove both from the sphere of effective popular participation, with the party acting as a proxy for the public in the practical-democratic
sphere, and the government monopolising the technical-administrative side. The limited development of a public sphere, defined as 'a realm of social life where matters of general interest can
be discussed, where differences of opinion can be settled by rational argumentation and not by
recourse to established dogma or customs',[21] removed both from the purview of popular accountability and allowed technocratic 'hyper-rationality' to run unhindered. It permitted ruling
elites to advance their own status and power under the guise of an alleged technical rationality.[22]
While popular participation everywhere might have little to do with the actual process of government and administration, the absence of a public sphere undermined Soviet local government
and effective participation. The encouragement of *glasnost* was an essential aspect of the revival
of a public sphere and with it the regeneration of participation. In the event, however, the revival
of politics soon went beyond the framework of Soviet power.

Institutional forms of participation

Participation can be divided into institutional and non-institutional forms. The institutional focuses on the formal mechanisms for socialisation and for channelling public activity. In any political system there is a balance between voluntary and coerced participation in the structures of social organisation, a distinction which in the Soviet context is usually seen in terms of mobilised or autonomous participation. Soviet theory distinguished between state bodies, such as the ministries, the military and the police; state committees and commissions and so on; and the mass, voluntary organisations, of which the party was supreme, but joined by the trade unions, Komsomol and other bodies. The soviets were unique in that they were designed to mediate between the two. Of all the participatory mechanisms in the USSR party membership was the most widespread, and for some the most effective. The contrast between the party official and the rank-and-file membership has already been described: at higher levels the party official wielded power, while at lower levels the party member exerted influence.

The designation of participatory mechanisms as solely downward transmission belts became less true as they also allowed the upward transmission of information and complaints. The major bodies in this respect were the trade unions, some of the most important mass institutions. Early hopes that the unions would ultimately take over the management of the economy gave way after the Civil War to stressing their educative and defensive functions, especially under the mixed economy of the NEP. With the onset of rapid industrialisation the tasks of the unions again changed. In 1933 the separate labour ministry was abolished and the unions took over a wide range of functions which they retained to the end. They were responsible for the observance of safety regulations, administered social insurance, managed the complaints procedure, oversaw the factory food-distribution network (*zakazi*), ran a massive network of social clubs, sports complexes and housing, and owned major resorts and rest homes. They were closely involved in efforts to raise labour productivity and to maintain labour discipline.

There were about 125 million union members in 1988, including virtually all those employed, with the exception of the military. Soviet unions were organised on production rather than on craft principles. Whole industries belonged to a single union rather than being divided between electricians, welders and so on. Nevertheless, the massive Soviet trade union movement had feet of clay in that it played only an advisory role in production issues and lacked real powers in setting wages, although formally this was one of its major concerns. The status of the unions was comparable to that of a delegate at a conference with consultative rather than voting powers. The unions followed the line set by the government and had little input in policy formation, illustrated by the lack of trade union leaders in the Politburo. The post of trade union leader was used as a staging post for those going up (Grishin, 1956–67) or going down (Shelepin, 1968–75), and was firmly within the *nomenklatura* of the party. Unions did have an important, and often effective, part to play in defending the social rights of workers, and it was this role that Gorbachev urged the February 1987 congress of Soviet trade unions to fulfil more vigorously.

Socialisation of a child is the essential mechanism whereby a society reproduces its values and mores. In the USSR a variety of institutions had been established for this purpose and participation in them was encouraged from an early age. Between the ages of 7 and 10 all children joined the Young Octobrists, which had a membership of about 25 million in 1974. At age 10 children became Young Pioneers until the age of 14, with activities geared towards nature and social participation. The Pioneers owned houses and palaces, organising summer camps in the countryside for urban children, rich and poor alike: the first post-Soviet generation retained bitter-sweet memories of these, and their passing was one of the most lamented features of the old order. The organisation was based in the classroom and involved almost all children of the relevant age group. Its socialisation effort, like Soviet education itself, was highly politicised, with vows to love Lenin and to serve the communist party. The emphasis from the earliest age was on the group and support for the *kollektiv*, while individualism was frowned upon as a residue of bourgeois consciousness.

Both the above bodies were universal, but from age 14 the All-Union Leninist Communist League of Youth (VLKSM, or Komsomol) was more selective (although less stringent than the Communist party) and membership was formally optional. Membership in 1987 was 38.4 million, organised in the place of study or work. There were major advantages to active participation and many a Soviet career began here by displays of political loyalty. The role of Komsomol activist was often the first step on a career in Soviet public life, as was the case with Andropov and Gorbachev. The Komsomol played a major role in the socialisation effort to inculcate party values among youth through such activities as lectures, meetings and wall-newspapers in factories, offices and colleges. The organisation published one of the more lively Soviet daily newspapers (*Komsomolskaya Pravda*) with a circulation of 10 million, and it ran three publishing houses, the major one being Molodaya Gvardiya (The Young Guard), which in the last decades assumed an increasingly Russian nationalist tone.

Komsomol acted as the junior branch of the CPSU for those between the ages of 14 and 28, with the party organisations at all levels taking a major supervisory role. A key function of Komsomol was as a preparation for party membership, and all those under 25 wishing to join the party required formal approval by the Komsomol. About 1.5 million Komsomol members also belonged to the party and the majority of party recruits came via the Komsomol. As with the unions, the leadership of Komsomol was firmly part of the *nomenklatura* system. The top position was usually occupied by an older party figure, such as Shelepin between 1952 and 1958 when in his forties. In many ways the Komsomol was an extension of the party apparatus. In foreign affairs the Komsomol acted as the public representative among youth organisations of Soviet policies. International youth festivals provided an opportunity for the Soviet Union to proclaim its message. However, it is clear that genuinely voluntary participation was rare and too often the organisation was used as a career path. Few were real enthusiasts and most did what was required of them for fear of reprisals.[23] Reports from the Urals in the early 1980s suggested that over a third of young workers failed to join their factory Komsomol organisation, claiming that it was a waste of time. The problem became a matter of acute leadership concern, and Chernenko sought to combat the alleged indiscipline of Soviet youth of the 1980s by the imaginative application of the methods of the 1930s. In the period of *glasnost* the first secretary of Komsomol admitted at its twentieth congress in April 1987 that the organisation failed to connect with a large proportion of youth. Gorbachev's view at the congress that there could be no socialism without genuine democracy was applied immediately. For the first time since the ascendancy of Stalin voting was not unanimous, with a split vote over amendments to the Komsomol rules.

A further form of mass participation which sould be mentioned was military or police activity. Every year nearly 2 million Soviet men between the ages of 18 and 20 were conscripted to serve two years of military service. The army played an important part in educating and socialising Soviet youth in collective values and Soviet patriotism. In addition, the highly developed civil defence programme, with reserve training and exercises, involved a large proportion of the population under 30. There was enormous participation in policing through the *druzhiny*, the irregular militia groups organised by local soviets. The DOSAAF organisation for voluntary assistance for the Soviet armed forces by 1988 claimed a membership of 80 million, or two-thirds of the entire adult population.

These major forms of institutional participation were designed by the regime to serve its own ends and did not necessarily reflect any fundamental underlying sense of unity. They were not intended to articulate social interests but to further the cohesion of the one-party state. At times of political breakdown the aggregation of social interests in Soviet-type regimes spontaneously took on different forms. Among the commonest alternative 'genuine' participatory institutions were the workers' councils, institutionalised in Yugoslavia in the form of workers' self-management, emerging in Hungary and Poland in 1956 and Czechoslovakia in 1968. In the last the youth organisation was thoroughly reformed, and in Poland in 1980–81 the official trade union movement was abandoned as worthless. As the USSR headed for oblivion, its participatory institutions appeared more resilient but nothing like workers' councils emerged: they appeared to be instruments for the humanisation of socialism, whereas now the task appeared to be its transcendence.

Non-institutional forms of participation

These were formalised but generated in a broad variety of anonymous and individual ways. Most important in this respect was the role of letters, which since the early 1960s had become an important link between the party and the population. In addition to the thousands of citizens received personally at the Central Committee offices in Moscow and in local soviets, letters to the press, party and soviet institutions provided an important forum for public opinion. There was a rising flood of letters, with over 3.5 million received between 1981 and 1986, and regulations stipulated that every one was to be answered. They were all carefully indexed to provide the government with a measure of public concerns. Complaints predominated in the party's postbag, with the major issue being housing. Most appealed to party and state bodies for redress of grievances. Letters were also sent to state bodies, especially to the Supreme Soviet and local soviets, and to the various ministries, particularly those responsible for fields like health. Clearly, for every letter sent several more remained unposted, and the sheer scale of this activity revealed the extent of grievances and the highly centralised nature of the system where local complaints could only be resolved in Moscow.

By far the largest number of letters were sent to the press, reaching some 60 to 70 million a year by the mid-1980s. Radio and television studios receive some 2 million letters annually, while a national newspaper received an average of 75,000. The two major papers (*Pravda* and *Izvestiya*) each received nearly two-thirds of a million in 1987, with the numbers rising with the onset of *glasnost*. Complaints predominated, with housing the major issue, but with poor organisation in factories also important and other concerns associated with *perestroika*. Even before *glasnost* the press had acted as a massive para-political mechanism. The importance of these letters lies both in the symbolic value of the few that were published, and in the fact that they were forwarded to the relevant agency to be dealt with. The press increasingly emerged as a fourth estate using the mirror of *glasnost* to amplify the themes of *perestroika*. The primary means to heal the many sores that festered under Brezhnev was a more active media which encouraged the participation of the population in the struggle against corrupt and inefficient bureaucracies. The press, nevertheless, almost to the end remained under strict party control and there were limits to what and how it could express criticism.

The same applied to letter-writers if they wished to have their complaints dealt with. They had to avoid directly implicating their immediate superiors since it was not uncommon for writers to be victimised as a result of drawing attention to inadequacies. Anonymity was no cover, since unsigned letters under Gorbachev were automatically discounted. The required tone was to write in the spirit of a common dedication to improving the Soviet system. Letters played an ombudsman role in Soviet politics and in the absence of other mechanisms they indicated the mood of grass-roots opinion. They also provided a legitimating role, giving the appearance that citizens' requests were actually being considered. Letter-writers came from a wide spectrum of Soviet citizens, and the act of writing could enhance a sense of community with the feeling that justice was attainable.[24]

A range of voluntary or special interest societies made up another kind of participation. By 1987 there were at least 135,000 of these, stimulated by a new law on 'Amateur Associations and Hobby Clubs' of May 1986. Formal groups had long been encouraged, but they had always been highly regulated and severely circumscribed by regulations and controls by the local soviet. Already in 1920 Alexandra Kollontai complained in her pamphlet *The Workers' Opposition* that the most minor of public activities was being stifled by a mass of bureaucratic regulation. Almost to the end an approved sponsoring organisation had to be found, such as trade unions, farms or cultural departments of local soviets. Those lacking formal approval gained the sobriquet of 'informals' (*neformaly*) because of their unofficial status. Most activities were covered by an official organisation, especially with sports activities and games clubs, and they often had workplace branches. Here, as elsewhere, party members in them formed their own group. Groups concerned with environmental issues proliferated. These societies acted in turn as 'transmission belts', sending the party's message down and transmitting popular concerns upward. As Jim Riordan points out, Soviet sport was highly politicised, encouraged as a patriotic endeavour and used to implement and propagate official policy. Literary policy was channelled through the Union of Soviet Writers, film policy through the Union of Film-Makers, and so on. All these activities were part of the attempt to create the 'New Soviet Person'.

Brezhnev particularly favoured mass discussion before the adoption of new legislation. This reached its apogee before the adoption of the 1977 constitution, and was revived by Chernenko to air views on the draft legislation for the educational reform of 1984. Although a reported 130 million people took part, it was formal to say the least, although some changes were introduced in the final version of the legislation. The quality of this kind of participation was particularly low, although designed to allow citizens to feel responsible for the legislation. To a lesser extent these discussions were encouraged on a range of practical issues, such as housing and alcoholism, which were of special concern to the regime. In June 1986 the Supreme Soviet adopted a law formalising national discussions on major issues. Mass discussions were restricted to topics permitted by the authorities and could not be taken to denote the existence of a public sphere.

In addition to the above, a system of complaints procedures allowed citizens to participate in the correction of abuses. Further, an extensive programme of meetings and lectures was organised to expound the party's views on current issues. Local party organisations and local soviet agitprop committees organised formal and informal meetings in the workplaces. A speaker expounded on a current topic, such as 'recent events in China', or 'American imperialism in Central America'. A less political form of lecture programme was offered by the *Znanie*

(Knowledge) Society under whose auspices about 30 milion lectures a year were organised. Another common form of participation was the officially organised mass demonstration to support Soviet policies and condemn the United States. These really were 'demonstrations' – called to show the West that the Soviet Union also had demonstrations and to be reported in the press as examples of mass support for regime policies. Several times a year, especially after the winter snows, a further form of participation was organised through the *subbotniks*, unpaid work on a Saturday, established to inculcate a sense of 'communist' labour for the common good and to generate a sense of civic consciousness but also performing a useful service, especially when cleaning up after blizzards.

The list is by no means complete but it is enough to give an indication of the range and nature of participation in the Soviet Union. Clearly, the Soviet Union had become a participatory society that no longer needed to rule primarily by coercion but had achieved a high degree of acquiescence for its policies. However, there was only a small degree of bargaining between the rulers and the ruled. In an over-administered society even the participatory mechanisms were highly regulated. As Burks puts it, 'The regime, while promoting a high degree of mass-participation at all levels, fears such participation equally. Participation may become effective "interference" in the prerogatives of the established authorities.'[25] Such was the danger of the participation encouraged by Khrushchev. The threat was removed by Brezhnev but the penalty was a widespread cynicism which came to replace fear as the cement of the polity. Participation in the Soviet Union was both voluntary and effective, but there were some missing ingredients: the freedom to refuse to participate; obstacles to the formation of groups; and tight limits to lobbying. Dramatisation of support for an issue through public protests, leaflets or pickets was strictly beyond the bounds of tolerated participation. The authorities set the agenda for participation. The ban on group activity reflected the politically atomised society. From the first days the Soviet regime closely monitored lateral contacts between citizens (and indeed within the party) to suppress the sin of horizontalism. Democratic centralism ensured that participation was directed vertically between the individual citizen and the authorities.

The official emphasis on mass participation was a legacy of the commune principles on which the Soviet state was built. Attempts to combine participation and administration, paradoxically, led to the radical separation of the two. It is not an inherent feature of the technical administration of modern society to require participatory institutions; extended bureaucracy inhibits the development of effective participation. For most of Soviet history popular participation in decision-making was largely formalised and had little impact on the decisions themselves, although at the social level participatory networks were important. Political participation did not ensure that authority was controlled by the populace but that the populace consented to being governed by others. Only with the onset of Gorbachev's reforms did the extension in the scope of mass participation since Stalin's death begin to alter the conduct of politics.

KEY TEXTS

Jacobs, Everett M., *Soviet Local Politics and Government* (London, George Allen & Unwin, 1983).

Friedgut, Theodore H., *Political Participation in the USSR* (Princeton, NJ, Princeton University Press, 1979).

Zaslavsky, V. and R. Brym, 'The Function of Elections in the USSR', *Soviet Studies*, Vol. 30, No. 3 (July 1978), pp. 362–71.

Part III
Politics

10 Power and policy-making

Politics, narrowly defined, is a contest over the distribution of political power. However, in the Soviet context such a definition is barely applicable since policy arose out of the total political and cultural context of the polity, not only of the present but burdened by the past and coloured by a vision of the future (we shall examine the role of ideology in the next chapter). The policy process in the USSR was clouded by the divergence between constitutional provisions and informal practices, changing over time and over the type of issue involved. Policy-making can be analysed in various ways. The focus can be on the policy process at the local level, or on a specific field, such as foreign policy, which has received a generous share of attention. The focus can be on the institutions involved, on the process of policy initiation, policy resolution or on the way that policy is implemented, which often subtly changes the policy itself. In the absence of convincing methodological approaches the emphasis has tended to focus on specific case studies. Our focus in this part will be on the role of leadership, various models of the Soviet polity, the role of ideology, and the general issues of legitimacy, political culture and the nature of power, the class and social nature of the system and the emergence of resistance in the form of dissent.

Until the very end of the Soviet Union's existence, and indeed to this day, the debate continued over the political nature of the regime. There were, broadly speaking, three main phases of analysis. The first, predominant in the first two post-war decades but by no means universally accepted, focused on the 'totalitarian' nature of the regime. Policy was seen as emerging largely as calculated responses by a monolithic power structure to domestic or foreign challenges. This 'rational actor' model then gave way to 'revisionist' approaches which highlighted the nascent pluralistic elements. Policy was now seen as emanating from the interaction of various individuals, institutions and groups representing a variety of perspectives and interests. How these interests were integrated and articulated remained a matter of debate since policy-making still took place largely behind closed doors. In the third and final phase in the 1980s the failure of the Soviet regime to engage in constructive reform for so long prompted a return to the themes of closure, political blockage and instrumental use of power resources by particular elites that had characterised the totalitarian approach earlier. When reforms finally did begin under Gorbachev many of the radical reformers adopted the language of totalitarianism, too, to describe their own past, but failed seriously to engage with the problem of structuring the more democratic system to which they aspired.

THE ROLE OF LEADERSHIP

Marxism emphasises the role of objective socio-economic processes in the development of human societies. Lenin's achievement was to assert the role of human will, or consciousness, in the revolutionary process, although he always placed his voluntarism within the framework of impersonal laws of development. Soviet history convincingly demonstrated the decisive role that leadership and individuals play in the development of social systems. A movement that was meant to be based on impersonal class forces took its name from its founders, Marx and Lenin. Lenin's own contribution cannot be overestimated, Stalin's personal dominance over policy for over two decades stamped a whole era, while the personal characteristics of Gorbachev's leadership contributed immeasurably to the denouement of the system. The personality of the leader did make a significant difference and the leadership principle appeared to be an integral part of the Leninist power system. However, this impact was mediated through the party and other institutions and moderated by social processes. Soviet society, however, was never able to impose political constraints on leadership, although it was able to subvert policies in myriad acts of personal resistance and adaptation.

The exaltation of the leader was an inalienable part of the Soviet political process after Lenin's death in 1924 unleashed the leader cult. The leadership principle played an important part in the functioning of the system itself; the charisma of the leader bolstered the legitimacy of the whole system. However, while Bolshevik ideology stressed the role of human intervention in history it was never a theory of individual dominance. The cult of leadership was in conflict with the formally collectivist nature both of the Bolshevik political system and of the ideology of Marxism. Stalin's personality cult from 1929 offended both principles and was forced to justify itself by appealing to new bases of legitimacy: Stalin's closeness to Lenin; his achievements in building socialism; and his skills as a theoretician. Stalin's cult sought to establish its pedigree from Marxism–Leninism by claiming that 'Stalin is the Lenin of today'.[1] The history of the party itself had to be rewritten to eliminate any trace of an earlier ethos of debate and collective leadership. Those who had entered into controversy with Lenin were portrayed not as errant colleagues but as wicked counter-revolutionaries.

The leadership principle is an essential mechanism through which the original revolutionary ideology can be modified to take into account new circumstances and adapt itself to new challenges. In their very different ways, both Napoleon and Yeltsin are examples of this, while E. H. Carr argued that without Stalin the Russian revolution would have run into the sands of history. Leadership therefore acts as a means of ideological adaptation, and it is for this reason that communist leaders designated themselves as theoreticians and published multi-volume editions of their works. Gill makes the important observation that the more grandiose the ambitions of the revolution, the more magnified a leadership cult is liable to appear as a focus of orientation in a time of turbulent change. As revolutionary enthusiasm subsides the full-blown version of the leadership cult becomes a liability, and so when Khrushchev developed a minor personality cult of his own he was ousted. The leadership principle was redefined in the light of the bitter experience of Stalin and to suit a mature industrial society. In this context the inflation of Brezhnev's personality cult was a grotesque confirmation of Marx's dictum that in history tragedy repeats itself as farce. The cult of Brezhnev was largely a personal affair designed to buttress his own power and that of his coterie rather than to allow the system to adapt to new challenges. In that sense Brezhnev was an accurate personification of the ills that increasingly besieged the system. Gorbachev's rule was initially marked by personal modesty and open impatience with the trappings of the leadership cult, like extended ovations and exaggerated obeisance, yet ultimately he sought to institutionalise his personal leadership in a strengthened presidency.

The personalities of Soviet leaders and the choice of policies were closely related. The classic example was the decision to embark on accelerated industrialisation and full collectivi-sation of agriculture in 1928–29. The policy was always an option in the 1920s, but the par-ticular way that it was implemented was very much of Stalin's choosing. Khrushchev's denunciation of the excesses of Stalin was to be expected, but it nonetheless represented a major act of personal courage. Brezhnev's personal commitment to détente in the 1970s was a factor in its relative success, and Andropov's insistence on discipline was a reflection of his own preferences and background. Gorbachev's bold policies displayed a great deal of personal policy initiation and his individual style of conviction politics.

Formally, however, there was no constitutional basis to the exaggerated forms of Soviet leadership. The communist party's General Secretary was not formally vested with executive power, as the President is in the USA, but was constrained by the principle of collective lead-ership. In theory he was only *primus inter pares*, but in practice led the Politburo and the country. After 1953 the personal rule of the individual General Secretary was played down and the Politburo was careful to restrict his powers. The 1986 party Rules explicitly stressed collective party leadership as a guarantee against a revival of the cult of personality. However, the Gorbachev succession was exceptional in that there was very little public emphasis on the principle of collective leadership, as there had been in the first years of both Khrushchev's and Brezhnev's rule. Throughout the emphasis was on the collective rule of the CPSU marked by unity and continuity, with policy allegedly immutably established by ideology, the economic system, geo-political situation and historical traditions – the only rational outcome in the circumstances. However, in the absence of constitutional limitations a Soviet leader had great scope for policy innovations and was able to stamp his personality on a period.

After 1953 all leaders were constrained by the general framework of 'neo-Stalinism', not breaking out into liberalism or reverting to Stalinism. There was a continuity in goals and methods, although the emphasis changed between leaders. Voslensky argues that in fact the General Secretary was a 'prisoner', unable to stray too far from representing the interests of the party machine for fear that the apparatus would dismiss him, as it did Khrushchev in 1964. The elaborate rules against factionalism, such as the provision passed in 1964 that no two members of the Politburo could meet alone (to prevent plotting), ensured that leadership links were focused on the party machinery itself.[2] This view perhaps has a tendency to reify the *nomenklatura* system, to give it a personality as if it had a life of its own. It downplays the degree to which a General Secretary might launch independent initiatives not wholly consonant with the interests of the *nomenklatura* office-holders.

There was no settled succession mechanism as such in the Soviet Union for the simple reason that theoretically there was no succession. Nowhere was it decreed that the leader of the party would be the leader of the country. There were no general elections for the party leader-ship and of course no choice between parties. The creation of an executive presidency, at first elected by the Congress of People's Deputies, regularised the position of the Soviet leader, but Gorbachev's attempts to combine the advantages of both the traditional system of party power with democratic legitimacy ultimately deprived him of both.

The three successions of 1924, 1953 and 1964 were accompanied by bitter contests, but overall the six successions of Soviet power saw a diminution in the intensity of the struggle. Formally, it was the Central Committee that selected the General Secretary, but the real choice was made in the Politburo. The Brezhnev succession confirmed the pattern whereby the successful contender was conventionally simultaneously a member of the Politburo and the Secretariat. The nomination procedure worked effectively in the 1980s, confounding some of the more alarmist predictions that chaos would follow Brezhnev's death. The lack of a constitutional mechanism, however, reflected the absence of an open way of integrating conflicting interests. While not resolved, they were settled behind closed doors, giving rise to much Kremlinological speculation. While many Western social scientists called for more attention to be paid to long-term developmental processes such as changes in social mobility, education and general sociological factors rather than the minute study of the entrails of power struggles within the Kremlin, these pleas were undermined by the absence of open policy debate and the continued inability to formalise leadership practices. While the role of leadership in the post-Stalin years might not have been all that exaggerated in comparison with that in many liberal democracies, it was the absence of a formal institutional context (selection procedure, length of term in office, and so on) that made it appear so. As growth faltered and resources declined, these informal mechanisms of conflict resolution put an intolerable strain on the system.

There was no established term for remaining in power. With the exception of Khrushchev all pre-Gorbachev party leaders died in office. The lack of a tradition of honourable retirement had dire consequences for the country since, as Brezhnev proved, the leader refused to give up his job for fear of being discredited by his successor. At the same time, no Soviet leader was formally able to designate his successor, and the emergence of an individual as heir-apparent usually presaged his downfall as the other pretenders united to destroy him. Lenin in his Last Testament seems to have deliberately set his putative successors at each other's throats by the inflammatory and derogatory terms in which he described them all without exception. By surrounding himself with men his own age Brezhnev tried to ensure that any heir-apparent would be too old to displace him before his death, as he himself had ousted Khrushchev in 1964. Only Andropov appeared openly to favour Gorbachev as his successor, and even then Chernenko's brief rule created an interregnum.

The role of leadership in the Soviet political system was an independent variable which waxed and waned. It was not derived from institutional sources of power alone but from a combination of personality factors, the tradition of the 'strong Tsar' and the presidential factor: the ability to inaugurate and promote policy initiatives in a system which had a tendency towards immobilism and inertia. The posts themselves rose and fell depending on the personalities of the incumbent. A distinction should be drawn between the 'power' of a leader and his 'powers'. The formal powers did not derive from any constitutional provisions since the Soviet leader was more like a British prime minister than an American president. Actual power, which can be termed authority, depended on convention and the personality of the leader. Stalin had virtually complete mastery over policy-making, while Khrushchev's dual position as head of both party and government from early 1958 gave him great leverage. His formal powers were considerable, but his authority waned because of his inability to solve problems or to maintain a coalition of support. Brezhnev's leadership rested on a consensual approach, the building of policy coalitions and the gradual consolidation of his own personal position. There was constant faction-fighting at the top of the Soviet political system, but the power of the leader depended on shifting balances between individuals, factions and institutions.[3]

The successions of the early 1980s demonstrated the Politburo's fears that someone would be chosen who would rise to far above them. Once elected, each General Secretary sought to consolidate his position. The real substance of a General Secretary's power came from a combination of control over personnel and policy. Peter Frank pointed out that a new leader inherited a government rather than created a new one,[4] and Bunce illustrated that 'Soviet leaders campaign after coming to office'.[5] Power came from the ability to manipulate personnel; authority came from success in policy.

The leader's first priority was to build a power base. The initial emphasis on collective leadership gradually gave way to the emergence of personalised rule. Stalin's bloodthirsty purges of the leadership were only the most dramatic expressions of the pattern whereby every major leader tried to remould the Politburo and the party apparatus to suit his needs. Before 1957 Khrushchev was able to replace a significant proportion of the Central Committee, and after 1957 much of the Politburo and regional party leaderships. Brezhnev moved slowly and required six or seven years to consolidate his personal position. In this period some observers considered that a stable system of oligarchical rule had developed based on the collective leadership of Brezhnev, Podgorny, Kosygin, Suslov and Kirilenko.[6] However, Brezhnev gradually emerged as the dominant figure and upset the balance. In policy terms also the rejection from 1976 of Kirilenko's high industrial-investment strategy saw his demotion and the rise of Chernenko as the CC Secretary in charge of personnel.

Allied to the personalism of Brezhnev's political style a broad network of patron–client relations was allowed to develop which threatened the anonymous rule-governed aspects of the system. Patronage groups emerged at all levels in which loyalty was rewarded by political and social benefits, bypassing the *nomenklatura* system and often degenerating into plain corruption. Brezhnev's group focused on the 'Dnepropetrovsk Mafia' but also included many other institutional and regional interests (especially from Moldavia), marking his progress through the Soviet political system. Such networks provided an important channel for the aspiring politician. Gorbachev's own rise from Stavropol to the Politburo as a client of Kulakov and ultimately Suslov is a case in point. At its worst, there 'was a trend to promote people often on the grounds of personal devotion' giving rise to a 'cult of mediocrity'.[7] Brezhnev's policies represented the lowest common denominator of general agreement among the elite and reflected the conservative consensus; he sought to smooth over conflicts rather than to resolve them. For the patron these networks helped consolidate their control over institutions and politicians. For a Soviet leader like Brezhnev they provided a way of integrating the formation of policy with its implementation and the general supervision of the governmental and party machinery. Of course, the existence of competing patronage networks acted as a check on his leadership and justified his consensual approach.[8] Gorbachev's early strategy focused precisely on breaking up local patronage networks by 'parachuting in' outsiders.

However much power any individual General Secretary may have wielded, he had to be able to establish his authority by posing as a successful problem-solver. Brezhnev had conspicuously failed to do this by the late 1970s, and while his power appeared to be at a peak, his authority was waning and he began to lose his hold over the policy agenda. In the 1980s leaders tried to consolidate their positions very fast. Andropov launched several policy initiatives, such as the discipline campaign, and consolidated his power through substantial though not dramatic personnel changes. Andropov's many years away from the party apparatus in the relative backwater of the KGB meant that he lacked an extensive clientele network on whom he could rely and found himself in the strange position of a patron without clients. He quickly promoted his own supporters such as Aliev, Chebrikov and Shevardnadze, but for the rest he had to turn to the former supporters of Kirilenko, those who had supported greater investment in industry in the 1970s, such as Ligachev, Vorotnikov and Ryzhkov with a technical or economic background. During his fifteen months in power 35 of the then 155 *obkom* first secretaries (22 per cent of the total), 25 ministers (20 per cent) and a quarter of the Politburo were replaced, dismissed or retired. Andropov had to force through these changes against the Brezhnevites and their still active leader Chernenko. Andropov had much authority but relatively little power, despite taking on the presidency.

Following his death it was clear that there was considerable resistance to the appointment of the functionary Chernenko. His appointment took several days, compared to the two days required to select Andropov and the few hours to confirm Gorbachev. The latter came to power with much authority and substantial power, which he moved fast to consolidate. The sense of crisis provided an atmosphere conducive to the exercise of an activist leadership. In personnel terms Gorbachev was exceptionally fortunate since a series of deaths left a number of vacancies on the Politburo which he could fill with like-minded people. Ryzhkov was appointed Premier, and Gorbachev took on greater personal responsibility for foreign policy by nominating the veteran foreign minister Andrei Gromyko President and replacing him with Shevardnadze. There was little emphasis on collective leadership but Gorbachev was forced to reckon with some of Andropov's appointments, above all Ligachev (responsible for ideology) and Viktor Chebrikov (the head of the KGB). He launched a major challenge on the Council of Ministers, scathingly condemning the industrial ministries. Capitalising on the need to rejuvenate the elite, the twenty-seventh party congress in March 1986 replaced 44 per cent of Central Committee members. The rapid consolidation of Gorbachev's power was achieved by the traditional means of creating a patronage network loyal to himself by the extensive transfer of personnel. His demand for loyalty, however, was tempered by an insistence on ability which took primacy over the principle of 'stability of cadres'. However, part of the reason for Boris Yeltsin's dismissal from the post of Moscow party leader in November 1987 was his obsession with moving personnel around, giving rise to a dangerous 'instability of cadres'. In personnel policy and in policy formation Gorbachev placed himself in a strong and, with the accumulation of the office of presidency, apparently unassailable position. His authority, however, could only be sustained by success in the fields in which he had chosen to invest his prestige (the rejuvenation of the Soviet economy and polity), and when these signally failed to bear fruit (despite successes in foreign policy), his authority rapidly declined.

In the post-Stalinist Soviet political system the leader could no longer simply impose his will on his colleagues but had to operate within consensus politics. Policy emerged through the interaction of the leader, the leadership group and certain vested interests. The General Secretary was more than first among equals but had to take into account the views of colleagues over policy and appointments (or dismissals) from the Politburo. Archie Brown has summed up the general position: 'Each General Secretary has wielded less individual power over policy than his predecessor, but within his period in office has increased his power vis-à-vis his colleagues during his time in office.'[9] The concentration of power accelerated after Brezhnev because of the onset (with the exception of Chernenko) of a period of policy dynamism. Within nine months Andropov was wielding more power and had accumulated as much authority as Brezhnev had in nearly a decade. Chernenko was an anomaly and too sick to do more than hold back the tide of change for a year. The rapid consolidation of Gorbachev's power and authority, due as much to his dynamic personality and intrinsic abilities as to the undefined powers of his office, created the novel situation of an 'imperial General Secretary', comparable to the 'imperial presidency' in the USA. Just as the liberals in the New Deal and the 1960s put their faith in a strong president to push through a reform programme, so it appeared that solutions to the USSR's problems required the concentration of power to overcome vested interests. Already under Brezhnev the General Secretary had begun to maintain his personal staff, and Gorbachev quickly gathered around himself a group of advisers on whom he greatly relied, including economists and political scientists.

There was unprecedented rapid leadership turnover, and yet Gorbachev felt himself opposed at all levels of the leadership and polity. His fight in his first years of power to implement a reform programme illustrates the limits to the power of the General Secretary. His struggle was rather like Lenin's attempt in the immediate post-1917 years to carry his policies. Such struggles increasingly entailed the revival of some of the features of Civil War internal party life, such as open discussions, that were terminated so abruptly by the tenth party congress in March 1921. The CPSU in its last days moved from no formalised internal oppositions to a surfeit, falling prey to bitter faction-fighting. To compensate, Gorbachev created the executive presidency to provide an institutional framework for his personalised and relatively authoritarian leadership style. The shift from party to state leadership, however, had barely been established before the state itself had collapsed.

The issue of generational change was closely associated with the political changes of the 1980s. The succession was as much an actuarial as a political revolution. The old generation came to power as a result of the massive upward social and political mobility of the early Stalin years, and they came to maturity managing his system in war and post-war reconstruction. This generation greyed under Khrushchev, and slowly slipped into senility under Brezhnev. The new generation, represented by Gorbachev, began to take up major posts in significant numbers under Andropov. They were children during the war and came to maturity against the background of destalinisation and the threat of nuclear war. They were better educated and had a broader view of the world than their predecessors. They were aware of the need for dynamism and international contacts to overcome economic and social inertia, but the form of their preferred dynamism is unclear. There is little evidence that they were necessarily more liberal than the old generation. The no-nonsense authoritarian style of the 1930s and the war gave way to the no less dirigiste style of the cold-blooded technocrat; the leather-jacketed Chekist gave way to the reformer in the business suit. The changing sociology of leadership might have made some differences in style and tone, but changes in content were acts of political will rather than generational change.

The broader context in which policy was formulated had changed. The Soviet people itself had matured: the population was better educated and had achieved a basic Western standard of living. Having achieved economic welfare, this people increasingly resented their exclusion from meaningful political participation and the hollow formality of so much that passed for political life in the Soviet system. The neo-Stalinist compromise broke down both because the regime was no longer able to offer improving standards of living, and because the people no longer tolerated their political exclusion. A generational change of mood had taken place. After Stalin political society seemed to cry out for a leader who could invigorate the moribund political and social processes. In Khrushchev they found a dynamic personality, but after his ouster they looked for calm. Brezhnev's stability, however, was taken to excess and once again in the 1980s the mood was ready for change.

From the above account it is clear that new leaders do make a difference in the Soviet Union. Weber was clearly right in arguing that individual charisma is a historical force in its own right. Too often, however, charisma is ground down by institutionalisation. The concentration of power in the Soviet system was such that despite elements of collective leadership and continuity the accession of a new leader broadened the scope for policy innovation over and against the vast apparatus. Individual leadership in the USSR reflected the fundamental dirigisme of the system as a whole. Policy change in some cases flowed directly from struggles within the elite. Bunce illustrates that in the 'honeymoon' period following accession to office a new leader makes major policy innovations. These innovations then become routine until a new leader begins the process anew, dubbed by Bunce the 'policy cycle'.[10] However, in certain important respects a new Soviet leader did not make that much of a difference. The 'policy cycle' inaugurated by the October revolution had become routinised; a change of leader allowed some tilts to the rudder but not a fundamental change of course. Despite six changes of leadership there was little fundamental change in the relationship between the state and society until Gorbachev inaugurated a new policy cycle. No leader was prepared, or allowed, to concede a role for associations beyond the aegis of the state–party apparatus. Until Gorbachev permitted an unprecedented debate over policy options all leaders shared the same fundamental views on the nature of the system, the role of the ideology and the way that the system should operate. Post-Stalin leaders had been appointed to preserve the party's leading role, not to preside over its dismemberment.

MODELS OF SOVIET POWER

The various models on offer imply different understandings of the dynamics of the Soviet state and each has both its own contribution to make to understanding the system, and its drawbacks. There are three main types of model: those that emphasise the concentration of power; those that stress its diffusion; and those that try to combine an understanding of the centralist elements of the Soviet system with the apparent devolution of influence.

Totalitarianism and concentration models

Totalitarianism can be taken as representative of concentration models. The term was first used by Benito Mussolini in the 1920s in Italy to signify his intention to consolidate power in a one-party state. In the late 1930s Western social scientists began to apply the term to describe the phenomenon of the massively expanded powers of the state in Germany and the USSR. It was developed into a political philosophy by Franz Borkenau, and Hannah Arendt argued that a new social form had emerged in Germany under Hitler and in the Soviet Union that was not synonymous with traditional forms of tyranny, dictatorship or authoritarianism.

The classic definition of totalitarianism was provided by Carl Friedrich and Zbigniew Brzezinski.[11] They identified six key elements:

1 an official ideology to which adherence was demanded: the ideology was intended to achieve a 'perfect final stage of mankind';
2 a single mass party, hierarchically organised, closely interwoven with the state bureaucracy and typically led by one man, the *Führerprinzip*;
3 monopolistic control of the military by the party (as opposed to the state);
4 a similar monopoly of the means of effective communication;
5 a system of terroristic police control;
6 central direction and control of the entire economy.

The original version very much stressed the role of the leader, known as the *vozhd* in Russian, and the mass party brooking no opposition and extending its tentacles into all other organisations. The role of terror, an aggressive ideology with a dynamic of external expansion and a mass movement were also highlighted. Of the six points some (like state management of the economy in emergencies) have been present in states that are not considered totalitarian; while some features (like the systematic denigration of whole peoples or classes up to the attempt to achieve their total destruction) that might be thought to be the characteristic feature of twentieth-century totalitarianism are not forcefully reflected in the six-point syndrome outlined above.

Two novel features lie at the centre of totalitarianism which distinguish it from run-of-the-mill authoritarianism. The first is the nature of the relationship at the heart of the system, between the totalitarian party and its supporters. Adherence is gained out of psychological 'impulses' as much as out of political belief, and even less out of personal greed. It is an impersonal appeal for loyalty to a higher goal in which loyalty is ideologically structured. When more base motivations become dominant then one can talk of the decline of totalitarianism. Under Stalin the charismatic personality cult focused these ties on the leader, who was seen as fulfilling the historical needs of the movement. The unique feature of Stalin's rule was his control over the mass movement and the downgrading of the principles on which a party operates, namely routine, established procedures and the dominance of organisation over personal arbitrariness. The clash between charismatic and bureaucratic principles was resolved by the great purges, which firmly subordinated the bureaucracy to the cult of personality while allowing the latter to triumph over society.

The second feature is the relationship between the totalitarian apparatus and society. Totalitarianism focuses on the structure and application of power at the centre and stresses the destruction of alternative sources of power and influence ('islands of separatism') in society. In a totalitarian society all intermediate institutions between the party and the masses are eliminated. Among other things, law becomes subordinate to the power centre and in practice loses any semblance of independence from the state and party. There are no legal, political or moral restraints on power. This is usually described by the term atomisation, the destruction of all social ties and groups not necessary for the maintenance of the totalitarian system. The regime obliterates the distinction between private and public spheres and individuals are marked by loneliness, anomie and alienation.

Parallels are often drawn between totalitarian theory and the organisation of 'hydraulic societies'. In his *Oriental Despotism* Karl Wittfogel argued that Russia was never fundamentally a Western-type society but was instead characterised by the 'Asiatic Mode of Production'. This was marked by the dominance of the state over society, the absence of intermediary proprietors, the prominent role of the state in organising or regulating production, and the concentration of economic surpluses in the hands of the state through taxation. This model was profoundly subversive of Soviet power (and indeed of Marxism) for it suggested that Soviet communism's transcendence of the market and the private ownership of the means of production could lead backwards to 'oriental despotism' rather than forwards to socialism.

The concept of totalitarianism was never wholeheartedly adopted by sovietologists, and has been under severe attack since the 1960s. As part of the movement to strip the social sciences of their normative connotations and to make them more value free and objective, Western scholars tried to reduce the earlier stress on the USSR's exceptionalism and to study it within the terms of general social science methods applicable to any other society. The criticisms of totalitarianism can be summarised as follows. The theory tended to equate not Stalinism and fascism, but communism and fascism, and therefore was not easily able to conceptualise the differences that may have existed between Lenin's regime and Stalin's, or between Khrushchev's and Brezhnev's, let alone Gorbachev's. Even under Stalin the concept tried to bring together two very different systems, communism and fascism, whose internal dynamics were very different. Totalitarianism, moreover, was held to have described the state of affairs under Stalin and had therefore become anachronistic. With the era of mass terror giving way to the less arbitrary application of coercion against specific targets, there was at least a change from terroristic totalitarianism to 'totalitarianism without terror', or simple totalitarianism. The mass of the population were now allowed to get on with their own affairs as long as they did not make untoward political demands on the system. The era of mass mobilisations from above and the demand for belief gave way to a less demanding approach. The concentration of power in the hands of a single leader declined significantly, thus weakening the *Führerprinzip*. Khrushchev retained elements of one-person dominance, while Brezhnev was firmly constrained by the collective leadership. The interplay between the leader, the leadership and some institutions increased.

The fundamental idea of totalitarianism, that social relations become atomised and that rule becomes anomic and direct, is questionable. Arendt's idea of totalitarianism was associated with the theory of mass society which posits that atomisation increases as group and class loyalties dissolve.[12] Atomisation is a vague concept and begs the question whether such a condition, even if it existed, could be maintained for long. Natural solidarity remains as in family relations, subcultural networks, religious affiliations and societies of friendship. The fundamental tenet of totalitarianism – that a monolithic regime dominates a passive population – was belied by evidence of popular resistance and even political struggles throughout the Soviet period. Vera Dunham demonstrated that even under Stalin a Soviet middle class emerged with which the regime made a 'Big Deal'. The theory of totalitarianism exaggerated the success of official socialisation, and tended to take the regime's self-evaluation at face value. With the fall of the regime more and more evidence emerged that the party's ability to control popular beliefs and values was not as effective as its ability to control overt political behaviour. The resistance of society at all stages of Soviet power continued in more or less subtle ways (see Chapter 13). At worst, resistance derived from atomisation took the form identified by Alexander Zinoviev, an active though cynical participation in political structures combined with the concentration on enhancing one's own life chances within smaller groups, or 'communes', in a Hobbesian war of all against all.[13] At best, resistance took the form of the personal affirmation of certain inalienable human values.

Totalitarianism stressed the monolithic unity of the party and its partners in ruling the Soviet polity. As we have seen, there were considerable shifts over time and the tensions between institutions and their fragmented interaction can hardly be called monolithic. While the dominance of the institutions of the power elite over society is undoubted, this also can barely be called monolithic. In the Polish context, for example, intermediary forces remained between the state and society in the form of the Roman Catholic church and an independent peasantry. In the post-Stalinist Soviet system, too, power relations were mediated by clan relations and other forms of traditional societal relations. To describe this reality, B. Wolfe Jancar rejected the term totalitarianism in favour of the term 'absolute monopoly', implying *exclusive* rather than *total* control.

The main charge against totalitarianism was that it was too static.[14] It failed to take into account not only social and economic developments, but political changes since Stalin. The theory did not have a way of explaining political change other than through the leadership mechanism and thus it ignored the sources of change in Soviet-type systems. The policy process was limited to the top leadership. An associated criticism is that the theory of totalitarianism overemphasised formal institutions at the expense of locating Soviet-type power systems within their national and cultural contexts. Totalitarianism, it was argued, looked very different in Vilnius to how it looked in Baku, let alone in Warsaw or in Tirana. Even if different societies approximate to the ideal type of totalitarianism, marked by omnipotent control and all-pervasive power, they had various distinctive features.[15]

The dynamics of industrial society themselves are considered to undermine the long-term viability of the more overt forms of totalitarianism. The classic totalitarianism of high Stalinism was allegedly undermined by a threefold process: organisational changes encouraged various forms of bureaucratic pluralism; social factors brought to the fore the specialists and the huge class of the technical intelligentsia; and cultural interpenetration meant that totalitarian regimes could no longer insulate themselves from the non-communist world. Given the changes in communist systems and the increasing national and cultural diversity, either the model had to keep being modified or one remained loyal to the original model, the 'ideal type', and measured the distance the Soviet Union deviated from it.

The theory of totalitarianism would appear to be riddled with insurmountable weaknesses. However, a solid case can be made in favour of retaining the concept. While its defenders on the whole admit that the model has flaws, they argue that in the absence of anything better it remains the best existing model of Soviet politics and should not be discarded lightly. Totalitarianism, they argue, emphasises what was truly important in Soviet politics, above all the pervasive level of political and ideological controls, together with fluidity and arbitrariness of government, a feature shared with Nazi Germany and identified by Arendt in her original formulation of the concept in the early 1950s. Totalitarianism in common usage was ultimately about the quality of political relationships. There remained a vast coercive apparatus which was unleashed once more against dissent after 1979. There were no effective safeguards for the Soviet citizen against arbitrary police powers. While the authorities on occasion relaxed their control over intellectual life, overt rival intellectual currents were not tolerated. The policy process remained highly centralised and usually operated in secrecy, and the state administrative apparatus pervaded society. The division between public and personal was tolerated but not legitimised by a concept of privacy. The system remained a 'dictatorship over needs' in that the social project of equality, full employment and so on retained priority over narrowly political concepts of individual freedom.[16] The defenders insist that totalitarianism is capable of acting as a comparative concept to analyse other communist systems. Totalitarianism, it is argued, should be defined more as the aspiration to obtain total control rather than its achievement. Above all, they argue, it would be difficult to study the early to middle years of the Soviet system without using the concept. For the later stages, it focused attention on the factors that made the system less totalitarian.[17] This point allows totalitarianism to be used to analyse the changes, weakening the argument that the theory was too static. Of the original six points only two points had changed substantially: the role of the leader and the decline in terror. It would be difficult to study Soviet-type systems without the concept of totalitarianism, or some version of it, to understand their authoritarian features. The decline in impersonal loyalty and the implicit appeal to self-interest under Brezhnev represented the social modification of totalitarianism while its political structures remained relatively intact.

Hence the concept of totalitarianism returned with a vengeance. In the 1960s it was often dropped for the wrong reasons. The concept had connotations not of academic study but of crude anti-communist politics. However, the division over the use of the term was never simply a split between the left and the right. Those who favoured describing the Soviet Union as totalitarian included Soviet dissenters, East European critical intellectuals, democratic socialists, exiles from communist lands, Western conservatives and, ultimately, the reform-minded Soviet leadership itself. The term was sometimes used by Western socialists to describe the West, and by the Soviet Union to describe systems it found odious. It was applied by Trotsky to describe the Soviet Union under Stalin. The concept is a broad one, but as Archie Brown points out, the social sciences are full of key concepts that are not susceptible to simple definitions. Above all, the theory of totalitarianism was revived because the earlier optimism about the reform of these systems was disappointed. The theory of convergence from the 1950s predicted that social and economic developments would act to weaken the concentration of power in Soviet-type systems. In fact, communist leaderships tried to co-opt advances in technology (such as computers) to consolidate their power within the 'mono-organisational' system. Václav Havel in his *Power of the Powerless* referred to 'post-totalitarianism', but later dropped the 'post' in the belief that the crude totalitarianism of Stalin only foreshadowed the more subtle totalitarianism practised later. The leading role of the party was consolidated and communist political power remained remarkably impervious to social and technological changes. Gorbachev's reforms could be interpreted both ways: to demonstrate that the Soviet system retained the capacity for radical renewal and to break decisively with totalitarianism; but the very fact that the reforms broke the regime revealed the brittleness of the system.

The group approach and diffusion models

The theory of totalitarianism was challenged by the group approach to Soviet politics. In the 1950s American political scientists, led by David Truman in his *The Governmental Process* (1951), inspired by Arthur F. Bentley's *The Process of Government* (1908), moved away from the study of legal structures and state institutions to focus more on informal processes and society. Analysis shifted to societal inputs to the policy process, above all the role of organized groups. In the 1960s the approach was applied to the Soviet Union in an explicit attempt to minimise Soviet uniqueness and to integrate Soviet studies into mainstream social science. Totalitarianism tended to focus on the formal structures of Soviet politics, whereas the group approach focused on how the system actually worked in practice. The shift in interest was part of what was known as the behavioural revolution in political science, away from political institutions to informal processes and individuals, from government to politics. At its most developed the group approach was the basis for a pluralistic theory of politics, although the two are not synonymous. Pluralism implies conflict over political power and policies whereas the group approach specifies only that groups are an important factor in this competition.

Stalinist totalitarianism had allegedly been its own gravedigger as the society born of rapid industrialisation matured. The revolution was consolidated and there was a growing institutionalisation of Soviet political life. Although Soviet politics lacked an overtly competitive dynamic typical of liberal democracies, there were nevertheless contestatory processes involved in the allocation of resources and in the enjoyment of the fruits of power. Under Gorbachev the terminology of reformists and conservatives indicated the *de facto* emergence of two 'parties', although not legitimised in any way. It is clear that any open debate about policies entails a degree of lobbying, if not 'factionalism'. There was considerable conflict and diversity beneath the formalised surface of Soviet political life, and in particular there was much evidence of bureaucratic or group activity. An element of pluralist competition was pursued between individuals, groups and the various offices and departments of the party and government. However, while the group approach highlighted an important facet of Soviet political life, there remained major limits to the diffusion of power. As Skilling warned, pluralism was not a group theory of politics, but a theory of groups in Soviet politics.[18]

Beneath the veneer of monolithic unity the USSR was as divided into national, class, professional or religious groups as any other society. The actual classification of groups could take different forms. Skilling divided them into occupational and opinion groups. Occupational groups could be both bureaucratic and intellectual, while opinion formations cut across other groups and tended towards more unified views. Three categories can be derived from the occupational groups: leadership groups or factions involved in policy-making; official or bureaucratic groups, including the military, police, party apparatus and industrial managers; and a broad group of brain workers such as scientists, writers, journalists, scholars and other specialists and intellectuals. A fourth category encompasses a range of broadly based but not institutionalised social forces such as workers, peasants, nationalities, religious groups, regional, age and gender groups, and at the most general level social interests like consumers. The weakness of autonomous interests meant that the focus in the Soviet context was very much on institutionalised interests and professional groupings such as economic managers and planners, teachers and lawyers, rather than general groupings such as age, gender, race or religion.[19]

Pluralism shifts the emphasis away from the concentration of power and the 'output' side of politics (the policies) and from supports (how the regime maintains itself in power) to the input side of politics, the demands that groups and individuals make on the system. Policies are initiated not only from above but also from below, and in their implementation are modified. Skilling insisted that groups acted on the leadership as much as they were acted upon. However, while it is easy to name groups, the immediate problem with the group approach is how to define a group and how to define an interest. An interest group, according to Skilling, is a collection of people who share a common position on an issue and act to fulfil their group ambitions. There is a question over how the imputed interests can be articulated. In the Soviet context groups were forced to behave in informal ways, with overt lobbying forbidden but discreet bargaining possible. The point, however, was not whether the demands were made, but whether they were, to some degree, to be satisfied, and indeed on the mechanism whereby they could be satisfied. While power was clearly concentrated in the USSR, the concept of 'more' and 'less' power suggested an element of diffusion. The role of leadership at all levels meant that the aggregation of interest took place in a fundamentally different way from in the West, and even there few claim that policy flows simply out of the clash of groups. Bentley argued that once you have looked at the groups you have looked at everything: but the suggestion that politics, including the government and parties, does not exist outside group processes is clearly exaggerated.[20]

Groups have always played an important role in Soviet politics. From Lenin's time the notion of 'departmentalism' (or localism), where institutions or groups put their interests above those of society as a whole, was condemned. There is evidence that groups influenced policy in the 1930s and 1940s even at the height of Stalinism. It is clear that policy conflicts are as endemic to the Soviet system as to any other. Skilling characterises the Stalin period as quasi-totalitarian, on the grounds that pure totalitarianism is a practical impossibility. Groups existed, but had little capacity for independent action and were manipulated by the leadership.[21]

Douglas Weiner has shown that under Stalin a sustained covert struggle raged between the defenders of ecological *zapovedniki* (reserves) and a range of opponents led by the 'industry first' lobby.[22] The fundamental principle of the right of scientists to pursue their own research independent of state direction was never abandoned, despite the depredations of a charlatan like Lysenko. Dunmore and others have shown that under the ferocious though weakening gaze of the dictator in his declining years there were pluralist and bureaucratic elements in Soviet politics, with conflicts over consumer goods and agricultural policy, cultural and foreign policy. The Zhdanov 'party revivalist' faction was opposed by Malenkov, who put greater emphasis on state procedures as they had developed during the war years. Such factional activity is a reflection of personal conflicts, institutional jealousies, and genuine policy debate.

Under Khrushchev the professional and institutional groupings came into their own, despite continued support for Lysenko. The decline in political terror and mass mobilisation permitted a degree of political competition between groups pursuing their own interests. The debate over the Virgin Lands Scheme showed the possibility of intra-elite conflict, and the 1958 educational reform demonstrated that a professional grouping could influence policy between its inception and implementation. Specific specialist interest groups and inchoate social resistance were able to modify the policies of the leader of an allegedly totalitarian state. The education reform revealed the limits to policy group activity as well, such as the need to build support within the apparatus, the need to avoid openly challenging party policy, that objections had to be voiced in a non-political 'technocratic' language, and that success was possible only over relatively uncontroversial policy issues.[23] It perhaps showed less the importance of interest groups than the centrality of bureaucratic politics, and indeed the strength of the social groups whose privileges were under attack. The announcement of the state of all the people limited the concept of 'one class – one party – one truth' and broadened the theoretical scope of group politics. The bureaucracy and the military, with the approval of other elite factions, played a key role in ousting Khrushchev in 1964.

Skilling characterised the Soviet Union under Brezhnev as post-totalitarianism, a form of 'consultative authoritarianism' or 'imperfect monism' in which the political leadership was secure but willing to consult experts. The long-anticipated next stage predicted more vigorous group activity that would be able occasionally to challenge official policies.[24] Under Brezhnev group activity was able to establish itself as a constraining rather than as an active promotional force. Stewart argued that Soviet interest groups lacked the associational element found in the USA and instead institutional interest groups, lacking independent resources and yet consulted by the leadership in the making of policy, became key actors.[25] Hough identified the development of an 'institutional pluralism', which permitted a degree of administrative devolution to certain 'complexes' (termed 'policy whirlpools') as part of the larger corporatist style of politics, with a leadership effectively neutralised by Brezhnev's occupancy.[26] The currency of exchange with the leadership was specialised information, but the value of the currency depended on the group's strategic position within the system. The increasing complexity of administration made it more difficult for the checking mechanisms, primarily achieved through the party, to monitor the apparatus. This allowed officials to carve out areas of relative autonomy amidst the forest of rules and regulations, a form of bureaucratic pluralism. Andropov's accession showed the importance of the KGB both as an interest group and as a checking mechanism, while Gorbachev admitted that certain groups were able to impede his policy of *perestroika*. The military was to exert considerable influence on policy simply by the fact that they represented a cardinal concern of the whole body politic. Under Gorbachev this gave way to the primacy of civilian economic interests, the party apparatus, and the liberal intelligentsia. Groups like lawyers and environmentalists also achieved some success in influencing policy.

Despite the undoubted role of groups in Soviet politics there are strong arguments against the application of the idea of pluralism to the Soviet Union. Above all, there was the lack of formal legitimacy for group activity. The Soviet party and its allies did not accept political pluralism as either desirable or permissible. Pluralism ran directly counter to the foundations of Soviet ideology and organisation, and there was no accepted philosophical basis for group activity. The concept of socialist pluralism became acceptable as part of Gorbachev's reform process, yet was only beginning to be politically institutionalised when the system fell. Societal groups were weak and non-inclusive and were not able to overcome the element of 'mass society' in Soviet politics. Some ruling parties, as in Poland, had to accommodate the realities of pluralistic forces, such as the church, but overt threats to the leading role of the party up to 1989 were suppressed. Under Dubček the Action Programme envisaged only a limited form of political pluralism, and even that was intolerable to the Brezhnev leadership. The 'normalisation' process under Gustav Husak, following the invasion, was designed to root out all the shoots of pluralism that had emerged during the Prague Spring. Normalisation was indeed the normal state of Soviet politics. Even in Yugoslavia, where relatively independent social organisations were sanctioned, the political leadership retained wide discretionary powers. While the theory of 'one class – one party' had given way to a state of all the people, this did not signify an autonomous role for social forces or particularities in Soviet-type societies.

As far as policy formation is concerned, lack of formal legitimacy reduced the effectiveness of groups. Group interests could only be articulated through personal solicitation or indirect access to channels of influence. The group approach reacted against the study of formal institutional structures of political regimes in favour of the informal processes which determine decision-making. However, as Griffiths pointed out, groups were not central to the policy process in the USSR. The approach assumes that a polity is 'sub-system-dominant', where the whole can be explained by the sum of the parts or sub-systems, with interaction between autonomous interest groups, the government and the party, whereas in the Soviet Union this was far from being the case. The Soviet polity was clearly system-dominant, and interaction with groups was not central to policy outcomes.[27] The group approach exaggerated the role of sub-system relationships and underestimated overarching factors such as leadership or ideology. Skilling and Griffiths concluded that groups influenced only the form of policies, not the policies themselves, and then only on non-sensitive issues.

By definition pluralism is a system where political power is dispersed and yet the 'dictatorship' of the Politburo remained. In the context of weak legal traditions and a diffuse constitutionality there was a tendency for groups to form on the basis of 'patronage' (clientship) or professional ties. However, the CPSU until very nearly the end was able to avoid degenerating into competing factions based on these groups. There was a need for specialist advice, but the system was able to incorporate various pressures and conflicting influences. The integrated power system was preserved almost in its entirety, buttressed by democratic centralism and the continued ban on factions. The bonds of adherence at the heart of the regime, although tempered by corruption, did not give way to a non-ideological loyalty to the group or faction, and hence the system retained, in this respect at least, the totalitarian emphasis on impersonal ties.

Group activity in the USSR operated within the context of universal nationalised property and was therefore based not on ownership but on a politically mediated differential access and role in the operation of the means of production. To a degree Soviet group activity simply reflected the division of labour within a single system. Intra-class differentiation became a permitted field of sociological study but contradictions were regarded as non-antagonistic and therefore not the site of class struggle.

The cohesion of groups was open to question. Those like the party *apparat*, military or state bureaucrats did not necessarily have a single view – as became apparent during *perestroika*. In the Soviet Union, as in the West, there were concerns that cut across simple institutional divisions, such as ideological, national, generational, religious, gender and social alignments which to some extent moderated the fundamental division between state and society. The boundaries between groups were blurred and members often acted in several simultaneously. No organisation could consolidate group identity by openly advancing its interests, and interaction between members was limited. Their views as a group were not sanctioned by any formal arrangements such as ballots or elections. There was always the danger of reifying groups, giving them personalities and characteristics, such as selfishness, and forgetting that they were no more than abstract categories.

There was little role for groups beyond the institutional system, although this changed rapidly under Gorbachev. They operated within the framework of the administrative structure rather than appealing to society for support. The imperfect monism was reflected in the 'pluralism of elites' whereby competing forces and interests could be articulated by their leaders within the party and state mechanism. The emphasis on informal groups tended to neglect the centrality of the official groups. The analysis of groups has to be supplemented by analysis of the institutional context in which they operated, and by more nebulous concepts like political culture. The highly formalised but non-constitutionalised nature of political relations endowed Soviet politics with a fluidity that inhibited the consolidation of a patterned structure of group relations. Under Gorbachev groups could take on a more formal identity, but the parallel decay of the constitutional order meant that once again they lacked a juridical framework in which to formulate and pursue their interests and concerns.

The group approach was developed to describe the realities of Western, and above all American, liberal democracy, and hence there is some doubt over its applicability to the Soviet Union. Pluralism *a priori* studies the diffusion of power, which in the Soviet Union is a questionable assumption. The use of the term is a case of what Giovanni Sartori called 'conceptual stretching'. It forces an inappropriate conceptual framework on to a system in which conflicting group influence on policy was both theoretically and practically denigrated, and where power was monopolised to a great extent by a single institution, the communist party. Interest groups in the Soviet Union operated in a very different way from those in the United States. The proliferation of terms – institutional pluralism, bureaucratic pluralism – reflected the hesitancies and qualifications required to apply the concept to the Soviet Union. While the totalitarian approach threatened to reduce the United States and the Soviet Union to mirror images of each other, there was an equal danger in applying the group approach in that the enthusiasm for a value-free approach to the study of the changing Soviet polity led to the exaggeration of similarities between the two. There is a danger of ethnocentrism as familiar images are projected on to the 'other' to tame it. The ethnocentricity in the context of group politics comes down to the belief that groups by definition must be contestatory, the American pattern, whereas in other cultures and political systems groups may be compatible with overall integrative structures. The Farmers' Solidarity in 1980–81 in Poland, for example, refused to see itself simply as a 'lobby' working on behalf of its membership but wished to participate in the general social renewal process.

The theory of pluralism as applied to the Soviet Union does not focus on the autonomy of society but examines fragmentation within the power structure. Divisions could take various forms (individual, professional or institutional) but their ability to influence policy was severely circumscribed. There was some diffusion of influence to specialist and other groupings, but the overwhelming fact about the Soviet political system remained its centralisation. The long-awaited revival of the soviets, for example, came about not through the initiative of the soviets themselves but from the party leadership. The political system historically was able to retain a degree of autonomy from the socio-economic 'base' on which it rested. Social pluralism does not necessarily entail political pluralism: economic and social developments were not automatically reflected in political change in the Soviet system.

Corporatism and other models

The emergence of a number of non-dictatorial but authoritarian one-party systems in the wake of decolonisation stimulated the search for new approaches. A number of theories sought to reconcile the insights of concentration and diffusion models. If totalitarianism was associated with the institutional approach to politics, and group theory with the 'behavioural revolution', then the intermediate models can schematically be identified with the methodology of functionalism which argues that while political systems institutionally may vary widely, certain functions are common to all. Inputs in the form of demands and supports pass through the gatekeeper (parties or interest groups) to the political system, whose outputs take the form of authoritative decisions, which in turn are connected with the inputs by a feedback loop.[28] Functions include political recruitment and socialisation through to policy-making and implementation. Functionalism provides a ready-made arsenal of terms to analyse the Soviet system, though too often the wood got lost in the trees of the verbiage of structural functionalism.

Corporatism is a way of combining 'output' models (totalitarianism) and 'input' models (pluralism). A distinction can be made between 'state corporatism' as practised in Latin America or the USSR, and 'societal corporatist systems' as in Great Britain in the 1970s. The difference is that in the latter the corporatist actors (such as trade unions or employers' organisations) retain the right to organise themselves and choose their own leaders, whereas in state corporatist systems the mass bodies act largely as state organisations, or transmission belts with their leaders imposed on them by the state. But the similarity of corporatism and pluralism is clear since both stress group input in policy formation. However, the theory obviates the necessity of developing a competitive theory of interest participation in the policy process and instead focuses on co-ordination and co-optation.

Corporatism came to take the place of pluralism as a key concept in studying the Soviet polity. In particular, it was applied to explain the compromise between the leadership and various interests during the Brezhnev years. The lifting of Khrushchev's threats to the party and state bureaucrats in 1964 was consolidated by the lack of vigour in pursuing the aims of the 1965 economic reform against the vested interests of the economic bureaucrats. The compromise was broadened during the era of détente to satisfy most sectors of society. The major casualty was labour and factory productivity as incentives were inadequate and industrial investment lagged. Brezhnev's conciliatory policy did little to change the structure of power. The major interests such as the KGB, trade unions, industrial ministries, republican party organisations or research institutes of the USSR Academy of Sciences did not gain the ability either to select their own leaders or openly to articulate their own interests. Their heads were appointed by the *nomenklatura* system, and policy was formed elsewhere. Corporatism developed the furthest in Yugoslavia and to a lesser extent in Hungary and provided a more accurate description of political reality than pluralism: groups were given more autonomy but not freed from the restraints of directed politics. The value of the corporatist model is that it reveals the central paradox of the power system in the Soviet Union: the multiplicity of institutions operating in an uninstitutionalised framework. It helps explain the diversity of groups in the Soviet Union and the limits of group activity. However, it seems anomalous to talk of corporatism, whether societal or state, in the Soviet context given the ideological and organisational strictures against political corporations of any form beyond the direct control of the party. The same 'conceptual stretching' as with pluralism is involved here.

Monist models are similar to corporatism but focus more on the power centre. They incorporate some of the insights of diffusion theories by modifying the idea of the concentration of power while avoiding the pitfalls of totalitarianism. Monist societies are those in which all power is public and rests in the hands of the state, which itself is controlled by a single political ruling group which manages the economy and society. This is rather similar to Rigby's mono-organisational model which examines the means whereby the dominant party and leadership integrated the multiplicity of elites that emerged as society became more diverse under the impact of technological and social change. The pluralism of elites was reflected in the party leadership as the post-totalitarian system developed.

The move away from totalitarianism was accompanied by great interest in convergence models.[29] In the 1960s the idea of convergence seemed to offer a theoretical framework for the common evaluation of industrial societies. Analysis took on a sociological flavour with the emergence of the 'development' model and of the 'mature industrial model'.[30] Classical versions of convergence theory placed American-style pluralism and Soviet-style totalitarianism at opposite ends of an implicit continuum, and suggested that they were moving towards each other as the capitalist state took on more of the functions of planning and social welfare, and the socialist state shed some of its ideology and allowed a certain play to market forces. One of the earliest theorists of this view, impressed by Khrushchev's relative liberalisation and apparent move away from totalitarianism, was Talcott Parsons, whose functionalist approach to world history moved through three stages: primitive, intermediate and modern. The modern stage affected communist countries as much as capitalist ones with new patterns of industrial production and life characterised by state interventionism, bureaucratisation, differentiation of functions and competing interest groups.[31] Parsons argued that pluralist democracy was an 'evolutionary universal', essential to sustain a degree of consensus in a complex system composed of various groups. Such a consensus, he insisted, cannot be achieved in an authoritarian system and thus the efficiency of the system is reduced by the lack of legitimacy.[32]

A gloomier version of convergence was advanced by Herbert Marcuse who saw technological imperatives as integrating the mass of the population not only into the rhythms of factory production but also into the mental condition acceptable to industrial labour processes. The need for overt coercion in East and West decreases as individuals internalise the necessary discipline. People repress themselves and become one-dimensional individuals.[33] Elements of this view, although not from the perspective of convergence, are contained in the idea of a dictatorship over needs. The theory suggests a radical governmental manipulation not only over the physical needs of human beings, but also over their mental lives.[34]

There were many different versions of convergence, yet they all suffered from an economic and political determinism. The argument is a crucial one, since Soviet studies was long haunted by the determinism that asserted that the backwardness of Russian conditions forced the expansion of the state as a substitute for broader social movements such as entrepreneurs or revolutionary workers. The era of stagnation graphically illustrated that industrial development on its own does not weaken the power of a dirigiste power system. The same criticism of determinism can be made of those who hold that the Soviet Union was a transitional society whose development had been arrested midway between capitalism and socialism. From a Marxist perspective the sequence of change from feudalism through capitalism to socialism was historically determined, but the time sequence was not. The whole problem of a prolonged transitional society has been finessed by those who argue in favour of convergence: instead of socialist societies marking a radical divergence, they turn back on themselves to share certain features with capitalist states. The problem remains, even in a post-communist world, to understand what industrial societies have in common while remaining sensitive to their political differences.

One of the more interesting models of Soviet-type societies was the idea of communist neo-traditionalism. The approach accepted the total set of structures pertaining to communist systems as unique and evolving, while stressing the distinctive features employed to achieve the high level of social control typical of these systems. In contrast to the totalitarian emphasis on coercive means of control, it focused on the positive incentives for compliance. The fusion of economic and political power allowed neo-traditionalist systems to reward political loyalty with a patterned system of favours such as career advancement, privileges and status. The theory explored the ambiguity between the demands at the heart of the system for impersonal loyalty and ideological standards of behaviour, and the dense network of patron–client relations through which this loyalty was rewarded. Hence a clientship system was the unintended social effect of party policies. Moreover, this loyalty–reward relationship was posited to be at the heart of regime–society relations. Despite running counter to the party's ideological and organisational principles, the operation of the system encourages 'a rich subculture of instrumental–personal ties through which individuals circumvent formal regulations' to obtain goods, income and career opportunities.[35] These are to be found in political relations and at the workplace. Employment is not primarily a market relationship but the source both of work and of a variety of benefits, cultural life and services. The workplace is also the centre of informal subcultural networks with other workers.

The neo-traditional argument accepted the group approach's view of competition and conflict for resources, but reasserted the centrality of communist political institutions not only in overt political processes but also in social consciousness itself. There was a creative tension between group loyalties and vertical allegiances. Perhaps the greatest insight offered by the neo-traditional image was the rejection of visions of convergence with the advanced capitalist state. It focused on the uniqueness and complexity of communist patterns of rule. There was evolution and change in communist systems, but towards a historically distinctive social formation. The actual features of this formation can be disputed. For neo-traditionalists, the novelty lay in the authority pattern of clientship, characterised by a citizenry dependent on social institutions and leaders.[36] These were modernising societies, but were transformed from within by 'their pattern of economic organisation and the ambiguities of their official ideology and political institutions'.[37] This evolutionary process was set in train from the very first days of the system and hence the model rejected any fundamental contrast between the 'mobilisation' and 'post-mobilisation' phases of Soviet history.

The theory of neo-traditionalism is not used to suggest a system that is not yet 'modern'. Instead, it refers to the changes in Western Europe from the eighteenth century, analysed by Emile Durkheim, Talcott Parsons and others, in which 'the term *tradition* has come to be associated with dependence, deference, and particularism, and the term *modern* with independence, contract and universalism' marked by impersonality and anonymity.[38] The theory of the dictatorship over needs also makes the point that the Soviet system was stamped by a fundamentally pre-Enlightenment set of authority relationships and mindset locked on to a modern industrial context.

We have looked at some of the models which seek to explain the operation of the Soviet political system. All highlight aspects of the system, but each has major drawbacks. Between models which stress the concentration of power and those which highlight its diffusion, intermediary concepts which stress the uniqueness of the Soviet system and take note of the distinctive pattern of evolution seem to be the strongest. In particular, the theory of neo-traditionalism helps explain the fundamental continuity in Soviet politics and the totality of the interaction between the party, ideology and economic organisation and developments in society. This review of models, however, would be incomplete without raising the issue of the nature of the Soviet state and referring back once again to the role of leadership. The pluralist view, which focuses on the societal input into policy formation, clearly must be tempered. The state-dominated structure of power was more than the arena of group conflict: it had interests of its own standing far above all other groups.

The models do highlight various aspects of the operation of the party-state and its relationship to groups and individuals in society. The fundamental paradox is that the diversification of economic, social and political life undermined the classical features of totalitarianism, but there was no breakthrough into a liberalisation of social life or the institutionalisation of pluralism. The state (whose social nature will be examined in Chapter 12) remained absolutely dominant, it was in certain respects not a state at all, permeated by the state-party and deprived of autonomy. Faced with political indeterminacy on a grand scale there was plenty of scope for the proliferation of models. What does appear to be clear, however, is that the Soviet Union can only be understood in its own terms as a unique and changing political formation. The power structure (or regime) was a semi-autonomous actor with interests of its own. Soviet politics was largely the history of state initiatives to control and restructure society, from collectivisation to high-rise housing, and the story of the impact of state policies on society. It was a hitherto unique system where a section of society, the Bolshevik party, took control of the state and proceeded to use it to inaugurate a massive programme of social and political change. Soviet politics was also the story of how, in fits and starts, socio-economic forces and society gradually reduced the autonomy of the state-party and decreased the scope and effectiveness of state initiatives. When these forces took on overtly political forms, the system collapsed. The story of the fall will be the subject of Part V.

KEY TEXTS

Brown, Archie, *Soviet Politics and Political Science* (London, Macmillan, 1974).

Brown, Archie, 'Political Power and the Soviet State', in Neil Harding (ed.), *The State in Socialist Society* (London, Macmillan, 1984), pp. 51–103

Brown, Archie (ed.), *Political Leadership in the Soviet Union* (London, Macmillan, 1988).

Fehér, Ferenc, Agnes Heller and Gyorgy Markus, *Dictatorship over Needs: An Analysis of Soviet Societies* (Oxford, Blackwell, 1983).

Gleason, Abbott, *Totalitarianism: The Inner History of the Cold War* (Oxford, Oxford University Press, 1995).

Harasymiw, Bohdan, *Political Elite Recruitment in the Soviet Union* (London, Macmillan, 1984).

Hough, J., *The Soviet Union and Social Science Theory* (Cambridge, MA, Harvard University Press, 1977).

Janos, A. (ed.), *Authoritarian Politics in Communist Europe* (Berkeley, CA, University of California Press, 1976).

Johnson, Chalmers (ed.), *Change in Communist Systems* (Stanford, CA, Stanford University Press, 1970).

11 Ideology and authority

In the Soviet system power and ideology were explicitly linked. As Lenin put it in *What Is To Be Done?*, 'Without theory there can be no revolutionary movement.' In the pre-revolutionary and Soviet traditions not only did ideas matter, but intellectuals were listened to and respected, if not feared and imprisoned. Censorship can be seen as a back-handed compliment to the power of ideas, something the Old Bolsheviks (those of Lenin's generation) very well understood since many of them were intellectuals themselves. Under Stalin ideas and ideology were gutted of any living content and reduced to mere instruments of power. While Khrushchev might have revived the party, his failure to revive a sphere for open policy debate and to legalise the limited intellectual openings of the thaw period condemned the system to the stagnation of his successors. Under Gorbachev *glasnost* was at first defined in instrumental terms but soon the intellectual ferment burst beyond any bounds that the authorities tried to impose. Lenin's link between ideology and authority was broken, and the system collapsed.

THE MEANING OF IDEOLOGY

The Bolsheviks combined a view of the world made up of three cardinal features. The first, reminiscent of the Populists, was what Bauman calls 'the intellectual idiom', the belief that the world must be changed and that intellectuals know how to change it.[1] The second aspect concerned the actual content of their beliefs, derived from Marxism. The third feature was the distinctively Leninist understanding of a mechanism to make the necessary changes, the revolutionary party. When these three factors came together in the Bolshevik party they were to have an explosive impact on the twentieth century. The Bolsheviks came to power in the service of an idea since they represented, in Bauman's telling phrase, 'the despotism of the enlightened':[2] the belief that they, guided by reason, knew what was best for the people, and the people, once the dark clouds of ignorance were dispelled by education and agitprop, would gladly embrace this vision. Those who failed enthusiastically to respond to the glorious utopia opened up by the Bolshevik revolution were self-evidently not only deluded but criminal, and had to be swept away to allow the people to enter the communist paradise.

The party itself acted, in Antonio Gramsci's words, as the 'collective intellectual', representing, in another of his telling phrases, 'the modern prince'. Hence any analysis of the party's novel organisational features must be supplemented by stressing its intellectual resources. The Bolsheviks were initially intellectuals in power, but even as Stalin destroyed the intellectuals the party clung even more tenaciously to a dogmatised and shrivelled version of the original idea and to the belief that there should be a ruling idea. Ideology and organisation were merged in the body of the party: it was not simply that the ideology buttressed the leading role of the party; or that the party supported the dominance of an ideology. They were organically linked and the one could not survive without the other, although both were susceptible to change.

The problem remains, however, to define the meaning of ideology. Is it a system of beliefs or a mode of action? Marxists talk of *praxis*, the unity of theory and action. In this sense one can talk of the Soviet Union as the active utopia (Bauman) where certain goals were being implemented. In the United States there is a liberal tradition derived from Locke and based on individualism, but when one studies the actual operation of American politics it is clear that the ideology is modified by various class, social, gender, race and other power factors. There were similar if not greater problems in the Soviet Union, with the major difference that Soviet ideology specified its own pre-eminence and explanatory role not only of the present but of the future. The Soviet Union had an official state ideology, believed by some and tolerated by many more, which refers to both what is and what will be, usually adding a rosier hue to both. Anthony Black distinguishes between ethos, the spontaneous convictions of everyday life that Gramsci called 'commonsense'; ideology, the *ad hoc* (and according to Marx not necessarily conscious) presentation of a case; and philosophy, the systematic, rational examination of political norms.[3] Ideology in capitalist societies, according to Marxists, is a system of thought that reflects class interests while professing to express a universal world view. Ideology, in other words, masks the domination of the ruling class.[4] Did ideology play a similar role in the Soviet Union? We will try to use philosophy to understand the relationship between ideology and authority in the USSR.

The elements of Soviet ideology can be summarised in nine bundles of related issues.

1   Soviet ideology was based on dialectical materialism, denoting a philosophical methodology critical of idealism (transcendent or God-based views of humanity) which stresses the notion of continual interaction, of movement and dynamism, in the development of nature, human society and thought. In the dialectical method the thesis comes into contradiction with an antithesis and results in a synthesis at a higher level. The practical application of this methodology is historical materialism in which the changes in society are considered to be derived from the fundamental contradiction between classes based on their different relationship to the means of production. Marx uses the base/superstructure metaphor to illustrate the dependence of the political on the economic. The final stage of the class struggle, according to Marx, was the overthrow of the bourgeoisie (thesis) by the proletariat (antithesis) to result in the transcendence of both (synthesis) in communism.

2   Lenin's major contribution to Marxism was the notion of consciousness, which underlay his theory of party organisation. As we have seen, by 1902 Lenin was impatient with the slow development of the Russian working class and insisted on the need to imbue it with revolutionary class consciousness. This would have to come from outside, which in effect meant intellectuals. For Lenin ideology was not simply a reflection of the material base, the implication of Marx's base/superstructure metaphor, but instead he drew attention to the conscious application of change in history, sometimes called voluntarism. Lenin insisted that revolutions have to be organised, whereas Marx tended to think that history itself would bring the working class to power. Lenin's voluntarism, however, was located firmly in the historicist, or determinist, framework: the revolution was inevitable but needed active assistance. On coming to power Lenin's historicism revealed itself in the belief that since working-class power was inevitable the problems that arose *must* have a solution in history itself, and hence his rudimentary approach to the structure of working-class political power. Lenin was the original exponent of 'guided

democracy' practised under the direction of a vanguard party. Under Stalin the idea of consciousness became an exaggerated theory of Bolshevik activism typified by his statement that there are 'no fortresses that a Bolshevik cannot storm'.

3   Soviet ideology was marked by economism, the belief that the economic substructure of society determines the social relations within that society. Nationalisation of the means of production, for instance, is taken to mean the establishment of socialism since the exploiting classes have been abolished. The idea that new forms of exploitation could emerge based on the social relations within a socialised economy was hardly considered other than by some dissidents. Economism stresses the relationship betwen *things* and not the social relationships between *people*. It subordinates politics to economics, to so-called objective laws. Economism was triumphant during War Communism and lies at the heart of Stalinism. Gorbachev's reform programme stressing the 'human factor' and the quality of social relationships was an explicit condemnation of economism and an implicit rejection of Stalinism. The human face was at last being put back on to socialism.

4   Marxism–Leninism was the cornerstone of Soviet ideology and provided the rationale for the existence of a dominant ruling party. It was said to embody scientific truths about society, and the CPSU claimed that it, and it alone, clearly and correctly understood these truths. The role of the party was defined by the ideology, but the party constantly modified the ideology to take into account changing circumstances. The important point is that, however much it might have changed, Marxism–Leninism was held to represent the truth at any particular time. The concept of a single 'truth' rejects the pluralist conception of partial and many truths. The party was the bearer of revolutionary tradition, hence it had a moral right to rule. The official elements of that tradition, and in particular the history of the CPSU, were incorporated into the Soviet version of Marxism–Leninism to establish a mutually reinforcing relationship between the ideology and party authority. The party became the only legitimate mouthpiece of the working class, even if the working class disagreed with it, because the party claimed to know what was in its best interests. The party alone could decode the processes of history and interpret Marxist ideology. In the absence of war, overriding national tasks, free elections or charismatic leadership, Soviet ideology became ever more important to justify the party's leading role. Marxism–Leninism provided the rationale for the rule of a militant vanguard party taking power in the name of the movement and nation.

5   Marx's great achievement had been to put socialism on an allegedly scientific basis, dispensing with the idealistic dreams of a Robert Owen or a Proudhon, and instead establishing the basis for 'scientific communism' from his study of material life. Marx never tried to provide detailed guidance on the organisation of communist society, and dismissed such attempts as utopian. Scientific communism came to denote the short-range pronouncements on the detailed management of communist states. The revolution underwent many metamorphoses as the domestic commitment to far-reaching change gradually focused on maintaining stability. The 1961 party Programme, for example, talked of the 'comprehensive building of communism by 1980', but as we have seen his successors dropped Khrushchev's grandiose perspectives in favour of more modest ambitions. This was expressed above all in Brezhnev's concept of 'developed socialism', or 'developed socialist society'. After the storms of Stalinism and Khrushchev's flirtation with populism it signalled that the ethos of the new era was technology, professionalism and controlled administrative change.

6   The technocratic element in Soviet ideology should be singled out more specifically. It is a crucial part of the concept of developed socialism and signalled the adaptation of the 'intel-

lectual idiom' to modern industrial society. The increasingly technocratic bias to Soviet ideology suggested that society was no longer to be transformed but to be managed. Brezhnev's concept of developed socialism embodied the 'scientism' implicit in the technocratic ideal buttressed by two supplementary concepts. The first was the 'scientific-technological revolution' (STR) and the second the 'scientific management of society'. The STR reiterated the Marxist and Soviet belief in the leading role of technology in social change, but modified economism by stressing a scientific approach to enterprise management and labour relations. The notion of the scientific management of society only confirmed the role of scientific communism in providing the key to managing social processes. Political and economic management was restricted to a group of 'experts' with a privileged understanding of the allegedly real forces operating at any given time. However, the political restrictions on technocratic power (with a limited autonomy for technical specialists and professionals of whatever stripe) meant that even under Brezhnev one could not talk of the triumph of the technocracy, the allegedly rational and depoliticised solution of existing problems. In the USSR problems were dealt with as political issues rather than as technical problems subject to instrumental rationality alone. Gorbachev condemned the technocratic elements in Brezhnev's rule (the belief that social problems could be resolved by technical means *alone*) and suggested that the concept of developed socialism was premature, but freed the technical and cultural intelligentsia from the restrictions under which they had laboured since the late 1920s.

7   Stalin promoted the fusion of political ideology with social ethos, particularly during the Great Patriotic War when for the first time at the mass level the interests of the regime and the state were seen to correspond. The Brezhnev years witnessed the consolidation of what can be called an official patriotic traditionalism, the merging of an uncritical and bombastic (unreflexive) Russian and Soviet nationalism. The existing was raised to the level of the eternal, stifling critical responses to emerging problems. This was accompanied in Brezhnev's later years by the idea of 'the Soviet way of life' which closed the gap between doctrine and practice by lending the vision of communism a thoroughly Soviet face. The 'Soviet way of life' was a conservative mixture of patriotic xenophobia and self-praise which combined a contempt for 'Western' (liberal–democratic) values with an aggressive nationalism and a submission to paternalistic authority.

8   Soviet ideology was always marked by a strong teleological element, the belief that society was directed towards a historical goal and shaped by a purpose. The view of a rational world to come can lead to de-enlightenment, or irrationality, in the present. During War Communism Soviet communists believed that the future could be attained immediately. After the low-key NEP Stalin used the teleological elements in Soviet ideology to whip the population into a frenzy of expectations which appeared to justify the sacrifices and cruelties. Post-Stalin expectations declined, and Khrushchev's vision of communism in the 1961 Programme was a fairly tame Sovietised version of consumer industrialism. Brezhnev's rule was marked by a sharp decline in ideological enthusiasm and represented a further turn in the downward spiral of expectations: the aim remained 'communism', but the concept appeared more to fulfil the function of filling discursive space rather than having any substantive content or influence on the day-to-day practices of the regime. The stress under Gorbachev returned to the problems of real or existing socialism rather than the socialism of the future. The replacement of enthusiasm with scepticism can be seen as a process of re-enlightenment as rational analysis took the place of irrational expectations, and philosophy the place of ideology.

9   This survey of Soviet ideology is enough to illustrate yet another of its major characteristics, what might be called its rigid flexibility (analogous to the organised chaos in the

administrative sphere): the 'party line' might change, but at every juncture total and uncritical obedience was demanded. It is not clear whether the many shifts witnessed by the ideology since 1917 represented fundamental changes or simply the adaptation of the old ideology to new circumstances. The very premiss of dialectical materialism permits flexible, or dialectical, responses to actual processes. Hence, as Basily pointed out in 1938, the communist party 'differs from ordinary political bodies just as much by the rigidity of its doctrines as by the extreme instability of its immediate programme'.[5] Zaslavsky attributes the combination of stability and flexibility to the extraordinary explanatory strength and absorptive capacity of Marxism, its role as the sole official ideology in a single-party system (organised factions and feuds within the party were banned and hence intellectual debate limited), and the role that Marxism played as the dominant ideology of the international communist movement.[6] The operating ideology underwent change whereas the solid core provided stability.

Marxism–Leninism remained the hegemonic force in cultural and political life, but its hegemony was not derived from its innate dynamism but from its institutionalisation as the 'state religion'. While weakened as a rational explicatory or predictive force, it remained at the centre of the Soviet power system. Marxism–Leninism contributed to a novel body of thought and belief termed Soviet ideology, an amalgam of Marxism, traditional socialist precepts, the Bolshevik (or Leninist) interpretation of Marxism, and the traditions and experience of seventy years of Soviet power. It operated within the context of a socialist economic basis, the political monopoly of the CPSU, a leadership cult focused on Lenin, the universal application of the principle of democratic centralism, and the memory of the revolutionary and Soviet past. The stability of Soviet ideology was derived in part from the fact that it was not primarily used as a means of intellectual exchange or debate but as part of a structure of authority. It was modified in response to the needs of the power system rather than to new currents of intellectual thought. The Soviet ideology as here defined was synonymous with the beliefs and actions of the Soviet power system. Over the years Soviet ideology became transformed into the ethos of the system, and by the same token lost some of the characteristics of philosophy.

THE IDEOLOGICAL APPARATUS

Historical materialism is determinist in its belief that people are conditioned by their social environment; or as Marx put it, 'being determines consciousness'. The new communist society would produce a new person as the previous one had produced the old. However, instead of a new social consciousness arising spontaneously, the Soviet Union maintained a massive apparatus of ideological persuasion and control to make the 'new Soviet person'. Soviet practice conceded that consciousness could be changed irrespective of material conditions. The ideology which once inspired a small group of revolutionaries was now, with modifications, imposed upon the rest of society as the only truth. The ideology was binding; otherwise it would become ineffective. Just as in the administrative sphere Soviet democracy called for the guidance of an elite political organisation, so in the realm of ideas guidance was similarly required.

The ideological apparatus that emerged under Lenin was massively strengthened under Stalin. The party intervened directly, for example, in literary politics. In 1925 the party's Central Committee declared that the class war had not ended on the literary front, and pronounced that neutral art was impossible. This resulted in draconian measures to impose unity on literature. During the cultural revolution from 1928 cultural and intellectual life was mobilised in a systematic way. Only after the cultural revolution had spent its energy by about 1931, however, did all spheres of academic and cultural life, in economics, philosophy, psychology, education and history, become subordinated to the needs of the party apparatus and Stalin personally. In 1932 socialist realism was proclaimed as the only acceptable form of literature and in 1934 this was given organisational status by the formation of the Union of Soviet Writers. In biology this period saw the triumph of Trofim Lysenko's spurious genetic theories. In history Mikhail Pokrovskii's school of historiography, which concentrated on the role of the masses and revolutionary traditions in Russian history, was replaced by a greater stress on the national progressive role of monarchs, implying that Stalin the Great was carrying on the traditions of a Peter or Catherine. The consolidation of Stalinism was accompanied by the uneasy coalescence of patriotic traditionalism with Marxism–Leninism. The ideological apparatus was designed to propagate the ideology, popularise the current shifts and to ensure that the leadership could control the direction and degree of its flexibility.

Censorship lay at the heart of the system of ideological restriction, even though it had been strongly opposed by Marx, and Rosa Luxemburg argued that 'Freedom only for the supporters of the government, only for the members of one party – however numerous they may be – is no freedom at all. Freedom is always and exclusively for the one who thinks differently.'[7] Lenin from the first took a radically diffferent view, and one of his first acts on coming to power in October 1917 was to close down the bourgeois press to control the flow of ideas. Victory in the Civil War saw the final suffocation of an independent press. Cultural and literary restrictions to varying degrees stultified Soviet intellectual life from then onwards. Glavlit (the Main Administration for Safeguarding State Secrets in the Press) was the organiser of censorship. Formed in 1922, by 1934 it had the power to control the press and journals, to remove books from libraries, decide which books would be published, and license imported publications. In libraries and museums there were 'special stores' in which allegedly controversial matter was kept for the use of trusted people. The methods of the censorship can be compared to the Black Book of Polish Censorship, a publication smuggled to the West in the late 1970s giving detailed instructions to the censors. Censorship is at its most effective when it is invisible, giving life an impression of immutable reality rather than being contingent on the whims of a bevy of censors. Once the censorship becomes visible, with blank spaces in papers, it loses its credibility. A law on the mass media in Gorbachev's early years shifted the emphasis away from direct censorship towards more subtle forms of editorial control. Glavlit's functions were reduced and were supplemented by a council of editors which monitored the 8,000 newspapers and 5,000 magazines published in the USSR in 1988. Only in July 1990 did a new law on the press effectively abolish preliminary censorship.

One of the main functions of the ideological apparatus was to insulate the Soviet Union from foreign influences. The trial of Sinyavsky and Daniel in February 1966, marking the end of Khrushchev's relative liberalism, was prompted by the publication of their works abroad. Already Boris Pasternak had been viciously criticised in the Soviet press in 1958 for having published his masterpiece, *Doctor Zhivago*, abroad, a work for which he received (but was not able to collect in person) the Nobel Prize for Literature. Laws passed in 1966 included the new Article 190 of the RSFSR Criminal Code, making it an offence to disseminate in oral or written form 'conscious fabrication discrediting the Soviet state'. The definition of 'fabrication' was left to the authorities. Post from abroad was strictly controlled and foreign radio stations, in particular broadcasts by the CIA-sponsored Radio Liberty based in Munich, jammed, despite the enormous expense involved.

Political education and the agitprop apparatus were used to mobilise the population to build communism. As noted in Chapter 9, mass organisations such as the trade unions and Komsomol were vehicles not only of participation but also of socialisation. Each major party committee had ideology and agitprop sections. At the local level the PPOs (Primary Party Organisations) played a key role, supplemented by a widespread system of closed lectures delivered at workplaces and a network of circles (*kruzhki*) for political and party enlightenment. Socialisation was reinforced through the Soviet festival and ritual system, notably the May Day and 7 November (the anniversary of the Bolshevik seizure of power, New Style calendar) parades, which inculcated the ideology in a particularly vivid manner. The Soviet victory in the Second World War was used to imbue the population with patriotic values in the system of civic education.

The ideology was used as a social integrator and acted as a supra-national unifying force over and above national, religious and ethnic divisions. The language and mission of socialist transformation served to establish the parameters of acceptable behaviour and beliefs. It was axiomatic in Soviet ideology that dissent would naturally wither away as the social basis for it disappeared. But in keeping with Bolshevik voluntarism, and the inevitable authoritarianism of the 'despotism of the enlightened', the stubborn persistence of dissent was ascribed to the pathological inadequacies of individuals rather than manifestations of social imbalance. A massive apparatus existed to ensure the withering away of alternative ways of thought through both coercion and by socialisation. The ideological apparatus tried to inculcate in social consciousness not only hopes for a better tomorrow but also the view that the Soviet present was, despite its shortcomings, preferable to any other system. Under Gorbachev this increasingly hollow 'propaganda of success' gave way to a more sober examination of past and present inadequacies while looking with growing pessimism towards the future.

The socialisation effort was clearly flawed and, while not without success in shaping the attitudes of a broad swathe of the population, increasingly lost its grip on reality. It competed with a variety of other influences such as material life, careers and family interests. By the 1980s it became increasingly clear that the years in which the agitprop apparatus had claimed growing numbers of meetings both organised and attended, and more propaganda pamphlets published had not seen the development of the desired new person. The sheer statistical enumeration of agitprop activity said little about its effectiveness. Respect for ideology among the young appeared extremely low: classes in Marxist–Leninist ideology were to be endured rather than enjoyed. The younger generation numbed by Brezhnevite crassness was a particularly alienated group.[8] Becoming aware of the problem, the Politburo in September 1987 called for 'drastic improvements' in the system of political education, but the time had passed when such exhortations could influence social processes.

Cultural policy during *perestroika* revealed a tremulous uncertainty about the degree to which the party could allow the various cultural associations greater freedom. Brezhnevite functionaries were replaced, often by people who had seen their work shelved during the era of stagnation. The removal of the minister of culture, Peter Demichev, in 1986 was accompanied by criticism that the ministry had usurped some of the rights of the CC Secretariat in cultural affairs; the attempt to overcome the administrative autonomy devolved to ministries under Brezhnev was accompanied by attempts to enhance the authority of the party. The intervention by leading writers in public issues was encouraged as long as it was supportive of the broader goals of *perestroika*. The lessons of the Khrushchev years, which capitalised on the writers' ability to mobilise popular feelings in the destalinisation campaign but unleashed forces that it could not control, had been learned.

Rosa Luxemburg's main argument against censorship was that the lack of criticism would lead to bureaucratism and corruption. In this she was amply proved correct, and Gorbachev's *glasnost* campaign was clearly an instrumental attempt to use greater openness to expose corruption and inadequacies. *Glasnost* did not signify the end of censorship or editorial control; it did mean, though, a greater willingness to tolerate the public expression of ideas as long as it remained within a broadly constructive framework. It represented the reconstitution of the rationality implied in Marxism, the belief that the ideology was a scientific doctrine rather than a utopian project. *Glasnost* represented a weakening of the demand for belief in the infallibility of the party or the interpreters of ideology and thus broadened the scope for debate. Only when *glasnost* gave way to freedom of spech, however, did the residue of party instrumentalism give way to a genuinely free public sphere. By then, unfortunately, financial and other pressures forced editors to play more to the gallery to increase circulation, and the familiar problems of the Western media came to haunt Russia.

THE ROLE OF IDEOLOGY

Ideologies inspire, justify and inhibit actions, but the precise combination of the three always remains a matter of judgement. The Marxist classics and Lenin offered no detailed guidelines about the policy choices of an urbanised, educated and increasingly computer-literate society. While there was no doubt about the centrality of ideology to the Soviet system, its precise role remains a matter of controversy. Was it a set of fundamental principles, a doctrine, remaining in the background, or was it an action programme determining policy? These contrasting views were reflected in the debate between Solzhenitsyn and Sakharov. Solzhenitsyn argued that the Soviet state was guided by the overarching influence of Marxist ideology and that it had been responsible for all the disasters that had befallen the Soviet people. The only way forward lay in the country's liberation from the stifling ideology.[9] These views were echoed by commentators such as Vladimir Bukovskii, Alexander Shtromas, Robert Conquest and Richard Pipes, who insisted that the West's reluctance to take Soviet ideology seriously imperilled its own security. They argued that it was an act of naivety to project Western values on to the 'power seekers' and 'hegemonists' in the Kremlin. On the other hand, Sakharov argued that the official state ideology was dead and that it was no longer taken seriously. It was therefore ridiculous to imagine that it could guide and shape practical policies. From this perspective R. V. Daniels argued that Marxism–Leninism was very much subordinate to factors like Russian political culture in shaping policy.

Both views reflect aspects of the truth, but any analysis which does not place ideology at the centre of the Soviet power system distorts the reality of Soviet politics. The Soviet state had ideology built into its foundations to inspire and legitimise its actions and its very existence. The government itself justified the political system in terms of its relationship to Marxism–Leninism. And yet too often, even when the centrality of ideology was recognised, it was applied as a very blunt explanatory instrument. The antinomies expressed by the Sakharov–Solzhenitsyn debate are fundamentally misleading. Ideology was not an external device to be utilised as circumstances permitted but lay at the heart of the system of power.

The relationship of ideology to policy-making remains ambivalent. The question arises whether the ideology was a guide to action or its justification: inspirational (sincere) or instrumental (hypocritical)? Did it inspire policies or was it simply used to justify them? Was it inhibitive (preventing certain things happening) or proactive? One thing is clear: the ideology was absolutely indispensable to the operation of the Soviet system irrespective of how seriously it was taken or how crudely it was presented. This does not mean that in each and every decision ideological considerations were dominant. Decisions were taken within the context of an evolving Soviet ideology which continually modified Marxism–Leninism in the light of current needs. Marxism–Leninism was part of the power structure of the Soviet Union but it did not serve as a blueprint for building communist society. The most that it could do was to identify the broad goals and assess the policies that were compatible with the building of communism. Just as the ideology retained a certain autonomy from the power structure, so the structure of decision-making was not wholly dependent on the ideology.

All policies were expressed in ideological terms, their alleged contribution to the strengthening of communism, but in detailed policy-making there was a balance between ideological and practical influences. Soviet policy was always severely practical in foreign and domestic policies. The operating ideology restricted the type of demands that could be made by society, but it did not significantly reduce the freedom of manoeuvre of the power elite. Soviet history is the story of the flexible application of 'communist ideology', and indeed Stalinism can be defined as the subordination of the means to the end. Few, if any, policy options were excluded (inhibited) by the ideology as long as they could be made compatible with an evolving ideology of socialism. While the decollectivisation of agriculture or the denationalisation of industry would have been difficult to square with Soviet ideology, a way (as in Poland) might have been found in case of necessity. In foreign policy the ideology did not prevent a pact with Hitler's Germany or the invasion of fellow socialist states. The ideology as such did not specify the preponderance of heavy over light industry: that was a consequence of the preferences of a specific leadership group. A distinction is to be drawn between the ideology and the party line, the current political expedient based on immediate political considerations. A broad flexibility in tactics was permitted within the general strategic line. However, rather than practice determining ideology, the ideology offered a way of identifying the interests and demands compatible with the overall goal. The flexibility of the ideology was often manifest in current policies, but its rigidity derived from the idea of an ideal society towards which the present society should be guided. Marxism–Leninism became less of a prescription for action than a set of loose goals.

Alfred Meyer defined Soviet ideology as operating in two distinctive modes. In the first the ideology provided a language or a code for communication in the political sphere; and in the second it affirmed certain values which served to legitimate the role of leadership.[10] The philosopher Leszek Kolakowski argues that the ideology in Soviet-type systems was used primarily to legitimise the monopoly of power.[11] The irreducible element of Soviet ideology was the maintenance of the leading role of the party. The formulation of this changed from the dictatorship of the proletariat to the state of all the people, but in the Soviet Union as elsewhere no communist system challenged this fundamental idea, although in practice Stalin and other charismatic leaders displaced the party as a functioning political institution. However, while it is probably unduly restrictive to argue that the main role of Soviet ideology was to maintain the existing political system, it is difficult to see how the regime could have survived without an explicit ideology. Its abandonment (as urged by Solzhenitsyn) might well have strengthened a modified system, but that system would already have been a long way towards becoming something else. In Eastern Europe major changes did take place, but the operative ideology had been *Soviet*, generated by an alien historical and political experience. Although communist ideology in the Soviet Union was increasingly buttressed by other legitimating factors such as victory in the war or rising standards of living, the party's special relationship to ideology continued to justify its dominant role in the system. Its task remained to interpret and fulfil the laws of social development.

From at least the 1950s there was much talk about the end of ideology in the Soviet Union. Such statements meant several things. First, it depends on what aspect of ideology one has in mind, whether Marxism, Leninism, generically communist or Soviet ideology. One could mean that no one believes in the ideology any more. For the Soviet Union this would probably have been an exaggeration, although in the sense that Marxism–Leninism in the Soviet Union was no longer regarded as infallible, that the communist utopia for an increasing number of Soviet citizens was no longer considered desirable, let alone achievable, the statement that ideology was dead was correct. The process has been seen as the 'rationalisation' or 'de-ideologisation' of the communist movement as it lost its earlier chiliasm in favour of more limited and incremental objectives.[12] Communist rule changed from mobilising to managing the society through rational organisation. The Soviet Union, according to this view, shared certain aspects of modernity and could be studied in comparative political science terms. This process, if anything, accelerated under Gorbachev's practical and flexible approach, although the reforms remained situated in the old ideological framework. While teleology had become a minor chord in the symphony of Soviet ideology, the dirigiste implications of the planned transformation of society remained.

Convergence theory and concepts of advanced industrial society hold that ideology will decline as power is devolved to specialist groupings and government becomes more instrumental. Daniel Bell in the late 1950s predicted that 'The STR [scientific-technical revolution] … inevitably leads to the end of ideology … It always and everywhere produces commonality in technology and methods of industrial leadership, the development of similar ways of life among all peoples, and common social problems.'[13] This may well have been correct, but it was at least thirty years premature. It presupposed a convergence of industrial societies, whereas two very different models of advanced industrial society existed, the Western and the Soviet type. In the West the emergence of a relatively affluent consumer-based economy eased class conflicts compared to the first stages of industrialisation, but in the Soviet Union ideology was not rooted in the conflict of social classes but in the supremacy of the communist party reinforced by the vitality of Soviet patriotic traditionalism. The ideology became vested in a cohesive, bureaucratic, autonomous ruling elite, although the role of ideology cannot be reduced to the exercise of power. The component parts of Soviet ideology affected different groups in different ways, but as the coherence of the ideology declined each separate element became magnified and acted as the basis of intensified group or class conflict. John Dunlop saw the decay of Marxist–Leninist ideology taking a path towards the development of nationalist and religious feelings.[14] Hough argued that the ideology was declining and that its growing ambiguity allowed the increased vitality of public policy debate.[15] In the event it became clear that greater debate signified not greater confidence on the part of the power structure or any change in the role of ideology but an attempt to broaden the regime's base faced with the decay of its own rule. Growing ideological flexibility did not signify the reconstitution of a public sphere.

The death of Brezhnev permitted a profound debate over the content and role of ideology in the Soviet Union. Shortly after his accession in his speech on the hundredth anniversary of the death of Marx in January 1983, Andropov revealed a slightly more pragmatic approach in arguing for a re-evaluation of the role of ideology:

> To verify one's actions by the principles of Marx, of Marxism–Leninism, is by no means to
> compare mechanically the process of life with certain formulas. We would be worthless

followers of our teachers if we satisfied ourselves with a repetition of truths they had discovered and relied on the magic power of quotations once learned by heart. Marxism is not a dogma but a living guide to action, to independent work on complicated problems we are faced with at every new turn of history … We Soviet communists are proud to belong to the most influential ideological movement in the entire history of world civilisation – Marxism–Leninism.[16]

While he asserted that all the antagonistic contradictions had been resolved by the transition from capitalism to socialism, non-antagonistic ones remained that could not be ignored. Battle was joined at the June 1983 'ideological plenum' of the CC. Andropov spoke in favour of the 'creative use of ideology'. Marxism, he argued, does not give answers in ideology once and for all. Chernenko countered, however, by asserting that 'there are eternal verities, some truths which cannot be changed'. His was the voice of an old generation unremittingly hostile to the modernisation of the ideology. Andropov, in contrast, insisted that changes in the productive forces required changes in production relations and he attacked 'formalism' and 'mechanical repetition'. Gorbachev continued Andropov's arguments with a renewed vigour. At the January 1987 CC plenum he argued that the party's theory was fixed in an outdated mould dating from the 1930s, implying that it was marked by Stalinist dogmatism and authoritarianism buttressing a conservative bureaucratic machinery. Gorbachev insisted that the Soviet system required democracy like 'the air we breathe'. However, at the plenum he insisted that he was not proposing a new theory for the period. Hence, as Zhores Medvedev notes, 'although Gorbachev did talk about theory, he did not actually talk theoretically'.[17] This might well be regarded as the epitaph of his reforms, with Gorbachev never really coming to grips with the profound theoretical questions raised by what he assumed could be simultaneously radical *and* incremental reforms. Lacking a clear sense of direction other than trying to humanise the existing system, by 1990 he had lost his ideological way entirely.

Much of the fascination of the Soviet system (and the source of its early dynamism) was the combination of incompatible elements, such as Marx's condemnation of censorship with one of the most severe censorship regimes in the world, the belief in popular self-management combined with the radical negation of popular control, and the belief in communism as a world system while confined to a single country. The Andropov–Chernenko debate and Gorbachev's vigorous approach illustrate that Soviet ideology retained the capacity for critical reflection. It was forced to adapt as an act of survival in order to avoid suffocating from its own complacency. Paradoxically, in the final debate over reform, ideology, considered the force most resistant to change, proved to be the sphere where reformers achieved their greatest successes in reinterpreting the demands of the Soviet polity. Alexander Yakovlev's thinking represented a sharp break with Suslov's dogmatic inflexibility, yet this failed to compensate for the failure to build a sustainable reform coalition encompassing the groups who would most radically become the subjects of reform, above all the governmental and party bureaucracy itself. Gorbachev's greatest achievement was not to bury the ideology, but to make it responsive to the requirements of modern Soviet society. But for too long all statements about beliefs and policies were still couched in the language of Marx and cast in terms of their loyalty to Lenin's bequest, and despite the greater sense of possibilities of interpretation of the sacred canon this proved insufficient to reforge belief in the Soviet project. The discussion was over means not ends and until the Soviet system passed away it was premature to speak of the end of ideology.

POWER, POLITICAL CULTURE AND LEGITIMACY

Soviet ideology exercised a mobilising function to justify the common ownership and management of large-scale property. It legitimated a fundamentally asocial political practice in which social forms of life were subordinated to goals generated beyond the real-life experience of the people. At its most violent peaks in the 1930s (comparable to the Chinese cultural revolution of 1966–76) the system lurched towards its own self-destruction and was forced to modify the extremism of its other-worldliness. From the first, the enthusiasm of enlightenment, couched in the language of development and historical progress, provided the Soviet system with enormous reserves of popular support, even during its most sanguinary periods. Stalinism was not based purely on coercion but on a great degree of popular support for policies such as collectivisation and industrialisation. The image of a totalitarian regime dominating an atomised society through power techniques alone is exaggerated. The element of coercion in the Stalinist polity was projected as a necessary response to external crises and domestic emergency within the context of a culture of despotism buttressed by the *dirigisme* implicit in the ideology. Stalinist 'order' and paternalism, even in post-communist Russia, still evoke a certain nostalgia.

Gramsci's insights on the role of hegemony in capitalist society are applicable to the Soviet system. Gramsci modified the traditional Marxist view of the state as an instrument of coercion and in its place developed an expanded view of the state as based on both coercion and consent. Consent was achieved through hegemony, described by Gramsci as intellectual and moral leadership as opposed to dictatorship or domination. His ideas were taken up by Eurocommunists in the notion of a 'democratic' road to socialism eschewing the need for insurrectionary politics, and were reflected in the Action Programme of the Czechoslovak communists in 1968. Domination gives way to leadership, and the idea of the dictatorship of the proletariat was replaced by the concept of the hegemony of the working people. Yet in the context of the reaffirmation of the leading role of the party, the formal nature of much participation and the sustained low level of coercion, the achievement of consent operated in a radically different way from in the West.[18] The immediate aspirations of the population and the welfare and paternalistic policies of the regime at a basic level coincided. Prices until 1988 remained reasonably stable and the disciplinarian policies of the government gave the appearance of sustaining a high degree of 'law and order'. If democracy is defined as consent to rule, then the USSR was clearly a highly democratic system: open dissent was restricted to the margins of political life. To a degree, however, this consent was manufactured: the ideological apparatus was responsible for the bureaucratic organisation of consensus, while the coercive apparatus mopped up the rest. Yet that is not the whole story. Consent to state policies does not take place in a vacuum but within the context of social, economic and psychological relations. Models of the state based on consent or coercion, dictatorship or democracy, bureaucracy or participation are designed to further the analysis of how precisely the state under socialism really functioned.

The concept of political culture is a broad one and is used in many senses. Political culture should be distinguished from Soviet ideology, the belief system of the authority structure. Political culture refers to both the operational pattern of decision-makers and the general psychological attitudes of the public. It is a concept that can be tested in specific cases of decision-making only with great difficulty. For example, the decision to invade Czechoslovakia in 1968 can be cited as an expression of Russian political culture in its attitude to neighbouring peoples. But such a statement is fairly meaningless; the Russian people were not asked about the invasion, and a small group protested against it in Red Square. The term is usually restricted to analysis of the general context of decisions and processes. Tucker retreats from using the concept of political culture to explain specific processes, and refers to it as 'a complex of real and ideal culture patterns, including political roles and their inter-relations, political structures, and so on'.[19] Archie Brown stresses that the best way to use the term is in terms of subjective orientation. Beliefs and values are to be kept distinct from behaviour.[20]

The study of Soviet politics suffered grievously from the tendency to replace ideological determinism by a historical determinism based on political culture. The practices of the present were monolithically ascribed to the traditions of the past. The alleged congruence between elite values and popular aspirations was ascribed to the influence of a historically determined political culture whose major features were listed in Chapter 1. The historical experience of leadership from above and lack of formal restraints on the state within a centralised power structure, with few formal channels for popular involvement in politics and the lack of accountability of rulers, were the key features of the continuity theorists. Other factors included common attitudes towards authority and the state and the sense that there was a primordial legitimacy vested in a powerful Russian state as defender of the borders and provider in a paternalistic way of security and economic welfare. Another feature is the weakness of individualism in an economic and social sense. This was reflected in the under development of representative institutions and a traditional lack of focus on the role of law. In particular, hierarchy and bureaucratism are argued to have been transferred from Tsarism to the Soviet Union.

It would be more accurate to focus on the distinctive Bolshevik combination of ideology and organisation rather than on Russian political culture. The new system borrowed the elements of the old regime which were considered necessary for its own survival, rather than being burdened by a choiceless past. Even though Stalin has been seen as the 'Red Tsar' continuing a tradition of strong monarchs, he achieved a radical transformation of society that would have been incomprehensible to the Romanovs with their religious and traditional values. The Tsars aimed to conserve and defend, whereas the Bolsheviks aimed to destroy and transform.[21]

The Russian past was made up of many contradictory elements and the concept of political culture cannot explain why some traditional patterns were incorporated into modern social and institutional structures, while others were undermined and destroyed. Survival or destruction of earlier forms depended on their relationship to institutional or cultural patterns that served to perpetuate the Soviet system. The mechanics of this relationship must be examined. The fundamental question is whether modern forms were grafted on to traditional structures or cultural norms and were thus subverted by them and forced to conform to older forms; or whether the older forms only survived because of their utility to the new social formation. The answer probably lies somewhere in between. Thoroughly modern functions were performed in the guise of traditional institutions. In any case, a very large proportion of Soviet practices had no counterpart in pre-revolutionary traditions.

The debate over political culture contains an apologetic element: that Soviet socialism may well have worked better if only Russia had been been different, if it had had more democratic institutions, and if it had not been tainted by oriental despotism and Byzantine mysticism, and if the working class had been stronger and the peasantry less numerous. This is the argument put forward by Trotskyists and others who seek to distance socialism as a world movement from its specific fate in the Soviet Union. For them Soviet communism was 'Marxism reflected in a samovar'. This simply will not do: the form that socialism took in the Soviet Union was one possible evolutionary path contained within it – not inevitable, but nor was it totally contingent on factors pertaining to Russia alone.

An important facet of political culture is the relationship between popular attitudes and the structure of political power, a question that can be examined under the heading of legitimacy. It is clear that major changes had taken place since the era of high Stalinism and that the basis of the legitimacy of the Soviet regime had to some extent changed. Max Weber identified three main 'pure' types of legitimacy. The first is based on 'traditional domination', sanctioned by the preservation of ancient customs and based on patrimonial and patriarchal values. In a Soviet-type system traditional legitimacy 'is not seen as rooted in an "eternal past" but in the promise of a "better tomorrow"'. It is based on the 'belief in the inevitability and immutability of a given order, in the idea that no alternative to it can be conceived'.[22] The second is charismatic legitimation, where the individual leader, endowed with almost supernatural gifts, is venerated in the religious and political spheres. Examples are prophets, elected war lords, or political party leaders. The third type is based on 'legality', the acceptance of legal norms and a rational order in which each performs functions based on rules. The executives of the modern state and its bureaucracy fall within this category. The cult of personality under Stalin represented a form of charismatic rule. However, even under Lenin and towards the end of the USSR elements of charismatic legitimation were 'routinised' in the collective personality of the communist party. The charisma of the post-Stalin leader, in theory, was only the reflected brilliance of the party. In addition, as time passed there was an increasing development of legitimation based on the 'legal' processes of party governance in a developed and stable society. However, the bureaucratic nature of Soviet rule, one of its most distinctive features, never fully became rule in a bureaucratic way, marked by clearly delineated rules, the demarcation of functions and an end to arbitrariness in administrative and judicial procedures. At that stage the legitimacy of the Soviet regime would have been based on legality, and the charismatic or 'heroic' features would have correspondingly declined. Instead, the Soviet system increasingly adopted the characteristics of a fourth form of legitimation identified by Leslie Holmes as 'eudaemonism', based on performance in achieving certain (increasingly materially based) goals.[23]

The basis of the Soviet regime's legitimacy changed over time. It shifted away from ideological and programmatic grounds to the regime's identification with the creation of the industrial basis of socialism. The growing complexity of the system generated a thick web of social relationships relatively independent of the power relations of the system, and the purely ideological forms of legitimation necessarily waned. The third type of Weberian legitimacy, the rational-legal, became increasingly important, accompanied by increasing prominence for relatively de-ideologised eudaemonic goals. Here social demands could be given a legal orientation with rules and procedures for achieving consensus, the elements of a genuine social contract. But in the absence of the full emergence of a rational-legal order a series of socially generated forms of legitimation arose to fill the gap, such as defence of the national territory and patriotic traditionalism. Gorbachev's attempts to create a socialist legal state provided opportunities for philosophical challenges to be mounted against Soviet ideology on the grounds of rationality.

Among the latter-day bases of legitimacy was a characteristic identified by F. Fehér, the role of paternalism as a mode of legitimation. The regime acted as a benevolent and protective entity which removed both the fear of disorder and constituted (to use Eric Fromm's expression) a 'fear of freedom'. The terror meant death for many, but for others the Stalinist system obviated the need for independent thought or initiative. The death of Stalin allowed the emergence of paternalism to replace charismatic legitimation. As part of the neo-Stalinist compromise, paternalistic dictatorship helped consolidate a fundamentally authoritarian system by making it responsive to the needs of the population. Arbitrary terror was removed but a degree of paternalistic coercion was ingrained in the system. The neo-Stalinist compromise permitted a slow improvement in living standards, but at the price of the continued depoliticisation of society as the state retained a monopoly of political life. State paternalism was allied to the maintenance of a conservative family pattern which, according to Fehér, sustains the 'authoritarian personality'.[24]

The battle for legality, socialist or otherwise, gained the support of all post-Stalin leaders. This can be given a sociological perspective, with the rising modern strata of officialdom and technical specialists seeking to consolidate their gains in legal form. For the polity also, legality became an increasing political necessity as the period of revolutions from above came to an end. The consolidation of legality became the concern of one of the most effective of the Soviet Union's 'interest groups', the jurists.[25] Whether consciously or not, the jurists provided the basis for the development of the Soviet system into a state governed by law, a socialist *Rechtsstaat*. Gorbachev's own legal training helped make legal reform an essential part of *perestroika*.

By Brezhnev's last years indications of a fundamental 'legitimacy crisis' became apparent in the Soviet Union. For Habermas a legitimation crisis (as applied to advanced capitalist states) is marked by the increasing inability of the political-administrative system to manage the economy.[26] The Soviet Union for a long time managed to avert a moment of fundamental breakdown caused by a legitimacy crisis comparable to Hungary in 1956 or Poland in 1980–81. Disappointed expectations gave rise to general dissatisfaction but whether this constituted a full-scale crisis in political legitimacy remains debated. The strength of the communist vote in early post-communist Russia and of the old elites in most other republics suggests otherwise. Gorbachev's reforms posed new challenges and it might be argued that it was their very incoherence that hastened the collapse. We shall return to these questions in Chapter 17.

For Pye and Verba political culture represents the structure of popular attitudes which provide the context in which the authority system operates,[27] although the two may or may not be congruent. Almond and Verba went on to provide a threefold classification of political culture: parochial, subject and participant. In the parochial culture the political system is regarded as something outside the individual's life experience. In the subject culture individuals have passive relationships to politics, and while they are aware of government they do not participate in it but simply react to political output. A participant culture entails interest and involvement in policy-making.[28] Soviet political culture in this scheme had changed from being overwhelmingly subject-parochial towards a more subject-participant form – a civic culture supportive of democratisation was emerging.

The measurement of change in the USSR is hampered by the lack of broad social survey data, yet there was sufficient evidence to permit broad generalisations. Emigré studies of the 1950s showed that there was a basic level of support among the Soviet population for the Soviet system and a belief in the Soviet future. They showed a great deal of support for ideas of discipline, authority and welfare, and civil liberties did not rank highly among their preoccupations.[29] While economic concerns remained dominant, human rights took on a much higher profile following the Helsinki process. The Soviet Interview Project of the 1980s showed that despite a generally high level of satisfaction in the USSR there were some worrying features, especially the sense of alienation provoked by the lack of incentives and poor work organisation among the 'brightest and the best', those at the educational and professional peaks.[30] The old ideological input was increasingly ineffective and could no longer project an attractive vision of the future. The 1980s in particular were marked by a decline in optimism. This was marked among intellectuals, disappointed by the reversal of destalinisation, the crushing of the liberalisation processes in Czechoslovakia and Poland, and the general tightening of political controls up to the mid-1980s. The falling growth rate depressed living standards, but the main criticisms were directed against the poor level of public services, in particular health, education and social welfare. There was a shift of interest to the personal sphere. The regime was unable to shed its heavy-handed paternalism while retaining the popularly approved 'order'. Stephen White's review of Soviet and Western materials confirmed the conclusion of the earlier survey that the Soviet 'system' achieved a broad degree of legitimacy, in that such policies as high welfare provision and public ownership of the means of production were popular, but the 'regime' or the institutions of the political system failed to gain a similar legitimacy.[31]

The rationality crisis over resolving the conflicting demands of various sections of society became ever sharper. The myth of 'non-antagonistic' interests managed for the good of all by the communist party finally gave way to the realisation that the effective crisis management of the system was achieved by damping down various demands rather than by integrating them to strengthen the system. In contrast to most East European countries, which could draw on national traditions, the absence of a vision of what the alternative order could be in the Soviet Union sustained the legitimacy of the existing system until Gorbachev's reforms allowed new national subjects to emerge in the Soviet political process – above all the fifteen national republics. Soviet-type regimes ultimately were more concerned with staying in power than with maintaining their legitimacy, a short-sighted approach that led to their downfall. They abandoned mass terror, but in its place had recourse to more subtle but no less sustained forms of oppression.[32] They were unable to turn the evolutionary potential of society into the creative renewal of the regime; instead, each new idea and social initiative was considered subversive and destroyed.

Such an approach helps explain the apparent paralysis and schematic nature of reforms in Soviet-type systems: reforms endangered the political and social supremacy of the political and administrative elites even though they would have considerably enhanced the legitimacy of the socialist system. The socialist idea itself was weakened by coming to mean no more than what the ruling group said it meant. Not surprisingly, the ideology became artificial and increasingly took the form of the politics of pretence. Not only opponents of the existing systems were repressed, but even, or indeed especially, overenthusiastic reformers. It was enough for Gorbachev to talk of reforms to infuse the Soviet system with a legitimacy that had been waning under Brezhnev. In the event, this was too little and too late to save the system. As Pareto noted, an elite falls apart when it no longer believes in its own rationality, and this was certainly the case in the last days of the Soviet Union.

KEY TEXT

White, Stephen and Alex Pravda (eds), *Ideology and Soviet Politics* (London, Macmillan, 1988).

12 Class and gender

One of the paradoxes of the Soviet system was that the abolition of private property in the means of production, considered by Marxists to be the main source of exploitation, did not eliminate inequality or hierarchy. New sources of economic, social and political inequality rapidly emerged whose causes and operation, and indeed whose very existence, were long denied by Soviet commentators. The nationalisation of economic life itself gave rise to new forms of stratification. At the same time, while the exploitative relations of capitalism might have been abolished, social relations remained stamped by hierarchy and inequalities. This was nowhere more apparent than in relations between the sexes. While capitalism might have been abolished, patriarchy remained deep-rooted.

NEW CLASS AND SOCIETY

The defeat of Khrushchev's challenge to elite status during the educational reform of 1958 illustrated the strength of the new hierarchy. By the time Brezhnev died there were clear signs that the defence of elite privileges had given rise to widespread social corruption. On 13 February 1986 *Pravda* published a review of readers' letters which sharply condemned party privilege:

> When considering social justice, it is impossible to close our eyes to the fact that party, soviet, trade union, economic and even Komsomol leaders sometimes objectively intensify social inequality by their enjoyment of all kinds of special buffets, special shops, special hospitals and so on.[1]

The call for a thorough purge of the *apparat* was supported by Boris Yeltsin, and was partly responsible for his fall in November 1987. Even under *glasnost* direct attacks on official privileges were rare at first, although the general problem was frequently discussed. Gorbachev himself admitted that there had been an 'erosion of the ideological and moral values of our people'.[2]

A number of theories try to explain the nature and structure of the dominant 'new class', as it was first termed by Milovan Djilas. The new class can be considered in two ways: first, in political terms, an elite in whose hands power is concentrated; second, in social terms, focusing on the privileges enjoyed by this class and the general inequalities in society. The political and social characteristics of the new class often coincided, enjoying a monopoly on power while taking an inordinate share of the surplus generated by the state-dominated economic system. The question was not so much one of the 'erosion of ideological and moral values' of the individuals concerned since the social ownership of property and the accompanying division of labour itself generated a class structure irrespective of the greed or asceticism of the new class. The privileges granted to the Stalinist elite are well known, with factory managers enjoying sumptuous accommodation while their workers lived in squalor.[3]

In capitalist countries social stratification derives from the working of the market and ownership of private property. Classes, according to Marx, derive from the ownership (and non-ownership) of property and the relationship of individuals and groups to the means of production. What this means in practice is not entirely clear. Even under capitalism the institutions of modern political society cannot be reduced to the class relations of the capitalist mode of production. In the Soviet Union the state owned almost all property and the market had been all but abolished. Differentials in wages and stratification were generated primarily by political rather than economic forces, making the application of Marxist class theory problematic. The political and administrative system was itself the major source of stratification and power. The problem in the Soviet context is to distinguish between the occupational structure, based on the necessary division of labour, and a class structure, which can be defined broadly in either political or economic terms.

The unification of political and economic power was foreshadowed during War Communism when, as Karl Kautsky pointed out, the state's attempt to organise all of social life forced it to substitute for social classes. The new state and party officialdom took over the functions of the former capitalist managers and owners.[4] The ruling party selects goals and implements them, legislates and enforces, all without accountability to society. In communist societies the state is the owner of almost all the economy and so there is no institutional separation, as there is in capitalist societies, between the influence of property-holders and control by the incumbents of political offices. Bauman distinguishes between officialdom and class. The officialdom is generated by the political structures and is sustained above all by the unquestioned authority over all appointments to office exercised through the party's *nomenklatura* system. The class structure is based on the inequalities that arise from the operation of the economic system and the black economy.[5] In practice, however, the officialdom and class were to a large extent one and the same, the new class. In the Soviet Union there was an integrated hierarchy of power and privilege which Nove called a unihierarchical society. The outcome of the marketisation of the economy after the fall of communism was the formal separation of officialdom and class to create a dual-type hierarchy, but even here the two remain closely interpenetrated.

The official Soviet view maintained that in the Soviet Union there were only two friendly classes, the peasantry and working class, and one stratum, the intelligentsia, in the process of evolution towards the classless society of communism. Officially, in 1987, 61.8 per cent were classified as workers, 23.5 per cent as intelligentsia and 15.1 per cent as collective farmers.[6] The pattern was similar to that in other societies with a shift from agriculture to industry, and from factory to service work. There was allegedly no class antagonism or class stratification. The classes were based on different types of property: the working class was associated with state property (considered the highest form); the collective farm peasantry with co-operative property; and the intelligentsia, a broad category which included employees, was designated as a stratum rather than a class since its members did not have property. The intelligentsia is a very broad catch-all category lacking much analytical precision. Under Stalin there was no pretence that this was an egalitarian society. Indeed, from 1932 there was a struggle against *uravnilovka* (wage-levelling or equality-mongering). The aim was to use monetary incentives to increase production, and the resulting substantial inequalities were held to reflect not class or strata privileges but different contributions to production.

Soviet writing later introduced new ideas into the discussion but without repudiating the earlier image. Soviet society was seen as a hierarchical structure of social groups ranked according to 'higher' or 'lower' status, especially marked on the mental–manual labour continuum. The literature talked of various socio-occupational groups of different economic status, cultural level and so on, including internal differentiation within classes. The general goal of 'developed socialism' was equality, but the pace of equalising work and rewards towards a fully homogeneous society was to be controlled. There was a sharp rejection of group struggles for the improvement of conditions. Social equality was considered part of the larger problem of 'social management', the application by the party of 'scientific socialism' to social processes. The image of society as a set of functional, non-antagonistic social groups remained dominant. The Soviet interpretation did not explain why substantial inequality continued to exist long after the elimination of private property and the bourgeoisie.[7] Just as the political equalisation that was expected to result from commune democracy failed to materialise, so social inequality persisted and, indeed, was partly derived from political stratification. Soviet Marxists provided few analyses of the sources of economic and social differentiation in a socialist society. Too often it was ascribed to legacies of the past, economic backwardness and the social division of labour, destined to disappear once the society of abundance was achieved. However, during *perestroika* there was an increased willingness to concede that socialist society would not become more uniform as it advanced towards communism, but that, on the contrary, it would become more complex and differentiated.

Theories of bureaucracy make up one of the most influential schools of thought in the study of class and power in the Soviet Union. Most were inspired in one way or another by Max Weber or by Trotskyist analyses. The term 'bureaucracy' can be used in three broad senses: it can describe a style of administrative management; a social group of functionaries; or more narrowly a political elite who rule rather than govern. Hence, a political bureaucracy could rule in a bureaucratic way, but they would not comprise a bureaucracy in the Weberian sense (see below).

The conditions for the consolidation of the bureaucracy were identified long ago by Luxemburg:

> With the repression of political life in the land as a whole, life in the soviets must also become more and more crippled. Without general elections, without unrestricted freedom of the press and assembly, without a free struggle of opinion, life dies out in every public institution, becomes a mere semblance of life, in which only the bureaucracy remains as the active element.[8]

Trotsky developed his theory of the Soviet Union as a degenerated workers' state after his exclusion from power in the mid-1920s. He identified the growth of a privileged bureaucracy, whose representative was Stalin, as the cause of the 'degeneration'. This was provoked, Trotsky argued, by Russia's isolation and economic backwardness, and resulted not in the emergence of a new capitalist ruling class but in a ruling bureaucratic caste living off the socialist foundations of nationalised property. It was a caste rather than a ruling class because its position and benefits derived from malfunctions in the distributive mechanism rather than through exploitation based on the system of production, as under capitalism. There was a certain lack of credibility in Trotsky's criticism of such features as lack of democracy within the party when he contributed so much to its destruction. There is the further problem of explaining the persistence of the bureaucratic caste, based on the state as the surrogate for capitalist industri-alisation, once backwardness had been overcome and isolation reduced. The degeneration of the workers' state was based on the idea of impermanence, and yet the position of the working class in institutional terms changed little over the years. According to Rudolf Bahro the 'bur-eaucratic superstructure' continued to exist because the 'industrial underdevelopment' of socialist states remained in comparison with more mature capitalist countries and because of the pressures of competition with them.[9] Bureaucratic hierarchies by definition anyway have a self-perpetuating quality.

The bureaucratic interpretation expounded by Tony Cliff asserts that the Soviet Union was state capitalist. According to him capitalism was restored in the Soviet Union about 1928 in a new amalgamated form of state property. Under Stalin the national economy became the business run as one large enterprise headed by a collective capitalist, the Soviet elite or the bureaucracy, who forced through collectivisation and industrialisation. The state acted as the substitute for market forces. The major problem with this approach is how one can call the system capitalist when the major features of capitalism were lacking, such as profits and market competition between rival capitalist groupings, and the category of 'capital' was by no means predominant. Production was controlled by and in the interests of a unified state and most production was not for sale on competitive markets, hence it was traditionally an economy of waste. Market regulation was replaced by attempts at the direct administration of economic life. Until 1988 there was no market competition between enterprises, so strictly speaking only export material was produced capitalistically in competition with other states. Cliff answers that the major spur to economic accumulation was the operation of a 'permanent arms economy' in competition with capitalist states, forcing the Soviet leaders to improve the efficiency of their giant factory. The concept of state capitalism tends to blur the distinctive pattern of Soviet development. Trotsky himself refused to label the Soviet Union as state capitalist since he insisted that state property remained socialist. In reducing socialism to property relations Trotsky was as guilty of economism as Stalin.

In 1965 two Poles, J. Kuron and K. Modzelewski, rebutted the view that there could be no antagonistic contradictions between workers and 'their' state after the nationalisation of the means of production. Their analysis of officialdom and class in a bureaucratic context led them to conclude that the state ownership of the means of production is secondary to the exercise of the powers associated with ownership by the social groups in control of the state. Political power was consolidated by control over production and distribution. At the heart of the power system was the central political bureaucracy (CPB) which determined basic political and economic policy. They did not analyse the size or structure of the CPB, but stressed its role in society and in the social process of production. The bureaucratic elite identified itself with the state and, in a perverse resuscitation of peasant commune principles, held property collec-tively in the name of the state, a fact which determined their internal structure as a class. Its class nature derived from the relationship as a group to the means of production and the relationship to other social classes, principally the working class. The privileges of consump-tion and power were by-products of the ability to control production.

The bureaucratic interpretation of class has a managerial version. Bruno Rizzi in 1934 foresaw the fascist and communist states developing into a new type of 'bureaucratic collectivist' society in which the new class collectively owned the state and its economic apparatus. This perspective was developed by the American socialist James Burnham in 1941. From his studies of European countries he came to believe, contrary to his original intention, that modern managers had a positive role to play in the technocratic systems of modern 'managerial societies'. The number of managers increases to keep pace with the changing nature of production, and they secure their position by taking over the state. By the 1960s the emphasis had shifted from the concept of totalitarianism towards an organisational approach focusing on 'rationality' and 'efficiency' stripped of the need for terror. Managerial theories now talked in terms of 'administered societies' (Kassof). The major problem with managerial and/or bureaucratic theories was that they blurred the differences between industrial societies, irrespective of whether they were capitalist or socialist. This sort of reductionism led to the palpably absurd assertion that from the class point of view there was no difference between an American worker in Detroit and a Soviet worker in Volgograd. This was neither analytically accurate nor politically helpful since the life expectations and possibilities, the nature of class struggle and the type of issues involved differed radically in the two systems. The theory, moreover, exaggerated the level of unity in the managerial class.

The term 'bureaucracy' fulfils a multitude of purposes but on its own tells us little about the nature of Soviet society. The Soviets usually used the term primarily to denote 'inadequacies of the mechanism', petty bureaucratic failings in an otherwise splendidly functioning system. In the West the term is usually understood in the Weberian sense of an apparatus of professional officials operating according to hierarchical principles and constrained by rules and regulations. It is difficult to characterise the Soviet bureaucracy as bureaucratic in a Weberian sense. Most elements of rationality, professionalism, established procedures and steadiness of expectations were missing. Hough points out that the bureaucracy in the Soviet Union was plagued by particularism and irrationality. The involvement of party officials in administration prevented clear lines of authority becoming established, a process Hough considered positive.[10] Rules were plentiful but acted not so much to regulate procedures as to consolidate the control of superior bodies over inferior ones.[11] To understand the phenomenon, sociological investigation or studies in social administration have to be supplemented by more narrowly political analysis.

The division between a political level, represented by the leadership, and the social level, focused on the bureaucracy, is a crucial one for evaluating the political independence of the bureaucracy in the USSR. Trotsky's major point was that in the Soviet Union a 'sovereign bureaucracy' had emerged which did not compete with other bureaucracies. The declining role of charismatic leadership and the consolidation of an institutionalised style of governance, accompanied by the decay of the teleological ideology, allowed the bureaucracy to consolidate itself. Soviet ideology gradually lost its anti-bureaucratic and egalitarian elements and emerged in a symbiotic and mutually supportive relationship with the bureaucracy. As Bauman pointed out, the bureaucracy was no longer simply the 'civil service' that implemented the policies of a force beyond it, such as the charismatic leader, but became an intrinsic part of the structure of power itself.[12] Its subordination to the political elite was questionable, and some even came to argue that the political elite itself became not much more than an emanation of the bureaucracy.[13] The argument is questionable since the party continued to dominate the administrative system and, despite much elision, never came to fuse with it: the party retained its autonomy. The bureaucratic or managerial class had been in existence since 1918, but under Stalin it grew in social power but it depended, and ultimately continued to depend, on the political elite's favour for its continued privileges: its role was derivative. The cultural revolution in China served as a warning to theories of bureaucratic power in communist systems. The political officialdom during *perestroika* once again assaulted the privileges of the bureaucratic and managerial class to achieve economic and political reform, although Gorbachev avoided using the language of Maoist cultural revolution. The managerial class received stipends and privileges for its work, but this was meant for personal consumption rather than accumulation or investment. Political functionaries remained dominant over the social bureaucracy: the latter were not able to usurp the party and translate their privileges into political power. In fact, in the end game the reverse took place: political officialdom converted its power into property and privileged insider dealings in the new market-oriented dispensation.

Another major theory of class in the Soviet Union focuses on the role of the intellectuals. At the turn of the century the Russian-born Pole Jan Waclaw Machajski systematised Bakunin's earlier nostrums against the intelligentsia and warned of the dangers of the intellectual domination of the working class by the social democratic intelligentsia. He claimed that Marxism was used first to mobilise the masses to achieve power, and then to legitimate the rule of the intelligentsia over them.[14] Such a development was implicit, as Luxemburg and Trotsky had warned, in Lenin's theory of consciousness. The ideological expropriation of the working class later led on to its political exploitation. The Workers' Opposition during War Communism took up the theme, in particular in baiting the so-called *spetsy*, although their call for the increased workerisation of administrative structures in no way reduced the gulf between managerial and administrative elites and the masses. Bureaucrats with worker roots behaved no differently to those of intellectual origin.

While theorists like Trotsky, Djilas and Kuron considered the state and party bureaucracy the main force opposing the working class, Konrad and Szelenyi argued that this contrast was secondary to the overriding contradiction between the working class and the intellectuals, of which the bureaucracy was only a part. They argued that the ideal of the planned society was a project of the intellectual imagination imposed on the actual producers, giving rise to what was called earlier the 'despotism of the enlightened'. Gouldner claimed that intellectuals are not as selfless and free-floating as they like to portray themselves but a class with specific interests. There is a form of critical discourse in the currency of scientific and cultural communication within the Soviet elite that distinguished them from the consumers of their product. This intelligentsia appeared to enjoy a relatively high degree of social group consciousness, and their internal communication acted as a functional substitute for a public sphere. The intelligentsia, or specialists, had been produced in greater numbers than the unreformed Soviet socio-political system could absorb, rising from 10 per cent of the population to 20 per cent during Brezhnev's rule, and while this might have given greater substance to the nascent Soviet middle class, weakening employment opportunities led to increasing alienation from the system.

The major problem with theories that put the intellectual at the heart of class analysis was that they worked within the 'economistic' critical categories of Marxist class analysis, although the subject was shifted from the working class to the intellectuals. By arguing that the main forms of stratification are class based they remained lodged in a methodology that was questionable in the Soviet context of the dominance of 'political' and non-class-based forms of hierarchy. All class theories are assailed by the boundary problem: at what point does one class end and another begin in the endless series of gradations which typify a modern functionally differentiated society. Were the millions of low-paid workers by brain, such as the 2.2 million teachers, to be included as part of the ruling class? In the jigsaw of society class boundaries do not always coincide with professional demarcations, and politically an individual may simultaneously be a teacher and a member of the CPSU and a trade union.

Elite theory is an alternative to class approaches to understanding the dynamics of social conflict. Vilfredo Pareto denied the viability of social democracy in modern societies by arguing that they will inevitably generate elites of two sorts: a governing elite dominating politics and a non-governing elite dominant in society. Gaetano Mosca insisted that human history is characterised by the emergence of 'a class that rules and a class that is ruled'. All societies, he argued, were dominated by a minority, with the rulers being a cohesive and self-conscious category. The theory was far too static and impermeable to understanding the process of change. It confused the ruling class and the political elite, who actually do the ruling. Pareto took a more complex systems approach identifying a fixed hierarchy, an aristocracy, which is an inalienable part of human society. Both views have been criticised on the grounds that modern industrial societies are fragmented into a multiplicity of elites. The plurality of competing elites took a distinctive form in the USSR since it was expressed in institutional forms and was mitigated by the unified system of political control. The hierarchies of wealth, power and status were to a degree one and the same. There was some functional differentiation within the system, but ultimately political power was concentrated in a single hierarchy.

Mosca's follower Robert Michels directly confronted the notion of commune or participatory democracy, arguing that the 'iron law of oligarchy' operated in socialist political parties no less than in other human organisations. Classical elite theorists pointed out that the Bolshevik revolution in Russia only 'bureaucratised' the revolution. The fusion of economic and political power engendered a unified elite with expanded powers. Pareto's notion of the circulation of elites saw lions alternating with foxes: lions rule by force, foxes by cunning. Soviet politics was marked by a shift from the lions like Stalin to the foxes, ruling by subtlety and persuasion, like Gorbachev. The circulation of elites did not stop there for long, however, and a new more cunning elite generation emerged.

The existence of the *nomenklatura* should have made it fairly easy to identify the political elite in the Soviet Union; its existence clearly indicated who the system considered important. However, the task was not so easy since the list covered an enormous spectrum of posts. Was the elite the Politburo alone, the party apparatus, or the whole *nomenklatura*? Even if we restrict ourselves to the top section we learn nothing about the cohesion of the bureaucrats staffing various parts of the machinery. Mosca stressed the importance of sub-elites mediating between the government and the masses. In the Soviet context, given the traditional importance of the intelligentsia in Russian society, this would clearly include leading cultural figures and possibly the cultural intelligentsia as a whole.

The traditional picture of the Soviet Union as a country of high social mobility stimulated by rapid industrialisation, the expansion of the working class and the creation of a new intelligentsia gave way to an increasingly rigid class structure. The word caste, however, is inadequate to describe the elite because it suggests fixed hereditary status. For proponents of state capitalist theories the absence of significant private property inheritance did not nullify the fact that the dominant class collectively controlled property through the state and hence only had to reproduce itself to maintain its position. In this respect the 'new class' embodied 'human capital', characterised, according to Gouldner, by its intellectual traits.[15] The educational system tended to fix people in their class position. Mobility was supplemented by the party, the military and other apparatuses, and yet the educational system remained the fundamental channel for advancement, and all the more so in the context of declining economic growth rates. The party under Khrushchev consciously tried to boost social fluidity, while under Brezhnev the jump between secondary and higher education was increasingly monopolised by the elite, especially at a time of a slowdown in the growth of higher education. The over-supply of educated people in comparison with the number of suitable jobs led the authorities from the 1960s to try to lower the expectations of school pupils. This was partially the aim of the 1984 educational reform. Between 1966 and 1986 the gainfully employed population increased by 55 per cent while the number of specialists with higher education increased fourfold. Brezhnev tried to ease blockages on upward mobility by establishing programmes to encourage working-class participation in higher education, by combating bribery in access to higher education, and by increasing the attractiveness of technical-vocational schools and blue-collar professions by raising wages. In a direct sense, education became associated with state or party office as a new technocratic class emerged whose ability counted as much as ideological acceptability. The Soviet Union like other advanced industrial countries witnessed an ever-growing propor-tion of the educated elite: the traditional worker and peasant classes lost status as the society 'post-industrialised'. There was a significant level of inherited privilege, but the elite was still far from becoming a self-perpetuating caste.

The above discussion clearly shows the problem of defining class in the Soviet context and the need to distinguish between political and social relationships. For Marxists there is a clear logic of class formation in the differentiated access of various groups to control over the means of production. This does not fully explain the relationship between 'the masses' and the 'elite'. Is it a subjective 'we–they' relationship or simply a gradation of more or less power? Should this entire dominant group be considered a political category (an elite), or a social one as well (a class). The decline of the totalitarian model increased awareness about elements of plural-ism, but was the alleged dispersion of power accompanied by a dispersion of privilege? Hough urged the abandonment of the 'all or nothing' concept of political power and instead stressed the importance of the nature and quality of political relationships.[16] Effective social and politi-cal power was concentrated in the hands of an elite, but their rule is very difficult to define in class terms.

The division in the Soviet Union between officialdom and class remained central. Andropov's anti-corruption campaign sought to reverse the dangerous trend for the party's leading role to be confused with the social dominance of the *nomenklatura*, while under Gorbachev the bur-eaucracy was less secure than it was during the Brezhnev years. The various theories posit the rise of a new group whose very existence was dependent on the political regime. Its actual name is not important: new class, stratum, caste, elite, bureaucracy, *nomenklatura*, partocracy or central political bureaucracy. Ultimately we are talking about a ruling group whose power derived from a combination of ideological factors, the belief that society was moving towards a final end, and the institutional relationship to the means of production. Non-economic forms of stratification and domination allowed the Soviet Union to evolve into a hierarchical society where status and power depend on rank. Rule was enjoyed by a political elite, but their privi-leges were incidental to the fundamental juridical relationship to the mass of social workers. The dominance of the political elite simply reflected the dominance of the state-party over society.

THE POLITICS OF GENDER

The politics of gender in any society helps identify the fundamental political and social proc-esses within that society. Whether these politics are universal, however, is a hotly contested issue; one must be sensitive to cultural differences. While the symptoms of gender exploitation between the West and the USSR might have been similar, the processes whereby inequalities were practised in each society were very different. There are major difficulties in applying Western concepts of feminism to the Soviet Union, a country which underwent decades of socialist transformation. Feminism itself must be defined and can be categorised into three broad tendencies: liberal, radical and Marxist. A distinction can further be made between movements for 'women's rights', in the sense of civil and political equality; and 'women's emancipation', in the sense of a broader striving for freedom from patriarchy and oppressive restrictions imposed by sex and for self-determination and autonomy. The first definition, the liberal view, does not necessarily imply an equality of roles between men and women; it can be seen as an equality in terms of moral and rational worth. The second definition, closer to the radical view, implies a sustained difference, since self-determination and autonomy might well emphasise the separation between the sexes. Self-determination was possible but autonomy was illusory in the Soviet context.

The Soviet view, derived from the writings of Marx, Engels and August Bebel, was balanced between the two concepts – rights and emancipation. Western feminist notions were often rejected in the Soviet Union, as in much of the non-Western world today, as part of imperialism and derided as 'bourgeois feminism'. Bebel condemned women's struggles for equality as essentially bourgeois, and the struggle for sexual liberation was regarded as a distraction from the main task – the class struggle. Soviet theory was a variation of the general socialist programme which argued that gender exploitation could only be overcome as part of the socialist transformation of society. The abolition of class exploitation would entail the ending of gender divisions. This might not take place immediately, but as the state promotes development the changes in the economic sphere would wreak changes in the social sphere. But, in a dialectical manner, changes in the social sphere were seen as a way of accelerating developments in the economic sphere. Hence the USSR took women's emancipation as far as it was useful for economic development, namely to release the economic potential of women in the labour force.

The first act of most socialist countries was to remove restrictions on female employment and legal status. The economic and political modernisation of the USSR required the mobilisation of a number of previously disadvantaged groups as part of the broader process of social transformation. Equality for women, as much as egalitarianism, was a basic socialist goal; but it was also seen as part of the developmental goals. To a degree these two principles were in conflict. In contrast to theories that rely on naturalistic and biological causation, but in keeping with the economism of much of Soviet theory, women's historical subordination was seen as deriving from economic causes. But even in Soviet practice there was much emphasis on 'women's qualities' in the nurturing and caring professions. The induction of women into the labour force was considered an act of economic, and hence social, liberation, but at the same time women retained primary responsibility for the domestic sphere. This was the theoretical and practical origin of the notorious 'double-shift' for women: a full-time job combined with responsibility for the home. Women's emancipation in Soviet theory did not take the crucial step of analysing the ideological factors that gave rise to the subordination of women in work and in the home.

The history of the women's movement in the Soviet Union covers several phases. During the Civil War the various pre-revolutionary 'bourgeois feminist' movements were destroyed but a wide range of experiments in recasting social arrangements was conducted. From 1919 special women's departments (*zhenotdely*) began to be formed under Bolshevik party committees, although they were starved of resources and encountered much male communist scorn. The outstanding figure of this period was Aleksandra Kollontai, who played an active part in the Workers' Opposition of 1920–21. The organised women's movement in Soviet Russia gained very limited autonomy. As Lenin put it: 'We derive our organisational ideas from our ideological conceptions. We want no separate organisations of communist women. She who is a communist belongs as a member of the party, just as he who is a communist.'[17] Bolshevik and feminist policy in this first phase was designed to break up the patterns of life inherited from the old regime, such as the family, and to create a 'new Soviet woman'. Under the impetus of War Communist ideological enthusiasm all sorts of experimental ideas were tried out. In Vladimir in 1918 a decree was issued proclaiming all women state property on reaching the age of 18.[18] There was a great boom in companionate marriage.

The *zhenotdel* activists sought to stimulate a growing women's movement to support the Bolsheviks, but were wary of any autonomous developments that might challenge party hegemony. The women's organisation was subordinated to the party since, quite apart from any political threat that it may have represented, an independent women's movement would have challenged male complacency. Working women, and especially peasant women, of this period were often considered 'backward' and unreceptive to Bolshevik ideas. As the years passed the image of the 'new woman' was gradually modified to fit in with changes in Soviet reality, above all with a greater stress on the nurturing role, to be all things – worker, wife and mother. As Clements points out, whatever the changing content, the image of the 'new Soviet woman' was always at the service of the new regime.[19] In *Literature and Revolution*, published in 1924, Trotsky took a typically male Bolshevik condescending view of the poets Anna Akhmatova and Marina Tsvetaeva. In the 1920s Kollontai's own subordination to Stalin was typical of the submissive attitude of the *zhenotdely* to the consolidation of the authoritarian regime. The *zhenotdely* tried to change the *byt* (daily life) of women through the organisation of canteens and emphasising the social functions of the place of work. They believed that under socialism it was the duty of the state to take over the major functions of the family. Communal facilities staffed by paid labourers would free women of the burden of domestic labour and endow them with economic and social independence.

This was the time of major campaigns in Soviet Central Asia against what were considered obscurantist Muslim practices in regard to women, such as seclusion and the wearing of the *chaydor*. This provoked religious anti-Bolshevik crusades and reinforced the *basmachi* resistance to the regime. Bolshevik policy had two purposes: to weaken the Islamic male dominance over women and to establish legal equality and access to education; and to weaken the structures of traditional authority to facilitate the consolidation of Bolshevik power in these areas. Women's emancipation was part of the process of advancing the revolution.

The consolidation of Stalinism was accompanied by the stabilisation of the Soviet family. The 1926 Code of Common Law placed a multitude of obligations on the husband and wife, but above all guaranteed child support and alimony to spouses in common law marriages, whereas the 1918 marriage law stated that alimony was only available for state marriages. The 1926 alimony law was designed to strengthen the family and placed the burden of child-rearing on women. The care of children was now the responsibility of the family. From that point the official representation of women stressed their child-bearing and nurturing roles. The dialectic of production and reproduction saw a narrowing of the scope for specifically feminist ideas. The abolition of even the semi-autonomous *zhenotdely* in 1930 set the tone for the massive uptake of women in employment during Stalin's five-year plans. A booklet published in 1934 in the USSR stated that the women's question was solved. A decree of 8 July 1944 recognised civil marriage alone as legal and, reversing the 1926 law, no longer accepted common law marriages. The consolidation of the state and the family were parallel processes, though no automatic relationship can be drawn between the authoritarian state and the patriarchal family. Both, however, can be seen as part of the attempt of the post-revolutionary regime to find an optimum means of sustaining its power. Following Stalin's death more flexible methods were sought to achieve the regime's aims in family and gender policy. Soviet practices can be examined under the four major headings of education, work, politics and the family.

1   Education was the basic means of building the new society and the curriculum of schools was moulded to meet the needs of socialist development. Socialisation in schools stressed the advantages of female employment both as a means of self-development and as a patriotic duty. Strong gender-typing began at an early age, reinforced by the fact that the majority of teachers were women. There was equal access for men and women to education, and indeed the educational accomplishments of women were the same as men's, but the type of course chosen revealed a divergent pattern. Women dominated in the caring professions such as education, health and welfare. As in most industrialised countries, the top posts in engineering remained a male preserve, even though women made up 40 per cent of the profession.

2   Women represented a 'reserve army' to be drafted into the economy to sustain rapid economic growth and to overcome the huge demographic losses of collectivisation, war and purges (see Table 6). An exceptionally high proportion of women worked outside the family, rising from 19 million in 1950 to 51 million in 1974. Between 1959 and 1970 the number of women exclusively involved in homemaking fell from 18 million to 6 million. In the 1980s women made up 53 per cent of the total population and 51 per cent of the Soviet labour force, compared to 42 per cent in Britain, constituting the highest proportion of any country. The participation rate for women aged between 15 and 64 in employment was 87 per cent in 1980 (7.5 per cent were students), compared to 48.5 per cent in the European OECD countries and 59.7 per cent in the USA. Some 44 per cent of the total female population were employed, of whom 80 per cent were between 20 and 39 years old, the period of highest fertility. Given the low average wages, there was enormous pressure for women to go to work to make up a living family wage, especially if there were dependent children.

Entrance of women to paid employment was seen as the key to the success of the emancipation of women, but it was also convenient in stimulating the socialist economy. There was usually equal pay for equal work, but the occupational status of employed Soviet women was generally inferior to that of men. The pursuit of economic growth led to the denigration of the

Table 6 Gender composition of the population

Year	Total population (millions)	Men	Women	Men (%)	Women (%)
1913	159.2	79.1	80.1	49.7	50.3
1940	194.1	93.0	101.1	47.9	52.1
1959	208.8	94.0	114.8	45.0	55.0
1970	241.7	111.4	130.3	46.1	53.9
1979	262.4	122.3	140.1	46.6	53.4
1981	266.6	124.5	142.1	46.7	53.3
1987	281.7	132.5	149.2	47.0	53.0

Source: *SSSR vtsifrakh v 1986 godu* (Moscow, 1987), p. 27.

idea of equality. For example, two-thirds of female manual workers were classified as unskilled, but only one-fifth of men. Many manual, unskilled occupations were reserved for women, especially in the countryside. Most dairy operatives were women, whereas most tractor drivers were men: men were lathe operators; women were auxiliaries. On average women did 50 per cent more manual work than men. In the non-manual sector gender divisions were as persistent but less obvious. Women tended to fall behind in terms of career advancement – the Soviet 'glass ceiling' was no more permeable than elsewhere. Even though women made up 77 per cent of the medical profession, they comprised only 52 per cent of head doctors. Women were considered an unstable element in the labour force, as they are in many societies. Productivity tends to be lower and there was a higher absenteeism rate as the burden of the 'double shift' forced women to stay at home to look after sick children. As the proportion of women rose in an occupation, like education or medicine, it tended to become 'deskilled'. Status devaluation took place as men moved out and pay levels fell. Women's earnings were an average 30–35 per cent below men's. This took place not only between sectors of the economy but also within particular professions. Where women were concentrated, wages and prestige were lower, as in the service sectors of the economy where average wages were one-third lower than in male-dominated professions. Women's representation at the higher levels of economic decision-making was minimal. Only 9 per cent of enterprise directors in 1975 were women, but this was a great improvement over the 1 per cent of 1956. It is clear that the sexual division of labour in socialist countries in both form and effect was similar to that in capitalist countries. Although Gorbachev led the drive to improve the status of such professions as teaching and medicine, the prospect of the loss of job security as the economic reforms began to bite led the official image once again to stress the 'womanly mission' of homemaking to prepare women for unemployment.

3   In politics the traditional Western pattern of women playing a secondary role in terms of political participation, especially in the higher echelons of administration and political leadership, was replicated. The low percentage of women in the party was compounded by the fact that only 5 per cent of women between 31 and 60 were members compared to 22 per cent of men. There were great variations in female participation depending on geographical factors and field. The higher the executive body, the lower the proportion of women, with a relatively low female impact in policy-making bodies. In 1986 only 3.5 per cent of the Central Committee were women, and only one woman was ever on the Politburo, Ekaterina Furtsova (1956–61), and then only as a candidate member. The appointment of Alexandra Biryukova to the CC Secretariat in 1986 broke a long tradition, but was redolent of tokenism as she was assigned responsibility for the 'nurturing' field of social welfare. The only two female ministers since the 1920s were Furtsova (minister of culture, 1960–74) and Maria D. Kovrigina (minister of health in the mid-1950s). There were very few top women in the republican and *oblast* leaderships, and none of the regional party secretaries were ever women. To balance the picture, there was high participation in policy bodies with high formal authority but little actual power. Women comprised one-third of the Supreme Soviet, and the proportion rose to half in local soviets. There was high participation in the trade unions and the Komsomol, but neither body was ever led by a woman. In general, the impact of women was marked in such policy areas as health, education and welfare, and they achieved influence at the very summit of these bodies, especially in the localities. Women were well represented in certain professions which influence policy such as college teachers, scientists, journalists and writers, economists and planners.

There are many reasons for the low achievement of women in politics. Rejection of the idea of 'mechanical equalisation' inhibited the development of positive equal opportunities programmes. The burdens of combining full-time work with running the home inhibited the participation of women in public life and hampered their acquisition of the necessary education and experience. In Muslim areas this burden was reinforced by tradition. Weighed down by a multitude of responsibilities, women were reluctant to take on extra commitments that would take up precious time and constitute a triple burden. The overall level of female participation declined precipitously with marriage and especially with the birth of a child. At the same time, political structures and male prejudices themselves screened out women. Party recruitment policies stressed the activist and leadership image, which, given their socialisation and lack of time, discouraged women. There may simply have not been enough women with the necessary experience and education.

Following the abolition of the *zhenotdely* in 1930 there was no organised women's movement as such in the USSR, and the Soviet women's committee played a largely decorative role. In 1969 special commissions for women were set up under the trade unions (*zhensovety*), but there was no separate mass women's movement under the party. The reason for this arose from the party's conviction that the women's question had been settled and that sexual inequalities no longer existed. However, under Gorbachev the women's question was put back on the agenda of Soviet politics. A nationwide system of women's councils was formed in workplaces and neighbourhoods intended to become actively involved in 'managing the affairs of state and society'.

There was no tolerance for unofficial women's organisations until the very end. In 1979 a group of Leningrad women, including Tatyana Mamonova, published an almanac entitled *Women and Russia* which disagreed with the official view that the women's question had been solved. The magazine was banned and the authors persecuted, though it still appeared clandestinely. The journal dealt with some of the main problems women faced, such as the lack of sex education, male brutality in the home and intimate relations, a repressive official puritanism and a pervasive hypocrisy about stymied career opportunities. The authorities response revealed once again that feminism was regarded as subversive. With the onset of *glasnost*, informal women's groups emerged to take up the themes of the Leningrad group.

4   The official Soviet definition of femininity was a farrago of sex-role stereotypes which was used to reconcile women to their domestic and employment roles. Traditional Marxism predicted that the family would ultimately disappear, although it would remain in the transition to socialism. Engels dismissed the bourgeois family as a microcosm of capitalist class relations and as organised prostitution. The father represented the bourgeoisie while the wife and children were the proletariat. Under socialism the family was to be stripped of its economic functions. The Bolsheviks expected that all the problems would be solved by instituting legal equality between the sexes and economic emancipation for women. This economistic thinking led the Bolsheviks to perpetuate traditional values on the division of power and labour within the family. Soviet family legislation reinforced heterosexual monogamy and tried to ensure its stability. In 1970, 90 per cent of the Soviet population lived in a family.

Government policy towards the family reflected demographic concerns. The Soviet Union pursued strongly pro-natalist policies to compensate for demographic disasters caused by war and famine by providing incentives for marriage, and tried to mould social values in favour of large families. The reproductive functions of the family were often painted in glowing patriotic terms, and Stalin inaugurated the order of Mother Heroine for mothers of ten children or more. The politics of population is a sensitive issue, since the attempts to increase fertility by improving living standards and other such measures were clearly oriented towards the European part of the Soviet Union. A population explosion was taking place in Soviet Central Asia, whereas one-child families were the norm in European USSR. A variety of incentives were offered for large families. One of the major taxes was the 'childlessness tax' levied on married women and men. There was little individual choice in the question of contraception. Abortion was legalised in 1920, banned in 1936, and once again legalised in 1955. Abortion was free, and indeed was the major form of contraception. It is estimated that 67 per cent of women who had been pregnant had an abortion, with the average Soviet woman having six to eight abortions in her lifetime, giving rise to a host of complications, not least of which is sterility. Concern over the spread of AIDS encouraged the greater provision of condoms. Women were encouraged to enter paid labour and so the state took on the provision of certain child-care facilities, although their quality and availablity were very uneven.

The birth-rate in European USSR was depressed by a variety of social and economic factors. The burden of domestic labour weighed heavily in the absence of the broad availability of labour-saving devices of adequate quality. Men played a small part in domestic tasks, though official policy encouraged the redistribution of the burden between other family members, especially between the sexes. This met with the greatest success among the intelligentsia. Little encouragement was given to alternative forms of household management, and Khrushchev's communal apartments, not surprisingly, fell into disfavour. The majority of families (34 million out of 59 million) lived in towns, often in apartments where several generations lived together. Marriages were put under severe strain, adding to the high divorce rate. Between one-third and one-half of marriages ended in divorce, the rate being especially high in the early years of marriage. When no children were involved the procedure involved no more than a simple three months' wait.

The dual image of women as paid workers and primary homemakers was reflected in the dual burden that fell to them. Women entered employment in great numbers and the routes of political advancement were opened. However, they suffered from material disadvantages in comparison to men in terms of lower average wages and depressed career opportunities. Inequalities persisted beneath formal equality and the official view of the female question and the family was conservative. The sexual division of labour persisted and the burden of domestic work fell on women. Legal and professional equality, economic independence, the socialisation of the means of production and the abolition of the directly economic functions of the family had not of their own created equality for women. The developmental functions of female emancipation took priority over examination of the psychological and social aspects of inequality.

Was there a 'women's problem' in the USSR, or was the official view that it had been solved correct? Gorbachev's speech to the twenty-seventh party congress conceded the need to improve the context of women's lives by supporting the family and improving social and work conditions. There was widespread dissatisfaction among women over unfair treatment at work, poor promotion prospects, income differentials and the burden of housework. Much has been published in the Soviet Union on the hardness of the woman's lot. Especially noteworthy is Natalia Baranskaya's *A Week Like Any Other*, published in the journal *Novy Mir*, which broke with the tradition of Soviet socialist realism to depict the awful difficulties of daily life, the inner life of women, and the dehumanising effects of the double burden. However, perhaps surprisingly, this dissatisfaction did not usually take the form of a sense of grievance as found among Western feminists. Despite her description of the patriarchal oppression imposed by the authoritarian state and in marriage to an uncouth husband, Baranskaya herself denied ever having any feminist motives. The story was intended, she stated later, to portray the 'power of love', and she went on to criticise Western women's efforts to displace men from their position of 'natural superiority' and condemned the 'unfeminine' attitudes of Western women.[20]

Not much more could be achieved through legislation in the Soviet Union on a formal level of equality. There was a broad acceptance that further advances could be achieved only through cultural changes rather than political acts. Soviet women, even intellectuals, knew little of the substantive arguments of Western feminists and were often prepared to accept differences of treatment on 'common-sense' grounds: for instance, that teachers' wages in a profession domi-nated by women can be low since they usually represented a second wage. There was much greater acceptance of the conventional image of the 'biological essence' of women and their motherly mission as teachers and trainers. There was a profound cultural difference between Soviet women and their Western counterparts. Whether this represented a success for govern-ment socialisation, political culture or something more profound is not clear. For better or worse the Soviet Union missed out on the 1960s sexual revolution and increased female mili-tancy of the West. Despite the massive social changes, beneath the carapace of Soviet power society was to some extent shielded from the constant changes engendered by capitalism. This was above all true in the area of gender relations. There was little real pressure from within the socialist state, or indeed society, for radical change. The impression is that liberal reforms limited to bringing the man into the family rather than taking the woman out would have been the limit of most Soviet women's ambitions.

The major reason for the general lack of resonance of radical feminism in the Soviet Union was that it did not mesh with Soviet socio-political realities. The Soviet family was no longer an economically productive unit (though this was to a degree reversed by the emergence of family-based businesses) but provided a variety of functions. From a demographic point of view it reproduced workers and soldiers, and it acted as the major unit of consumption. The family was to some extent co-opted into the Soviet state, typified by the glorification of Pavlik Morozov who informed on his parents during collectivisation. And yet the family, ultimately, was a bastion of social autonomy against the pervasive state, and hence any theory that threatened this last rebut of independence would not resonate in a society that needed to cling on to these vestigial 'islands of separatism'.[21] Whatever the external political circumstances, families pre-served a relative autonomy: their formation, growth or dissolution all depended in the last analysis on personal decisions. The socialisation that a child received in the family was often at variance from that received from the state. The family was often a crucial psychological haven. A radical feminism which seeks to dissolve the family may well be socially progressive, but in the Soviet context it was profoundly politically reactionary.

KEY TEXTS

Atkinson, Dorothy, Alexander Dallin and Gail Warhofsky Lapidus (eds), *Women in Russia* (Brighton, Harvester Press, 1978).
Buckley, Mary, *Women and Ideology in the Soviet Union* (Brighton, Wheatsheaf, 1988).
Holland, B. (ed.), *Soviet Sisterhood: British Feminists on Women in the USSR* (London, Fourth Estate, 1985).
Lapidus, G. W. (ed.), *Women, Work and Family in the Soviet Union: Equality, Development and Social Change* (New York, M. E. Sharpe, 1982).
Nove, Alec, 'Is There a Ruling Class in the USSR?', *Soviet Studies*, Vol. 27, No. 4 (October 1975), pp. 615–38.
Nove, Alec, 'The Class Nature of the Soviet Union Revisited', *Soviet Studies*, Vol. 35, No. 3 (July 1983), pp. 298–312.
Yanowitch, Murray, *The Social Structure of the USSR* (Boulder, CO, Westview Press, 1987).

13 From dissent to pluralism

The emergence of overt dissent following Stalin's death revealed that the Soviet Union was no longer an oppositionless state, even though it remained a one-party state. Political life was dominated by a single party which monopolised institutional and ideological life, and yet the view of the Soviet Union as a sea of grey immobility and passivity was clearly mistaken. Soviet society was marked by many currents of autonomous activity, including those in favour of continuing destalinisation, various trends of intellectual dissent and elements of working-class resistance. The Soviet regime, as much as those in Eastern Europe, was faced with economic and social challenges which could less and less be contained within the bounds of economic reform alone. Dissent acted as a litmus test of the degree to which the Soviet Union had changed since the death of Stalin. Unfortunately for the regime itself, the failure to integrate some of the ideas bubbling beneath the country's placid surface into the regime's social and intellectual operation left it increasingly isolated and exposed, and ultimately reduced its evolutionary potential.

POLITICAL DISSENT AND THE STATE

Barghoorn points out that dissent is endemic to political systems, but in the Soviet system it tended to be equated with opposition and under Stalin was treated as tantamount to treason.[1] Shtromas distinguishes between those who aim to change the system from within, and those who reject the system, and stresses the importance of the *overt* nature of dissent.[2] The term dissent is rather restricted, covering a few thousand active protesters, and associated with disagreement only to certain of the regime's actions or policies. Another common term is opposition, the word used to describe the various tendencies that racked the party under Lenin. Medvedev revived the term to talk of a 'loyal opposition'. Some of this was tolerated, and indeed some of the demands, since they coincided with the further rational development of the regime, have been discussed earlier. Historically, the Leninist form of organisation has been authoritarian, but Medvedev insisted that the participatory side of Leninism, the side represented by the debates of the early years, would permit the emergence of a modified and more inclusive regime. Medvedev's hopes were disappointed, but his views reflected those who believed in the system's capacity to regenerate itself. The term opposition, moreover, was clearly inadequate since it suggested something akin to oppositions in parliamentary systems, movements with an alternative programme wishing to replace the existing government or state. This exaggerated both the possibilities and ambitions of most dissenters.

The term preferred by most activists in the Soviet Union was 'other-thinker' (*inakomyslyashchii*), denoting being of a different mind or heterodox. The term highlighted the ideological challenge posed by such concerns as human rights and religious freedom. It challenged official-dom precisely where it was most sensitive, the ideological claims that buttressed their rule. With the state as the universal employer, resistance had no autonomous socio-economic base and thus challenges were focused on the ideological sphere. No rising class could couch its own demands in the language of universal truths: the demands of other-thinkers could only be cast in the language of intellectual and social demands. It was primarily cerebral. However, while illuminating an important aspect of regime-society relations, the term is too restrictive in ex-cluding the influence of sociological factors in resistance and the play of social forces. As we saw in the previous chapter, tensions were emerging in the dynamics of relations between 'officialdom' and 'class'. Other thinking, moreover, was not restricted to those outside the system but was to be found in most nooks and crannies within it as well; it was, in addition, not a black and white issue but spread along a whole spectrum from the mildly critical, the reform-ist, to the out-and-out hostile.

A more encompassing concept (although not without its own drawbacks) which covers all groups in society and permits a more subtle gradation of oppositional activity is the term resistance. The word refuses to accept the ghetto imposed by the term dissent or other-thinker. It recognises that resistance was a widespread phenomenon in Soviet society, inside the regime and out, and took many different forms, from mild criticism to outright rejection of the system. Resistance encompassed small acts operating in the 'fifth column of social consciousness', the struggle for personal truth against the universal 'lie' sustained by the propaganda of success and the distortion of the past, to the societal struggle for the restoration of the public sphere, the area of life in which people behave as citizens engaged in free expression on matters of general interest. Resistance includes all kinds of activities which challenged the prevailing norms and uncritical obedience. Resistance could be political, social and economic. The second economy, for example, can be seen as a mark of resistance to the exclusivity and inefficiency of the command economy, representing the emergence of the economic basis of civil society. Resistance could be found from the highest echelons of the party to the caretaker of an apart-ment block.

The terminology reflects various facets of the phenomenon, and we shall use each where appropriate. Whereas overt dissent operated in the public sphere, personal resistance entailed fewer risks but by the same token its impact was less striking, if no less effective in the long run. Personal resistance took on political significance very rapidly in the Soviet Union. The concept of resistance includes the concept of 'internal emigration', focusing on personal mental and spiritual concerns.[3] It would be inaccurate to describe this as 'private' since much was shared with people of similar beliefs in subcultural ties of friendship and had a profound impact on society as a whole. It is for this reason that the word 'personal' is used in preference to the term 'private'. By putting the individual at the heart of the social project, the dissenters sought to regain some of the advances of liberalism. They were re-enacting the centuries-long struggle for the creation of a public sphere.

THE EVOLUTION OF DISSENT

While Stalin lived dissent was not only brave but suicidal. Under Khrushchev the secret police apparatus was partially dismantled and the relaxation allowed the thaw to begin. The emer-gence of overt resistance revealed the strains generated by the command economy and dirigiste politics. Khrushchev's Secret Speech in February 1956 was only the most famous incident in a ferment that questioned Stalinist orthodoxies. Gradually a cultural opposition emerged consisting of small groups of students and writers who focused on artistic and intellectual issues rather than on political criticism of the regime. Khrushchev tolerated and to a degree even encouraged such activity as long as it was restricted to condemning Stalinist practices, hoping thereby to strengthen his position against the conservatives. Following the renewed anti-Stalinist campaign at the twenty-second party congress Khrushchev in 1961 approved the publication of Solzhenitsyn's and Yevtushenko's works. This was the high tide of officially tolerated literary opposition, called by Diane Spechler 'permitted dissent', especially in the pages of *Novy Mir* edited by Alexander Tvardovskii. By the early 1960s the concerns of the critical intelligentsia began to broaden from mainly literary issues to encompass political criticism encouraging genuine destalinisation. This was accompanied by the emergence of *samizdat* (a play on the name of the state publishing house, Gosizdat), or the underground publication of materials bypassing official censorship. The period saw the emergence of a democratic opposition which focused on political issues.

The last years of Khrushchev saw a clampdown on dissent, including the trial of the poet Joseph Brodsky in 1964. The new Brezhnev leadership from October 1964 continued the trend towards stifling the opportunities for open criticism. Dozens of intellectuals were tried in the Ukraine in 1965. The attempt to suppress overt resistance culminated in the trials of the writers Andrei Sinyavskii and Yulii Daniel in the spring of 1966. The harsh sentences set the precedent of criminal prosecution for the publication of works abroad (a fate Pasternak escaped for his *Doctor Zhivago*). The trial stimulated a new wave of dissent, focused now on questioning the system that had allowed such a trial to take place in the first place. On a modest scale Ted Gurr's ideas on *Why Men Rebel* are applicable here, since the law of 'relative deprivation' ensured that resisters who had become accustomed to certain freedoms compared their status not with conditions under Stalin but under Khrushchev.

The high point of this phase came in 1968 when demonstrations against the Warsaw Pact forces' invasion of Czechoslovakia were accompanied by petitions and the emergence of the *Chronicle of Current Events*. The unifying motif of this activity was the demand for legality, especially for the democratic freedoms of assembly and association, and for the Soviet regime to obey its own laws and constitution. The regime's response was uncompromising but now more subtle, masterminded by Yurii Andropov who had become head of the KGB in 1967. The partial rehabilitation of Stalin was accompanied by the increased repression of active dissent. By 1972 organised opposition was largely crushed through a combination of repression and by splits within the resistance. The regime stifled the aspirations of the democratic movement by imprisonment or exile to the West. In 1974 Alexander Solzhenitsyn was exiled and two years later Vladimir Bukovsky was exchanged for the Chilean communist leader Luis Corvalan.

Repression against dissent only reflected the increasing rigidity of political structures under Brezhnev. In relative terms the years between 1972 and 1979 were a period of tolerance, with no large-scale arrests but steady pressure. By choice or by necessity a generation of talented Soviet intellectuals was forced out of the mainstream of Soviet life and into menial jobs such as caretakers and stokers. The Jackson-Vannik and Stevenson amendments of 1974 tried to exert pressure on the Soviet government to allow greater Jewish emigration, in part successfully for a time. Soviet agreement to the 'third basket' of humanitarian issues at Helsinki in August 1975 provided its domestic critics with a powerful new weapon, an international commitment by the Soviet government itself to maintain certain standards of human rights. However, a number of well-publicised cases did Soviet standing in the international community much damage. The arrest of Yurii Orlov in December 1976 was a signal to Washington of Moscow's refusal to alter domestic policies in response to external pressure, what the US secretary of state under presidents Nixon and Ford, Henry Kissinger, had called 'entanglement': the attempt to influence Soviet behaviour by enmeshing it in Western policy concerns. The replacement of Kissinger's realist approach by Carter's idealistic if inconsistent campaign for human rights in 1977 ultimately proved incompatible with the continuance of détente. The staging of trials as a snub to Carter's human rights campaign in the summer of 1977 stretched the limits of toleration within the bounds of détente to the limit, especially when accompanied by an active Soviet foreign policy in Africa (Angola, Ethiopia). Anatolii Shcharanskii was tried and sentenced on a patently false charge. It showed more than anything the limits of 'soft linkage', associated with the name of Marshal Shulman, to moderate Soviet behaviour not by direct pressure but by subtle influence appealing to 'progressive' elements in the Soviet hierarchy. The policy of 'hard linkage', as expressed through the amendments, however, fared little better.

Soviet behaviour towards overt dissent was not primarily a function of the cycles of the Cold War, despite assertions to the contrary by Western socialists.[4] While attitudes might at times have coincided with foreign policy cycles, the Soviet Union always preserved its autonomy and rejected what it saw as interference in its domestic affairs. In the battle against non-conformity the authorities condoned the breaking of its own laws, constitutional provisions and (after Helsinki) its international commitments. The inability of détente to be transformed into a genuine breakthrough into respect for Soviet legality and an acceptance of the right of criticism of regime actions was one of the major reasons not only for the failure but also the widespread discrediting of détente. A strong case could be made for the proposition that détente was not lost, as Brzezinski put it, in the 'sands of the Ogaden' (the Soviet intervention to support Ethiopia against Somalian attack) but in the KGB's Lefortovo Prison, the main pre-trial detention centre in Moscow for political cases. In the 1980s neither of the superpowers was willing to see a revival of détente in its old form. More than ever it provoked the Eurocommunist challenge that democracy was an essential part of the socialist programme. Under Brezhnev the increased consultation of expert and interested opinion in policy-making and a certain tolerance of diversity of opinion on less sensitive issues were unable to offset the increasingly stifling atmosphere.

In mid-1979 the Soviet regime decided on a final push to eliminate dissent. Among the reasons for the new hardline policy was the non-ratification by the USA of SALT II, inner-party struggles for the Brezhnev succession, with Andropov above all bidding for power, and the traditional Soviet response of conducting a purge of potential opposition prior to a major international gathering, given the forthcoming Olympics in Moscow in summer 1980. The government clearly considered that it had nothing more to lose with the dissolution of détente. The invasion of Afghanistan in December 1979 and the onset of the second Cold War were accompanied by harsh repression, including the exile of the dissident physicist Andrei Sakharov to Gorkii (now Nizhnii Novgorod). There were limits to Soviet tolerance of developments in Poland, and Jaruzelski claimed that his imposition of martial law in December 1981 and the banning of Solidarity were to pre-empt a Soviet invasion. This hardline policy, both at home and abroad, continued under Andropov and Chernenko. By 1985 the Soviet Union's standing in the international community was at an unprecedented low point.

Gorbachev's early years were marked by several major initiatives towards dissent which improved the atmosphere both at home and abroad and helped pave the way for more constructive engagement, including arms-control agreements. Shcharanskii was released in exchange for three Soviet spies in early 1986 and shortly afterwards the poet Irina Ratushinskaya was released from labour camp and allowed to emigrate. In December 1986 Andrei Sakharov was not only released but 'rehabilitated'. In early 1987 about 170 of the 600 known imprisoned dissidents were 'pardoned' after pressure to recant and to sign documents stating that they would no longer participate in unofficial activities. The tempo of Jewish emigration significantly increased, including a number of leading refuseniks (those refused exit visas), which deprived the *aliya* (the return to Israel) movement of its leadership.

The multifaceted character of resistance is reflected in the absence of a single policy carried out by the state to control it in the post-Stalin years. The authorities tried to isolate the most active dissenters, to split the movement and to deal with various issues individually. Overt resisters were usually dismissed from their jobs and attempts were made to turn them into social pariahs. Dissidents were vilified more often than not for their individual moral failings, and an almost obsessive emphasis was placed on their usually fabricated links with Western powers and the CIA. The more subtle tactic of the KGB was to intimidate potential resistance by calling people in for 'talks' (*besedy*) at KGB headquarters. The tone of these *besedy* was of a stern parent with a wayward child. If the individual proved obdurate there was a gradual escalation in the level of coercion. Some of the more active or isolated dissidents were incarcerated in psychiatric institutions. Notable examples were Petr Grigorenko, Zhores Medvedev, Bukovsky and Koryagin. Another method was the use of exile, applied against Solzhenitsyn. Medvedev had a taste of both, being held in a psychiatric hospital before being exiled to the West.

STRANDS OF RESISTANCE

The hopes raised by the Khrushchev thaw and their suffocation under Brezhnev once again raised the dilemma faced by the Polish resistance of the nineteenth century: the choice between 'organic work', the steady devotion to the cause but working through the system, and insurrection. In the Soviet context, given the regime's overwhelming preponderance in physical force, insurrection was not a viable alternative; but, given the impermeable nature of Soviet power, organic work for many resisters was not an option either, although some chose to try to effect changes from within. A third path tried to negotiate between a range of activities which as far as possible was insulated from official structures. The embryo of an 'alternative society' began to emerge which was not so much counterposed to the official world but rather ignored it.[5] This process had developed much further in countries like Poland, but in Russia the weakness of society and the intelligentsia's traditional concern with national destiny meant that oppositional thinking was focused much more on the fate of the state than elsewhere. Patterns of resistance, moreover, differed in each of the fifteen union republics and we can no more than hint at this variety. In the absence of an overriding national component comparable to the struggle for liberation in nineteenth-century Poland (except in the Baltic republics, parts of Ukraine and elsewhere), Soviet resistance can be categorised into four very broad strands.

1   The first was the idea of genuine Marxism–Leninism, the belief that the system had the capacity to be regenerated to provide a viable path of development, a view that evolved into the reform communism of the early *perestroika*. This was close to the 'organic work' view which asserted that there was nothing fundamentally wrong with the system and all that was required were some adjustments to eliminate the distortions of the past and to return to Leninist ideals. This had something in common with Trotsky's idea of the degenerated workers' state, which

held Stalin and the bureaucracy responsible for deviating from the true Soviet path. The approach accepted the basic propositions of the Soviet system: private property was seen as the source of exploitation and the establishment of collective or nationalised property was considered an achievement. The end of bourgeois parliamentarianism was regarded as progressive, although they accepted that major distortions had taken place in Soviet legality which required only an act of political will to remedy. At the margin this was the view of some of the within-system reformers and ultimately Gorbachev himself. This stance had been defended earlier by Grigorenko, Roy Medvedev and was supported by Lev Kopelev. Medvedev argued that a neo-Stalinist formation had taken power in the USSR and that its elimination would allow the genuinely socialist system to emerge.

Medvedev's view of 'reformism' from above denied the need for a revolution or mass movement from below. Stalinism, for him, was a distinctive power system opposed to the correct principles of Leninism. Grigorenko, on the other hand, fought for the maximum political and organisational independence of the democratic movement from the ruling system; he characterised the leadership as a ruling caste. After enjoying some popularity in the 1950s and 1960s, especially when the belief in reform from above was stimulated by Khrushchev's denunciation of Stalin, this Marxist–Leninist tendency declined markedly. Its fundamental proposition on the inherent reformability of Marxist–Leninist regimes was dealt a severe blow by the crushing after 1968 in Czechoslovakia not only of the reforms but of the ideas that had inspired them. Following the ban on Solidarity in Poland the tendency almost completely disappeared, although in both cases the attempts at reform were halted by outside influences – a factor which did not apply to the Soviet Union. In many respects the Brezhnev years saw the extinction of Marxism–Leninism as a meaningful political philosophy in the Soviet Union and Eastern Europe. It became transformed, according to its critics, into a dogma supportive of the existing regimes. It no longer appeared to have any explanatory power. Leninist oppositions to Soviet-type regimes shared too many assumptions with them to be able to sustain effective critiques. This was the case with Gorbachev's own reforms, which became trapped between trying to save the system and transcending its limitations, giving rise to compromises that not only satisfied no one, but that undermined the system and the reform communism that tried to save it.

2   The second major tendency in resistance thought was the role of religion as a counter-ideology. A religious belief system acted as a filter, screening the attempts at political socialisation by the regime. Of necessity under Soviet conditions this took place mainly in the family. While Islam was as persecuted as any religion in the USSR, leaving few mosques still functioning, Islamic faith was widespread among Soviet Muslims (concentrated in Central Asia, some of the Volga republics, the North Caucasus and Azerbaijan) and provided an effective alternative source of socialisation and moral support. In Lithuania the Roman Catholic church was strong and created a situation analogous to that pertaining in Poland. The Baptists were particularly strong in the Ukraine, while the Uniates (Orthodox owing loyalty to the Pope) in the Western part of that country remained strong underground and kept alive the spirit of Ukrainian national resistance to Soviet subjugation. The Russian Orthodox Church (ROC) from the 1970s witnessed a revival in attendance but perhaps more importantly in its spiritual life. The notable figure in this respect was Fr Dmitrii Dudko, who tried to forge a link between Orthodoxy and intellectual criticism. While the ROC had been devastated by Lenin's early struggle against religion, Stalin's persecution and Khrushchev's renewed anti-religious crusade, and its hierarchy was severely compromised by collaboration with the authorities and the secret police, there remained an undercurrent of resistance. In almost all Soviet religion there was a

mixture of belief and nationalism. This was particularly important among active Jews where religion was the basis of ethnic identity. In Georgia and Armenia Christian churches of great antiquity bestowed a spiritual element to the proud nationalism. In Russia itself Solzhenitsyn represented a fusion of Orthodox belief and Russian patriotism.

3   The third strand follows on from the second, broadly represented as national dissent, which can be further divided into linguistic, cultural and other sub-groups. The Armenian groups of the 1970s were some of the few who resorted to terrorist acts. Ethnic politics were represented by the nationalist expatriate groups such as the Crimean Tatars. There were elements of militant Islam in Central Asia, taking on a radical nationalist hue. Jews made up a special group because of their concern with emigration and extra-national links with the state of Israel. They provided one of the most consistent, vocal, sustained and effective sources of resistance to the regime. The Volga Germans achieved one of their aims, the ability to emigrate, but failed to re-establish their national republic on the Volga destroyed by Stalin in the early days of the Second World War. The resurgence of a Russian national consciousness divided into many streams, ranging from an authoritarian (even fascist) right wing to a moderate Russian nationalism best exemplified by Solzhenitsyn. His views reflected the *pochvennik* (soil-bound) tradition in nineteenth-century Russian thinking, the view that Russia should abandon its imperial pretensions and concentrate on developing its own customs and practices. This will be discussed further in Chapter 15.

4   The fourth major trend in the resistance was liberal ideology, or a belief in the values of liberal democracy in the broadest sense. The major representative of this tendency was Andrei Sakharov. These were the successors to the nineteenth-century Westernisers, especially in their support for a transition to a Western-style democracy. Sakharov himself rejected the division of ideas into Western or Slavophile as false; for him, there were only true or false ideas. Like classical liberals everywhere, they rejected ideologies that placed social justice above political liberty, although this did not exclude support for 'social liberal' views on the welfare responsibilities of the state. They rejected the view of some believers that religious community comes above individuality. They condemned the Soviet Union for having failed to achieve social justice, individual liberty or community; and insisted that economic development required the liberation of individuals from state tutelage.

These four major strands were communicated to the Soviet public and the world in a number of different ways. The creation of civil and human rights groups gathered pace in the 1970s, including the Helsinki Watch Group established in the mid-1970s and broken up in the early 1980s. The group of the early 1980s to Establish Trust Between the USA and the USSR enjoyed a tenuous existence until Gorbachev's accession. One of the unwitting side-effects of Andropov's peace campaign (directed against the deployment of Cruise and Pershing missiles in Europe) was the emergence of groups within the Soviet bloc itself asking provocative questions about the relationship of 'peace' to human and civil rights. Major cities were full of small 'circles' (*kruzhki*) of 'other-thinkers' pursuing literary, religious or national preoccupations, often all three together. Cultural associations played a key role in harbouring heterodox thinking that burst into the open after 1985. The Writers' Congress of 1986, for example, heralded a cultural thaw, while the Cinematographers' Union took the lead in restoring formerly censored works to the screen.

Glasnost permitted the exposure of religious, national and class tensions that took the form of the *neformaly*, new social movements numbering hundreds, if not thousands (see below). They were initially concerned with unofficial art or music but broadened into cultural, gender, social, historical and ecological issues and finally into overt political concerns. Many of the groups concerned with gender politics came from a dissident background disappointed to find that most dissidents failed to take their concerns seriously. Feminist dissent shifted attention from political to social oppression. Homosexuality remained illegal in the Soviet Union and thus it was well-nigh impossible to organise effectively to advance gay rights. (Since lesbianism was not recognised as existing it was not illegal.) The wide variety of groups concerned with environmental issues became one of the few genuine mass movements in the Soviet Union, reflecting the growing resistance to the continued degradation and despoliation of the Soviet environment. They sought to ensure compliance to the impressive Soviet laws on the protection of the environment, but the ability to hold enterprises and ministries responsible for their actions in this field (as in others) required a general improvement in the USSR's legal system and the development of a civil litigation system.

The standard image of Soviet workers as divided, demoralised and depoliticised was broadly accurate. The working class found itself in a particularly difficult position since the regime nominally ruled in its name. Worker organisations became institutionalised as the basis of the Soviet regime and hence working-class organisations and ideology were colonised by the regime. Attempts at independent organisation had emerged in the stagnation period, as in the attempt by Klebanov to form the Free Trade Union (SMOT). Low-level worker resistance was prevalent, usually focusing on local issues; only seventy-five strikes were documented between 1953 and 1983. Most strikes were spontaneous occurrences provoked by exceptional circumstances, such as a cut in rations or increased work norms. The major incident of worker unrest took place in Novocherkassk in 1962, sparked off by food price increases and raised work norms. The strikers carried banners of Lenin, just as the demonstrators in 1905 carried pictures of the Tsar. The strike lasted three days before the authorities crushed it with tanks. National factors and level of development play their part in the incidence of strikes, with a disproportionate number in the Ukraine and the Baltic states, with a corresponding quiescence in the Russian republic. In Soviet circumstances a strike could not remain economic for long and was seen by the officialdom as a political challenge. A strike acted as a way of appealing for redress to a level above the local management or party authorities. Most strikes were localised affairs with the strikers usually remaining in the factories. The authorities usually conceded immediate demands and then dealt with the 'ringleaders' at leisure. With the onset of *perestroika* strikes grew in number, although at first they decreased in intensity. The full-scale revival of a workers' movement came with the miners' strikes of July 1989, signalling the moment when Gorbachev lost control of *perestroika* as a movement of reform from above and its transformation into a challenge from below.

While in the 1950s the opposition, in its cultural phase, was made up overwhelmingly of the urban intelligentsia, the demand for cultural freedom had a resonance far beyond the parochial concerns of intellectuals and into society beyond. The links with the working class were at one time weak but the repression of many dissidents forced them to manual work, if not into the larger industrial enterprises. In the Soviet Union there was fairly free movement between workers and intellectuals, and a large proportion of Soviet intellectuals was less than a generation away from the working class. Barghoorn demonstrates that intellectuals supported workers' demands, and Alexeyeva notes the lack of correlation in Soviet dissident activity between class identity and movement demands. In other words a social component was added to the earlier concerns of the cultural opposition and then the human rights movement. The struggles for the right to strike and against social injustice were increasingly seen as connected. At the same time, the belief in workerism – the view that the working class possessed certain innate virtues and that politics can be based on this alone – was discredited by the experience of Stalinism. It would no longer be possible to repeat the Bolsheviks' own pattern of coming to power by agitation among workers under the guidance of intellectuals.

THE RETURN OF PLURALISM

Since at least the death of Stalin there had been growing social pressure, led by intellectuals, for greater autonomy. Ultimately, the Soviet regime never found a way of integrating the growing pluralisation of society into the institutions of the system. Instead, dissent and the later explosion of social activism during *perestroika* contributed to the downfall of communism in Russia and the other republics. The reason for this, it might be argued, is that Leninist forms of rule by definition exclude the contestation and bargaining typical of politics. For Lenin, politics (like the state itself) emerged from the conflict of classes, and under socialism politics was destined gradually to give way to the 'administration of things' as classes disappeared. Gorbachev's rejection of the centrality of class conflict allowed the revival of politics, and party rule became monopolistic rather than monolithic, but the new pluralism became institutionalised in ways that destroyed the integrity of the Soviet system.

Civil society can be defined as a sphere independent of and legally guaranteed by the state. A civil society is one where rights are effectively secured and in which civil associations and interest groups can assert themselves. It is a pluralist approach to society. Civil society in the Soviet context represented the nascent entrepreneurial class, the independent groupings, freedom of expression, religious freedom and a thousand other forces that were harassed and suffocated after October 1917. Despite persecution, elements of civil society and a sense of what constitutes 'normal life' and decent human relations survived to take revenge on Lenin–Stalinism and all its works. The civil society that had been gathering strength in myriad covert ways came out into the open under Gorbachev, and this gathering force of individual and group initiative burst the bounds that mere 'democratisation' placed on them.

Despite the rhetoric, attempts to revive effective participation (see Chapter 9) under Khrushchev and Brezhnev had failed. The period of stagnation saw the gradual disengagement of the population from enthusiastic involvement in the procedures of Soviet democracy. Participation became instrumental, to achieve limited aims in housing or for career advancement. Disengagement became most pronounced among a whole generation of the best intellectuals of all professions.[6] When *perestroika* finally allowed popular re-engagement with the political process, the institutional framework was lacking to structure this activity and to allow it to take system-integrative forms. Even the many 'within-system reformers', possibly including Gorbachev himself, were forced to destroy faster than they could create, provoking the new freedoms to take on increasingly dangerous 'anarchistic' forms.

The line between official and unofficial activity practically disappeared. Gorbachev came to power after a period of severe repression against the so-called dissident movement, and while the rapid pace of reform increasingly made the term anachronistic the success of the earlier repression left no deeply embedded structures ready to emerge. Even the Russian Orthodox Church found itself deeply mired in the legacy of collaboration, and although it flourished institutionally as churches were reopened and it became a presence in national life, the taint of earlier years was by no means expunged. Dissent had always been an ambiguous term and operated at several levels ranging from resistance within the system to the brave actions of a small group of overt dissidents. *Glasnost* brought hitherto heterodox views and critical opinions into the mainstream of Soviet political life, but the legacy of the past cast a shadow over this springtime of the people.

The rebirth of politics witnessed the growth of a multitude of groups and civic organisations, known as informal associations (*neformaly*), which forced the pace of the pluralisation of Soviet politics. A law on associations came into effect in spring 1986, establishing a procedure for registration under the sponsorship of an official organisation, but most groups simply ignored the bureaucratic procedure involved and hence remained 'informal'. In August 1987 a conference of about 600 independent left-wing groups was sanctioned by the authorities in an unprecedented break with tradition. The conference was co-ordinated by the Club of Social Initiatives (CSI), formed in late 1986 to transform the reforms from above into activism from below. The emergence of these political clubs attested to the new atmosphere in which the authorities were willing to listen to some of the broad range of criticisms put forward by resisters and to learn about the true situation in the country. The conference called for the erection of a monument to Stalin's victims and warned of the dangers of right-wing nationalist extremism. It also formalised the CSI, which registered officially as a member of the Soviet Sociological Association headed by Tatyana Zaslavskaya. Toleration of such groups reflected the overdue official recognition that as society becomes more complex it becomes more differentiated, and hence becomes more difficult to control from above. New forms of social and political management were required in which participation had to become less formal and more effective.

By 1989 the informal groups had developed into a dense network of some 60,000 organisations, many concerned with sporting and other leisure activities, but a large number were involved in political life. The founding congress of the Democratic Union, the first formal opposition party since the 1920s, was held on 7–9 May 1988 amid police disruption. The congress condemned the system of rule instituted by the October revolution and Leninism, both of which in its view led to totalitarianism, and called for genuine political pluralism encompassing a multi-party system and parliamentarianism. By 1990 at least 500 parties had been founded, most no more than 'couch' parties whose entire membership could fit comfortably on a single divan. The miners' strikes from summer 1989 signalled the re-emergence of a militant labour movement, while in most non-Russian republics national movements gained ground. Environmental concern gave rise to one of the largest mass movements, with a wide range of groups promoting, defending or protesting a number of issues. A second polity emerged to challenge the official political system.

While the aims of some of the new organisations coincided with those of the reformist leadership, the mere existence of a growing independent movement combined with the underdevelopment of parties left politics increasingly fragmented, and even the communist party itself (as we saw in Chapter 6) began to disintegrate. The majority of the groups tended to represent ideas rather than interests as such, and it was to be a long time before the Western pattern of interest group formation began to be reproduced. This is characterised by a division into economic groups, which 'protect and promote the specific economic interests of their members', and ideological groups, which 'promote or defend legislative or administrative change for ideological reasons rather than to forward their members' particular financial interests'.[7] Ultimately this period of popular insurgency helped push communist rule to extinction, but it failed sufficiently to institutionalise itself in effective parties and organisations to act as a counterweight to the reassertion of post-communist rule by 'democratic' bureaucrats.[8] The popular democratic aspirations of this period have still to find an effective political form.

DISSENT IN PERSPECTIVE

The Soviet system was a guided one but within it there was much social activity of one form or another. Resistance came in many forms, from civil liberties groups, nationalist movements, religious believers, or simply individuals calling for greater truth in Soviet policy and an honest appraisal of the Stalin period. Increasingly these concerns were joined by calls for social, political and national justice. But the question remains of why resistance appeared to be so much less widespread in the Soviet Union than in Eastern Europe. One major reason is that in the Soviet Union (taken as a whole) nationalism and the Soviet regime tended to be integrated, whereas in Eastern Europe nationalist tendencies ran counter to regimes supported by the USSR. But that is only part of the answer. The reality in the Soviet Union was more complex, and the society that had emerged over seven decades of Soviet power had established a unique relationship with the regime which consisted of opposition but also a great degree of inter-action.

Some of the weaknesses of Soviet dissent can be noted. While resistance may have been widespread, it remained unfocused. There was no meta-dissent (except in some of the republics) like nationalism or religion in Poland. No single mass movement, even under *perestroika*, emerged, and the opposition remained fragmented. Overt dissent was restricted to a small minority while the rest of the population was not so much passive as demobilised, seeing no effective or purposeful way of becoming involved. The resources available to the state to mould social consciousness were buttressed by the patrimonial relationship between a nation of employees and the state as the universal employer. It is also clear that the regime was more competent than the one in the 1970s in Poland. It managed to avoid such acts of bravado, or ineptitude, as raising food prices on the eve of major holidays. The price of social peace, however, was the continued stagnation of the economy and society.

Those who had specific grievances did complain, and there were channels to incorporate such complaints. The regime was always careful to keep its finger on the pulse on public opinion and was willing to pay almost any price to avoid having to use overt and widespread coercion. To some extent dissent was too bound up with single issues, and perhaps too intro-spective. Much overt dissent was concerned with the persecutions against dissenters themselves in the late 1960s and 1970s. The concerns of many dissenters did not appeal to the mass of the Soviet people and appeared too parochial, with the exception of the issue of Jewish emigration, to make much of an impact on the rest of the world. The fate of Solzhenitsyn in the West appears to show that the issues that worried the alternative Russian society made little impact on Western public opinion. The absence of mass support clearly reflected the success of the regime in isolating dissent. Repression was accompanied by the portrayal of dissenters in a wholly unfavourable light: as maladjusted people bearing some sort of grudge against society, threatening the achievements of the republic and acting as conduits for foreign powers and influences.

Much overt dissent was concentrated among the intelligentsia, a relatively small group divided among themselves. However, the whole movement of overt resistance cannot be dismissed as the demands of a section of the elite for the privileges of the bourgeois intelligentsia in the West. The crisis of the late Brezhnev years appeared to confirm the dissident argument that social justice could not be achieved without political justice. A major weakness was that there was no clear alternative programme or idea of what might follow the Soviet regime. Effective opposition needs at least a minimum common programme around which to organise and mobilise. Reform-communist rhetoric was weakened by its identification with the regime, and the distinction between some purer socialism and the 'real socialism' practised by the government was too arcane to seize the popular imagination. Even such fundamental issues as support for basic civil rights and free elections were contested, although the almost universal condemnation of violence inhibited the emergence of terroristic resistance groups.

A further weakness was that Soviet resistance had few international links: it was largely isolated within the Soviet Union (with the exception of the Jewish, Volga German, Armenian and some other groups). Support in the West was crucial for the success of any Soviet movement, and indeed for the physical survival of many of the individuals concerned, but their departure for the West invariably weakened the movement they left behind. Some of the isolation was transcended by the rise of transnational issues, such as feminism and ecological concerns, especially after the disaster at the Chernobyl nuclear power station in 1986. The rise of a Soviet peace movement established issues of common concern legitimated by the human rights groups and the Helsinki monitoring process. These developments internationalised Soviet dissent, but links with Eastern European resistance movements remained weak.

Soviet dissent was unable to capitalise on splits within the bureaucracy itself. Some dissidents, however, were shielded by patrons in the political establishment, and it is remarkable how many of the key dissenters come from elite families. The deep conflicts within the Soviet political establishment under Khrushchev gave way to the bland façade of the Brezhnev leadership, although policy divisions remained acute. The success of the Czechoslovak reform movement in 1968 was prepared by the emergence of a group of reformers within the party itself over a period of years who were willing to respond to the profound crisis in relations between the regime and society. Conditions in the Soviet Union were different in that the pressures from society were more diffuse and even tended to neutralise each other. The group of reformers who emerged around Gorbachev gives the lie to the view that the leadership was populated only by cynics and careerists, but they, too, lacked any single coherent view of the way forward. Moreover, the new generation of official reformers (as under Khrushchev) did not appear to speak the same language as the majority of dissidents.

Resistance needs to establish some form of organisational identity to succeed, but in the Soviet Union any such organisational achievement was the signal for repression. In contrast, movements in Poland were not only able to survive but grew in strength, while even Charter 77 in Czechoslovakia was able to survive for several years. It is not surprising that the organised resistance was weak in the Soviet Union (both in the centre and the republics), when faced with such ferocious repression, managed for so many years by Andropov. The regime, especially after 1968 and with renewed intensity from 1979, was committed to suppressing overt acts of resistance and to a large extent succeeded. However, the main result of this was that the regime drove resistance deep into society, where it emerged in random acts of violent despair, poor work discipline, alcoholism, and in a profound popular distrust of the regime. Gorbachev's reforms no sooner began to overcome some of this distrust than they were engulfed by a wave of self-provoked hostility.

The achievements of dissent were not negligible. The ferment of the post-Stalin years left its mark on Soviet society. It was the first opposition of any seriousness since the elimination of Trotsky in the late 1920s. It demonstrated that apathy was not universal and that some people were willing to stand up for rights and truth. There was a broad political continuity between the concerns of the Bolshevik oppositions in the early years of Soviet power and the revived cultural and democratic opposition in the 1950s. They represented an undercurrent of resistance to the monopoly of political power that neither Stalin nor, later, Andropov could wipe out entirely.

The resistance provided alternative sources of information and ideas through underground printing (*samizdat*), sending material abroad to be published (*tamizdat*), and through audio-cassettes of popular chansonniers (*magnitizdat*), such as Vladimir Vysotsky, Alexander Galich and Mikhail Zhvanetskii. The increasing availability of VCRs was accompanied by the emergence of *videoizdat*, and gradually *computizdat*, or *PCizdat*, appeared. The resistance also provided an important source of information for the West, much of which was beamed back through the BBC and Radio Liberty. The magazine *Glasnost* tested the limits of Gorbachev's strategy of that name, yet the editor's (Sergei Grigoryants) contacts with the West exposed the magazine to the attention of the KGB. These various methods broke the regime's monopoly on information. Bolshevism as an idea in power had to be challenged in the realm of ideas to achieve a breakthrough; philosophy was to take the place of ideology. The Bolsheviks, representing the fusion of ideology and organisation, had no time, and indeed saw no need, for independent intellectual activity. The emergence of overt resistance reconstituted the Enlightenment tradition of autonomy for intellectual endeavour, the search for the rational and the reasonable (however idealistic the project might be). Intellectual resistance established the foundations for a reconstituted public sphere, an arena of intellectual debate free of state tutelage. This in itself did not signify the reconstitution of civil society, an arena of free action and the interplay of social forces and groups, but it was the essential prerequisite.

Resistance activity was far more than simply opposition to the regime. Its works enriched Russian and national cultures with books, songs and scholarly works, sometimes of a very high standard. It gave birth to a number of subcultures. It kept the national memory alive, especially by revealing the undistorted history of the Soviet Union and its peoples. The outstanding works in this respect are Solzhenitsyn's *Gulag Archipelago* and Roy Medvedev's *Let History Judge*, both focusing on the hidden history of Stalinism and repression. Indeed, one of the major achievements of the resistance was to prevent the rehabilitation of Stalin. In 1969 resistance to Brezhnev's plans expanded to include significant sections of the elite, joined by Eastern and Western European communist leaders. They also achieved an improved status for certain categories of political prisoners. Among the other successes of resistance currents have been the exoneration of the Crimean Tatars in 1967, the mass emigration of Jews in the 1970s and the waiving of the education tax on emigrants.

Dissent can be seen as a conflict within the elite (though not within the leadership), since the intelligentsia (and indeed the working class) was largely the product of regime policies. While overt political dissent did not gain much sympathy, the fight, for example, for cultural integrity cut across elite–society lines. Jeffrey Goldfarb has convincingly demonstrated that in communist societies cultural freedom was realised not simply as dissent in opposition to the prevailing order, but within the official institutions of creative life. The revival of Soviet cultural organisations during *perestroika* illustrated that the persistence of freedom in the aesthetic sphere, despite censorship and the whole vast apparatus of social control, survived in the interstices of *official* policy and institutions.[9] This probably applies to the whole range of Soviet official institutions. The argument undermines not only the logic of totalitarian theory, but theories which stress the unified nature of the communist apparatus. The fault lines that were inherent in the system were eventually unable to withstand the pressure of social and artistic forces.

The fundamental cleavage was between the communist party and other groups. In economic terms the Soviet Union became an advanced industrial society, but the existence of informal resistance and dissent illustrated the slowness of the regime to undergo political modernisation. The absence of effective formal means of conflict resolution and claims to a monopoly on legitimate intellectual debate created an underground market of ideas. In other countries many of the groups mentioned above, such as feminists and peace groups, would have become interest or lobby groups. In the Soviet Union they were forced to become dissident groupings; dissent was a product of the system itself. By legitimating the concept of socialist pluralism Gorbachev recognised that these movements did not pose a mortal threat to the Soviet regime but only to its most obscurantist features, hence he sought to enlist them in his own struggle for change. The regime accepted that it could no longer mould society but that it had to work within society and achieve its ends through patience and negotiation rather than confrontation and storming. Resistance placed limits on the bureaucracy's dream of remoulding society in its own image.

Resistance in the Soviet Union made a significant impact on Soviet politics. The resistance of a group of economists and sociologists under Brezhnev, for example, acted as the catalyst of change under Gorbachev. Many elements of the programme proposed by Sakharov and his associates became key features of the reform programme of Gorbachev, albeit in a controlled and limited form. The existence of a vigilant public opinion expressed by dissenters ensured a modicum of lawfulness of the Soviet regime and restrained some of the excessive arbitrariness. Dissent acted as the conduit to the West, which then acted as the loudspeaker, the substitute for an active society within the Soviet Union itself. The resistance ultimately placed limits on the power of the Politburo. The government could no longer push through genuinely unpopular legislation since it would encounter too much resistance: public opinion became a factor in policy-making.

Dissident activity and the state's response to it kept the focus on Khrushchev's promises of establishing socialist legality to prevent the recurrence of Stalin's arbitrary and murderous rule. Socialist legality was the Soviet equivalent of a bill of rights without the backing of the force of law. Dissent, of course, was an artificial construct since the boundary of permitted activity and thought was temporally and spatially defined: the 'healthy' criticism of a Novosibirsk academic becomes 'dissent' in the mouth of a Moscow intellectual. The resistance broadened those limits and raised them to the level of political consciousness. The fundamental impact of the activities of dissenters was initially on society itself; it kept alive the memory of the past and hopes for other ways of living. Gradually society in the form of grass-roots pressure affected the state; resistance represented an incipient pluralism. Above all overt dissent was a massive indictment of the authorities and challenged the moral authority of the government to govern in the old way. Dissidents achieved something simply by continuing to exist. Dissent was ineradicable because it was an inalienable part of Soviet reality. There were no guarantees for individual inviolability, no real restraints on state power, no irreversible process of democratisation, so dissent continued to exist. The existence of dissent is a reminder that, contrary to the arguments of modernisation theories, there is no automatic link between socio-economic change and the political system. In this respect Gorbachev was in the Leninist tradition: political change required conscious political intervention. The failure to transform and channel dissent into a 'loyal opposition' ultimately turned the whole society into dissenters and the regime was swamped by the tidal wave of opposition.

Soviet and East European resistance in general helped reformulate issues not only for their own countries but for the intellectual life of the Western political tradition. In asking the most pertinent questions about their own society, the resistance also raised issues of concern to all industrial societies. Among the cardinal questions were the restraint of authoritarianism, the possibilities of non-capitalist forms of democracy and the relationship between political and social democracy. Above all, the conviction borne of the Soviet experience that in the absence of political freedom there can be no social justice is of more than national significance, together with the renewed stress on the Kantian conviction that the individual is an end in him- or herself, not to be a nameless sacrifice on the alter of utopia. Soviet resistance pointed to the dangers of unrestrained social engineering, political dirigisme, ideological utopianism and technocratic wilfulness. These lessons, sadly, were trodden underfoot (or taken to their opposite extremes) in the rush to find the exit from communism in the early 1990s.

KEY TEXTS

Barghoorn, Frederick C., 'Regime–Dissenter Relations after Khrushchev', in Susan Solomon (ed.), *Pluralism in the Soviet Union* (London, Macmillan, 1983), pp. 131–68.

Havel, Vaclav, 'The Power of the Powerless', in Václav Havel (ed.), *Living in Truth* (London, Faber & Faber, 1987), pp. 36–122.

Medvedev, Roy, *On Soviet Dissent*, interviews with Piero Ostellino (New York, Columbia University Press, 1980).

Reddaway, Peter, 'Dissent in the Soviet Union', *Problems of Communism*, Vol. 32, No. 6 (November–December 1983), pp. 1–15.

Shtromas, A. Y., 'Dissent and Political Change in the Soviet Union', *Studies in Comparative Communism*, Vol. 12, Nos 2–3 (Summer–Autumn 1979), pp. 212–76.

Part IV
Policies

14 The command economy and reform

While human emancipation might have been the goal of Marxism, Leninism in power soon became an ideology of development. Industrialisation became the *raison d'être* of the Soviet state. This was not simply a matter of 'modernisation', since the process was as contradictory as the term itself: while the Soviet Union built the basic infrastructure of a modern medium-developed society, many of the social attributes typically associated with a 'modernised' society were missing – above all the openness to innovation in the technological and political spheres. The Soviet economy was able to achieve most of the goals it set itself and joined the front ranks of industrial powers through its ability to mobilise resources. Prestige projects like the great steel city of Magnitogorsk, the Kama River truck plant (KAMaz) or the Baikal–Amur Mainline railroad (BAM) stand as testimonies to the Soviet pattern of development. This campaign approach to economic development led Oskar Lange to liken the Soviet economy to a war economy, where all resources are concentrated on certain narrow ends, but of human emancipation little remained.

PLANNING AND POLITICAL ECONOMY

Political economy is related to historical materialism and seeks to explain the relationship between economics and politics. Marx believed that after the revolution political economy as a subject would become redundant since, in the absence of capitalist exploitation, socialist economic relations would become transparent. Reluctantly, however, Soviet scholars were forced to concede the need to study their own political economy. This was made all the more urgent since instead of inheriting a mature economic system ripe for socialism, the Bolsheviks took over from capitalism an unevenly developed country dislocated by years of war. The Soviet Union became what Alexander Eckstein called a mobilisation regime devoted to rapid economic progress. Economic performance and governmental practice became linked.

The Soviet economy was dominated by the centralised planning mechanism. About 80 per cent of all the ministries in the USSR Council of Ministers had a primarily economic function. Dedicated branch ministries, such as those for steel or power, were joined by sectoral ones covering statistics or finances. Above all, there was the Gosplan (state plan) committee, responsible for co-ordinating the whole economic life of the country. The five-year plan established general priorities, such as the balance between heavy and consumer goods, and set more detailed directives to individual plants. By 1987 Gosplan had the unenviable task of reconciling the interests of over 37,000 enterprises and production associations, and 26,300 collective and

Figure 6 USSR: natural resources

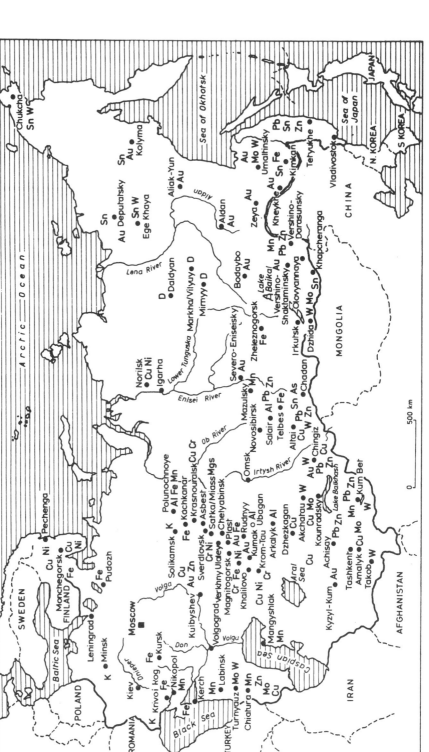

Key to minerals: Al aluminium, *As* asbestos, *Cr* chrome, *Cu* copper, *D* diamonds, *Au* gold, *Fe* iron, *Pb* lead, *Mgs* manganese, *Mo* molybdenum, *Ni* nickel, *K* potash, *Sn* tin, *W* tungsten, *Zn* zinc.

23,000 state farms, with a total workforce of 128 million dealing with over 300,000 major priorities of the government.

Direct administration increasingly gave way to directive planning (setting broad targets rather than itemised tasks) as elements of the market crept in. From the very beginning, however, the USSR was less of a planned economy than a command one; it was a society with a plan but not necessarily a planned economy. It increasingly became an administered economy, with the plans in a constant state of revision while enterprises adapted their behaviour to survive in a system marked by shortages, bottlenecks and mismanaged investment. One can talk of the anti-plan process whereby to fulfil the official plan lower bodies engaged in a variety of unorthodox strategems. To make up lost time due to supply bottlenecks, for example, enterprises engaged in 'storming' at the end of plan periods. The problems of detailed centralised planning became more acute as the economy grew in size and complexity. Despite endless exhortations to 'improve the planning mechanism', the problems required more radical changes. Most reform ideas challenged the efficacy of the direct link, established by Stalin, between production and consumption without the mediation of the market.

The party acted as the general co-ordinator and implementer of economic plans. Economic management and public administration formed a seamless web and both were equally liable to political interference. Party control over the economy was ensured through the *nomenklatura* system and the other methods outlined in Chapter 6. About half of the Central Committee's twenty-four departments up to 1988 were concerned with economic matters, such as agriculture, chemicals and defence industries. They acted as shadow ministries responsible for the supervision of economic affairs. The governmental economic bureaucracy was buttressed by a specifically party hierarchy which reviewed the state plans and budgets. In an unprecedented move in 1985 the plan proposed by Gosplan was rejected by the party. The vast network of party committees down to the primary party organisation oversaw the implementation of the plan, and the survival of a party secretary usually depended on successful plan fulfilment. It is still not clear whether party involvement actually promoted economic performance (Hough's view in *The Soviet Prefects*) or whether it engendered chronic instability and disorganisation. In 1988 the CC departments were replaced by an economic and social commission restricted to the general oversight over the economy. Whatever co-ordination the economy might have had was lost, and a decade of economic decline set in.

In the mid-1950s the achievements of the Stalinist industrial system were the admiration of socialists and non-socialists alike. The launching of the first Sputnik in 1957 seemed to support Khrushchev's contention that production per capita could exceed that of Western countries by the 1970s. Stalin's aim of 'catching up and overtaking' the West seemed to be imminent. Khrushchev's ouster in 1964 led to a more modest assessment, and by the late 1970s the talk more frequently was one of crisis. Food shortages, the lack of consumer goods, the massive waste of materials and labour power, the over-reliance on technologically obsolete coal-based industries, the poor utilisation of managerial skills, a growing budget deficit and so on became the currency of discussions about the Soviet economy. Although during the Soviet period industrial output increased sevenfold, agricultural output grew by 5.4 times, GNP quadrupled, and per capita consumption tripled,[1] critics such as Alain Besançon point out that despite the enormous sacrifices the average Soviet wage in terms of purchasing power was half that in Brazil. The great number of workers on the land, double that of Western Europe and North America combined, could not feed the country.[2] Peasant personal plots covered 4 per cent of the cultivated land and yet produced an estimated 60 per cent of potatoes, 30 per cent of

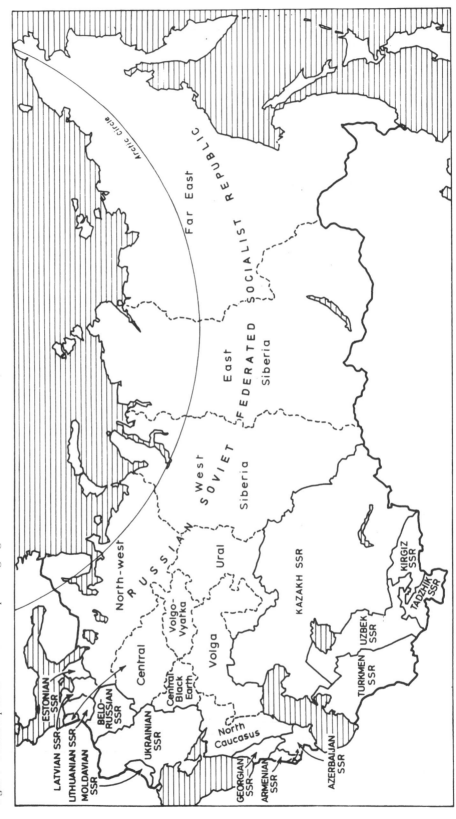

Figure 7 USSR: republics and economic planning regions

vegetables, and a large proportion of meat, milk and eggs. Moreover, the figures of Soviet economic growth were probably highly exaggerated, as some Soviet economists themselves admitted during *perestroika*.[3]

It became increasingly difficult for the USSR to sustain its global aspirations at a time when the gap between the world economy and the level of Soviet development was widening. There was a secular decline in the growth rate of the Soviet economy, especially marked from the 1960s. Annual growth rates during the first five-year plan reached 21 per cent, falling to 6.4 per cent between 1958 and 1967, 3.7 per cent between 1967 and 1973, and tailing off to under 2 per cent for most of the 1980s. Soviet GNP at the end, despite Khrushchev's hopes of overtaking the USA by the late 1960s, was still only 54 per cent of the USA's (falling from 58 per cent in 1975), and the USSR's position as the world's second largest economy was usurped by Japan, with less than half its population. Per capita GNP of the Soviet people was 48 per cent of the US level and fell from fifty-sixth place in the world in 1976 to seventieth in 1982 (see Table 7). By late 1988 some 24,000 out of 46,000 state enterprises were officially recorded as loss-making. For most of the 1980s living standards stagnated. The productivity of Soviet industrial labour was 55 per cent that of the USA, and in agriculture a quarter. The technological gap between the Soviet Union and the West was at least a decade, and growing as the USSR lagged ever further behind. It was obvious that the economic reforms of the mid-1960s had not gone far enough, and from the 1970s the economy was kept afloat by the economic benefits (however meagre) gained through détente and the exploitation of the huge new natural resources in Siberia, above all oil and gas which were exported to the West for foreign currency. Even here the Soviet Union squandered these resources, lacking the capital, technology, infrastructure, managerial skills and personnel to develop them effectively.

The pattern of Soviet economic development was unbalanced. During the first five-year plan Stalin set the country the ambitious task of 'catching up and overtaking' the West; by the 1960s this was achieved – but in terms of already outmoded indices. The emphasis had been on heavy industry, and the annual production of steel, oil, cement, pig iron and fertilisers

Table 7 Comparison of the Soviet economy and the world, 1986

Country	Population (millions)	GNP US$ (billions)	GNP USA=100	Per capita GNP US $	Per capita GNP USA=100	GNP per employee US$	GNP per employee USA=100
USA	234.5	3,310.5	100.0	14,120	100.0	29,400	100.0
USSR	272.5	1,843.4	55.7	6,760	47.9	13,600	46.3
Japan	119.3	1,157.0	34.9	9,700	68.7	20,000	68.0
West Germany	61.5	657.7	19.9	10,690	75.7	23,000	78.2
France	54.7	514.9	15.6	9,410	66.6	21,900	74.5
Great Britain	56.0	448.2	13.6	8,020	56.8	16,900	57.5
China	1,020.9	341.7	10.3	335	2.4	–	–
Canada	24.9	326.9	9.9	13,130	93.9	27,500	93.5
Brazil	131.3	296.8	9.0	2,260	16.0	–	–

Note: US dollars at 1983 values.
Sources: *Handbook of Economic Statistics* (Washington DC, National Foreign Assessment Centre, 1984), pp. 22ff.; calculated in *Soviet Union, 1984–85: Events, Problems, Perspectives*, ed. Federal Institute for East European and International Studies (Boulder, CO, Westview Press, 1986), p. 326; and using same data to compare the Soviet and American economies, see Paul R. Gregory and R. C. Stuart, *Soviet Economic Structure and Performance*, 3rd edn (New York, Harper & Row, 1986), p. 18.

surpassed the United States, and massive achievements were registered in the astronautics and military fields. However, consumer goods and services were neglected, and the information revolution lagged far behind the West. The USSR was strong in precisely those areas that characterise an emerging economy, and weak in areas that mark out a mature economy. Just at the moment when all the sacrifices of the Soviet people should have come to fruition, the definition of modernisation changed and condemned the Soviet Union to yet more exertions. Instead of decreasing, as predicted by Khrushchev, the gap between the developed capitalist countries and the USSR widened. Gorbachev constantly stressed the depth of the economic crisis bequeathed by the era of stagnation. The Soviet Union had become industrialised when the advanced countries were moving into the post-industrial era where services and information are more important than smokestack industries. Alvin and Heidi Toffler describe this as the 'third wave', following on from the agricultural and industrial revolutions, and representing a shift away from the dominance of industrialism. While aware of the issue from at least the mid-1970s, the regime under Brezhnev lacked the will to grapple with the problem. To compete, the Soviet Union needed a freer flow of information and initiative, but this would strike at the heart of the centralised political system.

The problems were not confined to the economy but amounted to a crisis in Soviet society. Leading Soviet and Western commentators identified a weakening in the political and social coherence and integrity of the Soviet polity. One of the key concepts in Gorbachev's twenty-seventh congress speech in 1986 was the idea of 'social justice', which focuses on receiving income only for work performed, but also includes a range of values such as rights to labour, education, medical assistance and social security. It also suggests such concepts as equality before the law, strengthened discipline and morality, and respect for the dignity of the person irrespective of social position or nationality. In other words, Soviet political stability was perceived as resting upon a commitment to social justice. It is in this context that the campaigns against corruption, against carbuncular architecture and the destruction of historic monuments, and against the excessive privileges of the elite have to be considered. Duty had given way to privilege, and the rhetoric of service that sustains rulers in power had weakened. It is for this reason that Gorbachev's reforms were more than a narrow attempt to improve economic performance: they were meant to affirm certain basic values to enhance the viability of society and thus the viability of the political system.

The organisation of the Soviet economy was under challenge. The suitability of a system designed to achieve the first stages of industrialisation in the more complex circumstances of the late twentieth century was questioned. The historical conjuncture was the transition from an extensive economy to an intensive one: from one concerned with building steel plants, railroads and such like, to one focused on what goes on inside the factory, the productivity of labour, the effectiveness of the machine tools, and the quality of the goods produced – not more shoes, but better shoes. The problem facing the country was to move from a labour-intensive economy to a technologically advanced capital-intensive labour-productive economy.

The economic sociologist Tatyana Zaslavskaya, in her important discussion paper of April 1983 dubbed the Novosibirsk Report, argued that the system of management created for the old-style command economy of fifty years ago remained in operation in very different circumstances. It now held back the further development of the country's economy. Her analysis was a rare example of the application of a critical Marxism to the operation of the Soviet system itself. Her argument was based on Marx's famous passage: 'At a certain stage of their development, the material production forces of society come into conflict with the existing relations of production … From forms of development of productive forces these relations turn into their fetters.'⁴ This was a theme taken up by Andropov at this time.⁵ The underlying premise was a Soviet version of convergence whereby the imperatives of industrial society forced changes in the political system. Zaslavskaya castigated the overconcentration of decision-making in the hands of central institutions, diminishing opportunities for participation from below. Popular initiative was no longer considered a luxury but essential for the further development of the economy and polity. On the grounds of rationality she argued that a more complex economy required a more responsive managing centre. The very legitimacy of the government was jeopardised by its lack of adaptability to the new circumstances, giving rise to morbid symptoms and the crisis in social justice. The existing economic arrangements, she argued, had appalling social consequences, a theme taken up by Gorbachev. She called for a shift to the market to complement the administrative allocation of resources. The nationalised economy had to take on more socialised forms.

The balance established in the post-Stalin years between economic development and political stability disintegrated. The neo-Stalinist compromise from 1953 was based on an implicit deal whereby political opposition was subdued by the state's commitment to improving the standard of living. Now the post-Stalin era came to an end as the enormous economic and social costs of sustaining the bargain became apparent. The compromise indeed had to be broken to reinvigorate the economy and to tackle the roots of the Brezhnevite malaise. As the experience of Poland demonstrated, however, the attempt to impose the burden of economic restructuring on to the population was fraught with political dangers. The state's direct responsibility for the economy at a time of declining economic performance and stagnation in living standards meant that economic resentments were directed against the political leadership. Moreover, there was a fundamental social, or class, dimension to the problem identified by Zaslavskaya. With political control over the means of production an unusually direct one in the USSR, it followed that economic reform entailed a fundamental adjustment in political relations. According to Marx a revolution takes place when the political superstructure is out of alignment with the economic base. Gorbachev's 'revolution without shots' reflected just such a fundamental realignment.

HISTORY OF ECONOMIC REFORM

In its final years the Soviet economy was faced with two types of problem. The first comprised general conjunctural issues, including such factors as demographic changes, labour shortages, technological modernisation and changes in the global economy. The second included systemic difficulties arising from problems internal to the socialist economy, and which could be remedied by actions taken by the leadership itself. Most of the latter arose from the pattern of Stalinist super-industrialisation which created a vast top-heavy bureaucracy managing the country's economic life. At a certain stage the enormous costs and wastage involved in maintaining the managing mechanism, the heart of the command economy, condemned Soviet-type economies to relative stagnation. In the absence of the invisible hand of capitalist market forces, and the increasingly palsied condition of the visible hand of command planning, such economies had no self-sustaining mechanism to imbue them with dynamism. They did not operate, at root, by cumulative gains and benefits, but by constant wasteful exertion. Instead of performing as a stimulant for the growth of the rest of the economy, for example, the expansion of the consumer sector acted as a depressant and was considered a diversion of investment from other sectors. Instead of mutually sustaining one another, they struggled for scarce resources.

These problems were not new, and the issue of economic reform had been at or near the top of the agenda at least since the death of Stalin. In 1957 Khrushchev focused on decentralisation by breaking up the ministries and creating over one hundred local economic councils (*sovnarkhozy*) (see Chapter 4). The highly centralised economic ministries, and some of their bureaucrats, were abolished. However, no effective way was found to integrate the councils and by 1962–63 there was a recentralisation and the full ministerial system was recreated by Brezhnev. Khrushchev's attempt to improve efficiency by deconcentration proved a failure and was dismissed as one of his 'hare-brained schemes'.

The debate continued, however, and the 1960s saw a boom in socialist reform economics. There was agreement that the old ministerial network had been guilty of excessive centralisation, but there was also a consensus that Khrushchev's decentralisation had not been an effective solution. At one pole reformers called for market socialism; others for cybernetic planning through the increased application of computers; while the conservatives insisted on the return of the old centralised system. Under Khrushchev a series of reforms to the old Stalinist economic model had been proposed by Yevsei Liberman; their main aim was to free the enterprises from centralised administrative control and give them greater freedom and responsibility. Planning was to retreat and concern itself with the major decisions. Industry was to be decentralised and influenced by the internal, and even the external, market. Liberman proposed replacing 'gross output' by a 'profit on total assets' as the main indicator of enterprise performance. Output as a measure of performance led to the hoarding of labour as managers produced more labour-intensive goods, and in general tried to avoid increases in their production norms. Similar ideas were put forward by Ota Sik in Czechoslovakia and had been taken the furthest in Yugoslavia, and to a lesser extent in Hungary.

In September 1965 the prime minister, Aleksei Kosygin, introduced an economic reform which incorporated some of Liberman's ideas: the regional economic councils were abolished; a system of managerial incentives was introduced; efficiency and technical rationality were to replace 'voluntarism'; and plans were to be 'directive' rather than specific.[6] The main aim of the 1965 economic reform was to give greater responsibility to individual enterprises by decreasing central direction from the ministries to improve efficiency and raise output. Managerial success was to be judged primarily by criteria of sales and profitability rather than the old method based on gross output. Managers were given some powers to allocate local resources and promote technological innovation. The reform itself was fairly limited in scope, failing to challenge any of the core principles of the Stalinist command economy, and restricted itself to altering institutional relationships. The reforms soon ran out of steam and were quickly forgotten. Bureaucratic reforms are always easy prey to 'sabotage' by bureaucrats. The leadership, and Kosygin personally, mindful of Khrushchev's recent fate, did not press the reforms out of fear of endangering their political control. Economic reform once again lost out to political considerations.

A follow-up to the 1965 economic reform was a more narrow attempt to deal administratively with low labour productivity and underemployment. The Shchekino experiment of 1967 was conducted in a chemical plant near Tula in which wage and bonus funds were integrated and managers given the right to make workers redundant without having to find them alternative employment. They were permitted to use half of the resulting wage savings to increase incentive payments to the remaining workers. The local soviets expanded their job centres to find alternative employment for those made redundant. The results were impressive as a reduced workforce increased output, productivity and wage levels. By 1980 Shchekino methods had been introduced in over 2,000 production associations, and another 7,250 used aspects of the method, but still this only covered 10 per cent of the Soviet economy. It was only reluctantly introduced by the central ministries, well aware of the broad social and political implications of the reform. Large-scale redundancies could turn into high unemployment. The reform was constrained by the 1977 constitution's guarantee of a job for every citizen, a commitment at the heart of Soviet labour policy since 1929. The attempt to achieve greater efficiency by giving more autonomy to the enterprises met with resistance from the central economic and political bureaucracy.

Brezhnev launched a small reform in 1973 in the form of production associations. These were created by the amalgamation of several allied enterprises to give them more autonomy than the individual enterprises. The reform represented an attempt to eliminate some bureaucratic duplication and to improve managerial efficiency. It presented an implicit challenge to the ministries who correspondingly dragged their feet in implementing the measure. By 1980 the associations produced only about half of Soviet industrial output with half the industrial workers. The same fate befell the Zlobin contract brigade method in the construction industry whereby payment depended on the performance of the financially autonomous brigade. There is some evidence that a group around Kirilenko in the 1970s was working towards an economic reform which would have introduced higher productive investment and wider differentials amongst workers, but the regime settled for social stability at the cost of economic stagnation. A new faith in long-range planning and computerisation of planning and economic management promised great rewards while leaving social relationships undisturbed. Continuing weak Soviet economic performance, however, forced Brezhnev to launch a mini-reform in 1979. The aim was to improve planning indicators, but in effect simple quantitative indicators were restored by a stress on quantity and the amount of goods sold. The last two decades saw a slow drift towards cost-accounting or self-financing (*khozraschyot*) principles. The clear pattern of the last thirty years of Soviet economic reforms was that they and the associated avalanche of edicts not only failed to solve the problems but in many cases exacerbated them.

The hesitancy in launching economic reforms after Khrushchev stemmed in part not only from the lack of political will but from the inability to decide the appropriate course of action. Marx and Lenin had little to offer in the new circumstances. The Hungarian New Economic Mechanism (NEM), launched in 1968, met with some success but could not be simply copied; Hungary had only some 800 enterprises and a relatively homogeneous population of 11 million, whereas the Soviet Union had a population closer to 290 million and was made up of over one hundred nationalities. In any case, the NEM suffered from certain major drawbacks of its own and was not immune to bureaucratic backsliding. The East German reforms of industry and the planning system made its economy one of the most successful in Eastern Europe, though the problem of low productivity had not been overcome. A comparison with the Chinese reforms is instructive. With ever greater conviction after 1978, the Chinese leadership under Deng Xiaoping condemned the harm caused by tight planning and called for economic decentralisation and the introduction of market mechanisms of managing the economy. By the late 1980s only about 30 per cent of the economy was still run by the state; but demands to extend the reforms to political and social life were crushed in Tiananmen Square in June 1989. Gorbachev in any case had warned that the Chinese approach to solving the problems of mature socialist economies was not applicable to the Soviet Union. There were no easy options and any reform carried its own risks; a huge economy places its own limitations on reform.

Berliner identified four models of reform. The conservative model followed by Brezhnev retained the *status quo* while making some piecemeal reforms. It focused on administrative reforms such as creating or dismantling the production associations, changing the success indicators for managers, increasing the emphasis on profit and improvements to the planning mechanism. It condemned the Soviet Union to permanent technological backwardness and consigned the Soviet population to a low standard of living. The second approach was the reactionary model which retained the basic Stalinist economic system but reversed some of the changes in social relations introduced since Stalin's death. Increased police power and coercion would have ensured discipline and order. A frequent reaction when facing mounting problems in a Soviet-type system was to reassert central control rather than to decrease it. High investment and a low standard of living would accompany the emphasis on large centralised enterprises. The third model is that of radical reform, somewhat along the lines of Yugoslavia and Hungary. It entails the decentralisation of planning and management, with the emphasis on profit, and the greater dominance of market forces, but it would be restricted by considerations of job security and limitations on income differentiation. The fourth model was the liberal one, a compromise solution since it retained the traditional planning methods for most of the economy while liberalising the restrictions on private initiative. It was reminiscent of the NEP and its mixed economy, with planning restricted to the commanding heights of the economy while allowing private initiative in certain sectors, such as services, handicrafts, retailing and construction.[7] The first two models enhance the powers of the bureaucracy, the second two undermine them.

Gorbachev's reforms combined the radical and liberal models, laced with a large dose of indecision. The Brezhnevite pattern of piecemeal adjustments of the 'economic mechanism' was replaced by broad-ranging initiatives, focusing in particular on *khozraschyot*. Gorbachev stressed the 'intensification' of the economy, the 'acceleration' (*uskorenie*) and 'invigoration' of social and economic changes. The focus at first was on modernising the machine-building complex. Institutional changes included the creation of super-ministries to co-ordinate long-term development, the shedding of some of the bureaucracy, greater powers for individual enterprises and their increased participation in drafting plans, restructuring the managerial system, increasing the participation of workers in management and dealing with the social problems of Soviet society to create social justice, though not equality. The anti-alcohol campaign from May 1985 deprived the treasury of a huge tribute from its citizens, with revenues from alcohol sales having increased fourfold in twenty years to reach 53 billion roubles in 1984. The government's growing financial difficulties and protests from the wine-growing regions caused the government to drop the campaign.[8]

Gorbachev's economic policies revived some of the practices of the NEP, including elements of the market and the equivalent of a tax in kind to replace the delivery quotas. For Gorbachev, *perestroika* above all meant the rationalisation of the Soviet administered economy to take advantage of the scientific–technological revolution. The aim was to realise the potential of socialism through the use of the 'human factor'. Gorbachev called all this 'revolutionary' and admitted that there would be a struggle to achieve it, just as Lenin had to fight for the introduction of the NEP. In the event, the attempt to raise the tempo of economic growth through acceleration while conducting reforms prevented the achievement of both.

The June 1987 CC plenum saw the radicalisation of the reforms. The document 'Main Provisions for Fundamentally Reorganising Economic Management' sought to tackle the inertia caused by fifty years of Stalinist centralisation. Gorbachev realised that his earlier reforms would fail unless carried further. This conviction was supported by his reform economists, his travels round the country and by the flood of letters complaining about the slow pace of improvements. The reforms adopted in June 1987 focused on four key features: reshaping the central planning system into a long-range mechanism giving guidance rather than specific orders; giving managers and enterprises more independence and allowing competition, with the uncompetitive ones going to the wall; eliminating the government-controlled pricing system and subsidies; and greater labour mobility, including redundancies. One of the leading reformers, Abel Aganbegyan, sought to shift the economy towards intensive rather than extensive growth, making it more receptive to technological developments, oriented towards the consumer and marked by democratic public self-management. The strategy was for the development of the 'socialist market', which Soviet commentators insisted was not to be confused with market socialism: the stress was on socialism rather than the market. Ultimately it was this that undermined Gorbachev's economic reforms in their entirety. In broad terms, Gorbachev advocated an extreme form of shock therapy yet insisted that there be no ideological or economic shock.

The rights of Soviet enterprises and farms were to be expanded and partially released from plans handed down from Moscow. The state plan was to become a general guideline while factories could deal with each other on the basis of contracts on negotiated prices rather than by prices set by state agencies. From 1 January 1988 about 60 per cent of Soviet industry began to go over to the *khozraschyot* or self-financing system. An estimated 13 per cent of enterprises operated at a loss, and thousands were in danger of going bankrupt if *khozraschyot* was seriously introduced. The details of bankruptcy proceedings remained vague, however, and were never implemented. The reform was accompanied by the radical reorganisation of foreign trade and greater freedom for the financial sector. Direct links were encouraged between enterprises and Western trading partners, allowing the establishment of joint ventures between them. By May 1988 about thirty-five had been set up by foreign corporations owning up to 49 per cent of the venture. Factory managers were forced to change the habits of a lifetime in a matter of months and sought continued guidance from the centre. The economic ministries only reluctantly relinquished their control.

The problems of agriculture typified those of the economy as a whole. Some 90 million (34 per cent) of the Soviet population lived in rural areas, and 24 million (19 per cent) of the workforce of 128 million actually worked on the land, much higher than the 2 to 5 per cent in advanced capitalist countries. And yet, far from being a net exporter of grain as before the revolution, the Soviet Union was forced to spend valuable hard currency on the purchase of foreign foodstuffs. Agriculture was no longer exploited for industry and instead under Brezhnev it became a burden on the rest of the Soviet economy, devouring 27 per cent of total investment between 1976 and 1980. The poor harvests from 1979 revealed that its problems were structural and social rather than due to any single factor such as lack of capital or infrastructure. The formation of about 9,000 agro-industrial complexes from the early 1970s as part of the attempt to industrialise farming created even more bureaucracy and restricted the rights of farm management. Administrative reforms were often used as a way of avoiding political reforms. This was clearly illustrated by the response to the Akchi experiment in Central Asia in the 1960s, which combined administrative and labour reorganisation. It was an attempt to change the political relationships on the farm by establishing new patterns of authority, with the rotation of offices and elections to fixed terms. The results were impressive, but the experiment was aborted and its organiser Khudenko imprisoned.

Gorbachev raised the status and power of the agriculture ministry by creating the new 'super-ministry' *agroprom*, cutting 22,000 bureaucrats at the same time. The reforms moved timidly beyond purely administrative changes and permitted some devolution of authority to the farms to allow more local decision-making over what to produce to overcome excessive centralised direction and misplanning. Under Gorbachev this never went so far as full decollectivisation. The Chinese experiment in decommunalising agriculture was rewarded by massive increases in output and a significant rise in rural incomes. The emphasis in the USSR was on labour reorganisation, especially the development of the autonomous work tier, or link (*beznaryadnoe zveno*). In earlier versions a small group of about five or six people worked a piece of land collectively and was paid by results. The system under Gorbachev was called *kollektivnyi podryad*, or group contract work, and was actively encouraged by him. The June 1987 CC plenum adopted measures that would expand small-scale family farming with only loose affiliation with the collective or state farms. The groups, however, did not receive the necessary support from farm managers, whose powers and prestige were threatened by the reforms. In the final period agricultural production grew much faster than industry's, giving farmers the advantage for the first time since 1929, but agriculture still devoured a subsidy of $90 billion between 1989 and 1991.

Agricultural reforms were accompanied by the planned phasing out of subsidised prices, one of the linchpins of Soviet socialism. Food price subsidies by 1987 cost the Soviet government an annual 57 billion roubles, 13.2 per cent of the state budget of 430 billion roubles. In 1986 the prices of 200,000 commodities were still set centrally. The plan was to raise salaries while decreasing subsidies for items ranging from bread to housing, remaining only for medicine, education, care for the elderly and book publishing. Each family would be entitled to a minimal apartment with subsidised rents, but prices would soar for extra space and amenities. The savings on consumer subsidies would release funds for investment elsewhere. None of this was implemented, however, and it was left to the successor regimes to tackle the huge distortions of Soviet prices.

The example of Poland in the 1970s illustrates that investment strategy is at the root of political and social stability. Spending on consumer welfare in communist states could no longer be considered a luxury; it was an integral part of improving general economic performance. In any economic system there are basically three demands on national resources: capital investment, consumption and defence. During *perestroika* the government pursued a policy of dizzy investment in industry, planning between 1986 and 1990 to lay out 175 billion roubles in capital investments, almost 50 per cent more than in the preceding five years. Gorbachev set ambitious tasks for the economy but it was never clear how he planned to achieve them. The necessary dramatic improvements in labour and capital productivity could only be achieved by giving enterprises and ministries a much greater stake in achieving profitability, otherwise the lack of correspondence between increased capital investment and steady defence spending would have meant a squeeze on social consumption in 'non-productive' sectors such as health, education, housing and culture.

Soviet technology proved its worth in the armed forces and space exploration, and yet most of the civilian economy suffered from backwardness. The introduction of new technology was inhibited by institutional conservatism, a restrictive price system and poor incentives. As elsewhere, the problem was the transition from extensive to intensive economic growth, but it was exacerbated in the sphere of semiconductor technology by the rapid pace of change in the rest of the world. The old cumbersome central planning machinery became a brake on development. The USSR was challenged by the need of modern economies for the free and rapid flow of information. The major experiment of the mid-1970s in developing a post-industrial service sector was the *Fakel'* (Torch) combine, established to provide enterprises with tailor-made software programs and various forms of consultancy work. The group was suppressed and its leader jailed. The failure of the Soviet Union to sustain an effective alternative form of social and technological organisation condemned it to sterility as an economic formation. In most areas the Soviet Union was condemned to the role of perpetual runner-up, always catching up on a world that always moved on. Information is the key to any advanced economy; however, technological advance does not operate in a social vacuum but is tied ever more closely to culture and to social structure. *Glasnost* reflected the need for the free movement of information, if not ideas. The challenge of what Daniel Bell calls post-industrialism, where the emphasis is on services and information, entailed a psychological shift of perceptions away from the USSR's romance with smoke-stack industrial development.

Perestroika aimed to give the Soviet employment structure less of a blue-collar look and make it conform more to a 'post-industrial' pattern. In 1988, 96 million (including 24 million farm workers) of the USSR's 128 million workers were in what Soviet economists called material production. While the Soviet social structure broadly approximated that of the West, there was a much slower shift from the primary to the secondary and tertiary sectors of employment. Gorbachev's reforms in the short term tended to increase the already disproportionate share of labour in the machine-building and metalworking sectors of industry. Furthermore, about 18 million people, or 14 per cent of those employed, were in administrative posts, of whom 2.5 million were in various administrative bodies such as ministries, while the rest were in the management of production associations, enterprises and offices (see Table 8). To compensate for the perceived shortage of labour, the number of administrators fell for the first time in many years in 1986.

The surfeit of labour gave way to labour scarcity, and when combined with declining returns on capital investment as the economy matured the only remaining source of economic growth was from increases in labour productivity. While the Stalinist command economy ended open unemployment, it failed to create a self-sustaining mechanism for achieving gains in labour productivity or for rewarding the productive workers, leading to the misuse of labour resources and underemployment. The participation rate (i.e. the proportion of the population aged between 15 and 64 who were employed) was 86.6 per cent in 1980, compared to 66.5 per cent in the European OECD countries and 70.9 per cent in the USA; for women, the proportion was 87 per cent, compared to 48.5 and 59.7 per cent, respectively.

Table 8   Distribution of the workforce according to sectors (%)

Sector	1940	1965	1970	1979	1984
Primary (agriculture and forestry)	54	31	25	21	20
Secondary (including construction, transport and communication)	28	44	46	48	47
Tertiary (including trade, finance, health, education, science, administration)	18	25	29	31	33
Total	100	100	100	100	100

Source: L. G. Churchward, *Soviet Socialism: Social and Political Essays* (London, Routledge, 1987), p. 30.

Despite a system of labour allocation for graduates, with the exception of the war years there had been a relatively free labour market in the USSR. Workers not only had the right to work but were obliged to do so, for most purposes they could choose where, for how long and how hard. The trend until 1987 was for the greater equalisation in earned incomes, leading to the weakening of material incentives. Zaslavskaya stressed the social repercussions of an economy which encouraged cheating and made people dishonest. The majority of economic reformers advocated pay differentials to provide incentives for more productive workers and managers alike. The promise of guaranteed employment came into conflict with the strategy of economic reform and the need to raise labour productivity. The threat of redundancy and unemployment weakened the legitimating ideology, while alternative strategies avoiding marketisation and selective incentives as a means of raising labour productivity remained vague.

The Soviet system devoted itself to suppressing individual initiative for most of its existence. A case in point is the long campaign waged on ideological grounds by the government against the *shabashniki*, the itinerant freelance construction teams active in the countryside. Gorbachev conceded that people had lost the habit of thinking and acting responsibly on their own initiative. His strategy was based on the attempt to apply the 'human factor' in the economy by freeing people's capacity to work and to stimulate economic and social initiative. These attempts conflicted with fears of the social and political consequences of growing inequality and personal enrichment. This was revealed at its starkest when measures to stimulate official economic initiative were preceded by harsh measures against unofficial private initiative. The Supreme Soviet in July 1986 passed a law against unearned income aimed at a section of the population who survived on the margins of society, especially a generation of semi-dissidents who lived by giving private lessons. From May 1987 the 'Law on Individual Enterprise' sanctioned certain kinds of businesses. Groups of family members living under the same roof, working in their time off from state jobs, were permitted to open small businesses from restaurants to toy factories, and to provide a range of services from repairs to tuition and translation. These activities were to be brought out of the twilight second economy to be monitored and taxed by the government. These moves by 1988 had been broadened to allow the development of co-operatives in a range of service industries. The co-operatives, however, tended to recycle goods from the state to the private sector at inflated prices but added very little to the net supply of goods or services.

Andropov had earlier expanded the contract brigade experiment of the 1970s. A law on worker collectives gave workers' groups certain rights to participate in the organisation of their work and to discipline their members. The 'brigade method' of shopfloor organisation was endorsed by the twenty-seventh congress, but its results were ambiguous. The aim was to overcome the chronic problems of low pay and poor working conditions by stimulating greater worker autonomy in the workplace. It shared the drawbacks typical of participation as a whole in the USSR.

The degree to which the workplace could be transformed into a democratic and egalitarian venue was as much a political as an economic question. The economic measures were accompanied by the extension of voting rights. Furthermore, under *glasnost* the unions were to take a more active role in defending the social rights of workers, ending the situation condemned by Gorbachev at the eighteenth Soviet trade union conference in February 1985 of 'trade union officials dancing cheek to cheek with economic managers'. They were to counteract the technocratic tendencies in the economy. In the struggle, as Gorbachev put it, between democracy and social inertia and conservatism the unions were to take the lead in reinvigorating self-management.

In its own terms the Soviet economy had registered massive achievements, albeit at equally massive costs. Steady, though declining, growth had been maintained. The Soviet economy suffered both from certain problems specific to itself and from others which reflected social or international factors and the quickening pace of change in all industrial societies. Above all, the problem was overcentralisation and lack of responsiveness to new demands, new technologies and new ideas. The problem was not one so much of economic collapse (until the final phase of Gorbachev's reforms) but of reducing the economic and social costs of an antiquated command system.

THE FAILURE OF REFORM

The era of stagnation saw the development of what Gorbachev called a 'pre-crisis', which would lead on to full-blown crisis if remedial action was not taken. By the late 1980s the Soviet Union had reached one of those turning points in history, like 1861 or 1905, when the need for reform was apparent to all. But, as on earlier occasions, this opportunity was embraced so half-heartedly and with so many caveats that events led on inexorably to the Soviet Union's own 1917.

Economic and allied reforms had come to the fore in the third of Russia's 'great debates', taking up the themes of the previous two of the late nineteenth century and the 1920s. The 1980s debate focused on the balance to be drawn between 'plan' and 'market' and the scope to be allowed in the private sector. The fundamental problem was the growing irrationality of the attempt to maintain the command economy and the administrative allocation of resources in a society and economy making increasingly complex claims on the system. Demands for high-quality goods and services were supplemented by calls for greater individual autonomy. The regime was faced with the problem of a lack of meaningful information in a system overburdened with information. If the economic issues, if not solutions, were clear, the political issue, as under Khrushchev, came down to a contest between the forces of reform and political conservatism.

While the restructuring of this period is linked indissolubly with Gorbachev personally, the rationale for the reforms was self-evident. Gorbachev pointed out to the Italian Communist Party newspaper *L'Unita* in June 1987 that '*perestroika* was not an enlightenment that came all of a sudden, within a single night'. The growing links between the Soviet and the world economies revealed ever more starkly the former's own shortcomings and pushed the country towards more reforms. The concept of interdependence within a single world economy implied that the weaker had to adapt to the stronger. However, while the necessity for change had become self-evident, this did not mean that the reforms were destined to succeed. The need for reform had been evident for at least thirty years, and yet they were resisted and a policy of 'muddling through' adopted. While necessity might be the mother of invention, she often goes barren.

The course of economic reform was anything but smooth. The opposition at the very heart of the process from cautious reformers such as Ligachev undermined whatever logic the reforms might have had, as in the law on unearned income of July 1986 and the restrictions hedging the law on individual enterprise of May 1987. Party and state bureaucrats did not take kindly to the torrent of abuse launched against them, with Gorbachev condemning lethargy, incompetence and corruption among party, public and economic officials. In his Krasnodar speech of September 1986 he noted the opposition to restructuring on the part of workers, peasants and even 'leading people in the apparatus. They can even be found among our intelligentsia.' In a speech of late October 1986 he argued that the bureaucracy was threatening the whole plan for the future.[9] The economic reform process was enmeshed in five major problems.

1   The first concerned the social consequences of reform: how could economic dynamism be combined with a commitment to social justice? While the attractions of the market mechanism were often proposed as a universal panacea, reform threatened to provoke social instability. The reduction in job security through the wholesale application of Shchekino methods would give rise to unemployment. At the June 1987 plenum Gorbachev pledged that new jobs would be found for the 15 million industrial workers that would be made redundant over the next decade, while women (it appeared) would be pushed back into the home. Marketisation would affect equality in incomes and services and bring out into the open existing privileges and inequalities. The monetisation of privilege would to some extent establish a new hierarchy of status. Economic reform undermines wage levelling and benefits the most skilled and best educated. A weakening of the centralised economic controls could be seen as corrosive of workers' economic rights, exposing them to the arbitrariness of the local economic and state authorities. Low prices were at the heart of the social contract between the regime and the people, while marketisation raised the spectre of inflation as managers fought to remain solvent. Price increases carried a political danger, as the authorities in Poland discovered several times, especially if lower-income groups were not adequately compensated from the very beginning. Some, moreover, would perhaps do too well out of reform, with the emergence of prosperous latter-day NEPmen and Soviet yuppies attracting the envy of the less successful, the phenomenon that later occurred, creating a group known as the 'new Russians'.

2   The second problem concerns the political consequences of reform. The decentralisation of authority threatened political fragmentation, especially in the non-Russian republics. Meaningful economic reform would raise the question of the party's dominance over political and economic life, and it would certainly change the context of the party's leading role. Economic reforms leading to the market would inexorably give rise to a pluralism in society that would sooner or later seek political expression. Chinese experience demonstrates that effective reforms entail the loosening of political controls over economic organisations. These economic organisations, producers and consumers then have to find a way of relating to each other, functioning as economic interest groups. The extent to which these groups could interact in a pluralist manner, defending not only economic but also political interests, would be a matter of concern to the political leadership. It was a political tightrope act to reap the benefits of an economic reform while containing its political implications. The Chinese reform process to date suggests that it can be done with adroit leadership.

3   The third factor was the influence of strategic and defence issues on domestic change. The Soviet reform process was traditionally hostage to the international environment. The argument that the 'international situation' does not permit reform was always a sure winner for conservatives, and it was Gorbachev's achievement to change the rules in this respect. Nevertheless, however pressing the need for reform, success is contingent upon stability in world affairs: a stability to which the USSR under Gorbachev contributed much. The arms race was converted into a process of disarmament.

4   The fourth factor which shaped the economic reforms was the role of ideology. How could the market be used in a Soviet system which had devoted seventy years to its elimination? The ideology stressed production for use rather than exchange as a commodity on the market. Party conservatives were increasingly alarmed about the ideological implications of an economic reform which increased the role of the market and raised the spectre of the restoration of capitalism. Socialism long had an intrinsic bias against 'consumerism' in which individually defined needs were regarded as frivolous in comparison with the allegedly rationally defined needs of the producers. In China the conservative reformer Chen Yun put forward his famous 'birdcage theory' which asserted that economic reform is like a bird which must be contained within the cage of socialist planning. The market deprives the central political elite of control over individual needs and gives rise to income differentials. The remnants of 'leftism' in China hindered the programme of reform and defended the rights of the party in economic management. Such 'leftism' was much more deeply entrenched in the Soviet Union and was more difficult to overcome than in China, where it was discredited by the excesses of the cultural revolution.

The basic argument focused on what was and what was not socialism. Would a partial restoration of market relations undermine the fundamental ideological premise of Marxism that there is a rational alternative to capitalism? The conservatives argued that liberal or radical economic reforms of Soviet-type systems undermined Marx's belief that communism is an alternative in which a community of producers could in a conscious way shape social relations and organise production. The reformers argued that economic reform was precisely the prerequisite for the fulfilment of this ideal, and in addition it would help alleviate the evident alienation in Soviet society. Marxism–Leninism in any case proved to be relatively flexible, permitting the personal plot and the free peasant market, the use of the incentive system from the 1930s and great inequality. The black economy of market relations already existed, caused by the disparity between supply and demand. There was furthermore the ideological current of 'advanced modernisation' (encompassing the scientific–technological revolution – STR), the economic equivalent of developed socialism, which was used to justify reform. But the ideology did place limits on economic reform. Gorbachev was careful to guard himself against accusations of 'revisionism', the worst charge in the communist lexicon of abuse. He insisted that the changes were not to be seen as a repudiation of principles but that, on the contrary, they were designed to develop, in his words, the potential and superiority of the socialist system.

5   The fifth factor on which restructuring depended was its ability to overcome opposition. Strategies can be considered in terms of the social forces that are served by one or another reform programme and, perhaps more importantly, whose interests are threatened. Opposition to reform was both social and political: the social elite defended its privileges; and political resistance took the form of the defence of ideological traditions. Resistance focused on four key groups: the economic bureaucrats; the political elite; the military; and the industrial workers. The opposition of the economic and political bureaucrats to the reforms in Hungary and China has been well documented. Their powers and privileges were eroded by the marketisation of the economy. Zaslavskaya argued that there was a social basis to opposition to economic reform, in effect admitting that there were contradictory social antagonisms in the Soviet system. Among bureaucrats she located the main source of opposition as the middle level of economic management in the ministries. Gorbachev criticised the ministries, to whom power had devolved under Brezhnev to create what Hough dubbed a type of 'feudalistic socialism'. The major contradiction of the first phase of *perestroika* was between the rights granted to

enterprises by the Law on State Enterprises of January 1988 and the existing powers of the ministries. The conversion of the huge Gosplan agency, used to directing the operations of the economy with thousands of employees, to a long-range planning agency was particularly ambitious, not least because of the lack of long-range planners. Sections of the political elite were clearly against liberal or radical reform. The very unpredictability and loss of control over social processes ran against the grain of the Soviet system. An increased role for the market presupposed the impartial rule of law, greater autonomy of the state from the political system, a growing divergence between the party and the government, and a relatively free flow of information and access to accurate government statistics, implying a reduction in the government's monopoly of information.

Opposition to reform was fragmented and could not unite on an alternative policy; yet, for radical or liberal reforms to succeed, a 'reform coalition' had to be created, sustained by a convincing rationale and marked by effective leadership. This ultimately was not forthcoming. The whole notion of 'economic reform', moreover, itself perpetuated top-down change. The problem, however, of how there could be organic growth of capitalism in a country where the very bases of neo-classical economic development had been extirpated (above all property rights, a legally regulated market and an entrepreneurial middle class) remains unresolved to this day.

KEY TEXTS

Aganbegyan, Abel, *The Challenge: Economics of Perestroika* (London, Hutchinson, 1988).

Colton, T. J., *The Dilemma of Reform in the Soviet Union*, rev. edn (New York, Council on Foreign Relations, 1986).

Lane, David, *Soviet Economy and Society* (Oxford, Basil Blackwell, 1985).

Nove, Alec, *An Economic History of the USSR* (Harmondsworth, Penguin, 1972).

Nove, Alec, *The Soviet Economic System*, 3rd edn (London, Unwin Hyman, 1981).

Zaslavskaya, Tatyana, 'The Novosibirsk Report', introduced by Phil Hanson, *Survey*, Vol. 28, No. 1 (Spring 1984), pp. 83–108.

15 Nationality politics

The Tsarist empire was dubbed by Marx 'the prison house of peoples', and yet the Soviet Union recreated a multinational state made up of some 126 registered nationalities and 170 languages. Only a few of the peoples, however, made a significant impact on the Soviet polity. According to the 1989 census there were twenty-two ethnic groups with over a million members (see Table 9), fifteen of whom had their own union republics. The viability of such a state in an era of nationalism and the dismemberment of empires was much debated, often posed in terms of whether there was a nationality 'question' or a nationality 'problem' in the Soviet Union. If the latter, then the state was threatened by centrifugal nationalist pressures, whereas the former implied no more than a manageable policy issue. The Soviet view was clear. The revised party Programme adopted in 1986 proclaimed that, 'The national question, a legacy of the past, has been successfully solved in the USSR.' This somewhat dismissive view was modified by the Soviet leadership in the light of the many contentious issues in nationality politics revealed by *glasnost*.

National sensitivities were revealed by the ousting of the long-time head of the party organisation in Kazakhstan, D. Kunaev, in December 1986 and the parachuting in of a Russian replacement, G. Kolbin, leading to riots in which several people died. At the January 1987 CC plenum Gorbachev spoke with obvious concern about the threat to the integrity of the USSR posed by nationalist groups. Demonstrations in the Baltic republics from 1987 illustrated the strength of national feelings in areas with recent memories of independent statehood. The vote in February 1988 of the Supreme Soviet of the Nagorno-Karabakh autonomous region to leave Azerbaijan to unite with Armenia brought inter-ethnic conflicts to the fore in the last period of Soviet politics. The dynamic between national reawakening and democratisation revealed the bitter conflicts lurking not far below the surface of the Soviet polity.

SOVIET CONSTITUTIONS AND FEDERALISM

In his pamphlet of 1916 *The Socialist Revolution and the Right of Nations to Self-determination* Lenin argued in favour of self-determination for peoples, in part to encourage the break up of empires but also reflecting traditional socialist anti-colonialism. His thinking reflected another socialist tradition, the belief that class should take precedence over national interests, a view expressed most forcefully by Rosa Luxemburg. Lenin remained loyal to this proletarian internationalist vision of socialism during the First World War, in contrast to the compromises with nationalism made by many other socialist leaders. After coming to power the long-term goal of

Table 9   Ethnic composition of the population, 1959–89

Ethnic group	No. (000s)			As percentage of total population		
	1959	*1979*	*1989*	*1959*	*1979*	*1989*
1 Russians	114,114 (1)	137,397 (1)	145,071	54.6	52.5	50.6
2 Ukrainians	37,253 (2)	42,347 (2)	44,135	17.8	16.2	15.4
3 Uzbeks	6,015 (4)	12,456 (3)	16,686	2.9	4.8	5.8
4 Belorussians	7,913 (3)	9,463 (4)	10,304	3.8	3.6	3.6
5 Kazakhs	3,622 (6)	6,556 (5)	8,137	1.7	2.5	2.8
6 Azerbaijanis	2,940 (7)	5,447 (6)	6,791	1.4	2.1	2.4
7 Tatars	4,968 (5)	6,317 (7)	6,645	2.4	2.4	2.3
8 Armenians	2,787 (8)	4,151 (8)	4,627	1.3	1.6	1.6
9 Tajiks	1,397 (16)	2,898 (11)	4,216	0.7	1.1	1.5
10 Georgians	2,692 (9)	3,571 (9)	3,983	1.3	1.4	1.4
11 Moldavians	2,214 (12)	2,968 (10)	3,355	1.1	1.1	1.2
12 Lithuanians	2,326 (10)	2,851 (12)	3,068	1.1	1.1	1.1
13 Turkmens	1,002 (19)	2,028 (13)	2,718	0.5	0.8	0.9
14 Kyrgyz	969 (22)	1,906 (15)	2,530	0.5	0.7	0.9
15 Germans	1,620 (13)	1,936 (14)	2,035	0.7	0.7	0.7
16 Jews	2,268 (11)	1,811 (16)	1,376	1.1	0.7	0.5
17 Latvians	1,400 (15)	1,439 (18)	1,459	0.7	0.5	0.5
18 Bashkirs	989 (20)	1,371 (19)	1,449	0.5	0.5	0.5
19 Mordvins	1,285 (18)	1,192 (20)	1,153	0.6	0.5	0.4
20 Poles	1,380 (17)	1,151 (21)	1,126	0.7	0.4	0.4
21 Estonians	989 (21)	1,020 (22)	1,027	0.5	0.4	0.4
22 Chuvash	1,400 (14)	1,751 (17)	839	0.7	0.7	0.4
Total	208,827	262,085	286,717	100.0	100.0	100.0

Notes: Figures in brackets refer to ranking order in 1959 and 1979. Figures for 1979 refer to permanently resident population as distinct from the population resident on the day of the census, 17 January 1979. The table excludes the 1.66 million ethnically heterogeneous Dagestanis.
Sources: *Narodnoe khozyaistvo SSSR v 1959 godu* (Moscow, 1960), p. 14; *SSSR v tsifrakh v 1986 godu* (Moscow, 1987), p. 32; *Chislennost' i sostav naseleniya SSSR* (Moscow, 1985), p. 71; *Natsional'nyi sostav naseleniya* (Moscow, Goskomstat, 1991), pp. 3–4.

Soviet communism was not merely to draw nations together but to bring about their merger. The distinction outlined by Lenin between the 'drawing together' (*sblizhenie*) of nations and their 'merger' (*sliyanie*) was a crucial one for later developments.

Soviet constitutions

The first years of Soviet power were marked by debates over the constitutional form that the new republic should take. The July 1918 constitution created a federal state (although within a centralised political framework), known as the Russian Soviet Federated Socialist Republic (RSFSR), covering the Russian heartlands. By the end of the Civil War most of the historical lands of the old Russian empire were under Soviet control (with the exception of Poland, the Baltic republics, Finland and the Far Eastern republic of Tuva), and hence the problem arose over how to administer the territory now under Soviet rule. Lenin gave short shrift to the ideas of the Austrians Karl Renner and Otto Bauer in favour of non-territorial cultural autonomy for national communities within the framework of a single state. Stalin, the long-time Bolshevik specialist on national affairs and commissar of nationalities, envisaged a unitary state with some autonomy for the regions and nationalities (the autonomisation plan). This would have made the regions units of a centralised Soviet state. Stalin insisted that the minority peoples should not be allowed to regress to a more backward system once they had become socialist. Hence, he argued, there was no need for the self-determination as earlier propounded by Lenin. The communist party itself was organised on unitary principles with its centre in Moscow and branches in the republics. Attempts by the Ukrainian Bolshevik party in 1920 to achieve some autonomy were vigorously suppressed by the Moscow leadership. Lenin rejected Stalin's autonomisation plan, bitterly distressed as he was at the time by what he called 'Great Russian chauvinism' displayed by Stalin, Orjonikidze and Felix Dzerzhinsky (none of whom was an ethnic Russian) towards the Georgian communists, and insisted on the association of formally equal nations in a federal system.

The Union of Soviet Socialist Republics (USSR) came into being in December 1922 with four founding republics: the RSFSR, Belorussia, Ukraine and the Transcaucasian Federation (Armenia, Azerbaijan and Georgia). A new constitution was adopted in January 1924, outlining the system which remained at the base of Soviet federalism. It was not as loose a federation as was the case in the USA, Canada or Australia; the central authorities in Moscow reserved certain powers such as the right to declare war, make treaties and develop a general economic plan for the country as a whole. The guiding principle of Soviet federalism, as Stalin put it, was to be 'national in form but socialist in content'. Although the word 'union' (*soyuz*) in Russian denotes 'alliance', the right to secede was only nominal. The structure of the USSR was replicated at lower levels since most of the constituent republics were themselves federated (see Table 10). The fifteen 'union republics' in principle had the right to manage their own affairs, and even the right of seceding from the union. The twenty autonomous Soviet socialist republics (ASSRs) belonged to one or another union republic and were populated by national groups who gave their name to a particular ASSR and were thus known as the titular nationality in that republic. They enjoyed a degree of local self-management and were represented in the affairs of the local republic and in the Soviet of Nationalities of the USSR Supreme Soviet. The eight autonomous regions (*oblasts*) and ten autonomous districts (*okrugs*) represented enclaves of national minorities and had few powers to manage their own affairs.

In the 1920s nationality politics were conducted in a relatively tolerant climate under the slogan of 'nativisation' (*korenizatsiya*). A Latinised alphabet was devised for the Turkic languages of Central Asia to replace the Arabic script, on the pattern adopted by Turkey itself. However, with the consolidation of Stalin's dominance, even though he was a Georgian, nationality policy took on a more chauvinistic and Russian face. The Turkic peoples were compelled to change their alphabet yet again and adopt the Cyrillic script. A peculiarly Stalinist cult of Russian glory was launched, and the historical and cultural traditions of minority peoples were undermined. Marxism–Leninism was combined with a Russianised version of Soviet communism to sustain a distinctive type of Soviet nationalism. As in Stalinist Eastern Europe after the Second World War, national cultures were reduced to folklore, and intellectual traditions that proved intractable were repressed. The accord with Russian nationalism and the Russian Orthodox Church during the Second World War proved temporary, but it ensured the identification of Soviet power with Russian national interests for the duration of the emergency. Stalin's Russification policy was not one pursued out of respect for Russian traditions but for perceived state interests.

Under Khrushchev policy emphasised the imminent merger (*sliyanie*) of nationalities. The concept of the New Soviet Person was promoted as a supranational entity whose loyalty to the

Table 10 Ethno-federal units of the USSR

Union republics	Autonomous republics (ASSR)	Autonomous oblasts (regions)	Autonomous okrugs (districts)
USSR			
RSFSR	Bashkiria	Adyegai	Agin-Buryat
	Buryatia	Gorno-Altai	Komi-Permyat
	Chechnya-Ingushetia	Jewish (Birobijan)	Koryak
	Chuvashia	Karachaevo-Cherkessia	Nenets
	Dagestan	Khakassia	Taimyr
	Kabardino-Balkiria		Ust-Ordyn-Buryat
	Kalmykia		Khanty-Mansi
	Karelia		
	Komi		
	Mari		Chukot
	Mordvinia		Evenk
	North Ossetia		Yamalo-Nenets
	Tatar		
	Tuva		
	Udmurtia		
	Yakutia		
Ukraine			
Belorussia			
Moldavia			
Transcaucasia			
Azerbaijan	Nakhichevan	Nagorno-Karabakh	
Georgia	Abkhazia	South Ossetia	
	Ajaria		
Armenia			
Central Asia			
Uzbekistan	Karakalpak		
Kazakhstan			
Tajikistan		Gorno-Badakhshan	
Kyrgyzstan			
Turkmenistan			
Baltic			
Lithuania			
Latvia			
Estonia			

socialist commonwealth would take precedence over ethnic affiliation. The concept of *rassvet*, cultural unification on a higher level, joined the lexicon of Soviet nationality policy. Economic concerns also encouraged closer national integration since the existing republican boundaries were not logical from the point of view of economic planning.

The tension between an ethno-federal state and a unitary political system was reflected in the discussions from 1959 leading to the adoption of the 1977 constitution. Certain officials sought to change the system on the grounds of institutional parallelism, unclear jurisdictional boundaries and the fact that demographic changes had made several titular nationalities minorities in their own republics, as in Kyrgyzia and Kazakhstan. Brezhnev admitted that proposals had been made to abolish federal divisions to create a unitary state, but fears of an ethnic backlash and charges of Russification prevented their implementation. The language issue in the Caucasian republics (Georgia, Armenia and Azerbaijan) revealed the sensitivity of the national problem in the region. Earlier local constitutions had stipulated that the national language was the 'state language of the republic', whereas the new draft republican constitutions implied that official status should be shared with Russian. The proposals evoked a sharp response, including demonstrations in Tbilisi in April 1978 in which a reported 20,000 demonstrators took to the streets demanding the restoration of Georgian to its former status. In an unprecedented concession to popular opinion, the demonstrators achieved their demands in the three republics and the languages of the titular nationalities were restored to prominence. The Brezhnev period as a whole saw the strengthening of ethno-federalism as the dominant mode of managing the national question; the titular peoples were allowed to strengthen their hold over the politics of the particular union or autonomous republic. A centralising ethos, however, ensured that republican powers were left vague while those of the union were consolidated, especially in economic affairs. The ethno-federal structure was retained as a concession to national feelings but did not contradict the goal of integration, the 'drawing together of nations' (*sblizhenie*).

Soviet federalism

The 1977 Soviet constitution recognised a large degree of local autonomy, and yet because of the superimposition of various overlapping administrative structures, between which there was no clear demarcation, local autonomy was often weakened. The ministerial system, for example, was highly centralised and allowed little scope for the republican or union-republican ministries. The rights of the republics were always subordinated to the larger interests of the Soviet state. As in other areas, the ethos of Soviet federalism was democratic centralism.

The criteria for inclusion as a republic were established by Stalin in 1936, when some autonomous republics were elevated to union-republic status. He listed three necessary factors to become a republic: sufficient population, considered to be over 1 million; compactness of population, which excluded the Jews who were scattered throughout the USSR; and location on the borders of the USSR, in case of secession. This latter provision excluded the Tatars and Bashkirs, who in terms of size and compactness of population deserved to become republics. It has also been suggested that these criteria were supplemented by whether peoples had resisted Soviet power, as in Central Asia, or had accepted the change relatively peacefully (Tatars and Bashkirs) and thus posed no threat. The fragility of Soviet constitutional guarantees for the rights of republics and peoples was demonstrated by the wholesale deportations during the Second World War and the summary dissolution of the Finno-Karelian republic by Khrushchev in 1956 once hopes were abandoned of the incorporation of Finland into the Soviet Union.

The right to secede remained a legacy of early Bolshevik ideas on the national question. It was a symbolic right and underlined the claim of the 1977 constitution that union republics were sovereign. Nevertheless, the constitution's emphasis on the unity of the Soviet state made the right virtually meaningless in practice. From 1957 union republics had the legal right to enact their own codes of law (a power that had been lost in 1936). The powers in this respect were very limited and allowed only some small regional variations to take into account local customs and traditions. Compared to American states the budgetary rights of Soviet republics were very weak. They were not permitted to raise taxes other than sales taxes or to dispose of their own revenues. The central government adopted a budget for the whole nation and allocated a share to each republic. In 1944 union republics were authorised to conduct their own foreign relations and allowed diplomatic representation. The aim was to gain extra seats in the

United Nations, being formed at that time. In the event only two republics achieved this right, the Ukraine and Belorussia, while Russia remained subsumed into the larger USSR. The same provisions in 1944 permitted union republics to maintain military forces, albeit with the centre retaining ultimate control. The 1977 constitution dropped all reference to this right, even though all the other symbols of republican sovereignty were retained. The army, like the party, was confirmed as being centralised and unitary.

Soviet federalism was marked by the notion of a 'new historical community of people' in the process of creation, the Soviet people, to which distinctive ethnic feelings were to be subordinated. While the Soviet Union never accepted the 'melting pot' theory of national assimilation, the idea of *sblizhenie* suggested that Soviet nations would be expected to mould themselves to the norms of their Russian 'elder brother'. Notions of Soviet patriotism and socialist internationalism downgraded pride in ethnicity. Nevertheless, the government was careful not to force the pace of *sliyanie* and instead under Brezhnev talked of 'complete unity' (*polnoe edinstvo*), which excluded biological homogenisation. The fear of a 'yellowing' of the Slavic peoples was an element in Soviet policy.

Tensions in the Soviet practice of federalism were apparent. As Bialer points out, there was a potentially fatal dualism in a Soviet federalism which in practice denied any but the slimmest margin of autonomy to the constituent nationalities and yet provided them with the symbolic institutions and administrative framework for autonomy.[1] Each union republic had the trappings of its own nationhood, which, given the collapse of central political authority in 1991, formed the core of a revived independent national identity. The 'dialectic of nationality' in the Soviet Union therefore emphasised unity and the struggle against centrifugal tendencies, while in practice tolerating the institutional framework of proto-statehood. The fear of centrifugal forces provided the rationale for the centralised unitary party dominating society. Nationalist tendencies also affected the nature and scope of economic reform and political democratisation. A formula was sought that did not weaken the unity of the state while reflecting the size and diversity of the nation. This formula was never found, and the centralised rule of the communist party acted as a substitute for a genuinely viable state system that could have forged unity out of diversity.

NATIONALISM IN THE USSR

While the regime claimed to have solved the national problem in the USSR, the question of what the Kazakh writer Olzhas Suleimenov called 'inter-nation relations' remained sharp. Nationalism in the Soviet context was particularly difficult to define. The two entries in the Soviet passport for citizenship and nationality reflected and perpetuated the dual nature of nationality in the USSR. In 1932 Stalin included a question on nationality in the new domestic passports. The fifth point specified the national identity of the holder in addition to the general rubric of Soviet citizenship. The entry was determined by the passport nationality of either parent, and a child at the age of sixteen could choose either (if those of the parents differed) but not another one, and thereafter it was almost impossible to change. The system erected rigid boundaries between ethnic groups and inhibited the development of a common sense of nationality, let alone Russification. If nationalism is above all subjective affiliation, then the fact of formal identification for life with a particular ethnic group decided by the parents at birth clearly caused much confusion as felt ethnic identification diverged from that inscribed in the passport.

The debate over whether the USSR was an empire continues to this day.[2] For the subjugated peoples of the Baltic, Western Ukraine and some other places there is little to be discussed: the Soviet regime perpetuated (and indeed intensified) Russian imperial dominance. For the rest, however, the question is not so clear cut. The USSR certainly differed from the Austro-Hungarian empire or even the British empire, which were based on very different dynamics. Rutland even went so far as to argue that it was quite possible that 'national identity can be channelled in ways that are integrative and system-supporting, rather than constituting a purely negative political force',[3] an argument that is not entirely invalidated by the disintegration of the USSR in 1991. Just as ethnic pride in the USA does not always pose a political challenge, so a rise in both Russian and minority nationalism was seen as not necessarily threatening the stability of the USSR; a renegotiated (con)federation remained Gorbachev's ambition to the end. The USSR was an 'empire' without a core, and although the other nationalities considered that Russia filled this role, the Russians themselves felt no less hard done by than any other nationality. It is clear that in the Soviet context nationalism was an evolving concept, just as was the notion of 'empire'.

Nationalism operated in a vertical or horizontal manner: vertically when counterposed to the central authorities; and horizontally when taking the form of inter-ethnic rivalry or conflict. Rakowska-Harmstone divided late Soviet nationalism into two categories: orthodox, or within the system; and unorthodox, which in some way challenged the system. The distinction between the two is flexible, with much of the ambiguity deriving from the dynamics of the relationship between Russians and non-Russians. Orthodox nationalism could take many forms, and during *perestroika* the issue of 'national justice' became the counterpart of social justice as various peoples sought to redress long-standing grievances. National elites were permitted within certain bounds to defend the interests of their locality. This could take the form of encouraging acceptable expressions of cultural nationalism, local arts and traditions. But above all orthodox nationalism took the form of defending regional economic interests. In a centralised system such as the USSR this was reflected in attempts to achieve some local autonomy to manage the economy, to gain a greater share of investment from the centre, to obtain preferential access to scarce consumer goods, and in general to modify national economic policy to the advantage of the republic.

The national implications of military deployment were illustrated in the case of the war in Afghanistan. The initial assignment of Central Asian forces in Afghanistan proved unsuccessful and they were replaced by non-Muslim forces. Hopes of creating local militia forces founded on the fear that they would be unreliable in case of disturbances in their own areas. During the 1956 riots in Tbilisi following the denunciation of Stalin the predominantly Georgian units in the locality were not used. The worker unrest in Novocherkassk in 1962 could only be suppressed after the local forces were replaced by loyal troops brought in from outside. Requests by Estonia for their recruits to be deployed in their republic were refused, although a similar request in Kazakhstan was regarded more favourably.

Investment policy in particular was bound up with national sentiments. If resources were assigned to the Slavic parts of the country the anger of the non-Slavs was aroused, and if to other republics, the Slavs felt aggrieved. This sort of elite nationalism often merged into unorthodoxy. For example, under Khrushchev Latvian officials opposed the expansion of the republic's heavy industry on the grounds that it would lead to the further dilution of the Latvian population in the republic. This led to a purge of top officials. The warnings by local officials opposed to the Virgin Lands Scheme that it would mean a vast influx of Russians proved correct and Kazakhs became an even smaller minority in their own republic (see Table 11). In

Table 11 Titular nationalities in the USSR

Republic	Population of republic (000s) 1979	1989	Percentage urban, 1979	Ethnic composition 1989 (%) Titular nationality	Russian
USSR	262,436	286,717	66	–	51.4
Moldavia	3,947	4,341	47	64.5	13.0
Slavic					
RSFSR	137,551	147,386	74	81.3	81.3
Ukraine	49,755	51,704	67	72.7	22.1
Belorussia	9,560	10,200	65	77.9	13.2
Transcaucasia	14,074	15,761			
Azerbaijan	6,028	7,029	54	82.7	5.6
Georgia	5,015	5,449	56	70.1	6.3
Armenia	3,031	3,283	68	93.3	1.6
Central Asia	40,165	49,381			
Uzbekistan	15,391	19,906	41	71.4	8.3
Kazakhstan	14,685	16,538	57	39.7	37.8
Tajikistan	3,801	5,112	33	62.3	7.6
Kyrgyzstan	3,529	4,291	38	52.4	21.5
Turkmenistan	2,759	3,534	45	72.0	9.5
Baltic	7,385	7,944			
Lithuania	3,398	3,690	68	79.6	9.4
Latvia	2,521	2,681	71	52.0	34.0
Estonia	1,466	1,573	71	61.5	30.3

Sources: *Naselenie SSR: po vsesoyuznoi perepisi naseleniya 1979 goda* (Moscow, Politicheskoi literatury, 1980), pp. 23–6; *Izvestiya*, 28 April 1989; *Pravda*, 29 April 1989; *USSR: Facts and Figures Annual*, ed. Alan P. Pollard, Vol. 15 (Gulf Breeze, FL, Academic International Press, 1991), pp. 499–502.

the case of Armenia, however, such considerations were respected and the Yerevan subway system was built by Russian *Gastarbeiters* (guestworkers) housed in tents so that they would not stay after the job was completed. The Ukrainian first secretary Peter Shelest opposed large-scale investment in Siberia and the North on the grounds that it would divert resources from the industrial heartlands of the Ukraine. He also sought to defend Ukrainian intellectuals from persecution by central authorities until he was purged himself. Such nationalism was not only manifested by minorities but applied equally to Russians. Politburo members D. Polyanskii and A. Shelepin allegedly headed a 'Russia first' faction, a position which Leningrad party boss G. Romanov was reputed to share and which may have contributed to his fall on Gorbachev's accession in 1985.

Unorthodox nationalism took many forms and was reflected in a mass of *samizdat* (self-published) literature, much of which came out into the open with the onset of *glasnost*. Most was based on religious, cultural or historical concerns, and to a lesser extent posed a directly political challenge to existing policies. There was an upsurge of national self-consciousness in all the republics focusing on language and ecological issues. This was not restricted to students and intellectuals but penetrated the mass of the population, and much went beyond the tolerated limits. At the extreme there was the rise of militant nationalism which challenged the very principles of Soviet federalism. In places there were demands for the independence of certain republics or support for long-standing irredentist demands.

The largest single national group in the USSR was Russian, with a population in 1989 of 145 million, representing 50.6 per cent of the Soviet population (see Table 9, p. 238). The declining birth-rate in Russia from 1960 meant that Russians became an ever-smaller proportion of the total Soviet population, and already by 1979 the ethnic Russian part of the population was less than half if the number of mixed marriages and children opting to have Russian as the nationality placed into their passports are taken into consideration. This represented a major psychological turning point and emphasised even more clearly the multinational character of the Soviet Union. The second largest group comprised the Ukrainians with 44 million (15.4 per cent); So, with the inclusion of the Belorussians at 10.3 million (3.6 per cent), Slavs made up nearly three-quarters of the total population.

Russian nationalism in the Soviet era took many forms and ranged from orthodoxy into unorthodoxy. The extreme right stressed racial purity of the Slavs in a language couched in anti-Semitic allusions and imbued with militaristic patriotism. They were particularly harsh in warning against the Chinese threat. Less extreme but still on the right was a tendency called National Bolshevism, derived from Nikolai Ustrialov who in 1920 reversed the official slogan and argued that the new regime was 'socialist in form, nationalist in content'. Stalinism was imbued with a sense of militant nationalism, but Mussolini was mistaken when he argued that Bolshevism had disappeared in Russia and in its place a Slav form of fascism had emerged. Soviet nationalism on the whole had little in common with the fascist type since it was not based on the militant projection of one ethnic group at the expense of others. The Russification that did occur was more of an administrative process rather than an attempt to glorify Russia proper. Latter-day national Bolsheviks praised the Soviet regime for having recreated the old Russian empire and restored Russia to great power status. Soviet nationalism certainly projected its Russian credentials, but at the same time forms of Russian patriotism that deviated from the Soviet path were persecuted as much as any other national deviancy – and in certain respects more so since many of the other nationalities had their own republican party leaderships to shelter behind whereas Russia lacked its own communist party and other attributes of statehood.

The conservative nationalists, like the group around the Molodaya Gvardiya publishing house of the Komsomol organisation, can be characterised as Russites and neo-Slavophiles. They worked within the establishment and were shielded by Polyanskii and allegedly by the KGB since they served as a counterweight to unorthodox Russian nationalists, who focused on religious or human rights issues. The semi-fascist and anti-Semitic features of this tendency represented morbid symptoms of the stifling immobility of the later Brezhnev years. In a long article in the November 1972 issue of *Literaturnaya gazeta* Alexander Yakovlev, then acting head of the Propaganda Department of the CPSU's Central Committee, in an article entitled 'On Antihistoricism', condemned the anti-Leninist stance adopted by nationalists and neo-Stalinists in some official publications, and denounced the awakening of Russian self-consciousness as 'patriarchal mentality, nationalism and chauvinism'. In response, in 1973 he was dismissed from his post and sent into 'exile' in Canada to serve as Soviet ambassador until recalled by Gorbachev. He was made a member of the Politburo and developed the increasingly liberal ideology of *perestroika* – for which he earned the hatred of the Soviet Russophiles. During *perestroika* a number of 'historical-patriotic' groups among ethnic Russians emerged such as Pamyat (Memory), Otechestvo (Fatherland) and Spasenie (Salvation). These groups found their support among intellectuals and, perhaps surprisingly, among scientists, but gained little support among the mass of Russians when they submitted to the test of the ballot box. Alexander

Yanov argued that the alleged erosion of Marxist–Leninist ideology would not automatically give way to the triumph of Western rationalist or liberal ideas but instead cleared the space for a variety of nationalist theories while permitting a revival of the Slavophile versus Westernisers debate of the nineteenth century over the path of Russian development. He argued that a so-called Russian party, the fusion of unofficial and official Russian nationalism, could come together as the basis of an authoritarian but 'sanitised' (i.e. non Marxist–Leninist) new ruling ideology.[4] To a degree he was right and what we call the Soviet Russophile trend remains strong, but he failed to note the enormous diversity of the Russian national reawakening.

The moderate orthodox nationalists were represented by the 'village school' of Russian writers such as Vladimir Soloukhin, the author of *Vladimir Back Roads*, and Valentin Rasputin, who actively campaigned over ecological issues (above all to preserve the purity of the world's largest fresh-water environmental treasure, Lake Baikal), joined by the painter Ilya Glazunov. They criticised the over-rapid pace of industrialisation which caused great damage to the environment and Russian village life. The Moscow Headquarters of the All-Russian Society for the Preservation of Historical and Cultural Monuments (VOOPIK) was familiarly known as the 'Russian Club' for its exposition of Russian nationalist sentiments. On certain issues this tendency was mobilised as a powerful lobby, notably to protest against the environmental degradation of Lake Baikal by the building of a cellulose plant. Similarly, the widespread anxiety provoked by the scheme to divert the flow of the Siberian rivers from North to South was acknowledged by Gorbachev to have contributed towards the plan's cancellation in August 1986. Major figures like Academician Dmitrii Likhachev gained official approval to start a fund to preserve Russian cultural artefacts. In the union republics protests helped prevent major projects, like the Daugavpils hydroelectric scheme in Latvia, and provoked a major debate over building the Danube–Dneiper canal in Ukraine.

Russian nationalism was coloured by the paradox that while the Soviet state ensured Russian political pre-eminence, in economic terms Russia was far from being the most prosperous republic (see Table 12). Unorthodox Russian nationalists condemned the persecution of the Russian Orthodox Church, the excessive internationalism whose burden fell disproportionately on Russian shoulders, the distortion of Russian history, and the imposition of socialist realism in place of Russian romanticism. National Bolshevism was condemned by more religious nationalists for espousing a Russian patriotism without a Christian foundation, based purely on the great power status of the Russian part of the Soviet Union – communism with a national face. Religious patriots stressed that Soviet nationalism was in fact antithetical to genuine Russian traditions; the Russian patriotism incorporated into Soviet nationalism, they insisted, served to buttress the power system but had little to do with genuine national traditions.

Solzhenitsyn argued that Russians should be permitted to pursue their destiny freed from the burden of empire. Liberal nationalists like him argued for the conversion of Russia from a military superpower to a spiritual great power, which they insisted would pose no threat to non-Russians or the outside world. Russian patriots of this sort were contemptuous of Western democracy but merciless in their condemnation of Soviet totalitarianism. The authoritarian implications of such views derive from their sense of moral absolutism; the attempt once again to remove politics from society and instead impose an organic theocratic government of justice and order.[5] The All-Russian Social Christian Union for the Liberation of the People (VSKhSON) of the 1960s tried to sustain a uniquely Russian path, not democratic but benignly authoritarian, and endowed with a theocratic vision of Russian uniqueness. These themes were taken up

Table 12 Comparative economic development of the union republics

Republic	Per capita nominal income (1978: USSR=100)	Per capita fixed capital (1975: USSR=100)	Growth of industrial production (1970=100)		Persons having higher or secondary education (1984)	
			1980	*1986*	Per 1,000 Aged 10 or over	Per 1,000 employed population
USSR	100.0	100	178	224	686	868
RSFSR	100.9	115	174	216	691	863
Ukraine	95.9	90	172	212	681	877
Belorussia	97.9	80	232	323	653	839
Moldavia	89.9	69	205	276	620	811
Transcaucasia						
Azerbaijan	63.6	64	220	300	723	886
Georgia	93.6	75	194	264	743	902
Armenia	86.7	73	212	298	749	915
Central Asia						
Uzbekistan	71.6	54	192	256	684	907
Kazakhstan	88.4	102	168	211	678	869
Tajikistan	59.5	51	180	224	632	843
Kyrgyzstan	69.7	60	192	255	665	869
Turkmenistan	75.1	73	173	208	669	889
Baltic						
Lithuania	115.1	101	187	246	626	806
Latvia	113.7	117	164	201	696	855
Estonia	126.7	137	174	207	680	857

Sources: First two columns from Paul R. Gregory and R. C. Stuart, *Soviet Economic Structure and Performance* 3rd edn (New York, Harper & Row, 1986), p. 7; third and fourth columns from *SSSR v tsifrakh v 1986 godu* (Moscow, 1987), p. 94; last two columns from M. Ryan and R. Prentice, *Social Trends in the USSR from 1950* (London, Macmillan, 1987), p. 74.

by the journal *Veche*, edited by Vladimir Osipov, which between 1971 to 1974 proclaimed itself the voice of the 'loyal opposition'. It was marked by a liberal nationalism which condemned 'the bureaucracy' and was concerned with the regeneration of Russia based on the church and village traditions, and focused on Siberia as the rampart of a reborn nation from which the threats from China and the West could be rebuffed.

If nationalism was strong in Soviet Russia itself, the issue was much more intractable in other republics. Non-Russian unorthodox nationalism also took diverse forms and in its extreme form adopted separatist demands. Issues ranged across cultural and linguistic concerns, job opportunities and governmental priorities. The Baltic provinces protested against the regime's witting and unwitting Russification policies. Several trials were staged in Latvia and Estonia of secessionist groups and opponents of assimilation. In Lithuania nationalist demands were buttressed by the strong Roman Catholic attachments of the population.

In Moldavia there was also much anti-Russian feeling but Ceausescu's dictatorship in Romania tempered their desire to be associated with that country. Nationalist feelings in Belorussia were weakened by the relative success of the economy, and by what many perceived to be the somewhat artificial nature of Belorussian nationalism, long divided between Russia and Poland. Ukrainian protest, on the other hand, was frequent and voluble, especially in the Western areas around Lvov taken from Poland in September 1939 and then brutally Sovietised. Some Ukrainian aspirations were covertly supported by their political leaders, like Shelest. The Uniate church of Orthodox converts to Catholicism was intensely persecuted in the Western Ukraine yet flourished in the forests and underground. In the Caucasus, groups condemned the persecution of the Georgian Orthodox Church and the corruption of high officials. There was some emigration of Armenians but their main effort was devoted to the preservation of the language and culture. Anti-Soviet Armenian nationalism was kept in check by memory of the genocide perpetrated by the Turks in 1915 and by the dispute with Azerbaijan over Nagorno-Karabakh. Far from all manifestations of nationalism challenged the regime vertically, but most could spill out horizontally in inter-ethnic clashes.

The total population of the five Sunni Muslim republics (Uzbekistan, Kazakhstan, Tajikistan, Turkmenistan and Kyrgyzia) in 1989 was 49.4 million, or one Soviet citizen in six. The area witnessed major population growth at an average rate of 3 per cent per annum over the last fifteen Soviet years compared to the national average of 1 per cent. Single-child families were the norm in the European areas of the USSR, whereas in Central Asia four or five children were common. The birth-rate of Uzbekistan in 1983, for example, was double that of the RSFSR. By 1970 Central Asia provided 20 per cent of all births in the USSR, and in 1989 the five indigenous populations of 34.2 million comprised 11.9 per cent of the USSR's population. The area therefore contained a relatively high proportion of the nation's young, and their demographic weight began to be reflected in a greater assertiveness. The nationalism of the five Turkic republics, however, was problematic – differing in Tajikistan in any case from the other four. It is not clear whether religion (Sunni Islam), language (Turkic), ethnicity (Mongol) or other factors would act as the unifying force to replace Soviet citizenship for these essentially artificially constructed republics, hewn out of an area marked by centuries of nomadic pastoral herding life.

Several cases of ethnic disturbances took place in Central Asia. In Uzbekistan the Tajik minority protested against changes in their internal passports which renamed them Uzbeks, while from 1989 murderous inter-ethnic clashes claimed hundreds of lives in Osh and the Fergana valley. The impact of the war in Afghanistan and the revival of Islamic fundamentalism in Iran and elsewhere eroded the legitimacy of the Soviet atheist state and encouraged the proliferation of various Muslim brotherhoods. Gorbachev responded at first with a renewed anti-religious campaign against Islam. Anti-Russian demonstrations took place in Tashkent in 1969 and in Alma Ata in 1986 but there is some evidence that nationalist feelings were kept in check by the proximity of these areas to China. Mao Zedong's attempts at Sinification of the Chinese Turkic minorities (above all the Uighurs across the border in Xinxiang) made the post-Stalin Soviet model of nationality politics look mild in comparison. Literacy, health care and economic development were promoted by the Soviet regime and were highly visible, whereas their losses, in terms of the destruction of the old cultural elite, religious freedoms and old way of life, were less obvious.

Repatriatory movements represented a major form of unorthodox nationalism. This 'homeless nationalism' was made up by various deported nationalities and the Jews. For some, their indeterminate social and political status led to poor integration into Soviet life (with the partial exception of the Jews) and hence their struggles were at the forefront of the nationality question. In the 1930s a Jewish autonomous region called Birobijan was established in the Soviet Far East, lying between two rivers in a sparse and rocky part of Siberia. According to the 1979 census the area contained 10,166 Jews and 170,000 Russians. Clearly the majority of the

USSR's 2 million Jews did not consider Birobijan their homeland. Soviet authorities insisted that Yiddish, and not Hebrew, was the language of Soviet Jews and thus hoped to drive a wedge between Soviet Jews and those in Israel. The Jewish movement to leave for Israel (the *aliya* movement) received a massive boost after the Israeli victories in the Six Day War of June 1967. Between 1968 and 1985, 265,657 Jews were able to emigrate, peaking at 51,330 in 1979 as the US Congress debated the SALT II accord and whether to grant the USSR most favoured nation (MFN) trading status. Despite the sharp cutback in emigration following the invasion of Afghanistan the *aliya* movement continued. About 400,000 Jews asked for invitations to Israel but had not formally applied, while some 10,000 applied and had been refused visas (and were thus known as *refuseniks*), a refusal which was usually accompanied by loss of job and by myriad petty and not so petty restrictions. Some of the better-known *refuseniks* were allowed to leave in 1987 in an attempt by Gorbachev to defuse the Jewish issue as part of the arms-control process, and in the late 1980s emigration rose dramatically. Many Soviet Jews were highly assimilated and, indeed, Russified, and evinced no desire to leave.

The Crimean Tatar issue was one of the most painful in Soviet nationality politics. They waged a prolonged struggle to return from Uzbekistan and other areas to the Crimean peninsula, from whence they hade been forcibly deported in 1944 for allegedly collaborating with the German occupiers. Brezhnev 'rehabilitated' them for their alleged collaboration but did not permit them to return to their homes, by then occupied by Slavs. Individual Tatars who returned were forcibly removed and returned to Central Asia. They became one of the best-organised unofficial groups in the USSR and the most vocal, culminating in a series of demonstrations in Red Square in July 1987. Over a million Volga Germans were deported by Stalin to the East in the early days of the Second World War, and though 'rehabilitated' by Khrushchev were not allowed to return to their homes on the Volga. Some 75,000 out of 2 million had emigrated, mainly to the Federal Republic of Germany, by 1989. Other deported nationalities included a sizeable group of Soviet Koreans, some deported Greeks who were relatively successful in emigrating to Greece, and the Meskhetians, a Turkic national minority from the Georgian republic who were also deported at the end of the Second World War.

Unorthodox nationalism sometimes took the form of inter-ethnic conflict and racism. While strongly condemned by official policy, racism was seldom admitted and thus little was done to combat it. At times the regime itself was guilty of officially sponsored racism as in the confused line drawn between anti-Zionism and anti-Semitism. Inter-ethnic conflicts were revealed at their starkest in the struggle over the status of the autonomous region of Nagorno-Karabakh. In 1921 Lenin had promised the area to Armenia, but in 1923 Stalin reversed the decision in favour of Azerbaijan, a region with which he had long been associated, even though the population of Nagorno-Karabakh was 90 per cent Armenian. Over the years the proportion of Armenians fell to 75 per cent and their language and culture were stifled. The onset of *glasnost* allowed the long-standing tensions to emerge, and from February 1988 the area demanded unification with Armenia from which it is separated by only six kilometres at the closest point. The ensuing struggle represented the most serious challenge to Soviet nationality policy and, in Gorbachev's words, a 'sword at the throat of *perestroika*'. In Sumgait on 27 February 1988 the tensions erupted into a full-scale pogrom of Armenians by Azerbaijanis in which at least thirty people died. In the course of the struggle communist party authority effectively disintegrated in Nagorno-Karabakh as nationalist organizations, with the overwhelming support of the Armenian population, organised the most sustained strikes in Soviet history. Since the constitution stated that territorial changes can only be made with the agreement of all parties concerned the conflict became insoluble. The Supreme Soviet, afraid of setting a precedent, resolutely refused to redraw the country's internal borders.

As in other countries, the Soviet Union at its own peril underestimated the tenacity of nationalist sentiments. The roots of modern nationalism lie in the nineteenth century, but the source of tension in such areas as the Caucasus reach back not only centuries but millennia. Nationalism is fed by memories of greatness, of having survived successive invasions and deportations by clinging to religious and cultural traditions. In modern times the urge to autonomy and independence appears unquenchable, yet the social roots and psychological tenacity of nationalism are still little understood.

THE POLITICS OF NATIONALISM

Regime strategies to manage the multinational Soviet state reflected the Russian substance of Soviet nationalism. The problem appeared to be one of managing the relationship between a Russian centre and a non-Russian periphery. The centre in Moscow was dominated by Slavs, as was much of the machinery of government in the republics. The government applied a mixture of coercion and concessions to ethnic feelings, but after 1985 began to lose control over inter-ethnic dynamics and relations between national groups and the centre. A greater role for the market and economic decentralisation, moreover, stimulated national feelings. The centrifugal tendencies unleashed by marketisation in Yugoslavia were little understood by the Soviet leadership.

Unity in the pre-Gorbachev system was achieved above all through the mechanism of party rule. The party, as we have seen, was a unitary body and, although divided into republican parties (with the exception of Russia), it was not based on federal principles. The absence of a separate party organization for the RSFSR, and indeed the abolition of the bureau that used to manage its affairs after Khrushchev's ouster, only accentuated the administrative nature of the fourteen republican parties. In the Politburo Slavs were traditionally greatly overrepresented, although under Brezhnev there was significant minority representation with the Turkic population supplying Kunaev from Kazakhstan, Rashidov from Uzbekistan and Aliev from Azerbaijan. The early Gorbachev Politburo strengthened Russian dominance, lacking a representative from Central Asia and with Shevardnadze the only non-Slav. The pattern underlined the principle that no nationality (or indeed post) had *ex officio* membership derived from holding a specific job. The stress was on individual merit, which in effect meant suitability as seen from the point of view of the General Secretary. Certain patterns recurred, like representation from the Ukraine, but this was convention rather than law. Party recruitment tried to ensure adequate representation for the nationalities, although there were certain imbalances (see Chapter 6), above all the overrepresentation of Russians. In his speech on the sixtieth anniversary of the founding of the USSR Andropov argued against mechanical or mathematical affirmative action. Recruitment was to be based on criteria of suitability and the individual qualities of the person, rather than by ethnic or other attributes (the qota principle).

Investment policy was an important element in managing inter-ethnic relations, while economic growth, albeit decreasing, to some extent neutralised the sharp edge of the nationality question. The government tried to equalise levels of economic development between republics through the centralised allocation of resources. The least economically developed regions gained most economically from incorporation in the USSR. It has, as noted, created some tension in economically more advanced areas such as the Ukraine. Economic growth gave rise to rapid upward social mobility. Peasants leave the field and women leave the home (although in smaller numbers in Central Asia) and enter factories where they gain new skills and are socialised to the demands of industrial life. Whole peoples moved from yak-hide yurts to high-rise apartment blocks in the space of a generation. In the towns their children gained an education and training in modern skills. Students from the titular nationality were a higher proportion in full-time courses than other groups in the republics, indicating some preferential access, while expenditure on schools in Central Asia was higher than the national average to iron out historic inequalities. In Central Asia industrial jobs tended to be taken by Russians, but the long-term trend, as an indigenous working class and technical elite developed, was towards greater equality.

Social mobility in Soviet nationality areas was more rapid for those who adopted Soviet ideology and the Russian language. The 'Khrushchev theses' of November 1958 increased the pressure to adopt Russian as the language of education and intellectual life. Russian was the *lingua franca* of the nation, but local elites were sharply divided over whether it should be used only for conversing with outsiders or for work and study within a non-Russian group. Parents had the option of sending their children to elementary or high schools with instruction either in Russian or in the native language, and both were recognized as official languages (but not always as state languages) in each republic. If a Russian was present in a party committee then discussion tended to be conducted in Russian since it was unlikely that he or she would speak the local language. An obligation for Russians to take courses in the local language would have acted as a disincentive against taking short-term jobs in the non-Russian republics, but by the same token would have eased some of the resentment provoked against incomers. In the 1950s republics were given the option of teaching higher-education courses in the native language, but the concentration of the most prestigious institutes and universities in Moscow meant that the most talented elite offspring spent a period of effective socialisation in the nation's capital.

Economic development and upward social and educational mobility led to the creation of thoroughly Sovietised local political elites. Russians largely ruled the Soviet Union, but the indigenous ethnic elites to varying extents governed their own regions. Having been promoted by the existing system, they tended to have a strong commitment to its maintenance until the final period of *perestroika* forced them to secure their futures at the head of the national insurgency against the Soviet state. The careers of Stalin, Mikoyan, Beria, Kaganovich, Khrushchev and Shevardnadze demonstrated that non-Russians could rise high in the politics of the USSR. Within a national republic, membership of the titular nationality usually conferred a definite advantage in obtaining official positions and places in higher-educational institutions. This helps explain the unsatisfactory position in leading echelons of government of Tatars, Bashkirs, Jews and other nationalities without their own republics.

The *nomenklatura* system of appointments provided a powerful lever for the centre to manage nationality issues. The principles of positive or negative discrimination in principle were not applied, with allegiance to the Soviet system rather than ethnic identity being the crucial factor in advancement. Jews, however, were subject to a range of restrictions and in the late Brezhnev years were largely excluded from diplomatic, foreign trade and some military posts, while it was not easy for many other minority groups to be promoted. There was a conscious attempt to balance the proportion of nationalities but not in a 'mechanical' way. In the national republics Russians were found in many key posts but not usually at the expense of the local elite. There were great differences between republics reflecting patterns of historical development, with the Georgians and Estonians, for example, dominating their own hierarchy to a much greater extent than the Central Asian peoples like the Kazakhs or Turkmens.

The influence of native political elites on policy-making also varied. Khrushchev appointed Russians to head the five Central Asian republics whereas Brezhnev allowed the local elites to dominate to a degree that ultimately proved threatening to central control. Gorbachev reverted to Khrushchev's practice with the appointment of a Russian to head the Kazakh party organisation. A Russian was usually appointed as second in command and was generally moved on to another posting before developing local allegiances or mastering the local language. An important channel of information for Moscow was provided through the republican KGBs, which were nearly always headed by Russians. Military forces were naturally part of a highly centralised command system. The two years of conscript service in the army was intended to foster a multinational Soviet identity, but often had the opposite effect. One of the republics' major functions was to provide a forum for local social mobility and a framework for local elites to express themselves. It is clear, however, that the latitude allowed under Brezhnev permitted widespread corruption. The crackdown under Andropov and later, especially in the Caucasus and Central Asia, was accompanied by attempts to re-establish greater central control. Native social elites emerged in all the republics. With the destruction of the old intelligentsia by Stalin, the new native intelligentsia and middle class owed their existence and privileges to Soviet power. However, the Sovietisation of the cultural intelligentsia was far from complete, and many later went on to act as the proponents of independence.

The internal passport system acted as a powerful instrument of social control but undermined the development of a common Soviet identity. Physical mobility was always subject to the passport and registration (*propiska*) laws, although the choice of a place to live, like the place of work, remained largely a matter of personal preference, national temperament or social class. While 96 per cent of all Georgians and 95 per cent of all Georgian graduates lived in Georgia, only 51 per cent of Armenian graduates lived in Armenia and 35 per cent of Armenians were scattered across the nation. The Baltic republics tended to retain most of their citizens, while the career patterns of Ukrainians and Belorussians were almost indistinguishable from those of Russians.

Coercive measures were always available, and in the labour camps up to half of all political prisoners were nationalists of one sort or another. This sanction was tempered by its likely effect on international opinion, and the regime's nationality policies were influenced by their effect on the world at large. Armenians had a broad range of links with their compatriots around the world, while relations with the Central Asian republics were monitored by the Islamic nations of the Middle East. Central Asian developmental patterns were lauded in the Third World, and contrasted with the brutal policies of the Chinese leadership. However, unresolved problems reflected in the repatriatory movements could not be kept off the diplomatic agenda. Groups lobbying to emigrate, such as the Jews or Volga Germans, or to return to their homelands, such as the Crimean Tatars, influenced the Soviet Union's human rights image abroad and affected the success of its diplomatic initiatives. International lobbying on behalf of Jews seeking to emigrate, in particular, exerted a powerful hold on American policy-makers.

Soviet ideology provided a supranational rationale for the maintenance of the multi-ethnic state but operated in various ways in different republics. In the Baltic provinces and the Caucasus Sovietised elites rode hostile populations, whereas in Central Asia the ideology was a greater extent assimilated into indigenous social and political cultural patterns. In the USSR even the smallest nationality could share pride in the superpower status of a mighty state, but once this achievement began to pall, so too a process of national disaffiliation with the failing

Soviet project began to accelerate. The Soviet pattern of development had improved standards of living, education, health care and general social welfare, and as long as comparisons were made only with their own past, then the achievements were tangible enough, but if they were made with other developing countries, then the successes looked increasingly less impressive. The commitment to social justice (like universal health care and education), moreover, was not enough to offset declining economic performance given the enormous privileges enjoyed by the elite and the gross underfunding of public services. The onset of economic reforms disturbed whatever equilibrium there might have been, while creeping Russification provoked an ever-stronger reaction. The image of the Russian people as the 'elder brother' might have been a credible proposition in Central Asia, but counterproductive when applied to the developed regions of the Baltic and the Ukraine. It was particularly galling when history was rewritten to emphasise the progressive role played by Russia in the past, and to highlight the backwardness of the incorporated regions.

Soviet federalism was national in form but supranational in content; however, there was always the possibility that it would become national in content also. The dualism which granted the symbols of nationhood to republics while insisting on the supremacy of the central state and the end of national separateness was an inherently unstable compromise. Beneath the Sovietisation effort there remained a powerful undercurrent strengthening the autonomy of the basic national groups. The institutions of this autonomy replicated almost the entire range of central cultural and economic institutions. They were administered by local indigenous elites on behalf of the central authorities, but there was always the tendency for this to be transformed into rule on their own behalf. The Soviet system was built for crisis management but once the regime at the centre began to crumble, then it did not take long for the incipient states to voice their grievances and take the path of independence. Although at the root of Soviet nationality policy there was no systematic sustained economic exploitation by one nation of another, and the process of Sovietisation was very different from the Russification pursued by the autocracy or by other classical empires, the Soviet state lacked enough positive content to act as a dynamic pole of attraction. While Sovietisation weakened traditional patterns, it did not deny a role for redefined national identities within the modernising Soviet context. The concept of empire to describe the Soviet multinational state is misleading, although for many nationalists subjectively accurate, because of the lack of a dominant national core exploiting the rest; but it is objectively accurate in so far as it describes a political system based not on nation-state but on supra-ethnic principles. Nationalism was co-opted but not denied, and in the late 1980s emerged to claim in content the sovereignty that it had been promised in form.

KEY TEXTS

Carrère d'Encausse, Hélène, *The End of the Soviet Empire: The Triumph of the Nations* (London, Basic Books, 1994).

Conquest, R. (ed.), *The Last Empire: Nationality and the Soviet Future* (Stanford, CA, Hoover Institution Press, 1986).

Fowkes, Ben, *The Disintegration of the Soviet Union: A Study in the Rise and Triumph of Nationalism* (London, Macmillan, 1996).

Hajda, Lubomyr and Mark Beissinger (eds), *The Nationalities Factor in Soviet Politics and Society* (Boulder, CO, Westview Press, 1990).

16 Foreign and defence policy

Soviet foreign policy was dominated by the concept of peaceful coexistence. The term, coined by Lenin at the close of the Russian Civil War, passed through three main stages. From the end of the Civil War to 1944 the Soviet regime was primarily concerned with *defensive* peaceful coexistence, notwithstanding adventures in Mongolia and the conquests allowed by the Nazi–Soviet Pact of 1939. The Soviet regime was concerned primarily with its own survival, and competition with capitalist states did not necessarily mean war with them. From 1944 to 1985 Soviet foreign policy was characterised by an *expansive* peaceful coexistence, in which policy was stamped by an expansionist dynamic, although this does not mean that every opportunity for expansion was taken or exploited. With the coming to power of Gorbachev in 1985 the third and final phase of Soviet foreign policy was *co-operative* peaceful coexistence whereby the Soviet regime planned to develop in parallel with the Western capitalist system while retaining the essential features of its alternative and, Gorbachev hoped, equally vibrant modernity. One essential feature of co-operative peaceful coexistence was the relaxation of bloc discipline entailing, among other things, the dissolution of Soviet hegemony in Eastern Europe and an exit from the war in Afghanistan.

THE COURSE OF SOVIET FOREIGN POLICY

Soviet foreign policy traditionally emerged from the interplay between national interest and the idea of communism as a world system. Marx believed that the proletariat had no national home and that as classes disappeared so, too, would the state. There was therefore a tension between the internationalism of communism and the form in which it was contained, the national state. Soviet foreign policy was stamped by a dualism, torn between defensive concerns and the thoroughly expansive theory of communism whose spread was considered only a matter of time. In practice, however, apart from the debate over the Treaty of Brest-Litovsk, no destructive conflict between the two principles arose and the defence of the socialist achievements at home was never threatened directly by attempts to export the communist revolution abroad. Soviet foreign policy can be interpreted through the realist school of international relations theory.

In keeping with Lenin's theory of imperialism the new leaders after the October revolution expected the revolution to spread rapidly once the 'weakest link' in the imperialist chain had been broken. Trotsky, the first commissar of foreign affairs, indeed took a dim view of his new post, reflecting as it did the contemptible secret diplomacy and shady deals by the great powers which had, in the Bolshevik view, provoked and marked the First World War. He entered his new offices only after a considerable delay, and a few days after the revolution announced, 'I will issue a few revolutionary proclamations to the peoples of the world and then shut up shop.' Just as Lenin and the Bolsheviks considered that traditional politics would disappear after the revolution as the whole revolutionary nation set about managing its own affairs, so in the international sphere it was expected that diplomacy would give way to fraternal relations between the free countries of a socialist commonwealth. The concept of the 'permanent revolution' (in its external aspects) was not Trotsky's alone: the whole Bolshevik party believed that the revolution in Russia was but the harbinger of the world revolution. However, the revolution did not spread to industrially developed countries and the Soviet republic remained isolated, apart from Mongolia, between 1917 and 1939. The emphasis on defence industries in the industrialisation drive of the first five-year plans was justified by this isolation.

The tension between world revolution and socialism in one country was particularly marked while Lenin lived. The controversy in the Bolshevik party in 1918 over whether to accept the German peace terms at Brest-Litovsk was bitterly divisive (see Chapter 2). Bukharin and the Left Communists insisted that a revolutionary war should be launched, accompanied by appeals to the German soldiers and working class. Lenin's approach was a pragmatic one given Russia's military weakness; he no doubt realised that the war had contributed to the fall of Tsarism and the Provisional Government in 1917. He accepted the need to make concessions (bartering land for time) and, much to the anger of the left, appeared willing to put the survival of the Soviet state above utopian hopes of international revolution. The conflict between Soviet nationalism and world communism thus appeared in its sharpest form at this time. It is a moot point whether the calls for revolutionary war would have been effective against the might of the German war machine, but a Bolshevik call in March 1918 to rally to the defence of the nation against Germany might well have gained the Bolsheviks much support at home.

With the collapse of Germany in November 1918 Lenin's tactic proved partially justified, and the territories of the old Russian empire, with the exception of Poland, Finland and the Baltic republics, were recovered by the end of the Civil War. The creation of a number of short-lived 'soviet republics' in 1919 in Hungary, Slovakia and Bavaria seemed to confirm the belief that the Russian revolution was only the first break in the imperialist chain. The establishment of the Third Communist International (Comintern) in March 1919 was designed to assist the spread of the world revolution. At a time of civil war and foreign intervention the Comintern was an attempt to utilise all the means at the disposal of the Bolsheviks to take the war to the enemy. The Comintern, however, was soon subordinated to Soviet state interests and became an instrument of Bolshevik policy. The '21 Conditions' adopted at the second Comintern congress in July 1920 were imposed on all other communist parties wishing to join the organisation and reflected Soviet's communism's sectarianism and violence. The coexistence of the Comintern with a Commissariat of Foreign Affairs symbolised the tension between ideology and expediency. In 1920 certain elements of the revolutionary war strategy were revived with the war against Poland, which was seen as a bridge to the resources and support of the German economy. The Polish war of 1920 saw the emergence of a 'revolutionary jingoism' as socialist internationalism merged with Soviet nationalism.

Lenin's foreign policy in general was marked by a pragmatism that was to become the hallmark of Soviet foreign policy. Already in 1918 the Soviet state had begun to practise the art of diplomacy, albeit rather crudely at first with Trotsky's tirades against the German generals at Brest-Litovsk. At the peace conference at Versailles in 1919–20 (from which Soviet Russia was excluded) the French premier Georges Clemenceau hoped to establish a *cordon sanitaire* around the Soviet republic. The Russo-German treaty signed at Rapallo in 1922 between the two outcast nations of interwar Europe signalled the end of Soviet Russia's diplomatic isolation. Lenin had sent his foreign minister, Chicherin, to negotiate within the framework of 'peaceful coexistence': the view that the struggle with the bourgeoisie did not preclude dealing with them while waiting for capitalism's demise. The Bolsheviks still expected revolution in the West, and their diplomatic initiatives were regarded as little more than holding actions. With the final defeat of the German revolution in October 1923 the isolation of Soviet communism was confirmed, although the Soviet state was recognised by a number of countries in the early 1920s. A new balance was required between Soviet diplomacy and world revolution.

The two aims, however, were in many ways incompatible. Lenin was cautious in his foreign policy but he remained a committed internationalist in that he saw international relations through the prism of the class struggle. Although Stalin remained contemptuous of the long-term prospects of peace with the capitalist states, under his leadership the USSR unequivocally defined its policies towards other states in terms of Soviet national interests, which he claimed represented the highest interests of the international working class at the given stage of development. Stalin's policy of 'socialism in one country' from 1924 led to the subordination of the workers' revolution to the needs of Soviet diplomacy. The Comintern was launched in the belief that a revolutionary wave would destroy capitalism, but in the 1920s it was forced to accommodate itself to a period of revolutionary stagnation. Under Stalin almost every internal change of policy was reflected by shifts in foreign policy. The NEP in particular was marked by compromises, with relative class peace at home accompanied by compromises abroad. During the ten-day general strike of May 1926 in Britain the Soviet Union supported the more moderate TUC through the Anglo-Russian Trade Union Council. In China Stalin insisted on the continuation of the alliance of the Chinese communists with the Nationalist Guomindang under Jiang Jieshi (Chiang Kai-shek). Comintern moderation was discredited by the Nationalist massacres of communists in Shanghai in April 1927.

Only three Comintern conferences met under Stalin, whereas under Lenin four were held in a much shorter period. The fifth congress in 1924 ordered the denunciation of Trotsky throughout the communist parties of the world. The sixth in 1928 eliminated the influence of Bukharin and the 'Right Deviation'. In December 1927, following the Chinese debacle and his turn to the left against the NEP, Stalin declared that the 'stabilisation of capitalism' had come to an end, and the congress inaugurated the notorious Third Phase in Soviet foreign relations of 1929–34. The policy was marked internally by collectivisation and externally by the denunciation of social democracy. The bizarre reflection of murderous internal policies in the extreme leftist foreign policy proved a disaster. In Germany the condemnation of the Social Democratic Party as 'social fascists', the most dangerous enemies of communism, smoothed the path of the Nazis to power under Hitler in January 1933.

With the consolidation of the virulently anti-communist Nazis in Germany Soviet policy dropped the extremism of the Third Phase and began a search for security. The seventh Comintern congress in 1934 inaugurated the era of the popular fronts whose aim was to forge defensive alliances and internal blocs against fascism. The USSR joined the League of Nations at this time and the Soviet foreign minister, Maxim Litvinov, sought to use the forum to establish 'collective security' against aggressors. A Russo-French agreement was reached at Locarno, but Soviet hopes of an 'Eastern Locarno' of defensive pacts with its bordering states of East Europe was hampered by news of the great purges at home. Internal purges and external security agreements proved incompatible, and indeed at this time the purges took on an international dimension. In the Spanish Civil War of 1936–39 Stalin fought a second war, organised by his secret services, against Republican forces who did not owe primary allegiance to the Soviet Union. The destruction of the Trotskyist POUM in Barcelona, described by George Orwell in *Homage to Catalonia*, was only the most publicised case.

Stalin's search for security was not an unambiguous policy. The destruction of the anti-German Tukhachevskii and the Soviet High Command in the purges of 1937–38 was perhaps an attempt to keep his options open to Germany. Following the Munich agreement of September 1938, in which Britain and France capitulated to German demands and granted Czechoslovakia's German-populated Sudetenland to Hitler, there was a gradual realignment of Soviet foreign policy. Stalin considered Munich an inducement by the West for Germany to look eastwards. Soviet assertions of readiness to go to war over Czechoslovakia appear rather unrealistic given the condition and disposition of Soviet forces. There was now little talk of collective security as Stalin understood Chamberlain's policy as an attempt to keep Russia out of Europe. Stalin increasingly saw advantages in reviving the spirit of Rapallo. At the eighteenth party congress in March 1939 he attacked the forthcoming 'imperialist war' while simultaneously denouncing appeasement and urging France and Britain to prepare for war with Germany. The months prior to open hostilities offered the undignified spectacle of all major powers hoping to divert the attention of the Nazi Moloch to their opponents. In mid-1939 Hitler talked of attacking Poland but not Russia, and in May Stalin replaced his Jewish foreign minister, Litvinov, with Molotov. On 23 August 1939 the Soviet Union and Germany signed the Molotov–Ribbentrop non-aggression pact at the expense of Poland and Western Europe. A Secret Protocol provided for the reversion of the Baltic republics, Eastern Poland, Bessarabia and Finland to the USSR (see Figure 8). Like Alexander I at Tilsit, Stalin hoped thereby to gain time. Nine days later Germany invaded Poland and the Second World War began.

Soviet expansionism in the period following the Nazi–Soviet pact can, at a pinch, be understood as fuelled by the search for security. Less understandable, however, is the thoroughness with which Stalin pacified the regions brought under his control. The Nazi *Blitzkrieg* from 1 September swiftly brought Poland to its knees. On 17 September Soviet forces entered Poland, and while the Nazis committed genocide in the western area, Soviet forces conducted 'classicide' in the east. About 1.5 million Poles, in particular the intelligentsia, were deported to Soviet labour camps, and 15,000 Polish officers were murdered at Katyn and other camps near Smolensk in 1940. The damage inflicted on the Soviet Army by the purges was reflected in its poor performance against the Finns in the Winter War of 1939–40. Early in 1940 Soviet forces occupied Latvia, Lithuania and Estonia and shortly afterwards incorporated them into the Soviet Union. Communism was exported at the point of a bayonet but socialism remained in one country, albeit an enlarged one. The breathing space bought by the Nazi–Soviet pact was not used effectively to prepare for war. Defences along the old border were dismantled but, for fear of offending Hitler, the new border was left almost defenceless. Stalin was dismayed by the 'phoney war' in the West, and suspected that Britain and France (cowering behind the 'impregnable' Maginot Line) were waiting for Germany to attack the Soviet Union. He therefore compensated by redoubled assurances of good faith in holding to the Nazi–Soviet pact, delivering enormous quantities of oil and grain. His dismay was completed by the rapid collapse of France under the impact of *Blitzkrieg* in May 1940.

Stalin's attempts to appease Hitler proved of no avail and on 22 June 1941 German forces launched a massive assault. Stalin appears to have had a nervous collapse at this betrayal (although this is now disputed) and disappeared for ten days. He had ignored Allied warnings

Figure 8 Territorial changes in the west, 1939–41

BARENTS SEA

Petsamo
Murmansk

Salla
Kuolayarvi

WHITE
SEA

N. Dvina River

NORWAY

SWEDEN

Oulo

FINLAND

Kirov

Viipuri
Helsinki

Lake
Ladoga

Vologda
Kostroma
Kazan

Volga River

Tallinn
Leningrad

ESTONIA

Kalinin

R U S S I A

Riga
LATVIA

W. Dvina River

LITHUANIA
Kaunas

Moscow

Königsberg
Danzig

Vilna

Smolensk

Saratov

EAST
PRUSSIA

Minsk

Don River

POLAND
Warsaw

Pinsk

Kursk

GERMANY

Kiev

Stalingrad

Krakow
Lvov

Dnieper River

Kharkov

SLOVAKIA

Dnepropetrovsk

Dniester River

Rostov-on-
Don

BESSARABIA

HUNGARY

Kishinev

SEA OF
AZOV

Odessa

CRIMEA

Novorossiisk

WALLACHIA

ROMANIA

BLACK   SEA

▨ Seized from Poland Sept. 1939	▥ Lithuania, Latvia and Estonia annexed August 1940
▦ Portions of Poland seized by Germany 1939	—— Russian boundary 1 September 1939
▨ Seized from Finland March 1940	– – – Other international boundaries 1 September 1939
▨ Seized from Romania June 1940	••••••• Russian boundaries 6 August 1940

and those of his own secret service (especially those from the Soviet agent Richard Sorge in Tokyo) of the impending German attack. In his desperate attempts to maintain the agreement he had continued to supply Germany with fuel and food. Stalin's role as a war leader has been much debated, and as we have seen it was criticised by Khrushchev in his Secret Speech. His conduct was marked by the wasteful use of human resources and petty interference in operational questions. He refused to allow a retreat in the first days of the war, even though the German forces were better armed and more numerous, leading to the destruction of elite divisions and a vast amount of military equipment. He refused to sign the Geneva Convention on Prisoners of War causing Soviet soldiers untold extra sufferings in German camps, while Soviet labour camps were full of people who could have fought. Soviet forces waited at the gates of Warsaw from the summer of 1944 to early 1945 while the uprising was destroyed. Victory was marked by the deportation of whole nations accused of collaboration with the occupying forces, even though the German Army had not reached some of them.

Nevertheless, as a symbolic rallying force and overall strategist Stalin played a powerful role in the Allied defeat of the Nazis. The industrial base in the eastern areas developed during his five-year plans, reinforced by the evacuation of factories from the west at the beginning of the war, became the vital manufactory of war *matériel*. Stalin became a symbol of Soviet resolve, epitomised by the Battle of Stalingrad from September 1942 which halted the German advance. He did not wage the war as a revolutionary war or under the banner of revolution, but was able to exploit the emotional power of Russian nationalism. In May 1943 the Comintern was abolished and a concordat was reached with the Russian Orthodox Church. The battle was fought as a national war with great prestige accruing to the army. Pre-revolutionary ranks and insignia were restored to stress the continuity with Russian traditions. Some of the restrictions on the peasant personal plots were relaxed for the duration. At this time Soviet nationalism became solidly based on Russian themes. Stalin promoted new commanders like Zhukov and Konev and dropped the incompetent ones such as his long-time supporters Voroshilov and Budennyi. From 1942 he downgraded the political commissars and introduced a unified command under regular officers.

The German attack was so powerful that it appeared in the first weeks of the war that the regime would collapse. However, any sympathy that the Germans might have been able to exploit in favour of the overthrow of Soviet power (above all in Ukraine, where memories of the collectivisation famine were still vivid, and the struggle against incorporation of the western parts still continued) swiftly turned to hostility as the bestial nature of Nazi policies and practices became clear. The sheer size of the country, the harsh winter of 1941–42 which blunted the German advance at the gates of Moscow, and the policies pursued by Stalin were able to defeat the aggressor. The alliance forged with the Western powers provided the USSR with vital supplies. However, Stalin was haunted by fears of a separate peace between Germany and the Allies, or that the West would remain on the sidelines as the Soviet Union and Germany exhausted each other. Stalin sought guarantees by insisting on the speedy creation of a second front, and fought for Allied recognition of the 1941 frontiers (that is, the inclusion of parts of Poland and Finland, Bessarabia and the Baltic states). The suspicions among the Allies during the war were the seeds that grew into the Cold War.

Stalin's bargaining position grew ever stronger as the eastern front advanced from Stalingrad in early 1943 through Kursk and to Germany's borders by late 1944. In May 1945 the Soviet flag was raised over Berlin, and during the few days in July 1945 that the Soviet Union was at war with Japan it was able to gain the Kurile Islands. The victory raised Stalin to unprecedented heights, and the Soviet Union emerged as a major power on the world stage. The communist regime had finally found a national legitimacy as the organiser of the defence of the motherland against the German attack. However, the losses were devastating, with at least 27 million dead and vast tracts of the country devastated. Soviet forces occupied most of Eastern Europe and promoted the spread of communist power. Once again, as in 1917, the revolution had not developed as predicted by Marx. Victory meant the end of socialism in one country, but the transplantation of Soviet communism to Eastern Europe was a long and complex affair. The dialectic between socialism and Soviet armed force was to give rise to an ongoing instability in Eastern Europe as nationalism and communism contended.

Three conferences between the Allies tried to establish a viable post-war settlement. At Teheran in late 1943 agreement was reached over Poland and for an offensive either in the Balkans (Churchill) or France (Stalin and Roosevelt). In October 1944 at a meeting between Churchill and Stalin in Moscow the idea of zones of influence was accepted with the infamous 'percentages agreement' giving, for example, the USSR an 80 per cent stake in Hungary to the West's 20 per cent. The Warsaw uprising from August 1944 strained relations between the Allies. The fate of post-war Eastern Europe was settled at the meeting of Stalin, Churchill and Roosevelt at Yalta in February 1945. Soviet foreign policy interests in Eastern Europe were legitimated and the basic design of the division of Europe into spheres of influence was accepted. The plan was imposed at Potsdam in July–August 1945, in the shadow of the first nuclear explosion on 16 July 1945. The war ended with the major elements of the post-war world in place: the advent of nuclear weapons (used against Hiroshima on 3 August and Nagasaki on 6 August 1945); Soviet–American rivalry to gain world ascendancy to replace a debilitated Europe; disputes over the institutionalisation of Soviet influence in Eastern Europe; and a divided Germany symbolised by the partition of Berlin.

With the demise of the common enemy that had provided the bond for coalition, the Cold War developed with an inexorable logic based on irreconcilable conflicts of interest between the former allies and a profound ideological incompatibility. The Cold War, however, did not spring full-blown from the defeat of Nazi Germany but emerged only over a period of years. Controversy over the fate of Germany was compounded by conflicts over Eastern Europe; the course of East–West and Soviet–Eastern European relations mirrored each other. The first period of Soviet occupation of Eastern Europe saw the establishment of coalition governments designated people's democracies: the avoidance of the term 'dictatorship of the proletariat' signalled that these regimes were to be coalitions of workers, peasants and intelligentsia. The establishment of a Soviet-type regime in Poland, however, particularly exacerbated relations between the former Allies. The elections promised at Yalta were delayed until January 1947, by which time the communists were able to manipulate the result to defeat the popular Peasants' Party led by Deputy Prime Minister Stanislaw Mikolajczyk. Following the victory over fascism each country hoped to find its own path to socialism and hence there was an implicit contradiction with the Soviet Union as a great power – all the more so since the Second World War was a battle of nationalities against the supranational policy of the Germans. National paths had been legitimated by the dissolution of the Comintern and seemed to augur greater autonomy for individual communist parties. Between 1945 and 1948 various 'national roads to communism' were tried out. Wladislaw Gomulka in Poland, for instance, hoped to achieve a distinctively national form of communism in the shadow of a Soviet Union aspiring to regional hegemony.

Alarmed by the ruthlessness with which Soviet power had been consolidated in Poland and elsewhere, in a speech in Fulton, Missouri, on 5 March 1946 Churchill warned that, 'From

Stettin in the Baltic to Trieste in the Adriatic, an iron curtain has descended across the continent.' He called for an Anglo-American alliance to contain the Soviet threat. The announcement of the Truman Doctrine in March 1947 for the 'containment' of the USSR, followed by the Marshall Plan for the economic reconstruction of Europe, was delivered under the nuclear umbrella. The doctrine was based on the idea that the Soviet Union had a messianic urge to conquer the world, a view which argued that traditional Russian expansionism was bolstered by aggressive Marxist–Leninist ideology. George Kennan provided the most coherent rationale for this belief in his famous 'Mr X' article 'The Sources of Soviet Conduct' in July 1947, although he insisted later that he meant a political rather than a military response.[1] The Cold War represented the sharpening of pre-war conflicts by the struggle for mastery over Europe and ultimately the world.

As long as Stalin hoped to maintain elements of the wartime coalition he tolerated some national autonomy in Eastern Europe. With the deterioration in East–West relations he perceived a growing divergence between national roads and Soviet security interests, and thus from late 1947 to 1948 there was the imposition of the Stalinist model irrespective of local conditions. In Yugoslavia in mid-1948 the attempt to establish Stalinist hegemony met with resistance from Josif Broz-Tito and the Yugoslav communists. They had come to power largely by their own efforts and were not dependent on the Red Army. Stalin had no model of how to conduct relations between communist countries other than by the methods he had used to consolidate his power within the Soviet Union. But such methods raised powerful emotions when applied to relations between sovereign nation-states and with peoples who had never been part of the Russian empire. The break between Yugoslavia and the Soviet Union owed little to ideology, and everything to the dialectics of nationalism. It was the first major example of an Eastern European state seeking to pursue its national interests within a communist framework. Similar problems were to appear following the coming to power of Mao Zedong and the Chinese communists in 1949. The spread of communism was not an unmitigated blessing for Stalin as Moscow's position as the centre of the ideology was eroded by the development of other models of socialism in Belgrade and Beijing. The spread of communism came into contradiction with the Soviet Union's great power status. The wheel had come full circle as socialism in one country gave way to a multinational communist movement in power.

The spread of communism, however, did not alter the manner in which Stalin ruled, and he chose Soviet state interests over the formation of a socialist commonwealth. Shocked by the temerity of the Yugoslav communists, Stalin proceeded to impose draconian regimes in the countries within the Soviet sphere of influence. Already the Communist Information Bureau (Cominform) had been established as a successor to the Comintern at a conference of European communist leaders in the Polish Silesian town of Sklarska Poreba in September 1947. The creation of the Cominform reflected frustration at the failure of communist parties to come to power in France and Italy, but above all it was designed to contain Western influence in the East rather than to advance communism in Western Europe. National paths to socialism were discredited, and its exponents, such as Gomulka in Poland, were lucky if they escaped with their lives. 'Little Stalins' emerged in most East European countries between 1948 and 1953 – Mátyás Rákosi in Hungary, Boleslaw Beirut in Poland, Klement Gottwald in Czechoslovakia – who proceeded to stage their own show trials. The Soviet model of development was imposed on these countries irrespective of local conditions or their previous level of development. Collectivisation of agriculture was accompanied by the same irrational concentration on heavy industry that had marked the Soviet pattern of development. In the Soviet Union this was merely wasteful, but in more developed countries such as Czechoslovakia it proved disastrous and entailed regression to a more primitive pattern of economic development. In addition, the imposition of the Soviet political system in such relatively advanced countries as Poland and Czechoslovakia, with Western-oriented political cultures dating back a millennium, imposed massive political strains. The Soviet bloc was formed as a defensive barrier for the USSR and hence these countries' own internal revolutionary development was subordinated to the state interests of the USSR. The extension of Stalinism was validated by the international power structure, confirmed at Yalta, and was reinforced by the Soviet Union's emergence as the supreme military power in the East (see Figure 9).

The death of Stalin in March 1953 marked the onset of a new period in international relations. The deployment of nuclear weapons forced a re-evaluation of the 'inevitability of war' between the superpowers. Stalin himself in his last work, *Economic Problems of Socialism in the USSR*, had modified his position on the grounds that 'powerful popular forces had come forward in defence of peace'. The doctrine of peaceful coexistence now came to mean not that conflict between East and West had ended but only that its forms had changed – the emphasis was now on ideological rather than military struggle. The basic premiss was that there had been a shift in the 'correlation of forces' in favour of the USSR: socialism had been extended to Eastern Europe, creating a socialist bloc of 'peace-loving' states; the colonial powers had declined and their empires were challenged by socialist or nationalist movements opposed to imperialism; and the military and economic power of the USSR had increased and it possessed thermo-nuclear weapons to counter 'imperialist aggression'. The view of peaceful coexistence as the active pursuit of Soviet interests as socialism allegedly became the ascendant historical force was to lie at the root of the failure of détente in the 1970s.

The change from the defensive coexistence of 1917–44 was marked by a much more forward Soviet posture in the Third World, symbolised by the extension of Soviet influence in Egypt and Ghana. Khrushchev's rule saw a temporary breakdown of the synthesis of communism and Soviet nationalism as scarce funds were expended in support of the world revolution. The Soviet Union underwrote the completion of the Aswan High Dam in Egypt, provided considerable assistance to India, and then burdened itself with subsidising the Cuban revolution. Stalin's death allowed relations to be improved with Yugoslavia. Tito was rehabilitated and the Belgrade Declaration of 1955 acknowledged the diversity of national paths to socialism. The creation of the Warsaw Treaty Organisation in 1955, together with the revival of the Council for Mutual Economic Assistance (Comecon), was an attempt to depersonalise Soviet–East European relations. Khrushchev hoped to provide a more reciprocal, multinational institutional framework to replace Stalin's pattern of exploitative bilateral relations. At the twentieth party congress in February 1956 Khrushchev's denunciation of Stalin's cult of personality was accompanied by an attack on his heavy-handed dominance over Eastern Europe. Destalinisation in Eastern Europe released pent-up resentments (see Chapter 4). The attempt to reconcile nationalism with socialism in a specifically Hungarian way was crushed by Soviet tanks. A paradoxical effect of the liberalisation under Khrushchev was that some national leaders, notably in Albania and China, joined later by Romania, became anti-Soviet Stalinists.

In foreign policy, as in domestic policy, Khrushchev followed a zigzag path. In 1958 Yugoslavia was once again condemned. In 1960 came the momentous break with China precipitated by Khrushchev's sudden withdrawal of Soviet experts and assistance. Here again, as with Yugoslavia, national suspicions played a much greater part in provoking the split than ideology.

Figure 9 USSR and Eastern Europe, 1945–91

Soviet occupied zones in Germany 1945-1949 and Austria 1945-1955

British, French and American occupied zones 1945-1955

'Iron Curtain' since 1955

Former German and Czechoslovak territory annexed by USSR 1945

Former German territory annexed by Poland 1945

Principal areas of protest and revolt 1953-1988

The ongoing Berlin confrontation was exacerbated between 1958 and 1961 by Khrushchev's aggressive posturing, culminating in the building of the Berlin Wall which divided the city in August 1961. Khrushchev's erratic behaviour climaxed with the confrontation over the placing of Soviet strategic missiles in Cuba in October 1962. The world came to the brink of nuclear war but Khrushchev's retreat with the face-saving formula of an American commitment not to invade the island or place new missiles in Turkey in return for the removal of the Soviet missiles averted the catastrophe. Amidst widespread alarm at the near-disaster, a 'hot line' was installed between Moscow and Washington, and in 1963 the Partial Test Ban Treaty prohibited atmospheric testing of atomic weapons.

The reformism associated with Khrushchev served to throw the communist parties of Eastern Europe back on to their own national communist traditions and to weaken their dependence on the Soviet Union. This was a period of the slow dissolution of the blocs as Western Europe grew stronger in relation to the USA and the Cold War thawed slightly. The relatively slow economic progress of the USSR, its setback in Cuba in 1962, the failure over Berlin, the split with China, all accelerated moves towards greater independence and polycentrism. Khrushchev's foreign policy saw the extension of Soviet influence around the globe, but the failures, as over Cuba and China, were cited as part of the reason for his overthrow in 1964. His major achievement was to establish a new framework for East–West relations and to modify relations with Eastern Europe.

The Brezhnev era saw the transformation of the Soviet Union from a regional to a world power. Soviet military potential increased steadily from the early 1960s as Soviet military planners sought to remedy the perceived weakness revealed by the Cuban missile crisis. By the end of Brezhnev's rule the Soviet Union had fulfilled its post-war ambition to achieve strategic parity with the United States and to become a truly global power. The decision to invade Czechoslovakia in 1968 and thus to abort the reform process under Dubček reflected Soviet domestic conservatism as much as its desire to maintain hegemony over Eastern Europe. The 'Brezhnev doctrine' of limited sovereignty underwrote bloc cohesion in Eastern Europe. Soviet gains were legitimised internationally by the Helsinki Conference on Security and Co-operation in Europe in August 1975. The conference ratified the post-war borders, but the Soviet Union was forced to make human rights commitments that were later used by dissidents to contrast the divergence between the USSR's formal commitments and practices.

Under Stalin foreign policy played a primarily defensive role, even when the Soviet Union was expanding. Khrushchev's peaceful coexistence saw the shifting of the struggle between East and West on to the ideological sphere, but it did not eliminate the conflicts on other levels. Starting then, and even more under Brezhnev, Soviet foreign policy changed its bearings and became more active and more visible, and in some ways more independent of domestic concerns. The slogan of peaceful coexistence under Brezhnev was continued under the name of détente. The Basic Principles Agreement and SALT I (Strategic Arms Limitation Talks placing limits on the *growth* of nuclear arms) of 1972 laid the basis of détente. The policy ultimately failed because the USA and the USSR had different perceptions of what it meant. For the USA, it meant Soviet restraint in the Third World, a slow-down of military growth, and some liberalisation of human rights. From the Soviet point of view détente meant that recognition of strategic parity with the USA would also lead to political equality and co-responsibility for managing world affairs. Détente failed to provide the expected economic rewards. The USA did not grant the USSR most favoured nation trading status or low-cost trade credits. Détente did not prevent the United States from pursuing a resolute policy of excluding the Soviet

Union from the Middle East peace process or from playing the China 'card' in a remorselessly hostile manner. As far as the Soviet Union was concerned, détente did not mean stepping aside from the world revolutionary process, and when the revolutionary forces in Angola, Ethiopia or elsewhere demanded Soviet assistance, it was provided. In late 1979 it became increasingly clear that the US Congress would not ratify SALT II. In addition, as the Soviet leaders saw it, détente gave the United States the illusion that under the guise of concern for dissidents it could interfere in the Soviet Union's domestic affairs. With hindsight it can be seen that détente permitted technological and economic exchange with the West which delayed domestic economic reform.

Despite many successes in the international arena, the Brezhnev era ended in discord and failure as a new Cold War took the place of détente. From 1979 East–West relations deteriorated markedly. The Soviet invasion of Afghanistan in December 1979 was not the cause of the end of détente but a symptom. Opposition in the West to détente was marked by the coming to power of Margaret Thatcher in Britain in 1979 and Ronald Reagan in the USA in 1980. The imposition of martial law in Poland on 13 December 1981 further worsened relations. Soviet perceptions were marked by the fear of a 'new encirclement' by the USA, China, Japan and Western Europe. The US use of economic warfare against the Soviet Union further exacerbated relations. Reagan's announcement of the Strategic Defence Initiative (Star Wars) in 1982 and talk of the winnability of nuclear war both increased tension, as did the gross mishandling by the Soviet Union of the shooting down of a Korean airliner (KAL 007) in September 1983. The dissolution of détente, economic problems, indebtedness, world recession, arguments over the placing of US intermediate nuclear forces (INF), Cruise and Pershing II, in response to the Soviet deployment of SS20 missiles all marked a thirty-year low in East–West relations. The succession struggles in the Soviet Union furthermore led to a paralysis of Soviet decision-making. By 1985 the USSR had achieved the remarkable feat of alienating almost every country in the world, communist and non-communist alike.

Of necessity Gorbachev was forced to retrieve the situation and develop the policy of co-operative peaceful coexistence. His accession radically changed the international atmosphere and established a new context for East–West dialogue. The succession was over and the scene was set for a period of new realism in Soviet foreign policy. Gorbachev's rule was immediately marked by a new vigour. The attempts to re-establish some sort of arms-control agreement were matched by a series of concrete proposals which were no longer directed mainly at Western public opinion but to policy-makers. In the United States Reagan's fading presidency prepared to enter into a series of arms-reduction agreements. The meeting between Reagan and Gorbachev in Geneva in late 1985 was the first summit for nearly a decade. The encounter between them in Reykjavik in October 1986 saw astonishing proposals and counter-proposals for the complete elimination of nuclear weapons. An INF treaty completely eliminating categories of nuclear weapons was signed at the Washington summit in December 1987. The arms-control process continued towards a START (Strategic Arms Reduction Talks) treaty at the Moscow summit of May 1988. Gorbachev's spirit of revived détente differed significantly from that pursued by Brezhnev. While for Brezhnev the inflow of Western technology was of crucial importance, for Gorbachev it was designed as a complement rather than a substitute for domestic reform. Under Gorbachev, 'Foreign policy would be the locomotive pulling the Soviet Union into the international system and providing the time and energy necessary for economic resurgence.'[2]

Gorbachev's foreign policy was conducted under the banner of New Political Thinking (NPT), drawing on earlier Soviet academic analysis and Western writings on interdependence and mutual security regimes. The problem with the NPT, however, was that it still remained heavily ideological, still propounding the view of foreign policy as a crusade for a new world. It represented not the end of ideology in foreign policy, but a more benevolent and indeed utopian version. Gorbachev's strategy was to reform Soviet society to achieve political comparability with the West in international affairs. Tragically for him, his successes in foreign policy were not accompanied by equal achievements at home.

THE MAKING OF FOREIGN POLICY

With the assumption of a global role Soviet policy-makers had to pay far more attention to foreign issues. Except in wartime, policy-making is not usually dominated by a single overriding ambition but arises out of the interplay of various motives and factors, not all of which are compatible. Western analysis of Soviet foreign policy veered between, on the one hand, the Riga axioms (named after a hostile group of inter-war specialists in Latvia) which emphasised the Soviet desire for world hegemony; and, on the other, the Yalta axioms which stressed the Soviet search for accommodation and the desire to be recognised as an equal and legitimate great power. Factors contributing to Soviet foreign policy included the following.

1   Certain geopolitical constraints were in the tradition of Tsarist foreign policy, giving rise to the view that 'communism was Tsarism in overalls', reflecting certain constants influencing policy-makers based in Moscow of whatever hue – factors that remained with the fall of communism. These include threats from insecure borders and the geopolitical imperatives for a power based on the Eurasian land mass. An associated feature is the role of political culture, a view which often suggests that Russia has an irresistible urge to expand, owing to the nature of the country itself. Arrogant leaders combined with a boorish xenophobic people, Kennan argued in 1947, provide the conditions for expansionism. R. V. Daniels stressed the continuity in centralised, autocratic rule buttressed by an official belief system, police control and the absence of effective law restraining the state as lending Soviet foreign policy its Tsarist colours.[3] The problems associated with a concept of political culture, which confuses Tsarist authoritarianism with Bolshevik totalitarianism, have been noted, and the idea does little to illuminate the specific concerns of Soviet policy.

2   Analysis of Soviet foreign policy is complicated to a greater extent than in most other countries by the ambiguous role of ideology. Did adherence to Marxism–Leninism reinforce traditional Russian concerns and drive the Soviet Union to establish a Pax Sovietica across the globe? The Soviet Union became a world power in military terms, but it also had a world, or universalistic, ideology whose precise role in Soviet foreign policy was ambivalent. Every great power develops an imperial creed to justify its actions as a world historical mission. However, whether Soviet ideology was used in an instrumental way to justify an expansionism based on its traditional great power interests, or whether it was itself the major motor in a logic of expansionism is not clear. Soviet ideology was an amalgam of Marxism–Leninism and pragmatic considerations which tempered the chiliastic ambitions for a world united under the banner of socialism.

The original Leninist ideology was internationalist, committed to the goal of world socialism, though the means of achieving it were the subject of controversy. It was stamped by a loathing for other social systems, but the persistence of socialism in one country necessitated dealings with them. The ideology therefore took on a nationalist colour expressed in terms of loyalty to the Soviet state. From the political culture point of view, Marxism was redundant in explaining Soviet foreign policy. However, the Soviet view of the world was still tempered by the contribution of its ideological foundations. International affairs were not viewed simply as the interplay of nation-states, the nineteenth-century view, but as a continuing struggle among various domestic and international interests. For most of Soviet history international relations were seen as class struggles waged in the international arena in the form of contests for global dominance between imperialism and socialism. Under Stalin the theory of the 'two camps' saw the world polarised at two hostile axes, neither of which could destroy the other, and so war was inevitable but not necessarily imminent. The associated theory of capitalist encirclement helped explain the ideological inconsistency between hopes of the withering away of the state and its monstrous strengthening under Stalin. Neither theory altogether precluded a notion of stable relations between the rival systems since Soviet foreign policy always aimed at securing the best possible conditions for the building of socialism at home and abroad. As in domestic ideology, Marxist–Leninist doctrine was combined with great power nationalism to sustain the hybrid Soviet ideology as the legitimating and motivating force of policy-making and popular support. Ideology was not the determining but a conditioning factor in Soviet foreign policy.

3   Another view would see Soviet foreign policy as the straightforward defence of national interest in which ideology played a subordinate role. As Churchill put it in a radio broadcast of 1 October 1939: 'I cannot forecast to you the action of Russia. It is a riddle wrapped in a mystery inside an enigma; but perhaps there is a key. That key is Russian national interest.' It was at this period that the USSR was maintaining a pact with its sworn ideological enemy, Nazi Germany. The concept of national interest is a contentious one at the best of times, and policy-making often reflects short-term elite interests. There is no final court of appeal which can establish what in the long-term comprises national interest.

4   A common view of Soviet foreign policy sees it as being driven by a relentless opportunism which exploited and exacerbated regional conflicts for its own ends. Such a view is not incompatible with the opinion which sees Soviet policy as simply crisis management, a reactive approach to developing challenges. This minimalist view of the policy process allows little scope for leadership initiative or long-term strategic goals. Soviet foreign policy can be seen as the search for recognition and equality in the world order of sovereign nation-states. This it largely achieved, and its aim then became to gain a commensurate status in the management of the evolving international system.

5   Another view sees the Soviet Union as an authoritarian system in which the external threats, real or imagined, were required by the power system to justify its own dominance over the polity. An ambitious foreign policy served to redirect the force of popular frustrations from domestic shortcomings to an external foe. The constant threat of the 'enemy without', imperialism, justified repression against the 'enemy within' and the maintenance of the security state.

These views of the factors contributing to Soviet foreign policy are reflected in three major models of how the Soviet Union dealt with foreign policy decisions. The first is the counterpart of totalitarianism applied in international relations, the rational actor model (RAM) located in the realist school of foreign policy analysis. It identifies a single centralised monolithic policy-making process which plans foreign policy moves and responses. This centre is considered unbuffeted by departmental, institutional or interest group pressures and is devoid of personality. The model plays down disagreements within the Soviet foreign policy establishment. The RAM model suffers from conflating centralisation of policy-making with the suggestion that policy outcomes will therefore be rational. Under Stalin the Soviet foreign policy process was highly centralised, but

Stalin's policies were not thereby any more coherent. Indeed, it has now become clear that Stalin was far from being the cold, calculating and far-sighted leader that his propaganda made him out to be. As John Lewis Gaddis argues, his decisions were often based on emotions, as in his view that with a socialist base in eastern Germany after the war, the western part would soon fall under his sway. Similarly, his authorisation of Kim Il Sung's invasion of South Korea in June 1950 was based on a totally unrealistic assessment of the changed balance of forces achieved by the coming to power of Mao Zedong in China a few months earlier.[4]

Pluralist models take the opposite view and see foreign policy as emerging out of the interplay of various forces. Graham Allison provided two alternatives to what he had identified as the rational actor model. In the 'organisation process' model decisions emerge less as a matter of deliberate choice but out of political bargaining between various bureaucratic and specialist groups 'functioning according to standard patterns of behaviour'; while in the 'bureaucratic politics' model rational choices by leaders at the top are discounted in favour of intense competition among players in the government – with decisions emerging as a result of bargaining between bureaucratic agencies and leaders.[5] In a Soviet-type system the subtle differences between pluralistic alternatives were minimal. Decisions were not always the rational ones but the result of a particular balance of forces at any one time; a group's ability to put forward its own interests counted for more than the long-term interests of the country. Brezhnev's consensual style of policy management certainly encouraged these tendencies, with the military and its associated industrial complex growing in influence. But as with interest group theory in general there is a tendency to exaggerate the cohesion of groups, although the theory when applied to the West does include bargaining within organisations. The autonomy of the decision-making centres from social or institutional interests tends to be underrated. Even under Brezhnev the decision-making process was not disjointed or fragmented among individuals and groups but remained firmly in the hands of the Politburo.

The style of policy-making does not necessarily have any automatic effect on the type of policies that emerge. Consensual pluralism, for example, does not mean that Soviet foreign policy becomes more conservative or marked by greater restraint. The decision to invade Czechoslovakia in August 1968 is a classic case of policy resulting from the vigorous interplay of bureaucratic institutions and personalities. With his own position apparently in jeopardy, Brezhnev was forced to side with the emerging consensus view of the military, KGB and party leaders in the western USSR afraid of being contaminated by 'socialism with a human face'.[6] One can assume, however, that interests such as agriculture or consumer industries are in favour of a less ambitious foreign policy.

The third model takes a mid-path and suggests an emerging controlled pluralism in which interest groups expressed certain views but within strict limits. In the political bargaining model policy outcomes are dependent on the interplay of the participants and what is acceptable as a politically viable solution. This sort of pluralism can be termed structural bureaucratic and is confined to certain institutions and elites involved in foreign policy formation. This model most closely approximates to Soviet reality.[7]

The new realism in foreign policy after 1985 was reflected in the modernisation of the Soviet foreign policy establishment. The bodies involved in foreign policy-making included the Defence Council and the Ministry of Defence itself which, with the KGB, provided a major channel for information, monitoring and formulation of policy options. The purge of Soviet military officers in the western military district during the Polish crisis of 1980–81 indicated a taming of military ambitions and influence. The role of the military has been discussed earlier

(Chapter 8), but it is worth stressing that under *perestroika* the emphasis on shifting resources from defence to the modernisation of the Soviet civilian economy meant that military influence on policy formation declined. The dominance of the military over the arms-control process, for example, was broken by the creation of a civilian arms-control section within the International Department of the Central Committee Secretariat.

The CPSU Central Committee Secretariat had departments covering the main foreign policy fields and together they constituted the nerve-centre of decision-making. Gorbachev placed diplomats acquainted with the West in key positions at home. Anatolii Dobrynin, the long-serving Soviet ambassador to Washington, was recalled to Moscow and played a key role at the head of a revitalised International Department, advising on East–West relations. Alexander Yakovlev, who spent ten years as ambassador to Canada and then headed IMEMO (the Institute of World Economy and International Relations), became a full member of the Politburo and head of the Secretariat's propaganda department, taking a keen interest in relations with the Third World. Relations with the socialist world were handled by the Department for Relations with Communist and Workers' Parties of Socialist Countries. The Ministry of Foreign Affairs (MFA) under Shevardnadze was revitalised and given more autonomy from direct party interference in international affairs. Some of the old anomalies like placing the Australian and New Zealand desks under Britain, the legacy of empire, were done away with and they were placed in a remodelled South Pacific section.

Academic institutions like IMEMO and the USA and Canada Institute, long headed by Georgii Arbatov, became increasingly important sources of specialised information and advice to the leadership. The move away from the old obsession with US–Soviet relations was reflected in the creation of a new Institute of European Affairs under the USSR Academy of Sciences. The new institute, significantly, studied not only Western but also Eastern Europe. Relations with the East moved away from the old party-to-party basis towards a broader state-to-state footing. These institutes played a critical role in the modernisation of Soviet diplomacy under Gorbachev.

THE POLITICS OF SECURITY

After 1945 Soviet socialism was no longer restricted to one country but became first a regional and later a global force. The Soviet Union's own role changed dramatically as it became one of the superpowers with a voice and influence matching in many respects that of the United States. The Gorbachev period saw a spate of unprecedented foreign policy initiatives, particularly in the sphere of arms control. Gorbachev clearly demonstrated that he was a prisoner neither of his foreign policy establishment nor of interest group pressures. There was a clear desire to exploit new opportunities to develop trade and technology, to establish a peaceful international environment to allow domestic modernisation, and to raise Soviet prestige on the world stage. This was to be achieved by establishing formal limits to East–West competition to reforge the concept of peaceful coexistence away from a crude image of international class struggle into a new model of co-operative relations between different social systems. As far as Gorbachev was concerned, each system could remain true to its own principles without having to come into conflict with the other. The competitive dynamic inherent in the concept of peaceful coexistence remained, but this was now tempered by a co-operative ethic. This position was clearly theoretically incoherent but it did allow Soviet foreign policy to be refined if not fundamentally reshaped.

The new political thinking modified the Soviet view of international relations and the role of the USSR was rethought. International politics was no longer seen as the playing out of the class struggle in the international arena and instead the leadership focused on the world's common problems. The NPT was motivated by a new sense of the unwinnable nature of nuclear war and by a re-evaluation of détente. The strengthening of the military power of the Soviet Union did not on its own automatically strengthen peace, and indeed threatened it. Too much attention and excessive resources were devoted to the military aspects of countering 'imperialism', Gorbachev argued at the June 1988 party conference, leading to the failure to take advantage of new political opportunities in the world. The nuclear threat was rethought and the idea of 'reasonable sufficiency' advanced, allowing a certain amount of 'disarmament for development': deterrence was played down and to a degree nuclear weapons were delegitimised. The NPT prompted a new analysis of the military, economic and political interdependence between East and West. Above all, the emphasis shifted to the interdependence of the human race for survival, accompanied by the stress on international economic security. The 'correlation of forces' was no longer seen as ineluctably tilting in the USSR's favour. The old definition of peaceful coexistence and détente were underpinned by the Soviet belief that the long-term struggle between the two systems would inevitably be won by the progressive forces led by the USSR, whereas the co-operative version suggested that the Soviet and capitalist worlds would continue to develop in parallel indefinitely. The evaporation of the old optimism encouraged the new realism of the NPT. This was accompanied by modifications to the notion of 'imperialism'; it was no longer seen in quite the stark terms as previously and thus allowed the moderation of inter-system rivalries. The new thinking, it should be stressed, was far from being universally accepted, with Ligachev, for example, stressing that Soviet diplomacy should continue to base itself on the 'class character of international relations'.

Just as there was no single motive to Soviet foreign policy, there was no single focus either: Soviet decision-makers were faced by a multiplicity of issues and problems. At the top of the list in the 1980s was the debate between economic reform and military commitments. The achievement of the Soviet Union's global status was at huge domestic cost in financial and political terms. Shevardnadze talked in terms of what can be called *khozraschyot* in the international sphere, to make foreign policy more cost effective by avoiding wasteful expenditure on defence and excessive foreign commitments. The defence sector, the nineteenth party conference resolved, had to concentrate not on quantity alone, but on improving quality through science and technology. Closely related was the crucial issue of arms control. Gorbachev's overriding aim was to free both economic and foreign policy from the burdens imposed by the arms race. The nuclear threat meant, in Gorbachev's words, that 'the human race has lost its immortality'. This understanding, together with the decline in the old optimism that history was working in the Soviet Union's favour, led to a shift away from the view that peace could be assured only by the advance of socialism and that, on the contrary, peace was a condition of socialist development. The emphasis now was on 'necessary military sufficiency' for defence rather than an open-ended commitment to military expenditure. The Strategic Defence Initiative, however, struck directly at this doctrine by extending the arms race to space and converting it into a race of technologies. The START negotiations faced formidable obstacles because of the complexity of the issues invloved and the balance to be drawn between nuclear and conventional forces. The NPT opened the door to fruitful talks since the USSR now accepted the need for deep, and not necessarily symmetrical, cuts in weaponry and the need for extensive verification.

Another major concern of Soviet foreign policy was more narrowly the relationship with the

United States. Both were guarantors of world security, and had the capacity not only to destroy themselves but the rest of the world with them. The two superpowers long saw the mirror image of themselves in the other, but there was much evidence that the bipolar structure of international relations established at Yalta in February 1945 was declining. The consolidation of the European Community (EC, now the European Union) and the emergence of regional powers, such as China and Japan, Brazil and India, created a more complex world. Soviet foreign policy after the Second World War was based on the premise that international relations were determined by two contending camps. The Soviet Union was content to dominate its own camp and tolerated United States' domination of the industrialised non-communist world since it provided a mechanism to control German revanchism and Japanese militarism. Under Andropov there was a shift to a more multipolar view, and under Gorbachev relations improved with Germany, Japan, the EC and Latin America. The veteran foreign minister Gromyko, the main proponent of the bipolar view, was relieved of his foreign affairs portfolio. The German question was no longer such a divisive issue, and Japan had turned its energies to economic development. Gorbachev had hoped to remove ideological rivalry from superpower relations and by implication to return to a nineteeth-century model of balance-of-power diplomacy, no longer confined to the concert of Europe but enacted on a world stage. Until Gorbachev's final period there was little to indicate the imminent dissolution of the blocs; but between 1989 and 1991 the USSR's alliance system disintegrated with extraordinary rapidity.

Under Shevardnadze Soviet foreign policy became much more sophisticated. It was no longer obsessed with relations with Washington as it had been for so many years under Gromyko. Far from retreating into some form of 'socialist isolationism', a range of regional policies was developed for most parts of the globe. Closer ties in particular were established with Western Europe, but traditional attempts to drive a wedge between the two wings of the Atlantic alliance were pursued with rather more tact than previously. The Soviet Union sought to acquire a voice in a Middle East settlement, and to develop multilateral security systems for everywhere from Latin America to South Asia. There was no scaling down of Soviet ambitions although they were no longer couched in the messianic terms of world revolution. Gorbachev increased the range and scope of the Soviet Union's global concerns. The long neglect of the Pacific littoral, for example, was remedied by Gorbachev's sharp reminder in a speech in Vladivostok in July 1986 that the Soviet Union regarded itself as 'an Asian and Pacific country'. Soviet relations with the Third World moved into a new phase. In the immediate post-war years the USSR was more concerned with its relations with the West and with consolidating its power in Eastern Europe. Under Khrushchev a new period of activism was launched and from the late 1960s the Soviet Union was willing to use its growing military power in Africa and Asia. During the interventionist phase Soviet policy appears not to have been the outcome of an expansionist design but the opportunistic exploitation of favourable local and international circumstances: the disarray of the USA following its defeat in Vietnam and the crises in Angola, Ethiopia and Afghanistan. One of the major factors precipitating the US's disillusionment with détente in the 1970s was direct Soviet involvement in a number of Third World conflicts. Whether intervention was justified is a matter of debate, but in *realpolitik* terms all that had changed was that Soviet capabilities could now match those of the USA. The Soviet Union took advantage of opportunities rather than actively seeking avenues of advancement. However, it became clear to the Gorbachev leadership that Soviet activism in the Third World damaged its other foreign policy goals, above all good relations with the West.

Soviet arms transfers helped to cement political ties, but increasingly also became a source of foreign currency. Even where Soviet military or economic assistance was crucial it would be a mistake to characterise the recipients as 'client states', however limited their room for ma-noeuvre might be. The Soviet Union had to deal with formidable nationalisms from Cuba to Ethiopia and Vietnam. In Afghanistan, however, the revolutionary forces became almost en-tirely dependent on the Soviet Union. Bitter disputes among warring factions in the ruling party, combined with the nature of the terrain and the dedication of the resistance, led to defeat in what has been called the Soviet Union's Vietnam. By the beginning of the withdrawal of the 'limited contingent' of some 115,000 men in May 1988 Soviet forces had lost 13,310 men killed and 35,478 wounded.

The heavy burden of client states led to a significant shift in Soviet relations with the Third World. Interventionism gave way to a greater concentration on economic relations and domes-tic reform. The grudging support to the Sandinista regime in Nicaragua revealed the wish to avoid an onerous open-ended commitment to 'another Cuba'. Revolutions, it was now argued, required a sufficiently developed economic base to be viable, otherwise they would require Soviet assistance. According to the Rand Corporation the USSR spent up to $40 billion annu-ally in supporting dependent states, rising from $14 billion in the early 1970s. Soviet attention now shifted to the industrialising and newly industrialised countries. In November 1986 *Pravda* warned Third World Marxist movements that violence may no longer be justified in over-throwing capitalism because of the dangers posed by nuclear weapons. The world revolution-ary process, in other words, was to be subordinated to Soviet developmental and security needs. Under Gorbachev there was a clear intention to reduce Soviet global military expenditure and to avoid superpower confrontation in the Third World. The weakening of bipolarity was re-flected in much greater Soviet tolerance of the Non-Aligned Movement.

The relationship of the Soviet Union to the world communist movement underwent signifi-cant changes. The USSR renounced its claims to be the directing centre, and there was now a degree of acceptance of polycentrism and for each country to find its own road to socialism. Sino-Soviet relations in the 1980s improved steadily as both countries launched ambitious reform programmes. Ideological denunciations gave way to the practical development of eco-nomic contacts. Soviet policy traditionally had two main aims in Eastern Europe: to maintain the cohesion of what used to be called the Soviet bloc; and to ensure the stability of the individual regimes. These goals were not always compatible since the enforcement of bloc unity was destabilising in terms of popular support. The association of socialism with the state interests of the Soviet Union undermined the legitimacy of the local governments. The whole region suffered from declining economic dynamism. The Eastern European countries illus-trated that the attempt to 'muddle through' had exhausted itself as an option and that more comprehensive reform efforts were unavoidable to achieve regime stability. *Perestroika* led to changes in Comecon focusing on the development of economic co-operation between mem-ber countries, improving its own organisation and working out strategic perspectives for long-term co-operation. The aim of economic integration, espoused by Khrushchev, was shelved.

The Soviet link prior to Gorbachev acted as a brake on the political renewal of these coun-tries. Soviet–East European relations were long governed by the principle of proletarian inter-nationalism which severely limited the policy options and allowed a high level of Soviet interventionism in day-to-day affairs. During *perestroika* relations began to be described by the term 'socialist internationalism', implying a looser form of unity and greater consultation. Alliance dynamics had never been simply the imposition of Soviet views, although the USSR as the senior partner and major supplier of arms clearly dominated relations. In the Warsaw

Pact, as in other areas, the national factor increasingly cut across broader ties of ideology, institutional structures and military necessity. The nineteenth party conference propounded the doctrine of 'freedom of choice' for states to choose their own social systems, though the degree to which this allowed Eastern European states to choose their own destinies at the time remained unclear, with Gorbachev insisting that they would remain within the framework of 'the socialist choice'. The old pattern of power politics in the region gave way to attempts to develop a 'socialist commonwealth'. The Stalinist concept of direct power through military occupation and party control gave way to a model whereby the Soviet Union limited its influence to more informal mechanisms. The principles governing such a relationship of independence of parties and socialist countries were adopted in the Soviet–Yugoslav declaration of March 1988 at the end of Gorbachev's visit. The declaration represented a formal repudiation of the Brezhnev doctrine of limited sovereignty. The Soviet leadership under Gorbachev did not repeat the mistake of the post-Stalin leadership in forcing allied countries to follow each twist and turn of Soviet domestic struggles. *Glasnost*, however, ultimately did have the same impact on Eastern Europe as destalinisation. Gorbachev allowed the indigenous leaderships to adopt their own policy towards reform, but increasingly warned that delay would be fatal for their rule. Even Vietnam, long suffering from a particularly virulent and typically disastrous form of War Communism, adopted economic reform policies. When change did come in Eastern Europe in 1989, it came as a tidal wave that swept away the regimes in their entirety.

Prior to *perestroika* the completeness of the USSR as a superpower was questioned. Its military power was not matched by economic creativity or cultural dynamism. While the USA had myriad non-military ways of extending its power and influence, from Coca-Cola to culture and computers, Moscow's global status was forced to rely more unequivocally on military power in the absence of the proven success of its economic system or ideology. It was a one-dimensional world power.[8] Soviet foreign policy even under Gorbachev continued to be torn by the tension between Soviet nationalism and communism as an international phenomenon. Even at a time of profound reform the question remained of which vision of the Soviet role in the world was most applicable: the 'hawks' of the Riga school who stressed 'communist expansionism', or the 'doves' of Yalta who emphasised the legitimate interests of a major state continuing the traditions of Russia. Both views suffered from a narrowness of vision, since it is clear that Soviet foreign policy derived from the complex interaction of ideology and opportunities, elite perceptions and economic realities. The freedom of manoeuvre of superpowers in the age of nuclear weapons was limited. Gorbachev stressed the problems the USSR had in developing its own territories, let alone expanding to control more. Nevertheless, while Soviet policy became undoubtedly defensive in character, the definition of 'defence' is problematic. The USSR traditionally saw the world as a hostile and alien place and therefore maintained an aggressive and absolute concept of defence, which the rest of the world correctly saw as threatening. It was Gorbachev's achievement to tame the world in the perceptions of the Soviet leadership and thus open the door to fruitful diplomacy. Gorbachev was the first Soviet leader to have broken out of the narrow definition of Soviet interests to accept the implications of the increasing interdependence and integrity of the world as a global system. Despite this, Soviet perceptions of the world remained within a strong ideological framework which, while not determining foreign policy, created the framework in which foreign policy was determined. It fell to Gorbachev's successors finally to dismantle the ideological state and to return to the pursuit of Russian national interests – if they could agree on how these interests were to be defined.

KEY TEXTS

Gorbachev, Mikhail S., *Perestroika: New Thinking for our Country and the World*, part 2 (London, Collins, 1987) pp. 135–252.

Gorodetsky, Gabriel (ed.), *Soviet Foreign Policy 1917–1991: A Retrospective* (London, Frank Cass, 1994).

Light, Margot, *The Soviet Theory of International Politics* (Brighton, Wheatsheaf, 1987).

Lynch, Allen, *The Soviet Study of International Relations* (Cambridge, Cambridge University Press, 1987).

Nogee, J. L. and R. H. Donaldson, *Soviet Foreign Policy since World War II*, 3rd edn (New York, Pergamon, 1987).

Petro, Nicolai N. and Alvin Z. Rubinstein, *Russian Foreign Policy: From Empire to Nation State* (Harlow, Addison Wesley Longman, 1996).

Rubinstein, Alvin Z., *Soviet Foreign Policy since World War II: Imperial and Global*, 2nd edn (Boston, Little, Brown & Co., 1985).

Ulam, Adam, *Expansion and Coexistence: Soviet Foreign Policy, 1917–1973* (New York, Holt, Rinehart & Winston, 1974).

Part V
Perspectives

17 Rise and fall of the Soviet system

The Soviet Union was born in war, it was forged in war, and it was tempered by war, but it did not, surprisingly enough, die in war. It was the First World War that made possible Lenin's seizure of power; during the Civil War the essential features of the system emerged; the Great Patriotic War (the Second World War) acted to relegitimate the system; and although the USSR's engagement in the war in Afghanistan from 1979 to 1988 brought it no honour, it did not seriously precipitate its downfall. Some might argue that the USSR's enormous commitment of resources to fight the Cold War debilitated it to the point of collapse, but the argument that the Soviet Union collapsed in a time of peace remains valid.

MAIN FEATURES

It was a relatively easy matter for the Bolsheviks to seize power, but how they would organise that power and what they would do with it was, however, never satisfactorily resolved. Within an extraordinarily short period of coming to power the main features of the system were in place: the high degree of coercion; the marginalisation of popular representation in the soviets; an uncomfortable relationship with the working class – even though the system continued to rule in the name of the workers; ideological maximalism combined with theoretical flexibility when it suited the leadership; and the death of politics not only in society at large but also within the party itself. In key areas fundamental problems dogged the system to the end. Let us examine each in turn.[1]

International relations

Revolutionary socialism of the Leninist type is internationalist by its very definition, believing that only communism as a world system can be viable. This was the belief Lenin outlined in his booklet on *Imperialism*, and one to which he remained committed despite the failure of the revolution to spread very far after 1917. The contradiction between the universal ideology of revolutionary socialism and the form in which it was contained, an isolated nation-state, was never resolved, despite the expansion of communism into Eastern Europe, China and elsewhere after the Second World War. This tension between ideology and circumstances was vividly manifested during the period of War Communism, but later was to take the form of a Cold War not only between East and West but also within the state – between the universal aims of communist internationalism and the national interests of the country itself.

Following Lenin's death in January 1924, Stalin was to make a virtue of necessity and proclaimed the doctrine of 'socialism in one country', insisting that Soviet Russia could not only begin the building of socialism but could go on by its own efforts to complete it without the help of the developed West. This was a far cry from Lenin's, and even more Marx's, view that socialism was an international system or it was nothing. Stalin later went even further by announcing that the interests of the Soviet Union *were* the interests of socialism, thus preventing a creative partnership with the international socialist movement. It was on this subordinate basis that relations with the 'satellite states' in Eastern Europe after the Second World War were based, leading to endless conflicts and stifling any creative renewal of the Soviet system by contact with the relatively more developed Central and East European societies. The Soviet bloc states soon moved from being a security and economic asset into becoming a liability, sowing mistrust between the USSR and the rest of the world and ultimately destabilising the Soviet Union itself. Bolshevik militancy became Soviet militarism, marked not so much by external expansionism as by the militarisation of Soviet society and external relations.

Economic development

Marx had anticipated that communism would inherit a developed industrial infrastructure together with a sophisticated social system and the experience of 'bourgeois' democracy. Socialism in Russia, however, felt constrained to take upon itself the developmental tasks that it was to have inherited from a mature capitalist system. This was to have momentous consequences for the whole trajectory of the communist experiment in Russia, giving the system an 'economistic' twist and undermining the humanistic aspirations of the original Marxian project. Development and production became the substitute for the implied original emancipatory goals of Marxian socialism. In addition, as L. Kritsman had noted in his work on War Communism, commodity-capitalist societies were characterised by surpluses whereas a proletarian-natural economy was stamped by generalised shortages: indeed, the Soviet system was dubbed an 'economy of shortages'.

The attempt to eliminate capitalist property relations in their entirety and to build an industrial society without a market represented one of the greatest social experiments known to humanity. During War Communism money itself came close to being abolished in its entirety, and then during the mass collectivisation of the peasantry from December 1929, when Stalin sought to 'liquidate the kulaks as a class', an unprecedented war of the town against the countryside was unleashed, provoking untold misery and famine in the short term, and a continuing crisis in the agricultural sector that lasts to this day. The whole system of planning was a misnomer, and in practice took the form of commands from the centre, and all sorts of evasive techniques by managers in the enterprises. The planning system was designed less to match resources to capacity as a way of stimulating economic growth by setting targets. This was not a planned economy but a command economy.

The emphasis, moreover, was less on balanced growth than on the development of heavy industry. This it achieved, although at enormous cost in wasted lives and resources, and laid the basis for the armaments industries that helped achieve victory in the Second World War. Oskar Lange had argued that communism was the war organisation of capitalism.[2] Stalinist industrialisation, however, led to an extremely unbalanced pattern of economic development: agriculture remained no more than a tributary of industry; heavy industry was privileged over light industry; the service sector was neglected; and innovation in science and technology was inhibited. While reasonably effective in the relatively simple 'extensive' phase of industrial development, where quantity takes priority over quality, the 'intensive' phase posed challenges to the command economy that it ultimately could not meet.

Nationality policy

Despite the endless 'propaganda of success' in this field, the USSR never found a satisfactory way of integrating its multinational community into an effective polity. Established by the Union Treaty of December 1922 and regulated by the constitution adopted in January 1924, the USSR combined the principles of national autonomy with federalism. Certain national areas were granted the privilege of becoming ethno-federal units based on a titular nationality ranked hierarchically. Thus by the end there were fifteen union republics enjoying many of the privileges of sovereign states, including the formal right to secession; a number of autonomous republics with rather fewer rights; and various smaller autonomous provinces and regions. The Russian Soviet Federative Socialist Republic (RSFSR) was just one of the fifteen union republics but was in the anomalous position of lacking its own party organisation, academy of sciences and some other institutions enjoyed by the other republics. All-union Soviet bodies served the whole country and the RSFSR, creating a disequilibrium that angered Russian nationalists while offending the sensibilities of the other republics in implying that Russia and the Soviet Union were one and the same, something that was far from the truth.

Developed by Stalin as part of his policy of divide and rule, where the borders between ethno-federal units were often demarcated precisely to cause maximum aggravation between peoples, the Soviet Union catastrophically failed to build itself as a viable national polity. The fifth point of the internal passport system forced people to state their nationality and fostered an ethnicised sense of national identity that might otherwise have been eroded. The definition of nationhood was thus institutionalised in two main ways: territorial and political on the one hand, and ethnocultural and personal on the other, an incompatible dual formulation whose legacy still shapes nationality politics in Russia today.[3] The extraordinarily careless stimulation and maintenance of nationalism through the construction of an unwieldy ethno-federal state structure while failing to provide a national basis to the regime proved to be the Achilles heel of Soviet power.

The emphasis on Soviet citizenship ultimately proved insufficient to compensate for the lack of a Soviet *national* identity. The forced incorporation of the Baltic republics, Moldavia and the western regions of Ukraine during and after the Second World War, moreover, added peoples to the USSR who proved impossible to assimilate. Napoleon's dictum that 'all empires die of indigestion' was once again confirmed. In conditions of relative freedom under Gorbachev, the many tensions in the Soviet national and federal system came into the open. More adroit leadership might have contained them and transformed the Soviet Union into a confederation, but this would have taken leadership of a rare calibre. By 1990 Russia itself, by far the largest republic, was stirring. Elections to Russia's Congress of People's Deputies in March 1990 brought a large swathe of the opposition into the republic's parliament. In May of that year Boris Yeltsin was elected Chairman of the Russian Congress, and became the symbol of Russia's new-found attempt to reforge its identity. The Declaration of State Sovereignty on 12 June 1990 placed Russian laws above those of the party and the USSR. Russia began to reconstitute itself as a sovereign state, a process that accelerated after the failed coup of August 1991, provoking the disintegration of the Soviet Union in December of that year.

Politics and the state

Marx had never anticipated the dominance of the single party, believing that the proletariat as a whole would be mature enough to rule on its own without an intermediary organisation. The creation of the party as an instrument of rule on behalf of the working class was what turned Marxism into Marxism–Leninism. In his 1917 pamphlet *The State and Revolution* Lenin had toyed with the idea of socialism as a vast anti-bureaucratic self-managing society based on the power of the soviets, but he gave little indication of how this would work in practice. In the event, the Bolshevik party took over, in the words of the infamous Article 6 of the 1977 Soviet constitution, as the 'leading and guiding force of Soviet society and the nucleus of its political system, of all state and public organisations'. The Bolshevik party, with a membership of a few thousand in 1917, had by 1988 (at its peak) become an organisation with nearly 20 million members. Renamed the Communist Party of the Soviet Union (CPSU) in 1952, the party was at the heart of the *nomenklatura* system of appointments, placing its nominees in positions of responsibility at all levels of state and economic administration.

We have noted that theories of convergence suggested that while the structures differed, the political process in the USSR was essentially similar to that in other modern industrial states. The whole thrust of Gorbachev's reforms was an admission that this was in fact not the case. The issue is not even the dominance of a single monopolistic party, since other countries like Mexico, Singapore and (earlier) South Korea were one-party systems, but the refusal of the party to allow elements of social self-organisation, independent large-scale economic activity and civil society. The 'party' as such, moreover, was a fiction: all major decisions were taken by its staff of full-time functionaries, known collectively as the *apparat* (hence the word *apparatchik*, a communist official). Power was concentrated in the hands of the General Secretary, officially designated by the Central Committee of some three hundred members but often dominating the party's key decision-making body, the Politburo of about a dozen members. The Central Committee was at the head of a huge administrative system run by its Secretariat. The CPSU was in effect a parallel administration, shadowing the official departments of state: a party-state emerged undermining the functional adaptability of both.

Despite the Marxist view that under socialism the state would (as Engels put it) 'wither away', in practice all twentieth-century revolutionary socialist systems have increased the powers of the state. As Stalin put it, 'We advance towards the abolition of the state by way of strengthening of the state.' Once all the liberal safeguards for individual freedom had been swept away after October 1917, and with the suffocation of all intermediary civil associations between the state and society, there was nothing to prevent the massive aggrandisement of state power. The individual stood isolated and unprotected under the 'iron heel' (in Jack London's phrase) of the state. But this contradiction between the intended abolition of the state and its actual leviathan-like growth does not exhaust the paradoxes of the Soviet state. While all-powerful with respect to society and the individual, the 'state', as such, under revolutionary socialism hardly existed, and certainly lacked any autonomy. The state was colonised by the parasitic party organism and, although highly institutionalised and marked by a degree of bureaucratic pluralism, remained shapeless. Although bureaucratised, the Soviet administrative system was not 'bureaucratic' in any recognisably Weberian sense. For Max Weber, the bureaucracy was the engine room of the modern state, based on a clearly defined division of labour, impersonal rules, stable expectations, job security and with selection based on competence not patronage and with procedures based on an ordered hierarchy of authority. The

Soviet system remained arbitrary and irregular, based on ideological goal achievement rather than legal norms and the application of rules. Rigby argued that Stalinism gave rise to a mono-organisational society.[4] Entwined with the party, the collapse of the CPSU in 1991 was accompanied by the relative immobilisation of the state, deprived now of its guiding mechanism.

Leadership

While Marxism is a theory of collective class action, in practice the Soviet experience was based on the exaggerated role of leadership, first through the party and then of individuals. Although always formally ruling through collective party or state institutions, the Soviet years are stamped by the character of individual leaders: this is how history will remember each stage of Soviet development. As early as under Lenin government became personalised, although the party's institutional life remained vigorous. Following Lenin's death, however, it became clear that Stalin, appointed General Secretary of the Bolshevik party in 1922, had gathered the reins of power in his hands. By a process of deft manoeuvring against other claimants to Lenin's mantle Stalin emerged as the unchallenged leader by 1929 and ruled without serious challenge until his death in March 1953. Condemned by his successor Nikita Khrushchev in his 'Secret Speech' at the twentieth party congress in February 1956 for having developed a 'cult of the personality', this hardly begins to describe the enormous power Stalin enjoyed over the life and death of citizens and over the fate of the country. Khrushchev re-established the party as a functioning institution, but he too ruled on the basis of his personal authority and policy initiatives.

Following Khrushchev's ouster in a 'palace coup' in October 1964, his successor, Leonid Ilich Brezhnev, ruled in a much more restrained but in ultimately a no less influential way. His consensual style and muddling through policies allowed the country to slip into what was later called the era of stagnation (*zastoi*). Politics was dominated by an oligarchy composed of a narrow range of elite interests operating, in public at least, according to the principle of unanimity. The concept of developed socialism appeared to be little more than the ideology of stagnation. Indeed, stagnation appears to be part of the 'iron law' of Soviet development, alternating with periods of mobilisation: what is absent is steady progressive development. The Brezhnev period was characterised by growth without modernisation; while the economic percentages, numbers and statistics in all respects appeared to improve, development was not rooted into adaptive social processes. Brezhnev's death in November 1982 opened the way for the brief rule of two very different, but equally old, men. In the few months allowed to him Yurii Andropov launched a programme of authoritarian reform based on the tightening of discipline in the workplace, soviets and the party. His successor from February 1984, Konstantin Chernenko, was a man more in the Brezhnev mould, but his death in March 1985 opened the door for the accession of Gorbachev to head the CPSU, and to launch his own brand of increasingly radical reforms under the slogan of *perestroika*.

Models and modernity

The theory of totalitarianism, developed by Hannah Arendt and others from the 1950s, sought to place Soviet coercion in the larger perspective of German Nazism and Italian Fascism. The differences should be stressed, however, and while fascism sought to reject modernity, communism represented an attempt to reforge modernity. As we saw in Chapter 10, the theory of totalitarianism according to Friedrich and Brzezinski focuses on the imposition of a single ideology, the dominance of a single mass party, the leadership principle (Hitler, Stalin), party control over the military, a monopoly over the means of effective communication, a terroristic system of police control and central direction of the economy. The main feature is the attempt to impose a single source of authority over all aspects of society. The concept of totalitarianism reflects the ideology and not the system, the aspiration and not necessarily the achievement. While in many respects unattainable, the attempt to impose total control is the defining feature of high totalitarianism.

Following Stalin's death the Soviet system, while not quite mellowing, certainly relaxed its terroristic control over society. This is not the same, however, as granting society any autonomy. Independent civil associations, let alone political organisations or organised dissenting groups, continued to be ruthlessly crushed. Thus, when Gorbachev relaxed the totalitarian impulse, society found itself ill prepared for the relatively liberal regime, lacking a structured civil society and unaccustomed to the conventions of pluralistic social life or a competitive political system. There was no shadow democratic political order waiting in the wings to take over. This was to cast a long shadow over post-communist politics.

PATTERNS OF SOVIET RULE

Three main stages of Soviet politics can be identified. The first was the period of *system building*, lasting from 1917 to 1953, when the main outlines of the political and economic organisation of the society were established. Lenin's imposition of the Bolshevik party at the centre of Soviet life was accompanied later by Stalin's collectivisation, industrialisation and cultural revolution. This phase was marked by enormous achievements in establishing the foundations of an industrialised economy, changing the face of the country from a predominantly peasant to an urbanised, literate and educated society. Yet the system built in this period had some major problems including a resistance to technological innovation, wasteful use of material and human resources and a debilitated agriculture. Above all, the attempt to reforge modernity in the furnace of Soviet industrialisation left out of account what during *perestroika* was called 'the human factor', the need to reward (not necessarily only materially) individual enthusiasm.

The second stage of Soviet politics between 1953 and 1985 was marked by attempts at *system consolidation*. It was precisely the failure to find an effective form of polity and economy in this period that gave rise to a chronic struggle between attempts to remobilise society and stagnation, a tension that prompted reformist bursts under Khrushchev and Andropov but which effectively gave way to the entropic elements in the Soviet system under Brezhnev. The very definition of the system in the Brezhnev period as 'developed socialism' suggested that it represented the apogee of Soviet development. While there were notable advances in these years in terms of standards of living and the achievement of strategic parity with the United States, the whole post-Stalin period is sometimes characterised as a 'neo-Stalinist compromise'. This suggests that in return for the state promising an end to indiscriminate mass terror and improved welfare, the people would limit their political demands such as elections with a free choice of candidates. As noted in Chapter 5, a type of 'welfare-state authoritarianism' (Breslauer) emerged. This unstated compromise broke down when the system was no longer able to deliver on its promises of improving the quality of life. The courage and importance of the relatively few political dissidents who demanded a genuine opening of the system should not be forgotten, yet the mass of the people was reconciled to its enforced political infantilism – not allowed to think for themselves in the political sphere. Dissent played an important part in alerting the world and the country's own rulers to problems, but on its own did not act as the catalyst for the far-reaching changes launched by Gorbachev.

The third stage, between 1985 and 1991, can be characterised as a dual process of *system dissolution* and *national disintegration* when the fundamentals of the regime were radically transformed and then destroyed, while the country itself disintegrated by December 1991. The distinction between the two processes should be noted: while clearly linked, the logic of the two was different. The Soviet political system collapsed for a distinctive set of reasons (which will be examined below), while the break-up of the Soviet Union (with the exception of certain areas like the Baltic republics and Moldavia) appeared contingent on the dissolution of the CPSU. What is clear, however, is that Gorbachev's attempt to unlink ideology from state organisation proved fatal to both: the Soviet system had survived as a peculiar amalgam of power and claims to special knowledge on the development of societies and the future. Without a privileged relationship to knowledge, what was the point of Soviet power?

Lenin's suppression of the ability of party members themselves to participate in organised political lobbying began the process whereby the communist party became little more than a bureaucratised administrative agency. The defeat of external opponents was one thing, but the crushing of internal opposition another. The 'ban on factions', and in general the prohibition of horizontal contacts and the suffocation of internal debate through democratic centralism and other forms of control, stifled internal sources of renewal. At the same time, the growth of state power was ambivalent; the Soviet state was strong yet 'disorganised'. George Kennan had pointed out soon after the Second World War that Soviet power 'bears within it the seeds of its own decay'. He warned that if 'anything were ever to disrupt the unity and the efficacy of the Party as a political instrument, Soviet Russia might be changed overnight from one of the strongest to one of the weakest and most pitiable of national societies'.[5] This indeed was to occur when the August 1991 coup tried to reverse some of Gorbachev's reforms to restore elements of the old authoritarian order. The failure of the coup and the accompanying self-destruction of the party revealed the fragility of the entire system. The whole edifice of communist power came tumbling down, followed in December by the disintegration of the USSR itself.

REASONS FOR THE FALL

From at least 1975 it was clear that the Soviet economy was under pressure. The Soviet growth rate was falling and there were deep structural problems that suggested continued decline and probably stagnation. Muddling through was no longer a viable option. Declining productivity was depressing the economy, reducing living standards and exacerbating the widespread cynicism about the system. Although the CIA estimated that Soviet GNP had reached about 58 per cent of the USA's, the comparison was to a degree meaningless (as the CIA itself recognised). Quite apart from the problem of finding convincing rates of exchange and comparative price equivalents, it was difficult to measure things like the quality and availability of goods. Above all, the overall GNP figure included the enormous military sector that did little for the domestic economy, while the exploitation of raw materials became an ever larger proportion of the total economy. Thus the size of the Soviet economy masked major distortions, above all the distribution between defence and consumer goods, raw materials and energy extraction compared to manufacturing output. In short, the Soviet economy increasingly looked not so much an advanced economy as a less-developed one.

From its very early days the Soviet system entered a cycle of reform and reaction. It should be stressed that profound elements of continuity remained despite the many changes in forms of rule and the personalities of the leaders. The attempt to eliminate capitalism during War Communism gave way to the reformist period of the New Economic Policy (NEP) from 1921 to 1928. This reformism, however, was of a special type, concentrating on some economic concessions to the peasants to allow the restoration of elements of the market while consolidating the single-party Bolshevik dictatorship. The very success of NEP in a sense led to its downfall, having helped achieve economic recovery at the price of social inequality and unemployment. The NEP was always vulnerable to changes in Bolshevik policy, and while as an economic system it might have provided an effective framework for Soviet development, the consolidation of Stalin's rule at the end of the 1920s saw a renewed onslaught against the market, religion and political deviancy. The second reformist period took place under Khrushchev, but once again his experimentation with popular participation and economic deconcentration was hostage to the changing fortunes of Soviet political leadership. His ouster in 1964 inaugurated a long period of decline. The third period of change under Gorbachev saw the system reform itself out of existence.

Perestroika represented the last and greatest reform period, yet the polity quite simply was unable to withstand reform. Indeed, the system had been created to withstand dynamic open-ended change, endowing it with the brittleness identified by Kennan. Although reform was in the air throughout the system-consolidation years, there was an equally strong 'conservative' trend which insisted that the system established by Lenin and Stalin required little, if any, change. Just as revolution can be seen as the functional outcome of a crisis of state and society, so reform can be seen as a way of adjusting the revolution; it might equally be seen, however, as an indication of the bankruptcy of the revolution. The very notion of reform suggests an underlying recognition of flaws in the system. The dynamic of Soviet reform always tended towards a transcendence of the system, undermining the very order it was intended to save. It is in this implacable circular logic that Gorbachev found himself trapped.

By the time Gorbachev came to power traditional Soviet methods for controlling unrest and imbuing the system with dynamism, like 'discipline', were unlikely to restore the economy's fortunes. The burden of the defence sector, moreover, distorted the whole pattern of economic development. There were no easy options for any reformer. A further dilemma of reform was that the very measures required to deal with the accumulation of problems would undermine the political mechanism (above all, the power of the *nomenklatura* and the party *apparat*) that gave the reformer the political muscle to bring about change. In the event Gorbachev's attempts to restructure the system alienated conservatives in the bureaucracy and a large part of the intelligentsia while failing to deliver the economic results that might have sustained political support. The reforms became increasingly radical in the political sphere, epitomised above all by the restructuring of the system of party rule in September 1988 and the reform of the constitution in December of that year, leading to relatively free elections in March 1989 and the convocation of the new legislature, the Congress of People's Deputies, two months later. A deeper process, however, was taking place as sections of the managerial and ministerial bureaucracy began to take advantage of the opportunities opened up by the onset of the market to convert their power and privileges into property, preparing to take their share of state assets as privatisation developed.

Three main approaches in the study of the fall of the Soviet Union can be identified. The first focuses on the notion of an *ontological* (or structural) failure of Soviet politics. Simply put, this means that the Soviet system dissolved because of certain inherent shortcomings of the system itself, including the structural flaws identified above. Above all, the extirpation of the market deprived the authorities of any sense of what was really happening in the economy. Central planning proved effective in the first stages of industrialisation, able to concentrate resources on the limited tasks of developing extractive industries, building steel works, and establishing a military-industrial complex rivalled only by that of the USA. As the economy became more sophisticated the planning system was unable to cope with the myriad demands and decisions required of it. The system remained locked in a primitive model of an industrial society. As Western societies moved towards post-industrial service economies the Soviet system still concentrated on supplying producer goods and meeting centrally formulated targets that bore little relation to the needs of society. On the political side, too, ontological approaches suggest that the lack of a dynamic and open-ended relationship between the regime and society foreclosed the evolutionary option of societal development. Society itself became a jungle of informal relationships while the polity became reduced to a set of neo-feudal patron–client relations.

Already Vladimir Dudintsev's novella, *Not by Bread Alone*, published in *Novy Mir* in 1956, suggested that the problems lay not just in the arrogance of the bureaucracy but in the system itself. If we accept this view then Gorbachev's predicament becomes almost inescapable. While he may well have been pursuing a deep strategy, at the tactical level his endless tacking and turning disoriented the party, undermined the economy and ultimately destroyed the union. It might have been better simply to have taken any decision and stuck to it. In his *The Wisdom of Solomon* Jon Elster cites the example of child-custody cases where there can be no painless choices; it might appear most rational simply to toss a coin, providing at least a rapid decision. The question remains, however, that even with the wisdom of Solomon, rational choice theory and modelling of policy formation, were there optimal 'correct' choices for Gorbachev to have taken? From the ontological perspective, all choices would have been wrong if they perpetuated a fundamentally irrational system; but the 'right' choices could only be destructive and thus from the perspective of political leadership, that seeks to enhance state capacity and perpetuate a political system, 'wrong'. It was in these dilemmas that Gorbachev found himself ensnared.

Ontological arguments are challenged by those who espouse *conjunctural* approaches to the fall, suggesting that the system did have an evolutionary potential that might have allowed it in time to adapt to changing economic and political circumstances. The emergence of a reformer like Gorbachev from within the system suggests that there remained a hidden intellectual potential in the communist system responsive to the challenges of information technology, the more sophisticated requirements of an educated and urbanised population, and a more open relationship with the world and other communist states. Gorbachev's ultimate failure and the collapse of the system are ascribed to contingent factors, including the strength of internal party opposition, the alleged opportunism of the Russian leadership under Boris Yeltsin (apparently willing to bring down the whole Soviet Union in its ruthless quest for power), and the failure of the West to commit enough resources to support Soviet reforms.[6]

A third approach would concede that the two earlier views reflect important elements of the truth but would stress that some middle-level theory more accurately encompasses the various dimensions of the fall. Such a theory might be called *decisional*, stressing that particular decisions at particular times precipitated the collapse, but that these political choices were made in the context of a system that could only be made viable by a thorough transformation of social, economic and political relations. This transformation could have been a long-term gradual process, but required a genuine understanding of the needs of the country. This approach is less than absolutely deterministic about the inevitability of a Soviet collapse but is more than a contingent reading of circumstantial facts.

Yegor Ligachev is an exponent of this view, arguing 'we were led to the brink of the abyss not only by the scope and complexity of the accumulated problems but also by the gross errors made by the leaders of *perestroika* … Is the answer in the crisis of the system, or in the blunders and mistakes of the leaders of *perestroika*?'[7] The decisional approach does justice to the mix of factors bringing down the Soviet system. It focuses on particular factors of leadership, the external situation (in particular, the emergence of a resolute foe in the form of Ronald Reagan's USA), but stresses that the policy responses at the time of crisis precipitated the fall. Above all, the very decision-making mechanism was weakened by Gorbachev. The former ambassador to Washington, Anatolii Dobrynin, argued that Gorbachev had become a 'virtual monarch, bypassing the traditional policymaking institutions'.[8] The powers of the existing institutions were weakened, but there was a failure to create legitimate new bodies, creating an institutional vacuum that Gorbachev sought to fill by personal activism.

The structuralist would look at the USSR's declining international competitiveness to argue that the actually existing 'communist' systems by the 1980s could no longer compete with the West in terms of standards of living or technological dynamism, allowing a widening gap to open up between the USSR and developed Western economies. This lack of international viability, the decisionalist would counter, was not the key factor leading to the fall. Despite claims that the American rearmament programme of the 1980s brought the Soviet Union to its knees, there is no particular reason for the USSR to have responded in kind, especially since the technological limitations of Star Wars were well known to the Soviet military. Despite being faced by a host of problems – including declining rates of economic growth since the 1960s (falling to an average 2 per cent per annum in the 1980s), declining productivity, increasing grain imports, lagging oil production, and the failure to keep abreast of scientific and technological developments in the West – other countries in the 1970s had also stagnated but had pulled out of the crisis.

Structuralists would counter to argue that Soviet problems were far more deep-rooted than those of comparable industrial systems. The command economy was increasingly dysfunctional, suppressing social dynamism and ultimately inhibiting technological and social innovation. The Soviet economic system drew its inspiration from the nineteenth-century smoke-stack model of industrial society rather than the knowledge-based service economies of the advanced capitalist societies. Despite numerous attempts at economic reform, the fundamentals of the system established in the 1930s remained. But even here it has been argued that the Soviet economy might have been able to limp on indefinitely. According to Ellman and Kontorovich, 'The immediate causes of the partial collapse were the actions of the leadership itself, its destabilising institutional changes and economic policies.'[9] The highly concentrated decision-making mechanism in this sphere, as in others, focused policy-making in the hands of a few people who little understood the nature of the problem and whose unshakeable belief in the reformability of the system led to incompetent decisions.

Even in nationality politics the disintegration of the USSR was not, it might be argued, structurally determined. If, for example, Gorbachev had been able to find a common language with the leader of Lithuania, Algirdas Brazauskas, once the latter was elected as the reformist communist leader there in late 1988, then the USSR might well have been able to transform itself into a free confederation of states. After all, Brazauskas had taken Gorbachev at his word and was at first a loyal exponent of *perestroika*. Instead, Gorbachev appeared to require subordinates rather than colleagues and partners, and Soviet–Lithuanian relations entered into a cycle of distrust and recriminations ending ultimately with the declaration of Lithuanian independence in April 1991.[10]

In politics the argument might be put that if Gorbachev had allowed the genuine emergence of free elections, created a workable constitutional system and parliament and, when faced with opposition from within the CPSU, split the party in time and placed himself at the head of a reformist social democratic party that could then have gone to the country to gain the legitimacy conferred by democratic elections, then the outcome might have been very different. The rump conservatives would then have been isolated and marginalised, while the new Gorbachevian party could have implemented gradual policies of economic reform and marketisation, avoiding the catastrophic economic collapse and social difficulties that came later. This is speculation, but developments along this line appear perfectly feasible. In China an evolutionary exit from communism appears to be working, with the emergence of a dynamic market economy within the carapace of a barely reformed communist system.

It is at this point that we must try to reconcile the view that there were irremedial flaws in the Soviet system with the argument that its fall was not structurally determined. The apparent paradox can be resolved by focusing precisely on decisional structures. The distinction between policy and polity, between the various policy spheres (foreign, nationality and economic) and the decision-making element itself, something that can broadly be called the polity, is standard in political science but in the Soviet system took on extreme forms. While collapse in the various policy spheres might have been avoided, the ontological incapacity of the Soviet polity to 'normalise' itself ultimately destroyed the whole project. Thus while more skilful leadership might have averted various policy crises, the polity itself was incapable of reform.

The regime that had been able to modernise the country was unable to transform itself. From the perspective of modernisation, social and political dynamism were stifled by the suffocating tutelage of the communist authorities: 'The one-party regime ultimately fell owing to its inability to respond to immense social changes that had taken place in Soviet society – ironically, social changes that the Party itself had set in motion.'[11] The gutting of the very sources of radical socialist approaches to human organisation undermined the legitimacy of communist aspirations (like egalitarianism and collectivism) in their entirety. More prosaically, the Soviet polity itself appeared to suffer from a permanent crisis of governance. The party itself was never designed as an instrument of government and the formulation that 'the party rules but the government governs' allowed endless overlapping jurisdictions, while the state itself remained formless and subject to constant arbitrary interventions by the party. The collapse of the party in 1991 led to a crisis of the state whose legacy has not yet been overcome.

At least three crucial differences between the different exit paths from communism in the USSR and China help put our distinction beteen polity and policies in perspective. The first focuses on differences between the polity and the nation. In China the subject of reform, the Chinese national state, is barely contested, whereas in the former USSR the political system of Soviet socialism reigned over the other fifteen union republics as some sort of free-floating 'sixteenth republic'. While Chinese leaders have never hesitated to pursue identifiable Chinese national interests, the national interests of the abstract 'Soviet' sixteenth republic could never be reduced to the specific interests of countries called 'Russia', 'Ukraine' and the others. This confusion between the polity called the USSR and the particular national states was reflected in the way that the democratic insurgents in Russia from the late 1980s spoke simply of 'the country' rather than any particular state entity. Lacking a national base, the Soviet polity simply could not sink roots in any particular country. It appears that Gorbachev came to accept Solzhenitsyn's argument that Soviet leaders had sacrificed Russia on the pyre of world revolution and ideology, and this fatally undermined his self-confidence in the final struggle with Yeltsin and the resurgent Russia.[12] Whereas a reformed China is still China, reform of the USSR meant transcending the USSR.

Following on from this, we can distinguish between the polity and the state. Even within each national area the Soviet polity only tangentially corresponded to the state interests of any particular country: in some places more (Central Asia) and in some less (the Baltic republics), but everywhere there remained a tension between the polity and the state. In his 1973 *Letter to the Soviet Leaders* Solzhenitsyn urged that the Soviet leaders *themselves* should transform the supranational communist empire into a normal nation-state.[13] The third major difference was the USSR's place in the international system, with the Soviet polity representing the major geopolitical alternative to Western hegemony. This challenge demanded an ever greater proportion of domestic resources leading to a classic case of what Paul Kennedy has called 'imperial overstretch', the attempt to maintain a military capacity beyond what is economically viable at the expense of economic and social modernisation.[14]

The Soviet Union represented the first and most sustained attempt to implement the principles of Marxian revolutionary socialism, above all the attempt to abolish the market and private property in the means of production. Although these principles were drastically modified by the harsh encounter with the realities of Russia in the twentieth century and by the needs of various elite groups, they remained a recognisable element in the system that fell in 1991. The system was characterised by a sustained tension between the polity and society, a tension that took economic, national and political forms. The social modernisation of the society, accompanied by the growing divergence between the living standards and cultural norms of Soviet and Western societies, exposed the inadequacies of the system built by Lenin and Stalin and the failure to achieve a viable consolidation by Khrushchev and Brezhnev. The relative liberalisation of *perestroika* allowed these tensions to surface, but while more adroit leadership and an earlier recognition of the necessary transformatory measures might have allowed the resolution of certain policy issues, an evolutionary outcome to the crisis of the Soviet polity itself was always unlikely.

KEY TEXTS

Arnason, Johann P., *The Future that Failed: Origins and Destinies of the Soviet Model* (London, Routledge, 1993).

Daniels, Robert V., *The End of the Communist Revolution* (London, Routledge, 1993).

Jowitt, Ken, *New World Disorder: The Leninist Extinction* (Berkeley, CA, University of California Press, 1992).

Remnick, David, *Lenin's Tomb: The Last Days of the Soviet Empire* (New York, Random House, 1993).

18 Conclusion: Soviet politics in perspective

Soviet socialism was not the successor to developed capitalism but its alternative. Instead of inheriting a developed economy and a mature democracy, Soviet power was faced with a relatively underdeveloped industrial infrastructure and a society that had barely tasted of the cup of democracy before it was dashed away. *Perestroika* initially appeared to prove that systemic change was possible in the Soviet system, but as the contradiction between the aim of reviving Soviet socialism and the pressure for a more open-ended form of political evolution became ever stronger, it ended up demonstrating the opposite – rather than saving the system, reform proved its gravedigger. The system appeared to lack evolutionary potential, a mechanism that would have allowed the enormous changes in society wrought by the regime itself to modify the political superstructure.

Perestroika not only proved that change was possible in the Soviet Union, but confirmed the fears of those who warned that radical reform would threaten the survival of the system itself. In his book *Perestroika* Gorbachev in effect admitted that what had been built in the USSR was not socialism as outlined in its more humanistic variants but a grotesquely centralised and alienating administrative-bureaucratic system. Gorbachev sought to transform a decayed totalitarian system into an authoritarian one, guided by what was meant to become the benevolent rule of the communist party, but the growing pressure from below, combined with challenges from within the elite system, above all from the republics, forced greater moves towards democratisation. The constitution was modified to allow the establishment of a parliamentary system, then the electoral process was gradually disengaged from party control, and finally the leading role of the party itself was removed to allow the emergence of multiparty democracy. *Perestroika* represented the redemocratisation of the socialist project, but came to demonstrate not only the failings of revolutionary socialism but also the incoherence of a 'third way' of non-market democratic socialism. The contradiction lying at the heart of *perestroika*, however, was that it appeared to offer democratisation, but no choice was offered over the type of political or economic system that was to replace the old system.

Gorbachev's reforms had been provoked by numerous factors, above all by the maturation of society, the perceived inability of the USSR to move into the stage of advanced 'post-industrial' modernisation, the ideological crisis of the party and the type of rule that its dominance represented, and by the growing sense that Soviet rule and the command economy were no longer viable in an increasingly interdependent world. The dynamic development of the West, both in economic and cultural terms, challenged the legitimacy of communist rule. *Perestroika* encountered growing opposition from all sides, and the attempt to reform the Soviet system while keeping many of its key features led to compromises that satisfied no one. Gorbachev never lost his belief in the superiority of socialism as an alternative form of modernity developing in parallel and no longer locked in conflict with the West. He sought to undermine the messianic belief about the immutable victory of socialism over capitalism while retaining what he would have defined as the achievements of socialism.

Perestroika sought to change a system designed to withstand change. The system established by Lenin and consolidated by Stalin was tested in famine and war and resisted repeated attempts at reform. Nearly everybody had learned to live with the old system and got something out of it, not only the elite but the common people. Moreover, a large part of society was compromised in the crimes, excesses and follies of the past, from Stalin's torturers to Khrushchev's enthusiasts and Brezhnev's bureaucrats. Faced with entrenched structures, a gradualist strategy of piecemeal reforms might have allowed an evolutionary exit out of communism. Instead, Gorbachev launched a frontal assault on the very structures of the party and the state bureaucracy that sustained his rule. He refused, however, to adopt a Maoist strategy of calling on the masses to overthrow the bureaucracy, and thus found himself dangerously short of allies. The Soviet system stood or fell as one piece, and the attempt to change some of its building blocks brought the whole edifice crashing down.

Gorbachev's reforms should be seen in the larger context of Russian and Soviet politics. The country is unique in many respects, but one feature in particular is striking, namely the periodic attempt to change itself. These regular bouts of reform, arising out of a sense of dissatisfaction with itself and its place in the world, have been of two sorts. The first is the imposed modernisation from above of the type of Peter the Great and Stalin, despots who sacrificed society in order to modernise it. The second type of reform is that launched by Alexander II and Gorbachev. These have been long-term programmes which sought to activate society and encourage the development of a vigorous civil society as the basis for a viable state and an effective economic system. The parallels with the 'Great Reforms' of the mid-nineteenth century under Alexander II are striking. The earlier reforms included the abolition of serfdom, the creation of elected local government, the relaxation of censorship and the development of a modern legal system. In both periods an active citizenry with regulated duties and protected rights began to emerge. At the end of War Communism the sociologist Peter Sorokin characterised Soviet power as a 'new serfdom' of the Soviet citizenry in thrall to a ubiquitous political and economic bureaucracy. Just as the great reforms of Alexander II began with the abolition of serfdom in 1861, so Gorbachev began to overcome the 'new serfdom' imposed by the administrative command model of socialism.

The fate of the earlier reforms and those of Gorbachev are also instructive. The historian Alexander Yanov has advanced a theory of Russian history based on the cycle of despotism, reform and stagnation. In the first phase a reforming but authoritarian leader imposes modernisation on society. This gives way to a phase of more rational reform in which the tyrant is denounced and his victims rehabilitated. This period then peters out amidst corruption and bureaucratic inertia which gives rise to yet another push from above to overcome the stagnation, and thus the cycle is renewed. Alexander II himself was blown up by a terrorist bomb in 1881, and his opening-up of society was reversed by his son, Alexander III, while the opportunities for establishing a new relationship between state and society under his successor from 1894, Nicholas II, were squandered and ended with the revolutions of 1917. The Bolsheviks had no time for an active civil society or the rule of law, and thus only now, with the fall of communism, is the challenge posed by the Great Reforms once again being taken up.

It should be stressed, however, that while there are indeed parallels between patterns in Tsarist and Soviet history, the differences are perhaps even greater. Sergei Pushkarev notes that while in his practical politics Lenin was a follower of the revolutionary methods of Nechaev and Tkachev, his social and political philosophy was decidedly of a Western origin. He quotes Arnold Toynbee as follows:

> Communism is a weapon of Western origin. If it had not been invented by a couple of nineteenth century Westerners, Karl Marx and Friedrich Engels, communism could never have become Russia's official ideology. There was nothing in the Russian tradition that could have led the Russians to invent communism for themselves.[1]

The Soviet experiment can now be seen as no more than an interlude in the larger pattern of Russian history. It would be an exaggeration to see it as an 'aberration', since the Russian revolution was clearly rooted in the crisis of autocratic development and reflected tensions and elements in Russian political culture and society. At the same time, it would be equally false to see the communist period as a manifestation of an innate Russian authoritarianism. It is still too early to judge whether constitutional liberal democracy will take root in post-communist Russia, and any overall judgement of the Soviet period will inevitably be coloured by later developments.

Stephen Cohen saw post-Stalinist history as torn between reformist and conservative traditions. His conclusion was that the USSR's political culture inhibited reform rather than stimulated it.[2] The rationality of the Soviet system ran counter to that of liberalising reforms. Gorbachev was therefore forced to undertake a reform contrary to the flow of Soviet politics and could not even build on the various strands of a reform tradition. His predecessors had been too effective in stifling the regenerative forces that did arise within the system, from the Democratic Centralists to the dissidents. When examining the roots of Stalinism, Soviet commentators wondered why it was so easy to create an administrative command system but so hard to dismantle it.[3]

The enormously powerful system proved to have a fault in its design that reduced its adaptive and evolutionary potential: the fall was programmed into the origins of the Soviet system itself. The seizure of power in October 1917 was a revolution, encompassing the aspirations of large sectors of society for 'bread, peace and land', but at the same time the attempt to impose political dominance over the revolution as well as society meant that it was also a *coup d'état*.[4] For Marx a revolution reflects the emergence of a latent new socio-economic order in the womb of the old, whereas a coup is a response to a political crisis and is difficult to institutionalise in an ordered system of government and economy. The political form of the social revolution of 1917 was the system of soviets, but under the Bolsheviks they were soon marginalised. Lenin made the 1917 revolution a specifically *Bolshevik* revolution, giving the social movement political leadership and an ideological perspective – the destruction of capitalist economic relations in their entirety under the guidance of a small group of committed revolutionaries who claimed a unique relationship to the body of theory that later became known as Marxism–Leninism. But Lenin's genius was flawed, brilliant at seizing and keeping power but less effective at devising an effective system of governance. The combination of exhaustively detailed bureaucratic regulation of society and politics with personalised arbitrariness came to characterise the whole Soviet period.

In broader terms W. W. Rostow has characterised twentieth-century communism as a 'disease of the transition' from a rural to an urban society.[5] All successful communist revolutions have taken place not in advanced capitalist societies but in countries only embarking on capitalist transformation. The Soviet regime could fulfil a historically progressive function as long as there remained modernisation tasks, but having created an educated middle class, a sophisticated urban society and a relatively modern economic infrastructure it had outlived its usefulness. By 1979 over half the population lived in cities with populations over 20,000. Sociologically determinist explanations of the rise and fall of Soviet communism do not reveal the whole picture, but modernisation arguments are certainly part of the story.

The twentieth century has been stamped by the Soviet experience. The Soviet system sought to fulfil the Marxist promise that, freed of the exploitative narrowness of capitalist private property, human beings could achieve their full potential in a co-operative 'communist' society. Instead, the attempt to achieve absolute freedom led to the imposition of absolute servitude – something that liberal theory had always predicted would happen when 'negative freedoms' are abolished. The absence of a developed concept of politics in Marx's thinking, the belief that once class exploitation had been abolished there would no longer be any contradictory interests in society requiring mediation through political bargaining and compromise, left the door open for a ruthless leader like Lenin to impose his iron will on society. Soviet communism failed either to release the full potential of individuals or the productive potential of a collective economy, but even though the Soviet experiment in most respects failed to fulfil even its own promises, the search for a humanistic alternative to unbridled global capitalism is by no means over. The Soviet experience at least tells us how it should not be done.

Notes

1 THE RUSSIAN LEGACY

1 R. Pipes, *Russia under the Old Regime* (Harmondsworth, Pelican, 1974), p. xvii.
2 Nicolai N. Petro, *The Rebirth of Russian Democracy: An Interpretation of Political Culture* (Cambridge, MA, Harvard University Press, 1995), Chapter 2.
3 See Robert B. McKean, *St Petersburg between the Revolutions* (London, Yale University Press, 1990).
4 See Robert W. Thurston, *Liberal City, Conservative State: Moscow and Russia's Urban Crisis, 1906–1914* (Oxford, Oxford University Press, 1987).
5 Max Weber, *Politics as a Vocation*, in H. H. Gerth and C. W. Mills (eds), *From Max Weber: Essays in Sociology* (New York, Oxford University Press, 1956), p. 77.
6 Letter from Marx to Danielson, 15 November 1878, quoted in Haruki Wada, 'Marx and Revolutionary Russia', in T. Shanin (ed.), *Late Marx and the Russian Road: Marx and the 'Peripheries of Capitalism'* (London, Routledge & Kegan Paul, 1984), p. 58.
7 *Ibid.*, pp. 98–126.
8 Leon Trotsky, 'Our Political Tasks' (*Nashi politicheskie zadachi*) (Geneva, 1904).

2 THE CREATION OF THE SOVIET STATE

1 For a fine analysis, see Evan Mawdsley, *The Russian Civil War* (London, George Allen & Unwin, 1987).
2 Cf. Thomas F. Remington, *Building Socialism in Bolshevik Russia: Ideology and Industrial Organisation, 1917–1921* (Pittsburgh, PA, University of Pittsburgh Press, 1984).

3 STALIN AND STALINISM

1 V. I. Lenin, *Polnoe sobranie sochinenii*, 5th edn (Moscow, Politicheskai literatury, 1975), Vol. 45, p. 345.
2 For a discussion of this, see C. Lefort, *The Political Forms of Modern Society: Bureaucracy, Democracy, Totalitarianism* (Cambridge, MA, MIT Press, 1986), p. 40.
3 Leon Trotsky, *The Revolution Betrayed* (London, New Park, 1973).
4 Nadezhda Mandelstam, *Hope against Hope* (Harmondsworth, Penguin, 1970), p. 167.
5 Robert Redfield, *Peasant Society and Culture* (Chicago, IL, University of Chicago Press, 1956), pp. 17–20, 40–45.
6 Bukharin's views in *Notes of an Economist* (*Pravda*, 30 September 1928) are discussed by M. Lewin, *Political Undercurrents in Soviet Economic Debates* (London, Pluto, 1975), pp. 49–72.
7 For a classic statement of this view, see Stephen F. Cohen, *Bukharin and the Bolshevik Revolution* (New York, Vintage Books, 1975), chapter IX.
8 G. Grossman, 'Notes for a Theory of the Planned Economy', *Soviet Studies*, Vol. 15 (1963), pp. 101–23.
9 Moshe Lewin, 'Society and the Stalinist State in the Period of the Five-Year Plans', *Social History* Vol. 1, No. 2 (May 1976), p. 148.
10 L. Viola, '*Bab'i bunty* and Peasant Women's Protest during Collectivisation', *Russian Review*, Vol. 45, No. 4 (1986), pp. 23–42.
11 L. Viola *The Best Sons of the Fatherland* (Oxford, Oxford University Press, 1987).

12　Official figures cited by Roy Medvedev, 'New Pages from the Political Biography of Stalin', in R. C. Tucker (ed.), *Stalinism: Essays in Historical Interpretation* (New York, W. W. Norton, 1977), p. 211.

13　Vladimir Tikhenov, *Literaturnaya gazeta*, No. 31, 3 August 1988.

14　See Robert Conquest, *The Harvest of Sorrow* (London, Hutchinson, 1986).

15　D. Joravsky, 'The Construction of the Stalinist Psyche', in S. Fitzpatrick (ed.), *Cultural Revolution in Russia, 1928–1931* (Bloomington, IN, Indiana University Press, 1978), pp. 105–28.

16　J. H. Hough, 'The Cultural Revolution and Western Understanding of the Soviet System', in Fitzpatrick (ed.) *Cultural Revolution*, pp. 241–53.

17　Stalin, 'The Tasks of Business Executives', speech at the First All-Union Conference of Managers of Socialist Industry, February 1931, in R. V. Daniels (ed.), *A Documentary History of Communism*, Vol. 1, *Communism in Russia*, (London, I. B. Tauris, 1987), pp. 229–32.

18　S. G. Wheatcroft, R. W. Davis and J. M. Cooper, 'Soviet Industrialization Reconsidered: Some Preliminary Conclusions about Economic Development between 1926 and 1941', *Economic History Review*, 2nd series, Vol. 39, No. 2 (1986), pp. 264–94.

19　R. and Z. Medvedev, *Khrushchev: The Years in Power* (New York, Columbia University Press, 1976), p. 28.

20　M. Lewin, 'Society and the Stalinist State', p. 15; 'Society, State and Ideology during the First Five-year Plan', in *The Making of the Soviet System* (New York, Pantheon Books, 1985), pp. 218–31.

21　*Ogonek*, No. 50, December 1987, p. 6.

22　For a contrary view of the Kirov murder, see J. A. Getty, *Origins of the Great Purges* (Cambridge, Cambridge University Press, 1985), pp. 207–10; and for an evaluation of the evidence, Robert Conquest, *The Great Terror* (Harmondsworth, Pelican, 1971), pp. 74–77.

23　The major articles by S. Rosefielde are 'An Assessment of the Sources and Uses of Gulag Forced Labour 1929–1956', *Soviet Studies*, Vol. 33, No. 1 (January 1981); 'Excess Mortality in the Soviet Union: A Reconsideration of the Demographic Consequences of Forced Industrialisation 1929–1949', *Soviet Studies*, Vol. 35, No. 2 (July 1983); 'Incriminating Evidence: Excess Deaths and Forced Labour under Stalin: A Final Reply to My Critics', *Soviet Studies*, Vol. 39, No. 2 (April 1987), pp. 292–313.

24　S. Wheatcroft, 'On Assessing the Size of Forced Concentration Camp Labour in the Soviet Union, 1929–56', *Soviet Studies*, Vol. 33, No. 2 (April 1981), pp. 265–95; 'A Note on Steven Rosefielde's Calculations of Excess Mortality in the USSR, 1929–49', *Soviet Studies*, Vol. 34, No. 2 (April 1984), pp. 277–81.

25　Figures from I. G. Dyadkin, *Unnatural Deaths in the USSR, 1928–54* (New Brunswick, NJ, Transaction Books, 1983), p. 60; Conquest, *Harvest of Sorrow*, p. 229; Conquest, *The Great Terror*, pp. 699–713.

26　On numbers of party victims, see A. L. Unger, 'Stalin's Renewal of the Leading Stratum', *Soviet Studies*, Vol. 20, No. 3 (July 1969), p. 321.

27　*Kommunist*, No. 13 (June 1987).

28　T. Dunmore, *Soviet Politics, 1945–53* (London, Macmillan, 1984), p. 2.

29　A. Solzhenitsyn, *From under the Rubble* (London, Fontana, 1976), pp. 10–11.

30　M. Hirszowicz, *The Bureaucratic Leviathan* (Oxford, Martin Robertson, 1980), p. 57.

31　Roy Medvedev, *Let History Judge* (Nottingham, Spokesman Books, 1976), p. 360.

32　R. C. Tucker, *Stalin as a Revolutionary: Essays in Historical Interpretation* (New York, W. W. Norton, 1977).

33　S. F. Cohen, 'Bolshevism and Stalinism', in *Rethinking the Soviet Experience* (Oxford, Oxford University Press, 1985), p. 48.

34　T. H. Rigby, 'Stalinism and the Mono-Organisational Society', in Tucker (ed.), *Stalinism*, pp. 53–76.

35　A. Janos (ed.), *Authoritarian Politics in Communist Europe* (Berkeley, CA, University of California Press, 1976), p. 9.

4　KHRUSHCHEV AND DESTALINISATION

1　M. S. Gorbachev, 2 November 1987 speech for the seventieth anniversary of the October revolution, *Soviet News*, 4 November 1987.

2　Tim Dunmore, *Soviet Politics, 1945–53* (London, Macmillan, 1984), p. 158.

3　Quoted by Robert Conquest, *Great Terror* (Harmondsworth, Pelican, 1971), p. 685.

4　Roy Medvedev, *Khrushchev* (Oxford, Basil Blackwell, 1982), p. 89.

5　M. McAuley, *Politics and the Soviet Union* (Harmondsworth, Penguin, 1977), ch. 7.

6　G. W. Breslauer, 'Khrushchev Reconsidered', in S. F. Cohen, A. Rabinowitch and R. Sharlet (eds), *The Soviet Union since Stalin* (London, Macmillan, 1980), pp. 51–2.

7 J. D. Grossman, 'Khrushchev's Anti-religious Policy', *Soviet Studies*, Vol. 24, No. 3 (1972–73), pp. 374–86.
8 G. W. Breslauer, *Khrushchev and Brezhnev as Leaders* (London, George Allen & Unwin, 1982), pp. 114–17, 133.
9 Quoted by Medvedev, *Khrushchev*, p. 245.
10 S. F. Cohen, 'The Friends and Foes of Change', in E. P. Hoffmann and R. F. Laird (eds), *The Soviet Polity in the Modern Era* (New York, Aldine, 1984), p. 85; also in his *Rethinking the Soviet Experience*.

5 FROM BREZHNEV TO GORBACHEV

1 V. Zaslavsky, *The Neo-Stalinist State: Class, Ethnicity and Consensus in Soviet Society* (Brighton, Harvester Press, 1982), pp. vii–x.
2 James R. Millar, 'The Little Deal: Brezhnev's Contribution to Acquisitive Socialism', *Slavic Review*, Vol. 44, No. 4 (Winter 1985), pp. 694–706.
3 G. W. Breslauer, 'On the Adaptability of Soviet Welfare-state Authoritarianism', in E. P. Hoffmann and R. F. Laird (eds), *The Soviet Polity* (New York, Aldine, 1984), p. 221. See also Linda Cook, *The Soviet Social Contract and Why it Failed* (Cambridge, MA, Harvard University Press, 1993).
4 George Breslauer, *Khrushchev and Brezhnev as Leaders: Building Authority in Soviet Politics*, (London: George Allen & Unwin, 1982) pp. 12–13.
5 V. Bunce, 'The Political Economy of the Brezhnev Era', *British Journal of Political Science*, Vol. 13 (April 1983), p. 134.
6 Bunce, 'The Political Economy of the Brezhnev Era', p. 145.
7 G. W. Breslauer, 'Khrushchev Reconsidered', *Problems of Communism*, Vol. 25, No. 5 (September–October 1976), p. 30.
8 J. Hough, 'The Brezhnev Era', *Problems of Communism*, Vol. 25, No. 2 (March–April 1976), p. 10.
9 Breslauer, 'Khrushchev Reconsidered', pp. 31–2.
10 Hough, 'The Brezhnev Era', p. 17.
11 Breslauer, 'Khrushchev Reconsidered', in S. F. Cohen *et al.*, (eds), *The Soviet Union since Stalin* (London, Macmillan, 1980), p. 60.
12 Yegor Ligachev, *Inside Gorbachev's Kremlin* (Boulder, CO, Westview Press, 1996), p. 34.
13 Speech to the June 1983 plenum of the Central Committee. For a discussion, see D. Sturman, 'Chernenko and Andropov: Ideological Perspectives', *Survey*, Vol. 28, No. 1 (Spring 1984), p. 17.
14 W. G. Hyland, 'Kto Kogo in the Kremlin', *Problems of Communism*, Vol. 31, No. 1 (January–February 1982), p. 24.
15 The prospect of 'evolution from above' was considered by G. W. Breslauer, *Five Images of the Soviet Future: A Critical Review and Synthesis* (Berkeley, CA, Institute of International Studies, University of California, 1978), p. 75.
16 M. S. Gorbachev, *Perestroika: New Thinking for Our Country and the World* (London, Collins, 1987), p, 25.

6 THE COMMUNIST PARTY

1 Jerry F. Hough and Merle Fainsod, *How the Soviet Union is Governed* (Cambridge, MA, Harvard University Press, 1979), pp. 324–8.
2 J. H. Miller, 'The Communist Party: Trends and Problems', in A. Brown and M. Kaser (eds), *Soviet Policy for the 1980s* (London, Macmillan, 1982), p. 5.
3 Philip Hanson and Elizabeth Teague, 'Soviet Communist Party Loses Members', *RFE/RL Report on the USSR*, Vol. 2, No. 18 (18 May 1990), pp. 103.
4 *Pravda*, 26 July 1991, p. 2.
5 *Partiinaya zhizn*, No. 14 (July 1986), p. 28.
6 *Ibid.*, p. 22.
7 *Ibid.*, p. 21.
8 *Ibid.*, p. 22.
9 *Izvestiya Tsk KPSS*, No. 4 (1990), pp. 113–15.
10 *Rules of the Communist Party of the Soviet Union: Approved by the 27th Congress of the CPSU, March 1, 1986* (Moscow, Novosti, 1986), p. 12.
11 See Thane Gustafson and Dawn Mann, 'Gorbachev's Next Gamble', *Problems of Communism*, Vol. 36, No. 4 (July–August 1987), pp. 1–20; J. F. Hough, 'Gorbachev Consolidates Power' in the same issue, pp. 21–43.

12 Yegor Ligachev, *Inside Gorbachev's Kremlin* (Boulder, CO, Westview Press, 1996), p. 84.

13 M. Voslenskii, *Nomenklatura: Anatomy of the Soviet Ruling Class* (London, Bodley Head, 1984), pp. 92–6; R. Hill and P. Frank, *The Soviet Communist Party*, 3rd edn (London, George Allen & Unwin, 1986), p. 89.

14 *Konstitutsiya (Osnovni Zakon) Soyuza Sovetskikh Sotsialisticheskikh Respublik* (Moscow, Yuridicheskaya Literatura, 1980), p. 6.

15 Hill and Frank, *Soviet Communist Party*, p. 108.

16 J. F. Hough, *The Soviet Prefects* (Cambridge, MA, Harvard University Press, 1969).

17 J. Habermas, *Legitimation Crisis* (London, Heineman, 1976), p. 49.

18 M. Croan, 'The Leading Role of the Party: Concepts and Contexts', in A. Janos (ed.), *Authoritarian Politics in Communist Europe* (Berkeley, CA, University of California Press, 1976), pp. 159–61.

19 *The Action Programme of the Czechoslovak Communist Party*, Spokesman Pamphlet No. 8 (Nottingham, Spokesman Pamphlet No. 8, 1968); see also Galia Golan, *The Czechoslovak Reform Movement* (Cambridge, Cambridge University Press, 1971); and H. Gordon Skilling, *Czechoslovakia's Interrupted Revolution* (Princeton, NJ, Princeton University Press, 1976).

20 R. Lowenthal, 'Development vs Utopia in Communist Policy', in Chalmers Johnson (ed.), *Change in Communist Systems* (Stanford, CA, Stanford University Press, 1970), pp. 33–116.

21 S. P. Huntington, 'Social and Institutional Dynamics of One-party Systems', in S. P. Huntington and C. H. Moore (eds), *Authoritarian Politics in Modern Societies* (New York and London, Basic Books, 1970), pp. 3–47; D. E. Apter, *The Politics of Modernisation* (Chicago, University of Chicago Press, 1965), pp. 394–6.

22 K. Jowitt, 'Inclusion and Mobilization in European Leninist Regimes', *World Politics*, Vol. 28, No. 1 (October 1975), pp. 69–96.

23 Z. Bauman, 'Systemic Crisis in Soviet-type Societies', *Problems of Communism*, Vol. 20, No. 6 (November–December 1971), pp. 45–53.

24 Roy Medvedev, *On Socialist Democracy* (Nottingham, Spokesman Books, 1977).

25 *Partiinaya zhizn*, No. 11 (1988), p. 15.

26 *Materialy XIX Vsesoyuznoi konferentsii, 28 iyunya–1 iyulya 1988 goda* (Moscow, Politizdat, 1988), pp. 70–2.

27 *Ibid,*, pp. 124–6.

28 *Izvestiya*, 11 June 1989.

29 'Socialism, Democracy, Progress', *Pravda*, 8 August, *Sovetskaya Rossiya*, 9 August 1991.

30 *Nezavisimaya gazeta*, 23 July 1991, p. 2; Mark Sandle, 'The Final Word: The Draft Party Programme of July/August 1991', *Europe–Asia Studies*, Vol. 48, No. 7 (1996), p. 1136.

7 THE STRUCTURE OF POWER

1 *Europe–Asia Studies*, Vol. 49, No. 4 (June 1997), p. 745.

2 S. White, 'Communist Systems and the Iron Law of Political Pluralism', *British Journal of Political Science*, Vol. 8 (1978), p. 111.

3 Andrei Sakharov, 'All Power to the Soviets', *XX Century and Peace*, No. 8 (1989), pp. 9–12.

4 *Partiinaya zhizn*, 4 February 1988, p. 19.

8 SECURITY AND JUSTICE

1 *Kommunist*, No. 7 (1978), p. 112.

2 See Mark Galeotti, *Afghanistan: The Soviet Union's Last War* (London, Frank Cass, 1995).

3 Cited by G. W. Breslauer, *Khrushchev and Brezhnev as Leaders: Building Authority in Soviet Politics* (London: George Allen & Unwin, 1982) pp. 284–5.

4 Cited by W. E. Odom, 'The "Militarisation" of Soviet Society', *Problems of Communism*, Vol. 25, No. 5 (September–October 1976), p. 34.

5 K. Gerner, *The Soviet Union and Central Europe in the Post-War Era* (Aldershot, Swedish Institute of International Affairs, 1985), p. 181.

6 T. Hasegawa, 'Soviets on Nuclear-war Fighting', *Problems of Communism*, Vol. 35, No. 4 (July–August 1986), pp. 68–79.

7 *Pravda*, 8 January 1987.

8 N. de Basily, *Russia under Soviet Rule: 20 Years of Bolshevik Experiment* (London, George Allen & Unwin, 1938), p. 171.

9 LOCAL GOVERNMENT AND PARTICIPATION

1 *Deputatu mestnogo soveta: sbornik normativnykh aktov*, chast' 1 (Moscow, 1985), p. 3.
2 *Ibid*.
3 R. Medvedev, *On Socialist Democracy* (Nottingham, Spokesman Books, 1977), pp. 140–41.
4 W. Taubman, *Governing Soviet Cities: Bureaucratic Politics and Urban Development in the USSR* (New York, Praeger, 1973), p. 4.
5 *Ibid.*, p. 9.
6 M. E. Urban, 'Information and Participation in Soviet Local Government', *The Journal of Politics*, Vol. 44 (1982), pp. 70, 85.
7 E. M. Jacobs, *Soviet Local Politics and Government* (London, George Allen & Unwin, 1983), p. 8.
8 Taubman, *Governing Soviet Cities*, p. 113.
9 *The Action Programme of the Czechoslovak Communist Party* (Nottingham, Spokesman Pamphlet No. 8, 1968), p. 12.
10 T. H. Rigby *et al.* (eds), *Authority, Power and Policy in the USSR* (London, Macmillan, 1982), p. 25.
11 For example, *Pravda*, 28 December 1986.
12 M. S. Gorbachev, *Perestroika* (London, Collins, 1987), p. 112.
13 'Towards the Full Power of Soviets', Gorbachev's report to the Supreme Soviet, 29 November 1988, *Soviet News*, 30 November 1988, p. 440.
14 V. Zaslavsky and R. J. Brym, 'The Function of Elections in the USSR', *Soviet Studies*, Vol. 30, No. 3 (July 1978), p. 36.
15 B. Racz, 'Political Participation and Developed Socialism: The Hungarian Elections of 1985', *Soviet Studies*, Vol. 39, No. 1 (January 1987), pp. 40–62.
16 See Jeffrey Hahn, 'An Experiment in Competition: The 1987 Elections to the Local Soviets', *Slavic Review*, Vol. 47, No. 2 (Fall 1988), pp. 434–47.
17 D. Little, 'Mass Political Party Participation in the US and USSR: A Conceptual Analysis', *Comparative Political Studies*, Vol. 8, No. 4 (January 1976), p. 437.
18 K. Marx, *The Civil War in France*, with F. Engels, *Selected Works* (London, Lawrence & Wishart, 1968).
19 See J. L. Talmon, *The Origins of Totalitarian Democracy* (London, Secker & Warburg, 1952).
20 Little, 'Mass Political Party Participation', p. 453.
21 Introduction to J. B. Thompson and D. Held (eds), *Habermas: Critical Debates* (Cambridge, MA, MIT Press, 1982), p. 4.
22 Cf. Urban, 'Information and Participation', pp. 65–67.
23 A. Unger, 'Political Participation in the USSR: YCL and CPSU', *Soviet Studies*, No. 1 (January 1981), p. 111.
24 S. White, 'Political Communications in the USSR: Letters to Party, State and Press', *Political Studies*, Vol. 31 (1983), p. 48.
25 R. V. Burks, 'Popular Participation under Socialism', *Studies in Comparative Communism*, Vol. 15, Nos 1–2 (Spring–Summer 1982), p. 149.

10 POWER AND POLICY-MAKING

1 G. Gill, 'Personal Dominance and the Collective Principle', in T. H. Rigby and F. Fehér (eds), *Political Legitimation in Communist States* (London, Macmillan, 1982), pp. 95–6.
2 M. Voslensky, *Nomenklatura* (London, Bodley Head, 1984), ch. 6.
3 On power and authority see T. H. Rigby, 'A Conceptual Approach to Authority, Power and Policy in the Soviet Union', in T. H. Rigby *et al.* (eds), *Authority, Power and Policy in the Soviet Union* (London, Macmillan, 1980); G. W. Breslauer, 'Power and Authority in Soviet Elite Politics', in J. L. Nogee (ed.), *Soviet Politics: Russia after Brezhnev* (New York, Praeger, 1985), pp. 15–33.
4 Peter Frank, 'Political Succession in the Soviet Union: Building a Power Base' (Colchester, University of Essex, Russian and Soviet Studies Centre, Discussion Paper No. 2, 1984), p. 1.
5 V. Bunce, 'The Political Economy of the Brezhnev Era', *British Journal of Political Science*, Vol. 13 (1983), p. 138.
6 T. H. Rigby, 'The Soviet Leadership: Towards a Self-stabilising Oligarchy?', *Soviet Studies*, Vol. 22 (October 1970), p. 2.
7 For a savage critique of the practices of the Brezhnev years, see *Kommunist*, No. 4 (1987), pp. 3–19.
8 See J. P. Willerton, 'Patronage Networks and Coalition-building in the Brezhnev Era', *Soviet Studies*, Vol. 39, No. 2 (April 1987), pp. 175–204.
9 In Rigby *et al.* (eds), *Authority, Power and Policy in the USSR*, p. 136.

10 V. Bunce, *Do New Leaders Make a Difference?* (Princeton, NJ, Princeton University Press, 1981).

11 C. Friedrich and Z. Brzezinski, *Totalitarian Dictatorship and Autocracy*, rev. edn (New York, Praeger, 1966), p. 22.

12 Hannah Arendt, *The Origins of Totalitarianism* (London, André Deutsch, 1986); on mass society, see W. Kornhauser, *The Politics of Mass Society* (London, Routledge & Kegan Paul, 1960).

13 Alexander Zinoviev, *The Yawning Heights* (Harmondsworth, Penguin, 1979); *The Radiant Future* (London, Bodley Head, 1981); *The Reality of Communism* (London, Gollancz, 1984); see also Philip Hanson, 'Alexander Zinoviev: Totalitarianism from Below', *Survey*, Vol. 26, No. 1 (Winter 1982), pp. 29–48.

14 For an analysis of this point, see Dankwart A. Rustow, 'Communism and Change', in Chalmers Johnson (ed.), *Change in Communist Systems* (Stanford, CA, Stanford University Press, 1970), pp. 343–58.

15 See Archie Brown, 'Political Power and the Soviet State: Western and Soviet Perspectives', in N. Harding (ed.), *The State in Socialist Society* (London, Macmillan, 1984), pp. 51–103.

16 F. Fehér *et al.* (eds), *Dictatorship over Needs* (Oxford, Blackwell, 1983).

17 W. Odom, 'A Dissenting View on the Group Approach to Soviet Politics', *World Politics*, Vol. 28 (July 1976), p. 567.

18 H. G. Skilling, 'Interest Groups and Communist Politics Revisited', *World Politics*, Vol. 36, No. 1 (1983), p. 5.

19 See H. G. Skilling and F. Griffiths (eds), *Interest Groups in Soviet Politics* (Princeton, NJ, Princeton University Press, 1971); S. Solomon (ed.), *Pluralism in the Soviet Union* (London, Macmillan, 1983).

20 A. F. Bentley *The Process of Government* (Chicago, 1908), pp. 330–6.

21 Skilling, 'Interest Groups and Communist Politics: an Introduction', in Skilling and Griffiths, *Interest Groups in Soviet Politics*, p. 17.

22 Douglas R. Weiner, *Models of Nature: Conservation and Community Ecology in the Soviet Union, 1917–1935* (Bloomington, IN, Indiana University Press, 1988).

23 J. J. Schwartz and W. R. Keech, 'Public Influence and Educational Policy in the Soviet Union', in R. E. Kanet (ed.), *The Behavioural Revolution and Communist Studies* (New York, The Free Press, 1971), pp. 151–86.

24 Skilling, 'Interest Groups and Communist Politics', p. 17.

25 P. Stewart, *Political Power in the Soviet Union* (Indianapolis, IN, Bobbs-Merrill, 1968), pp. 4–5.

26 Jerry F. Hough, 'The Man and the System', *Problems of Communism*, Vol. 25, No. 2 (March–April 1976), pp. 1–17 at p. 14.

27 F. Griffiths, 'A Tendency Analysis of Soviet Policy-making', in Skilling and Griffiths, *Interest Groups in Soviet Politics*, p. 335.

28 D. Easton, *A Framework for Political Analysis* (Englewood Cliffs, NJ, Prentice-Hall, 1965); G. Almond and G. Powell, *Comparative Politics: System, Process and Policy* (Boston, Little, Brown, 1978).

29 See Alfred G. Meyer, 'Theories of Convergence', in Chalmers Johnson (ed.), *Change in Communist Systems* (Stanford, CA, Stanford University Press, 1970), pp. 313–41.

30 Alex Inkeles, 'Models and Issues in the Analysis of Soviet Society', *Survey*, Vol. 60 (July 1966), pp. 3–19.

31 Talcott Parsons, *Structures and Process in Modern Societies* (Glencoe, IL, Free Press, 1960).

32 Talcott Parsons, 'Evolutionary Universals in Society', *American Sociological Review* Vol. 29, No. 3 (June 1964), pp. 339–57.

33 Herbert Marcuse, *One-dimensional Man* (London, Spere Books, 1968).

34 Fehér *et al.*, *Dictatorship over Needs*.

35 A. G. Walder, *Communist Neo-Traditionalism: Work and Authority in Chinese Industry* (Berkeley, CA, University of California Press, 1986), pp. 5–8.

36 *Ibid.*, p. 8.

37 K. Jowitt, 'Soviet Neotraditionalism: The Political Corruption of a Leninist Regime', *Soviet Studies*, Vol. 35, No. 3 (July 1983), pp. 275–97.

38 Walder, *Communist Neo-traditionalism*, p. 10.

11 IDEOLOGY AND AUTHORITY

1 Zygmunt Bauman, 'Intellectuals in East-Central Europe: Continuity and Change', *Eastern European Politics and Societies*, Vol. 1, No. 2 (Spring 1987), pp. 165–66.

2 *Ibid.* p. 174.

3 Anthony Black, *Guilds and Civil Society in European Political Thought from the Twelfth Century to the Present* (London, Macmillan, 1984), p. xiii.

4 See David McLellan, *Ideology* (Milton Keynes, Open University Press, 1986).

5 N. de Basily, *Russia under Soviet Rule* (London, George Allen & Unwin, 1938), p. 105.

6 V. Zaslavsky, 'Socioeconomic Inequality and Changes in Soviet Ideology', *Theory and Society*, Vol. 2, No. 9 (March 1980), p. 395.

7 Rosa Luxemburg, *The Russian Revolution* (Ann Arbor, MI, University of Michigan Press, 1961), p. 69.

8 James R. Millar and Peter Donhowe, 'Life, Work and Politics in Soviet Cities: First Findings of the Soviet Interview Project', *Problems of Communism*, Vol. 36, No. 1 (January–February 1987), pp. 46–55.

9 A. Solzhenitsyn, *Warning to the West* (New York, Farrar, Straus and Giroux, 1976), p. 114.

10 A. Meyer, 'The Functions of Ideology in the Soviet Political System', *Soviet Studies*, Vol. 17, No. 3 (July 1966), pp. 273–85.

11 Leszek Kolakowski, 'Ideology in Eastern Europe', in Milorach Drachkowitch (ed.), *East Central Europe: Yesterday – Today – Tomorrow* (Stanford, CA, Hoover Institution Press, 1982), p. 45.

12 A. Janos, 'Systemic Models and the Theory of Change in the Comparative Study of Communist Politics', in A. Janos (ed.), *Authoritarian Politics in Communist Europe* (Berkeley, CA, University of California Press, 1976), p. 19.

13 D. Bell, *The End of Ideology*, cited by J. F. Hough, *The Soviet Union and Social Science Theory* (Cambridge, MA, Harvard University Press, 1977), p. 197.

14 John B. Dunlop, *The New Russian Revolutionaries* (Massachusetts, Nordland, 1976).

15 Hough, *The Soviet Union and Social Science Theory*, p. 35.

16 Yu. V. Andropov, 'The Teaching of Karl Marx and Some Problems of Socialist Construction', *Speeches and Writings*, 2nd edn (Oxford, Pergamon Press, 1983), pp. 276–98, at pp. 296–97.

17 Z. Medvedev, *Labour Focus on Eastern Europe*, Vol. 8, No. 2 (May 1986), pp. 3–9.

18 John Hoffman, 'The Coercion/Consent Analysis of the State under Socialism', in N. Harding (ed.), *The State in Socialist Society* (London, Macmillan, 1984), pp. 129–49.

19 R. C. Tucker, 'Culture, Political Culture and Communist Society', *Political Science Quarterly*, Vol. 88, No. 2 (June 1973), pp. 173–90.

20 A. Brown (ed.), *Political Culture and Communist Studies* (London, Macmillan, 1984), pp. 1–12.

21 For a view of Tsarism as 'constrained autocracy', see Nicolai Petro, *The Rebirth of Russian Democracy: An Interpretation of Political Culture* (Cambridge, MA, Harvard University Press, 1995), ch. 2.

22 A. Jasinska-Kania, 'Rationalization and Legitimation Crisis: The Relevance of Marxian and Weberian Works for an Explanation of the Political Order's Legitimacy Crisis in Poland', *Sociology*, Vol. 17, No. 2 (May 1983), p. 161.

23 Leslie Holmes, *The End of Communist Power: Anti-corruption Campaigns and Legitimation Crisis* (Cambridge, Polity Press, 1993), pp. 15–17 and *passim*.

24 F. Fehér, 'Paternalism as a Mode of Legitimation in Soviet-type Societies', in T. H. Rigby and F. Fehér (eds), *Political Legitimation in Communist States* (London, Macmillan, 1982), p. 77.

25 D. Barry and H. Dernan, 'The Jurists', in H. G. Skilling and F. Griffiths (eds), *Interest Groups in Soviet Politics* (Princeton, NJ, Princeton University Press, 1971).

26 J. Habermas, *Legitimation Crisis* (London, Heinemann, 1976), pp. 46–49.

27 L. W. Pye and S. Verba, *Political Culture and Political Development* Princeton, NJ, Princeton University Press, 1969).

28 G. A. Almond and S. Verba, *The Civic Culture* (Princeton, NJ, Princeton University Press, 1963).

29 A. Inkeles and R. A. Bauer, *The Soviet Citizen* (Cambridge, MA, Harvard University Press, 1959).

30 James R. Millar, *Politics, Work and Daily Life in the USSR: A Survey of Former Soviet Citizens* (Cambridge, Cambridge University Press, 1988).

31 Stephen White, *Political Culture and Soviet Politics* (London, Macmillan, 1979), p. 189.

32 See Mark Wright, 'Ideology and Power in the Czechoslovak Political System', in Paul Lewis (ed.), *Eastern Europe: Political Crisis and Legitimation* (London, Croom Helm, 1984), pp. 111–53.

12 CLASS AND GENDER

1 See Peter Frank, 'Gorbachev's Dilemma: Social Justice or Political Instability?', *The World Today*, Vol. 42, No. 6 (June 1986), p. 94.

2 Gorbachev, *Perestroika*, (London, Collins, 1987) p. 21.

3 For a vivid description, see Victor Kravchenko, *I Chose Freedom* (London, Robert Hale, 1947), ch. 12.

4 Karl Kautsky, *Terrorism and Communism* (London, George Allen & Unwin, 1920).

5 Z. Bauman, 'Officialdom and Class', in F. Parkin (ed.), *The Social Analysis of Class Structure* (London, Tavistock, 1974).

6 *The USSR in Figures: 1917–1987* (Moscow, 1987).

7 See M. S. Yanowitch, *Social and Economic Inequality in the USSR* (London, Martin Robertson, 1977), pp. 5–20; D. Lane and F. O'Dell, *The Soviet Industrial Worker: Social Class, Education and Control* (London, Martin Robertson, 1978).

8 Rosa Luxemburg, *The Russian Revolution* (Ann Arbor, MI, University of Michigan Press, 1961), p. 71.

9 Rudolf Bahro, *The Alternative in Eastern Europe* (London, New Left Books/Verso, 1978).

10 J. F. Hough, *The Soviet Prefects: Local Party Organs in Industrial Decision-making* (Cambridge, MA, Harvard University Press, 1969) p. 3.

11 M. Hirszowicz, *The Bureaucratic Leviathan* (Oxford, Martin Robertson, 1980), p. 26.

12 Z. Bauman in A. Janos (ed.), *Authoritarian Politics in Communist Europe* (Berkeley, CA, University of California Press, 1976) pp. 83–4.

13 Hirszowicz, *The Bureaucratic Leviathan*, pp. 16–17.

14 See Marshall S. Shatz, *Jan Waclaw Machajski: A Radical Critic of the Russian Intelligentsia and Socialism* (Pittsburgh, PA, University of Pittsburgh Press, 1989).

15 Alvin Gouldner, *The Future of Intellectuals and the Rise of the New Class* (London, Macmillan, 1979).

16 J. F. Hough, *The Soviet Union and Social Science Theory* (Cambridge, MA, Harvard University Press, 1977) pp. 203, 215, 217.

17 Cited by Alistair McAuley, *Women's Work and Wages in the Soviet Union* (London, George Allen & Unwin, 1981).

18 B. Kerblay, *Modern Soviet Society* (London, Methuen, 1983), p. 113.

19 B. A. Clements, 'Birth of New Soviet Woman', in A. Gleason *et al.* (eds), *Bolshevik Culture* (Bloomington, IN, Indiana University Press, 1985), pp. 230, 233.

20 Helen Goscilo, 'Domostroika or Perestroika?' in Thomas Lahusen and Gene Kupman (eds), *Late Soviet Culture: From Perestroika to Novostroika* (Durham, NC, Duke University Press, 1993), pp. 233–4; the point is developed by Judith Armstrong, 'Cultural Difference – Russia's Putative Entry into the European Union', in Richard Sakwa (ed.), *The Experience of Democratisation in Eastern Europe* (London, Macmillan, 1998).

21 For Western feminist views of the family, see Michele Barrett and Mary McIntosh, *The Anti-social Family* (London, Verso/New Left Books, 1982).

13 FROM DISSENT TO PLURALISM

1 F. C. Barghoorn, 'Regime–Dissenter Relations after Khrushchev', in S. Solomon (ed.), *Pluralism in the Soviet Union* (London, Macmillan, 1983), p. 131.

2 A. Y. Shtromas, 'Dissent and Political Change in the Soviet Union', *Studies in Comparative Communism*, Vol. 12, Nos 2–3 (Summer–Autumn 1979), p. 213.

3 For an exploration of these themes, see the collection of essays by Vaclav Havel, *Living in Truth* (London, Faber & Faber, 1987).

4 For example, E. P. Thompson, *The Heavy Dancers* (Manchester, Merlin Press, 1982), pp. 125–26.

5 For a discussion of these perspectives see Adam Michnik, *Letters from Prison and Other Essays* (Berkeley, CA, University of California Press, 1985), in particular the crucial essay of 1974 'A New Evolutionism'; and V. Havel, *Power of the Powerless: Citizens against the State in Central-Eastern Europe* (London, Hutchinson, 1985).

6 James R. Miller (ed.), *Politics, Work and Daily Life in the USSR* (Cambridge, Cambridge University Press, 1987).

7 David Marsh (ed.), *Pressure Politics: Interest Groups in Britain* (London, Junction Books, 1983), p. 3.

8 See M. Stephen Fish, *Democracy from Scratch: Opposition and Regime in the New Russian Revolution* (Princeton, NJ, Princeton University Press, 1995); and Michael Urban, with Vyacheslav Igrunov and Sergei Mitrokhin, *The Rebirth of Politics in Russia* (Cambridge, Cambridge University Press, 1997).

9 J. Goldfarb, *The Persistence of Freedom: The Sociological Implications of Polish Student Theater* (Boulder, CO, Westview Press, 1980), p. 1.

14 THE COMMAND ECONOMY AND REFORM

1 M. I. Goldman, *USSR in Crisis: The Failure of an Economic System* (New York, W. W. Norton, 1983), p. 174.

2 Alain Besançon, 'Andropov and His Soviet Union', *Policy Review*, Vol. 25, No. 1 (Summer 1983), pp. 21–23.

3 For a radical downwards revision of official figures on economic growth between 1928 and 1985, see V. Selyunin and G. Khanin, 'Lukovaya tsifra', *Novy Mir*, No. 2 (February 1987), pp. 191–201. The figures have possibly been exaggerated by a factor of ten, see Alec Nove, 'A Further Note on Hidden Inflation and its Statistical Consequences', *Soviet Studies*, Vol. 40, No. 1 (January 1988), p. 136.
4 K. Marx, *Contribution to the Critique of Political Economy, Selected Works* (Moscow, 1968), p. 182.
5 Yu. V. Andropov, 'The Teaching of Karl Marx and Some Problems of Socialist Construction', *Speeches and Writings*, 2nd edn (Oxford, Pergamon Press, 1983); from *Kommunist*, No. 3 (1983).
6 For details, see John Keep, *Last of the Empires: A History of the Soviet Union, 1945–1991* (Oxford, Oxford University Press, 1996), pp. 233–37.
7 J. S. Berliner, 'Managing the USSR Economy: Alternative Models', *Problems of Communism*, Vol. 32, No. 1 (January–February 1983), pp. 40–56.
8 See Stephen White, *Russia Goes Dry* (Cambridge, Cambridge University Press, 1996).
9 *Pravda*, 30 October 1986.

15 NATIONALITY POLITICS

1 S. Bialer, *Stalin's Successors: Leadership, Stability, and Change in the Soviet Union*, (Cambridge, Cambridge University Press, 1980) p. 210.
2 Mark Beissinger, 'The Persisting Ambiguity of Empire', *Post-Soviet Affairs*, Vol. 11, No. 2 (1995), pp. 149–84.
3 P. Rutland, 'The "Nationality Problem" and the Soviet State', in N. Harding (ed.) *The State in Socialist Society* (London, Macmillan, 1984), p. 151.
4 A. Yanov, *The Russian New Right* (Berkeley, CA, Institute of International Studies, University of California Press, 1978).
5 The liberal-nationalist view is advanced in the collection edited by Alexander Solzhenitsyn, *From under the Rubble* (London, Fontana, 1974).

16 FOREIGN AND DEFENCE POLICY

1 George Kennan, 'The Sources of Soviet Conduct', *Foreign Affairs*, Vol. 25, No. 4 (July 1947). This article develops the themes of Kennan's 'long telegram' of 22 February 1946.
2 Carolyn McGiffert Ekedahl and Melvin A. Goodman, *The Wars of Eduard Shevardnadze* (University Park, PA, Pennsylvania State University Press, 1997), p. 59.
3 Robert V. Daniels, *Russia: The Roots of Confrontation* (Cambridge, MA, Harvard University Press, 1985).
4 John Lewis Gaddis, *We Now Know: Rethinking Cold War History* (Oxford, Oxford University Press, 1997).
5 Graham T. Allison, *Essence of Decision: Explaining the Cuban Missile Crisis* (Boston, MA, Little, Brown & Co., 1971).
6 See Jiri Valenta, 'Soviet Decision-making and the Czechoslovak Crisis of 1968', *Studies in Comparative Communism*, Vol. 8, Nos 1/2 (Spring/Summer 1975), pp. 147–73.
7 The three basic models are discussed in D. Simes, 'The Politics of Defence in the Soviet Union', in J. Valenta and W. Potter (eds), *Soviet Decision-making for National Security* (London, George Allen & Unwin, 1984), pp. 74–84.
8 See S. Bialer, *The Soviet Paradox: External Expansion, Internal Decline* (London, Tauris, 1986); Paul Dibb, *The Soviet Union: The Incomplete Superpower* (London, Macmillan, 1986).

17 RISE AND FALL OF THE SOVIET SYSTEM

1 Some of the themes of this chapter are outlined in Richard Sakwa, 'From the USSR to Postcommunist Russia', in Stephen White, Alex Pravda and Zvi Gitelman (eds), *Developments in Russian Politics* (London, Macmillan, 1997), pp. 1–18.
2 Cited by Kristian Gerner and Stefan Hedlund, *Ideology and Rationality in the Soviet Model: A Legacy for Gorbachev* (London, Routledge, 1989), p. 35.
3 Rogers Brubaker, 'Nationhood and the National Question in the Soviet Union and Post-Soviet Eurasia: An Institutionalist Account', *Theory and Society*, Vol. 23 (1994), pp. 47–78.

4 T. H. Rigby, 'Stalinism and the Mono-organisational Society', in T. H. Rigby, *The Changing Soviet System* (Aldershot, Edward Elgar, 1990), pp. 82–112.

5 George Kennan ('X'), 'The Sources of Soviet Conduct', *Foreign Affairs*, Vol. 25, (July 1947), p. 580.

6 Jack F. Matlock, *Autopsy on an Empire* (New York, Random House, 1995), discusses the relationship between structural and circumstantial factors in the fall.

7 Yegor Ligachev, *Inside Gorbachev's Kremlin* (Boulder, CO, Westview Press, 1996), p. 313.

8 Anatoly Dobrynin, *In Confidence* (New York, Times Books, 1995), p. 628.

9 Michael Ellman and Vladimir Kontorovich (eds), *The Disintegration of the Soviet Economic System* (London, Routledge, 1992), p. 27.

10 Alfred Erich Senn, *Gorbachev's Failure in Lithuania* (New York, St Martin's Press, 1995).

11 Philip G. Roeder, *Red Sunset: The Failure of Soviet Politics* (Princeton, NJ, Princeton University Press, 1993), p. 3.

12 Anatolii S. Chernyaev, *Shest' let s Gorbachevym* (Moscow, Progress, 1993), pp. 277–79.

13 Alexander Solzhenitsyn, *Letter to the Soviet Leaders* (New York, Harper and Row, 1975).

14 Paul Kennedy, *The Rise and Fall of the Great Powers: Economic Change and Military Conflict from 1500 to 2000* (London, Unwin Hyman, 1988), pp. 488–514.

18 CONCLUSION: SOVIET POLITICS IN PERSPECTIVE

1 Sergei Pushkarev, *The Emergence of Modern Russia, 1801–1917* (New York, Holt, 1963), p. 423.

2 Stephen F. Cohen, 'The Friends and Foes of Change: Soviet Reformism and Conservatism', in his *Rethinking the Soviet Experience: Politics and History since 1917* (Oxford, Oxford University Press, 1985), pp. 128–57.

3 *Pravda*, 30 September 1988.

4 A theme developed by Richard Pipes, *The Russian Revolution 1899–1919* (London, Harvill, 1990), ch. 11.

5 W. W. Rostow, *The Stages of Economic Growth: A Non-communist Manifesto* (Cambridge, Cambridge University Press, 1960), pp. 162–64.

Bibliography

GENERAL WORKS

Acton, Edward, *Russia: The Tsarist and Soviet Legacy*, 2nd edn (Harlow, Longman, 1995).

Adelman, Jonathan A., *Torrents of Spring: Soviet and Post-Soviet Politics* (New York, McGraw-Hill, 1995).

Amalrik, Andrei, *Will the Soviet Union Survive until 1984?* (Harmondsworth, Penguin, 1970).

Andrle, Vladimir, *A Social History of Twentieth Century Russia* (London, Edward Arnold, 1994).

Armstrong, John A., *Ideology, Politics, and Government in the Soviet Union, An Introduction*, 4th edn (Lanham, MD, University Press of America, 1976/1986).

Baradat, Leon P., *Soviet Political Society*, 3rd edn (Englewood Cliffs, NJ, Prentice-Hall, 1992).

Barghoorn, Frederick C. and Thomas F. Remington, *Politics in the USSR*, 3rd edn (Boston, MA, Little, Brown & Co., 1986).

Barry, Donald D. and Carol Barner-Barry, *Contemporary Soviet Politics, An Introduction*, 3rd edn (Englewood Cliffs, NJ, Prentice-Hall, 1987).

Basily, N. de, *Russia under Soviet Rule, 20 Years of Bolshevik Experiment* (London, George Allen & Unwin, 1938).

Bialer, Seweryn, *Stalin's Successors: Leadership, Stability, and Change in the Soviet Union* (Cambridge, Cambridge University Press, 1980).

Bialer, Seweryn (ed.), *The Domestic Context of Soviet Foreign Policy*, 2nd edn (Boulder, CO, Westview Press, 1988).

Billington, James H., *The Icon and the Axe: An Interpretive History of Russian Culture* (New York, Vintage Books, 1970).

Black, Cyril E. (ed.), *The Transformation of Russian Society: Aspects of Social Change since 1861* (Cambridge, MA, Harvard University Press, 1960).

Breslauer, G. W., *Five Images of the Soviet Future, A Critical Review and Synthesis* (Berkeley, CA, Institute of International Studies, University of California Press, 1978).

Brown, Archie and Michael Kaser (eds), *The Soviet Union since the Fall of Khrushchev* (London, Macmillan, 1975, 2nd edn 1978).

Brown, Archie and Michael Kaser (eds), *Soviet Policy for the 1980s* (London, Macmillan, 1982).

Brown, Archie *et al.* (eds) *The Cambridge Encyclopedia of Russia and the Soviet Union* (Cambridge, Cambridge University Press, 1982).

Brzezinski, Z. (ed.) *Dilemmas of Change in Soviet Politics* (New York, Columbia University Press, 1969), especially ch. 1, 'The Soviet System, Transformation or Degeneration?'.

Brzezinski, Z. and S. P. Huntington, *Political Power USA/USSR* (Harmondsworth, Penguin, 1977).

Bunce, V. and J. M. Echols III, 'From Soviet Studies to Comparative Politics, the Unfinished Revolution', in S. White and D. Nelson (eds) *Communist Politics, A Reader* (London, Macmillan, 1986), pp. 317–25.

Byrnes, Robert (ed.), *After Brezhnev, Sources of Soviet Conduct in the 1980s* (Bloomington, IN, Indiana University Press, 1983).

Carew Hunt, R. N., *The Theory and Practice of Communism*, 5th edn (London, Macmillan, 1961).

Churchward, L. G., *Contemporary Soviet Government*, 2nd edn (London, Routledge & Kegan Paul, 1975).

Churchward, L. G. *Soviet Socialism, Social and Political Essays* (London, Routledge, 1987).

Cocks, Paul, R. V. Daniels and Nancy Whittier Heer (eds), *The Dynamics of Soviet Politics* (Cambridge, MA, Harvard University Press, 1976).

Cohen, Ariel, *Russian Imperialism: Development and Crisis* (New York, Praeger, 1996).

Cohen, Stephen F., *Rethinking the Soviet Experience, Politics and History since 1917* (Oxford, Oxford University Press, 1986).

Cohen, Stephen F., Alexander Rabinowitch and Robert Sharlet (eds), *The Soviet Union since Stalin* (London, Macmillan, 1980).

Colton, Timothy J., *The Dilemma of Reform in the Soviet Union*, rev. and expanded edn (New York, Council on Foreign Relations, 1986).

Colton, Timothy, *Moscow, Governing the Socialist Metropolis* (Cambridge, MA, Bellknap, 1995).

Connor, Walter D., *Socialism's Dilemmas, State and Society in the Soviet Bloc* (New York, Columbia University Press, 1988).

Cornel, R. (ed.) *The Soviet Political System* (Englewood Cliffs, NJ, Prentice-Hall, 1970).

Crouch, Martin, *Revolution and Evolution, Gorbachev and Soviet Politics* (London, Philip Allan, 1989).

Crummey, Robert O. (ed.), *Reform in Russia and the USSR: Past and Prospects* (Urbana, IL, University of Illinois Press, 1989).

Custine, Marquis de, *Letters from Russia*, trans. and ed. Robin Buss (London, Penguin Classics, 1991).

D'Agostino, Anthony, *Soviet Succession Struggles, Kremlinology and the Russian Question from Lenin to Gorbachev* (London, George Allen & Unwin, 1988).

Dallin, A. and G. W. Breslauer, *Political Terror in Communist Systems* (Stanford, CA, Stanford University Press, 1970).

Dallin, Alexander and Gail W. Lapidus (eds), *The Soviet System in Crisis: A Reader of Western and Soviet Views* (Boulder, CO, Westview Press, 1991).

Dallin, Alexander and Gail W. Lapidus (eds), *The Soviet System: From Crisis to Collapse*, rev. edn (Boulder, CO, Westview Press, 1995).

Dallin, Alexander and Condoleeza Rice (eds), *The Gorbachev Era* (Stanford, CA, Stanford Alumni Association, 1986).

Daniels, R. V. (ed.), *A Documentary History of Communism*, Vol. 1 *Communism in Russia* (London, I. B. Tauris, 1987).

Davies, R. W., *Soviet History in the Gorbachev Revolution* (London, Macmillan, 1989).

Davies, R. W. (ed.), *The Soviet Union*, 2nd edn (London, Unwin Hyman, 1989).

Davies, R. W., *Soviet History in the Yeltsin Era* (London, Macmillan, 1996).

Deutscher, Isaac, *The Unfinished Revolution, Russia, 1917–1967* (Oxford, Oxford University Press, 1967).

Dowlah, Alex F. and John E. Elliott, *The Life and Times of Soviet Socialism* (London, Praeger, 1997).

Dunlop, John B., *The Rise of Russia and the Fall of the Soviet Empire* (Princeton, NJ, Princeton University Press, 1993).

Fainsod, Merle, *How Russia is Ruled* (Oxford, Oxford University Press, 1963).

Field, Mark G. (ed.), *Social Consequences of Modernisation in Communist Societies* (Baltimore, MD, Johns Hopkins University Press, 1976).

Fitzpatrick, Sheila, *The Russian Revolution, 1917–32* (Oxford, Oxford University Press, 1982).

Gerner, K. and S. Hedlund, *Ideology and Rationality in the Soviet Model: A Legacy for Gorbachev* (London, Routledge, 1989).

Gooding, John, *Rulers and Subjects: Government and People in Russia 1801–1991* (London, Edward Arnold, 1996).

Hammer, Darrell P., *USSR: The Politics of Oligarchy*, 2nd edn (Boulder, CO, Westview Press, 1986).

Harding, N. (ed.), *The State in Socialist Society* (London, Macmillan, 1984).

Hazard, J. N., *The Soviet System of Government*, 5th edn (Chicago, IL, and London, University of Chicago Press, 1980).

Heller, Mikhail, *Cogs in the Soviet Wheel* (London, Collins, 1988).

Heller, Mikhail and Aleksandr Nekrich, *Utopia in Power, The History of the Soviet Union from 1917 to the Present*, trans. P. B. Carlos (New York, Summit Books, 1986).

Hill, Ronald J., *Soviet Politics, Political Science and Reform* (Oxford, Martin Robertson, 1980).

Hill, Ronald J., *Soviet Union, Politics, Economics and Society*, 2nd edn (London, Frances Pinter, 1989).

Hoffmann, E. P. and R. F. Laird *The Soviet Polity in the Modern Era* (New York, Aldine Publishing Company, 1984).

Holloway, David and Norman Naimark (eds), *Reexamining the Soviet Experience: Essays in Honor of Alexander Dallin* (Boulder, CO, Westview Press, 1996).

Hosking, Geoffrey, *A History of the Soviet Union* (London, Fontana, 1985/1990).

Hosking, Geoffrey, *The Awakening of the Soviet Union* (London, Heinemann, 1990).

Hosking, Geoffrey, *Russia: People and Empire 1552–1917* (London, HarperCollins, 1997).

Hough, J. F., *The Soviet Union and Social Science Theory* (Cambridge, MA, Harvard University Press, 1977).

Hough, J. F. and M. Fainsod *How the Soviet Union is Governed* (Cambridge, MA, Harvard University Press, 1979).

Huntington, Samuel P., 'Social and Institutional Dynamics of One-party Systems', in Samuel P. Huntington and Clement H. Moore (eds), *Authoritarian Politics in Modern Society, The Dynamics of Established One-party Systems* (New York, Basic Books, 1970).

Huntington, Samuel P. and Clement H. Moore (eds), *Authoritarian Politics in Modern Society, The Dynamics of Established One-party Systems* (New York, Basic Books, 1970).

Janos, A. (ed.), *Authoritarian Politics in Communist Europe* (Berkeley, CA, University of California Press, 1976).

Johnson, Chalmers (ed.), *Change in Communist Systems* (Stanford, CA, Stanford University Press, 1970).

Jowitt, K., 'Inclusion and Mobilization in European Leninist Regimes', *World Politics*, Vol. 28, No. 1 (October 1975), pp. 69–96.

Juviler, Peter H. and Henry W. Morton, *Soviet Policy-making: Studies of Communism in Transition* (New York, Praeger, 1967).

Kagarlitsky, Boris, *The Thinking Reed: Intellectuals and the Soviet State from 1917 to the Present*, trans. Brian Pearce (London, Verso, 1988).

Kagarlitsky, Boris, *Farewell Perestroika: A Soviet Chronicle* (London, Verso, 1990).

Kaiser, Robert G., *Russia: The People and Power* (New York, Atheneum, 1976).

Katkov, G. *et al.*, *Russia Enters the Twentieth Century* (London, Methuen, 1973).

Kautsky, John, *Communism and the Politics of Development* (New York, Wiley, 1968).

Keeble, Curtis (ed.), *The Soviet State: The Domestic Roots of Soviet Foreign Policy* (Aldershot, Gower, 1985).

Keep, John L. H., *Last of the Empires: A History of the Soviet Union, 1945–1991* (Oxford, Oxford University Press, 1996).

Kelley, Donald R., *Soviet Politics in the Brezhnev Era* (New York, Praeger, 1980).

Kelley, Donald R., *Politics of Developed Socialism* (New York, London, Greenwood, 1986).

Kennan, George, 'Communism in Russian History', *Foreign Affairs*, Vol. 71 (Winter 1990–91), pp. 168–86.

Kochan, Lionel and John Keep, *The Making of Modern Russia* (Harmondsworth, Penguin, 1997).

Kort, Michael, *The Soviet Colossus: The Rise and Fall of the USSR*, 4th edn (London, M. E. Sharpe, 1996).

Lane, David, *The Socialist Industrial State, towards a Political Sociology of State Socialism* (London, George Allen & Unwin, 1976).

Lane, David, *Soviet Economy and Society* (Oxford, Basil Blackwell, 1985).

Lane, David, *State and Politics in the USSR* (Oxford, Basil Blackwell, 1985).

Lane, David, *Soviet Society under Perestroika* (London, Unwin Hyman, 1990).

Lane, David, *The Rise and Fall of State Socialism* (Cambridge, Polity Press, 1996).

Lieberman, Sanford R. *et al.* (eds), *The Soviet Empire Reconsidered: Essays in Honor of Adam B. Ulam* (Boulder, CO, Westview Press, 1994).

Little, Richard D., *Governing the Soviet Union* (New York, Longman, 1989).

Lowenthal, Richard, 'Development versus Utopia in Communist Policy', in Chalmers Johnson (ed.), *Change in Communist Systems* (Stanford, CA, Stanford University Press, 1970), pp. 33–116.

Mackenzie, David, *A History of the Soviet Union*, 2nd edn (Belmont, Wadsworth, 1991).

Mackenzie, David and Michael W. Curran, *A History of Russia and the Soviet Union*, 3rd edn (Chicago, IL, The Dorsey Press, 1987).

Malia, Martin, *The Soviet Tragedy: A History of Socialism in Russia* (New York, The Free Press, 1994).

McAuley, Mary, *Politics and the Soviet Union* (Harmondsworth, Penguin Books, 1977).

McAuley, Mary, *Soviet Politics, 1917–1991* (Oxford, Oxford University Press, 1992).

McCauley, Martin, *The Soviet Union, 1917–1991*, 2nd edn (Harlow, Longman, 1993).

Medish, Vadim, *The Soviet Union*, 4th edn (Englewood Cliffs, NJ, Prentice-Hall, 1991).

Millar, James R., *Politics, Work and Daily Life in the USSR: A Survey of Former Soviet Citizens* (Cambridge, Cambridge University Press, 1988).

Morton, Henry W. and Rudolf L. Tokes (eds), *Soviet Politics and Society in the 1970s* (New York, The Free Press, 1974).

Nettl, J., *The Soviet Achievement* (London, Thames & Hudson, 1967).

Niiseki, K., *The Soviet Union in Transition* (London, Avebury, 1987).

Nogee, Joseph L., *Soviet Politics: Russia after Brezhnev* (New York, Praeger, 1985).

Pearson, Raymond, *The Russian Moderates and the Crisis of Tsarism, 1914–1917* (London, Macmillan, 1977).

Pipes, Richard, *Russia under the Old Regime* (Harmondsworth, Penguin, 1974).

Pipes, Richard, *The Russian Revolution* (New York, Random House, 1991).

Potichnyi, Peter J. (ed.), *Soviet Union, Party and Society* (Cambridge, Cambridge University Press, 1987).

Ragsdale, Hugh, *The Russian Tragedy: The Burden of History* (New York, M. E. Sharpe, 1996).

Rakowska, T. (ed.), *Perspectives for Change in Communist Societies* (Boulder, CO, Westview Press, 1979).

Remington, Thomas F. (ed.), *Politics and the Soviet System* (London, Macmillan, 1989).

Reshetar, John S. Jr, *The Soviet Polity* (New York and Toronto, Dodd, Mead, 1971).

Riasanovsky, Nicholas V., *A History of Russia*, 5th edn (Oxford, Oxford University Press, 1993).

Rigby, T. H., *The Changing Soviet System: Mono-organisational Socialism from its Origins to Gorbachev's Restructuring* (Aldershot, Edward Elgar, 1990).

Rigby, T. H., Archie Brown and Peter Reddaway (eds), *Authority, Power and Policy in the USSR* (London, Macmillan, 1980).

Roeder, Philip G., *Red Sunset: The Failure of Soviet Politics* (Princeton, NJ, Princeton University Press, 1993).

Rogger, H., *Russia in the Age of Modernisation and Revolution, 1881–1917* (London, Longman, 1983).

Rosenberg, W. and M. Young, *Transforming Russia and China, Revolutionary Struggle in the Twentieth Century* (Oxford, Oxford University Press, 1982).

Rothman, S. and George Breslauer, *Soviet Politics and Society* (St Paul, MI, West Publishing Co., 1978).

Ryavec, Karl W. (ed.), *Soviet Society and the Communist Party* (Amherst, MA, University of Massachusetts Press, 1978).

Sachs, Michael P. and Jerry G. Pankhurst (eds), *Understanding Soviet Society* (London, Unwin Hyman, 1988).

Sakwa, Richard, *Soviet Politics: An Introduction* (London and New York, Routledge, 1989).

Sakwa, Richard, *Gorbachev and His Reforms, 1985–1990* (London, Philip Allan, 1990).

Sandle, Mark, *A Short History of Soviet Socialism* (London, UCL Press, 1997).

Schapiro, Leonard, *The Government and Politics of the Soviet Union*, 2nd edn (London, Hutchinson, 1978).

Service, Robert, *A History of Twentieth-century Russia* (Harmondsworth, Penguin, 1997).

Shipler, D. K., *Russia: Broken Idols, Solemn Dreams* (London, MacDonald, 1983).

Shtromas, Alexander and Morton A. Kaplan (eds), *The Soviet Union and the Challenge of the Future*: Vol. 1, *The Soviet System, Stasis and Change* (New York, Paragon House Publishers, 1987); Vol. 2, *Economy and Society* (1989); Vol. 3, *Ideology, Culture and Nationality* (1989); Vol. 4, *Russia and the World* (1989).

Sik, Ota, *The Communist Power System* (New York, Praeger, 1981).

Skocpol, Theda, *States and Social Revolutions* (Cambridge, Cambridge University Press, 1979).

Smith, Gordon, *Soviet Politics*, 2nd edn, *Struggling with Change* (London, Macmillan, 1991).

Smith, Hedrick, *The Russians* (London, Sphere Books, 1976).

Taranovski, Theodore, *Reform in Modern Russian History, Progress or Cycle?* (Cambridge, Cambridge University Press, 1995).

Thatcher, Ian (ed.), *Regime and Society in Twentieth Century Russia* (London, Macmillan, 1997).

Thompson, John M., *Russia and the Soviet Union: An Historical Introduction from the Kievan State to the Present*, 3rd edn (Oxford, Westview Press, 1994).

Treadgold, Donald W., *Twentieth Century Russia*, 7th edn (Boulder, CO, Westview Press, 1989).

Treadgold, Donald W., *Twentieth Century Russia*, 8th edn (Oxford, Westview Press, 1994).

Ulam, Adam, *A History of Soviet Russia* (New York, Praeger, 1976).

Ulam, Adam, *The Unfinished Revolution* rev. edn (London, Longman, 1979).

Von Laue, Theodore H., *Why Lenin? Why Stalin?*, 2nd edn (Philadelphia, PA, Lippincott, 1971).

Von Laue, Theodore H., *Why Lenin? Why Stalin? Why Gorbachev? The Rise and Fall of the Soviet System*, 3rd edn (New York, HarperCollins College Publishers, 1993).

Walker, Martin, *The Waking Giant, The Soviet Union under Gorbachev* (London, Abacus, 1987).

Westwood, John, *Endurance and Endeavour: Russian History, 1812–1992*, 4th edn (Oxford, Oxford University Press, 1993).

White, Stephen and Daniel N. Nelson (eds), *Communist Politics: A Reader* (London, Macmillan, 1986).

White, Stephen, Alex Pravda and Zvi Gitelman (eds), *Developments in Soviet Politics* (London, Macmillan, 1990).

Zaslavsky, Viktor, *The Neo-Stalinist State: Class, Ethnicity and Consensus in Soviet Society* (Brighton, Harvester Press, 1982).

Zinoviev, Alexander, *The Reality of Communism* (London, Victor Gollancz, 1984).

Zinoviev, Alexander, *Homo Sovieticus* (London, Victor Gollancz, 1985).

1 THE RUSSIAN LEGACY

The old regime

Auty, R. and D. Obolensky (eds), *An Introduction to Russian History* (Cambridge, Cambridge University Press, 1976).

Black, C. E. (ed.), *The Transformation of Russian Society* (Cambridge, MA, Harvard University Press, 1960).

Charques, Richard, *The Twilight of Imperial Russia* (Oxford, Oxford University Press, 1958).

Emmons, T., *The Formation of Political Parties and the First National Elections in Russia* (Cambridge, MA, Harvard University Press, 1983).

Emmons, T. and W. Vucinich (eds), *The Zemstvo in Russia: An Experiment in Local Self-government* (Cambridge, Cambridge University Press, 1982).

Fuller, William C., *Strategy and Power in Russia, 1600–1914* (New York, The Free Press, 1992).

Haimson, Leopold H., 'The Problem of Social Stability in Urban Russia, 1905–1917', Part I, *Slavic Review*, Vol. 23, No. 4 (December 1964), pp. 619–42; Part II, *Slavic Review*, Vol. 24, No. 1 (March 1965), pp. 1–23.

Haimson, Leopold H. (ed.), *The Politics of Rural Russia, 1905–1914* (Bloomington, IN, Indiana University Press, 1979).

Hosking, Geoffrey, *The Russian Constitutional Experiment: Government and Duma, 1907–1914* (Cambridge, Cambridge University Press, 1973).

LeDonne, John P., *The Russian Empire and the World, 1700–1917: The Geopolitics of Expansion and Containment* (Oxford, Oxford University Press, 1997).

Lieven, D. C. B., *Russia and the Origins of the First World War* (London, Macmillan, 1983).

Lincoln, W. Bruce, *In the Vanguard of Reform: Russia's Enlightened Bureaucrats, 1825–1861* (DeKalb, IL, Northern Illinois University Press, 1982).

Lincoln, W. Bruce, *In War's Dark Shadow: The Russians before the Great War* (New York, Oxford University Press, 1994).

Lincoln, W. Bruce, *Passage through Armageddon: The Russians in War and Revolution, 1914–1918* (New York, Oxford University Press, 1994).

Maclean, Fitzroy, *Holy Russia: An Historical Companion to European Russia* (London, Century Publishing, 1978).

McCauley, Martin and Peter Waldron, *Octobrists to Bolsheviks: Imperial Russia, 1905–1917* (London, Edward Arnold, 1984).

Manning, Roberta T., *The Crisis of the Old Order in Russia: Gentry and Government* (Princeton, NJ, Princeton University Press, 1982).

Martin, Alexander M., *Romantics, Reformers, Reactionaries: Russian Conservative Thought and Politics in the Reign of Alexander I* (DeKalb, IL, Northern Illinois University Press, 1997).

Nichols, R. L. and T. G. Stavrou (eds), *Russian Orthodoxy under the Old Regime* (Minneapolis, MN, University of Minnesota Press, 1978).

Orlovsky, Daniel, *The Limits to Reform: The Ministry of Internal Affairs in Imperial Russia, 1801–1881* (Cambridge, MA, Harvard University Press, 1981).

Pipes, R., *Russia under the Old Regime* (Harmondsworth, Pelican, 1974).

Raeff, M., *The Decembrist Movement* (Englewood Cliffs, NJ, Prentice-Hall, 1966).

Raeff, M. *Understanding Imperial Russia: State and Society in the Old Regime*, trans. Arthur Goldhammer, foreword by John Keep (New York, Columbia University Press, 1984).

Rawson, Don C., *Russian Rightists and the Revolution of 1905* (Cambridge, Cambridge University Press, 1995).

Riasanovsky, Nicholas V., *A History of Russia*, 4th edn (Oxford, Oxford University Press, 1984).

Rogger, Hans, *Russia in the Age of Modernization and Revolution, 1881–1917* (London, Longman, 1983).

Seton-Watson, Hugh, *The Russian Empire, 1801–1917* (Oxford, Clarendon Press, 1967).

Seton-Watson, Hugh, *The Decline of Imperial Russia* (Boulder, CO, Westview Press, 1985).

Waldron, Peter, *Between Two Revolutions: Stolypin and the Politics of Renewal in Russia* (DeKalb, IL, Northern Illinois University Press, 1997).

Waldron, Peter, *The End of Imperial Russia, 1855–1917* (London, Macmillan, 1997).

Warth, Robert D., *Nicholas II: The Life and Reign of Russia's Last Monarch* (London, Praeger, 1997).

Weissman, N. B., *Reform in Tsarist Russia: The State Bureaucracy and Local Government, 1900–1914* (New Brunswick, NJ, Rutgers University Press, 1981).

Wortman, R. S., *The Development of a Russian Legal Consciousness* (Chicago, IL, University of Chicago Press, 1976).

Yaney, George L., *The Systematisation of Russian Government: Social Evolution in the Domestic Administration of Imperial Russia, 1711–1905* (Urbana, IL, University of Illinois Press, 1973).

Social and economic developments to 1917

Atkinson, Dorothy, *The End of the Russian Land Commune, 1905–1930* (Stanford, CA, Stanford University Press, 1983).

Bideleux, Robert, *Communism and Development* (London, Methuen, 1985).

Blackwell, W. L. (ed.), *Russian Economic Development from Peter the Great to Stalin* (New York, New View-points, 1974).

Bonnell, V. E., *Roots of Rebellion: Workers' Politics and Organisation in St Petersburg and Moscow, 1900–1914* (Berkeley, CA, University of California Press, 1983).

Crisp, Olga, *Studies in the Russian Economy before 1914* (London, Macmillan, 1976).

Davies, R. W. (ed.), *From Tsarism to the New Economic Policy: Continuity and Change in the Economy of the USSR* (London, Macmillan, 1990).

Eklof, Ben and Stephen P. Frank (eds), *The World of the Russian Peasant: Post-emancipation Culture and Society* (London, Unwin Hyman, 1990).

Emmons, Terence, *The Russian Landed Gentry and the Peasant Emancipation of 1861* (Cambridge, Cambridge University Press, 1968).

Falkus, M. E., *The Industrialisation of Russia, 1700–1914* (London, Macmillan, 1972).

Gatrell, Peter, *The Tsarist Economy, 1850–1917* (London, Batsford, 1986).

Gerschenkron, A., *Economic Backwardness in Historical Perspective* (Cambridge, Cambridge, MA, Harvard University Press, 1962).

Gregory, P. R., *Russian National Income, 1885–1913* (Cambridge University Press, 1982).

Haimson, Leopold H., 'The Problem of Social Stability in Urban Russia, 1905–1917', Part I, *Slavic Review*, Vol. 23, No. 4 (December 1964), pp. 619–42; Part II, *Slavic Review*, Vol. 24, No. 1 (March 1965), pp. 1–23.

Johnson, R. E., *Peasant and Proletarian: The Working Class of Moscow in the Late Nineteenth Century* (Leicester, Leicester University Press, 1979).

Kitching, G., *Development and Underdevelopment in Historical Perspective: Populism, Nationalism and Industrialisation* (London, Methuen, 1982).

McKean, Robert B., *St Petersburg between the Revolutions: Workers and Revolutionaries, June 1907–February 1917* (London, Yale University Press, 1990).

Rostow, W. W., *The Stages of Economic Growth: A Non-communist Manifesto* (Cambridge, Cambridge University Press, 1960).

Schapiro, Leonard, *Russian Studies* (London, Collins Harvill, 1986).

Shanin, Teodor, *The Roots of Otherness: Russia's Turn of the Century*. Vol. 1, *Russia as a 'Developing Society'*; Vol. 2, *Russia, 1905–1907: Revolution as a Moment of Truth* (London, Macmillan, 1985–86).

Schneiderman, Jeremiah, *Sergei Zubatov and Revolutionary Marxism: The Struggle for the Working Class in Tsarist Russia* (London/Ithaca, Cornell University Press, 1976).

Thurston, Robert W., *Liberal City, Conservative State: Moscow and Russia's Urban Crisis, 1906–1914* (Oxford, Oxford University Press, 1987).

Von Laue, T. H., *Sergei Witte and the Industrialisation of Russia* (New York, Columbia University Press, 1963).

Vucinich, W. (ed.), *The Peasant in Nineteenth-century Russia* (Stanford, CA, Stanford University Press, 1968).

Wirtschafter, Elise Kimerling, *Social Identity in Imperial Russia* (DeKalb, IL, Northern Illinois University Press, 1997).

Yaney, G. L., *The Urge to Mobilise: Agrarian Reform in Russia, 1861–1930* (Urbana, IL, University of Illinois Press, 1982).

Zelnik, Reginald E., *Labor and Society in Tsarist Russia: The Factory Workers of St Petersburg, 1855–1870* (Stanford, CA, Stanford University Press, 1971).

Revolutionary movements and Bolshevism

Ascher, Abraham, *Pavel Axelrod and the Development of Menshevism* (Cambridge, MA, Harvard University Press, 1972).

Ascher, Abraham, *The Revolution of 1905*: Vol. 1, *Russia in Disarray*; Vol. 2, *Authority Restored* (Stanford, CA, Stanford University Press, 1992).

Baron, S. H., *Plekhanov: The Father of Russian Marxism* (Stanford, CA, Stanford University Press, 1963).

Berdyaev, Nicolas, *The Origin of Russian Communism* (London, Geoffrey Bles, 1937).

Berlin, Isaiah, *Russian Thinkers* (Harmondsworth, Penguin, 1979).

Besançon, Alain, *The Rise of the Gulag: The Intellectual Origins of Leninism* (New York, Continuum, 1981).

Fischer, George, *Russian Liberalism: From Gentry to Intelligentsia* (Harvard, MA, Harvard University Press, 1958).

Getzler, Israel, *Martov: A Political Biography of a Russian Social Democrat* (Oxford, Oxford University Press, 1967).

Haimson, Leopold H., *The Russian Marxists and the Origins of Bolshevism* (Boston, MA, Beacon Press, 1966).

Harcave, Sidney, *The Russian Revolution of 1905* (London, Collier-MacMillan, 1964).
Harding, Neil, *Lenin's Political Thought* (2 vols) (London, Macmillan, 1981).
Harding, Neil, *Leninism* (London, Macmillan, 1996).
Harding, Neil (ed.), *Marxism in Russia: Key Documents, 1879–1906*, trans. Richard Taylor (Cambridge, Cambridge University Press, 1983).
Herzen, Alexander, *My Past and Thoughts* (New York, Alfred S. Knopf, 1973).
Keep, John, *The Rise of Social Democracy in Russia* (Oxford, Clarendon Press, 1963).
Kingston-Mann, Esther, *Lenin and the Problem of Marxist Peasant Revolution* (Oxford, Oxford University Press, 1983).
Lane, David, *The Roots of Russian Communism* (Assen, van Gorcum, 1969/75).
Lane, David, *Leninism: A Sociological Interpretation* (Cambridge, Cambridge University Press, 1981).
Lenin, V. I. Key writings include *What Is To Be Done?*; *Two Tactics of Social Democracy*; *Imperialism, The Highest Stage of Capitalism*; *The State and Revolution*.
Malia, Martin, *Alexander Herzen and the Birth of Russian Socialism* (Cambridge, MA, Harvard University Press, 1961).
Meyer, Alfred G., *Leninism* (New York, Praeger, 1957).
Perrie, Maureen, *The Agrarian Policy of the Russian Socialist Revolutionary Party, 1905–1907* (Cambridge, Cambridge University Press, 1976).
Pipes, Richard, *Struve: Liberal on the Left, 1870–1905* (Cambridge, MA, Harvard University Press, 1970).
Pipes, Richard, *Struve: Liberal on the Right, 1905–1944* (Cambridge, MA, Harvard University Press, 1980).
Rawson, Don C., *Russian Rightists and the Revolution of 1905* (Cambridge, Cambridge University Press, 1995).
Shub, David, *Lenin* (Harmondsworth, Pelican, 1966).
Swain, Geoffrey, *Russian Social Democracy and the Legal Labour Movement, 1906–1914* (London, Macmillan, 1983).
Szamuely, Tibor, *The Russian Tradition* (London, Secker & Warburg, 1974).
Tucker, Robert C., *The Marxian Revolutionary Idea* (London, George Allen & Unwin, 1970).
Ulam, Adam, *The Bolsheviks: The Intellectual and Political History of the Triumph of Communism in Russia* (New York, Macmillan, 1965).
Venturi, F., *Roots of Revolution: A History of the Populist and Socialist Movements in Nineteenth-century Russia* (London, Weidenfeld, 1961).
Walicki, Andrzez, *A History of Russian Thought: From the Enlightenment to Marxism* (Oxford, Oxford University Press, 1988).

2 THE CREATION OF THE SOVIET STATE

The revolutions of 1917

Abraham, Richard, *Alexander Kerensky: The First Love of the Revolution* (London, Sidgwick & Jackson, 1987).
Acton, Edward, *Rethinking the Russian Revolution* (London, Edward Arnold, 1990).
Acton, Edward and William G. Rosenberg (eds), *Critical Companion to the Russian Revolution 1914–1921* (London, Edward Arnold, 1997).
Anweiller, Oskar, *The Soviets: The Russian Workers', Peasants', and Soldiers' Councils* (New York, Pantheon Books, 1974).
Avrich, Paul, *The Russian Anarchists* (Princeton, NJ, Princeton University Press, 1967).
Brinton, Crane, *The Anatomy of Revolution* (New York, Vintage, 1952).
Carr, E. H., *The Bolshevik Revolution* Vols 1–3 (Harmondsworth, Pelican, 1966).
Carrère d'Encausse, H., *Lenin: Revolution and Power* (London, Longman, 1982).
Daniels, Robert V., *Red October: The Bolshevik Revolution of 1917* (New York, Scribner, 1967).
Dukes, Paul, *October and the World* (London, Macmillan, 1979).
Elwood, Ralph Carter (ed.), *Reconsiderations on the Russian Revolution* (Cambridge, MA, Slavica, 1976).
Ferro, Marc, *The Russian Revolution of February 1917* (London, Routledge, 1972).
Ferro, Marc, *The Bolshevik Revolution: A Social History of the Russian Revolution* (London, Routledge, 1985).
Fitzpatrick, Sheila, *The Russian Revolution, 1917–1932* (Oxford, Oxford University Press, 1982).
Frankel, Edith R., Jonathan Frankel and Baruch Knei-Paz (eds), *Revolution in Russia: Reassessments of 1917* (Cambridge, Cambridge University Press, 1992).
Gill, Graeme, *Peasants and Government in the Russian Revolution* (London, Macmillan, 1979).
Haimson, Leopold H. (ed.), *The Mensheviks: From the Revolution of 1917 to the Second World War* (Chicago, IL, Chicago University Press, 1974).

Harding, Neil, *Leninism* (London, Macmillan, 1996).

Hasegawa, Tsuyoshi, *The February Revolution: Petrograd 1917* (Seattle, WA, University of Washington Press, 1980).

Kaiser, Daniel (ed.), *The Workers' Revolution in Russia: The View from Below* (Cambridge, Cambridge University Press, 1987).

Katkov, George, *Russia 1917: The February Revolution* (London, Collins, 1967).

Keep, John L. H., *The Russian Revolution: A Study in Mass Mobilisation* (London, Weidenfeld & Nicolson, 1976).

Kochan, Lionel, *Russia in Revolution* (London, Paladin, 1970).

Koenker, Diane, *Moscow Workers and the 1917 Revolution* (Princeton, NJ, Princeton University Press, 1981).

Kowalski, Ronald, *The Russian Revolution, 1917–1921* (London, Routledge, 1997).

Mandel, David, *The Petrograd Workers and the Fall of the Old Regime: From the February Revolution to the July Days, 1917* (London, Macmillan, 1984).

Mandel, David, *Petrograd Workers and the Soviet Seizure of Power, July 1917–June 1918* (London, Macmillan, 1984).

Medvedev, Roy, *The October Revolution* (London, Constable, 1979).

Mstislavskii, Sergei, *Five Days which Transformed Russia* (London, I. B. Tauris, 1990).

Pearson, R., *The Russian Moderates and the Crisis of Tsardom* (London, Macmillan, 1977).

Pipes, R. (ed.), *Revolutionary Russia: A Symposium* (Cambridge, MA, Harvard University Press, 1968).

Pipes, Richard, *The Russian Revolution* (London, HarperCollins, 1992).

Rabinowitch, Alexander, *Prelude to Revolution: The Petrograd Bolsheviks and the July 1917 Uprising* (Bloomington, IN, Indiana University Press, 1968).

Rabinowich, Alexander, *The Bolsheviks Come to Power: The Revolution of 1917 in Petrograd* (New York, W. W. Norton, 1976).

Radkey, Oliver, *The Agrarian Foes of Bolshevism: Promise and Default of the Russian Socialist Revolutionaries, February to October 1917* (New York, Columbia University Press, 1958).

Radkey, Oliver, *The Sickle under the Hammer: The Russian Socialist Revolutionaries in the Early Months of Soviet Rule* (New York, Columbia University Press, 1963).

Raleigh, Donald J., *Revolution on the Volga: 1917 in Saratov* (Ithaca, NY, Cornell University Press, 1986).

Read, Christopher, *From Tsar to Soviets: The Russian People and their Revolution, 1917–1921* (London, UCL Press, 1996).

Reed, John, *Ten Days That Shook the World* (New York, Vintage, 1960).

Rosenberg, William G., *Liberals in the Russian Revolution: The Constitutional Democratic Party, 1917–1921* (Princeton, NJ, Princeton University Press, 1974).

Schapiro, Leonard, *The Russian Revolutions of 1917: The Origins of Modern Communism* (New York, Basic Books, 1984).

Service, Robert *The Bolshevik Party in Revolution: A Study in Organisational Change, 1917–1923* (London, Macmillan, 1979).

Service, Robert, *The Russian Revolution: Culminations, Beginnings, Disruptions* (London, Macmillan, 1986).

Service, Robert, *Lenin: A Political Life: Volume Two: Worlds in Collision* (London, Macmillan, 1991).

Service, Robert, *Lenin: A Political Life: Volume Three: The Iron Ring* (London, Macmillan, 1995).

Smith, S. A., *Red Petrograd: Revolution in the Factories, 1917–1918* (Cambridge, Cambridge University Press, 1983).

Steinberg, Mark D. and Vladimir M. Khrustalev, *The Fall of the Romanovs: Political Dreams and Personal Struggles in a Time of Revolution* (New Haven, CT, Yale University Press, 1995).

Suny, Ronald G., *The Baku Commune, 1917–1918: Class and Nationality in the Russian Revolution* (Princeton, NJ, Princeton University Press, 1972).

Suny, Ronald G., 'Towards a Social History of the October Revolution', *American Historical Review*, Vol. 88, No. 1 (February 1983), pp. 31–52.

Trotsky, Leon, *The History of the Russian Revolution*, trans. Max Eastman (London, Pluto Press, 1997).

Von Laue, Theodore H., *Why Lenin? Why Stalin?*, 2nd edn (Philadelphia, PA, Lippincott, 1971).

Wade, Rex A., *Red Guards and Workers' Militias: Spontaneity and Leadership in the Russian Revolution* (Stanford, CA, Stanford University Press, 1983).

White, James D., *The Russian Revolution 1917–1921: A Short History* (London, Edward Arnold, 1994).

Wildman, Alan, *The End of the Russian Imperial Army: The Old Army and the Soldiers' Revolt (March–April 1917)* (Princeton, NJ, Princeton University Press, 1980).

Wilson, Edmund, *To the Finland Station* (London, Collins, 1960).

Wolfe, Bertram, *Three Who Made a Revolution*, 4th edn (Harmondsworth, Penguin, 1966).

Wood, Alan, *The Origins of the Russian Revolution*, 2nd edn (London, Routledge, 1993).

The formation of the Soviet state, 1918–21

Aves, Jonathan, *Workers against Lenin: Labour Protest and the Bolshevik Dictatorship, 1920–22* (London, I. B. Tauris, 1996).

Bettelheim, Charles, *Class Struggles in the USSR: First Period, 1917–1923* (Brighton, Harvester Press, 1976).

Bradley, John, *Civil War in Russia, 1917–1920* (London, Batsford, 1975).

Broido, Vera, *Lenin and the Mensheviks: The Persecution of Socialists under Bolshevism* (Aldershot, Gower, 1987).

Bukharin, N. I. and E. A. Preobrazhensky, *The ABC of Communism*, ed. E. H. Carr (Harmondsworth, Penguin, 1969).

Carr, E. H., *The Russian Revolution from Lenin to Stalin, 1917–1929* (London, Macmillan, 1979).

Chamberlin, W. H., *The Russian Revolution, 1917–1921* (London, Macmillan, 1935).

Daniels, R. V., *The Conscience of the Revolution: Communist Opposition in Soviet Russia* (Oxford, Oxford University Press, 1960).

Farber, Samuel, *Before Stalinism: The Rise and Fall of Soviet Democracy* (London, Verso, 1990).

Gleason, Abbott, Peter Kenez and Richard Stites (eds), *Bolshevik Culture: Experiment and Order in the Russian Revolution* (Bloomington, IN, Indiana University Press, 1985).

Liebman, Marcel, *Leninism under Lenin* (London, Merlin Press, 1975).

Lovell, David W., *From Marx to Lenin: An Evaluation of Marx's Responsibility for Soviet Authoritarianism* (Cambridge, Cambridge University Press, 1984).

Malle, Silvana, *The Economic Organisation of War Communism, 1918–1921* (Cambridge, Cambridge University Press, 1985).

Mawdsley, Evan, *The Russian Civil War* (London, Allen & Unwin, 1987).

McCauley, Martin (ed.), *The Russian Revolution and the Soviet State, 1917–1921: Documents* (London, Macmillan, 1975).

Polan, A. J., *Lenin and the End of Politics* (London, Methuen, 1984).

Remington, Thomas F., *Building Socialism in Bolshevik Russia: Ideology and Industrial Organisation, 1917–1921* (Pittsburgh, PA, University of Pittsburgh Press, 1984).

Rigby, T, H., *Lenin's Government: Sovnarkom, 1917–1922* (Cambridge, Cambridge University Press, 1979).

Rosenberg, W. G. (ed.), *Bolshevik Visions: First Phase of the Cultural Revolution in Soviet Russia* (Ann Arbor, MI, Ardis Publishers, 1985).

Sakwa, Richard, *Soviet Communists in Power: A Study of Moscow during the Civil War, 1918–21* (London, Macmillan, 1988).

Schapiro, Leonard, *The Origin of the Communist Autocracy: Political Opposition in the Soviet State, 1917–1922* (London, Bell/LSE, 1955).

Sirianni, Carmen, *Workers' Control and Socialist Democracy: The Soviet Experience* (London, Verso/NLB, 1982).

Swain, Geoffrey, *The Origins of the Russian Civil War* (Harlow, Longman, 1995).

3 STALIN AND STALINISM

The NEP compromise

Bettelheim, Charles, *Class Struggles in the USSR: Second Period, 1923–1930* (Brighton, Harvester, 1978).

Bideleux, Robert, *Communism and Development* (London, Methuen, 1985).

Brovkin, Vladimir, *Russia after Lenin: Politics, Culture and Society, 1921–1929* (London, Routledge, 1998).

Carr, E. H., *The Bolshevik Revolution, 1917–1923*, Vol. 2 (London, Macmillan, 1952).

Carr, E. H., *The Interregnum, 1923–1924* (London, Macmillan, 1954).

Carr, E. H., *Socialism in One Country, 1924–1926*, Vol. 1 (London, Macmillan, 1958).

Carr, E. H., *The Russian Revolution from Lenin to Stalin, 1917–1929* (London, Macmillan, 1979).

Carr, E. H. and R. W. Davies, *Foundations of a Planned Economy, 1926–1929*, Vol. 1, 2 parts (London, Macmillan, 1969).

Chayanov, Alexander, *The Theory of Peasant Co-operatives* (London, I. B. Tauris, 1990).

Cohen, Stephen, *Bukharin and the Bolshevik Revolution: A Political Biography, 1888–1938* (New York, Vintage, 1975).

Cox, Terry and Gary Littlejohn (eds), *Kritsman and the Agrarian Marxists* (Library of Peasant Studies, No. 7) (London, Frank Cass & Co., 1984).

Danilov, Viktor P., *Rural Russia under the New Regime* (London, I. B. Tauris, 1988).

Davies, R. W., *The Socialist Offensive: The Collectivisation of Soviet Agriculture, 1929–1930* (London, Macmillan, 1980).

Davies, R. W., *The Soviet Collective Farm, 1929–1930* (London, Macmillan, 1980).

Davies, R. W., *Crisis and Progress in the Soviet Economy* (London, Macmillan, 1996).

Davies, R. W. (ed.), *From Tsarism to the New Economic Policy: Continuity and Change in the Economy of the USSR* (London, Macmillan, 1990).

Davies, R. W., Mark Harrison and S. G. Wheatcroft (eds), *The Economic Transformation of the Soviet Union, 1913–1945* (Cambridge, Cambridge University Press, 1993).

Day, Richard, *L. Trotsky and the Politics of Economic Isolation* (Cambridge, Cambridge University Press, 1973).

Deutscher, Isaac, *Trotsky: The Prophet Unarmed, 1921–1929* (Oxford, Oxford University Press, 1959).

Deutscher, Isaac, (ed.), *The Age of Permanent Revolution: A Trotsky Anthology* (New York, Dell, 1964).

Erlich, A., *The Soviet Industrialisation Debate, 1924–28* (Cambridge, MA, Harvard University Press, 1975).

Farber, Michael, *Before Stalinism: The Rise and Fall of Soviet Democracy* (Cambridge, Polity Press, 1990).

Fitzpatrick, Sheila, *The Commissariat of the Enlightenment* (Cambridge, Cambridge University Press, 1970).

Fitzpatrick, Sheila, *The Russian Revolution: 1917–1932* (Oxford, Oxford University Press, 1982).

Fitzpatrick, Sheila (ed.), *Cultural Revolution in Russia, 1928–1932* (Bloomington, IN, Indiana University Press, 1978).

Gerschenkron, A., *Economic Backwardness in Historical Perspective* (Cambridge, MA, Harvard University Press, 1962).

Gleason, Abbott, Peter Kenez and Richard Stites (eds), *Experiment and Order in the Russian Revolution* (Bloomington, IN, Indiana University Press, 1985).

Haynes, M., *Nikolai Bukharin and the Transition from Capitalism to Socialism* (Beckenham, Croom Helm, 1985).

Jasny, N., *Soviet Economists of the Twenties: Names to be Remembered* (Cambridge, Cambridge University Press, 1972).

Knei-Paz, B., *The Social and Political Thought of Leon Trotsky* (Oxford, Oxford University Press, 1978).

Kozlov, Nicholas N. and Eric D. Weitz, *Nikolai Ivanovich Bukharin: A Centenary Reappraisal* (London, Praeger Publishers, 1990).

Leibich, André, *From the Other Shore: Russian Social Democracy after 1921* (Cambridge, MA, Harvard University Press, 1997).

Lewin, Moshe, *Russian Peasants and Soviet Power* (Evanston, IL, Northwestern University Press, 1968).

Lewin, Moshe, *Lenin's Last Struggle* (London, Pluto, 1975).

Merridale, Catherine, *Moscow Politics and the Rise of Stalin: The Communist Party in the Capital, 1925–32* (London, Macmillan, 1990).

Molyneux, John, *Leon Trotsky's Theory of Revolution* (New York, St Martins Press, 1981).

Narkiewicz, Olga, *The Making of the Soviet State Apparatus* (Manchester, Manchester University Press, 1970).

Nove, Alec, *Economic Rationality and Soviet Politics, or Was Stalin Really Necessary?* (London, George Allen & Unwin, 1964).

Nove, Alec, *An Economic History of the USSR* (Harmondsworth, Pelican, 1972).

Pethybridge, Roger, *The Social Prelude to Stalinism* (London, Macmillan, 1974).

Pethybridge, Roger, *One Step Backwards, Two Steps Forward: Soviet Society and Politics under the New Economic Policy* (Oxford, Clarendon Press, 1990).

Preobrazhenskii, E. A., *The Decline of Capitalism*, trans. and ed. Richard B. Day (Armonk, NY, M. E. Sharpe, 1985).

Rakovsky, Christian, *Selected Writings on Opposition in the USSR, 1923–1930*, ed. Gus Fagan (London, Alison & Busby, 1980).

Siegelbaum, Lewis A., *Soviet State and Society between Revolutions, 1918–1929* (Cambridge, Cambridge University Press, 1992).

Ward, Chris, *Russia's Cotton Workers and the New Economic Policy: Shop Floor Culture and State Policy, 1921–1929* (Cambridge, Cambridge University Press, 1990).

Stalin and the Stalin period

Ali, Tariq (ed.), *The Stalinist Legacy* (Harmondsworth, Penguin, 1984).

Alliluyeva, Svetlana, *Twenty Letters to a Friend* (London, Hutchinson, 1967).

Andreyev, Catherine, *Vlasov and the Russian Liberation Movement: Soviet Reality and Emigré Theories* (Cambridge, Cambridge University Press, 1987).

Andrle, V., *Workers in Stalin's Russia: Industrialisation and Social Change in a Planned Economy* (Hemel Hempstead, Harvester Wheatsheaf, 1988).

Antonov-Ovseyenko, Anton, *The Time of Stalin: A Portrait of Tyranny* (New York, Harper and Row, 1981).

Avtorkhanov, A., *Stalin and the Soviet Communist Party: A Study in the Technology of Power* (London, Atlantic Books, 1959).

Barmine, Alexander, *One Who Survived* (New York, Putnam, 1945).

Bartov, Omer, *The Eastern Front, 1941–1945: German Troops and the Barbarisation of Warfare* (London, Macmillan, 1985).

Bialer, Seweryn, *Stalin and His Generals* (London, 1970).

Blank, Stephen, *The Sorcerer as Apprentice: Stalin as Commissar of Nationalities, 1917–1924* (London, Greenwood Press, 1994).

Boffa, Giuseppe, *The Stalin Phenomenon* (Ithaca, NY, Cornell University Press, 1992).

Brzezinski, Z., *The Permanent Purge* (Cambridge, MA, Harvard University Press, 1956).

Callinicos, Alex, *Trotskyism* (Milton Keynes, Open University Press, 1990).

Burlatsky, Fedor, *Khrushchev and the First Russian Spring: The Era of Khrushchev through the Eyes of His Adviser* (London, Weidenfeld & Nicolson, 1991).

Campeanu, Pavel, *The Origins of Stalinism: From Leninist Revolution to Stalinist Society* (London, M. E. Sharpe, 1986).

Campeanu, P., *The Genesis of the Stalinist Social Order* (London, M. E. Sharpe, 1988).

Carr, E. H., *Socialism in One Country, 1924–1926*, 3 vols (London, Macmillan, 1958–59).

Carr, E. H. (Vol. 1 with R. W. Davies), *Foundations of a Planned Economy, 1926–1929*, 3 vols (London, Macmillan, 1969).

Carrère d'Encausse, H., *Stalin: Order through Terror* (London, Longman, 1981).

Clark, A., *Barbarossa – The Russo-German Conflict, 1941–45* (London, Hutchinson, 1965).

Cohen, Stephen, *Bukharin and the Bolshevik Revolution: A Political Biography 1888–1938* (New York, Vintage Books, 1975).

Conquest, Robert, *The Great Terror: Stalin's Purge of the Thirties* (Harmondsworth, Pelican, 1971).

Conquest, Robert, *Inside Stalin's Secret Police: NKVD Politics, 1936–39* (London, Macmillan, 1985).

Conquest, Robert, *The Harvest of Sorrow: Soviet Collectivisation and the Terror Famine* (London, Hutchinson, 1986).

Conquest, Robert, *Stalin and the Kirov Murder* (London, Hutchinson, 1988).

Dallin, Alexander, *German Rule in Russia, 1941–45: A Study in Occupation Policies* (London, Macmillan, 1957; 2nd edn, 1981).

Dallin, Alexander and George W. Breslauer, *Political Terror in Communist Systems* (Stanford, CA, Stanford University Press, 1970).

Daniels, Robert V. (ed.), *The Stalin Revolution*, 3rd edn (Lexington, MA, D. C. Heath & Co., 1990).

Danilov, Viktor, *Rural Russia under the New Regime* (London, Hutchinson, 1988).

Davies, R. W., *The Industrialisation of Soviet Russia*: Vol. 1, *The Socialist Offensive: The Collectivisation of Soviet Agriculture, 1929–1930*; Vol. 2, *The Soviet Collective Farm*; Vol. 3, *The Soviet Economy in Turmoil, 1929–30*; Vol. 4, *Crisis and Progress in the Soviet Economy, 1931–33* (London, Macmillan, 1980).

Davies, Sarah, *Popular Opinion in Stalin's Russia: Terror, Propaganda and Dissent, 1934–41* (Cambridge, Cambridge University Press, 1997).

Day, Richard, *Leon Trotsky and the Politics of Economic Isolation* (Cambridge, Cambridge University Press, 1973).

Deutscher, Isaac, *The Prophet Armed: Trotsky, 1879–1921*; *The Prophet Unarmed: Trotsky, 1921–1929*; *The Prophet Outcast: Trotsky, 1929–1940* (Oxford, Oxford University Press, 1954/59/63).

Deutscher, Isaac, *Stalin: A Political Biography* (Harmondsworth, Penguin, 1966).

Deutscher, Isaac (ed.), *The Age of Permanent Revolution: A Trotsky Anthology* (New York, Dell Publishing, 1964).

Deutscher, Isaac and David King, *The Great Purges* (Oxford, Blackwell, 1984).

Djilas, Milovan, *Conversations with Stalin* (Harmondsworth, Pelican, 1962).

Dunham, Vera, *In Stalin's Time* (Cambridge, MA, Harvard University Press, 1979).

Dunmore, Tim, *The Stalinist Command Economy: The Soviet State Apparatus and Economic Policy, 1945–53* (London, Macmillan, 1980).

Dunmore, Tim, *Soviet Politics, 1945–1953* (London, Macmillan, 1984).

Ellenstein, Jean, *The Stalin Phenomenon* (London, Lawrence & Wishart, 1976).

Erlich, A., *The Soviet Industrialisation Debates, 1924–1928* (Cambridge, MA, Harvard University Press, 1975).

Fainsod, Merle, *Smolensk under Soviet Rule* (Cambridge, MA, Harvard University Press, 1958).

Filtzer, Donald, *Soviet Workers and Stalinist Industrialization* (London, Pluto Press, 1986).

Fitzpatrick, Sheila, *Stalin's Peasants: Resistance and Survival in the Russian Village after Collectivisation* (Oxford, Oxford University Press, 1994).

Fitzpatrick, S. (ed.), *Cultural Revolution in Russia, 1928–1931* (Bloomington, IN, and London, Indiana University Press, 1978).

Gerschenkron, Alexander, *Economic Backwardness in Historical Perspective* (Cambridge, MA, Harvard University Press, 1966).

Getty, J. Arch, 'Party and Purge in Smolensk: 1933–1937', *Slavic Review*, Vol. 42, No. 1 (Spring 1983), pp. 60–79.

Getty, J. Arch, *Origins of the Great Purges: The Soviet Communist Party Reconsidered, 1933–1938* (Cambridge, Cambridge University Press, 1985).

Getty, J. Arch and Roberta T. Manning (eds), *Stalinist Terror: New Perspectives* (Cambridge, Cambridge University Press, 1993).

Gill, Graeme, *The Origins of the Stalinist Political System* (Cambridge, Cambridge University Press, 1990).

Ginzburg, Eugenia, *Into the Whirlwind* (Harmondsworth, Penguin, 1968).

Gorbatov, A. V., *Years off my Life* (London, Constable, 1964).

Gouldner, Alvin W., 'Stalinism: A Study of Internal Colonialism', *Telos*, No. 34 (Winter 1977/78), pp. 5–48.

Grey, Ian, *Stalin: Man of History* (London, Weidenfeld & Nicolson, 1979).

Grossman, Vasily, *Forever Flowing* (London, Collins, 1988).

Grossman, Vasily, *Life and Fate* (London, Collins Harvill, 1995).

Hahn, Werner G., *Postwar Soviet Politics: The Fall of Zhdanov and the Defeat of Moderation, 1946–53* (Ithaca, NY, and London, Cornell University Press, 1982).

Harrison, Mark, *Soviet Planning in Peace and War, 1938–1945* (Cambridge, Cambridge University Press, 1985).

Haynes, M., *Nikolai Bukharin and the Transition from Capitalism to Socialism* (London, Croom Helm, 1985).

Hingley, R., *Joseph Stalin: Man and Legend* (London, Hutchinson, 1974).

Holloway, David, *Stalin and the Bomb* (New Haven, CT, Yale University Press, 1994).

Hughes, James, 'Patrimonialism and the Stalinist System: The Case of S. I. Syrtsov', *Europe–Asia Studies*, Vol. 48, No. 4 (June 1996), pp. 551–68.

Jasny, Naum, *Soviet Industrialization, 1928–1952* (Chicago, IL, Chicago University Press, 1961).

Katkov, George, *The Trial of Bukharin* (London, Batsford, 1969).

Kershaw, Ian and Moshe Lewin (eds), *Nazism, Stalinism and Dictatorship* (Cambridge, Cambridge University Press, 1997).

Khlevniuk, Oleg V., *In Stalin's Shadow: The Career of 'Sergo' Ordzhonikidze*, ed. Donald J. Raleigh (New York, M. E. Sharpe, 1995).

Knight, Amy, *Beria: Stalin's First Lieutenant* (Princeton, NJ, Princeton University Press, 1993).

Kotkin, Stephen, *Magnetic Mountain: Stalinism as a Civilisation* (Berkeley, CA, University of California Press, 1995).

Krasso, N. (ed.), *Trotsky: The Great Debate Renewed* (St Louis, MO, New Critics Press, 1972).

Kravchenko, Victor, *I Chose Freedom: The Personal and Political Life of a Soviet Official* (London, Robert Hale Limited, 1947).

Kuromiya, H., *Stalin's Industrial Revolution: Politics and Workers, 1928–32* (Cambridge, Cambridge University Press, 1988).

Lampert, N. and Gabor T. Rittersporn (eds), *Stalinism: Its Nature and Aftermath* (London, Macmillan, 1992).

Larina, Anna, *This I Cannot Forget: The Memoirs of Nikolai Bukharin's Widow* (London, Hutchinson, 1994).

Lewin, Moshe, *Russian Peasants and Soviet Power* (Evanston, IL, Northwestern University Press, 1968).

Lewin, Moshe, *Lenin's Last Struggle* (London, Pluto, 1975).

Lewin, Moshe, *Political Undercurrents in Soviet Economic Debates: From Bukharin to the Modern Reformers* (London, Pluto, 1975).

Lewin, Moshe, 'Society and the Stalinist State in the Period of the Five-Year Plans', *Social History*, Vol. 1, No. 2 (May 1976), pp. 139–75.

Lewin, Moshe, 'The Social Background of Stalinism', in R. C. Tucker (ed.), *Stalinism: Essays in Historical Interpretation* (New York, W. W. Norton, 1977).

Lewin, Moshe, *The Making of the Soviet System: Essays in the Social History of Inter-war Russia* (London, Methuen, 1985).

Linz, Susan J. (ed.), *The Impact of World War II on the Soviet Union* (Totowa, NJ, Rowman & Allanheld, 1985).

McCagg, W. O., *Stalin Embattled, 1943–48* (Detroit, MI, Wayne State University Press, 1978).

McCauley, Martin, *Stalin and Stalinism*, 2nd edn (Harlow, Longman, 1995).

McNeal, Robert H., 'The Decisions of the CPSU in the Great Purges', *Soviet Studies*, Vol. 23, No. 2 (October 1971), pp. 177–85.

McNeal, Robert H., *Stalin: Man and Ruler* (London, Macmillan, 1988).

Mandelstam, N., *Hope against Hope: A Memoir* and *Hope Abandoned* (Harmondsworth, Penguin, 1970).

Medvedev, Roy, *On Stalin and Stalinism* (Oxford, Oxford University Press, 1979).

Medvedev, Roy, *All Stalin's Men* (Oxford, Basil Blackwell, 1983).

Medvedev, Roy, *Let History Judge: The Origin and Consequences of Stalinism*, revised and expanded edn (Oxford, Oxford University Press, 1989).

Moore Jr, Barrington, *Soviet Politics: The Dilemma of Power* (Cambridge, MA, Harvard University Press, 1950).

Moore Jr, Barrington, *Terror and Progress USSR: Some Sources of Change and Stability in the Soviet Dictatorship*, (New York, Harper & Row, 1966).

Nicolaevsky, Boris, *Power and the Soviet Elite* (New York, Praeger, 1965) includes 'Letter of an Old Bolshevik' (Bukharin).

Nove, Alec, *Economic Rationality and Soviet Politics, or Was Stalin Really Necessary?* (London, George Allen & Unwin, 1964).

Nove, Alec, *Stalinism and after: The Road to Gorbachev*, 3rd edn (London, Unwin Hyman, 1988).

Orlov, Alexander, *The Secret History of Stalin's Crimes* (London, Jarrold's, 1954).

Ra'anan, Gavriel D., *International Policy Formation in the USSR: Factional 'Debates' during the Zhdanovshchina* (Hamden, CT, Archon Books, The Shoestring Press, 1983).

Rassweiler, Anne D., *The Generation of Power: The History of Dneprostroi* (Oxford, Oxford University Press, 1989).

Reiman, Michael, *The Birth of Stalinism: The USSR on the Eve of the 'Second Revolution'* (London, I. B. Tauris, 1987).

Rigby, T. H. (ed.), *Stalin* (Englewood Cliffs, NJ, Prentice-Hall, 1966).

Rigby, T. H., 'Stalinism and the Mono-Organisational Society', in R. C. Tucker (ed.), *Stalinism: Essays in Historical Interpretation* (New York, W. W. Norton, 1977).

Rigby, T. H., 'Was Stalin a Disloyal Patron?', *Soviet Studies*, Vol. 38, No. 3 (July 1986), pp. 311–24.

Rittersporn, G. T., 'Rethinking Stalinism', *Russian History/Histoire Russe*, Vol. 11, No. 4 (Winter 1984), pp. 343–61.

Roberts, Geoffrey, *The Unholy Alliance: Stalin's Pact with Hitler* (London, I. B. Tauris, 1989).

Rosefielde, Steven, 'An Assessment of the Sources and Uses of Gulag Forced Labour 1929–1956', *Soviet Studies*, Vol. 33, No. 1 (January 1981), pp. 51–87.

Rosefielde, Steven, 'Excess Mortality in the Soviet Union: A Reconsideration of the Demographic Consequences of Forced Industrialisation 1929–1949', *Soviet Studies*, Vol. 35, No. 3 (July 1983), pp. 385–409.

Rosefielde, Steven, 'Incriminating Evidence: Excess Deaths and Forced Labour under Stalin: A Final Reply to My Critics', *Soviet Studies*, Vol. 39, No. 2 (April 1987), pp. 292–313.

Rosenberg, Suzanne, *A Soviet Odyssey* (Oxford, Oxford University Press, 1989).

Rosenberg, William G. and Lewis H. Siegelbaum (eds), *Social Dimensions of Soviet Industrialisation* (Bloomington, IN, Indiana University Press, 1993).

Rosenfeldt, N. E., *Knowledge and Power: The Role of Stalin's Secret Chancellery in the Soviet System of Government* (Copenhagen, Rosenkilde and Bagger, 1978).

Salisbury, H. E., *The 900 Days: The Siege of Leningrad* (London, Macmillan, 1969).

Scott, John, *Behind the Urals: An American Worker in Russia's City of Steel* (London, Secker & Warburg, 1942).

Serge, Victor, *Memoirs of a Revolutionary*, trans. Peter Sedgwick (London, Writers and Readers, 1984).

Siegelbaum, Lewis H., *Stakhanovism and the Politics of Productivity in the USSR, 1935–1941* (Cambridge, Cambridge University Press, 1988).

Solzhenitsyn, Alexander, *The Gulag Archipelago: An Experiment in Literary Investigation*, 3 vols (Glasgow, Collins-Fontana, 1974–76).

Souvarine, Boris, *Stalin: A Critical Survey of Bolshevism* (London, Secker & Warburg, n.d.).

Thorniley, Daniel, *The Rise and Fall of the Soviet Rural Communist Party, 1927–39* (London, Macmillan, 1988).

Tokaev, Grigori, *Betrayal of an Ideal* (Bloomington, IN, Indiana University Press, 1955).

Tolstoy, N., *Stalin's Secret War* (London, Cape, 1981).

Trotsky, L., *Stalin* (London, Hollis and Carter, 1947).

Trotsky, L., *The Revolution Betrayed* (London, New Park Publications, 1973).

Tucker, R. C., *The Soviet Political Mind: Stalinism and Post-Stalin Change*, revised edn (London, George Allen & Unwin, 1972).

Tucker, R. C., *Stalin as a Revolutionary, 1879–1929* (London, Chatto & Windus, 1974).

Tucker, R. C., *Stalinism: Essays in Historical Interpretation* (New York, W. W. Norton, 1977).

Ulam, Adam, *Expansion and Coexistence: Soviet Foreign Policy, 1917–1973* (New York, Holt, Rinehart & Winston, 1974).

Ulam, Adam B., *Stalin: The Man and His Era* (London, I. B. Tauris, 1974/88).

Urban, G. R. (ed.), *Stalinism: Its Impact on Russia and the World* (Aldershot, Wildwood House, 1985).

Viola, Lynne, *The Best Sons of the Fatherland: Workers in the Vanguard of Soviet Collectivisation* (New York, Oxford University Press, 1987).

Vizulis, Izidors, *The Molotov–Ribbentrop Pact of 1939: The Baltic Case* (London, Praeger Publishers, 1990).

Von Laue, T. H., *Why Lenin? Why Stalin?*, 2nd edn (Philadelphia, PA, Lippincott, 1971).

Voznesensky, N., *The Economy of the Soviet Union during World War II* (Moscow, 1948).

Ward, Chris, *Stalin's Russia* (London, Edward Arnold, 1998).

Weissberg, Alexander, *The Accused* (New York, Simon & Schuster, 1951).

Werth, A., *Russia at War, 1941–45* (London, Barrie & Rockcliff, 1964).

Wheatcroft, Stephen, 'On Assessing the Size of Forced Concentration Camp Labour in the Soviet Union, 1929–56', *Soviet Studies*, Vol. 33, No. 2 (April 1981), pp. 265–95.

Wheatcroft, Stephen, 'A Note on Steven Rosefielde's Calculations of Excess Mortality in the USSR, 1929–49', *Soviet Studies*, Vol. 34, No. 2 (April 1984), pp. 277–81.

Wheatcroft, Stephen, 'The Scale and Nature of German and Soviet Repression and Mass Killings, 1930–1945', *Europe–Asia Studies*, Vol. 48, No. 8 (December 1996), pp. 1319–54.

Wolfe, B. (ed.), *Khrushchev and Stalin's Ghost* (London, Atlantic Press, 1957).

Wood, Alan, *Stalin and Stalinism* (London, Routledge, 1990).

Zubok, Vladislav and Constantine Pleshakov, *Inside the Kremlin's Cold War: From Stalin to Khrushchev* (Cambridge, MA, Harvard University Press, 1997).

4 KHRUSHCHEV AND DESTALINISATION

Bialer, Seweryn, *Stalin's Successors: Leadership, Stability and Change in the Soviet Union* (Cambridge, Cambridge University Press, 1980).

Breslauer, George, 'Khrushchev Reconsidered', *Problems of Communism*, Vol. 25, No. 3 (September–October 1976), pp. 18–33; also in S. F. Cohen, A. Rabinowich and R. Sharlet (eds), *The Soviet Union since Stalin* (London, Macmillan, 1980).

Breslauer, George, *Khrushchev and Brezhnev as Leaders: Building Authority in Soviet Politics* (London, George Allen & Unwin, 1982).

Brinkley, George A., 'Khrushchev Remembered: On the Theory of Soviet Statehood', *Soviet Studies*, Vol. 24, No. 3 (1972–73), pp. 387–401.

Brumberg, Abraham (ed.), *Russia under Khrushchev* (London, Methuen, 1982).

Chotiner, B. A., *Khrushchev's Party Reform: Coalition Building and Institutional Innovation* (Westport, CT, Greenwood Press, 1984).

Cohen, S. F., 'The Friends and Foes of Change: Reformism and Conservatism in the Soviet Union', in S. F. Cohen *et al.* (eds), *The Soviet Union since Stalin*; revised version in S. F. Cohen, *Rethinking the Soviet Experience* (Oxford, Oxford University Press, 1985).

Crankshaw, Edward, *Khrushchev's Russia* (Harmondsworth, Penguin, 1959).

Deutscher, Isaac, *Russia after Stalin* (London, Hamish Hamilton, 1953).

Frankland, Mark, *Khrushchev* (Harmondsworth, Penguin, 1966).

Goudoever, Albert P. van, *The Limits of Destalinisation in the Soviet Union: Political Rehabilitations in the Soviet Union since Stalin* (London, Routledge, 1986).

Grossman, Joan Delaney, 'Khrushchev's Anti-religious Policy and the Campaign of 1954', *Soviet Studies*, Vol. 24, No. 3 (1972–73), pp. 374–86.

Johnson, Priscilla and Leo Labedz, *Khrushchev and the Arts, 1962–64* (Cambridge, MA, MIT Press, 1965).

Khrushchev, Nikita, *Khrushchev Remembers*, includes the 'Secret Speech', introduced by Edward Crankshaw (London, Little, Brown, 1971).

Khrushchev, Nikita, *Khrushchev Remembers: The Glasnost Tapes*, foreword by Strobe Talbott (Boston, MA, Little, Brown, 1990).

Khrushchev, Sergei, *Khrushchev on Khrushchev* (Boston, MA, Little, Brown, 1991).

Leonhard, Wolfgang, *The Kremlin since Stalin* (New York, Praeger, 1962).

Linden, Carl A., *Khrushchev and the Soviet Leadership, 1957–1964* (Baltimore, MD, Johns Hopkins Press, 1966).

McCauley, Martin, *Khrushchev and the Development of Soviet Agriculture: The Debate on the Virgin Lands, 1953–64* (London, Macmillan, 1976).

McCauley, Martin, *The Khrushchev Era, 1953–1964* (Harlow, Longman, 1995).

McCauley, Martin (ed.), *Khrushchev and Khrushchevism* (London, Macmillan, 1987).
Medvedev, Roy, *Khrushchev*, trans. Brian Pearce (Oxford, Basil Blackwell, 1982).
Medvedev, Roy and Zhores Medvedev, *Khrushchev: The Years in Power* (Oxford, Oxford University Press, 1977).
Miller, R. F. and F. Feher (eds), *Khrushchev and the Communist World* (London, Croom Helm, 1984).
Pethybridge, R. W., *A Key to Soviet Politics: The Crisis of the Anti-party Group* (New York, Praeger, 1962).
Pethybridge, R. W., *A History of Post-war Russia* (London, Allen & Unwin, 1966).
Schapiro, Leonard (ed.), *The USSR and the Future: An Analysis of the New Programme of the CPSU* (New York, Praeger, 1963).
Tatu, Michel, *Power in the Kremlin: From Khrushchev's Decline to Collective Leadership* (Glasgow, Collins, 1969).
Tompson, William J., *Khrushchev: A Political Life* (London, Macmillan, 1995).
Werth, Alexander, *The Khrushchev Phase* (London, Robert Hale, 1961).
Wolfe, B. (ed.), *Khrushchev and Stalin's Ghost* (London, Greenwood Press, 1983).

5 FROM BREZHNEV TO GORBACHEV

Brezhnev

Bialer, Seweryn, *Stalin's Successors: Leadership, Stability and Change in the Soviet Union* (Cambridge, Cambridge University Press, 1980).
Breslauer, George, *Khrushchev and Brezhnev as Leaders: Building Authority in Soviet Politics* (London, George Allen & Unwin, 1982).
Brown, A. amd M. Kaser (eds), *Soviet Policy for the 1980s* (London, Macmillan, 1982).
Brown, A. and M. Kaser (eds), *The Soviet Union since the Fall of Khrushchev*, 2nd edn (London, Macmillan, 1982).
Brzezinski, Z. 'The Soviet Political System: Transformation or Degeneration', *Problems of Communism*, Vol. 15, No. 1 (January–February 1966), pp. 1–15; also in Z, Brzezinski (ed.), *Dilemmas of Change in Soviet Politics* (New York, Columbia University Press, 1969), pp. 1–34.
Bunce, V., 'The Political Economy of the Brezhnev Era', *British Journal of Political Science*, Vol. 13 (April 1983), pp. 129–58.
Bunce, V. and J. Echols 'Soviet Politics in the Brezhnev Era: "Pluralism" or "Corporatism"?', in D. Kelley (ed.), *Soviet Politics in the Brezhnev Era* (New York, Praeger, 1980).
Evans, A., 'Developed Socialism in Soviet Ideology', *Soviet Studies*, Vol. 26, No. 3 (July 1977), pp. 409–28.
Hazan, Baruch A., *From Brezhnev to Gorbachev: Infighting in the Kremlin* (Boulder, CO, Westview Press, 1987).
Hough, J., 'The Soviet Union: Petrification or Pluralism?', *Problems of Communism*, Vol. 21, No. 2 (March–April 1972), pp. 25–45.
Hough, J. 'The Brezhnev Era: The Man and the System', *Problems of Communism*, Vol. 25, No. 2 (March–April 1976), pp. 1–17.
Millar, James R., 'The Little Deal: Brezhnev's Contribution to Acquisitive Socialism', *Slavic Review* (Winter 1985), pp. 694–706.
Strong, J. W. (ed.), *The Soviet Union under Brezhnev and Kosygin* (New York, Van Nostrand Reinhold, 1971).
Veen, Hans-Joachim (ed.), *From Brezhnev to Gorbachev: Domestic Affairs and Soviet Foreign Policy* (Leamington Spa, Berg Publishers, 1987).

Andropov and Chernenko

Andropov, Yuri V., *Speeches and Writings*, 2nd enlarged edn (Oxford, Pergamon Press, 1983).
Beichman, Arnold and Mikhail S. Bernshtam, *Andropov: New Challenge to the West* (New York, Stein and Day, 1983).
Besançon, Alain, 'Andropov and His Soviet Union', *Policy Review*, Vol. 25, No. 1 (Summer 1983), pp. 21–23.
Brown, Archie, 'Andropov: Discipline *and* Reform', *Problems of Communism*, Vol. 32, No. 1 (January–February 1983), pp. 18–31.
Ebon, Martin, *The Andropov File* (London, Sidgwick & Jackson, 1983).
Elliot, Iain, 'Andropov Scrutinised', *Survey*, Vol. 28, No. 1 (Spring 1984), pp. 61–67.

Goodman, Elliot R., 'The Brezhnev–Andropov Legacy', *Survey*, Vol. 28, No. 2 (Spring 1984), pp. 34–69.

Heller, M., 'Andropov: A Retrospective View', *Survey*, Vol. 28, No. 1, (Spring 1984), pp. 46–60.

Hough, J. F., 'Andropov's First Year', *Problems of Communism*, Vol. 32, No. 6 (November–December 1983), pp. 49–64.

McCauley, Martin (ed.), *The Soviet Union after Brezhnev* (London, Heinemann, 1983).

Medvedev, Zhores, *Andropov: His Life and Death* (Oxford, Basil Blackwell, 1984).

Meissner, Boris, 'The Transition in the Kremlin', *Problems of Communism*, Vol. 32, No. 1 (January–February 1983), pp. 8–17.

Odom, W. E., 'Choice and Change in Soviet Politics', *Problems of Communism*, Vol. 32, No. 3 (May–June 1983).

Parker, John, *Kremlin in Transition*, Vol. 1 (London, Unwin Hyman, 1991).

Shtromas, A. *The Soviet Union in the 1980s* (Brighton, Wheatsheaf, 1987).

Steele, J. and E. Abraham, *Andropov in Power* (Oxford, Basil Blackwell, 1983).

Sturman, D., 'Chernenko and Andropov: Ideological Perspectives', *Survey*, Vol. 28, No. 1 (Spring 1984), pp. 9–21.

Zemtsov, Ilya, *Chernenko: The Last Bolshevik* (London, Transaction, 1989).

Zlotnik, Mark D., 'Chernenko's Platform', *Problems of Communism*, Vol. 31, No. 6 (November–December 1982), pp. 70–80.

Zlotnik, Mark D., 'Chernenko Succeeds', *Problems of Communism*, Vol. 33, No. 2 (March–April 1984), pp. 17–31.

Gorbachev

Aganbegyan, Abel, *The Challenge: Economics of Perestroika* (London, Hutchinson, 1988).

Ali, Tariq, *Revolution from above: Where is the Soviet Union Going?* (London, Hutchinson, 1988).

Aslund, Anders, *Gorbachev's Struggle for Economic Reform* (London, Pinter, 1989).

Balzer, Harley D. (ed.), *Five Years that Shook the World: Gorbachev's Unfinished Revolution* (Boulder, CO/Oxford, Westview Press, 1991).

Bialer, Seweryn (ed.), *Politics, Society and Nationality inside Gorbachev's Russia* (Boulder, CO, Westview Press, 1989).

Blacker, Coit D., *Hostage to Revolution: Gorbachev and Soviet Security Policy, 1985–1991* (New York, Council on Foreign Relations Press, 1993).

Boettke, Peter J., *Why Perestroika Failed: The Politics and Economics of Socialist Transformation* (London and New York, Routledge, 1993).

Boldin, Valery, *Ten Years that Shook the World* (London, Basic Books, 1994).

Breslauer, George, 'Evaluating Gorbachev as Leader', *Soviet Economy*, Vol. 5, No. 4 (1989), pp. 299–340.

Brown, Archie, 'Gorbachev: New Man in the Kremlin', *Problems of Communism*, Vol. 34, No. 3 (May–June 1985), pp. 1–23.

Brown, Archie, 'Change in the Soviet Union', *Foreign Affairs*, Vol. 64, No. 5 (1986), pp. 1048–65.

Brown, Archie, 'Gorbachev and the Reform of the Soviet System', *Political Quarterly*, Vol. 58, No. 2 (April–June 1987), pp. 139–51.

Brown, Archie, 'Soviet Political Developments and Prospects', *World Policy Journal*, Vol. 4, No. 1 (Winter 1987), pp. 55–87.

Brown, Archie, *The Gorbachev Factor* (Oxford, Oxford University Press, 1996).

Brown, Archie (ed.), *New Thinking in Soviet Politics* (London, Macmillan, 1992), revised as *The Demise of Marxism–Leninism in Russia, 1985–91* (London, Macmillan, 1997).

Cerf, Christopher and Marina Albee, *Voices of Glasnost: Letters from the Soviet People to Ogonyok Magazine, 1987–1990* (London, Kyle Cathie, 1990).

Chiesa, Giulietto with Douglas Taylor Northrop, *Transition to Democracy: Political Change in the Soviet Union, 1987–1991* (Hanover, University Press of New England, 1993).

Connor, Walter D., *The Accidental Proletariat: Workers, Politics, and Crisis in Gorbachev's Russia* (Princeton, NJ, Princeton University Press, 1991).

Cook, Linda J., *The Soviet Social Contract and Why it Failed: Welfare Policy and Workers' Politics from Brezhnev to Yeltsin* (Cambridge, MA, Harvard University Press, 1993).

Cooper, Leo, *Soviet Reforms and Beyond* (London, Macmillan, 1991).

Crouch, Martin, *Revolution and Evolution: Gorbachev and Soviet Politics* (Oxford, Philip Allan, 1989).

Dallin, Alexander and Gail W. Lapidus (eds), *The Soviet System: From Crisis to Collapse*, revised edn (Oxford, Westview Press, 1994).

Dellenbrant, Jan Ake and Ronald J. Hill (eds), *Gorbachev and Perestroika* (Aldershot, Elgar Publishing, 1989).

Doder, Dusko and Louise Branson, *Gorbachev: Heretic in the Kremlin* (London, Viking, 1990).

Dyker, David A. (ed.), *The Soviet Union under Gorbachev: Prospects for Reform* (London, Croom Helm, 1987).

Feher, Ferenc and Andrew Arato, *Gorbachev* (Cambridge, Polity Press, 1988).

Friedberg, Maurice, *Soviet Society under Gorbachev: Current Trends and the Prospect for Reform* (London, M. E. Sharpe, 1988).

Galeotti, Mark, *Gorbachev and His Revolution* (London, Macmillan, 1997).

Goldfarb, J. C., *Beyond Glasnost* (Chicago, IL, Chicago University Press, 1989).

Gooding, John, 'Gorbachev and Democracy', *Soviet Studies*, Vol. 42, No. 2 (1990), pp. 195–231.

Gooding, John, 'Perestroika and the Russian Revolution of 1991', *Slavonic and East European Review*, Vol. 71, No. 2 (April 1993), pp. 234–56.

Gorbachev, M. S., *Perestroika: New Thinking for Our Country and the World* (London, Collins, 1987).

Gustafson, Thane and Dawn Mann, 'Gorbachev's First Year: Building Power and Authority', *Problems of Communism*, Vol. 35, No. 3 (May–June 1986), pp. 1–19.

Gustafson, Thane and Dawn Mann, 'Gorbachev's Next Gamble', *Problems of Communism*, Vol. 36, No. 4 (July–August 1987), pp. 1–20.

Hart, Gary, *The Second Russian Revolution* (London, Hodder & Stoughton, 1991).

Hazan, Baruch A., *From Brezhnev to Gorbachev: Infighting in the Kremlin* (Boulder, CO, Westview/Praeger, 1987).

Hewett, E. H. and Victor H. Winston (eds), *Milestones in Glasnost and Perestroika: Politics and People* (Washington DC, The Brookings Institution, 1991).

Hewett, E. H. and Victor H. Winston (eds), *Milestones in Glasnost and Perestroika: The Economy* (Washington DC, The Brookings Institution, 1991).

Hough, J. F., 'Gorbachev's Strategy', *Foreign Affairs*, Vol. 64, No. 1 (Fall 1985), pp. 33–55.

Hough, J. F., 'Gorbachev Consolidating Power', *Problems of Communism*, Vol. 36, No. 4 (July–August 1987), pp. 21–43.

Hough, Jerry F., *Democratization and Revolution in the USSR, 1985–1991* (Washington DC, The Brookings Institution, 1997).

Huber, Robert T. and Donald R. Kelley (eds), *Perestroika-era Politics: The New Soviet Legislature and Gorbachev's Political Reforms* (Armonk/London, M. E. Sharpe, 1991).

Jowitt, Ken, 'Gorbachev: Bolshevik or Menshevik?', in Stephen White *et al.* (eds), *Developments in Soviet Politics* (London, Macmillan, 1990), ch. 14.

Juviler, Peter and Hiroshi Kimura (eds), *Gorbachev's Reforms: US and Japanese Assessments* (New York, Aldine, 1988).

Kagarlitsky, Boris, 'The Intelligentsia and the Changes', *New Left Review*, Vol. 164 (July–August 1987), pp. 5–26.

Kagarlitsky, Boris, '*Perestroika*: The Dialectics of Change', *New Left Review*, Vol. 169 (May–June 1988), pp. 63–83.

Kagarlitsky, Boris, *The Thinking Reed* (London, Verso, 1989).

Kagarlitsky, Boris, *Farewell Perestroika* (London, Verso, 1990).

Kagarlitsky, Boris, *The Dialectics of Change* (London, Verso, 1990).

Kagarlitsky, Boris, *The Disintegration of the Monolith* (London, Verso, 1992).

Kaiser, Robert G., 'Gorbachev: Triumph and Failure', *Foreign Affairs*, Vol. 70, No. 2 (Spring 1991), pp. 160–74.

Kaiser, Robert G., *Why Gorbachev Happened: His Triumphs and His Failure* (Hemel Hempstead, Simon & Schuster, 1992).

Lane, David, *Soviet Society under Perestroika* (London, Routledge, 1992).

Lane, David (ed.), *Russia in Flux: The Political and Social Consequences of Reform* (Aldershot, Edward Elgar, 1992).

Laqueur, Walter, *The Long Road to Freedom* (London, Unwin Hyman, 1989).

Lewin, Moshe, *The Gorbachev Phenomenon: A Historical Interpretation* (Berkeley, CA, University of California Press, 1988).

Ligachev, Yegor, *Inside Gorbachev's Kremlin: The Memoirs of Yegor Ligachev* (Boulder, CO, Westview Press, 1996).

Mandel, Ernest, *Beyond Perestroika: The Future of Gorbachev's USSR* (London, Verso, 1989).

McCauley, Martin (ed.), *The Soviet Union under Gorbachev* (London, Macmillan, 1987).

McCauley, Martin (ed.), *Gorbachev and Perestroika* (London, Macmillan, 1990).

Medvedev, Roy and Giulietto Chiesa, *Time of Change: An Insider's View of Russia's Transformation* (London, I. B. Tauris, 1990).

Medvedev, Zhores, *Gorbachev* (Oxford, Basil Blackwell, 1986).

Melville, A. and G. W. Lapidus (eds), *The Glasnost Papers: Voices on Reform from Moscow* (Boulder, CO, Westview Press, 1989).

Merridale, Catherine and Chris Ward (eds), *Perestroika: The Historical Perspective* (London, Edward Arnold, 1991).

Miller, John, *Mikhail Gorbachev and the End of Soviet Power* (London, Macmillan, 1993).

Miller, R. F. *et al.* (eds), *Gorbachev at the Helm: A New Era in Soviet Politics* (London, Croom Helm, 1987).

Nove, Alec, *Glasnost' in Action* (London, Unwin Hyman, 1989).

Palazchenko, Pavel, *My Years with Gorbachev and Shevardnadze: The Memoir of a Soviet Interpreter* (University Park, PA, The Pennsylvania State University Press, 1997).

Ploss, S. L., 'A New Soviet Era?', *Foreign Policy*, Vol. 62 (Spring 1986), pp. 46–60.

Rieber, Alfred J. and Alvin Z. Rubinstein, *Perestroika at the Crossroads* (London, M. E. Sharpe, 1991).

Robinson, Neil, *Ideology and the Collapse of the Soviet System: A Critical History of the Soviet Ideological Discourse* (Aldershot, Edward Elgar, 1995).

Ruge, Gerd, *Gorbachev* (London, Chatto & Windus, 1991).

Sakwa, Richard, 'Gorbachev and the New Soviet Foreign Policy', *Paradigms: The Kent Journal of International Relations*, Vol. 2, No. 1 (June 1988), pp. 18–29.

Sakwa, Richard, 'Commune Democracy and Gorbachev's Reforms', *Political Studies*, Vol. 37, No. 2 (June 1989), pp. 224–43.

Sakwa, Richard, *Gorbachev and His Reforms, 1985–90* (Hemel Hempstead, Philip Allan, 1990).

Schmidt-Hauer, Christian, *Gorbachev: The Path to Power* (London, I. B. Tauris, 1986).

Spring, D. W. (ed.), *The Impact of Gorbachev: The First Phase, 1985–90* (London, Pinter Publishers, 1991).

Urban, Michael E. (ed.), *Ideology and System Change in the USSR and Eastern Europe* (London, Macmillan, 1992).

Walker, Rachel, *Six Years that Changed the World: Perestroika the Impossible Project* (Manchester, Manchester University Press, 1993).

White, Stephen, *After Gorbachev*, 4th edn (Cambridge, Cambridge University Press, 1992).

Zaslavskaya, Tatyana, *The Second Socialist Revolution: An Alternative Soviet Strategy* (London, I. B. Tauris, 1990).

The August 1991 coup and the fall of the USSR

Bonnell, Victoria E., Ann Cooper and Gregory Friedin (eds), *Russia at the Barricades* (Armonk, NY, M. E. Sharpe, 1994).

Coleman, Fred, *The Decline and Fall of the Soviet Empire: Forty Years that Shook the World, from Stalin to Yeltsin* (New York, St Martin's Press, 1997).

Crawshaw, Steve, *Goodbye to the USSR: The Collapse of Soviet Power* (London, Bloomsbury, 1992).

Gorbachev, Mikhail, *The August Coup: The Truth and the Lessons* (London, HarperCollins, 1991).

Grachev, Andrei, *Final Days: The Inside Story of the Collapse of the Soviet Union* (Oxford, Westview Press, 1995).

Lukic, Reneo and Allen Lynch, *Europe from the Balkans to the Urals: The Disintegration of Yugoslavia and the Soviet Union* (Oxford, Oxford University Press/SIPRI, 1996).

McDonnell, Lawrence, *October Revolution* (Staplehurst, Spellmount Limited, 1994).

Matlock, Jack F., *Autopsy on an Empire* (New York, Random House, 1995).

Pankin, Boris, *The Last Hundred Days of the Soviet Union* (London, I. B. Tauris, 1995).

Roxburgh, Angus, *The Second Russian Revolution: The Struggle for Power in the Kremlin* (London, BBC Books, 1991).

Ruge, Gerd, *Der Putsch: Vier Tage, die die Welt veranderten* (Frankfurt, Fischer Taschenbuch Verlag, 1991).

Russian Information Agency, *Putsch. The Diary: Three Days that Collapsed the Empire* (Stevenage, SPA, 1993).

Sakwa, Richard, 'The Revolution of 1991 in Russia: Interpretations of the Moscow Coup', *Coexistence*, Vol. 29, No. 4 (December 1992), pp. 27–67.

Sakwa, Richard, 'A Cleansing Storm: The August Coup and the Triumph of Perestroika', *Journal of Communist Studies*, Vol. 9, No. 1 (Spring 1993), pp. 131–49.

Sixsmith, Martin, *Moscow Coup: The Death of the Soviet System* (London, Simon & Schuster, 1991).

6 THE COMMUNIST PARTY

Blackwell, Robert E., 'Cadres Policy in the Brezhnev Era', *Problems of Communism*, Vol. 28, No. 2 (March–April 1979), pp. 29–42.

CPSU Programme, 1986.

Gill, Graeme, *The Collapse of the Single-party System: The Disintegration of the Communist Party of the Soviet Union* (Cambridge, Cambridge University Press, 1994).

Gill, Graeme (ed.), *The Rules of the CPSU* (London, Macmillan, 1988).

Gill, Graeme and Roderic Pitty, *Power in the Party: The Organization of Power and Central–Republican Relations in the CPSU* (London, Macmillan, 1996).

Hill, R. J., 'Party–State Relations and Soviet Political Development', *British Journal of Political Science*, Vol. 10 (1980), pp. 149–65.

Hill, Ronald J., 'The CPSU: Decline and Collapse', *Irish Slavonic Studies*, No. 12 (1991), pp. 97–119.

Hill, Ronald J., 'The CPSU: From Monolith to Pluralist', *Soviet Studies*, Vol. 43, No. 2 (1991), pp. 217–35.

Hill, R. J. and P. Frank, *The Soviet Communist Party*, 3rd edn (London, George Allen & Unwin, 1986).

Hough, J. F., *The Soviet Prefects: The Local Party Organs in Industrial Decision-making* (Cambridge, MA, Harvard University Press, 1969).

Kassof, A., 'The Administered Society: Totalitarianism without Terror', *World Politics*, Vol. 16, No. 4 (July 1964), pp. 558–75.

Laird, Roy D., *The Politburo: Demographic Trends, Gorbachev and the Future* (Boulder, CO, Westview Press, 1986).

Löwenhardt, J., *The Soviet Politburo* (Edinburgh, Canongate, 1982).

Lowenthal, Richard, 'The Ruling Party in a Mature Society', in Mark G. Field (ed.), *Social Consequences of Modernization in Communist Societies* (Baltimore, MD, Johns Hopkins University Press, 1976), pp. 81–118.

McAuley, Mary, 'Party Recruitment and the Nationalities in the USSR', *British Journal of Political Science*, Vol. 10 (1980), pp. 461–87.

Matthews, Mervyn, 'Inside the CPSU Central Committe (Interview with A. Pravdin)', *Survey*, Vol. 20, No. 4 (Autumn 1974), pp. 94–104.

Millar, James R. (ed.), *Cracks in the Monolith: Party Power in the Brezhnev Era* (London, M. E. Sharpe, 1992).

Miller, J. H., 'The Communist Party: Trends and Problems', in A. Brown and M. Kaser (eds), *Soviet Policy for the 1980s* (London, Macmillan, 1982).

Rigby, T. H., *Communist Party Membership in the USSR, 1917–67* (Princeton, NJ, Princeton University Press, 1968).

Rigby, T. H., 'The Soviet Leadership: Towards a Self-Stabilising Oligarchy?', *Soviet Studies*, Vol. 22 (1970), pp. 167–91.

Sartori, Giovanni, *Parties and Party-systems: A Framework for Analysis* (Cambridge, Cambridge University Press, 1976).

Schapiro, Leonard, *The Communist Party of the Soviet Union*, 2nd edn (London, Methuen, 1970).

Shakhnazarov, Georgi, *The Role of the Communist Party in Socialist Society* (Moscow, Novosti, 1974).

Shevtsov, V. S., *The CPSU and the Soviet State in Developed Socialist Society* (Moscow, Progress, 1978).

Voslenskii, Mikhail, *Nomenklatura: Anatomy of the Soviet Ruling Class* (London, Bodley Head, 1984).

Waller, Michael, *Democratic Centralism: An Historical Commentary* (New York, St Martins Press, 1981).

White, Stephen, 'Rethinking the CPSU', *Soviet Studies*, Vol. 43, No. 3 (1991), pp. 405–28.

White, Stephen and Ian McAllister, 'The CPSU and its Members: Between Communism and Postcommunism', *British Journal of Political Science*, Vol. 26, No. 1 (January 1996), pp. 105–22.

White, Stephen and Daniel Nelson (eds), *Communist Politics: A Reader* (London, Macmillan, 1986), pp. 135–56.

7 THE STRUCTURE OF POWER

Ahdieh, Robert B., *Russia's Constitutional Revolution: Legal Consciousness and the Transition to Democracy, 1985–1996* (University Park, PA, Pennsylvania State University Press, 1997).

Barry, Donald D. (ed.), *Towards the 'Rule of Law' in Russia?: Political and Legal Reform in the Transition Period* (Armonk, NY, M. E. Sharpe, 1992).

Biryukov, Nikolai, and V. M. Sergeev, *Russia's Road to Democracy: Parliament, Communism and Traditional Culture* (Aldershot, Edward Elgar, 1993).

Hahn, Jeffrey W. (ed.), *Democratization in Russia: The Development of Legislative Institutions* (New York, M. E. Sharpe, 1995).

Hill, R., 'Party–State Relations and Soviet Political Development', *British Journal of Political Science*, Vol. 10 (April 1980), pp. 149–95.

Hough, J., 'Centralisation and Decentralisation in the Soviet System', in J. Hough, *The Soviet Union and Social Science Theory* (Cambridge, MA, Harvard University Press, 1977), pp. 159–70.

Hough, J. and M. Fainsod, *How the Soviet Union is Governed* (Cambridge, MA, Harvard University Press, 1979).

Huber, Robert T. (ed.), *Perestroika-era Politics: The New Soviet Legislature and Gorbachev's Political Reforms* (Armonk, NY, M. E. Sharpe, 1992).

Khasbulatov, Ruslan, *The Struggle for Russia: Power and Change in the Democratic Revolution*, ed. Richard Sakwa (London and New York, Routledge, 1993).

Kiernan, Brendan, *The End of Soviet Politics: Elections, Legislatures, and the Demise of the Communist Party* (Boulder, CO, Westview Press, 1993).

Little, D. Richard, 'Legislative Authority in the Soviet Political System', *Slavic Review*, Vol. 30, No. 1 (March 1971), pp. 57–73.

Little, D. Richard, 'Soviet Parliamentary Committees after Khrushchev: Obstacles and Opportunities', *Soviet Studies*, Vol. 24 (July 1972), pp. 41–60.

Matthews, Mervyn, *Soviet Government: A Selection of Official Documents on Internal Policies*, Part 2 (London, Cape, 1974).

Nelson, Daniel and Stephen White (eds), *Communist Legislatures in Comparative Perspective* (London, Macmillan, 1982).

Remington, Thomas F. (ed.), *Parliaments in Transition: The New Legislative Politics in the Former USSR and Eastern Europe* (Boulder, CO, Westview Press, 1994).

Schneider, Eberhard, 'The Discussion of the New All-Union Constitution of the USSR', *Soviet Studies*, Vol. 31, No. 4 (October 1979), pp. 523–41.

Sharlet, Robert, *The New Soviet Constitution of 1977: Analysis and Text* (Brunswick, OH, Kings Cross, 1978).

Sharlet, Robert, 'Constitutional Implementation and the Juridicization of the Soviet System', in D. R. Kelley (ed.), *Soviet Politics in the Brezhnev Era* (New York, Praeger, 1980).

Sharlet, Robert, *Soviet Constitutional Crisis: From De-Stalinisation to Disintegration* (Armonk, NY, M. E. Sharpe, 1992).

Szeftel, M., *The Russian Constitution of April 23 1906* (Brussels, 1976).

Unger, Aryeh L., *Constitutional Developments in the USSR: A Guide to the Soviet Constitutions* (London, Methuen, 1981).

Urban, Michael E., *More Power to the Soviets: The Democratic Revolution in the USSR* (Aldershot, Edward Elgar, 1990).

Vanneman, Peter, *The Supreme Soviet: Politics and the Legislative Process in the Soviet Political System* (Durham, NC, Duke University Press, 1977).

White, Stephen, 'The Supreme Soviet and Budgetary Politics in the USSR', in S. White and D. Nelson (eds), *Communist Politics: A Reader* (London, Macmillan, 1986), pp. 55–72.

Whitefield, Stephen, *Industrial Power and the Soviet State* (Oxford, Oxford University Press, 1993).

8 SECURITY AND JUSTICE

Military

Adelman, Jonathan R., *Prelude to the Cold War: The Tsarist, Soviet and US Armies in the Two World Wars* (London, Lynne Rienner, 1988).

Agursky, M. and H. Adomeit, 'The Soviet Military-industrial Complex', *Survey*, Vol. 24, No. 2 (1979), pp. 106–24

Baev, Pavel, *The Russian Army in a Time of Troubles* (London, Sage, 1996).

Barghoorn, F. and R. Kolkowicz, chapters in H. G. Skilling and F. Griffiths (eds), *Interest Groups in Soviet Politics* (Princeton, NJ, Princeton University Press, 1971).

Bluth, Christoph, *The Collapse of Soviet Military Power* (Aldershot, Dartmouth, 1995).

Colton, Timothy, *Commissars, Commanders and Civilian Authority: The Structure of Soviet Military Politics* (Cambridge, MA, Harvard University Press, 1979).

Colton, Timothy, 'The Impact of the Military on Soviet Society', in S. White and D. Nelson (eds), *Communist Politics: A Reader* (London, Macmillan, 1986), pp. 243–59.

Colton, Timothy J. and Thane Gustafson (eds), *Soldiers and the Soviet State: Civil–Military Relations from Brezhnev to Gorbachev* (Princeton, NJ, Princeton University Press, 1990).

Currie, Kenneth M., *Soviet Military Politics: Contemporary Issues* (New York, Paragon House, 1992).

Galeotti, Mark, *The Age of Anxiety: Security and Politics in Soviet and Post-Soviet Russia* (London, Longman, 1994).

Hasegawa, T., 'Soviets on Nuclear-war Fighting', *Problems of Communism*, Vol. 35, No. 4 (July–August 1986), pp. 68–79.
Herspring, Dale, *The Soviet High Command* (Princeton, NJ, Princeton University Press, 1990).
Herspring, D. R. and I. Volgyes (eds), *Civilian–Military Relations in Communist Systems* (Boulder, CO, Westview Press, 1978).
Holloway, David, *The Soviet Union and the Arms Race* (New Haven, CT, Yale University Press, 1983).
Holloway, David and T. J. Sharp (eds), *The Warsaw Pact: Alliance in Transition?* (London, Macmillan, 1984).
Jones, Ellen, *Red Army and Society: A Sociology of the Soviet Military* (London, George Allen & Unwin, 1985).
Kolkowicz, Roman, 'The Military and Soviet Foreign Policy', in R. Kanet (ed.), *Soviet Foreign Policy in the 1980s* (New York, Praeger, 1982).
Kolkowicz, Roman, 'The Political Role of the Soviet Military', in J. L. Nogee (ed.), *Soviet Politics: Russia after Brezhnev* (New York, Praeger, 1985).
Larabee, F. Stephen, 'Gorbachev and the Soviet Military', *Foreign Affairs*, Vol. 66, No. 5 (Summer 1988), pp. 1002–26.
Leebaert, Derek (ed.), *Soviet Military Thinking* (London, George Allen & Unwin, 1981).
Lepingwell, John, 'Soviet Civil–Military Relations and the August Coup', *World Politics*, Vol. 44, No. 4 (July 1992), pp. 539–72.
Odom, W. E., 'The "Militarisation" of Soviet Society', *Problems of Communism*, Vol. 25, No. 5 (September–October 1976), pp. 34–51.
Sadykiewicz, M., 'Soviet Military Politics', *Survey*, Vol. 26, No. 1 (Winter 1982), pp. 179–210.
Scott, H. F. and W. F. Scott, *The Armed Forces of the USSR*, 2nd rev. edn (Boulder, CO, Westview Press, 1984).
Simes, D. K., 'The Military and Militarism in Soviet Society', *International Security*, Vol. 6, No. 3 (1980–81), pp. 123–43.
Spielman, Karl F., 'Defence Industrialists in the USSR', *Problems of Communism*, Vol. 25, No. 5 (September–October 1976), pp. 52–69.
Warner, Edward L., *The Military in Contemporary Soviet Politics* (New York, Praeger, 1977).

KGB

Albats, Yevgenia, *KGB: State within a State: The Secret Police and its Hold on Russia's Past, Present and Future* (London, I. B. Tauris, 1995).
Barron, John, *KGB Today: The Hidden Hand* (London, Hodder & Stoughton, 1984).
Conquest, R., *The Soviet Police System* (New York, Praeger, 1968).
Corson, W. R. and R. T. Crowley, *The New KGB: Engine of Soviet Power* (Brighton, Wheatsheaf, 1985).
Dallin, A. and G. W. Breslauer, *Political Terror in Communist Systems* (Stanford, CA, Stanford University Press, 1970).
Hingley, Ronald, *The Russian Secret Police* (London, Hutchinson, 1970).
Knight, Amy, *The KGB: Police and Politics in the Soviet Union* (London, Unwin Hyman, 1988).
Knight, Amy, *Spies without Cloaks: The KGB's Successors* (Princeton, NJ, Princeton University Press, 1996).
Leggett, George H., *The Cheka: Lenin's Political Police* (Oxford, Oxford University Press, 1981).
Penkovsky, Oleg, *The Penkovsky Papers* (London, Collins, 1965).
Waller, J. Michael, *Secret Empire: The KGB in Russia Today* (Oxford, Westview Press, 1994).
Wolin, S. and R. Slusser, *The Soviet Secret Police* (London, Methuen, 1957).

Justice

Barry, D., G. Ginsburgs and P. Maggs (eds), *Soviet Law after Stalin* (Leiden, Sijthoff, 1977–79).
Berman, Harold, *Justice in the USSR: An Interpretation of Soviet Law*, rev. edn (Cambridge, MA, Harvard University Press, 1966).
Butler, W. E., *Soviet Law* (London, Butterworth, 1983).
Feldbrugge, F. and W. Simon (eds), *Perspectives on Soviet Law for the 1980s* (The Hague, Martinus Nijhoff, 1982).
Feofanov, Yuri and Donald D. Barry, *Politics and Justice in Russia: Major Trials of the Post-Stalin Era* (New York, M. E. Sharpe, 1996).
Huskey, Eugene, *Russian Lawyers and the Soviet State: The Origins and Development of the Soviet Bar, 1917–1939* (Princeton, NJ, Princeton University Press, 1986).

Ioffe, Olimpiad S., *Soviet Law and Soviet Reality* (Dordrecht, Martinus Nijhoff Publishers, 1985).

Ioffe, Olimpiad S. and Peter B. Maggs, *Soviet Law in Theory and Practice* (London, Oceana Publications, 1983).

Juviler, Peter, *Revolutionary Law and Order* (New York, Free Press, 1976).

Shelley, Louise I., *Policing Soviet Society: The Evolution of State Control* (London, Routledge, 1995).

Solomon, Peter, *Soviet Criminologists and Criminal Policy* (New York, Columbia University Press, 1978).

Solomon, Peter, 'Local Political Power and Soviet Criminal Justice, 1922–41', *Soviet Studies*, Vol. 37 (July 1985), pp. 305–29.

Solomon, Peter H. (ed.), *Reforming Justice in Russia, 1864–1994: Power, Culture and the Limits of Legal Order* (New York, M. E. Sharpe, 1997).

Vaksberg, Arkady, *The Soviet Mafia* (London, Weidenfeld & Nicolson, 1991).

Van den Berg, Ger P., *The Soviet System of Justice: Figures and Policy* (Dordrecht, Martinus Nijhoff Publishers, 1985).

9 LOCAL GOVERNMENT AND PARTICIPATION

Local soviets and administration

Andrusz, Greg, *Housing and Urban Development in the USSR* (London, Macmillan, 1984).

Cattell, David T., *Leningrad: A Case History of Soviet Urban Government* (New York, Praeger, 1968).

Friedgut, T. and J. Hahn (eds), Introduction to *Local Power and Post-Soviet Politics* (Armonk, NY, M. E. Sharpe, 1994).

Frolic, B. Michael, 'Decision-making in Soviet Cities', *American Political Science Review*, Vol. 66, No. 1 (March 1972), pp. 38–52.

Hill, Ronald J., 'Patterns of Deputy Selection to Local Soviets', *Soviet Studies*, Vol. 25 (1973), pp. 196–212.

Hill, Ronald J., *Soviet Political Elites: The Case of Tiraspol* (London, Martin Robertson, 1977).

Hough, Jerry F., *The Soviet Prefects: Local Party Organs in Industrial Decision-making* (Cambridge, MA, Harvard University Press, 1969).

Jacobs, Everett M., *Soviet Local Politics and Government* (London, George Allen & Unwin, 1983).

Lewis, Carol W. and S. Sternheimer, *Soviet Urban Management* (New York, Praeger, 1979).

Morton, H. W. and R. C. Stuart, *The Contemporary Soviet City* (London, Macmillan, 1984).

Nelson, Daniel N. (ed.), *Local Politics in Communist Countries* (Lexington, KY, University Press of Kentucky, 1980).

Oliver, J. H., 'Turnover and Family Circles in Soviet Administration', *Slavic Review*, No. 3 (September 1973), pp. 527–45.

Ross, Cameron, *Local Government in the Soviet Union* (London, Croom Helm, 1987).

Smith, Gordon B. (ed.), *Public Policy and Administration in the Soviet Union* (New York, Praeger, 1980).

Stewart, Philip D., *Political Power in the Soviet Union: A Study of Decision-making in Stalingrad* (Indianapolis, IN, and New York, Bobbs-Merrill, 1968).

Taubman, William, *Governing Soviet Cities: Bureaucratic Politics and Urban Development in the USSR* (New York, Praeger, 1973).

Urban, Michael E., 'Information and Participation in Soviet Local Government', *The Journal of Politics*, Vol. 44 (1982), pp. 64–85.

Urban, Michael E., *The Ideology of Administration: American and Soviet Cases* (Albany, NY, SUNY Press, 1982).

Urban, Michael E., *More Power to the Soviets: The Democratic Revolution in the USSR* (Aldershot, Edward Elgar, 1990).

Elections

Berezkin, A. V. *et al.*, 'The Geography of the 1989 Elections of People's Deputies of the USSR', *Soviet Geography*, Vol. 30, No. 8 (October 1989), pp. 607–34.

Colton, Timothy J., 'The Politics of Democratisation: The Moscow Election of 1990', *Soviet Economy*, Vol. 6, No. 4 (October–December 1990), pp. 285–344.

Furtak, Robert K. (ed.), *Elections in Socialist States* (London, Harvester Wheatsheaf, 1990).

Gilison, J. M., 'Soviet Elections as a Measure of Dissent: The Missing One Per Cent', *American Political Science Review*, Vol. 62 (1968), pp. 814–26.

Hahn, Jeffrey W., 'An Experiment in Competition: The 1987 Elections to the Local Soviets', *Slavic Review*, Vol. 47, No. 3 (Fall 1988), pp. 434–47.

Hahn, Werner G., 'Electoral "Choice" in the Soviet Bloc', *Problems of Communism*, Vol. 36, No. 2 (March–April 1987), pp. 29–39.

Helf, Gavin and Jeffrey W. Hahn, 'Old Dogs and New Tricks: Party Elites in the Russian Regional Elections of 1990', *Slavic Review*, Vol. 51, No. 3 (Fall 1992), pp. 511–30.

Hill, Ronald J., 'Soviet Literature on Electoral Reform', *Government and Opposition*, Vol. 11, No. 4 (October 1976), pp. 481–95.

Hill, Ronald J., 'The CPSU in a Soviet Election Campaign', *Soviet Studies*, Vol. 28, No. 4 (October 1976), pp. 590–8.

Jacobs, E. M., 'Soviet Local Elections: What They Are and What They Are Not', *Soviet Studies*, Vol. 22 (1970), pp. 61–76.

Kiernan, Brendan and Joseph Aistrup, 'The 1989 Elections to the Congress of People's Deputies in Moscow', *Soviet Studies*, Vol. 43, No. 6 (1991), pp. 1049–64.

Pravda, Alex, 'Elections in Communist Party States', in S. White and D. Nelson (eds), *Communist Politics: A Reader* (London, Macmillan, 1986), pp. 27–54.

Remington, Thomas, 'The March 1990 RSFSR Elections', in Darrell Slider (ed.), *Elections and Political Change in the Soviet Republics* (Durham, NC, Duke University Press, 1991).

Slider, Darrell (ed.), *Elections and Political Change in the Soviet Republics* (Durham, NC, Duke University Press, 1991).

White, Stephen, 'Reforming the Electoral System', *Journal of Communist Studies*, Vol. 5, No. 4 (1988), pp. 1–17.

White, Stephen, 'From Acclamation to Limited Choice: The Soviet Elections of 1989', *Coexistence*, Vol. 28, No. 4 (December 1991), pp. 77–103.

Zaslavsky, V. and R. Brym, 'The Function of Elections in the USSR', *Soviet Studies*, Vol. 30, No. 3 (July 1978), pp. 362–71.

Participation

Adams, Jan S., 'Citizen Participation in Community Decisions in the USSR', in P. J. Potichnyj and J. S. Zacek (eds), *Politics and Participation under Communist Rule* (New York, Praeger, 1983), pp. 178–95.

Biddulph, Howard L., 'Local Interest Articulation at CPSU Congress', *World Politics*, Vol. 36, No. 1 (October 1984), pp. 28–52.

Bielasiak, Jack, 'Party Leadership and Mass Participation in Developed Socialism', in J. Seroka and M. D. Simon (eds), *Developed Socialism in the Soviet Bloc: Political Theory and Political Reality* (Boulder, CO, Westview Press, 1982) pp. 121–53.

Burks, R. V., 'Popular Participation under Socialism', *Studies in Comparative Communism*, Vol. 15, Nos 1–2 (Spring–Summer 1982), pp. 141–50.

Friedgut, Theodore H., *Political Participation in the USSR* (Princeton, NJ, Princeton University Press, 1979).

Hahn, Jeffrey W., *Soviet Grassroots: Citizen Participation in Local Soviet Government* (Princeton, NJ, Princeton University Press, 1988).

Hough, Jerry F., 'Political Participation in the Soviet Union', *Soviet Studies*, Vol. 18, No. 1 (January 1976), pp. 3–20.

Lampert, Nicholas, *Whistleblowing in the Soviet Union: Complaints and Abuses under State Socialism* (London, Macmillan, 1985).

LaPalombara, Joseph, 'Monoliths or Plural Systems: Through Conceptual Lenses Darkly', *Studies in Comparative Communism*, Vol. 8, No. 3 (Autumn 1975), pp. 305–32.

Little, D., 'Mass Political Party Participation in the US and USSR: A Conceptual Analysis', *Comparative Political Studies*, Vol. 8, No. 4 (January 1976), pp. 437–60.

Rigby, T. H., 'Hough on Political Participation in the Soviet Union', *Soviet Studies*, Vol. 18, No. 2 (April 1976), pp. 257–61.

Riordan, Jim, *Sport in Soviet Society* (Cambridge, Cambridge University Press, 1977).

Ruble, Blair A., *Soviet Trade Unions* (Cambridge, Cambridge University Press, 1981).

Schulz, D. and Jan S. Adams (eds), *Political Participation in Communist Systems* (Oxford, Pergamon Press, 1981).

Unger, Aryeh, 'Political Participation in the USSR: YCL and CPSU', *Soviet Studies*, Vol. 33, No. 1 (January 1981), pp. 107–24.

White, Stephen, 'The Effectiveness of Political Propaganda in the USSR', *Soviet Studies*, Vol. 32 (1980), pp. 323–48.
White, Stephen, 'Political Communications in the USSR: Letters to Party, State and Press', *Political Studies*, Vol. 31 (1983), pp. 43–60.

10 POWER AND POLICY-MAKING

General

Brown, Archie, *Soviet Politics and Political Science* (London, Macmillan, 1974).
Brown, Archie, 'Political Power and the Soviet State', in Neil Harding (ed.), *The State in Socialist Society* (London, Macmillan, 1984), pp. 51–103
Fehér, Ferenc, Agnes Heller and Gyorgy Markus, *Dictatorship over Needs: An Analysis of Soviet Societies* (Oxford, Blackwell, 1983).
Hough, J., *The Soviet Union and Social Science Theory* (Cambridge, MA, Harvard University Press, 1977).

Leadership and elites

Blondel, Jean, *Political Leadership* (London, Sage, 1987).
Breslauer, G. W., *Khrushchev and Brezhnev as Leaders* (London, George Allen & Unwin, 1982).
Breslauer, G. W., 'Power and Authority in Soviet Politics', in J. L. Nogee (ed.), *Soviet Politics: Russia After Brezhnev* (New York, Praeger, 1985), pp. 15–33.
Brown, Archie, 'The Power of the General Secretary of the CPSU', in T. H. Rigby, Archie Brown and Peter Reddaway (eds), *Authority, Power and Policy in the USSR* (London, Macmillan, 1980).
Brown, Archie, 'Leadership Succession and Policy Innovation', in A. Brown and M. Kaser (eds) *Soviet Policy for the 1980s* (London, Macmillan, 1982), pp. 223–53.
Brown, Archie (ed.), *Political Leadership in the Soviet Union* (London, Macmillan, 1988).
Bunce, V., *Do New Leaders Make a Difference? Executive Succession and Public Policy under Capitalism and Socialism* (Princeton, NJ, Princeton University Press, 1981).
D'Agostino, Anthony, *Soviet Succession Struggles: Kremlinology and the Russian Question from Lenin to Gorbachev* (London, Unwin Hyman, 1988).
Gill, Graeme, 'Political Myth and Stalin's Search for Authority in the Party', in T. H. Rigby, Archie Brown and Peter Reddaway (eds), *Authority, Power and Policy in the USSR* (London, Macmillan, 1980).
Gill, Graeme, 'The Soviet Leader Cult: Reflections on the Structure of Leadership in the Soviet Union', *British Journal of Political Science*, Vol. 10 (April 1980), pp. 149–66.
Gill, Graeme, 'Personal Dominance and the Collective Principle: Individual Legitimacy in Marxist–Leninist Systems', in T. H. Rigby and F. Fehér (eds), *Political Legitimation in Communist States* (London, Macmillan, 1982), pp. 87–118.
Gustafson, Thane and Dawn Mann, 'Gorbachev's Next Gamble', *Problems of Communism*, Vol. 36, No. 4 (July–August 1987), pp. 1–20.
Hodnett, G., 'The Pattern of Leadership Politics', in S. Bialer (ed.), *The Domestic Context of Soviet Foreign Policy* (Boulder, CO, Westview Press, 1981), pp. 87–118.
Hoffman, E., 'Changing Soviet Perspectives on Leadership and Administration', in S. F. Cohen, Alexander Rabinowitch and Robert Sharlet (eds), *The Soviet Union since Stalin* (London, Macmillan, 1980).
Hough, Jerry, 'The Soviet Elite: Groups and Individuals', *Problems of Communism*, Vol. 16, No. 1 (January–February 1967), pp. 28–35.
Hough, Jerry, *Soviet Leadership in Transition* (Washington DC, Brookings Institution, 1980).
Hough, Jerry, 'Gorbachev Consolidating Power', *Problems of Communism*, Vol. 36, No. 4 (July–August 1987), pp. 21–43.
Janos, A. (ed.), *Authoritarian Politics in Communist Europe* (Berkeley, CA, University of California Press, 1976).
Johnson, Chalmers (ed.), *Change in Communist Systems* (Stanford, CA, Stanford University Press, 1970).
McCauley, Martin and Stephen Carter, *Leadership and Succession in the Soviet Union, Eastern Europe and China* (London, Macmillan, 1986).
Mills, Richard M., 'The Soviet Leadership Problem', *World Politics*, Vol. 33, No. 4 (July 1981), pp. 590–613.

Narkiewicz, Olga A., *Soviet Leaders: From the Cult of Personality to Collective Rule* (Brighton, Wheatsheaf Books, 1986).

Odom, W. E., 'Choice and Change in Soviet Politics', *Problems of Communism*, Vol. 32, No. 3 (May–June 1983), pp. 1–21.

Rigby, T. H., 'The Soviet Leadership: Towards a Self-stabilising Oligarchy?', *Soviet Studies*, Vol. 22, No. 2 (October 1970), pp. 167–91.

Rigby, T. H., 'The Soviet Politburo: A Comparative Profile, 1951–1971', *Soviet Studies*, Vol. 24, No. 1 (1972–73), pp. 3–23.

Rigby, T. H., 'Personal and Collective Leadership', in D. Simes *et al.* (eds), *Soviet Succession* (Beverly Hills, CA, and London, Sage, 1978).

Rigby, T. H., 'A Conceptual Approach to Authority, Power and Policy in the Soviet Union', in T. H. Rigby *et al.* (eds), *Authority, Power and Policy in the Soviet Union* (London, Macmillan, 1980).

Rigby, T. H. and Bohdan Harasymiw (eds), *Leadership Selection and Patron–Client Relations in the USSR and Yugoslavia* (London, George Allen & Unwin, 1983).

Tatu, Michel, *Power in the Kremlin* (New York, Viking, 1968).

Tucker, Robert C., 'The Rise of Stalin's Personality Cult', *American Historical Review*, Vol. 84 (1979), pp. 347–66.

Tumarkin, Nina, *Lenin Lives! The Lenin Cult in Soviet Russia*, enlarged edn (Cambridge, MA, Harvard University Press, 1997).

Zaslavsky, Victor, 'The Rebirth of the Stalin Cult in the USSR', in *The Neo-Stalinist State* (Brighton, Harvester Press, 1982), pp. 3–21.

The making of policy: general works

Aspaturian, Vernon V. (ed.), *Process and Power in Soviet Foreign Policy* (Boston, MA, Little, Brown, 1971).

Bell, Daniel, 'Ten Theories in Search of Reality', in Daniel Bell, *The End of Ideology*, revised edn (London, Collier-Macmillan, 1960).

Bruce, James B., *The Politics of Soviet Policy Formation: Khrushchev's Innovative Policies in Education and Agriculture*, Monograph Series in World Affairs, Vol. 13, Book 4, (Denver, CO, University of Denver, 1976).

Brzezinski, Zbigniew and Samuel P. Huntington, *Political Power: USA/USSR* (New York, Viking Press, 1965).

Cocks, P., R. Daniels and N. W. Heer (eds), *The Dynamics of Soviet Politics* (Cambridge, MA, Harvard University Press, 1976).

Conquest, Robert, *Power and Policy in the USSR* (New York, Harper and Row, 1967).

Etzioni, A., *Modern Organisations* (Englewood Cliffs, NJ, Prentice-Hall, 1964).

Fainsod, Merle, *How Russia is Ruled* (Cambridge, MA, Harvard University Press, 1953).

Hammer, D. P., *USSR: The Politics of Oligarchy* (New York, Praeger, 1974).

Hough, Jerry and Merle Fainsod, *How the Soviet Union is Governed* (Cambridge, MA, Harvard University Press, 1979), ch. 14

Gallagher, Matthew P. and Karl F. Spielman, Jr, *Soviet Decision-making for Defense: A Critique of US Perspectives on the Arms Race* (New York, Praeger, 1972).

Gustafson, Thane, *Reform and Power in Soviet Politics: Lessons of Recent Policies on Land and Water* (Cambridge, Cambridge University Press, 1981).

Jowitt, Kenneth, 'Inclusion and Mobilisation in Leninist Regimes', *World Politics*, Vol. 8, No. 1 (October 1975), pp. 69–96.

Juviler, Peter H. and Henry W. Morton (eds), *Soviet Policy-making: Studies of Communism in Transition* (New York, Praeger, 1967).

Lodge, Milton C., *Soviet Elite Attitudes since Stalin* (Columbus, OH, Merrill, 1969).

Löwenhardt, John, *Decision-making in Soviet Politics* (London, Macmillan, 1981).

Moses, Joel C., *Regional Party Leadership and Policy-making in the USSR* (New York, Praeger, 1974).

Ploss, Sidney, *Conflict and Decision-making in Soviet Russia: A Case Study of Agricultural Policy, 1953–1963* (Princeton, NJ, Princeton University Press, 1965).

Ploss, Sidney I. (ed.), *The Soviet Political Process* (Toronto/London, Ginn & Co., 1971).

Remnek, R. B. (ed.), *Social Scientists and Policy-making in the USSR* (New York, Praeger, 1977).

Stewart, Philip, *Political Power in the Soviet Union: A Study of Decision-making in Stalingrad* (Indianapolis, IN, Bobbs-Merrill, 1968).

Valenta, Jiri, 'Soviet Decision-making and the Czechoslovak Crisis of 1968', *Studies in Comparative Communism*, Vol. 8, Nos 1–2 (Spring–Summer 1975). pp. 147–73

Totalitarianism and concentration models

Arendt, Hannah, *The Origins of Totalitarianism* (London, André Deutsch, 1986).

Armstrong, J. A., *The Politics of Totalitarianism: The CPSU from 1934 to the Present* (New York, Random House, 1961).

Barber, B., 'Conceptual Foundations of Totalitarianism', in C. Friedrich, M. Curtis and B. Barber, *Totalitarianism in Perspective: Three Views* (London, Pall Mall Press, 1969), pp. 3–52.

Burrowes, Robert, 'Totalitarianism: The Revised Standard Version', *World Politics*, Vol. 21, No. 2 (January 1969), pp. 272–94.

Curtis, M., *Totalitarianism* (New Brunswick, NJ, Transaction Books, 1979).

Fehér, Ferenc and Agnes Heller, *Eastern Left, Western Left: Totalitarianism, Freedom and Democracy* (Cambridge, Polity Press, 1987).

Friedrich, C. J., 'Totalitarianism: Recent Trends', *Problems of Communism*, Vol. 17, No. 3 (May–June 1968), pp. 32–43.

Friedrich, Carl and Z. Brzezinski, *Totalitarian Dictatorship and Autocracy* (Cambridge, MA, Harvard University Press, 1956).

Gleason, Abbott, *Totalitarianism: The Inner History of the Cold War* (Oxford, Oxford University Press, 1995).

Havel, Vaclav, *et al.*, *The Power of the Powerless: Citizens against the State in Central-Eastern Europe* (London, Hutchinson, 1985).

Jancar, B. Wolfe, *Czechoslovakia and the Absolute Monopoly of Power* (New York, Praeger, 1971).

Kassof, A., 'The Administered Society? Totalitarianism without Terror', *World Politics*, Vol. 16, No. 4 (July 1964), pp. 558–75.

Kassof, A. (ed.), *Prospects for Soviet Society* (London, Pall Mall, 1968).

Lane, David *The Socialist Industrial State: Towards a Political Sociology of State Socialism* (London, George Allen & Unwin, 1972), ch. 2.

Meissner, B., 'Totalitarian Rule and Social Change', *Problems of Communism*, Vol. 15, No. 6 (November–December 1966), pp. 56–61.

Rigby, T. H., 'Traditional Market and Organisational Societies and the USSR', *World Politics*, Vol. 16, No. 4 (July 1964).

Rigby, T. H., '"Totalitarianism" and Change in Communist Societies', *Comparative Politics*, Vol. 4, No. 3 (April 1972), pp. 433–53.

Rigby, T. H., 'Politics in the Mono-organisational Society', in A. C. Janos (ed.), *Authoritarian Politics in Communist Europe* (Berkeley, CA, University of California Press, 1976), pp. 31–80.

Rigby, T. H., 'Stalinism and the Mono-organisational Society', in R. C. Tucker (ed.), *Stalinism: Essays in Historical Interpretation* (New York, W. W. Norton, 1977), pp. 53–76.

Schapiro, Leonard, *Totalitarianism* (London, Macmillan, 1972).

Schapiro, L., (ed.), *Political Opposition in One-party States* (London, Macmillan, 1972), especially pp. 241–76.

Tucker, R. C., *The Soviet Political Mind: Stalinism and Post-Stalin Change*, revised edn (London, George Allen & Unwin, 1972).

Wittfogel, K. A., *Oriental Despotism: A Comparative Study of Total Power* (London and New Haven, Yale University Press, 1957).

Group approach and diffusion models

Azrael, Jeremy, *Managerial Power and Soviet Politics* (Cambridge, MA, Harvard University Press, 1966).

Bentley, Arthur F., *The Process of Government* (Chicago, 1908).

Biddulph, Howard L., 'Local Interest Articulation at CPSU Congresses', *World Politics*, Vol. 26, No. 1 (October 1983), pp. 28–52.

Eckstein, Harry, 'Introduction: Group Theory and the Comparative Study of Pressure Groups', in H. Eckstein and D. E. Apter (eds), *Comparative Politics: A Reader* (New York, Free Press of Glencoe, 1963).

Groth, Alexander J., 'USSR: Pluralist Monolith?', *British Journal of Political Science*, Vol. 9 (1979), pp. 445–64.

Hough, Jerry F., 'The Soviet System: Petrification or Pluralism', *Problems of Communism*, Vol. 21, No. 2 (March–April 1972), pp. 25–45.

Hough, J. F., '"Interest Groups" and "Pluralism" in the Soviet Union', *Soviet Union/Union Sovietique*, Vol. 8, Part I (1981), pp. 103–09.

Janos, Andrew C., 'Group Politics in Communist Society: A Second Look at the Pluralistic Model', in S. P. Huntington and C. H. Moore (eds), *Authoritarian Politics in Modern Society* (New York, Basic Books, 1970), pp. 437–50.

Kelley, Donald R., 'Interest Groups in the USSR: The Impact of Political Sensitivity on Group Influence', *Journal of Politics*, Vol. 34, No. 3 (August 1972), pp. 860–88.

Langsam, David E. and David W. Paul, 'Soviet Politics and the Group Approach: A Conceptual Note', *Slavic Review*, Vol. 31, No. 1 (March 1972), pp. 136–41.

Odom, W., 'A Dissenting View on the Group Approach to Soviet Politics', *World Politics*, Vol. 28, No. 4 (July 1976), pp. 542–67.

Schwartz, Joel J. and William R. Keech, 'Group Influence and the Policy Process in the Soviet Union', in Frederic J. Fleron (ed.), *Communist Studies and the Social Sciences* (Chicago, IL, Rand McNally, 1969).

Skilling, H. Gordon, 'Interest Groups and Communist Politics', *World Politics*, Vol. 18, No. 3 (April 1966), pp. 435–51.

Skilling, H. Gordon, 'Group Conflict and Political Change', in Chalmers Johnson (ed.), *Change in Communist Systems* (Stanford, CA, Stanford University Press, 1970), pp. 215–34.

Skilling, H. Gordon, 'Interest Groups and Communist Politics Revisited', *World Politics*, Vol. 36, No. 1 (October 1983), pp. 1–27; revised version in S. White and D. Nelson (eds), *Communist Politics: A Reader* (London, Macmillan, 1986), pp. 221–42.

Skilling, H. Gordon and Franklin Griffiths, *Interest Groups in Soviet Politics* (Princeton, NJ, Princeton University Press, 1971).

Solomon, Peter, *Soviet Criminologists and Criminal Policy: Specialists in Policy-making* (New York, Columbia University Press, 1978).

Solomon, Susan (ed.), *Pluralism in the Soviet Union* (London, Macmillan, 1983).

Truman, David B., *The Governmental Process* (New York, Knopf, 1951).

White, S., 'Communist Systems and the Iron Law of Political Pluralism', *British Journal of Political Science*, Vol. 8 (January 1978), pp. 101–17.

Intermediate models

Bunce, Valerie, 'The Political Economy of the Brezhnev Era: The Rise and Fall of Corporatism', *British Journal of Political Science*, Vol. 13 (1983), pp. 129–58.

Jowitt, Kenneth, 'Soviet Neotraditionalism: The Political Corruption of a Leninist Regime', *Soviet Studies*, Vol. 35, No. 3 (July 1983), pp. 275–97.

McCain, Morrie A. Jr, 'Soviet Jurists Divided: A Case for Corporatism in the USSR?', *Comparative Politics*, Vol. 15 (1983), pp. 443–60.

Meyer, Alfred G., 'Theories of Convergence', in Chalmers Johnson (ed.), *Change in Communist Systems* (Stanford, CA, Stanford University Press, 1970), pp. 313–41.

Schmitter, Philippe, 'Still the Century of Corporatism?', *The Review of Politics*, Vol. 36, No. 1 (January 1974), pp. 85–131; and in Frederick B. Pike and Thomas Stritch (eds), *The New Corporatism* (Notre Dame, IN, Notre Dame University Press, 1974).

Walder, Andrew G., *Communist Neo-traditionalism: Work and Authority in Chinese Industry* (Berkeley, CA, University of California Press, 1986).

11 IDEOLOGY AND AUTHORITY

Soviet ideology

Amalrik, Andrei, 'Ideologies in Soviet Society', *Survey*, Vol. 22, No. 2 (Spring 1976), pp. 1–11.

Bell, Daniel, 'Ideology and Soviet Politics', *Slavic Review*, Vol. 24, No. 4 (December 1965), pp. 591–621.

Besançon, Alain, *The Rise of the Gulag: Intellectual Origins of Leninism* (New York, Continuum, 1981).

Brzezinski, Z., *Ideology and Power in Soviet Politics* (New York, Praeger, 1967).

Carew-Hunt, R. N., *The Theory and Practice of Communism* (Harmondsworth, Pelican, 1963).

Conquest, Robert, *The Politics of Ideas in the USSR* (New York, Praeger, 1967).

Evans, Alfred B., 'Developed Socialism in Soviet Ideology', *Soviet Studies*, Vol. 29, No. 3 (July 1977), pp. 409–28.

Evans, Alfred B., 'The Decline of Developed Socialism?: Some Trends in Recent Soviet Ideology', *Soviet Studies*, Vol. 38, No. 1 (January 1986), pp. 1–23.

Evans, Alfred B., 'The Polish Crisis in the 1980s and Adaptation in Soviet Ideology', *The Journal of Communist Studies*, Vol. 2, No. 3 (September 1986), pp. 263–85.

Kanet, R. E., 'The Rise and Fall of the All-People's State', *Soviet Studies*, Vol. 29, No. 1 (July 1968), pp. 81–93.

Kelley, D. R., 'Developments in Ideology', in D. R. Kelley (ed.), *Soviet Politics in the Brezhnev Era* (New York, Praeger, 1980).

Kolakowski, Leszek, *Main Currents of Marxism: Its Origin, Growth, and Dissolution*, Vol. 3, *The Breakdown* (Oxford, Clarendon Press, 1978).

Kuusinen, O. V. (ed.), *Fundamentals of Marxism–Leninism: Manual* (London, Lawrence and Wishart, 1961).

Leonhard, Wolfgang, *Three Faces of Marxism* (New York, Holt, Rinehart and Winston, 1974).

Marcuse, Herbert, *Soviet Marxism: A Critical Analysis* (Harmondsworth, Pelican, 1971).

Meyer, Alfred G., *Leninism* (Cambridge, MA, Harvard University Press, 1957).

Meyer, Alfred G., *Communism* (New York, Random House, 1960).

Meyer, Alfred G., 'The Function of Ideology in the Soviet Political System', *Soviet Studies*, Vol. 17, No. 3 (January 1966), pp. 273–85, and discussion in succeeding issues by Nove, Joravsky, Chambre, etc.

Meyers, Alfred G., 'Assessing the Ideological Commitment of a Regime', in J. L. Nogee (ed.), *Soviet Politics* (New York, Praeger, 1985), pp. 107–21.

Mills, C. Wright, *The Marxists* (Harmondsworth, Pelican, 1963).

Tiersky, Ronald, *Ordinary Stalinism: Democratic Centralism and the Question of Communist Political Development* (London, George Allen & Unwin, 1985).

Tucker, R. C. (ed.), *The Marx–Engels Reader* (New York, Norton, 1972).

Tucker, R. C. (ed.), *The Lenin Anthology* (New York, Norton, 1975).

White, Stephen and Alex Pravda (eds), *Ideology and Soviet Politics* (London, Macmillan, 1988).

Zaslavsky, V., 'Socioeconomic Inequality and Changes in Soviet Ideology', *Theory and Society*, Vol. 2, No. 9 (March 1980), pp. 383–407.

The ideological apparatus and political socialisation

Androunas, Elena, *Soviet Media in Transition: Structural and Economic Alternatives* (Westport, CT, Praeger, 1993).

Benn, David Wedgwood, '*Glasnost*' in the Soviet Media: Liberalization or Public Relations', *The Journal of Communist Studies*, Vol. 3, No. 3 (September 1987), pp. 267–76.

Benn, David Wedgwood, *From Glasnost to Freedom of Speech: Russian Openness and International Relations* (London, Pinter Publishers/RIIA, 1992).

Dewhirst, Martin and Robert Farrell (eds), *The Soviet Censorship* (Metuchen, NJ, Scarecrow Press, 1973).

Dzirkals, L., T. Gustafson and R. Johnson, *The Media and Intra-elite Communication* (Washington, DC, Rand, 1982).

Hollander, Gayle, *Soviet Political Indoctrination: Developments in the Mass Media and Propaganda since Stalin* (New York, Praeger, 1972).

Hopkins, Mark, *Mass Media in the Soviet Union* (New York, Pegasus, 1970).

Kenez, Peter, *The Birth of the Propaganda State: Soviet Methods of Mass Mobilisation, 1917–1929* (Cambridge, Cambridge University Press, 1986).

Lane, Christel, *The Rites of Rulers: Ritual in Industrial Society: The Soviet Case* (Cambridge, Cambridge University Press, 1981).

Mickiewicz, Ellen P., *Media and the Russian Public* (New York, Praeger, 1981).

Mickiewicz, Ellen, *Split Signals* (Oxford, Oxford University Press, 1988).

Murray, John, *The Russian Press from Brezhnev to Yeltsin: Behind the Paper Curtain* (Aldershot, Edward Elgar, 1994).

Nove, Alec, *Glasnost' in Action: Cultural Renaissance in Russia* (London, Unwin Hyman, 1989).

O'Dell, Felicity Ann, *Socialisation through Children's Literature: The Soviet Example* (Cambridge, Cambridge University Press, 1978).

Roxburgh, Angus, *Pravda: Inside the Soviet News Machine* (London, Gollancz, 1987).

Wettig, G., *Broadcasting and Detente* (London, Hurst, 1977).

White, Stephen, 'The Effectiveness of Political Propaganda in the USSR', *Soviet Studies*, Vol. 32 (1980), pp. 323–48.

White, Stephen, 'Propagating Communist Values in the USSR', *Problems of Communism*, Vol. 34, No. 6 (November–December 1985), pp. 1–17.

Political culture and legitimacy

Almond, Gabriel A., 'Communism and Political Culture Theory', *Comparative Politics*, No. 15, 1983, pp. 127–38.

Brown, Archie (ed.), *Political Culture and Communist Studies* (London, Macmillan, 1984).

Brown, A. and J. Gray (eds), *Political Culture and Change in Communist Systems* (London, Macmillan, 1977).

Brym, Robert J., 'Re-evaluating Mass Support for Political and Economic Change in Russia', *Europe–Asia Studies*, Vol. 48, No. 5 (1996), pp. 751–66.

Brzezinski, Z., 'Soviet Politics: From the Future to the Past', in P. Cocks *et al.* (eds), *The Dynamics of Soviet Politics* (Cambridge, MA, Harvard University Press, 1976), pp. 337–51.

Daniels, R. V., 'Russian Political Culture and the Post-revolutionary Impasse', *The Russian Review*, Vol. 46, No. 2 (April 1987), pp. 165–76.

Golan, Galia, 'Elements of Russian Tradition in Soviet Socialism', in S. N. Eisenstadt (ed.), *Socialism and Tradition* (Atlantic Highlands, NJ, Humanities Press, 1975).

Gozman, Leonid and Alexander Etkind, *The Psychology of Post-totalitarianism in Russia* (London, Centre for Research into Communist Economies, 1992).

Habermas, Jurgen, *Legitimation Crisis* (London, Heinemann, 1976).

Hahn, Jeffrey W., 'Continuity and Change in Russian Political Culture', *British Journal of Political Science*, Vol. 21 (1991), pp. 393–412.

Inkeles, A., *Public Opinion in Soviet Russia* (Cambridge, MA, Harvard University Press, 1950).

Jowitt, Kenneth, 'An Organisational Approach to the Study of Political Culture in Marxist–Leninist Systems', *American Political Science Review*, Vol. 68, No. 3 (September 1974), pp. 1171–91.

Millar, James R., *Politics, Work and Daily Life in the USSR: A Survey of Former Soviet Citizens* (Cambridge, Cambridge University Press, 1988).

Paul, D. W., 'Political Culture and the Socialist Purpose', in J. P. Shapiro and P. J. Potichnyj (eds), *Change and Adaptation in Soviet and East European Politics* (New York, Praeger, 1976).

Pye, Lucian W. and Sidney Verba (eds), *Political Culture and Political Development* (Princeton, NJ, Princeton University Press, 1965).

Rigby, T. H. and Ferenc Fehér (eds), *Political Legitimation in Communist States* (London, Macmillan, 1982).

Samuel, R. and G. Stedman-Jones (eds), *Culture, Ideology and Politics* (London, Routledge & Kegan Paul, 1982).

Szamuely, Tibor, *The Russian Tradition* (London, Secker & Warburg, 1974).

Tucker, R. C., 'Culture, Political Culture and Communist Society', *Political Science Quarterly*, Vol. 88, No. 2 (June 1973), pp. 173–90.

Tucker, R. C., *The Political Culture of Soviet Russia: From Lenin to Gorbachev* (Brighton, Wheatsheaf, 1987).

White, Stephen, *Political Culture and Soviet Politics* (London, Macmillan, 1979).

White, Stephen, 'The USSR: Patterns of Autocracy and Industrialisation', in A. Brown and J. Gray (eds), *Political Culture and Change in Communist Systems* (London, Macmillan, 1979), pp. 25–65.

Zaslavsky, V., 'The Problem of Legitimation in Soviet Society', in A. Vidich and R. Glassman (eds), *Conflict and Control: Challenge to Legitimacy of Modern Governments* (Beverly Hills, CA, and London, Sage, 1979).

Zinoviev, Alexander, *Homo Sovieticus* (London, Gollancz, 1985).

12 CLASS AND GENDER

New class and society

Adam, Jan (ed.), *Economic Reforms and Welfare Systems in the USSR, Poland and Hungary: Social Contract in Transformation* (London, Macmillan, 1991).

Balzer, Harley (ed.), *Russia's Missing Middle Class: The Professions in Russian History* (New York, M. E. Sharpe, 1996).

Burnham, James, *The Managerial Revolution* (London, Putnam, 1942).

Churchward, L. G., *The Soviet Intelligentsia* (London, Routledge, 1973).

Cliff, Tony, *Russia: A Marxist Analysis* (London, Socialist Review Publishers, 1964).

Cliff, Tony, *State Capitalism in Russia* (London, Pluto Press, 1974).

Crozier, M., *The Bureaucratic Phenomenon*, part IV (Chicago, Chicago University Press, 1964).

Dahrendorf, Ralph, *Class and Class Conflict in Industrial Society* (London, Routledge & Kegan Paul, 1959).

Djilas, Milovan, *The New Class: An Analysis of the Communist System* (New York, Praeger, 1957).

Gouldner, Alvin, *The Future of Intellectuals and the Rise of the New Class* (London, Macmillan, 1979).

Harasymiw, Bohdan, *Political Elite Recruitment in the Soviet Union* (London, Macmillan, 1984).

Herlemann, H. (ed.), *Quality of Life in the Soviet Union* (Boulder, CO, Westview Press, 1987).

Hirszowicz, Maria, *The Bureaucratic Leviathan: A Study in the Sociology of Communism* (Oxford, Martin Robertson, 1980).

Hough, J. H., 'The Soviet Elite: Groups and Individuals', *Problems of Communism*, Vol. 16, No. 1 (January–February 1967), pp. 28–35.

Inkeles, Alex, *Social Change in Soviet Russia* (Cambridge, MA, Harvard University Press, 1968).

Konrad, G. and I. Szelenyi, *The Intellectuals on the Road to Class Power* (Brighton, Harvester Press, 1979).

Kuron, Jacek and K. Modzelewski, *An Open Letter to the Party* (London, Pluto, n.d. [1965]).

Lane, David, *The End of Social Inequality?: Class, Status and Power under State Socialism* (London, George Allen & Unwin, 1982).

Littlejohn, Gary, *A Sociology of the Soviet Union* (London, Macmillan, 1984).

Makhaisky, Waclaw, *The Intellectual Worker* (Geneva, 1905).

Matthews, Mervyn, *Class and Society in Soviet Russia* (Harmondsworth, Penguin, 1972).

Matthews, Mervyn, *Privilege in the Soviet Union: A Study of Elite Lifestyles under Communism* (London, George Allen & Unwin, 1978).

Matthews, Mervyn, *Poverty in the Soviet Union: The Lifestyles of the Underprivileged in Recent Years* (Cambridge, Cambridge University Press, 1986).

Meissner, B., 'The Power Elite and the Intelligentsia', in K. London (ed.), *The Soviet Union* (Baltimore, MD, Johns Hopkins University Press, 1968).

Michels, Robert, *Political Parties* (Glencoe, IL, Free Press, 1958).

Millar, James R. and Sharon L. Wolchik (eds), *Social Legacies of Communism* (Cambridge, Cambridge University Press, 1994).

Mosca, Gaetano, *The Ruling Class* (New York, McGraw-Hill, 1939).

Nove, Alec, 'Is There a Ruling Class in the USSR?', *Soviet Studies*, Vol. 27, No. 4 (October 1975), pp. 615–38.

Nove, Alec, 'The Class Nature of the Soviet Union Revisited', *Soviet Studies*, Vol. 35, No. 3 (July 1983), pp. 298–312.

Pareto, Vilfredo, *The Mind and Society* (New York, Harcourt Brace, 1935).

Parkin, Frank, *Class, Inequality and Political Order: Social Stratification in Capitalist and Communist Countries* (London, McGibbon & Kee, 1971).

Rizzi, Bruno, *The Bureaucratization of the World*, trans. Adam Westoby (New York, Free Press, 1985).

Sik, Ota, *The Communist Power System* (New York, Praeger, 1981).

Simis, Konstantin, *USSR: Secrets of a Corrupt Society* (London, Dent, 1982).

Yanowitch, M., *Social and Economic Inequality in the USSR* (London, Martin Robertson, 1977).

Yanowitch, Murray, *The Social Structure of the USSR* (Boulder, CO, Westview Press, 1987).

Yanowitch, Murray, *New Directions in Soviet Social Thought* (New York, M. E. Sharpe, 1989).

Yanowitch, Murray, *Controversies in Soviet Social Thought: Democratisation, Social Justice and the Erosion of Official Ideology* (New York, M. E. Sharpe, 1991).

Zemtsov, Ilya, *Private Life of the Soviet Elite* (New York, Crane, Russak, 1985).

Gender politics

Atkinson, Dorothy, Alexander Dallin and Gail Warhofsky Lapidus (eds), *Women in Russia* (Brighton, Harvester Press, 1978).

Attwood, Lynne, *The New Soviet Man and Woman: Sex-role Socialisation in the USSR* (Bloomington, IN, Indiana University Press, 1991).

Bebel, August, *Woman under Socialism* (New York, Schocken Books, 1975).

Browning, Genia, *Women and Politics in the USSR: Consciousness Raising and Soviet Women's Groups* (Brighton, Wheatsheaf, 1987).

Buckley, Mary, 'Women in the Soviet Union', *Feminist Review*, No. 8 (Summer 1981), pp. 79–106.

Buckley, Mary, *Women and Ideology in the Soviet Union* (Brighton, Wheatsheaf, 1988).

Buckley, Mary (ed.), *Perestroika and Soviet Women* (Cambridge, Cambridge University Press, 1992).

Clements, Barbara Evans, *Bolshevik Feminist: The Life of Aleksandra Kollontai* (Bloomington, IN, and London, Indiana University Press, 1979)

Clements, Barbara Evans, 'The Birth of the New Soviet Woman', in Abbott Gleason *et al.* (eds), *Bolshevik Culture* (Bloomington, IN, Indiana University Press, 1985), pp. 220–37.

Clements, B. E., B. A. Engel and Christine D. Worobec (eds), *Russia's Women: Accommodation, Resistance, Transformation* (Berkeley, CA, University of California Press, 1991).

Danilova, Y. Z. *et al.* (eds), *Soviet Women: Some Aspects of the Status of Women in the USSR* (Moscow, Progress, 1975).

Edmondson, Linda, *Feminism in Russia, 1900–1917* (Stanford, CA, Stanford University Press, 1984).

Edmondson, Linda (ed.), *Women and Society in Russia and the Soviet Union* (Cambridge, Cambridge University Press, 1992).

Einhorn, Barbara and Maxine Molyneux (eds), *Feminist Review*, Special Issue, No. 39 (1991) on Soviet Union and Eastern Europe.

Engels, Barbara Alpern, *Mothers and Daughters: Women of the Intelligentsia in Nineteenth Century Russia* (Cambridge, Cambridge University Press, 1983).

Engels, F., *The Origin of the Family, Private Property and the State* (London, Lawrence & Wishart, 1972).

Farnsworth, Beatrice, *Aleksandra Kollontai: Socialism, Feminism and the Bolshevik Revolution* (Stanford, CA, Stanford University Press, 1980).

Glickman, Rose L., *Russian Factory Women: Workplace and Society, 1880–1914* (Berkeley, CA, University of California Press, 1984).

Gray, Francine du Plessix, *Soviet Women: Walking the Tightrope* (London, Virago Press, 1991).

Hannson, C. and K. Liden, *Moscow Women: 13 Interviews* (London, Alison & Busby, 1984).

Hayden, Carol Eubanks, 'The Zhenotdel and the Bolshevik Party', *Russian History*, Vol. 3, No. 2 (1976), pp. 150–73.

Heitlinger, Alena, *Women and State Socialism: Women in the Soviet Union and Czechoslovakia* (London, Macmillan, 1979).

Heitlinger, Alena, *Reproduction, Medicine and the Socialist State* (London, Macmillan, 1987).

Holland, B. (ed.), *Soviet Sisterhood: British Feminists on Women in the USSR* (London, Fourth Estate, 1985).

Holt, Alix (ed.), *Selected Writings of Aleksandra Kollontai* (Westport, CT, Lawrence Hill, 1977).

Jancar, B. W., 'Women and Soviet Politics', in H. Morton and R. Tokes (eds), *Soviet Politics and Society in the 1970s* (New York, Free Press, 1974).

Jancar, B. W., *Women under Communism* (Baltimore, MD, Johns Hopkins University Press, 1978).

Kerblay, Basile, *Modern Soviet Society* (London, Methuen, 1983).

Lapidus, Gail Warhofsky, 'Political Mobilisation, Participation and Leadership: Women in Soviet Politics', *Comparative Politics*, Vol. 8, No. 1 (October 1975), pp. 90–118.

Lapidus, Gail Warhofsky, *Women in Soviet Society: Equality, Development and Social Change* (Berkeley, CA, University of California Press, 1978).

Lapidus, G. W. (ed.), *Women, Work and Family in the Soviet Union: Equality, Development and Social Change* (New York, M. E. Sharpe, 1982).

Lenin, V. I., *On the Emancipation of Women* (Moscow, Progress, 1965).

Lubin, N., 'Women in Soviet Central Asia: Progress and Contradiction', *Soviet Studies*, Vol. 33, No. 2 (April 1981), pp. 182–203.

McAuley, Alistair, *Women's Work and Wages in the Soviet Union* (London, George Allen & Unwin, 1981).

Mamonova, Tatyana (ed.), *Women and Russia: Feminist Writings from the Soviet Union* (Oxford, Basil Blackwell, 1984).

Molyneux, M., 'Socialist Societies Old and New: Progress towards Women's Emancipation?', *Feminist Review*, No. 8 (Summer 1981), pp. 1–34.

Molyneux, Maxine, 'The "Woman Question" in the Age of Perestroika', *New Left Review*, No. 183 (September–October 1990), pp. 23–49.

Nikolayeva, Anna, 'Women in Soviet Society', *New World Review*, Vol. 53, No. 2 (March–April 1985).

Posadskaya, Anastasiya, *Women in Russia* (Oxford, Blackwell, 1994).

Pushkareva, Natalia, *Women in Russian History: From the Tenth to the Twentieth Century* (New York, M. E. Sharpe, 1997).

Rai, Shirin, Hilary Pilkington and Annie Phizacklea (eds), *Women in the Face of Change: The Soviet Union, Eastern Europe and China* (London, Routledge, 1992).

Rzhanitsina, L., *Female Labour under Socialism: The Socio-economic Aspects* (Moscow, Progress, 1983).

Sacks, Michael, *Women's Work in Soviet Russia* (New York, Praeger, 1976).

Sidorova, T. N. (ed.), *Soviet Women* (Moscow, Progress, 1975).

Stites, R., *The Women's Liberation Movement in Russia: Feminism, Nihilism and Bolshevism, 1860–1930* (Princeton, NJ, Princeton University Press, 1978).

13 FROM DISSENT TO PLURALISM

Dissent

Alexeyeva, Ludmilla, *Soviet Dissent: Contemporary Movements for National, Religious and Human Rights*, trans. Carol Pearce and John Glad (Middletown, CT, Wesleyan University Press, 1985).

Amalrik, Andrei, *Will the Soviet Union Survive until 1984?* (London, Penguin, 1970).

Barghoorn, F. C., *Détente and the Democratic Movement in the USSR* (New York, The Free Press, 1976).

Barghoorn, Frederick C., 'Regime–Dissenter Relations after Khrushchev', in Susan Solomon (ed.), *Pluralism in the Soviet Union* (London, Macmillan, 1983), pp. 131–68.

Bloch, S. and Peter Reddaway, *Psychiatric Terror: How Soviet Psychiatry is Used to Suppress Dissent* (New York, Basic Books, 1977).

Bukovsky, Vladimir, *To Build a Castle: My Life as a Dissenter* (London, André Deutsch, 1978).

Bukovsky, Vladimir, *To Choose Freedom* (Stanford, CA, Hoover Institution Press, 1987).

Chalidze, Valerii, *To Defend These Rights* (New York, Random House, 1974).

Cohen, Stephen F. (ed.), *An End to Silence: Uncensored Opinion in the Soviet Union*, from Roy Medvedev's underground magazine *Political Diary*, trans. George Saunders (London, W. W. Norton, 1982).

Cutler, R. M., 'Soviet Dissent under Khrushchev: An Analytical Study', *Comparative Politics*, Vol. 13, No. 1 (October 1980), pp. 15–36.

Dunlop, John, *The New Russian Revolutionaries* (Belmont, MA, Nordland Press, 1976).

Gerstenmaier, C. I., *The Voices of the Silent* (New York, Hart, 1972).

Gorbanevskaya, N., *The Demonstration in Red Square* (London, André Deutsch, 1972).

Havel, Václav, 'The Power of the Powerless', in Václav Havel (ed.), *Living in Truth* (London, Faber and Faber, 1987), pp. 36–122.

Hopkins, Mark, *Russia's Underground Press: The Chronicle of Current Events* (New York, Praeger, 1983).

Kowalewski, D., 'Trends in the Human Rights Movement', in D. R. Kelley (ed.), *Soviet Politics in the Brezhnev Era* (New York, Praeger, 1980), pp. 150–81.

Lane, D., 'Human Rights under State Socialism', in S. White and D. Nelson *Communist Politics: A Reader* (London, Macmillan, 1986), pp. 326–45.

Litvinov, P., *The Demonstration in Pushkin Square* (London, Harvill Press, 1968).

Marchenko, Anatolii, *My Testimony* (Harmondsworth, Penguin, 1971).

Medvedev, Roy, *Détente and Socialist Democracy: A Discussion with Roy Medvedev*, ed. Ken Coates (Nottingham, Spokesman Books, 1975).

Medvedev, Roy, *On Socialist Democracy* (London, Spokesman Books, 1975).

Medvedev, Roy, *On Soviet Dissent*, interviews with Piero Ostellino (New York, Columbia University Press, 1980).

Meerson-Aksenov, M. and B. Shragin (eds), *The Political, Social and Religious Thought of Russian Samizdat: An Anthology* (Belmont, MA, Nordland Press, 1977).

Michnik, Adam, *Letters from Prison and Other Essays* (Berkeley, CA, University of California Press, 1985).

Reddaway, Peter, 'The Development of Dissent and Opposition', in A. Brown and M. Kaser (eds), *The Soviet Union since the Fall of Khrushchev* (London, Macmillan, 1978), pp. 121–56.

Reddaway, Peter, 'Policy towards Dissent since Khrushchev', in T. F. Rigby, Archie Brown and Peter Reddaway (eds), *Authority, Power and Policy in the USSR* (London, Macmillan, 1980) pp. 158–92.

Reddaway, Peter, 'Dissent in the Soviet Union', *Problems of Communism*, Vol. 32, No. 6 (November–December 1983), pp. 1–15.

Reddaway, Peter (ed.), *Uncensored Russia: The Human Rights Movement in the Soviet Union: Documents* (London, Cape, 1972).

Rubenstein, J., *Soviet Dissidents: Their Struggle for Human Rights*, 2nd edn (Boston, MA, Beacon Press, 1985).

Sakharov, Andrei, *Progress, Coexistence and Intellectual Freedom* (New York, W. W. Norton, 1968).

Sakharov, A., *Sakharov Speaks* (New York, Alfred Knopf, 1974).

Sakharov, A., *My Country and the World* (London, Collins, 1975).

Saunders, George (ed.), *Samizdat: Voices of Soviet Opposition* (New York, Monad Press, 1974).

Schapiro, L. (ed.), *Political Opposition in One-party States* (London, Macmillan, 1972).

Shanov, D. R., *Behind the Lines: The Private War against Soviet Censorship* (New York, St Martin's Press, 1985).

Shatz, Marshall S., *Soviet Dissent in Historical Perspective* (Cambridge, Cambridge University Press, 1980).

Shtromas, A. Y., 'Dissent and Political Change in the Soviet Union', *Studies in Comparative Communism*, Vol. 12, Nos 2–3 (Summer–Autumn 1979), pp. 212–76.

Shtromas, Alexander, *Political Change and Social Development: The Case of the Soviet Union* (Frankfurt am Main, Peter Lang, 1981).

Solzhenitsyn, Alexander, *Open Letter to Soviet Leaders* (London, Collins-Harvill, 1974).
Spechler, D. R., *Permitted Dissent in the USSR* (New York, Praeger, 1982).
Tokes, Rudolf L. (ed.), *Dissent in the USSR: Politics, Ideology, and People* (Baltimore, MD, Johns Hopkins University Press, 1975).
Ulam, Adam, *Russia's Failed Revolutions: From the Decembrists to the Dissidents* (London, Weidenfeld & Nicolson, 1981).
Woll, Josephine, *Soviet Dissident Literature: A Critical Guide* (Boston, MA, G. K. Hall, 1983).

Religion

Anderson, John, *Religion, State and Politics in the Soviet Union and Successor States* (Cambridge, Cambridge University Press, 1994).
Bourdeaux, Michael, *Gorbachev, Glasnost and the Gospel* (London, Hodder & Stoughton, 1991).
Davis, Nathaniel, *A Long Walk to the Church: A Contemporary History of Russian Orthodoxy* (Oxford, Westview Press, 1994).
Ellis, Jane, *The Russian Orthodox Church: A Contemporary History* (London, Croom Helm, 1986).
Hill, Ken R., *The Puzzle of the Soviet Church: An Inside Look at Christianity and Glasnost* (Portland, Multnomah Press, 1989).
Moizes, Paul, *Religious Liberty in Eastern Europe and the USSR: Before and after the Great Transformation* (Boulder, CO, Westview Press, 1992).
Ramet, Sabrina Petra (ed.), *Religious Policy in the Soviet Union* (Cambridge, Cambridge University Press, 1992).
Shirley, Eugene B. and Michael Rowe (eds), *Candle in the Wind: Religion in the Soviet Union* (Washington, DC, University Press of America, 1989).
Weigel, George, *The Final Revolution: The Resistance Church and the Collapse of Communism* (Oxford, Oxford University Press, 1993).

The new pluralism

Babkina, M. A. (ed.), *New Political Parties and Movements in the Soviet Union* (Commack, NY, Nova Science Publishers, 1991).
Fish, M. Stephen, *Democracy from Scratch: Opposition and Regime in the New Russian Revolution* (Princeton, NJ, Princeton University Press, 1995).
Hosking, Geoffrey A., Jonathan Aves and Peter J. S. Duncan, *The Road to Post-communism: Independent Political Movements in the Soviet Union* (London, Pinter Publishers, 1992).
Kitschelt, Herbert, 'A Silent Revolution in Europe?', in Jack Hayward and Edward C. Page (eds), *Governing the New Europe* (Cambridge, Polity, 1995), pp. 123–65.
Kitschelt, Herbert, 'Formation of Party Cleavages in Post-communist Democracies: Theoretical Propositions', *Party Politics*, Vol. 1, No. 4 (1995), pp. 447–72.
Mandel, David, *Perestroika and the Soviet People: Rebirth of the Labour Movement* (Montreal, Black Rose Books, 1991).
Orttung, Robert W., 'The Russian Right and the Dilemmas of Party Organisation', *Soviet Studies*, Vol. 44, No. 3 (1992), pp. 445–78.
Sedaitis, Judith B. and Jim Butterfield (eds), *Perestroika from Below: Social Movements in the Soviet Union* (Boulder, CO, Westview Press, 1991).
Temkina, Anna, 'The Workers' Movement in Leningrad, 1986–91', *Soviet Studies*, Vol. 44, No. 2 (1992), pp. 209–36.
Tolz, Vera, *The USSR's Emerging Multiparty System* (New York, Praeger, 1990).

14 THE COMMAND ECONOMY AND REFORM

Aganbegyan, Abel, *The Challenge: Economics of Perestroika* (London, Hutchinson, 1988).
Amann, Ronald and Julian Cooper (eds), *Technical Progress and Soviet Economic Development* (Oxford, Basil Blackwell, 1986).
Arnot, Bob, *Controlling Soviet Labour: Experimental Change from Brezhnev to Gorbachev* (London, Macmillan, 1988).
Aslund, Anders, *Gorbachev's Struggle for Economic Reform*, 2nd edn (London, Pinter Publishers, 1991).

Bergson, A. and H. S. Levine (eds), *The Soviet Economy: Towards the Year 2000* (London, George Allen & Unwin, 1983).

Berliner, J., 'Managing the Soviet Economy: Alternative Models', *Problems of Communism*, Vol. 32 No. 1 (January–February 1983), pp. 40–56.

Bornstein, Morris (ed.), *The Soviet Economy: Continuity and Change* (Boulder, CO, Westview Press, 1981).

Brus, W., *The Economics and Politics of Socialism* (London, Routledge & Kegan Paul, 1973).

Cole, John and Trevor Buck, *Modern Soviet Economic Performance* (Oxford, Basil Blackwell, 1986).

Colton, T. J., *The Dilemma of Reform in the Soviet Union*, rev. edn (New York, Council on Foreign Relations, 1986).

Dobb, Maurice, *Soviet Economic Development since 1917* (New York, International Publishers, 1948).

Dyker, David A., *The Soviet Economy* (London, Crosby Lockwood Staples, 1976).

Dyker, David A., *The Future of the Soviet Economic Planning System* (Armonk, NY, M. E. Sharpe, 1985).

Dyker, David A., *Restructuring the Soviet Economy* (London, Routledge, 1992).

Ellman, Michael and Vladimir Kontorovich (eds), *The Disintegration of the Soviet Economic System* (London and New York, Routledge, 1992).

Gey, Peter, Jiri Kosta and Wolfgang Quaisser (eds), *Crisis and Reform in Socialist Economies* (Boulder, CO, Westview Press, 1987).

Goldman, Marshall I., *USSR in Crisis: The Failure of an Economic System* (New York, W. W. Norton, 1983).

Goldman, Marshall I., 'Gorbachev and Economic Reform', *Foreign Affairs*, Vol. 64, No. 1 (Fall 1985), pp. 56–73.

Goldman, Marshall I., *Lost Opportunity: Why Economic Reforms in Russia Have Not Worked* (London, W. W. Norton, 1995).

Gregory, Paul R. and Robert C. Stuart, *Soviet and Post-Soviet Economic Structure and Performance*, 5th edn (London, HarperCollins, 1993).

Grossman, Gregory, 'The "Second Economy" of the USSR', *Problems of Communism*, Vol. 26, No. 5 (September–October 1977), pp. 25–40.

Hirszowicz, Maria, *Coercion and Control in Communist Society: The Visible Hand in a Command Economy* (Brighton, Wheatsheaf, 1986).

Hoffmann, E. P. and R. F. Laird, *The Politics of Economic Modernisation in the Soviet Union* (Ithaca, NY, Cornell University Press, 1982).

Hoffmann, E. P. and R. F. Laird, *Technocratic Socialism: The Soviet Union in the Advanced Industrial Era* (Durham, NC, Duke University Press, 1985).

Hohmann, Hans-Hermann, Alec Nove, and Heinrich Vogel (eds), *Economics and Politics in the USSR: Problems of Interdependence* (Boulder, CO, Westview Press, 1986).

Ioffe, Olimpiad S. and Peter B. Maggs, *The Soviet Economic System: A Legal Analysis* (Boulder, CO, Westview Press, 1987).

Jones, Anthony and William Moskoff, *Ko-ops: The Rebirth of Entrepreneurship in the Soviet Union* (Bloomington, IN, Indiana University Press, 1991).

Jones, Anthony and William Moskoff (eds), *The Great Market Debate in Soviet Economics: An Anthology* (New York, M. E. Sharpe, 1992).

Kahan, A. and B. Ruble, *Industrial Labour in the USSR* (New York, Pergamon, 1979).

Kornai, Janos, *The Road to a Free Economy: Shifting from a Socialist System. The Example of Hungary* (New York, W. W. Norton, 1990).

Kushnirsky, F., 'The Limits of Soviet Economic Reform', *Problems of Communism*, Vol. 33, No. 4 (July–August 1984), pp. 33–43.

Lane, David, *Soviet Economy and Society* (Oxford, Basil Blackwell, 1985).

Lane, David (ed.), *Labour and Employment in the USSR* (Brighton, Wheatsheaf, 1986).

Lane, David and F. O'Dell, *The Soviet Industrial Worker* (Oxford, Martin Robertson, 1978).

Lavigne, Marie, *The Socialist Economies of the Soviet Union and Eastern Europe*, trans. T. G. Waywell (Oxford, Martin Robertson, 1974).

Lavigne, Marie, *The Economics of Transition: From Socialist Economy to Market Economy* (London, Macmillan, 1995).

Leites, Nathan, *Soviet Style in Management* (New York, Crane Russak, 1985).

Lewin, Moshe, *Political Undercurrents in Soviet Economic Debates: From Bukharin to the Modern Reformers* (London, Pluto Press, 1975).

Mau, Vladimir, '*Perestroika*: Theoretical and Political Problems of Economic Reforms in the USSR', *Europe–Asia Studies*, Vol. 47, No. 3 (1995), pp. 387–411.

Mau, Vladimir, 'The Road to *Perestroika*: Economics in the USSR and the Problems of Reforming the Soviet Economic Order', *Europe–Asia Studies*, Vol. 48, No. 2 (1996), pp. 207–24.

Nelson, Lynn D., *Property to the People: The Struggle for Radical Economic Reform in Russia* (Armonk, NY, M. E. Sharpe, 1994).

Nove, Alec, *An Economic History of the USSR* (Harmondsworth, Penguin, 1972).

Nove, Alec, *Political Economy and Soviet Socialism* (London, George Allen & Unwin, 1979).

Nove, Alec, *The Soviet Economic System*, 3rd edn (London, Unwin Hyman, 1981).

Nove, Alec, *The Economics of Feasible Socialism* (London, George Allen & Unwin, 1983).

Prybyla, Jan S., *Market and Plan under Socialism: The Bird in the Cage* (Stanford, CA, Hoover Institution Press, 1987).

Rutland, Peter, *The Myth of the Plan: Lessons of Soviet Planning Experience* (London, Hutchinson, 1985).

Rutland, Peter, *The Politics of Economic Stagnation in the Soviet Union: The Role of Local Party Organs in Economic Management* (Cambridge, Cambridge University Press, 1992).

Schapiro, L. and J. Godson (eds), *The Soviet Worker: From Lenin to Andropov* (London, Macmillan, 1984).

Selm, Bert van, *The Economics of Soviet Breakup* (London, Routledge, 1997).

Smith, Keith (ed.), *Soviet Industrialisation and Soviet Modernity* (London, Routledge & Kegan Paul, 1986).

Sutela, Pekka, *Economic Thought and Economic Reform in the Soviet Union* (Cambridge, Cambridge University Press, 1991).

Wiles, Peter, *The Political Economy of Communism* (Cambridge, MA, Harvard University Press, 1964).

Zaslavskaya, Tatyana, 'The Novosibirsk Report', introduced by Phil Hanson, *Survey*, Vol. 28, No. 1 (Spring 1984), pp. 83–108.

Zaslavsky, Victor, 'The Regime and the Working Class in the USSR', *Telos*, No. 42 (Winter 1979–80), pp. 5–20; also in his *The Neo-Stalinist State* (Brighton, Harvester, 1982), pp. 44–65.

Ziegler, Charles E., 'Worker Participation and Worker Discontent in the Soviet Union', *Political Science Quarterly*, Vol. 98, No. 2 (Summer 1983), pp. 235–53.

15 NATIONALITY POLITICS

Nationalism and the USSR

Agursky, Mikhail, *The Third Rome: National Bolshevism in the USSR* (Boulder and London, Westview Press, 1987).

Azrael, Jeremy (ed.), *Soviet Nationality Policies and Practices* (New York, Praeger, 1978).

Bahry, Donna, *Outside Moscow: Power, Politics and Budgetary Policy in the Soviet Republics* (New York, Columbia University Press, 1987).

Bialer, Seweryn (ed.), *Politics, Society and Nationality in Gorbachev's Russia*, (Boulder, CO, Westview Press, 1989).

Bremmer, Ian and Ray Taras (eds), *New States, New Politics: Building the Post-Soviet Nations*, 2nd edn (Cambridge, Cambridge University Press, 1996).

Brubaker, Rogers, *Nationalism Reframed: Nationhood and the National Question in the New Europe* (Cambridge, Cambridge University Press, 1996).

Buttino, Marco (ed.), *In a Collapsing Empire: Underdevelopment, Ethnic Conflicts and Nationalisms in the Soviet Union* (Milan, Feltrinelli, 1993).

Carrére d'Encausse, Héléne, *Decline of an Empire: The Soviet Socialist Republics in Revolt* (New York, Newsweek Books, 1979).

Carrére d'Encausse, Héléne, *The Great Challenge: Nationalities and the Bolshevik State, 1917–1930* (New York, Holmes & Meier, 1992).

Carrére d'Encausse, Héléne, *The End of the Soviet Empire: The Triumph of the Nations* (London, Basic Books, 1994).

Connor, Walker, *The National Question in Marxist–Leninist Theory and Strategy* (Princeton, NJ, Princeton University Press, 1984).

Conquest, Robert (ed.), *The Last Empire: Nationality and the Soviet Future* (Stanford, CA, Hoover Institution Press, 1986).

Dawisha, Karen and Bruce Parrott, *The End of Empire? The Transformation of the USSR in Comparative Perspective* (New York, M. E. Sharpe, 1996).

Denber, Rachel (ed.), *The Soviet Nationality Reader: The Disintegration in Context* (Boulder, CO, Westview Press, 1992).

Diuk, Nadia and Adrian Karatnycky, *The Hidden Nations: The People Challenge the Soviet Union* (New York, William Morrow, 1990).

Drobizheva, Leokadia *et al.* (eds), *Ethnic Conflict in the Post-Soviet World: Case Studies and Analysis* (New York, M. E. Sharpe, 1996).

Fowkes, Ben, *The Disintegration of the Soviet Union: A Study in the Rise and Triumph of Nationalism* (London, Macmillan, 1996).

Gleason, Gregory, *Federalism and Nationalism: The Struggle for Republican Rights in the USSR* (Boulder, CO, Westview Press, 1990).

Goble, Paul, 'Ethnic Politics in the USSR', *Problems of Communism*, Vol. 38 (1989), pp. 1–14.

Hajda, Lubomyr and Mark Beissinger (eds), *The Nationalities Factor in Soviet Politics and Society* (Boulder, CO, Westview Press, 1990).

Hosking, Geoffrey, *People and Empire, 1552–1917* (London, HarperCollins, 1997).

Karklins, Rasma, *Ethnic Relations in the USSR: The Perspective from below* (London, George Allen & Unwin, 1986).

Katz, Z. (ed.), *Handbook of Major Soviet Nationalities* (New York, Free Press, 1975).

Khazanov, Anatoly M., *After the USSR: Ethnicity, Nationalism and Politics in the Commonwealth of Independent States* (Madison, WI, University of Wisconsin Press, 1996).

Kozlov, Victor, *The Peoples of the Soviet Union* (London, Hutchinson, 1988).

Kux, Stephan, *Soviet Federalism: A Comparative Perspective* (New York, Westview Press, 1991).

Lapidus, Gail W., 'Ethnonationalism and Political Stability: The Soviet Case', *World Politics*, Vol. 4 (July 1984), pp. 555–80.

Lapidus, Gail W., Victor Zaslavsky and Philip Goldman (eds), *From Union to Commonwealth: Nationalism and Separatism in the Soviet Republics* (Cambridge, Cambridge University Press, 1992).

Lieberman, S. R. *et al.* (eds), *The Soviet Empire Reconsidered: Essays in Honor of Adam B. Ulam* (Boulder, CO, Westview, 1994).

McLean, Fitzroy, *All the Russias: The End of an Empire* (London, Viking, 1992).

Mandel, William, *Soviet but not Russia: The 'Other' Peoples of the Soviet Union* (Palo Alto, CA, Ramparts Press, 1985).

Motyl, Alexander J., *Will the Non-Russians Rebel? State, Ethnicity and Stability in the USSR* (Ithaca, NY, Cornell University Press, 1987).

Motyl, Alexander J., *The Post-Soviet Nations: Perspectives on the Demise of the USSR* (New York, Columbia University Press, 1992).

Motyl, Alexander J. (ed.), *Thinking Theoretically about Soviet Nationalities* (Oxford, Oxford University Press, 1992).

Nahaylo, Bohdan and Victor Swoboda, *Soviet Disunion: A History of the Nationalities Problem in the USSR* (London, Hamish Hamilton, 1990).

McAuley, Alistair (ed.), *Soviet Federalism: Nationalism and Economic Decentralisation* (Leicester and London, Leicester University Press, 1991).

Olcott, Martha Brill (ed.), *The Soviet Multinational State: Readings and Documents* (Armonk, NY, M. E. Sharpe, 1990).

Pavkovic, Aleksandar *et al.* (eds), *Nationalism and Post-Communism: A Collection of Essays* (Aldershot, Dartmouth, 1995).

Rakowska-Harmstone, T., 'The Dialectics of Nationalism in the USSR', *Problems of Communism*, Vol. 23, No. 3 (May–June 1974), pp. 1–22.

Rywkin, Michael, *Moscow's Lost Empire* (New York, M. E. Sharpe, 1994).

Simon, Gerhard, *Nationalism and Policy toward the Nationalities in the Soviet Union: From Totalitarian Dictatorship to Post-Stalinist Society* (Boulder, CO, Westview Press, 1991).

Smith, Graham (ed.), *The Nationalities Question in the Post-Soviet States*, 2nd edn (Harlow, Longman, 1995).

Suny, Ronald Grigor, *The Revenge of the Past: Nationalism, Revolution and the Collapse of the Soviet Union* (Stanford, CA, Stanford University Press, 1994).

Swoboda, Victor, 'Was the Soviet Union Really Necessary?', *Soviet Studies*, Vol. 44, No. 5 (1992), pp. 761–84.

Szporluk, Roman, *Communism and Nationalism: Karl Marx versus Friedrich List* (Oxford, Oxford University Press, 1988).

Tishkov, Valery, *Ethnicity, Nationalism and Conflict in and after the Soviet Union: The Mind Aflame* (London, Sage, 1996).

Zaslavsky, Victor, 'The Ethnic Question in the USSR', *Telos*, No. 45 (Fall 1980), pp. 45–76.

Zaslavsky, Victor, *The Neo-Stalinist State: Class, Ethnicity, and Consensus in Soviet Society* (Armonk, NY, M. E. Sharpe, 1982).

Zwick, Peter, *National Communism* (Boulder, CO, Westview Press, 1983).

Russian nationalism

Agursky, Mikhail, *The Third Rome: National Bolshevism in the USSR* (Boulder, CO, Westview Press, 1987).

Allworth, Edward (ed.), *Ethnic Russia in the USSR: The Dilemma of Dominance* (New York, Pergamon Press, 1980).

Barghoorn, Frederick C., *Soviet Russian Nationalism* (Westport, CT, Greenwood, 1976).

Berdyaev, Nikolai, *The Russian Idea* (London, Geoffrey Bles, 1947).

Carter, Stephen K., *The Politics of Solzhenitsyn* (London, Macmillan, 1977).

Carter, Stephen K., *Russian Nationalism: Yesterday, Today, Tomorrow* (London, Pinter Publishers, 1990).

Chinyaeva, Elena, 'A Eurasianist Model of Interethnic Relations Could Help Russia Find Harmony', *Transition*, 1 November 1996, pp. 30–35.

Duncan, W. Raymond and Paul Holman (eds), *Ethnic Nationalism and Regional Conflict: The Former Soviet Union and Yugoslavia* (Boulder, CO, Westview Press, 1994).

Dunlop, John B., *The New Russian Revolutionaries* (Massachusetts, Nordland, 1976).

Dunlop, John B., *The Faces of Contemporary Russian Nationalism* (Princeton, NJ, Princeton University Press, 1983).

Dunlop, John B., *The New Russian Nationalism* (New York, Praeger, 1985).

Hammer, D. P., 'Vladimir Osipov and the Veche Group, 1971–74', *The Russian Review*, Vol. 43 (1984) pp. 355–75.

Hammer, D. P., 'Russian Nationalism and Soviet Politics', in J. L. Nogee (ed.), *Soviet Politics* (New York, Praeger, 1985), pp. 122–49.

Hammer, D. P., *Russian Nationalism and Soviet Politics* (Boulder and London, Westview Press, 1989).

Hosking, Geoffrey A. (ed.), *Church, Nation and State in Russia and the Ukraine* (London, Macmillan, 1991).

Hughes, Michael, 'The Never-ending Story: Russian Nationalism, National Communism and Opposition to Reform in the USSR and Russia', *The Journal of Communist Studies*, Vol. 9, No. 2 (June 1993), pp. 41–61.

Krasnov, Vladislav, *Russia beyond Communism: A Chronicle of National Rebirth* (Boulder, CO, Westview Press, 1991).

Labedz, Leopold (ed.), *Solzhenitsyn: A Documentary Record* (London, Pelican, 1974).

Laqueur, Walter, *Black Hundred: The Rise of the Extreme Right in Russia* (New York, HarperCollins, 1993).

Likhachev, Dmitri S., *Reflections on Russia*, ed. Nicolai N. Petro, trans. Christina Sever (Boulder, CO, Westview Press, 1991).

Parland, Thomas, *The Rejection in Russia of Totalitarian Socialism and Liberal Democracy: A Study of the Russian New Right* (Helsinki, The Finnish Society of Sciences and Letters, 1993).

Petro, Nicolai N., '"The Project of the Century": A Case Study of Russian Nationalist Opposition', *Studies in Comparative Communism*, Vol. 20, No. 3/4 (Fall/Winter 1987), pp. 235–52.

Petro, Nicolai N. (ed.), *Christianity and Russian Culture in Soviet Society* (Boulder, CO, Westview Press, 1990).

Petro, Nicolai N., 'New Political Thinking and Russian Patriotism: The Dichotomy of Perestroika', *Comparative Strategy*, Vol. 9, No. 4 (1990), pp. 351–70.

Petro, Nicolai N., 'Rediscovering Russia', *Orbis*, Vol. 34, No. 1 (Winter 1990), pp. 33–50.

Petro, Nicolai M., *The Rebirth of Russian Democracy: An Interpretation of Political Culture* (Cambridge, MA, Harvard University Press, 1995).

Pospielovsky, Dimitry, 'Russian Nationalism and the Orthodox Revival', *Religion in Communist Lands*, Vol. 15, No. 3 (Winter 1987), pp. 291–309.

Pushkarev, Sergei, *Self-government and Freedom in Russia* (Boulder, CO, Westview Press, 1988).

Russian Nationalism Today, special edition of *Radio Liberty Research Bulletin*, 19 December 1988.

Scammell, Michael, *Solzhenitsyn: A Biography* (London, Hutchinson, 1985).

Smith, Hedrick, *The New Russians* (New York, Random House, 1991).

Solzhenitsyn, Alexander, *Rebuilding Russia* (London, Harvill, 1991).

Szporluk, Roman, 'Dilemmas of Russian Nationalism', *Problems of Communism*, Vol. 38, No. 4 (July–August 1989), pp. 15–35.

Szporluk, Roman (ed.), *National Identity and Ethnicity in Russia and the New States of Eurasia* (New York, M. E. Sharpe, 1994).

Walicki, A., *The Slavophile Controversy* (Oxford, Oxford University Press, 1975).

Yakunin, Gleb *et al.*, *Christianity and Government in Russia and the Soviet Union* (Boulder, CO, Westview Press, 1989).

Yanov, A., *The Russian New Right: Right-wing Ideologies in the Contemporary USSR* (Berkeley, CA, Institute of International Studies, University of California Press, 1978).

Yanov, A., *The Russian Challenge and the Year 2000* (Oxford, Basil Blackwell, 1987).

16 FOREIGN AND DEFENCE POLICY

Bialer, S., *The Soviet Paradox: External Expansion, Internal Decline* (London, Tauris, 1986).

Bialer, S. (ed.), *The Domestic Context of Soviet Foreign Policy*, 2nd edn (Boulder, CO, Westview Press, 1988).

Bowker, Mike, *Russian Foreign Policy and the End of the Cold War* (Aldershot, Ashgate, 1997).

Brzezinski, Zbigniew, 'The Cold War and its Aftermath', *Foreign Affairs*, Vol. 71, No. 4 (Fall 1992), pp. 31–49.

Carr, E. H., *The Twilight of Comintern, 1930–1935* (Macmillan, London, 1982).

Crockatt, Richard, *The Fifty Years War: The United States and the Soviet Union in World Politics, 1941–1991* (London, Routledge, 1994).

Daniels, Robert V., *Russia: The Roots of Confrontation* (Cambridge, MA, Harvard University Press, 1985).

Dawisha, Karen and Phil Hanson (eds), *Soviet–East European Dilemmas* (London, Heinemann, 1981).

Dawisha, Karen, *Eastern Europe, Gorbachev and Reform: The Great Challenge* (Cambridge, Cambridge University Press, 1988).

Dibb, Paul, *The Soviet Union: The Incomplete Superpower* (London, Macmillan, 1986).

Dobrynin, Anatoly, *In Confidence: Moscow's Ambassador to America's Six Cold War Presidents (1962–1986)* (New York, Times Books, 1995).

Donald, Robert H., *The Soviet Union in the Third World: Success and Failures* (London, Croom Helm, 1981).

Dukes, Paul, *The Last Great Game: USA versus USSR* (London, Pinter Publishers, 1989).

Dukes, Paul, *World Order in History: Russia and the West* (London, Routledge, 1995).

Dukes, Paul, *Russia, the West and the World: Problems of Historical Interpretation* (London, Routledge, 1996).

Duncan, W. R., *The Soviet Union and Cuba: Interests and Influence* (New York, Praeger, 1985).

Edmonds, R., *Soviet Foreign Policy: The Brezhnev Years* (Oxford, Oxford University Press, 1983).

Ekedahl, Carolyn McGiffert and Melvin A. Goodman, *The Wars of Eduard Shevardnadze* (University Park, PA, Pennsylvania State University Press, 1997).

Goldgeier, James M., *Leadership Style and Soviet Foreign Policy: Stalin, Khrushchev, Brezhnev and Gorbachev* (Baltimore, MD, Johns Hopkins University Press, 1994).

Hoffmann, E. P. and F. J. Fleron (eds), *The Conduct of Soviet Foreign Policy* (Chicago, IL, Aldine, 1980).

Fleron, Frederic J., Jr, Erik P. Hoffman and Robbin F. Laird (eds), *Soviet Foreign Policy: Classic and Contemporary Issues* (New York, Aldine de Gruyter, 1991); also published in two volumes as *Classic Issues in Soviet Foreign Policy: From Lenin to Brezhnev* and *Contemporary Issues in Soviet Foreign Policy: From Brezhnev to Gorbachev*.

Gaddis, John Lewis, *We Now Know: Rethinking Cold War History* (Oxford, Oxford University Press, 1997).

Galeotti, Mark, *The Age of Anxiety: Security and Politics in Soviet and Post-Soviet Russia* (London, Longman, 1994).

Galeotti, Mark, *Afghanistan: The Soviet Union's Last War* (London, Frank Cass, 1995).

Garthoff, Raymond, *Détente and Confrontation: American–Soviet Relations, Nixon to Reagan* (Washington DC, Brookings Institution, 1985).

Gelman, Harry, *The Brezhnev Politburo and the Decline of Detente* (Ithaca, NY, Cornell University Press, 1984).

George, Alexander L. (ed.), *Managing US–Soviet Rivalry* (Boulder, CO, Westview Press, 1983).

Girardet, E. R., *Afghanistan: The Soviet War* (London, Croom Helm, 1985).

Golan, Galia, *Moscow and the Middle East: New Thinking on Regional Conflict* (London, Pinter/RIIA, 1992).

Gorbachev, Mikhail S., *Perestroika: New Thinking for our Country and the World*, part 2 (London, Collins, 1987), pp. 135–252.

Gorodetsky, Gabriel (ed.), *Soviet Foreign Policy 1917–1991: A Retrospective* (London, Frank Cass, 1994).

Gupta, B. S., *Afghanistan: Politics, Economy and Society* (London, Pinter, 1985).

Haigh, R. H. *et al.* (eds), *Soviet Foreign Policy, the League of Nations and Europe, 1917–39* (Aldershot, Gower, 1986).

Halliday, Fred, *The Making of the Second Cold War*, 2nd edn (London, Verso, 1986).

Haslam, Jonathan, *The Soviet Union and the Struggle for Collective Security in Europe, 1933–1939* (London, Macmillan, 1984).

Haslam, Jonathan, *The Soviet Union and the Threat from the East, 1933–1941* (London, Macmillan, 1992).

Hauner, Milan, *What is Asia for Us? Russia's Asian Heartland Yesterday and Today* (London, Unwin Hyman, 1990).

Heller, Agnes and Ferenc Fehér, *From Yalta to Glasnost: The Dismantling of Stalin's Empire* (Oxford, Blackwell, 1990).

Hoffman, E. P. and F. J. Fleron (eds), *The Conduct of Soviet Foreign Policy* (Chicago, IL, Aldine, 1980).

Holloway, David, *The Soviet Union and the Arms Race*, 2nd edn (London and New Haven, CT, Yale University Press, 1984).

Hough, Jerry F., *The Struggle for the Third World: Soviet Debates and American Options* (Washington DC, Brookings Institution, 1986).

Hough, Jerry F., *Russia and the West: Gorbachev and the Politics of Reform* (New York, Simon and Schuster, 1988).

Kaldor, Mary, *The Imaginary War: Understanding the East–West Conflict* (Oxford, Blackwell, 1990).

Kaldor, Mary, *Europe from below: An East–West Dialogue* (London, Verso, 1991).

Kanet, Roger E. (ed.), *Soviet Foreign Policy and East–West Relations in the 1980s* (New York, Praeger, 1982).

Kanet, Roger E. (ed.), *The Soviet Union, Eastern Europe and the Third World* (Cambridge, Cambridge University Press, 1988).

Kennedy-Pipe, Caroline, *Russia and the World since 1917* (London, Edward Arnold, 1997).

Kubalkova, V. and A. A. Cruickshank, *Marxism–Leninism and the Theory of International Relations* (London, Routledge & Kegan Paul, 1980).

Kull, Steven, *Burying Lenin: The Soviet Revolution in Ideology and Foreign Policy* (Boulder, CO, Westview Press, 1992).

Lebow, Ned and Janice Gross, *We all Lost the Cold War* (Princeton, NJ, Princeton University Press, 1994).

Light, Margot, *The Soviet Theory of International Politics* (Brighton, Wheatsheaf, 1987).

Lynch, Allen, *The Soviet Study of International Relations* (Cambridge, Cambridge University Press, 1987).

Lynch, Allen, *The Cold War is Over – Again* (Boulder, CO, Westview Press, 1992).

McCauley, Martin, *The Origins of the Cold War* (London, Longman, 1983).

Mastny, Vojtech, *The Cold War and Soviet Insecurity: The Stalin Years* (Oxford, Oxford University Press, 1997).

Medvedev, Roy, *China and the Superpowers* (Oxford, Blackwell, 1986).

Miller, R. F., *Soviet Foreign Policy Today: Gorbachev and the New Political Thinking* (London, Unwin Hyman, 1991).

Naarden, Bruno, *Socialist Europe and Revolutionary Russia: Perception and Prejudice* (Cambridge, Cambridge University Press, 1992).

Neumann, Iver B., *Russia and the Idea of Europe* (London, Routledge, 1995).

Nogee, J. L. and R. H. Donaldson, *Soviet Foreign Policy since World War II*, 3rd edn (New York, Pergamon, 1987).

Papp, Daniel S., *Soviet Perceptions of the Developing World in the 1980s: The Ideological Basis* (Lexington, MA, Lexington Books, 1985).

Petro, Nicolai N. and Alvin Z. Rubinstein, *Russian Foreign Policy: From Empire to Nation State* (Harlow, Addison Wesley Longman, 1996).

Pick, Otto, *Soviet Foreign Policy: An Analysis of Power and Ideology* (Brighton, Wheatsheaf, 1987).

Pike, D., *Vietnam and the Soviet Union: Anatomy of an Alliance* (Boulder, CO, Westview Press, 1987).

Ragsdale, Hugh (ed.), *Imperial Russian Foreign Policy* (Cambridge, Cambridge University Press, 1993).

Roberts, G., *Soviet Union in World Politics* (London, Routledge, 1997).

Rubinstein, Alvin Z., *Soviet Foreign Policy since World War II: Imperial and Global*, 2nd edn (Boston, MA, Little, Brown & Co., 1985).

Saivetz, Carol R. and Sylvia Woodby, *Soviet–Third World Relations* (Boulder, CO, Westview Press, 1985).

Shearman, P., 'Gorbachev and the Third World: An Era of Reform', *Third World Quarterly*, Vol. 9, No. 4 (October 1987), pp. 1083–117.

Shearman, P., *The Soviet Union and Cuba* (Routledge, London, 1987).

Shearman, P. and Phil Williams (eds), *The Superpowers, Central America and the Middle East* (London, Brassey's, 1988).

Simes, Dimitri K., 'Gorbachev: A New Foreign Policy?', *Foreign Affairs*, Vol. 65, No. 3 (1987), pp. 477–500.

Steele, Jonathan, *The Limits of Soviet Power* (Harmondsworth, Penguin, 1985).

Stevenson, R. W., *The Rise and Fall of Detente* (London, Macmillan, 1985).

Terry, S. M. (ed.), *Soviet Policy in Eastern Europe* (New Haven, CT, and London, Yale University Press, 1984).

Ulam, Adam, *Expansion and Coexistence: Soviet Foreign Policy, 1917–1973* (New York, Holt, Rinehart & Winston, 1974).

Valenta, J. and W. Potter (eds), *Soviet Decisionmaking for National Security* (London, George Allen & Unwin, 1984).

Valkenier, Elizabeth, *The Soviet Union and the Third World: The Economic Bind* (New York, Praeger, 1983).

Von Beyme, Klaus, *The Soviet Union in World Politics* (Aldershot, Gower, 1987).

White, Stephen, *The Origins of Detente* (Cambridge, Cambridge University Press, 1986).

Williams, P. and M. Bowker, *Superpower Détente* (London, Routledge, 1988).

Yanov, A., *Detente after Brezhnev: The Domestic Roots of Soviet Foreign Policy* (Berkeley, CA, University of California Press, 1977).

Yergin, Daniel, *The Shattered Peace: The Origins of the Cold War and the National Security State* (Boston, MA, Houghton Mifflin, 1977).

Young, John W., *Cold War Europe, 1945–1989* (London, Edward Arnold, 1991).

Zubok, Vladislav and Constantine Pleshakov, *Inside the Kremlin's Cold War: From Stalin to Khrushchev* (Cambridge, MA, Harvard University Press, 1996).

Zwick, Peter, *Soviet Foreign Relations: Process and Policy* (New York, Prentice-Hall, 1990).

17 RISE AND FALL OF THE SOVIET UNION

Arnason, Johann P., *The Future that Failed: Origins and Destinies of the Soviet Model* (London, Routledge, 1993).

Brzezinski, Zbigniew, *The Grand Failure: The Birth and Death of Communism in the Twentieth Century* (London, Macdonald, 1989).

Charlton, Michael, *Footsteps from the Finland Station: Five Landmarks in the Collapse of Communism* (St Albans, Claridge Press, 1992).

Chirot, Daniel (ed.), *The Crisis of Leninism and the Decline of the Left* (Seattle, WA, University of Washington Press, 1991).

Cox, Michael (ed.), *Soviet Collpase and the Post-communist World* (London, Cassell Academic, 1998).

Cullen, Robert, *Twilight of Empire: Inside the Crumbling Soviet Bloc* (London, Bodley Head, 1991).

Daniels, Robert V., *The End of the Communist Revolution* (London, Routledge, 1993).

Daniels, Robert V. (ed.), *Soviet Communism from Reform to Collapse* (Lexington, MA, D. C. Heath, 1995).

Gill, Graeme, *The Collapse of the Single-party System: The Disintegration of the Communist Party of the Soviet Union* (Cambridge, Cambridge University Press, 1994).

Goldman, Marshall I., *What Went Wrong with Perestroika* (New York, W. W. Norton, 1991).

Holmes, Leslie, *The End of Communist Power: Anti-Corruption Campaigns and Legitimation Crisis* (Oxford, Polity Press, 1993).

Hudelson, Richard H., *The Rise and Fall of Communism* (Boulder, CO, Westview Press, 1993).

Jowitt, Ken, *New World Disorder: The Leninist Extinction* (Berkeley, CA, University of California Press, 1992).

Kagarlitsky, Boris, *The Disintegration of the Monolith* (London, Verso, 1992).

Kotz, David and Fred Weir, *Revolution from above: The Demise of the Soviet System* (London, Routledge, 1997).

Laqueur, Walter, *The Dream that Failed* (Oxford, Oxford University Press, 1994).

Malia, Martin ('Z'), 'To the Stalin Mausoleum', *Daedalus*, Vol. 119, No. 1 (Winter 1990), pp. 295–344.

Malia, Martin, 'Leninist Endgame', *Daedalus*, Vol. 121, No. 2 (Spring 1992), pp. 57–75.

National Interest, special issue devoted to the fall of the Soviet Union (Spring 1993).

Ray, Larry, *Social Theory and the Crisis of State Socialism* (Cheltenham, Edward Elgar, 1996).

Remnick, David, *Lenin's Tomb: The Last Days of the Soviet Empire* (New York, Random House, 1993).

Robinson, Neil, *Ideology and the Collapse of the Soviet System: A Critical History of the Soviet Ideological Discourse* (Aldershot, Edward Elgar, 1995).

Ticktin, Hillel, *Origins of the Crisis in the USSR: Essays on the Political Economy of a Disintegrating System* (Armonk, NY, M. E. Sharpe, 1992).

Tolz, Vera and Iain Elliot (eds), *The Demise of the USSR: From Communism to Independence* (London, Macmillan, 1994).

Ulam, Adam, *The Communists: The Story of Power and Lost Illusions, 1948–1991* (New York, Macmillan, 1993)

Waller, Michael, *The End of the Communist Power Monopoly* (Manchester, Manchester University Press, 1993).

White, Stephen, Graeme Gill and Darrell Slider, *The Politics of Transition: Shaping a Post-Soviet Future* (Cambridge, Cambridge University Press, 1993).

Index